Procedures & Theory

for Administrative Professionals

7e

Procedures & Theory for Administrative Professionals

Karin M. Stulz
Assistant Professor
Northern Michigan University
Marquette, MI

Kellie A. Shumack
Assistant Professor
Auburn University at Montgomery
Montgomery, AL

Patsy Fulton-Calkins
University of North Texas
Denton, TX

SOUTH-WESTERN
CENGAGE Learning

Australia • Brazil • Japan • Korea • Mexico • Singapore • Spain • United Kingdom • United States

SOUTH-WESTERN
CENGAGE Learning™

Procedures & Theory for Administrative Professionals, Seventh Edition
Karin M. Stulz , Kellie A. Shumack, Patsy Fulton-Calkins

Vice President of Editorial, Business: Jack W. Calhoun

Vice President/Editor-in-Chief: Karen Schmohe

Senior Acquisitions Editor: Jane Phelan

Senior Developmental Editor: Karen Caldwell

Associate Marketing Manager: Shanna Shelton

Production Management and Composition: PreMediaGlobal

Senior Media Editor: Mike Jackson

Manufacturing Planner: Charlene Taylor

Internal Designer: PreMediaGlobal

Cover Designer: Lou Ann Thesing

Cover Image: ©mediaphotos, iStock

Photo Researcher: Darren Wright

Library of Congress Control Number: 2011942387

ISBN-13: 978-1-111-57586-1

ISBN-10: 1-111-57586-X

South-Western
5191 Natorp Boulevard
Mason, OH 45040
USA

Cengage Learning products are represented in Canada by Nelson Education, Ltd.

For your course and learning solutions, visit **www.cengage.com/school**

Visit our company website at **www.cengage.com**

Printed in Canada
1 2 3 4 5 6 7 15 14 13 12 11

Brief Contents

Contents

On Target at the Office

INTRODUCING

Technology & Procedures for the Administrative Professional, 7e

This edition is sharp and focused. It targets the skills and best practices in the administrative professional's work world.

"Key skills have been addressed. Easy and very interesting reading. Excellent content!"

Deborah Franklin
Bryant & Stratton College

New to This Edition

- Reorganized for better coverage of key topics such as the changing workplace, personal finance, workplace teams, applied ethics, and customer service.
- Updated throughout to reflect new technologies, processes, and global communication.
- Specific 21st Century Skills are featured in each chapter and applied within the activities to help students recognize and improve those important soft skills that are required on the job.
- Tech Talk feature introduces students to a wide variety of emerging technologies in today's workplace.
- Plentiful, action-oriented, career-focused end-of-chapter activities.
- Value-added website with technology activities, videos, quizzing, audio, *PowerPoint* presentations, and an interactive eBook.

CHAPTER 2

Your Professional Image

LEARNING OBJECTIVES

1. Describe the characteristics that contribute to a positive professional image.
2. Identify the components of a professional appearance.
3. Understand the conventions of business etiquette.

© Photographer/Image Source

Characteristics of a Professional

You have probably heard the expressions "a picture is worth a thousand words" and "you never get a second chance to make a first impression." When it comes to how you present and conduct yourself in a business environment, whether it is in that first interview or every day on the job with coworkers and clients, these expressions ring far truer than most people would like to admit.

Appearance is only part of the equation when creating and maintaining your **professional image**. The impressions you make on others, your attitude toward your work and your coworkers, your work ethic, your professional dress, and your familiarity with business etiquette all work together to form your professional image. Your ability to get a job, keep a job, and advance in your career will hinge on your professional image.

Successful businesspeople are those that spend time cultivating their professional image. In survey after survey, business leaders are asked what they look for when seeking new employees, and the most common responses deal with professional image. Although skills, education, and certification in specialized areas are important, employers are looking for successful individuals who possess a variety of professional characteristics as well. Successful individuals work hard to make a good first impression,

25

...with Updates from the Professionals

Career Profiles introduce you to administrative professionals who share their passion and advice for managing their careers.

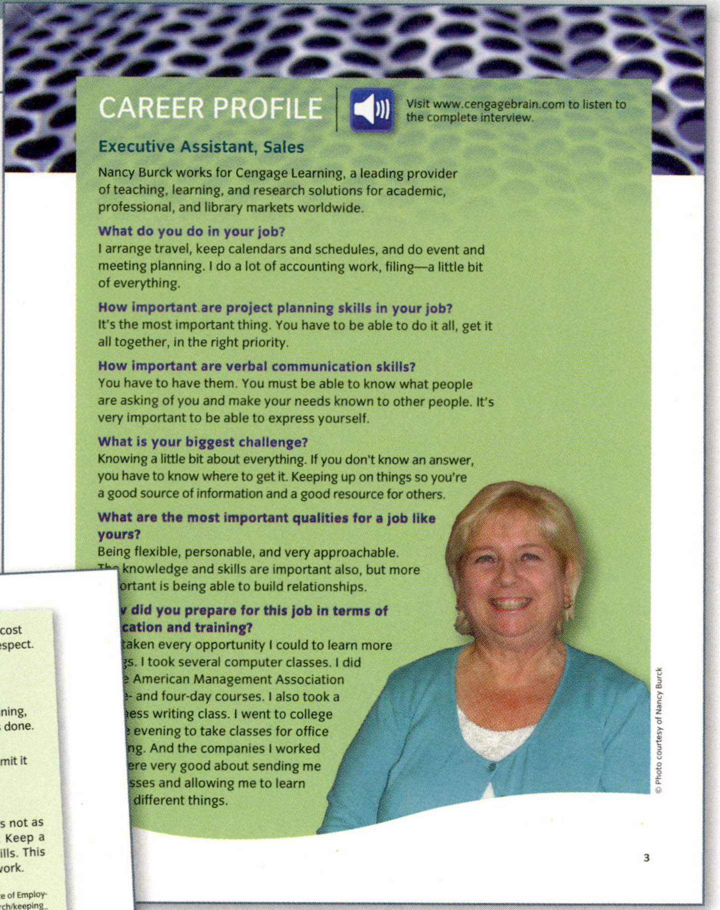

CAREER PROFILE

Visit www.cengagebrain.com to listen to the complete interview.

Executive Assistant, Sales

Nancy Burck works for Cengage Learning, a leading provider of teaching, learning, and research solutions for academic, professional, and library markets worldwide.

What do you do in your job?
I arrange travel, keep calendars and schedules, and do event and meeting planning. I do a lot of accounting work, filing—a little bit of everything.

How important are project planning skills in your job?
It's the most important thing. You have to be able to do it all, get it all together, in the right priority.

How important are verbal communication skills?
You have to have them. You must be able to know what people are asking of you and make your needs known to other people. It's very important to be able to express yourself.

What is your biggest challenge?
Knowing a little bit about everything. If you don't know an answer, you have to know where to get it. Keeping up on things so you're a good source of information and a good resource for others.

What are the most important qualities for a job like yours?
Being flexible, personable, and very approachable. The knowledge and skills are important also, but more ortant is being able to build relationships.

v did you prepare for this job in terms of cation and training?
taken every opportunity I could to learn more gs. I took several computer classes. I did e American Management Association - and four-day courses. I also took a ess writing class. I went to college e evening to take classes for office ng. And the companies I worked ere very good about sending me sses and allowing me to learn different things.

© Photo courtesy of Nancy Burck

3

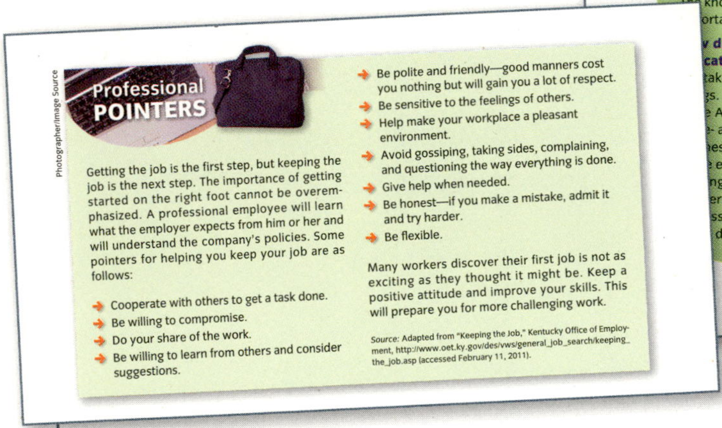

Professional POINTERS

Photographer/Image Source

Getting the job is the first step, but keeping the job is the next step. The importance of getting started on the right foot cannot be overemphasized. A professional employee will learn what the employer expects from him or her and will understand the company's policies. Some pointers for helping you keep your job are as follows:

- Cooperate with others to get a task done.
- Be willing to compromise.
- Do your share of the work.
- Be willing to learn from others and consider suggestions.
- Be polite and friendly—good manners cost you nothing but will gain you a lot of respect.
- Be sensitive to the feelings of others.
- Help make your workplace a pleasant environment.
- Avoid gossiping, taking sides, complaining, and questioning the way everything is done.
- Give help when needed.
- Be honest—if you make a mistake, admit it and try harder.
- Be flexible.

Many workers discover their first job is not as exciting as they thought it might be. Keep a positive attitude and improve your skills. This will prepare you for more challenging work.

Source: Adapted from "Keeping the Job," Kentucky Office of Employment, http://www.oet.ky.gov/des/vws/general_job_search/keeping_the_job.asp (accessed February 11, 2011).

Professional Pointers address tips for success.

"The Professional Pointers are right to the point and very easy to comprehend."

Monica Carmichael
Miller-Motte Technical College

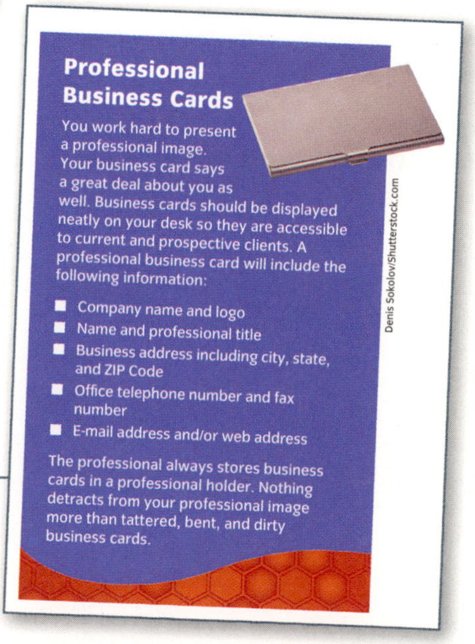

Professional Business Cards

You work hard to present a professional image. Your business card says a great deal about you as well. Business cards should be displayed neatly on your desk so they are accessible to current and prospective clients. A professional business card will include the following information:

- Company name and logo
- Name and professional title
- Business address including city, state, and ZIP Code
- Office telephone number and fax number
- E-mail address and/or web address

The professional always stores business cards in a professional holder. Nothing detracts from your professional image more than tattered, bent, and dirty business cards.

Denis Sokolov/Shutterstock.com

Special emphasis is given to topics that address professional habits and attitudes.

New Career-Focused Features

21st Century Skills discusses real-world competencies and applies them in multiple activities.

"The 21st Century Skills feature is extremely helpful . . . and not just for students."

Sherry Stanfield, RN
Miller-Motte Technical College

PARTNERSHIP FOR 21ST CENTURY SKILLS

Creativity/Innovation

Think Creatively Through Team Brainstorming

Thinking creatively and working creatively with others on a team are important skills for the 21st century workplace. **Brainstorming** is a technique that teams often use to get as many ideas as possible on the table. In a brainstorming session, team members build on what others say, and any and all ideas are encouraged. Generally, no idea is ever criticized or evaluated during the session; assessment takes place afterward. This approach helps promote the involvement of all team members and gets people to think outside established patterns.

Team members have to communicate ideas and also be open to new and diverse perspectives in an effort to benefit from a wide range of ideas. Software such as *Microsoft Office* and mind mapping tools are helpful as teams create and refine ideas. Mind mapping tools let you draw diagrams to show visually how information is organized. Links to several tools are available on the website for this text.

Activity

Creativity is a muscle you need to flex to keep in shape. Form a team of five or six and brainstorm ideas for one of the following topics. Rules: No ideas should be criticized in any way, and all ideas should be recorded. Be creative, and think outside the box! Outlandish ideas earn more creativity points.

- Texting while driving. How can we stop it?
- Tardiness to work. Too many people are coming in late. How can we solve this problem?
- Social networking on company time. What should company leaders do?
- A video game. Pick a popular game. Then come up with ideas for new games that will outsell it.
- A new mobile app. What is an app that no one has thought of yet that everybody needs?

DaveBolton/iStockphoto.com

DEVELOP WORKPLACE SKILLS

5. **Team examples** Form a team with a classmate. Use the Internet to search for at least three examples of how teams are used in the workplace, or use examples from this chapter. Using *Microsoft Word*, create a table with three columns and four rows. The first row will be the column headings: "Team Example," "Type of Team," and "Advice for Effective Teams." Give a brief explanation of each team example you found, determine which type of team it is, and use what you learned in this chapter to give the team two pieces of advice on how to be effective. The advice must be different for each example. Choose one of *Word's* preformatted tables for the design. (Learning Objectives 2 and 4)

PUT IT TO WORK

Team leader problem Ramirez & Shaw is a 15-year-old company providing computer services in the United States and Canada. The company has been very successful over the last ten years and attributes part of its success to its emphasis on solving problems through a team-based approach. Employees serve on project teams.

Benjamin Toulous was asked by his supervisor to serve on an eight-member team to examine the company's employee evaluation procedures. Benjamin is pleased about serving on this team. He believes he has several good suggestions that will improve the evaluation procedures. After he accepted the invitation to serve, he learned that the team leader was Alice Wong, the supervisor of the accounting department. Benjamin has little respect for Alice. He thinks she is a poor supervisor because he has heard stories from several of her employees about how unfair she is. Although Benjamin has never had direct experience with Alice as a supervisor and has actually never met her, he still believes she is an unacceptable team leader.

Technology Features

Tech Talk introduces emerging and useful technologies such as blogs, VoiceThreads, collaborative websites, and online portfolios.

Correlated end-of-chapter Tech Tools activities apply these concepts.

For additional practice, instructions, and links, visit CourseMate.

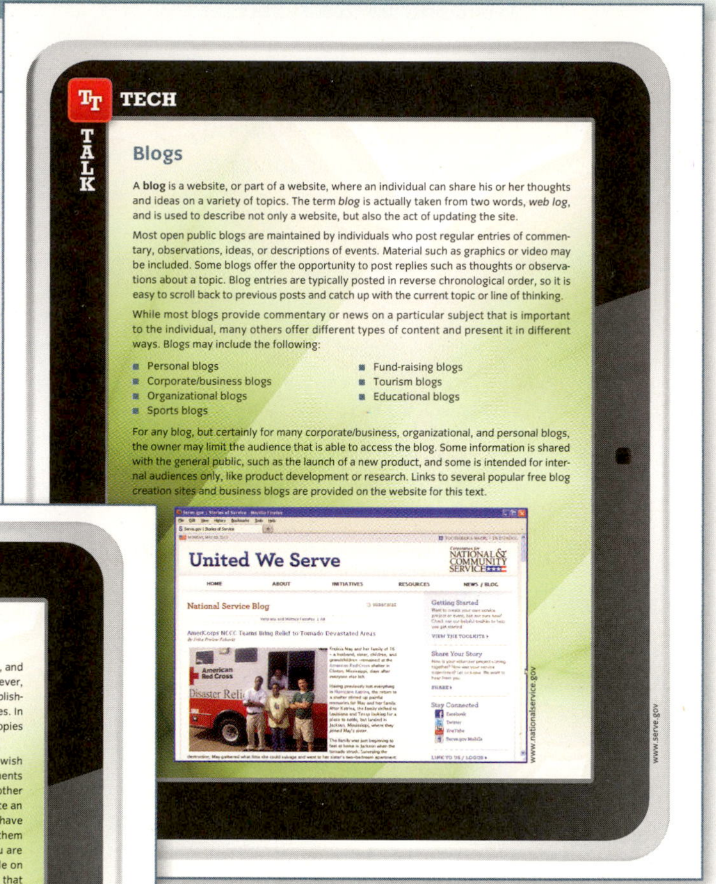

TECH TALK

Blogs

A **blog** is a website, or part of a website, where an individual can share his or her thoughts and ideas on a variety of topics. The term *blog* is actually taken from two words, *web log*, and is used to describe not only a website, but also the act of updating the site.

Most open public blogs are maintained by individuals who post regular entries of commentary, observations, ideas, or descriptions of events. Material such as graphics or video may be included. Some blogs offer the opportunity to post replies such as thoughts or observations about a topic. Blog entries are typically posted in reverse chronological order, so it is easy to scroll back to previous posts and catch up with the current topic or line of thinking.

While most blogs provide commentary or news on a particular subject that is important to the individual, many others offer different types of content and present it in different ways. Blogs may include the following:

- Personal blogs
- Corporate/business blogs
- Organizational blogs
- Sports blogs
- Fund-raising blogs
- Tourism blogs
- Educational blogs

For any blog, but certainly for many corporate/business, organizational, and personal blogs, the owner may limit the audience that is able to access the blog. Some information is shared with the general public, such as the launch of a new product, and some is intended for internal audiences only, like product development or research. Links to several popular free blog creation sites and business blogs are provided on the website for this text.

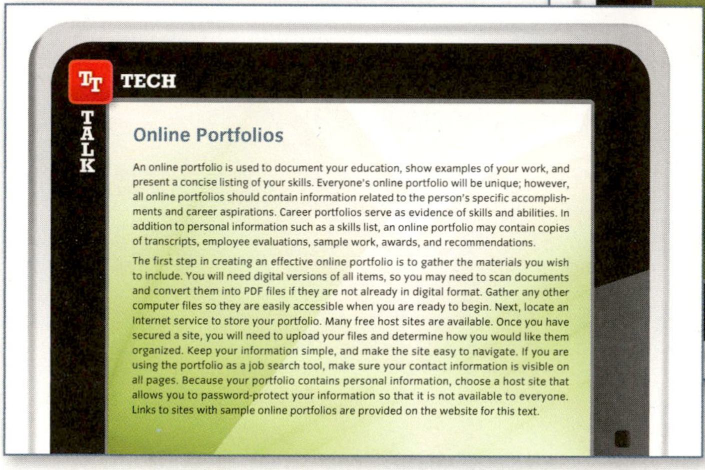

TECH TALK

Online Portfolios

An online portfolio is used to document your education, show examples of your work, and present a concise listing of your skills. Everyone's online portfolio will be unique; however, all online portfolios should contain information related to the person's specific accomplishments and career aspirations. Career portfolios serve as evidence of skills and abilities. In addition to personal information such as a skills list, an online portfolio may contain copies of transcripts, employee evaluations, sample work, awards, and recommendations.

The first step in creating an effective online portfolio is to gather the materials you wish to include. You will need digital versions of all items, so you may need to scan documents and convert them into PDF files if they are not already in digital format. Gather any other computer files so they are easily accessible when you are ready to begin. Next, locate an Internet service to store your portfolio. Many free host sites are available. Once you have secured a site, you will need to upload your files and determine how you would like them organized. Keep your information simple, and make the site easy to navigate. If you are using the portfolio as a job search tool, make sure your contact information is visible on all pages. Because your portfolio contains personal information, choose a host site that allows you to password-protect your information so that it is not available to everyone. Links to sites with sample online portfolios are provided on the website for this text.

USE TECH TOOLS

9. **Create a blog** Create a blog that you can use to post periodic reflection entries for this class. Compose a first entry in which you explain why you are taking this course and what you hope to learn. Use a blog site provided by your instructor or one of the free blog sites provided on the website for this text.

Blog

USE TECH TOOLS

7. **Online portfolio** Search the Internet to locate a free online portfolio service, or use one of the links provided on the website for this text. Create an account and design a home page to start building your professional online portfolio. Include professional images and words that would be appropriate for a potential employer. Create a portfolio that is flexible so that you can add information in the future.

e-Portfolio

...and Plentiful Activities That Bring it Together

"Excellent end-of-chapter activities; so many to pick from."

Deborah Franklin
Bryant & Stratton College

PUT IT TO WORK

Behaving like a professional Jose Garcia was hired six months ago in an entry-level sales position. Although Jose is interested in sales, he would eventually like to move into a management position. For the most part, Jose feels that he is getting along well with his sales team and his supervisor.

COMMUNICATE SUCCESSFULLY

1. **Making introductions** Write an appropriate introduction for each situation. (Learning Objective 3)
   - You are at a business dinner. You are introducing Kimberly Loukinen, a new student assistant, to your supervisor, Melody Hoover.

BUILD RELATIONSHIPS

6. **Getting along** Anna Chung has recently been hired to work with you. You know Anna from school; she has been in a few classes with you. Although you think Anna has good skills, she is difficult to work with because of her negative attitude toward everything—her personal life, her relationships, her job, and her supervisor. In fact, Anna is rarely positive about anyone or anything. After a few weeks on the job, you are beginning to have negative feelings, too. You like your work and your supervisor, and you can see there will be opportunities for advancement. What can you do to overcome your negative feelings? What can you do to make working with Anna more productive? (Learning Objective 1)

DEVELOP WORKPLACE SKILLS

4. **First impressions and workplace appearance** Your friend Elizabeth has been offered an interview for a teller position at a local bank. She is very excited and has asked for your advice on what to wear and how to make a good first impression. What suggestions can you give Elizabeth about appropriate professional dress for the interview? What tips can you give to help her make a positive first impression? (Learning Objectives 1 and 2)

NEW VALUE ADDED RESOURCES

www.cengagebrain.com

Procedures & Theory, 7e offers plentiful resources with tools and activities to enhance learning.

Instructor Resources available on the instructor's companion site or Instructor's Resource CD offer complete and customizable content, including the Instructor's Manual, **Exam***View*® test bank, and PowerPoint® presentations.

CENGAGE brain.com **Student Resources only available at CengageBrain.com**

On CengageBrain.com students will be able to save up to 60% on their course materials through our full spectrum of options. Students will have the option to rent their textbooks, purchase print textbooks, e-textbooks, or individual e-chapters and audio books all for substantial savings over average retail prices. CengageBrain.com also includes access to Cengage Learning's broad range of homework and study tools and features a selection of free content.

- Gain access to FREE book companion resources including learning objectives, flashcards, data files, chapter outlines, and more
- Try a demo chapter or access free content within CourseMate
- Study smarter, not harder

CourseMate **Engaging. Trackable. Affordable.**

Interested in a simple way to complement your text and course content with study and practice materials?

Cengage Learning's CourseMate brings course concepts to life with interactive learning, study, and exam preparation tools that support the printed textbook. Watch student comprehension soar as your class works with the printed textbook and the textbook-specific website. CourseMate for Procedures & Theory for Administrative Professionals goes beyond the book to deliver what you need!

CareerTransitions **Explore Career Interests. Achieve Employment Goals.**

Guide students in **exploring career interests** and **achieving employment goals** with the most valuable, complete career exploration and job-seeking online resource – ***Career Transitions***, now available through *CourseMate*. ***Career Transitions*** focuses on the entire career process – from initial career exploration and personal strength assessment to maximizing practical job-seeking tools, professional advice, and comprehensive job postings.

About the Authors

Karin M. Stulz, M.A.E., is an assistant professor in the College of Business at Northern Michigan University. Karin held several full-time administrative professional positions before starting her teaching career in 1989. Karin has been honored for her teaching expertise with an Outstanding Teacher Award from the College of Business, an Excellence in Teaching Award from Northern Michigan University, and a Postsecondary Business Teacher of the Year Award from the Michigan Business Education Association. She lives in Marquette, Michigan, with her husband Kevin and children Emily and Connor.

Kellie A. Shumack, Ph.D., is an assistant professor at Auburn University at Montgomery teaching Instructional Technology-related courses in the Department of Foundations and Secondary Education. Before joining the AUM faculty, Kellie worked as an administrative professional for five years and taught business at the secondary and postsecondary levels for 14 years. Kellie was awarded the 2010 Delta Pi Epsilon Outstanding Doctoral Research Award for her work in researching professional development needs in Business Education. She is also an Intel Certified Master Teacher. Follow Kellie's blog at http://techshumack.blogspot.com/.

Patsy Fulton-Calkins, Ph.D., C.P.S., has taught at the high school, community college, and university levels, including CPS review courses. Patsy has administrative experience at the college level, including division chairperson, vice-president of instruction, president, and chancellor.

Reviewers

Elaine Appelle
Educational Consultant
New York, New York

Monica L. Carmichael
Miller-Motte Technical College
N. Charleston, South Carolina

Siobhan Finnamore
Miller-Motte College
Raleigh, North Carolina

Deborah A. Franklin
Bryant & Stratton College
Orchard Park, New York

Andrea Robinson Hinsey
Ivy Tech Community College
Fort Wayne, Indiana

Rochelle A. Kunkel
Kankakee Community College
Kankakee, Illinois

Ronald M. Oler
Ivy Tech Community College
Richmond, Indiana

Debra W. Pressley
Blue Ridge Community College
Flat Rock, North Carolina

Judy Reiman
Columbia College
Sonora, California

Sherry Stanfield, RN, BSN, MSHPE
Miller-Motte Technical College
North Charleston, South Carolina

PART

1

The Dynamic Workplace

CAREER PROFILE

Visit www.cengagebrain.com to listen to the complete interview.

Executive Assistant, Sales

Nancy Burck works for Cengage Learning, a leading provider of teaching, learning, and research solutions for academic, professional, and library markets worldwide.

What do you do in your job?
I arrange travel, keep calendars and schedules, and do event and meeting planning. I do a lot of accounting work, filing—a little bit of everything.

How important are project planning skills in your job?
It's the most important thing. You have to be able to do it all, get it all together, in the right priority.

How important are verbal communication skills?
You have to have them. You must be able to know what people are asking of you and make your needs known to other people. It's very important to be able to express yourself.

What is your biggest challenge?
Knowing a little bit about everything. If you don't know an answer, you have to know where to get it. Keeping up on things so you're a good source of information and a good resource for others.

© Photo courtesy of Nancy Burck

What are the most important qualities for a job like yours?
Being flexible, personable, and very approachable. The knowledge and skills are important also, but more important is being able to build relationships.

How did you prepare for this job in terms of education and training?
I've taken every opportunity I could to learn more things. I took several computer classes. I did some American Management Association three- and four-day courses. I also took a business writing class. I went to college in the evening to take classes for office training. And the companies I worked for were very good about sending me to classes and allowing me to learn those different things.

CHAPTER 1

The Workplace—Constantly Changing

LEARNING OBJECTIVES

1. Identify changes that are occurring in the workplace.
2. Define common types of businesses and organizational structures.
3. Explain crucial skills and qualities of an effective administrative professional.

© Photographer/Image Source

The Dynamic Workplace

A constantly changing workplace is the expectation for administrative professionals today. A variety of factors contribute to this new and exciting work environment. Major changes in technology allow for faster and more efficient communication with established business partners in the same city, on the other side of the United States, or in another country. These emerging technologies also offer increased potential for organizations to develop new customers or work sites in untapped markets. People are living longer and staying in the workforce longer as well. Today's administrative professional interacts with people of different races, ages, cultures, and backgrounds on a daily basis.

Economic Globalization

The globalization of the world economy has changed businesses across the country. To remain competitive, many businesses must look outside their geographic regions for business partners and customers. Many choose to produce their goods or offer their services from operations in one country although their business operations may be headquartered in another country. This is commonly referred to as outsourcing.

Global interdependence has increased pressure on companies to streamline their operations. For this and other reasons, workers are less likely than they were in the past to stay with one employer throughout their careers. Companies are moving operations to locations where they can conduct business with lower costs, both within and outside the United States. Organizations may not invest as much money in employee training.

© Creative/Getty Images

Lifelong learning is essential in a changing business world.

As the cost of doing business increases, and as companies look to contain costs, they often seek to reorganize their operations. Cost-saving measures may take the form of downsizing by reducing the number of people who perform a certain duty; **cross-training**, which involves training personnel to complete differing tasks within a department or unit; or reassigning duties, which results from internal reorganization and restructuring of how the business operates from day to day.

All these changes have had an effect on the job duties of the administrative professional. While this type of change can be unsettling, it is inevitable. The administrative professional who is adaptable, confident, and a lifelong learner will be successful in the changing work environment.

Changing Technology

Today's administrative professional works in a fast-paced, high-tech world. Advances in technology have made it possible to conduct business across the globe almost instantly. In addition, reliance on new technology continues to expand in offices across the world. With this expansion of technology, the role of the administrative professional has changed drastically from several years ago. There is overwhelming evidence that technology will continue to change the way people work and live.

What does the rapid, constant evolution of technology mean for the administrative professional? One overarching answer is that due to technology, administrative professionals are able to accomplish more work in the same amount of time. This allows many administrative professionals to assume responsibilities once reserved for management, including providing training and support for new administrative professionals and supervising administrative professionals.

Because many of the job duties of the administrative professional involve human interaction, technology will not replace the administrative professional. Instead, the administrative professional will continue to be a vital part of the business world.

Workplace Diversity

Whether you are preparing to enter the workplace after finishing your studies or are presently employed either full- or part-time, the increased cultural diversity of the work environment is likely to be apparent to you. You may be working with people of many different ethnic, national, and racial backgrounds (and the clients and customers you serve may be correspondingly diverse). As laws have been passed to promote equal opportunities for women and minorities, this diversity has grown and is now embraced as a positive force in the job market.

People are living longer and working longer. Employees today can expect to work with individuals who are from 18 to 70 years old. Because of age differences, workers may have vastly different values and goals. Members of each generation view the world through a different lens according to the events that were taking place during their formative years. The effective administrative professional will recognize the positive effects of diversity and will embrace the opportunities that accompany a diverse workforce.

Job Outlook

Today both men and women are choosing office support positions as a career choice and as a way to advance within a company or field. For a career, the varied work and increase in job responsibilities can be very rewarding. Administrative professionals can work in a variety of fields such as sports, medicine, education, law, and government. They can specialize in work duties or choose a position that has a diverse set of responsibilities. Support positions can also serve as an introduction to a business or industry, from which the administrative professional can move to other positions or occupations.

The administrative professional of today supports organizations in many ways. Figure 1.1 lists some of the most common job responsibilities.

Administrative Professional Job Responsibilities
■ Using the Web to conduct research
■ Researching, identifying, and recommending equipment needed for the office
■ Providing training and support for new administrative professionals
■ Researching, preparing, and presenting on various topics of importance to the organization
■ Supervising one or more administrative professionals
■ Preparing presentation materials including researching the subject, writing significant content, and preparing visuals
■ Storing material on the computer and retrieving it for dissemination to staff and clients
■ Organizing and maintaining paper and electronic files
■ Creating spreadsheets, managing databases, and creating reports
■ Arranging conference calls and web seminars
■ Working in teams with other administrative professionals
■ Researching and preparing statistical reports
■ Reviewing journals, such as legal or technology journals
■ Writing and posting job vacancies
■ Ordering supplies
■ Preparing letters, memos, and e-mail
■ Scheduling appointments

FIGURE 1.1 The administrative professional has a wide range of job responsibilities.

The administrative professional's responsibilities have changed dramatically today. Continual changes that require additional management-related skills and increased technological knowledge are likely to occur in the future. These changes mean that as an administrative professional, you must:

- Continue to learn through attending appropriate workshops and seminars.
- Participate in professional organizations.
- Read about changes in your field in professional publications.
- Constantly improve your communication, time management, and critical-thinking skills.
- Accept new responsibilities with a positive attitude.

The U.S. Department of Labor (DOL) lists administrative assistant as one of the largest occupations in the United States, and it is among those expected to add the largest numbers of new jobs in the coming years. In 2008, administrative assistants held more than 4.3 million jobs. By 2018, some 471,600 new jobs are expected to become available. Figure 1.2 gives details about this projected growth.

This growth is predicted because administrative professionals work in areas of the economy that are expanding, such as health care, social services, and legal services. Some of this growth is occurring because the roles of administrative professionals are expanding as they take on more kinds of work that used to be completed by other professionals.

The DOL also reported that about 90 percent of administrative professionals worked in service industries. Service sector employment includes activities that provide a service rather than a product, such as health and legal services, hospitality and tourism, government, insurance and finance, education, the arts, and social services. Figure 1.3 shows administrative professional employment by specialty.

Projected Growth 2008–2018

Occupational Title	Employment 2008	Number Change	Percent Change
Secretaries and administrative assistants	4,348,100	471,600	11
Executive secretaries and administrative assistants	1,594,400	204,400	13
Legal secretaries	262,600	48,400	18
Medical secretaries	471,100	125,500	27
Secretaries, except legal, medical, and executive	2,020,000	93,300	5

FIGURE 1.2 Administrative Professional Job Growth Through 2018

Data from U.S. Department of Labor, *Occupational Outlook Handbook, 2010–11 Edition*, "Secretaries and Administrative Assistants," http://www.bls.gov/oco/ocos151.htm (accessed May 1, 2011).

Employment by Specialty	
Secretaries, except legal, medical, and executive	46%
Executive secretaries and administrative assistants	37%
Medical secretaries	11%
Legal secretaries	6%

FIGURE 1.3 Administrative Professional Employment by Specialty in 2008

Based on U.S. Department of Labor, *Occupational Outlook Handbook, 2010–11 Edition*, "Secretaries and Administrative Assistants," http://www.bls.gov/oco/ocos151.htm (accessed May 1, 2011).

Changing Workweek

Although a number of organizations still adhere to the traditional five-day workweek and 8 or 9 a.m. to 5 p.m. hours, the tradition is changing. Some companies have begun to establish flexible hours to accommodate changing family structures and needs. Several alternatives to the traditional workweek are gaining in popularity. These alternatives include the compressed workweek, flextime, and job sharing.

With a **compressed workweek**, employees work the usual number of hours (35 to 40) but work fewer

Varying Job Titles

Administrative professionals are known by many job titles. Although some administrative professionals see their jobs as opportunities to move into other positions, many choose this work as their profession. Many individuals change positions and expand their role and responsibilities as they progress through their career, but they remain in the profession they have selected. Other terms for administrative professional include the following:

- Administrative assistant
- Administrative associate
- Secretary
- Executive secretary
- Office manager
- Executive assistant

Other administrative professionals choose career paths that specialize in legal or medical professions. Here are two common titles for individuals in specialty fields:

- Medical secretary
- Legal secretary

Media Bakery 13/Shutterstock.com

than five days per week. For example, a 40-hour week may consist of four 10-hour days; a 36-hour week may be made up of three 12-hour days.

Flextime is another departure from the 8 a.m. to 5 p.m. workday. With flextime, working hours are staggered. Each employee must work the full quota of time but at periods convenient for the individual and the organization. Under this plan, all employees do not report to or leave work at the same time. For example, with a 40-hour week, one employee may come to work at 7:30 a.m. and work until 4 p.m. (with 30 minutes for lunch). Another employee may come to work at 9 a.m. and work until 5:30 p.m. Core hours (hours when everyone is in the office) may be from 9:30 a.m. until 2:30 p.m. Flextime helps reduce traffic congestion at traditional peak hours and allows employees flexibility in their schedules.

Still another departure from the traditional work schedule is **job sharing**. Under this arrangement, two or more part-time employees perform a job that one full-time employee might hold. For example, job sharing might be two people working five half days or one person working two full days and another person working three full days. Such a plan can be suitable for parents with small children when one or both spouses want to work on a part-time basis. In addition, job sharing can be suitable for workers who want to ease into retirement by reducing the length of their workday or workweek. Both employees and the organization can profit from job sharing. For instance, because full-time benefits are generally not paid to part-time employees, the company saves on benefit costs.

Physical Workplace

Today the physical workplace has changed drastically from the traditional office located in an established structure. The office exists in a variety of different forms, including the virtual office, mobile office, and home office.

The virtual office has no physical form and allows you to work from a variety of locations—at home, in your car, at a coffee shop, at an airport, or at an out-of-town location such as a hotel. The virtual office simulates a business location through the use of telecommunications and computer technologies. Technically, your office is wherever you are conducting business at the time.

Mobile offices are established using a variety of portable electronic equipment that duplicates the equipment of one's office. Mobile offices are created by individuals who regularly work outside their company office. They can take the form of temporary offices set up at almost any location that has a workspace available, including airport terminals, hotels, and coffee shops. A mobile office can also be created at a client's office. These offices are particularly convenient for people when they are traveling and need to communicate with their home work site. Additionally, with the continued growth of international businesses, workers have the potential for working at global sites owned and operated by U.S. businesses.

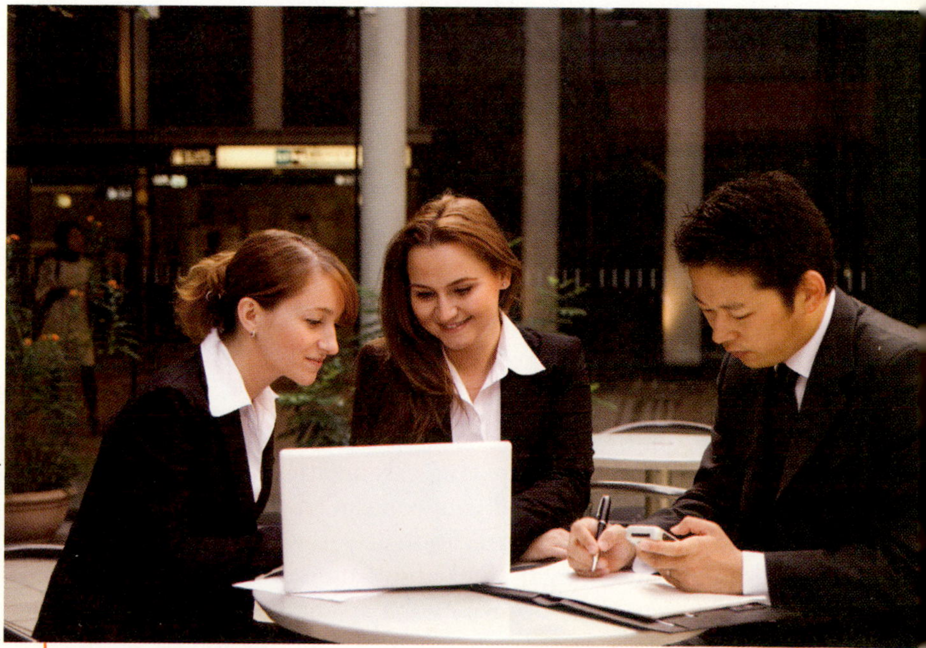

pierredesvarre/iStockphoto.com

Technology allows people to work in a variety of locations.

Home offices, as the name suggests, allow workers to work from their homes. Although a number of people who work at home are self-employed, a large number of home workers are employed by companies or organizations that allow employees to work full-time or even part-time from their homes.

With the ever-increasing technological capacity of our world, the types of workplaces will likely continue to expand, and new types will emerge. If you are to be successful as an administrative professional, you must be able to adapt to continual changes in the workplace environment.

Workplace Organization

In your career as an administrative professional, you may work for a number of different organizations. If you work in a business environment either now or when you complete your education goals, you should learn as much as possible about the organizational culture, the type of business, and the organizational structure. Although organizations operate differently, the major levels of an organization, along with an overview of the responsibilities of the individuals at these levels, are discussed in this section.

Organizational Culture

Every business has its own **organizational culture**, which reflects the key values, beliefs, and attitudes that describe the organization and the way it conducts business. It is sometimes described as the personality of the organization. Organizational cultures range from very formal and strict to extremely casual. Most cultures are somewhere in between.

The culture of an organization is often difficult to define in words. By paying careful attention to what is going on around you, you can learn about the culture of your organization as you work. For example, you can get clues about the culture of an organization by observing the arrangement of office furniture, the way people dress, and the way individuals interact with one another. To better understand an organization's culture, you should also pay attention to the unwritten rules. The unwritten rules may not be discussed but show up in employees' attitudes and behaviors.

A business with a healthy organizational culture is typically a more rewarding place to work. Employees are usually more productive and efficient. Try to find a job where the organizational cultural closely matches your own ethical values and standards.

Types of Business Organizations

The descriptions here are brief; however, they will provide you with insights into various types of organizations. As you continue your studies, you will want to learn as much as you can about various business entities. The principal types of business organizations are as follows:

- Sole proprietorships
- Partnerships
- Limited liability companies
- Corporations
- Nonprofit corporations
- Governmental entities

SOLE PROPRIETORSHIPS

A **sole proprietorship** is owned and controlled by an individual. This person may operate the business or hire managers and workers to operate it. All responsibilities, profits, and losses belong to the owner. A sole proprietor may be referred to as an independent contractor, consultant, or freelancer.

PARTNERSHIPS

A **partnership** consists of an association of two or more people as co-owners of a business. They may or may not take part in running the business and may hire managers and other workers. All profits and losses are distributed to the partners according to the terms of the partnership agreement. Partnerships are largely being replaced by limited liability companies.

LIMITED LIABILITY COMPANIES

A **limited liability company (LLC)** is a business form that combines the tax advantages of a partnership with the limited liability of a corporation. It must include two or more members. An LLC may conduct or promote any lawful business or purpose that a partnership or individual may conduct or promote. The LLC can own property, borrow or loan money, enter into contracts, and elect or appoint managers or agents. An advantage of an LLC is that members have limited personal liability from business activities. Professionals such as medical doctors, accountants, and lawyers may operate as an LLC.

CORPORATIONS

Corporations are legal entities formed by following a formal process of incorporation set forth by state statutes. A corporation may be publicly or privately owned. Corporations are owned by investors called stockholders who have purchased shares of stock in the company. Stockholders may or may not be involved in running the business. They are generally not responsible for the debts of the business and may receive part of its profits in the form of dividends.

An S-corporation is a type of corporation that must have 75 or fewer stockholders. The purpose of an S-corporation is to avoid double taxation of corporate income.

NONPROFIT CORPORATIONS

Nonprofit corporations are formed to promote a civic, charitable, or artistic purpose. These corporations are generally exempt from federal and state taxation on their income. However, they do have responsibilities for reporting their income, assets, and activities. They typically have fiduciary (holding in trust for another) responsibility to their members and contributors, and they must comply with federal and state laws governing nonprofit corporations. Numerous organizations, such as service organizations, performing arts groups, hospitals, faith-based organizations, charities, and private colleges, are set up as nonprofit corporations.

GOVERNMENTAL ENTITIES

Governmental entities are organizations funded and managed by a local, state, or national government in order to carry out its functions. Governmental units include city, county, state, and national services, such as regulatory agencies, public schools and universities, social services, and legislative bodies such as city councils. There are numerous departments, commissions, bureaus, and boards in all governmental units. These entities may be profit or nonprofit entities.

Organizational Structure

Organizational structure refers to the way that lines of authority, responsibility, and communication are arranged in order to accomplish the work of the business. When you join an organization, ask for an organizational chart if one is not made available to you. This chart will show you the organizational structure, the relationships between departments, and the levels of administrative authority. Certain portions of the chart may change from time to time, depending on projects of the company. These changes are usually reflected in dotted lines showing new relationships.

STOCKHOLDERS

Stockholders are investors in a business. A stockholder owns a portion or share of a corporation. Stockholders may be affected by the actions, decisions, policies, or practices of the business. For example, if the business is poorly managed or has financial problems, the value of the company stock may decrease. Thus, the stockholder loses money on the investment.

BOARD OF DIRECTORS

A **director** is an officer of a company who is charged with the management of its affairs and conduct. The number of board members varies based on the needs of the organization, with a board generally having approximately 12 to 15 members. Collectively, the group is referred to as a board of directors.

Theoretically, control of a company is divided between the board of directors and the sharehold-

Digital Vision/Getty Images

A board of directors establishes policies that guide the management of an organization.

ers. Large corporations have boards of directors that have the major responsibility of establishing policies to guide the management of the organization. Boards are composed of community, civic, and business leaders who meet monthly or every two or three months. In addition to making policy decisions, boards employ, evaluate, and dismiss (if necessary) the **chief executive officer (CEO)** of the corporation. A chief executive officer develops and implements strategic plans, makes major corporate decisions, and (often) oversees company operations. He or she is usually the highest-ranking person in a company and reports directly to the board of directors. Boards generally operate both as a unit and through committees that deal with specific aspects of the business, such as a personnel or finance committee. A director may not put himself or herself in a position in which personal or professional interests (e.g., making money for oneself) conflict with the duties the director owes the company. A board's bylaws or policies typically set rules regarding conflict of interest.

Board members of corporations deal with a variety of issues such as the following:

- Creating a strategic vision or mission for the organization
- Employing the CEO
- Assisting the CEO in determining the direction of the organization
- Holding the CEO responsible for profitability and overall performance

MANAGEMENT

Management refers to those individuals who are top or upper managers in a company, such as the CEO, chief operating officer, and vice presidents. Additionally, other administrators at lower levels are responsible for the day-to-day operations of the organization, with individuals having titles such as vice president of marketing, controller, treasurer, and sales representative.

At the beginning of your career as an administrative professional, you are not likely to manage other personnel. However, as you become an experienced and respected member of the office team, you may manage one or two administrative professionals who report to you. As you continue to grow in your job, you may be asked to take on additional management responsibilities.

Understanding Your Organization

The most valuable administrative professionals understand the organization where they work. One way to understand more about the organization is to learn how it is structured. Finding the answers to these questions will help you learn about your organization:

- Is it a nonprofit or profit-making organization?
- What is the organizational structure?
- Does it have stockholders?
- Does it have a board of directors?
- Who is the CEO? Who are the vice presidents?

Obtain a copy of the organizational chart so you can see the relationships in the organization.

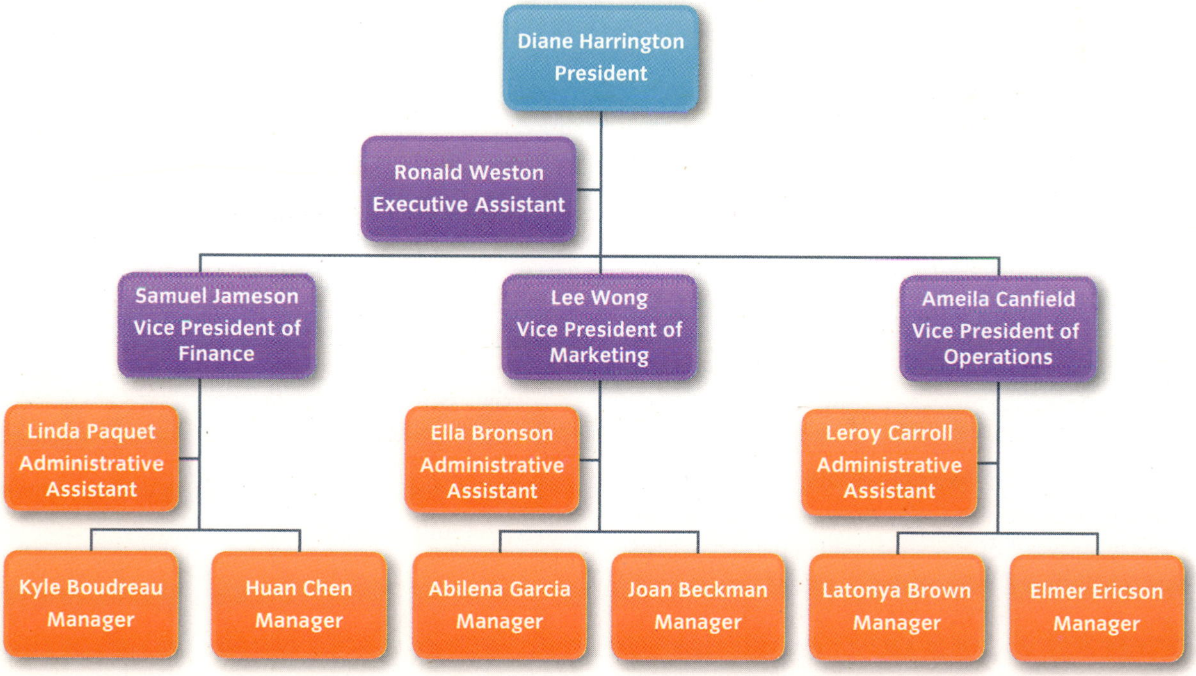

Administrative Professional Qualifications

Employers expect their employees to possess all the necessary skills and qualities to effectively do their jobs. A variety of professional skills and qualities are essential for success in an administrative professional position. This section identifies some of the major workplace requirements for being a successful and productive administrative professional.

Necessary Skills

Skills needed in all administrative professional positions include the following:

- Communication (listening, reading, verbal presentation, and writing)

- Interpersonal relations
- Time management
- Critical thinking
- Decision making
- Creative thinking
- Teamwork
- Technology
- Leadership
- Stress management
- Problem solving
- Customer focus

COMMUNICATION

Administrative professionals spend a major part of their time communicating with others. Communication takes the form of e-mails, letters, faxes, voice mail messages, telephone calls, written presentations, verbal presentations, and one-on-one conversations. As you assume greater responsibility in your job, you may be involved in presenting information to your peers and other groups of people both within and outside your organization. Regardless of the form communication takes, you must be extremely proficient in this area. You must express yourself accurately and concisely in written correspondence, and you must be clear, tactful, and straightforward in verbal communications. Part 3 of this textbook, Communication Essentials, will help you improve your communication skills.

INTERPERSONAL RELATIONS

You will interact with many people as an administrative professional. Within the company, you will have contact with coworkers, supervisors, and other executives. Contacts outside the company will include customers, clients, and visitors to the workplace. The people you encounter will be of different cultures, races, ethnicities, and ages. Additionally, you will interact with individuals who have diverse educational and professional backgrounds. If you are to be successful in working with these individuals, you need to be sensitive and accepting of their needs, cultures, and diverse backgrounds. Many chapters in this text address the importance of effective interpersonal relations. Throughout your life, you must continue to work on improving your human relations skills.

TIME MANAGEMENT

Time is a precious commodity for most people. The job of the administrative professional is busy, and you may find you do not have enough time to do all the tasks at your job or to relax and enjoy life. As an efficient administrative professional, you will need to organize your time, calendar, paper records, and electronic files so work flows smoothly and tasks are finished on time. Chapter 4 will help you improve your time management skills. Chapters 11 and 12 will help you learn how to manage your paper and electronic records.

CRITICAL THINKING

Critical thinking is a unique kind of purposeful thinking in which a person systematically chooses conscious and deliberate inquiry. *Critical* comes from the Greek word *krinein*, which means to separate or to choose. To think critically about an issue means to see it from all sides before coming to a conclusion.

As an administrative professional, you should think critically about the issues facing you. Doing so can save you time and can make you more productive. These skills can also make you a valuable employee for your organization—one who is recognized and promoted. As you are learning and practicing critical-thinking skills, a systematic process of asking appropriate questions will help you. Figure 1.4 lists

Critical-Thinking Questions
What is the purpose of my thinking?
What problem or question am I trying to answer?
What facts or information do I need?
How do I interpret the facts or information?
What conclusions can I draw from the facts or information?
Are my conclusions defensible?
Have I dealt with the complexity of the situation?
Have I avoided thinking in simple stereotypes?

FIGURE 1.4 Improving critical-thinking skills can help you be more productive.

several questions. Take a few moments to read them; then begin to practice and improve your critical-thinking skills.

DECISION MAKING

A decision is the outcome or product of a problem, concern, or issue that must be addressed and solved. In your role as an administrative professional, you will make decisions daily. It is important that you make good decisions. These decisions may range from recommending new technology to deciding how to handle a difficult client or customer. The decision-making process described in the 21st Century Skills feature on page 16 can help you learn how to make good decisions.

CREATIVE THINKING

Creativity is the ability to produce new ideas and to be original and imaginative. Creativity is a process. It is a way of thinking and doing. A creative person understands that multiple options exist in most situations and that he or she is free to choose from a wide variety of options. Creative individuals use more than one method or set of rules for getting a job done.

Take a few minutes to read and think about the tips given in Figure 1.5. Throughout this course, use these tips as you make decisions or solve problems. Then practice the tips on the job—the one you have now or the jobs you will have in the future.

Creative-Thinking Tips
■ Have faith in your own creativity.
■ Pay attention to everything around you.
■ Ask questions constantly.
■ Tackle tasks that are not easy and that require effort.
■ Do one thing at a time.
■ Stop worrying.
■ Pay attention to your intuition.

FIGURE 1.5 These tips will help you make decisions and solve problems.

TEAMWORK

The word *team* can be traced back to the Indo-European word *duek*, meaning to pull. Successful teams in the work environment include groups of people who work together to accomplish a given task. Chapter 3 discusses workplace teams.

Teamwork skills are similar to interpersonal skills in that they demand you understand, accept, and respect the differences among your team members. Teamwork also demands that you engage in the following behaviors:

- Treat all team members courteously.
- Build strong relationships with individual members of the team and the team as a whole.
- Learn collectively with the team. Start by developing self-knowledge and self-mastery; then look outward in developing knowledge and alignment with team members.
- Take responsibility for producing high-quality work as an individual team member and encouraging a high-quality team project.

TECHNOLOGY

If you are to succeed in the workplace, you must be competent and current in your knowledge of technology as it applies to your job and your skills in using it. You must develop the following:

- Proficiency with computers and current software
- Proficiency in telecommunications and wireless technologies
- Capability in researching on the Internet
- Competency in using printers, copiers, fax machines, and other office equipment
- Willingness to research and use new workplace technology

Later chapters in the textbook will help you develop these important skills.

LEADERSHIP

You can develop your leadership skills by seeking out and accepting opportunities that allow you to

PARTNERSHIP FOR 21ST CENTURY SKILLS

Critical Thinking/ Problem Solving

Make Effective Decisions: Five Steps

1. **Define the goal or problem.** This step may sound simple, but is usually the most difficult. What do you want to be different as a result of this decision? What purpose are you trying to achieve? Why is this decision necessary? What will be the outcome?
2. **Collect information.** Gather information related to the goal or problem. Ask people involved for their perspectives, and research the situation.
3. **Generate alternatives or possible solutions.** Brainstorm to generate options. If you identified any barriers in the previous step, discuss solutions.
4. **Assess the alternatives and make the decision.** Weigh the pros and cons of each alternative. Eliminate alternatives that are unrealistic or incompatible with your needs or criteria. Give additional thought to the best alternatives. Select the one that appears the most realistic, creative, challenging or satisfying.
5. **Evaluate the decision.** Evaluation helps you decide if you have made the right decision for the immediate situation. It also helps you improve your decision-making skills for the future. What was right about this decision? What was wrong? How did the decision-making process work? What improvements are necessary? What did you learn from the decision? What changes should you make for the future?

Activity

Think of a decision you will face in the next few months. Perhaps you need to find a summer job or place to live. Use the decision-making steps above to help you make this decision. As you move through the steps, write down your thoughts and responses to each step in the process.

© StockLite/Shutterstock.com

practice leadership. For example, you might accept a leadership position in one of your school's organizations or in your community. As you seek out and accept leadership opportunities, learn from each of them. Evaluate your performance or ask a close friend to do so. What did you do well? What did you not do well? How can you correct your mistakes? In Chapter 6, you will learn more about leadership and the application of leadership skills to your job.

Exercise and healthy eating habits will help you manage stress.

STRESS MANAGEMENT

You live in a fast-paced world—one where you may find yourself dealing with work-related stress. Chronic stress can cause serious health problems and can affect your work, not only in the way you perform when you are under stress, but also in the work you miss due to illness. Stress and time management are closely related. To be effective in your work and personal life, you need to understand how to manage your time so you do not become ill or chronically stressed. You will learn more about time and stress management in Chapter 4.

PROBLEM SOLVING

Every workplace has problems and challenges. Although it is always best to avoid problems, there will be times when you will not be able to avoid them. When that happens, you will be required to solve those problems. Understanding and implementing a problem-solving process will help you find appropriate solutions. Chapters 4 and 7 present a set of useful problem-solving steps. Study them and practice these skills throughout the course so you can handle problems effectively in the workplace.

CUSTOMER FOCUS

Employers are looking for administrative professionals who understand the importance of demonstrating a positive customer focus in all their actions. Establishing effective relationships with both internal and external customers is vital to the success of a business. Showing respect for customers, seeking customer input, and going the extra mile to maintain good relationships are all strategies that demonstrate customer focus. The successful administrative professional will demonstrate his or her commitment to customers through the use of effective problem-solving, listening, human relations, and communication skills.

Success Qualities

In addition to the skills identified in the previous section, certain qualities are essential for the success of an administrative professional. These qualities include the following:

- Openness to change
- Initiative and motivation
- Integrity and honesty
- Dependability
- Confidentiality
- Commitment to observing and learning

OPENNESS TO CHANGE

Change is constant in our society, and all indications are that change will continue to be a part of our world. An effective administrative professional not only will be able to cope with change but will embrace it.

TECH TALK

Blogs

A **blog** is a website, or part of a website, where an individual can share his or her thoughts and ideas on a variety of topics. The term *blog* is actually taken from two words, *web log*, and is used to describe not only a website, but also the act of updating the site.

Most open public blogs are maintained by individuals who post regular entries of commentary, observations, ideas, or descriptions of events. Material such as graphics or video may be included. Some blogs offer the opportunity to post replies such as thoughts or observations about a topic. Blog entries are typically posted in reverse chronological order, so it is easy to scroll back to previous posts and catch up with the current topic or line of thinking.

While most blogs provide commentary or news on a particular subject that is important to the individual, many others offer different types of content and present it in different ways. Blogs may include the following:

- Personal blogs
- Corporate/business blogs
- Organizational blogs
- Sports blogs
- Fund-raising blogs
- Tourism blogs
- Educational blogs

For any blog, but certainly for many corporate/business, organizational, and personal blogs, the owner may limit the audience that is able to access the blog. Some information is shared with the general public, such as the launch of a new product, and some is intended for internal audiences only, like product development or research. Links to several popular free blog creation sites and business blogs are provided on the website for this text.

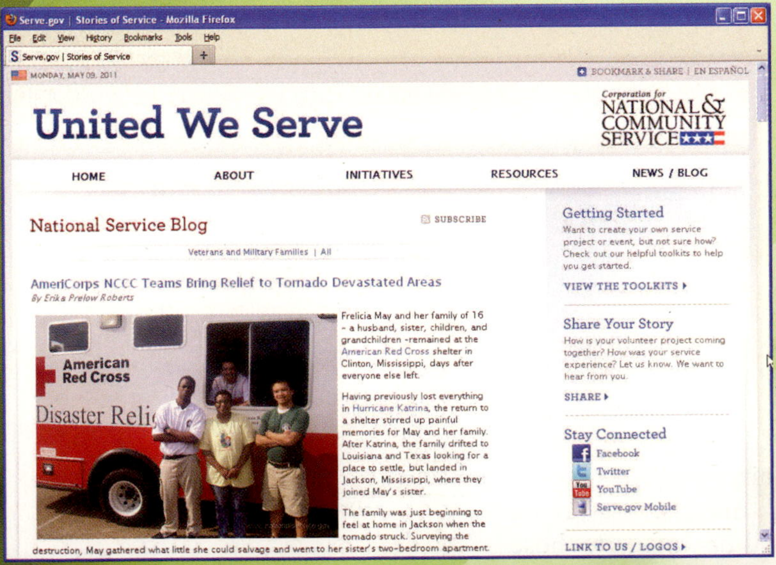

photo: www.nationalservice.gov
screenshot: www.serve.gov;

To help you with this challenge, seek to understand your organization well. Read documents that describe strategic directions for your organization; discuss these directions with your employer. Consistently learn new technologies and how you may be more effective in using them. Try to predict the changes you will face, and prepare yourself for them.

INITIATIVE AND MOTIVATION

Initiative is the ability not only to begin but also to follow through on a project. You demonstrate initiative by taking the projects that are given to you and completing them successfully. Additionally, you seek out tasks beyond those that have been assigned to you. You consistently analyze what needs to be done and then follow through on doing it.

Motivation is defined as an inducement to act—to get a task done. Motivation and initiative are closely related, with motivation providing the incentive to act and initiative providing the ability to get the task accomplished. You may be motivated *extrinsically* (from outside) or *intrinsically* (from within). For example, you may be motivated to perform a task because you are paid or because it provides external recognition from your supervisor. Additionally, you may be motivated to perform a task because you are committed to learning and growing. You understand that a new task provides you with an opportunity to learn and grow.

INTEGRITY AND HONESTY

In the workplace environment, *integrity* and *honesty* mean that you engage in the following behaviors:

- Adherence to a strict ethical code
- Truthfulness
- Sincerity

You do not engage in activities that provide an opportunity for others to question your values or morals. You are an ethical employee and demonstrate those ethics through thoughtful and appropriate behaviors. Ethics will be discussed in more detail in Chapter 5.

DEPENDABILITY

Dependability is defined as being trustworthy. In action, dependability means that you perform in the following manner in the workplace:

- You are productive and consistent in getting the tasks of your job done.
- You are thorough and timely in producing your work.
- You willingly put in additional time that is often needed for an important assignment.
- You do what you say you will do, when you say you will do it.

CONFIDENTIALITY

Confidentiality is defined as secrecy, privacy, or discretion. In the workplace, confidentiality means the ability to receive and keep certain information private. For example, if you work for a medical doctor, you will probably have access to highly personal and confidential information concerning health issues of various patients. You also may hear doctors discussing an illness of a particular patient. You are responsible for maintaining the confidentiality of

sjlocke/iStockphoto.com

You must protect confidential information.

this information. You must think carefully about what you say to others within and outside the organization about the information you have available to you because of your job. To give confidential information to others (except for the people who need to know) can cause irreparable harm to your organization, supervisor, and coworkers, as well as to patients, clients, and customers. You will learn more about confidentiality in Chapter 5.

COMMITMENT TO OBSERVING AND LEARNING

With the workplace constantly changing and new technologies being developed, your task as an administrative professional is to commit to continual learning. Several questions you should ask yourself as you go about this process are as follows:

- Do I make an effort to understand the directions of my organization?
- Do I understand what my employer expects of me?
- Do I listen to others?
- Do I live by a set of ethics and values?
- Do I respect diversity of people and ideas?
- Do I commit to learning new technologies?
- Am I reliable?
- Do I plan my daily and weekly schedule well?
- Am I flexible?
- Do I handle pressure well?
- Am I committed to continual learning?
- Am I productive at my job?

In the following chapters, you will learn the skills you need to succeed in your career as an administrative professional.

SUMMARY

To reinforce what you have learned in this chapter, study this summary.

- As administrative professionals gain more jobs and higher-level responsibilities, economic globalization and changing technology will continue to contribute to the changing work environment.
- As an administrative professional, you may work in various types of organizations with different structures and unique cultures. The major levels of large organizations include stockholders (for-profit organizations), a board of directors, and management.
- The effective administrative professional possesses a variety of necessary skills including communication, interpersonal relations, time management, critical thinking, decision making, creative thinking, teamwork, technology, leadership, stress management, problem solving, and customer focus skills. Success qualities include openness to change, initiative and motivation, integrity and honesty, dependability, confidentiality, and commitment to observing and learning.

KEY TERMS

blog, 18
chief executive officer (CEO), 12
compressed workweek, 8
confidentiality, 19
corporation, 11
cross-training, 5
director, 11
flextime, 9
government entity, 11
job sharing, 9
limited liability company (LLC), 11
nonprofit corporation, 11
organizational culture, 10
organizational structure, 11
partnership, 10
sole proprietorship, 10
stockholder, 11

1

STUDY Tools

Located at www.cengagebrain.com

- Chapter Outlines
- Flashcards
- Interactive Quizzes
- Tech Tools
- Video Segments
- and More!

LET'S DISCUSS

1. What effect has changing technology had on the job responsibilities of the administrative professional?
2. What is the job outlook for the administrative professional?
3. How important is organizational culture when seeking an administrative support position?
4. List and explain six skills necessary for a successful administrative professional.
5. Explain why confidentiality is an important quality for success.

PUT IT TO WORK

Correct a mistake Ricardo Mendoza accepted his first job as an administrative professional. He was interviewed by a team of individuals. Several days later, he received a letter welcoming him to the company. It was signed by Roger Athens, vice president of United Manufacturing. On his first day, Ricardo was introduced to Rebecca West. He extended his hand to her and said he was extremely pleased to work for United and was looking forward to meeting his boss. Ms. West smiled and said, "You have just met the boss; I am your supervisor." Ricardo was embarrassed and confused. He said, "I didn't expect to have a female boss; please forgive me for my assumption." Ms. West responded that he should not worry about what he had said and that she was looking forward to working with him.

Ricardo feels he has made a major mistake. He has never reported to a woman before and wonders how the situation will work out. However, he is willing to get to know her and learn what is expected of him.

Should Ricardo apologize to Ms. West? Should he attempt to forget what he said and show her he can be an asset to United? Should he quit immediately because he has made a major blunder?

COMMUNICATE SUCCESSFULLY

1. **Introduce a student** Find a student in the class whom you do not know. Interview each other so you can introduce one another to the rest of the class. Find out the following information: Why is your partner taking this course? What type of business organization does he or she hope to work for after graduation? What two crucial skills does your partner feel he or she possesses, and why? What are two qualities or skills the student hopes to improve through education? Learn one additional interesting fact about your partner. Use this information to introduce one another to the rest of the class. (Learning Objectives 2 and 3)

2. **Career goals** What do you hope to learn from this class? How will you use this knowledge in your career? Write a two-paragraph reflection paper that answers these questions. (Learning Objective 1)
3. **Find a job** Locate a job advertisement in a local print newspaper or online for a position that interests you. Review the required skills from the advertisement, and make a list of the skills you currently possess. Identify the areas where you need improvement, and describe your plans to improve your skills in these areas. (Learning Objective 3)

DEVELOP WORKPLACE SKILLS

4. **Assess your skills** Make a list of all the skills you currently possess that would make you an effective administrative professional. Include skills such as keyboarding, computer (listing the various computer competencies that you have), human relations, and so forth. Be honest with yourself; do not list skills you wish to have but do not at this point. Title the list "Skills I Currently Possess." (Learning Objective 3)
5. **Self-evaluation** Access the *Word* file *Ch01_Self-Evaluation* from the data files. Complete the form. Discuss your evaluation with a trusted friend, coworker, or family member to see if the person agrees with your ratings. Keep your self-evaluation; you will rate yourself again at the end of the course to determine the areas in which you have improved. (Learning Objective 3)
6. **Determine areas of growth** Using the list of skills you possess presently from Activity 4 and the self-evaluation chart from Activity 5, determine areas of growth you need to focus on in this course and throughout school. Develop a list of growth objectives you want to accomplish during this course and your education. Title the list "Areas of Growth for (add semester and date)." (Learning Objective 3)

BUILD RELATIONSHIPS

7. **Making decisions** Rocio Oxholm has completed her first year at Lincoln Hills Community College in Duluth, Minnesota. When she started college, she was not too certain of her career direction and took general education classes. She enjoyed all her classes, particularly her psychology and computer classes. She talked with one of the school counselors at the end of the year and took a personality test that indicated Rocio is an extrovert and a thinker.

   Rocio worked part-time in the president's office during the second semester. She answered the phone, made appointments, keyed reports, and handled complaints. She enjoyed every aspect of the job, especially the parts that dealt with people issues. The president's assistant complimented her several times on her decision-making ability and urged her to take office systems courses in the fall.

In a small group, discuss how Rocio should go about deciding what she should do. What should Rocio consider? What advice would you give her? Develop a plan you believe Rocio should follow, using the decision-making model presented in the 21st Century Skills feature on page 16. (Learning Objective 3)

8. **Organizational culture** A month ago, Chang Hu started an internship in a medical supplies office. Chang is excited about his job responsibilites and thinks they will be valuable when seeking a position after graduation. However, he is unsure if the internship is a good fit for him. For example, Chang is scheduled to work Mondays and Wednesdays from 8 a.m. until noon. Although Chang arrives at the office at 7:50 a.m., Mr. Reston, his supervisor, never arrives before 8:15 a.m. The office dress code is casual; many employees come to work in jeans and sweatshirts. Chang is used to a more formal structure and finds that when he wears jeans, his behavior is not as professional. He also notices he is making mistakes in his work.

   What advice would you give Chang? How important is organizational culture to his success? Should he quit and look for an internship that is a better match? (Learning Objective 2)

USE TECH TOOLS

9. **Create a blog** Create a blog that you can use to post periodic reflection entries for this class. Compose a first entry in which you explain why you are taking this course and what you hope to learn. Use a blog site provided by your instructor or one of the free blog sites provided on the website for this text.

Blog

PLAN AHEAD

Learn about a business Select a local business or large, nationally known company to research. Talk to employees, read newspaper or magazine articles, or do research on the Internet to find information about the company. Create a short report that gives the following information: (Learning Objective 2)

- Company name
- Type of business organization (partnership, corporation, etc.)
- Primary products or services offered
- Corporate culture (If you are doing research at the company website, look for a statement of values, mission statement, causes supported, or similar information.)
- A copy of the organizational chart (Create a chart if one is not available.)

CHAPTER 2

Your Professional Image

LEARNING OBJECTIVES

1. Describe the characteristics that contribute to a positive professional image.
2. Identify the components of a professional appearance.
3. Understand the conventions of business etiquette.

Characteristics of a Professional

You have probably heard the expressions "a picture is worth a thousand words" and "you never get a second chance to make a first impression." When it comes to how you present and conduct yourself in a business environment, whether it is in that first interview or every day on the job with coworkers and clients, these expressions ring far truer than most people would like to admit.

Appearance is only part of the equation when creating and maintaining your **professional image**. The impressions you make on others, your attitude toward your work and your coworkers, your work ethic, your professional dress, and your familiarity with business etiquette all work together to form your professional image. Your ability to get a job, keep a job, and advance in your career will hinge on your professional image.

Successful businesspeople are those that spend time cultivating their professional image. In survey after survey, business leaders are asked what they look for when seeking new employees, and the most common responses deal with professional image. Although skills, education, and certification in specialized areas are important, employers are looking for successful individuals who possess a variety of professional characteristics as well. Successful individuals work hard to make a good first impression, present a positive attitude, and demonstrate their professionalism through their exceptional work ethic.

First Impressions

The power of a first impression is immeasurable. Think back to the day when you first set foot on your college campus. You are very likely to recall, no matter how long ago it was, exactly how you felt, even if you do not remember all the details. Whether it was positive or negative, you remember the first impression that it made. Have you ever driven to a store or restaurant and decided not to enter because of the way it looked? Once again you made a decision based on a first impression.

Businesspeople also form a quick first impression of you, usually during the first 7 to 10 seconds of a meeting or interview. During that short period of time, you are being evaluated on your demeanor, mannerisms, **body language**, and grooming. The successful professional will not leave this first impression to chance. Instead, he or she will take the time to review his or her attitude, clothing, manners, and body language to ensure that the impression made is a positive one and one that will work to his or her advantage. What can you do to make a positive first impression?

- Be on time or arrive early. Arriving on time for an interview or meeting shows the person you are meeting with that the contact is important to you. When leaving for an appointment, allow extra time for traffic problems and other unforeseen delays. Although arriving early is always better than arriving late, do not arrive more than 15 minutes prior to your appointment time. If you have some extra time, get a cup of coffee, take a walk, or find a quiet place to review your notes. Timeliness is the first step in creating a positive first impression.
- Be comfortable and confident with your skills and abilities. If you are confident and comfortable with yourself, you will make the other person feel more at ease. This will help in presenting yourself in a positive light.
- Dress professionally. Whether you like it or not, people often make judgments based on the way you look. If the person you are meeting does not know you, your appearance is often their first clue to your personality. Pay careful attention to the section on professional dress and grooming that appears later in this chapter. What you wear and your personal hygiene make a strong statement about you.
- Smile. A warm and confident smile goes a long way toward making a good first impression. It will also put you and the other person at ease. Be careful not to seem insincere. Make sure your words and actions support the smile on your face.
- Be conscious of body language. You may have heard the expression "your actions speak louder than words." Standing tall, making eye contact, and greeting people with a firm handshake all go a long way toward making a good first impression. Avoid fidgeting, twirling your hair, and playing with your jewelry. Crossing your arms may signal that you are angry. Crossing your legs may show you in more of a casual light.
- Be positive. Remember, your attitude shows through in everything you do.
- Be courteous. Good manners and polite, courteous behavior help make a good first impression. In fact, anything less can ruin the one chance you have at making that first impression count. Give the person you are meeting with 100 percent of your attention. Turn off your cell phone, and do not become distracted by what is going on around you. Focus all your attention on the person with whom you are meeting.

Maridav/Shutterstock.com

You have only a few seconds to make a good first impression.

Photographer/Image Source

Getting the job is the first step, but keeping the job is the next step. The importance of getting started on the right foot cannot be overemphasized. A professional employee will learn what the employer expects from him or her and will understand the company's policies. Some pointers for helping you keep your job are as follows:

- Cooperate with others to get a task done.
- Be willing to compromise.
- Do your share of the work.
- Be willing to learn from others and consider suggestions.
- Be polite and friendly—good manners cost you nothing but will gain you a lot of respect.
- Be sensitive to the feelings of others.
- Help make your workplace a pleasant environment.
- Avoid gossiping, taking sides, complaining, and questioning the way everything is done.
- Give help when needed.
- Be honest—if you make a mistake, admit it and try harder.
- Be flexible.

Many workers discover their first job is not as exciting as they thought it might be. Keep a positive attitude and improve your skills. This will prepare you for more challenging work.

Source: Adapted from "Keeping the Job," Kentucky Office of Employment and Training, http://www.oet.ky.gov/des/vws/general_job_search/keeping_the_job.asp (accessed February 11, 2011).

Because you have just a few seconds to make a good first impression, it is important always to put your best foot forward. Whether you are meeting with prospective employers, colleagues, or other business associates, you must strive to make a positive first impression. Remember, it is almost impossible to change that first impression, so take the time and put forth the effort to make your first impression your best.

Positive Attitude

Attitude can be defined as disposition, feelings, or moods regarding events, circumstances, or people. Your attitude comes through in everything you do, from answering the phone to working with others in the office. Although attitude can be positive or negative, it is something a person can control. Every day a person has a choice as to what attitude to have. While there are things in life a person cannot change, individuals can change their attitudes and how they look at things.

Many people in business say attitude is more important than education. When an employer must decide between two equally qualified candidates, attitude is often the tiebreaker, and the person with the positive attitude comes out the winner. A positive attitude has other benefits as well. Research indicates that it promotes better health. Studies have shown that such an attitude actually retards aging, makes you healthier, and helps you develop better mechanisms for coping with stress.

Our attitude, whether positive or negative, affects those around us. People like to spend time with someone who is positive; they do not like to spend time with someone who is negative. Stay away from negative people. If possible, avoid places where negative people gather. If a conversation turns negative, politely excuse yourself. Also, a positive attitude is contagious. If you choose to project a confident, satisfied, positive image, those around you have a tendency to feel and act the same way.

How do you create a positive attitude? One way is to surround yourself with positive people who encourage you and believe in you. Spending time with positive people who make you feel good about yourself and your situation will help you maintain a positive attitude. Everyone can possess a positive attitude. A positive attitude begins with a healthy self-image. If you choose to love the way you are, and are satisfied, confident, and self-assured, you will make others around you feel the same way. Focus on the positive things in life, and you are more likely to exhibit a positive attitude.

Maintaining a positive attitude is not always easy. In fact, at times it is difficult to see things in a positive way. It helps to remember that not only is your positive attitude beneficial to you, but it is also valued and appreciated by those around you. You may find that you can accomplish more, and it can be accomplished more effectively, if you take on the task with a positive attitude. You are more likely to be offered the opportunity to take on important responsibilities, or even be considered for a promotion, if your attitude is positive.

Work Ethic

What is a work ethic? A **work ethic** is a set of values based on the merits of hard work and diligence. It is also a belief in the benefit of work and its ability to build a person's character. Coming to work on time, being prepared for meetings, and working cooperatively with others in your office says a lot about your work ethic. Exhibiting the right attitude, skills, and professional ethics is a positive start to developing an effective work ethic.

If you wish to be successful, you must develop a positive work ethic. Think about the type of work ethic you currently convey. Are you loyal to your employer? Do you take your job responsibilities seriously? Individuals with a strong work ethic typically display the following characteristics:

- Arrive at work on time and stay until their shift is over
- Meet all deadlines (both scheduled and unscheduled)
- Exhibit a sense of integrity and trustworthiness
- Follow established rules and procedures
- Make productive use of work time

A person with a strong work ethic demonstrates responsibility and initiative, is reliable, and maintains appropriate social skills. Individuals with a strong work ethic show their integrity by using their sick days only when they are sick and by taking vacation days only as scheduled. If a worker's lunch hour is scheduled for noon and a customer needs assistance at that time, the individual with the strong work ethic will take care of the customer's needs first. Always putting forth your best effort and doing your best work demonstrates a strong work ethic.

Having a strong work ethic does not mean that you are a **workaholic**—a person who is addicted to work. It equates to putting in a full day's work for a full day's pay; it does not mean that you are working overtime for free. Instead, the successful professional will find a comfortable and practical balance between work and personal life. Remember, individuals who exhibit a strong work ethic are often those who get the job, are given additional responsibility and higher wages, and are considered for promotions.

Other Professional Characteristics

Possessing and demonstrating the workplace skills discussed in Chapter 1 and throughout this text is important to your professional image. Possessing the skills necessary to effectively complete your job responsibilities is vital, but the ability to effectively manage your time, anger, and stress and to make decisions is equally important. Demonstrating to your supervisor, coworkers, and clients your expertise in the following workplace skills contributes positively to your professional image:

- Communication (listening, reading, verbal presentation, and writing)
- Interpersonal relations
- Time management
- Critical thinking
- Decision making
- Creative thinking
- Teamwork
- Technology
- Leadership

PARTNERSHIP FOR 21ST CENTURY SKILLS

Initiative/Self-Direction

Take Initiative

Every day in the office, there are many tasks and projects that need to be completed. An effective administrative professional has the ability to recognize what needs to be done. Putting paper in an empty printer tray, answering a telephone when the receptionist is busy, or volunteering to serve on a committee are all examples of initiative. You do not have to volunteer for the largest and most complex project to show initiative. You demonstrate initiative by taking the projects that are given to you and completing them successfully.

Some projects in an organization are large in scope and require the effort of many people. Another way to show initiative is to seek out tasks beyond those that have been assigned to you. Be aware of company projects, and take an active part in bringing these projects to completion. However, volunteer your skills or services only if you have the necessary expertise and time. Do not volunteer if you cannot fulfill the request.

Initiative is the ability not only to begin but also to follow through on a project. When you volunteer for a project, analyze what needs to be done, and then follow through with it. Make only promises you intend to keep. Although initiative is a personal and professional quality that can be hard to measure, it is a necessary trait for a successful administrative professional.

Activity

What does initiative mean to you? Describe how you can demonstrate initiative in your classes. How can you demonstrate initiative in achieving your goal of becoming an administrative professional? Create a list of ways a new employee can demonstrate initiative to his or her supervisor.

Dmitriy Shironosov/Shutterstock.com

- Stress management
- Problem solving
- Customer focus

As discussed in Chapter 1, the effective administrative professional possesses certain personal characteristics. If you wish to be successful, review the personal qualities listed in Chapter 1. These qualities include the following:

- Openness to change
- Initiative and motivation

Digital Vision/Getty Images

A neat, organized desk enhances your professional image.

- Integrity and honesty
- Dependability
- Discretion
- Commitment to observing and learning

Remember, these personal qualities and job skills in isolation will not make you successful. If you wish to be a successful administrative professional, you must integrate them with other personal success qualities. They are not your complete professional image; they are only a part of it.

Work Characteristics

Your work area is another avenue for you to present a positive professional image because it is an extension of your professional appearance. Whether you work at a desk in an open area of the office, in a cubicle among many cubicles, or in a small, enclosed office, the appearance of that workplace says a lot to others about your professionalism and your attitude toward your work. Careful attention should be focused on both your workspace and your desk.

YOUR WORKSPACE

The area around your desk, or your workspace, should be neat and orderly. In most instances it is acceptable to personalize this area, but make sure to keep it professional. It is still a place of business, not an extension of your home. A few personal photos and a small plant demonstrate that you are an employee who takes pride in your home and family, but do not make visitors feel as if they are uninvited guests in your living room.

To get a sense for how others view your workspace, periodically sit in the visitors' chair at your desk. Look around to see what your guests see. Things can look very different from the other side of the desk. Although it may be appropriate to display certificates or awards, do not overwhelm your space with these types of documents. A tasteful display of relevant certificates will enhance your professional image.

YOUR DESK

A professional has an organized desk. Your work supplies, including stapler, paper, envelopes, paper clips, and pens, should be organized and easily accessible. Keep current projects and completed projects organized as well. Being able to locate material quickly and efficiently demonstrates your professionalism.

Keep your desk clean. When something is no longer useful, move it from your desk to the garbage or the recycling bin. Keep food and drinks away from your computer and the papers on your desk. In addition to the potential for damaged equipment and messes, assorted cans and bottles do not present a professional image. Eating at your desk does not give you the necessary break most professionals need. In fact, some workplace policies prohibit individuals from having food items at their desks at any time.

YOUR DAILY WORK

What does the quality of your work say about you? Are coworkers likely to come to you for assistance with a project or problem? Their impression of how you work is an excellent indicator of how customers and clients view the work that you have done. Part of your professional image is based on the quality of the work you produce. Use accepted formats when creating business letters, reports, and other documents. An attractive and professional-looking document is a positive reflection on you and your organization.

Attention to detail is very important. Documents that are properly formatted and proofread, names and titles that are spelled correctly and used correctly, and papers that are clean and folded evenly all indicate the level of professionalism that is appreciated by your employer and your clients. You have probably heard the expression "don't sweat the small stuff." Although this may be good advice, generally do not ignore the small details related to your work. In the business world, the "small stuff" should never be done haphazardly! The way you complete small or routine tasks says a great deal about your attention to detail.

If you make a mistake, it is imperative that you take responsibility for the error and do your best to correct it. Acknowledge the error, apologize to those the error affects, and develop a plan to avoid repeating the mistake in the future. Not only will your supervisor appreciate this approach, but so will your coworkers, as all too often people try to blame others for their errors.

Professional Business Cards

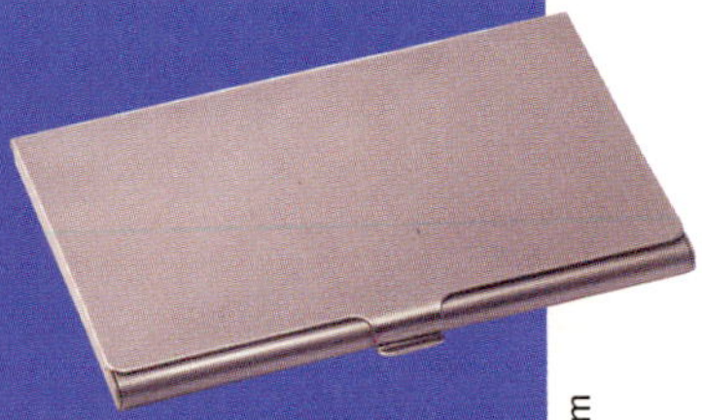

Denis Sokolov/Shutterstock.com

You work hard to present a professional image. Your business card says a great deal about you as well. Business cards should be displayed neatly on your desk so they are accessible to current and prospective clients. A professional business card will include the following information:

- Company name and logo
- Name and professional title
- Business address including city, state, and ZIP Code
- Office telephone number and fax number
- E-mail address and/or web address

The professional always stores business cards in a professional holder. Nothing detracts from your professional image more than tattered, bent, and dirty business cards.

Professional Organizations

Participating in professional organizations can help you improve your professional image. Through organizations such as the International Association of Administrative Professionals (IAAP) and ARMA International, administrative professionals can attain certifications that attest to their skills and knowledge in given areas. Professional organizations often provide websites, articles, newsletters, and seminars that can help you improve your skills. Knowing that you take the time and effort to try to improve your skills and knowledge will help give your superiors and coworkers a positive image of you.

You might also belong to a professional organization related to the industry or organization in which you work. For example, suppose you work as an administrative professional for a school system, and you deal largely with the system's adult education programs. You might join an organization such as the American Association for Adult and Continuing Education. Through the organization's publications and website, you could learn about research and current issues in this field that could be helpful to you in your work. Being knowledgeable about issues related to your organization's work enhances your professional image.

Business Networking

Networking is the process of exchanging information and building positive business relationships. Although networking is often discussed in the context of a job search, networking has become an accepted part of everyday business. If you have ever recommended a business based on the quality of its work, a restaurant, a movie, or even a gas station, you have networked.

Networking is often a deliberate, planned process. It involves the open exchange of leads and introductions. People network in many different settings: on the telephone, in hallways, at professional conferences, at company meetings, in classrooms, in elevators, on airplanes, in hotel lobbies, at athletic events, at symphonies, in supermarkets, or just about anywhere. Some networking is carefully planned, and some just happens. Regardless of how networking takes place, the most effective networker shows a genuine interest in other people. The savvy professional uses networking skills to help develop a positive professional image.

To enhance your professional network, you may consider joining an online professional network such as LinkedIn or BranchOut. These networks can help you stay connected to past and present colleagues and form associations with other individuals with similar interests. Professional networking sites provide an opportunity for you to network with others and encourage you to ask questions that can be answered by experts in your field. They are also helpful when looking for additional business contacts or opportunities.

Many people belong to one or more social networks, including Myspace, Facebook, and Twitter. Remember that the information you reveal, the words you use, and the images you post online are available to a wide audience. Make sure your images, profiles, and words are ones that you would want a potential employer and your coworkers to see. Making jokes that might be offensive, expressing yourself in an unprofessional way, or showing yourself in silly or compromising situations may seem like harmless fun when you are young. However, that sort of image can reflect badly on you in the workplace.

Your Professional Look

People may think that the quality of a person's work will match the quality of the person's appearance. Your appearance may indicate your attention to

TECH TALK

Online Portfolios

An online portfolio is used to document your education, show examples of your work, and present a concise listing of your skills. Everyone's online portfolio will be unique; however, all online portfolios should contain information related to the person's specific accomplishments and career aspirations. Career portfolios serve as evidence of skills and abilities. In addition to personal information such as a skills list, an online portfolio may contain copies of transcripts, employee evaluations, sample work, awards, and recommendations.

The first step in creating an effective online portfolio is to gather the materials you wish to include. You will need digital versions of all items, so you may need to scan documents and convert them into PDF files if they are not already in digital format. Gather any other computer files so they are easily accessible when you are ready to begin. Next, locate an Internet service to store your portfolio. Many free host sites are available. Once you have secured a site, you will need to upload your files and determine how you would like them organized. Keep your information simple, and make the site easy to navigate. If you are using the portfolio as a job search tool, make sure your contact information is visible on all pages. Because your portfolio contains personal information, choose a host site that allows you to password-protect your information so that it is not available to everyone. Links to sites with sample online portfolios are provided on the website for this text.

detail, your level of motivation, and your sense of professionalism. What you wear and how you present yourself says a lot about you and can damage or even destroy your chances of success in business.

Dressing the Part

People often make judgments about others based on how they look. Remember that people establish their first impressions during the first 7 to 10 seconds of an initial meeting. Because not much is said in this short time, this early judgment is based strictly on appearance. Although the person wearing jeans and a T-shirt may be both competent and intelligent, that person is often not taken as seriously as the person wearing a formal suit. In addition, your attitude and confidence level are affected by the clothes you wear. If you dress more casually, you may tend to behave more casually as well.

Professional dress also affects an individual's chances for promotion. You certainly should always follow the dress code. Make sure your clothes are clean and pressed. If you want to be respected as a professional and considered for promotion, dress the way that the individuals currently in that position dress. A good rule of thumb is to dress one step above your current level in the organization or to dress as well as the best-dressed person in the organization.

It may seem unfair, but your clothes, including your shoes, say a lot about the person you are. For example, a person wearing scuffed loafers may be viewed as lacking discipline and attention to detail. Therefore, understanding what is and is not appropriate for business dress in today's work world is an important first step to getting and keeping the job you really want. An appropriate business wardrobe is not the same in every organization. Some organizations have dress codes that are very conservative, while others have a more casual approach. The next two sections provide examples of a conservative professional wardrobe and casual business attire.

PROFESSIONAL BUSINESS ATTIRE

In the business world, professional business attire for women is typically a suit or tailored dress in a traditional color such as black, navy blue, brown, beige, or gray. The skirt should extend to the knee or below and should not have high slits or openings. A sleeved blouse in a light color that complements the color of the suit should be worn. Closed-toe, low-heeled, conservative pumps are also suggested. Women should avoid wearing spiked heels, sandals, and shoes with flashy beading or stitching. Hosiery should always be worn and should be neutral or skin-tone in color. Remember to make sure that your shoes and accessories are clean and polished.

Although pantsuits are becoming more acceptable in the business environment, do not assume that they are acceptable in all instances. Many conservative businesses still adhere to a strict professional dress code. If you have questions about the appropriateness of a particular type of clothing or accessory, check with someone in the organization or the human resources department first. If you are not sure, a traditional skirted suit is always the safest bet. Keep in mind that professional dress is always the best choice for an interview.

Professional business attire for men is a two-piece matched suit in a conservative color such as navy, dark gray, or black. A long-sleeved dress shirt in white or a light color is also required. Ties are mandatory, and men are encouraged to select a conservative tie that matches the suit. Shoes should be either brown or black leather and polished. Socks should match the suit and should pull up over the calves so skin does not show when sitting down. A simple leather belt that matches the color of the shoes should also be worn.

BUSINESS CASUAL ATTIRE

In the last several years, a new category of business dress has emerged. This new category, often referred to as **business casual dress**, has relaxed some of the conservative standards of the past. Although the business casual code allows an individual to dress in a more relaxed manner, it still means dressing professionally. Business casual is not a license to be sloppy or dress inappropriately; individuals are still required to have a neat and coordinated appearance.

For women, business casual may consist of a business skirt or casual pants. As with the professional category, the skirt should be at least knee length. Anything shorter is never appropriate in a

Yuri Arcurs/Shutterstock.com

A conservative suit is still the preferred professional attire in much of the business world.

business setting. Although casual slacks may be acceptable, in some instances khakis may be viewed as too casual for women. Typically short-sleeved shirts or blouses are considered more casual than the long-sleeved blouses worn with suits. Knit sweaters or sweater sets are also considered business casual. Leather shoes with a low or flat heel fit into this category.

Business casual does not mean that anything goes. Short skirts and sundresses are never considered appropriate business attire. Regardless of sleeve length, shirts should not be tight or expose too much skin. Although tennis shoes and flip-flops may be comfortable to wear during your leisure time, they are always considered too casual for a business setting.

In general, the best advice is to conduct research on the business before selecting your clothing. If you work for a company where there is no dress code, you will not be too far off if you study how those in senior management dress and emulate them. Also, do not be afraid to ask someone; it only shows that you care enough to get things right.

For men, business casual dress at a large corporation may mean a sport coat with a tie rather than a business suit. At a smaller company, business casual dress may mean khakis and a polo shirt. Once again, the best rule of thumb is not to make assumptions but rather to watch what others are wearing before making your clothing selections. Athletic shoes, hiking boots, and sandals are never appropriate (even in the summer). Men should wear leather shoes, dark socks that pull up over the calf, and a belt that matches the shoes. Research and find out exactly what business casual means for your organization.

OTHER DRESS CONSIDERATIONS

In addition to business standards or formalized dress codes, there are other variables that you may consider when deciding what to wear. Points to keep in mind when purchasing your business wardrobe may include the following:

- Climate. Wool suits may work well in northern climates where the weather is cool but would not be as appropriate in the sunshine states.
- Regional variations. Wall Street brokers may dress more conservatively than those working in a more trendy city such as Los Angeles.
- Business environment. When choosing clothing, you should consider what type of company you work for and the kind of work you will do. For example, if you are a woman working in the construction field, you would not want to be walking around a construction site wearing high heels.
- Type of occasion. The function you are attending should always be considered. If you are attending an evening event, your jewelry may be more elaborate than what you would wear to a breakfast meeting. The polo shirt that would

be acceptable when attending an outdoor event would certainly be out of place at an annual board meeting.

Appearance

Attention to personal appearance is just as important to your professional image as what you wear. In addition to selecting the right clothes, attention to personal hygiene is necessary. The checklist shown in Figure 2.1 will help you remember the important grooming issues that should be considered.

Remember, some individuals are allergic to fragrance. If you choose to wear perfume or cologne, make sure that it is never strong. In consideration of others, the best rule to follow is to use a little or not to use any at all.

Jewelry

For women, jewelry should not be gaudy or appear overpowering, and it should not be noisy. Some women are more relaxed when asked to shake hands if they don't have to worry about rings digging into someone's fingers. An easy guide for women suggests wearing no more than six or seven pieces of jewelry (earrings, a watch, two rings, a bracelet, and a necklace). For men, a conservative watch and wedding ring are appropriate. Even for business casual dress, jewelry should be minimal.

Appearance Guidelines	
Aftershave/ cologne	Little (light fragrance) or none at all
Body	Freshly bathed; deodorant; clean face and hands
Breath	Fresh
Facial hair (men)	Clean-shaven; mustache or beard neatly trimmed
Fingernails	Neat, clean, and trimmed; natural-looking
Hair	Clean, trimmed, and neatly combed and styled
Makeup	Not too much; fresh and natural-looking
Teeth	Brushed and clean

FIGURE 2.1 Paying careful attention to your appearance can help create a professional image.

Although multiple body piercings are becoming more common in today's society, in the strict world of business, unconventional body piercing is not always accepted. Many companies address the issue of body piercing in their dress codes. It is not uncommon for company policies to indicate that the only visible body piercing acceptable for male and female employees is the conventional earlobe piercing or piercing for cultural reasons. In fact, some business dress codes require employees to remove any visible jewelry for body piercing that does not fall into these categories.

Some dress codes also stipulate that employees cover any visible tattoos. If you wish to work in a conservative business setting, it is probably a good idea to remove jewelry from additional piercings on your ears or face during a job interview. If the issue of tattoos and piercings is important to you and it is not addressed during your interview, ask for a copy of the dress code from the human resources department before you leave the interview.

Understanding Business Etiquette

Presenting a professional image also requires that individuals utilize appropriate etiquette. **Etiquette** can be described as a code that governs acceptable behavior developed through customs and enforced by group pressure.[1] Business etiquette is the special code of behavior required in employment situations. Although these standards of behavior may vary slightly from business to business, it is important to understand the main categories of business etiquette in order to enhance your professional image. Understanding appropriate business etiquette helps people become successful and productive employees.

[1] "Etiquette," *Encyclopedia Britannica*, http://www.britannica.com/eb/article-9033150 (accessed February 12, 2011).

Good manners are important in maintaining effective relationships.

General Courtesy and Manners

One of the most common ways we judge an individual's grasp of etiquette is through his or her display of manners. **Manners** are the standards of conduct that show us how to behave in a cultured, polite, or refined way. Although there are no laws governing manners, social judgments are made based on whether or not we include courtesy and manners in our behavior toward others. Manners, then, are the general rules by which we need to live. They are the rules that guide us in our treatment of others.

A *courteous* person is respectful and considerate of others. Courtesy can be described as exhibiting excellent manners or polite behavior. Most of us learn about manners and courtesy when we are young. By the time children enter school, they are expected to behave politely in school and in other social settings. Much of what we learn can be summed up in the golden rule: Treat others as you would like to be treated.

Courtesy and good manners are important in maintaining effective business relationships. Unfortunately, instances of rudeness in the workplace continue to occur, and the effects go beyond just unease. According to an article in *Inc.* magazine, when individuals in the workplace are rude, people lose concentration and make mistakes.[2] In addition, research discussed in the *Harvard Business Review* states that in reaction to rudeness at work, employees decreased their work effort, their time at work, and their work quality.[3]

Good manners are based on consideration for other people. Three important phrases you should always remember to say are "please," "thank you," and "I'm sorry." Use the word *please* freely and with sincerity. If you do, you will find others more willing to work with you and assist you. Thank people for what they do for you. Whether it is as simple as opening a door for you or helping you carry a heavy box, say thank you with a smile and genuine feeling. Thanking others for their efforts goes a long way toward creating a positive working environment. If you know you have made a mistake, do not hesitate to apologize. Learn to say you are sorry for even the smallest mistake, and take responsibility for your behaviors or actions.

Greeting people appropriately is also a function of good manners. As we pass individuals in the hall, it is appropriate to acknowledge them and to greet them. Acknowledging someone's presence with a polite "hello" shows good manners. Asking how someone is doing shows an interest in that person. Acknowledging someone's existence shows that you care about that person and his or her well-being.

---

[2]Courtney Rubin, "The High Cost of Rudeness in the Workplace," *Inc.*, July 12, 2010, http://www.inc.com/news/articles/2010/07/how-rudeness-affects-the-workplace.html (accessed February 16, 2011).

[3]Christine Porath and Christine Pearson, "How Toxic Colleagues Corrode Performance," *Harvard Business Review*, April 2009, http://hbr.org/2009/04/how-toxic-colleagues-corrode-performance/ar/1 (accessed February 17, 2011).

If you are a smoker, good manners require that you do not smoke where you will cause discomfort to another person. In many public buildings, including workplaces, smoking is not allowed indoors. Smoking may be allowed outside the building in designated places. In some public buildings, smoking is allowed in designated areas. Be considerate of others who do not wish to be exposed to smoke by smoking only where you will not affect others.

Dining and Restaurant Etiquette

Much of today's business takes place during business meals. If you want to make a positive impression in a dining situation, you must use appropriate table manners. Regardless of whether you are having lunch with a business associate or dinner with a prospective client, your dining etiquette speaks volumes about you as a professional. There are different responsibilities you should assume if you are hosting the meal function or just attending as a guest. Review the following material to make sure you are presenting your best professional image during meal functions.

HOSTING A BUSINESS MEAL

If you are hosting a business meal, it is your responsibility to extend the invitation to your guests. You may offer your guests a few date or time alternatives and allow them to make the final selection of date, time, and restaurant. If possible, select a restaurant that will allow you to make reservations. As host, you should arrive 10 to 15 minutes early so you can greet your guests. Arriving early also gives you time to make arrangements as to how the bill will be paid.

As the host, you should be comfortable enough with the restaurant menu to make meal recommendations to your guests. If not, ask your server for suggestions. Allow your guests to order first, and encourage them to feel comfortable to order whatever they wish. As the host, order something easy to eat so you can carry on a conversation during the meal. If this is a business meal, it is appropriate to discuss business but not until the major portion of the meal is over.

Table manners play an important part in presenting a professional image during dining. Regardless of whether a person is dining with a business associate, a customer, or friends, manners say a lot about that person. Figure 2.2 lists table manners that should always be followed.

ATTENDING A BUSINESS MEAL

If you are the guest at a business meal, remember that the host should indicate the beginning of the meal by unfolding the napkin and placing it in his or her lap. The host should signal the end of the meal by placing the napkin back on the table. If the menu has not been preselected, the host will typically suggest that you order first. Avoid ordering the most expensive items on the menu or making several changes to a menu item.

When eating, remember to use your utensils in the order they are placed, from the outside moving inward toward the plate. A good rule to follow is to eat to your left and drink to your right. Your bread dish will be on your left, and your water goblet and wine glass will be on your right. Do not reach across the table or in front of others to get food or condiments. Pass food from the left to the right.

Table Manners
■ The guest should always order first.
■ Order items that are easy to eat.
■ Leave your cell phone behind or turn it off.
■ Sit up straight and keep your elbows off the table.
■ Do not eat too quickly or too slowly. Try to keep pace with the others at the table.
■ Never chew with your mouth open or try to speak with food in your mouth.
■ If you use the wrong piece of flatware, do not panic. Continue using it and ask the server for a replacement when you need it.
■ Once you pick up a piece of cutlery, it should never touch the table again. Put it on your dish, rather than leaning it half on and half off the dish.

FIGURE 2.2 Using proper table manners helps create a professional image.

iofoto/Shutterstock.com

Dining etiquette is an important component of your professional image.

When you are finished with your meal, do not push your plate away from you; instead, lay your fork and knife diagonally across your plate. If you are unsure about anything during the meal, watch your host or others around you. When the host signals the end of the meal, place your napkin on the table and thank your host.

The two typical dining styles are continental and American. With the American style of dining, the knife is used only for cutting. During cutting, the knife is held in the right hand and the fork in the left hand to help control the object being cut. The knife is then put down on the edge of the plate (blade facing in), and the fork is switched to the right hand to lift the cut food to the mouth. Remember to keep your hands in your lap when not being used.

With the continental dining style, the knife remains in the right hand and the fork in the left. After the food is cut, the knife is used to push the food onto the fork. The tines of the fork face downward when the cut food is lifted to the mouth. The hands remain above the table when they are not in use.

International Customs and Etiquette

For success in today's global economy, it is important to realize that appropriate etiquette can vary greatly among cultures. It would be foolish to assume that the behaviors considered appropriate for a business function in the United States are the same for all countries. Instead, it's important to take a proactive approach and research the country you are visiting so you are aware of its special customs.

INTERNATIONAL DINING ETIQUETTE

Appropriate dining etiquette varies widely by culture. For example, table etiquette in Japan involves saying traditional phrases before and after a meal to signal the beginning and ending of the meal. Also, when eating Western food, Japanese people use knives and forks. However, because chopsticks are the most frequently used utensils, be prepared to use them if traditional Japanese dishes are on the menu.[4] If you wish to be a successful businessperson in Japan, learn how to use chopsticks and how to eat Japanese food.

When you are invited to dinner in China, it is appropriate to sample every dish that is served. It is also polite to leave some food on your plate, to indicate that you have had enough to eat. However, when you are dining in Germany, leaving food on your plate is considered wasteful.

As you can see, dining etiquette varies by culture and country. The best advice is to do your research so that you are prepared for whatever situation you may encounter.

[4]Shizuko Mishima, "Japanese Table Manners," http://gojapan.about.com/cs/tablemanners/a/tablemanner.htm (accessed February 12, 2011).

INTERNATIONAL BUSINESS DRESS

The best suggestion for professional dress in countries outside the United States is to follow the most conservative professional standards found in the United States. Many countries expect this high level of formality in business dress.

In the Netherlands, conservative business attire is recommended at all times. Dark suits and ties for men and white blouses and dark suits or skirts for women are expected. Suits are required in Russia, and it is considered rude for men to remove their jackets during a business meeting. In Saudi Arabia, men are expected to wear long-sleeved shirts that button up to the collar. For women, high necklines with skirts that fall well below the knee are required.

Accessories should also be carefully researched and selected. In Saudi Arabia, men should avoid wearing any visible jewelry, especially around the neck. Although jewelry is acceptable in Germany, it should never be flashy or gaudy. Women must display manicured nails in Brazil. Men should never wear anything on the lapel in Chile. Make sure to research the customs of the country you are visiting to avoid embarrassment.

OTHER INTERNATIONAL ISSUES

It is impossible to list and describe all the cultural issues that may be relevant when conducting business in another country. Do not assume that one country is the same as all others. The best policy is to research the customs, culture, and etiquette of the country you are visiting so that you are prepared to act in a professional manner. Several items to consider when working with international colleagues, customers, or clients are listed here.

- Giving gifts may be an important ritual of business, or gifts may be strictly off-limits.
- Religious and national holidays and their customs may affect how and when business can be conducted.
- Business hours are not always the same as the typical hours observed in the United States. Businesses in other countries may start later, stay open later, or close in the afternoon for a rest period.
- Greetings vary by culture. Know when it is appropriate to shake hands, hug, or kiss.
- Time has different connotations in different cultures and countries. In some cultures, being late is expected, while in other cultures, tardiness is unacceptable.
- Be cognizant of your gestures and body language. It is possible to offend someone with a hand gesture that is acceptable in the United States but considered rude in other countries.

Visit a library or bookstore to learn about the country you will visit. You may also conduct research using the web. Some of these suggestions will also be helpful when interacting with a client or coworker from another culture. This topic will be discussed further in Chapters 3 and 7.

Making Introductions

The way you meet and greet individuals in business situations creates lasting impressions. Making appropriate introductions will put you and the people you are introducing at ease. Introductions are the first encounter an individual will have with others, so make sure to make them positive. Keep in mind that business introductions should be made based on professional rank, not gender. This means that the person of highest rank should be introduced first. Follow these guidelines when making introductions:

- Name the most important person first.
- Say each person's name clearly.
- In more formal introductions, use a courtesy or professional title (*Mr., Mrs., Ms., Miss, Dr.*) and last name. If you do not know what title a woman prefers, use *Ms.*
- Add interesting information (if you know something) about each person. "Terri Ruiz, please meet Robert Hailey, the vice president for Humber Electronics. Mr. Hailey transferred from Cleveland to the Detroit office. Mr. Hailey, Ms. Ruiz is the president of Mill Falls Electric."

The most important point to remember about introductions is to remember to make them. Failing to introduce a business customer to a colleague is

Put people at ease by making appropriate introductions.

embarrassing and rude. It may also cost your company business. Forgetting a person's name is not an acceptable excuse to skip an introduction. In fact, people would prefer you to make an incorrect introduction rather than to have them stand there unacknowledged and disregarded.

At times, you will be the person who is being introduced. When this is the case, follow these guidelines:

- Stand up (both men and women) when meeting someone.
- Smile and establish eye contact with the individual.
- Greet the other person; state your name and position.
- Shake hands firmly. However, you do not want to shake hands so firmly that the other person feels as though his or her hand is being crushed. Neither do you want to shake hands so limply that the other person feels no expression of warmth from you.
- Repeat the other person's name.
- Establish a conversation with the person. It does not need to be a lengthy conversation; a brief exchange of words is acceptable.
- After the conversation is over, let the person know you enjoyed meeting him or her. You might say, "I certainly enjoyed meeting you, and I look forward to seeing you in the future."

It is good manners and good etiquette to remember the names of work associates to whom you are introduced, even if you see them only occasionally. If you forget the name of a person, it is better to admit this than to guess and come up with the wrong name. Refer to Figure 2.3 to review how to introduce yourself.

Other Workplace Etiquette

Although proper etiquette in the workplace includes good manners, it does not stop there. Workplace etiquette includes learning how to behave around everyone you come in contact with including coworkers, superiors, and visitors in the office. It includes learning the appropriate behavior in a variety of business situations.

YOUR COWORKERS AND SUPERIORS

You must know how to establish cordial and respectful relationships with your coworkers. Not only do you need to work closely with them every day, but you often depend on them to get your job done. Do not use slang or inappropriate labels when speaking

Introducing Yourself
■ Stand.
■ Smile and establish eye contact with the individual.
■ Greet the other person; state your name and position.
■ Shake hands firmly.
■ Repeat the other person's name.

FIGURE 2.3 Acting appropriately during an introduction helps create a professional image.

International Greetings

Keep in mind that although the handshake is an acceptable greeting in the United States, other countries have different greeting customs.

Country	Greeting
China	Give a slight nod and bow; if people applaud, you should respond with applause.
Thailand	Place hands in a prayer position with your head slightly bowed (called the *Wai*); the higher your hands, the more respect shown.
Poland	Men may greet women by kissing their hands; women greet other women with a slight embrace and kiss on the cheek.
Colombia	Women hold forearms instead of shaking hands.

Source: "Handshaking," Operation STRIDE, Fort Detrick, Maryland, http://www.detrick.army.mil/stride/handshaking.cfm (accessed February 12, 2011).

It is important to complete your research before you conduct business in other countries. Learn the business customs and what constitutes an appropriate greeting or introduction.

with a coworker. Words like *honey* or *dear* have no place in the workplace. Do not ask a coworker to do something you would be uncomfortable or unwilling to do yourself. Remember, the best advice is to follow the golden rule and treat your coworkers as you would like to be treated.

The tone of the workplace and the formality of working relationships are typically determined by top management. This includes not only how people dress but how they address each other. Because this type of information is not written down anywhere, you will need to observe those around you. Typically, relationships in the business world are based on rank. A good rule of thumb is to address your superiors with a courtesy title followed by a surname. Do not use first names unless or until you are specifically invited to do so.

Some behaviors should be avoided. Swearing or using inappropriate language is never acceptable. Avoid telling gender, ethnic, or racial jokes. Hugging and kissing is never acceptable in a business situation. A good rule to follow is to refrain from doing anything that has the potential to make someone else uncomfortable.

GREETING VISITORS

When you receive a visitor in your office, remember that you are the host. Visitors will form their first impression of you and your company based on this initial meeting. How you treat a visitor says a lot about you and your company. Review Figure 2.4 to help you learn how to greet workplace visitors courteously and correctly.

Telephone Skills and Etiquette

Your use of the telephone and understanding of appropriate telephone etiquette also affect the professional image that you project. Often in an

Tips for Receiving Office Visitors

- When a visitor enters your office, greet the person graciously with a simple "good morning" or "good afternoon."
- Learn the visitor's name, and address the person by name.
- Determine the purpose of an unscheduled visit. Avoid blunt questions such as "What do you want?" A more appropriate question is "Could you please tell me what company you represent and the purpose of your visit?"
- Be pleasant to a difficult visitor. Be wary of visitors who try to avoid your inquiries with evasive answers such as "It's a personal matter." An appropriate response to such a statement is "My employer sees visitors only by appointment. I will be happy to set one up for you."
- Handle interruptions well. If you need to interrupt your employer with a message when a visitor is in his or her office, do so as unobtrusively as possible. You may call your employer on the phone or knock on the door and hand him or her a note.
- Let angry or upset visitors talk for a little while. Listen and try to understand the visitor's viewpoint. Usually the anger will dissipate after you have listened. Then you can help the person with the concern. If the visitor continues with inappropriate behavior, ask him or her to leave or call security personnel for help.

FIGURE 2.4 Be courteous and professional when greeting office visitors.

office situation, your calls may be overheard by others. Because of this, be mindful of the volume and tone of your voice, the language you use, and the content of your phone calls. You should avoid or limit personal calls while working. Telephone etiquette will be covered in greater detail in Chapters 9 and 10.

As you progress through this textbook, you will continue to be reminded about professional etiquette as it relates to business. E-mail etiquette is discussed in Chapter 8, "Written Communication"; telephone and cell phone etiquette are covered in Chapter 9, "Verbal Communication and Presentations," and Chapter 10, "Global Communication—Technology and Etiquette"; and behaviors and etiquette for meetings and events are discussed in Chapter 14, "Event and Meeting Planning."

SUMMARY

To reinforce what you have learned in this chapter, study this summary.

- Successful businesspeople spend time cultivating their professional image through making positive first impressions, presenting a positive attitude, exhibiting a strong work ethic, and demonstrating other professional and work characteristics.
- Because your appearance can help or damage your chances of success in business, research appropriate attire for business situations, and pay attention to grooming.
- Understanding and using appropriate business etiquette is an integral part of your professional image. Because appropriate etiquette varies greatly among cultures, research the country you are planning to visit to make sure you are ready to make a positive impression.

KEY TERMS

2

STUDY Tools

Located at www.cengagebrain.com

- Chapter Outlines
- Flashcards
- Interactive Quizzes
- Tech Tools
- Video Segments
- and More!

LET'S DISCUSS

1. Explain what you can do to make a positive first impression in a business situation.
2. Describe what is expected for professional dress for men and women in business.
3. Describe the appearance factors (other than clothing) that need to be considered when working in a conservative business environment.
4. Describe the responsibilities typically associated with hosting a business meal.
5. List four tips that will help you professionally greet office visitors.

PUT IT TO WORK

Behaving like a professional Jose Garcia was hired six months ago in an entry-level sales position. Although Jose is interested in sales, he would eventually like to move into a management position. For the most part, Jose feels that he is getting along well with his sales team and his supervisor.

Jose shares an office with Alex Franklin, one of his team members. Alex has made all his monthly sales quotas. His work habits, though, are not very professional. Jose notices that Alex arrives exactly at 8 a.m. and leaves immediately at 5 p.m. when the workday is over. He takes a coffee break at 10:15 and leaves for lunch exactly at noon, regardless of his workload. Last week when the phone rang at 11:50, Alex didn't answer because he had plans for lunch. When Alex was scheduled to attend a meeting on a Saturday morning, he called in "sick" the following Monday.

Jose has also noticed that in the last few weeks Alex has starting complaining about everything. He has made several negative comments about the required job duties. Last week Jose overheard Alex on the phone talking negatively about his supervisor. Jose has also noticed that people have started to avoid him when he is with Alex. In fact, yesterday when they walked into the break room, everyone left.

Next week, Alex has an interview in the marketing department with Eduardo Sanchez, the vice president for marketing. Alex has told Jose that he really wants this job and has asked Jose for help. Jose believes that Alex has great potential in sales and could be an effective employee with a little guidance. He agrees to meet Alex for dinner tomorrow to talk about the interview.

What tips can Jose give Alex for making a good first impression? What suggestions can Jose give Alex for showing a more positive attitude? What changes can Alex make to his work ethic that would help him present a more professional image? Think about both the advice Jose should give and the way he should give it. Jose wants to maintain his good working relationship with Alex and his professional image. (Learning Objective 1)

COMMUNICATE SUCCESSFULLY

1. **Making introductions** Write an appropriate introduction for each situation. (Learning Objective 3)
   - You are at a business dinner. You are introducing Kimberly Loukinen, a new student assistant, to your supervisor, Melody Hoover.
   - Leroy Sanchez, the president of the local Kiwanis club, is visiting your organization. You are introducing him to Thomas Lopez, the president of the organization.
   - You are shopping with your grandmother, Mrs. Bethany Rinaldi, and you run into your supervisor, Melody Hoover.
2. **Handshakes** As an administrative professional, you may be expected to greet customers or clients. Your supervisor has asked that you prepare a handout to distribute to new employees regarding appropriate business handshakes in the United States. Review the information you learned in this chapter, and conduct additional research if necessary. Create a handout that includes the steps to an appropriate handshake and at least five tips for conducting proper business handshakes. Select an appropriate document theme to create a professional-looking handout. (Learning Objective 3)
3. **Personal and work characteristics** Add a new post to the blog you created in Chapter 1. In this entry, reflect on the following statement: **This chapter has helped me recognize that I need to strengthen the following personal and work characteristics so that I portray a positive professional image.** (Learning Objective 1)

Blog

DEVELOP WORKPLACE SKILLS

4. **First impressions and workplace appearance** Your friend Elizabeth has been offered an interview for a teller position at a local bank. She is very excited and has asked for your advice on what to wear and how to make a good first impression. What suggestions can you give Elizabeth about appropriate professional dress for the interview? What tips can you give to help her make a positive first impression? (Learning Objectives 1 and 2)

5. **Professional image** Analyze the following situations. Describe in detail how you would handle each situation, and explain your reasoning. Key your answers. (Learning Objectives 1, 2, and 3)

- You are at a formal business luncheon with your supervisor. The waitress asks if you would like an alcoholic drink.
- A visitor whose appointment you forgot to cancel arrives as scheduled. Your supervisor is working under pressure to complete an important contract.
- You are invited to an outdoor picnic at your supervisor's house after work, and the invitation says business casual. You have an important meeting in the morning and need to wear a business suit to work; you will not have time to change before the party.
- You have made a rather serious error on a client's order. The client is not pleased about your error and calls your supervisor to complain.
- It is five minutes before you typically leave for lunch. Your supervisor asks you to make 50 copies of a 15-page report that he needs for a meeting immediately after lunch.
- You are on the elevator with several colleagues, and your cell phone rings.

BUILD RELATIONSHIPS

6. **Getting along** Anna Chung has recently been hired to work with you. You know Anna from school; she has been in a few classes with you. Although you think Anna has good skills, she is difficult to work with because of her negative attitude toward everything—her personal life, her relationships, her job, and her supervisor. In fact, Anna is rarely positive about anyone or anything. After a few weeks on the job, you are beginning to have negative feelings, too. You like your work and your supervisor, and you can see there will be opportunities for advancement. What can you do to overcome your negative feelings? What can you do to make working with Anna more productive? (Learning Objective 1)

USE TECH TOOLS

TT

7. **Online portfolio** Search the Internet to locate a free online portfolio service, or use one of the links provided on the website for this text. Create an account and design a home page to start building your professional online portfolio. Include professional images and words that would be appropriate for a potential employer. Create a portfolio that is flexible so that you can add information in the future.

e-Portfolio

PLAN AHEAD

Hiring practices Work with a classmate to complete this assignment. Identify someone from a local business who works in the human resources department or is responsible for hiring employees. Interview this person, asking him or her to respond to three of the following questions. Create two additional questions on your own.

- What personal qualities do you look for in an employee?
- What types of things do you first notice about an applicant?
- What do you look for when trying to determine an applicant's work ethic?
- Does your business have a formal dress code, or is there an unwritten policy?
- What standards are included in your dress code?
- How important is business etiquette?

Write a short report describing your findings, and be prepared to present them to the class. (Learning Objectives 1, 2, and 3)

CHAPTER 3

Workplace Teams

LEARNING OBJECTIVES

1. Develop an understanding of teamwork.
2. Develop an understanding of workplace team composition.
3. Understand the value of working with diverse people.
4. Describe the characteristics of effective workplace teams.
5. Discuss productive team communication.

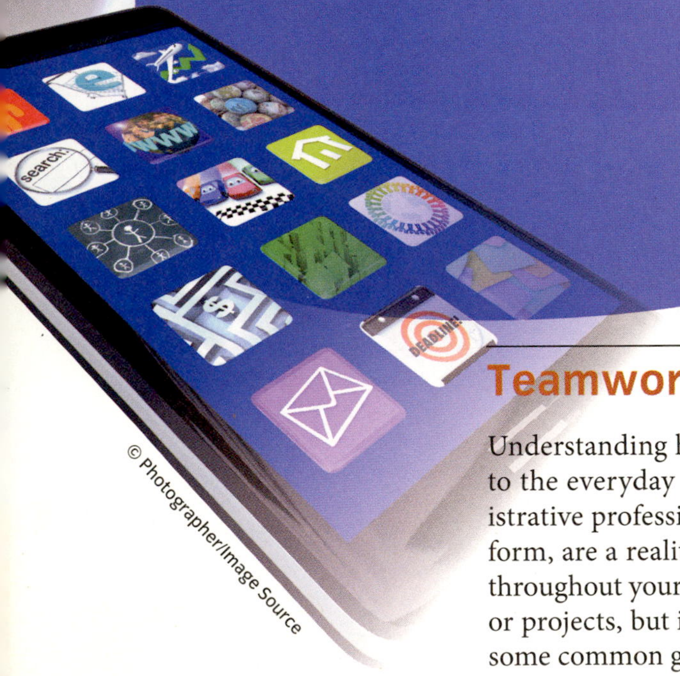

Teamwork

Understanding how teams function in the workplace and their significance to the everyday operations of an organization is important for the administrative professional. It is important because workplace teams, in whatever form, are a reality. You will be asked to work on formal and informal teams throughout your lifetime. Teams may take the form of groups or departments or projects, but in the long run, they all have one thing in common: there is some common goal, and everyone is working toward that goal.

Consider the example of a sports team. Each member is committed to the goal of winning, and team members collaborate and cooperate to achieve that goal. Individuals on a team work together for a common goal, they share resources, and they share many of the responsibilities. Ultimately, everyone gets the credit or the blame when the team succeeds or fails.

Teams are groups of employees who work together toward a common goal—simply put, people who work together to get a job done. The ideas you will read about in this chapter are generally transferable to any team situation you will encounter at work, at school, on sports teams, or at home. Teamwork is a very practical concept and an area in which you already have much experience.

Organizational Benefits

Employers consistently rank teamwork as one of the most important skills for an employee to possess. In fact, for several reasons, teams are vital to the health and efficiency of many organizations:

- Teams bring together skills and experiences that exceed those of an individual. Approaching a problem or process through the use of teams can result in greater creativity, more options, and better decisions and solutions, leading to improved productivity and quality.
- Studies show that effective teamwork increases worker productivity, decreases absenteeism, produces higher-quality products and services, and increases profits for organizations.
- Employees who serve on effective teams enjoy having greater responsibility and being able to contribute to the organization in a "bigger" or different way than they would normally in their jobs. As a consequence, they may have more job satisfaction, perform better, and be more likely to stay with the company.
- Teamwork is increasingly important as organizations continue to expand multinationally, adopt new technologies, and look for ways to decrease costs and improve profits.

Employee Benefits

Employees sometimes have mixed feelings about serving on teams. In fact, you may have experienced some negative feelings when asked to work on teams in school. You may have been concerned about having your time wasted, having teammates who wouldn't do their share of the work, or being held responsible along with the rest of the team for work that was not accomplished. Belonging to an effective team, however, can have several valuable benefits, especially in the workplace:

- You will gain insights, ideas, help, information, and more from team members, and they will gain insights, ideas, help, information, and more from you.
- Teams allow for cross-training on different tasks. Team members learn new skills that can make their jobs more interesting and can help them perform their jobs better. New skills can also be useful later in their careers.
- As a team collaborates on a project, all the members have the advantage of seeing the whole process, which makes the team better at problem solving and gives its members a new perspective on the tasks other people perform.
- Teams often get to see the big picture. Learning about the organization as a whole helps you in your job.
- They are fun. People on successful teams enjoy being a part of something bigger than themselves and get deep enjoyment and satisfaction from being on a team.

Yuri Arcurs/Shutterstock.com

Working well on a team is an essential skill for administrative professionals.

Successfully working on, supporting, and eventually leading a team are fundamental workplace skills. Regardless of how you participate, you will have unique challenges and opportunities as you seek to assist the team in accomplishing its goal.

Workplace Team Composition

Most administrative professionals work in a team environment, that is, in a small office, department, or division. They also support, serve on, and even lead committees, task forces, and other kinds of formal teams. Some of the skills presented in this chapter (such as leading and following) apply to serving on or leading a formal team. Others are generally applicable in any team environment. Other chapters examine skills that will also help immensely in a variety of team settings, such as leadership, time management, dependability, integrity, creativity, and communication skills.

Workplaces have many different types of teams. Some are ongoing and permanent, such as a finance committee. Others are temporary, set up for a specific task or purpose and disbanded once it has been achieved. An example is a task force set up to address the problem of increased employee absenteeism. Seven common types of workplace teams are described below. As you read about them, consider the common threads that emerge: communication, collaboration, a commitment to clearly defined goals, and shared responsibility for the outcome.

Project Teams and Task Forces

Teams that are developed for a clearly defined project with a beginning and an end are called **project teams**. A project team usually has a set budget and a schedule for how and when the work will be completed. Because companies constantly have to develop new products, services, or methods to stay productive, project teams are important and continue to gain in importance.[1] Examples of project teams are teams that find a new market niche, develop a new client service, or improve a process. As an administrative professional, you might be asked to serve on a project team established to find a more efficient way to pay vendors. In this case, you would bring your practical experience, knowledge, and expertise to the team.

A **task force** is a common type of project team set up to deal with a specific issue or problem. It usually conducts research and offers recommendations to a committee or organizational leader. An example given earlier was a task force established to examine employee absenteeism. An administrative professional might be asked to serve on a task force formed to recommend new database software for the organization.

Committee

A **committee** is set up to solve a problem, monitor an issue, or complete a task. It may be ongoing or have a definitive end. Your school, for example, may have a committee that is in charge of graduation. Your workplace may have a committee that meets regularly (perhaps every month) to identify and address safety issues. Since safety is an ongoing concern, the committee functions from year to year. A committee may have members who rotate on and off at particular times and who represent certain divisions of the organization.

Cross-Functional Teams

Cross-functional teams are composed of individuals from a number of different functional groups within an organization, such as the engineering, marketing, and quality control departments. They are typically brought together to solve a problem or work on a project that requires their expertise. A cross-functional team usually has resources that are borrowed temporarily from all over the company to accomplish a specific goal. As an administrative professional, you might be part of a cross-functional team established to plan for the implementation of a new e-mail system across the company.

[1]Anthony T. Cobb, *Leading Project Teams: An Introduction to the Basics of Project Management* (Thousand Oaks, Calif.: Sage, 2006), 2.

Photographer/Image Source

Here are some tips for working successfully in teams:

- Business is a team sport. No one individual can be successful without the support of fellow employees.
- Every member of a team must be involved. Keeping the lines of communication open and team members informed about the details of the team invites members to become involved or stay active.
- No one person has all the answers; all team members' opinions are valuable.
- There is no *I* in the word *team*.
- Teamwork is not about seeking credit for one's individual contributions; it is about the team succeeding.

Supervisor/Coworker Teams

Administrative professionals also form teams with supervisors and coworkers. Your relationship with your immediate supervisor is an important factor in your performance and productivity, as well as your overall job satisfaction. You and your supervisor work toward specific goals and must collaborate and cooperate. As part of this team, you make it possible for your supervisor to do his or her job well by providing support where needed.

Formal and informal teams consisting of you and a coworker or several coworkers are common in the workplace. These teams require the same commitment to a common goal and collaborative and cooperative skills. Maintain a good working relationship with all coworkers, regardless of whether they are on your team. The section on effective teams later in this chapter has techniques that will help the administrative professional function within any type of workplace team.

External Teams

An **external team** is formed when individuals within an organization work with individuals outside the organization to achieve specified goals. **Outsourcing** (using outside firms to perform certain functions of an organization) provides a good example of an external team. For example, an organization may outsource its website development. The administrative professional may be called upon in this case to work with the consulting firm to provide company information or images, proofread text before publishing, or serve as a liaison to executives. As is the case with any team, good communication and organizational skills are important when working on external teams.

Virtual Teams

Virtual teams primarily meet electronically and cross the boundaries of time and distance to operate. People often think of them in connection with national and international companies, but virtual teams are also used across regions, states, or even counties or cities.

Here are two examples:

- An insurance company wants to form a team of administrative professionals from its different offices all over the Southeast to develop a standard training program for new administrative professionals. Because the team will be meeting multiple times and is geographically separated, meeting virtually makes sense.
- Several executives in offices across town must meet frequently but are too busy to travel. They can save time and work more efficiently by meeting virtually.

Do's and Don'ts for Working With Your Supervisor

- Do learn what your boss expects and do it well.
- Do notice whether your boss asks for reports in writing or prefers to hear things orally. Then follow that approach. Strive to adapt your actions to your boss's way of doing things.
- Do watch others, and follow their lead. If no one knocks at your boss's door when it is closed, that's a sure sign that you shouldn't interrupt. If your coworkers stop in to see your boss when the door is open, you probably can, too.
- Do respect your boss's time. People in supervisory positions are busy. When communicating something to them, get right to the point. If they need more details, they'll ask.
- Do organize your thoughts before approaching your boss.
- Do respect your boss's authority. If you dislike some of his or her actions or behaviors, focus on the things you can respect. And, never go above your boss's head without his or her permission. That's a quick way to destroy any relationship you've built.
- Don't disturb your boss with problems that you can resolve. If you bring a problem to your boss's attention, have a solution ready to suggest.
- Don't complain to your boss about your coworkers. Try to work things out.
- Don't make your boss have to guess what you want. Communicate clearly and directly.
- Don't give insincere compliments. But do show appreciation and admiration when it is due.
- Don't take every harsh reply or unfriendly action personally. If you haven't done anything to deserve the action, most likely your boss was reacting to something else.

Source: Adapted from Doris Humphrey, *What Your Employer Expects* (Cincinnati: South-Western/Thomson Learning, 2002), 23–24.

Virtual teams are valuable to organizations for several reasons. They can save time and money, and they open up collaborative opportunities that wouldn't be possible or practical by any other means. An uncertain economy and a competitive marketplace also make virtual teams an attractive option.

Virtual teams need equipment, know-how, and some infrastructure for support. While the technology of *web conferencing* (meeting by means of the Internet) is not expensive or difficult, there is a learning curve that can be intimidating for someone unfamiliar with the possibilities. As you train in the administrative professional field, you should familiarize yourself with web conferencing tools, software, and equipment as much as possible. You will have an opportunity to use different technologies in the activities associated with this textbook. This will expand your experience and knowledge base and will help you feel more comfortable with a variety of technologies. Try to develop a curiosity when you see or hear about emerging technologies so you will be able to tackle them eagerly. Web conferencing will be discussed in more detail in Chapter 10.

Diversity in the Workplace

As the diversity of the U.S. workforce continues to grow, we must understand how to work with people from a wide range of different backgrounds. Administrative professionals who work well with a diverse group of individuals are an asset to any team. They will probably also experience greater present and future success on the job and will

TECH TALK

Collaborative Documents, Spreadsheets, and Presentations

Many web services are available that make team collaboration easy. Instead of sending multiple e-mails back and forth among team members, it is often easier to use a collaborative file that all users can access and edit. Here are three free and easy-to-use services:

- Google Docs allows a user to create and share documents, spreadsheets, forms, and presentations synchronously (at the same time) or asynchronously (at different times).
- Dropbox provides online storage space and lets users share documents stored "in the cloud."
- Windows Live® online services allow for online storage and sharing.

Both Google and Dropbox have mobile applications you can use to access their features via an Apple iPhone®, iPad®, or other mobile digital device.

Here's an example of how a team might collaborate on creating a presentation via the World Wide Web. The members decide they will all contribute and edit information before the next team meeting. This will save time and allow for a clear division of responsibilities. Using Google Docs, one member starts the presentation and then shares it with the others. Those members add slides, adjust content, and proofread. The finished presentation can be downloaded as a PDF file, a *Microsoft PowerPoint*® presentation, or a text file, or it can be presented from online using Google Docs.

generally be more comfortable in their work environment. An employee who works well with others is less likely to be terminated due to conflicts in the workplace and will be more satisfied with the work environment and thus desirous to stay.

Diversity has significant benefits for companies as well. Diverse groups of people bring different perspectives, values, and ideas to the workplace. Businesses use these new and creative ideas to enrich their products and services so they appeal to broader and different audiences. Groups and teams with diverse members are more creative and make better decisions. In addition, diversity helps a company attract and retain talented employees.

Seek to Understand Others

The differences an administrative professional can expect to meet in the workplace range from differences in ethnicity, race, nationality, age, sexual orientation, physical abilities, and gender to differences in values and backgrounds. The U.S. workforce today is more ethnically diverse than in the past, and it includes a higher proportion of older workers. Recognizing differences and then being intentional in your desire to understand those who are different from you will make you an effective team member in any situation. Here's an example to illustrate this point:

Jamie, who has cerebral palsy, is the newly hired administrative professional for a local insurance agency. Tonya and Rick are the two other administrative professionals in the office. Because of Jamie's physical limitations, she has a motorized wheelchair, but she also needs to walk short distances to use her muscles as much as possible. She has a slightly larger workspace since she needs room to maneuver her wheelchair.

Rick suggests that the office filing cabinets be moved closer to Jamie's work area so she can use the short walk for exercise. Tonya quickly notices that Jamie has excellent telephone skills as well as exceptional customer service skills. Tonya suggests that Jamie answer the telephone and allow Tonya to key the long reports often required by the agents at short notice. Because Jamie at times has some trouble with fine motor skills, she does not key as fast as Tonya, so this arrangement works well.

Before Jamie joined the informal team of administrative professionals, Tonya and Rick naturally divided up the duties that fit their interests, ability levels, and experience. They do the same when Jamie arrives. Jamie wants to be treated like everyone else and has coworkers who seek to understand her, her condition, and her abilities (and not to focus on her disability).

mediaphotos/iStockphoto.com

Diversity in the workplace brings new ideas and perspectives and benefits companies and individuals.

Show Respect the Way They Understand It

Being polite and showing respect is important in any culture and is a vital part of the business setting. As an administrative professional, you should show people respect the way they understand it. For example, Julie is an administrative professional in Mr. Gilchrist's engineering firm. When clients come in for meetings with Mr. Gilchrist, Julie usually offers them coffee, soft drinks, or bottled water. When Mr. Kim visits, Julie hands him his coffee using two hands. Mr. Kim is an older Korean gentleman, and Julie knows that when giving an item to someone, it is a sign of respect in the Korean culture to use two hands. Julie has adapted her own actions to fit Mr. Kim's understanding of respect.

Note that Julie took the time to learn how to show respect in the Korean culture. If you regularly come in contact with people from a different culture, you should learn something about that culture. Besides the suggestions given in Chapter 2, you can visit neighborhoods, observe what people from the culture say and do, and ask questions.

Image Source/Getty Images

Employees with disabilities want respect and the opportunity to work hard—just like those without disabilities.

Communicating Verbally Across Cultures

There are some general rules to remember when communicating verbally with someone from a different culture. Chapter 9 discusses verbal communication in detail, and Chapter 8 provides guidelines for writing for an international audience, some of which also apply to speech. The following items are foundational elements when communicating with people from other countries or cultures:

- Keep your language simple and to the point.
- Match your communication style to theirs.
- Avoid politics, religion, and other potentially sensitive topics.
- Be careful about using humor.
- With people for whom English isn't a first language, slow down a little and speak clearly.
- Don't correct people's English unless they have asked you to do so.

Effective Workplace Teams

On a team you are either the leader (you accept responsibility for guiding the team) or a follower (you accept responsibility for being a productive part of the team). Serving on or leading a team is a challenge and an effort that requires planning and thought. Knowing what is expected will help you be an effective leader or follower.

Leading a Team

As an administrative professional, you will be asked to serve on various teams and at times may be asked to lead a team. For example, you could be asked to lead a team that will plan the company-wide spring picnic or a team that will draft employee guidelines for social networking. It is important that you accept these leadership opportunities, as they will help you develop your skills in leading and managing people. Additionally, leading helps you progress in your job and allows you to be seen as a viable candidate for higher-paid positions involving more leadership.

Start by establishing clear expectations for your team and setting procedures for meetings and team communication. This will help you develop a rapport with team members and can eliminate problems in the future. People like to know what is expected of them and will generally strive to meet those expectations. You should also make sure the purpose of the team is clearly defined, both to you and to your team members. The purpose of the team will determine its focus. Without a clear purpose, you can be easily sidetracked and may waste time on unnecessary efforts. Some leaders start team meetings by reminding members of the purpose of the team, such as, "Remember, we're supposed to be researching how similar companies are implementing a four-day workweek." Talk to your supervisor if you are not sure of the purpose of the team and what it is expected to accomplish.

Set an example of service to your team. For instance, keep them informed about any changes or issues concerning the team's assignment. Do not wait until the last minute to schedule meetings. Let members know what will be discussed in advance of meetings. Make sure they realize this is a team effort and their input is valuable. Here are some other tasks of the team leader:

- Keep the team on schedule.
- Plan and organize meetings.
- Report team progress to supervisors.
- Make work assignments.
- Encourage openness and collaboration among team members.
- Be a trustworthy leader.
- Get to know the skills and strengths of each team member so they can be used effectively.
- Be a good listener.

Serving on a Team

Being a follower on a team may seem like an easy task. After all, you just need to do what you are told, right? No, a follower is a team member, and each member of the team has a role and purpose. Team members are chosen for a reason. They have skills, experience, or knowledge that will help the team accomplish its goal. The following actions and attitudes will help make you a good team member:

- Always be on time for meetings. This shows others that the team is a priority for you. Make sure meetings are on your calendar, and set your electronic calendar to remind you.
- Be prepared for meetings. Be aware of what will be discussed; read the agenda and any meeting materials. Was there anything you were supposed to do and then report to the team at this meeting?
- Have a folder dedicated to the team project, and take that folder to your meetings. This is a good

Expected Team Behaviors

To help establish an open, collaborative climate on your team, try setting ground rules such as these:

- Only one person talks at a time.
- Be on time for meetings.
- *Listen* to the person talking.
- No side discussions.
- Deal with issues, not personalities.
- Keep your commitments.

From James P. Lewis, *Team-Based Project Management* (New York: Amacom, 1998), 82.

way to keep information organized, and you will have documents ready if questions arise. It also shows others you take the team project seriously.

- Do the work the team assigns you to the best of your ability.
- Be willing to contribute to meetings and the work of the team. Volunteer for a task if you have the skills and time. This shows initiative and will make you stand out among your peers.

Leaders' and participants' responsibilities with respect to meetings are discussed in greater detail in Chapter 14. Leaders and followers both serve the team, just in different ways. Ultimately, both are working toward the common goal of accomplishing the tasks or objectives of the team.

Characteristics of Effective Teams

Not every team is effective, but when members take ownership of the team's performance and efficiency and work toward the common goal without focusing on personal goals, the overall effectiveness of the team increases. An effective team has the following characteristics:

- Individual members who focus on team goals rather than personal goals
- Good leadership
- Members with the skills, experience, and education to do the job
- Individual members who take responsibility for the success or failure of the team

Team Meeting Do's and Don'ts

- Do listen well to everyone.
- Do try to understand everyone's point of view.
- Don't interrupt anyone.
- Don't dominate the discussion.
- Don't talk off-topic.
- Don't demonstrate a negative attitude.
- Don't text, check e-mail, or surf the Internet on your cell phone or computer.

track5/iStockphoto.com

- The ability to work with a diverse group of people
- The capacity to reach an agreement when making decisions
- Goals that are practical and well defined
- Members who respect and trust one another

Teamwork Techniques

Members of a team are a working unit. Each individual works independently as well as interdependently to accomplish a variety of tasks. When you are working with others, it is helpful to practice some fundamental techniques.

BE RESPECTFUL

Respect is regard and appreciation that is shown toward others. It is an essential part of courteous behavior. Regardless of the position someone holds, you should show that person respect. A good rule to follow is to demonstrate the same degree of respect for a custodian that you do for the company president. This habit of being equally respectful toward everyone will not go unnoticed. It will earn you respect in return and will contribute to your professional image.

On a team, respect means regarding every member as valuable. Some people will be more vocal than others. Some members will demonstrate particular abilities, such as an amazing talent for solving problems. Remember that people who do not speak as often or show their talents as readily are still valuable contributors, with ideas or skills that may be useful to the team.

BE NONJUDGMENTAL

To be *nonjudgmental* means to avoid making judgments based on your personal belief system. In any situation involving others, you will face decisions, attitudes, and cultures that may be different from yours. This is inevitable, so cultivate a habit of being noncritical. You will often make personal value judgments based on your beliefs about right and wrong. However, being open-minded and suspending judgment when working with others is a professional approach that reflects respect for differences.

TAKE THE OTHER'S PERSPECTIVE

Perspective is the point of view from which something is considered. On a team, a helpful technique for working with others is to look at issues from their perspective. This goes along with being nonjudgmental. Taking the other person's perspective will go a long way toward preventing or resolving conflict, which will be discussed later in the chapter. For example, suppose a team member doesn't complete a task prior to the next meeting. Put yourself in that person's place and try to imagine why. Was the member out sick all week? Did a supervisor assign a task that took precedence over the team project? Did the leader effectively communicate the task and due date?

BE FLEXIBLE

This may be one of the hardest tasks to accomplish. *Flexibility* refers to the ability to "flex" or change when faced with a new situation. It is a valuable skill for any employee. Teams are not static entities, so they must be willing to adapt. Individuals on a team need to be flexible as new ideas, problems, and requirements arise that require rethinking and making changes. An inability to adapt can produce conflict, can lead to poor results, and can cause the team to stall in its efforts to meet its goals.

LISTEN

The ability to listen in such a way as to fully understand what others are saying is perhaps one of the most important requirements for working successfully on a team and as a team. Listening techniques will be discussed in more detail later, but it should be noted here that these skills and an appreciation of listening are invaluable assets to both the team leader and team members. Besides the obvious benefit of gaining information, being a good listener conveys respect and helps build trust and positive relationships.

Productive Team Communication

Communication is of the utmost importance in any team environment. Ineffective communication can mean that goals are not properly set or understood. Tasks may not be completed, or may be done incorrectly, because they have been poorly communicated. Progress may be halting or stalled. Misunderstanding, frustration, and low morale often result when employees believe they have not been properly understood or when they do not understand others. Poor communication can lead to poor decisions and the failure of the team to meet its goals.

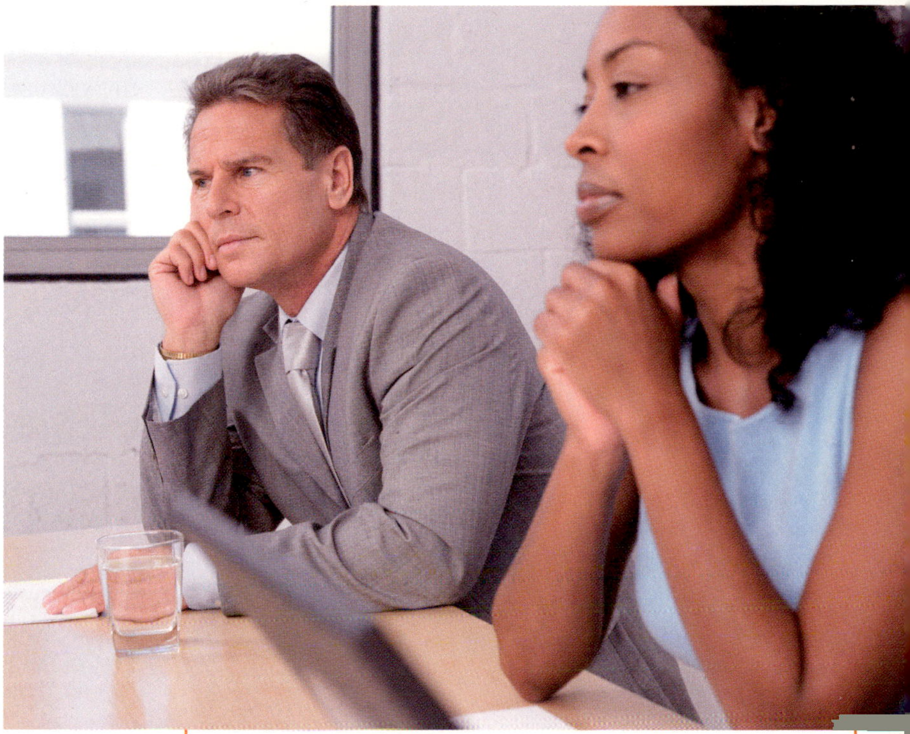
AISPIX/Shutterstock.com

Listening with an open mind to the ideas of others is an important teamwork skill.

Understanding the Organizational Structure

All organizations have both formal and informal communication channels. Your goal as an employee is to be productive in both channels.

FORMAL COMMUNICATION

Formal communication is communication through official channels. In an organization this may be downward, upward, or horizontal (see Figure 3.1 on page 60). **Downward communication** consists of messages that flow from management to employees of the company. **Upward communication** includes those messages that travel from employees to management. **Horizontal communication** involves messages flowing from coworker to coworker, from manager to manager, or within a team. Understanding the flow of communication will help you know whom to ask when you have questions and have a better understanding of how decisions are made within organizations and teams.

INFORMAL COMMUNICATION

In addition to formal communication in an organization, there are also informal channels (often called the grapevine). **Informal communication** includes unofficial communication, such as conversations in the hallway about the latest news on filling an open position or an exchange overheard in the elevator.

Informal communication is a natural and normal result of people working together. The negative aspect of this type of communication is the occasional rumor or untrue communication. Informal communication can result in a skewed perspective of an issue and should be viewed with suspicion, considering the accuracy of the source, the motive in the telling, and the relevance to other known facts. Since rumors and untruths cannot be entirely squelched, the best way to reduce them is with open lines of formal communication. As leaders keep team members informed, rumors and untruths have a tendency to fade.

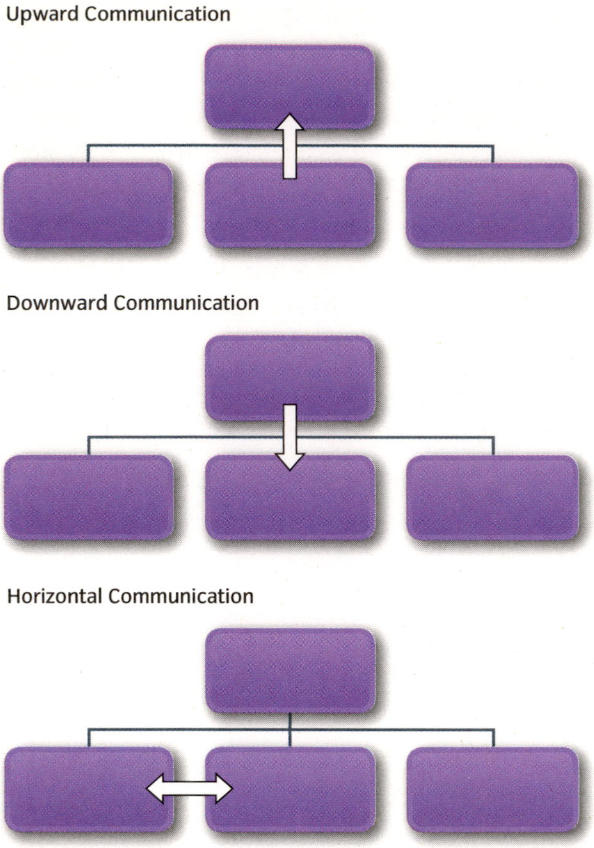

FIGURE 3.1 Formal Communication: Downward, Upward, and Horizontal

Interpersonal Skills

Interpersonal skills are critical to team communication and success. For team members, three of the most important interpersonal skills are the abilities to listen to each other effectively, work together collaboratively, and resolve any conflicts that occur. Other important interpersonal skills include building trust with others, practicing empathy (understanding or concern for someone's feelings or position), having a positive attitude, using appropriate etiquette, being appreciative, and paying attention to others. Your professional life will be affected by how well you connect with those around you.

LISTENING

Although workers spend a large portion of their time listening to others, they may not know how to listen effectively. Here is an example of poor listening:

Rick was explaining what he discovered when he researched a job candidate on a social networking site. Instead of actively seeking to understand what Rick was describing, Joan was thinking about what she was going to say regarding the evils of social networking as soon as Rick was finished. Did she really hear what Rick was saying about the candidate?

Listening effectively, also known as listening actively, requires you to focus on the speaker, instead of on what you want to say afterward. This is an important skill when working on a team, regardless of whether you are the leader or a team member, since team members need to feel their voices are being heard. Listening effectively also demands listening for feelings as well as for words. Figure 3.2 lists several techniques for active listening. Listening and understanding, including active listening, will be discussed in more detail in Chapter 9.

COLLABORATING

Collaboration is the act of working collectively with others on a shared project. This is, of course, the essence of teamwork. Here are some general suggestions for working together collaboratively, whether formally or informally:

- Define the purpose of the collaborative project at the first team meeting.

Effective Listening Techniques
■ Direct your attention to the speaker.
■ Maintain eye contact with the speaker.
■ Watch for nonverbal communication.
■ Ask questions that require more than a yes or no answer.
■ Organize what you hear.
■ Do not get angry.
■ Do not criticize.
■ Take notes if appropriate.

FIGURE 3.2 Using techniques like these will make you a better listener.

- Choose a chairperson or group leader if one has not already been assigned.
- Determine each group member's skills and expertise.
- Assign tasks to each group member.
- Establish guidelines for completing the task.
- Set a time for completion.
- Determine product evaluation standards.
- Set evaluation standards for group members.

RESOLVING CONFLICT

Conflict is a state of opposition or disagreement between persons, ideas, or interests. Even the most effective teams have conflicts. Understanding how to work through conflict is so important that team members may want to engage in a short session on conflict resolution at the beginning stages of a project. Communicating to prevent and resolve conflict will be discussed more fully in Chapter 9 on verbal communication. Here are several suggestions that can be effective in resolving conflicts on teams:

- Step back and try to identify what is causing the conflict. Be objective and put emotions aside if possible.
- Listen to all team members' viewpoints. Make true understanding your aim in listening.
- Identify points of agreement on the team.
- Work toward a solution in which all team members win.

Partnership for 21st Century Skills

Creativity/Innovation

Think Creatively Through Team Brainstorming

Thinking creatively and working creatively with others on a team are important skills for the 21st century workplace. **Brainstorming** is a technique that teams often use to get as many ideas as possible on the table. In a brainstorming session, team members build on what others say, and any and all ideas are encouraged. Generally, no idea is ever criticized or evaluated during the session; assessment takes place afterward. This approach helps promote the involvement of all team members and gets people to think outside established patterns.

Team members have to communicate ideas and also be open to new and diverse perspectives in an effort to benefit from a wide range of ideas. Software such as *Microsoft Office* and mind mapping tools are helpful as teams create and refine ideas. Mind mapping tools let you draw diagrams to show visually how information is organized. Links to several tools are available on the website for this text.

Activity

Creativity is a muscle you need to flex to keep in shape. Form a team of five or six and brainstorm ideas for one of the following topics. Rules: No ideas should be criticized in any way, and all ideas should be recorded. Be creative, and think outside the box! Outlandish ideas earn more creativity points.

- Texting while driving. How can we stop it?
- Tardiness to work. Too many people are coming in late. How can we solve this problem?
- Social networking on company time. What should company leaders do?
- A video game. Pick a popular game. Then come up with ideas for new games that will outsell it.
- A new mobile app. What is an app that no one has thought of yet that everybody needs?

DaveBolton/iStockphoto.com

SUMMARY

To reinforce what you have learned in this chapter, study this summary.

- Teams are a reality in the workplace, and they have numerous benefits for both organizations and employees.
- Most administrative professionals work in a team environment, and they also support, serve on, and lead formal teams.
- Two strategies for working successfully with many different kinds of people are to be intentional in your desire to understand them and to show respect the way they understand it.
- Team leaders and team members each have a distinct purpose and role on a team.
- Some fundamental teamwork techniques are to be respectful, be nonjudgmental, take the other's perspective, be flexible, and listen.
- For productive team communication, you should understand the organizational structure and develop interpersonal skills such as listening, collaborating, and resolving conflict.

KEY TERMS

brainstorming, 62
committee, 50
cross-functional team, 50
downward communication, 59
external team, 51
formal communication, 59
horizontal communication, 59
informal communication, 59
outsourcing, 51
project team, 50
task force, 50
team, 48
upward communication, 59
virtual team, 51

3

STUDY Tools

Located at www.cengagebrain.com

- Chapter Outlines
- Flashcards
- Interactive Quizzes
- Tech Tools
- Video Segments
- and More!

LET'S DISCUSS

1. What are some of the types of teams you have served on in the past? What was the purpose of those teams?
2. Explain some of the benefits to you as well as an organization when teams are used.
3. List and explain five types of teams.
4. Describe some of the characteristics of a good team leader.
5. Describe some of the characteristics of a good team member.
6. In your own words, explain what makes a team effective.
7. Explain two or three fundamental techniques for good teamwork.

PUT IT TO WORK

Team leader problem Ramirez & Shaw is a 15-year-old company providing computer services in the United States and Canada. The company has been very successful over the last ten years and attributes part of its success to its emphasis on solving problems through a team-based approach. Employees serve on project teams.

Benjamin Toulous was asked by his supervisor to serve on an eight-member team to examine the company's employee evaluation procedures. Benjamin is pleased about serving on this team. He believes he has several good suggestions that will improve the evaluation procedures. After he accepted the invitation to serve, he learned that the team leader was Alice Wong, the supervisor of the accounting department. Benjamin has little respect for Alice. He thinks she is a poor supervisor because he has heard stories from several of her employees about how unfair she is. Although Benjamin has never had direct experience with Alice as a supervisor and has actually never met her, he still believes she is an unacceptable team leader.

Benjamin is your friend and is wondering how he should handle this. Think through the choices he has. As you consider what he should do, be sure to examine the responsibilities of team leaders and followers, consider different techniques for working with others, and think about what role informal communication may have already played in this situation. Now, write a summary of the advice you would give Benjamin. (Learning Objectives 4 and 5)

COMMUNICATE SUCCESSFULLY

1. **Texting** Form a team with three or four classmates and formulate a list of the advantages and disadvantages of texting as a way to communicate. Individually, write a one-paragraph reflection on this team experience

using the following questions as a guide: In general, how did the team work? Did you remain on task the whole time, or did you stray from the team purpose? Were there conflicting opinions? Did everyone participate? Did you listen to everyone's opinion? (Learning Objectives 4 and 5)

2. **Team communication** You are the administrative professional for a vice president of the chamber of commerce in your city. Your boss, Cam Newton, directs the Ambassador/Membership Committee, which meets once a month. Mr. Newton would like you to send two regular monthly e-mails to committee members. The first will be a reminder about the next meeting (asking for a response so you can plan for the lunch that will be provided). The second will be an e-mail that provides a copy of the minutes after each meeting. Use the template feature of your e-mail software to compose the e-mails. Invent details as needed. (Learning Objective 5)

3. **International relations** In addition to its locations in the United States, Kapor Pharmaceuticals has locations in China and India. Because of this, your supervisor and colleagues spend a great deal of time working and communicating with employees from these countries. Your supervisor has decided to create a handout to help new employees understand some of the cultural differences that exist when communicating. Choose one of the international locations of Kapor Pharmaceuticals and research the following questions. Prepare a one-page handout your supervisor can share with new employees. Select an appropriate document theme to create a professional-looking handout. (Learning Objective 3)

   a. How do people in that country show respect?

   b. What are hand gestures or body language that could affect your message positively or negatively?

   c. What are some traditions of that culture?

   d. What language(s) are spoken?

4. **Most valuable concept** Add a new post to the blog you created in Chapter 1. In this entry, reflect on the following statement: **Name one concept you learned about teamwork in this chapter that you believe will benefit you the most in the workplace, and explain why.** (Learning Objective 3)

Blog

DEVELOP WORKPLACE SKILLS

5. **Team examples** Form a team with a classmate. Use the Internet to search for at least three examples of how teams are used in the workplace, or use examples from this chapter. Using *Microsoft Word*, create a table with three columns and four rows. The first row will be the column headings: "Team Example," "Type of Team," and "Advice for Effective Teams." Give a brief explanation of each team example you found, determine which type of team it is, and use what you learned in this chapter to give the team two pieces of advice on how to be effective. The advice must be different for each example. Choose a *Word* preformatted table for the design. (Learning Objectives 2 and 4)

6. **Team comparison** Form a team with a classmate. Share a team experience that each of you had in the past, and then compare those experiences. Use *Microsoft Word* to create a table in which you compare what was and wasn't effective about the teams. In making these evaluations, consider these topics from the Effective Workplace Teams section in this chapter: being a leader, serving on a team, characteristics of effective teams, and teamwork techniques. Then explain what benefits the team had for you and for the organization. Choose a *Word* preformatted table for the design. (Learning Objectives 1 and 4)

BUILD RELATIONSHIPS

7. **Conflict resolution** You have been placed on a two-person team with Jim, a coworker. Together, you are responsible for developing a short instructional video for your department. Jim is the expert in editing and shooting video, and your expertise is in getting information, finding suitable locations to shoot video, managing the budget, and keeping the project on schedule. Jim is good at what he does, but you two have already had some minor conflicts. Jim is at least 30 minutes late for work each day (he claims to stay late to make up for it). He doesn't tell you when he's spent money out of the project account, he never finishes when he says he will, and he's generally a loner. Develop a list of things you could do to resolve the issues at hand and possibly prevent further conflict. As you develop your list, review the tips for working successfully in teams and the technology tools that encourage collaboration and sharing of information. (Learning Objective 5)

USE TECH TOOLS

8. **Google Docs** Using Google Docs, prepare a group presentation about the characteristics of an effective workplace team. Address one of the characteristics mentioned in this chapter, and add at least two more your team agrees are necessary for team success. Do this activity outside class if possible, and do not meet face-to-face. Download your presentation in the format your instructor indicates (*PowerPoint*, PDF, or text format). (Learning Objective 4)

PLAN AHEAD

Website redesign Form a team with three or four classmates to review your school's website and make recommendations to redesign it. To be an effective team, you need to make sure everyone understands the purpose of the team and has a clear vision of what to do. As a team, you will analyze the current site to determine what works well and what needs to be changed. You will then discuss improvements that would make the site more user-friendly. You will consider the needs of four different groups of users—prospective students, current students, parents, and faculty/staff. Complete the following steps:

1. Using *Microsoft Word* or Google Docs, prepare a document that tracks the work of your team. Identify the purpose of the team and the specific goals to be accomplished.
2. As a team, discuss the following questions. Think of three or four additional questions to consider.
    - Should we survey users?
    - What do users complain about on the site?
    - What is great about the site?
    - Does the look need to be updated?
    - Is the search feature effective?
    - What characteristics of other sites would be appropriate?
3. Determine the responsibilities of team members, and add a section to the document that includes this information.
4. Discuss the needs of the four user groups. Create a table in the document that identifies these needs. Choose a *Word* preformatted table for the design.
5. Make a visual representation of the redesigned website, incorporating the information from the team discussions. You may use word processing tools or other tools you have available.
6. Prepare a presentation to show the class your proposed redesign and explain your recommendations.

PART

2

Workforce Behaviors

leezsnow/iStockphoto.com

CAREER PROFILE

Visit www.cengagebrain.com to listen to the complete interview.

Chancellor

Dr. Freida Hill is chancellor of the Alabama Community College System.

How important are project planning skills in your job such as time management?
They're very important. You have to be good at time management and scheduling. Fortunately for me I have the best admin anywhere, and she keeps me on schedule.

What do you see as your major responsibility?
Making sure I'm the best advocate for our community college system. I've told the people that work at the system office that their primary job is to provide good customer service to the colleges, and I think that's critically important.

How important is teamwork in the workplace?
Trying to manage at a time when your enrollment's going up and your budget is going down, it's critically important to work as a team. We have to put the right people at the table in decision making. When our students go out into the work environment, they need to know about good teamwork.

Could you comment on the value of a democratic leadership style?
I believe in shared decision making. I know that as a CEO or chancellor sometimes you have to make decisions in isolation, but it's my preference to get the right people together to look at the decision that has to be made and get input from those closest to it.

The Alabama Department of Postsecondary Education

How have previous administrative professional jobs you've held helped advance your career?
I've been a secretary, faculty member, president, and vice president, so I understand the challenges they go through. I see their perspective.

How did you prepare for your job in terms of education and training?
I knew I needed a higher degree, so I continued working toward that, and I've also taken some professional development—leadership skills, continued quality improvement courses, anything I thought would help me be better.

CHAPTER

4 Self-Management

LEARNING OBJECTIVES

1. Apply appropriate techniques for managing yourself in the work environment.
2. Understand and apply appropriate techniques for managing stress.
3. Describe strategies for managing your work.

© Photographer/Image Source

Manage Yourself

Part of self-management is your ability to meet goals and account for your productivity in the workplace. This requires self-discipline. **Self-discipline** is your own control over what you do, as well as how and when you do it. As you grow in experience throughout your career, you will gain a greater understanding of how to manage yourself. Applying this understanding can make all the difference in your personal as well as your professional life. In this chapter you will learn how to make self-discipline part of your own lifestyle.

Set Goals

Where do you want to be in your education or career in three years? In five years? What steps do you need to take to accomplish your objectives?

You may have heard the old saying that if you don't know where you are going, you are unlikely to get there. To get to your destination, you must set goals and make effective decisions about reaching them. Setting clear, attainable goals is a key to success in your private life as well as your work life, and each helps to support the other.

DETERMINE LONG- AND SHORT-TERM GOALS

To set goals, you need to determine what is important to you. Take an inventory of your needs, wants, interests, and abilities. Perhaps you will decide that you want your life to consist of career success, good health, financial security, and happiness. You must set some long-term goals that will help you realize these desires. Your goals, for example, may include becoming an administrative manager, having a family, and staying physically and mentally healthy. However, becoming a manager, having a family, and being healthy require hard work and the accomplishment of many short-term goals.

Your more ambitious goals will take some time to reach, which is why they are called long-term goals. Consider the long-term goal of becoming an administrative manager. Reaching it will require experience, commitment, hard work, and time. Thus, a logical short-term goal may be to get a job that will allow you to use the skills and knowledge you have gained, in addition to providing you with work experience for future opportunities. Salary in your first job may not be your highest priority as you work toward your long-term goal.

Your goals should be clear and concrete. Do not generalize or be vague. State them simply and specifically.

MAKE REALISTIC AND POSITIVE GOALS

Be realistic when specifying goals. Choose goals that are ambitious, but not beyond the realm of what is in your power to achieve. Often, much of the workday is taken up with routine tasks or interruptions that are out of your control. If something is going to take you eight hours to complete, don't expect to be able to complete it in one workday. Be willing to work hard to reach your goals, without discouraging yourself by overreaching.

Describe your goals in positive terms and with specific time frames. As a short-term goal, for example, instead of saying, "I will not waste time this afternoon," set the goal "I will finish this spreadsheet by 3 p.m." Instead of saying, "I will not wait until Friday to write the paper," set the goal "I will prepare the final draft on Friday."

Set goals that really matter to you—goals you really want to meet. There will be delays, obstacles, and setbacks, so stay flexible and be willing to adapt your plan. When you find yourself off the mark, reexamine and revise your strategies. Look upon missteps as temporary setbacks. Keep trying and do not give up.

Setting clear, attainable goals is a key to success.

Deklofenak/Shutterstock.com

Align and Adjust Your Goals

To be successful in your job, you need to align your goals with those of your coworkers, your supervisor, and the organization that employs you. Make sure you understand the mission of your organization and the goals of your department, and choose goals that contribute meaningfully to them. If goals are not aligned, they can work against one another, reducing the chances of success for others as well as you.

Remember that as an administrative professional, your role is to support others. You are part of a team working toward common goals that will be reached more easily if your own goals directly and indirectly support those of others. Knowing that you have made a significant contribution to other people's success can be very rewarding.

It is important to stick to the goals you have set. However, it would be a mistake to be too strict about this general rule. You need to be firm but flexible. Your priorities may change from day to day and from hour to hour depending on the needs of your company and department. Your top priority may have been completing the marketing report; however, if your supervisor asks you to do something he or she considers more urgent, realign your goals to match those of your supervisor. Move that marketing report down a notch. Finish your supervisor's priority as efficiently as you can, and then refocus on the marketing report.

Stay Motivated

It is also important to stay motivated and continue to move toward meeting your goals. Motivation is fed by progress as well as incentives. Progress means forward movement toward a goal. Stopping to measure your progress can encourage you to stay on track. Take time to focus on what you have accomplished rather than worrying about how far you have to go.

MEASURE YOUR PROGRESS

As you work toward your goals, you should pause from time to time to measure your progress. This will keep you focused on what you want to achieve, even if it is still a long way off. If you take the time to celebrate reaching short-term goals, long-term goals will seem more attainable. For example, if your goal is to earn an associate's degree, completing the first class with a good grade should encourage you to continue.

If you find that a certain step or strategy did not get you closer to your goal, it is time to reassess, rethink, and reenergize your efforts. Be flexible. If one strategy doesn't move you toward your goal, think of others that might.

REWARD YOURSELF

Make sure to reward yourself as you achieve your short-term goals. Use incentives to help you move forward toward achieving the next goal. An **incentive** is a reward or encouragement. It need not be a material reward such as a bonus or raise. Many strong incentives have no material value. Their value lies in the sense of accomplishment you feel. For example, impressing a client or your supervisor with excellent service reinforces your commitment to doing it again. The satisfaction of moving ahead can be one of the most powerful incentives to keep striving.

Also, there is no harm in promising and giving yourself small, tangible rewards. For example, you might say to yourself, "If I walk a mile after work, I'll have a frozen yogurt." The walk might also clear your mind to help you generate ideas for solving problems.

RESIST INTERFERENCE

Most offices are busy places where it is difficult to focus on a single task or project without interruptions and obstacles. It is the nature of office work that phones ring, visitors arrive, e-mail inboxes fill, coworkers ask questions, and your supervisor pages you. **Interference** is anything that stands in the way of progress, whether it is demands from other people or your own temptation to waste time on things that will not help you reach your goal.

Some types of interference can be avoided or minimized. Visit with your coworkers during lunch or on your break. Keep your phone conversations effective but brief. Activate the Internet only when necessary. Group like tasks together and handle them at the same time. Although you cannot eliminate all interference, you will stay motivated when you make progress toward your goals.

TAKE ADVANTAGE OF OPPORTUNITIES

Take advantage of opportunities as they come up. An *opportunity* is a good position, chance, or prospect. For example, if your long-term goal is to be an office manager, and the person doing that job offers to mentor you, take full advantage of the opportunity and learn all you can. Take advantage of opportunities to increase your skills and knowledge or to build your professional network. Attend workshops or seminars related to your current job responsibilities or a job you would like in the future. The increased knowledge might make you more marketable in your position or more qualified for future positions.

Maintain Your Physical Health and Energy

To be effective on the job, you need to feel well. An administrative professional's job is often a sedentary job. You will probably spend hours each day at a desk, with few breaks. Make sure you are eating a healthful diet, controlling your weight, exercising, and getting enough sleep.

vm/iStockphoto.com

Take advantage of workshops and seminars.

EAT WELL

What you eat or do not eat affects your overall health. Excessive intake of fat, sugar, or salt contributes to poor health and to certain diseases such as hypertension (high blood pressure) and heart disease. Excessive sugar consumption can result in an increase in triglyceride levels in the blood, which can lead to cardiovascular disease. Too much salt can lead to an increase in blood pressure and the development of hypertension. The wisest course of action is to lower the intake of fat, sugar, and salt in your diet.

It is vital to make healthy choices when selecting foods for your diet. Maintaining a diet rich in fruits and vegetables is important. Eating vegetables, fruits, cereals, and legumes helps you maintain high levels of nutrients and fiber in your diet. Decrease the amount of processed grains; instead, consume at least half of all grains as whole grains. Include a variety of lean protein foods such as seafood, eggs, beans, peas, soy products, and unsalted nuts and seeds. The *2010 Dietary Guidelines for Americans* provides the following tips for incorporating healthful eating habits into your lifestyle:

- Eat less.
- Avoid oversized portions.
- Make half your plate fruits and vegetables.
- Switch to fat-free or low-fat (1 percent) milk.
- Compare sodium in foods, and choose the foods with lower numbers.
- Drink water instead of sugary drinks.[1]

ADOPT AN EXERCISE PROGRAM

An important way to address the physical inactivity of your job is to establish an exercise program that you set as a top priority. Exercise is important not only to your physical health, but also to your mental health. Additionally, exercise provides other benefits such as keeping your weight at a healthful level, giving you more energy and endurance, allowing you to bounce back more quickly from injury or disease, and generally helping you to maintain good health. Figure 4.1 lists a number of benefits attributable to exercise. Along with exercise, you should commit to eating a healthful diet.

A few of the many types of exercise that are good for your body are swimming, bicycling, jogging, and walking. Participate in an activity you enjoy. Determine a regular time of day to exercise,

[1]U.S. Departments of Agriculture and Health and Human Services, *2010 Dietary Guidelines for Americans*, http://www.cnpp.usda.gov/DGAs2010-PolicyDocument.htm (accessed Feb. 24, 2011).

Benefits of Physical Activity
■ Reduces one's risk for heart attack, colon cancer, diabetes, stroke, and high blood pressure
■ Contributes to healthy bones, muscles, and joints
■ Promotes better balance that can reduce falls among older adults
■ Helps to relieve the pain of arthritis
■ Reduces symptoms of anxiety and depression
■ Decreases the need for hospitalizations, physician visits, and medications

FIGURE 4.1 Exercise is beneficial to your physical and mental health.

and commit to do it. When you begin exercising, go slowly. Train your body; do not strain it. If you have any medical problems, consult your doctor about the type of exercise that is best for you.

A number of companies throughout the United States recognize that employees need physical exercise. These companies may provide exercise rooms that are available at any time of the day. Employees may take a 30- to 60-minute break and go to the exercise room. Other organizations partner with a fitness club in their area to provide employees with free or reduced-rate memberships. If you work for a company that does not provide these opportunities, take time to exercise on your own. The benefits of consistent exercise far outweigh the time it takes from your day.

GET ENOUGH SLEEP

The proper amount of sleep is essential to mental and physical health. Although the amount of sleep needed varies by individuals, seven to nine hours per night is recommended for adults. In addition to making you more alert during the day, sufficient sleep is recognized as an important component of health promotion and disease prevention. Yet many people have trouble getting the proper amount of sleep due to busy schedules and stressful lives.

Even if you go to bed at an appropriate hour, you may have difficulty falling asleep. Perhaps you have trouble turning off your mind. Maybe you rethink what went wrong in your day or begin to plan for the next day. Practicing the following techniques will help you fall asleep:

- Go to bed at the same time each night, and get up at the same time each morning.
- Set aside the hour before bed for quiet activities such as reading.
- Take a hot bath.
- Turn off the TV in the bedroom and/or turn down the TV in an adjoining room.
- Practice deep-breathing exercises.
- Create a relaxing scene in your head—waves rolling up on a beach or a mountain stream.
- Be certain your mattress and pillow are right for you—the proper firmness or softness.
- Pay attention to the amount of coffee, tea, soda, and chocolate you are consuming. These items can lead to sleep deprivation.

Tyler Olson/Shutterstock.com

Daily exercise increases mental and physical abilities.

Manage Relationships

Successfully managing your relationships with different kinds of people is a skill that can be developed with time, experience, and thoughtful effort. Taking the time to think about yourself—to truly know what you want and what you don't, what you'll do and what you won't—is a good way to start. Knowing these things and being faithful to them will shape your interactions with others.

You should also spend time thinking about your negative emotions and what triggers them. When you understand what sorts of things make you impatient or angry, you can better control these emotions when they begin. Controlling your emotions is very important in both personal and work relationships. When you control your emotions, you can step back and consider the best way to respond, instead of mindlessly reacting.

Be sensitive to the needs of your employer and coworkers. Know what they expect of you. Know how you fit into the organizational structure. Accept people; be tolerant. Strive to communicate openly and honestly.

Get to know the people with whom you have relationships. Be interested, be observant, and pay attention to what they say and do. Try hard to understand their requests, problems, and so on, from their point of view. At work, strive to put your relationships on a professional level, adopting the professional attitude described in Chapter 2.

Balance Work and Home

Many people comment with a sense of pride that they work a 50- or 60-hour week. Are these people producing a large amount of work? Maybe not. Do they have demanding and challenging jobs? Perhaps. Are they appreciated and respected for their work contributions? Not necessarily. A relationship does exist between hours worked and productivity. Of course, individuals differ in the number of productive hours they can work. However, studies show that productivity decreases after extended periods. Most people realize immediately when they are not being productive. When they become fatigued, the amount of work they produce goes down and their error rate goes up.

You actually can gain new energy by taking time to play. As an adult, you may have forgotten how to relax and, with complete abandon, enjoy the world around you. Some experts writing in the field of creative energy recommend *joy breaks*—stopping for a few minutes to play when feeling overtired or nonproductive. When you take a few minutes for enjoyment a few times throughout the day, your mood becomes more positive, and you will become more productive and effective. Although the ultimate goal is for joy breaks to happen automatically, in the beginning you may need to write these daily breaks into your schedule.

sjlocke/iStockphoto.com

Strive to maintain a healthy balance between work and home demands.

TECH TALK

Digital Storytelling With *Windows Live Movie Maker*

Digital storytelling is simply telling a story using digital media. The practice of telling a story digitally has value because it requires careful planning, gathering of information, and creation of digital content. In addition, the final product demonstrates a person's ability to produce and create, as well as to use the technology. Many programs can be used to create a digital story, such as *Microsoft PowerPoint*, *Windows Live Movie Maker, Microsoft Photo Story*, and *Apple iMovie* software. Here is a quick description of a popular and commonly used program provided on most new personal computers: *Windows Live Movie Maker* software.

This program has a simple ribbon at the top with options to add images, video, and sound; choose a theme; and distribute or share the finished product in various ways. The first step is to add video or images. This opens an editing area where additions, deletions, and other types of changes can be made for sounds, images, video, and text.

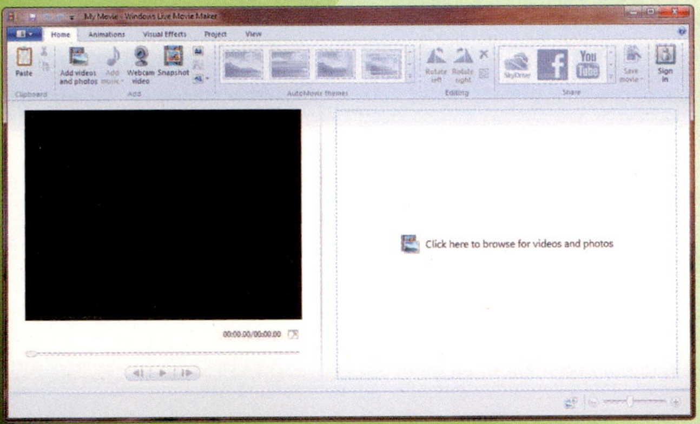

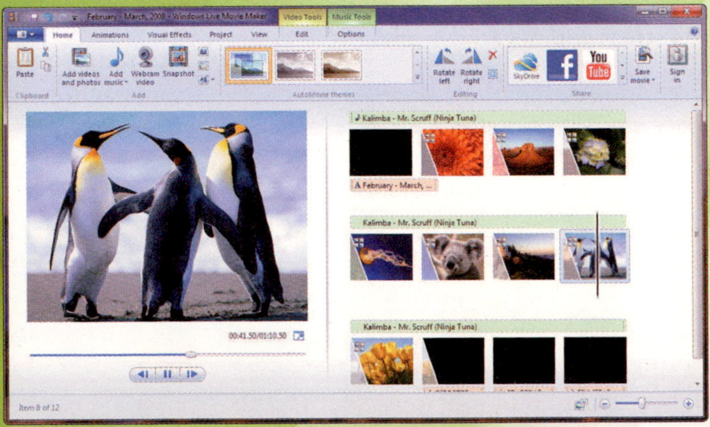

Another way to gain new energy is to take a short exercise break. You might keep athletic shoes at your desk for a short five- or ten-minute break to climb stairs or to take a brisk walk. Such physical activity allows you to release built-up tension, to open blocked thinking, and to trigger creative ideas.

If you are working from home, it is often difficult to maintain an appropriate balance between work and home demands. Discuss your work arrangements with your family and friends. Although some people will assume that you are not really working or that you are available to take on additional responsibilities, this is not true. Make sure family and friends know your working hours, and help them to understand when you cannot be disturbed. Let them know you have business responsibilities that you must complete.

Manage Stress

Stress is the worry and anxiety you feel when you react to pressure from others or yourself. The cost of stress is high for both the organization and the individual. For the organization, the price can be loss of productivity, poor work performance, and absenteeism or job turnover. For the individual, the price can be increased illness and temporary loss of work. Stress also has an impact on your interactions with others. If you are effective at managing your stress, it is more likely that you'll affect those around you in a positive way and less likely that other people's stress will negatively affect you.

Stress is inevitable, and it is safe to say that everyone at times experiences stress in life. However, the causes of stress are certainly individual. What may be stressful for you may have the opposite effect on someone else. For example, you may become tense when driving, while your friend may find driving a source of relaxation and enjoyment. Downhill skiing may cause fear in your friend, but may be something you look forward to after a day of studying. The first step in managing stress is to identify what stresses you. Once you have identified your stressors, it is critical to learn how to manage them.

Understanding Stress

Stress is sometimes positive. For example, you may feel stressed when you start a new job or feel pressure to meet a deadline. This stress can be helpful because it can encourage you to get your work done. It can give you a burst of energy and can prepare you to strive to meet challenges. However, negative stress can affect your mental and physical health.

One of the factors that contribute to workplace stress is role ambiguity. **Role ambiguity** exists when individuals have inadequate information about their work roles—when there is a lack of clarity about work objectives and expectations. As an administrative professional, you may experience role ambiguity. You may not understand exactly what is expected of you. When this situation occurs, you have the responsibility to find out what your job is. If a job description exists for your position, read it carefully. If there is no job description, ask your employer what he or she expects of you.

Another factor that contributes to stress is job insecurity. In a volatile economy, organizations are often in the process of downsizing. If your organization is doing so, it is normal to wonder, *Will I be the next to go?* If you have these thoughts, you probably are not able to give your best efforts to the job. Your productivity may suffer.

An important component of understanding stress is to learn what stresses you and what you can do to control the stress in your life. If you are unable to cope with stress, you can become physically, mentally, and/or emotionally ill. Therefore, you must achieve an appropriate balance between the stress in your life and your ability to cope with it.

Types of Stress

The most common types of stress are short-term and long-term stress. You may experience short-term stress when missing the bus, taking an exam, or going to a job interview. The workday of an administrative professional may be filled with short-term stress situations. Answering a busy telephone, meeting project deadlines, and handling clients and customers can all be causes of short-term stress in an

George Dolgikh/Shutterstock.com

There are many causes of short-term stress in an office.

office. Short-term stress can cause emotional issues including anxiety, irritability, and depression. It can also cause muscular problems including tension headaches or jaw pain and other physical problems including upset stomach, elevated blood pressure, and dizziness.

Long-term stress occurs when a stressful situation is prolonged with no rest or recuperation for the body. Examples of long-term stress include not getting along with coworkers, losing your job, and suffering from financial problems. Long-term stress has been linked to both heart disease and cancer, which are the two leading causes of death in the United States. In addition, prolonged stress can cause other physical problems such as these:

- Headaches
- Weight gain
- Elevated cholesterol
- Shortness of breath
- Chest pain
- Back pain
- Sleeping problems

Long-term stress can also cause emotional problems such as the following:

- Depression
- Withdrawal
- Anger
- Self-rejection
- Anxiety

Preventing and Coping With Stress

Many organizations offer stress reduction programs in the workplace. They include exercise, diet, and stress reduction techniques such as meditation, relaxation training, and changes in lifestyle management. Some organizations even offer programs designed to increase fun in the workplace.

As an individual, you can help decrease the effects of stress on your body by maintaining your physical health and energy. Follow the suggestions earlier in this chapter related to making healthy food choices. Establish and follow an exercise program. Make sure to get the proper amount of sleep. The better you feel, the better equipped you'll be to manage work stress without becoming overwhelmed.

USE VISUALIZATION

Visualization is the creation of a mental picture. Using visualization can help you relieve stress. Through visualization, you block out unwanted thoughts.

To achieve the maximum benefits from visualization, get into a comfortable position, relax any muscles that feel tense, and begin to visualize a sky of white fluffy clouds, ocean waves licking a golden beach, the sun glistening on a snow-covered mountain, or a beautiful sunset over your favorite lake. Focus on the scene for several minutes to block out the tensions of the day. You can also use visualization as soon as you begin to feel anxious, to avoid stress, or as a way to refocus yourself after a stressful situation.

RELAX

You can help to reduce the effects of stress by taking the time to relax. If you have been feeling stressed, spend some time each day doing something you enjoy like listening to music, reading a good book, or taking a walk. You can help to relax your muscles and decrease the stress and tension in your body by stretching or massaging your muscles.

Deep-breathing exercises are one of the quickest ways to relax your body. Begin by finding a comfortable position, sitting in a comfortable chair or lying down. You may close your eyes if that makes you feel more at ease. Next, slowly inhale through your nose until you feel your lungs fill with air. Then exhale slowly, breathing out through your nose or mouth. Repeat the process until you begin to feel a sense of relaxation.

USE POSITIVE SELF-TALK

When you are stressed, negative self-talk can escalate your feelings; positive self-talk, on the other hand, can produce positive results. For example, assume you are playing a game of tennis with a skilled opponent. You want to play your best. You miss a ball and say to yourself, *That was terrible; I can't even get a ball over the net*. You are engaging in negative self-talk, and negative self-talk on the tennis court can cause you to miss even more shots. In other words, your negative self-talk can become a self-fulfilling prophecy. You decide you are terrible, and you prove yourself right.

Now consider a positive self-talk response. When you miss a ball, you say to yourself, *No big deal; I'll get the next one*. And you do! You make a terrific shot that your opponent is unable to return. When you find yourself engaging in negative self-talk, stop. Make a deliberate effort to switch to positive self-talk.

WALK AWAY

Sometimes you can prevent stress by avoiding situations that typically cause you stress. For example, if you find driving in heavy traffic stressful, avoid driving during rush hours. While avoiding stressful situations is not always possible, you may be able to diminish stress by walking away from a stressful situation. For instance, if there is a lunchtime discussion at work that you find stressful, politely excuse yourself and walk away. If you cannot walk away physically, walk away emotionally or mentally. For example, count silently to ten, or envision yourself at one of your favorite places having a wonderful time.

TALK TO FRIENDS OR FAMILY MEMBERS

If a situation at school or work is making you feel stressed, talk about it with trusted friends or family members. Talking about your problems with people you trust can make you feel better. They might be able to help you understand what is causing your

Monkey Business Images/Shutterstock.com

Talking to a friend can sometimes help you feel better.

stress and help you decide what to do about the situation. They may be able to suggest solutions that have not occurred to you.

SOLVE THE PROBLEM

Make a list of the situations that cause you stress. From your list, determine which of these situations or problems you can solve. Ask yourself these questions:

- What is the problem?
- What are my alternatives?
- From the alternatives generated, what is the best alternative in this situation?

Once you have identified the problem and determined the best alternative in dealing with it, act and evaluate!

- Act on the best alternative—implement it.
- Evaluate the situation: Did the action I implemented solve the problem? If not, why not? Did I choose the wrong alternative? If so, what other alternative can I try?

Being able to solve the problem gives you some control over the situation and the confidence to continue to solve problems and tackle issues as they arise. That sense of confidence will help you feel less stressed. However, sometimes the situation is out of your control and there is nothing you can do. If that is the case, walk away. Follow the five steps listed in Figure 4.2 to assist you when solving problems.

Problem-Solving Steps
1. Define or identify the problem.
2. Collect and analyze information.
3. Generate alternatives or possible solutions.
4. Assess and implement an alternative.
5. Evaluate the solution.

FIGURE 4.2 Following logical steps will help you solve problems.

Manage Your Work

Time is a precious commodity for most people. They never have enough time for everything they want or need to do. Administrative professionals are no exception. You, as a busy person in a world of change, will find yourself often lamenting the fact that you do not have enough time—to do all the tasks at your job, to handle all the stressors of your professional and personal life, or to relax and enjoy yourself. By organizing your workspace, conducting a time audit, planning and organizing assignments, completing your work correctly, avoiding procrastination, handling paper and e-mail, streamlining tasks, managing large projects, and handling time wasters, you can make better use of the time you have available and have more time for the things you want or need to do.

Manage Your Workspace

The first step in managing your work is to organize your workspace. This may not be an easy task, but it is important. An organized work area saves you time and makes accomplishing your work easier. Knowing where things are and being able to lay your hands on what you need instantly helps you feel relaxed and in control. In addition, a clean, neat, and organized workspace demonstrates your professionalism.

Keep your desk neat and organized. Have items that you use frequently each day on your desk, and store other items away. Keep the drawers of your desk organized. Put frequently used supplies in top drawers where they are easily accessible. Discard items you do not use, and store items you use rarely somewhere else.

When you are working on a project, clear your desk of materials that relate to other projects. Put them away neatly, with any files clearly marked so you can find them again quickly. The key to keeping things in order is to put them away right after you use them. Review the information in Chapter 2 about maintaining a professional and organized work area.

Conduct a Time Audit

To utilize time more effectively, you must understand something about time. You never seem to have the time you need; yet you have all the time there is. Time is a resource you cannot buy, sell, rent, borrow, save, or manufacture. You cannot change it, convert it, or control it. It can only be spent. Everyone receives an equal amount of time every day. The term *managing time* is a misnomer. In actuality, *managing time* means managing yourself in relation to your time.

To make effective choices about your time, you need to know as much as you can about how you spend it. An effective way to discover this is to do an audit. Track the time you are spending on various activities for a few days. Once you know how you are spending your time, determine positive steps you can take to use your time more productively. For instance, you can practice and implement the effective time management strategies discussed in this chapter.

Albert H. Teich/Shutterstock.com

A cluttered desk can be a major time waster.

Plan and Organize Assignments

If you are trying to work without planning and organizing, you are doing yourself a great disservice. Even if you have a great memory and are very organized, it is still important to take the time to plan. Here are several reasons why you should manage your tasks with a planning system and a daily written to-do list:

- As an administrative professional, you will have lots of little details to remember as part of your regular work. Keeping a list of even routine tasks will help you make sure all tasks get done.
- As an administrative professional, you will also have to deal with several projects and tasks at the same time. It is easy to forget something when you are managing the details of your everyday work while incorporating the tasks associated with special projects and duties.
- Most people have difficulty planning and ordering items solely in their head. It is much easier to make decisions when things are written down.
- You may feel anxious or overwhelmed trying to remember the details of your tasks or projects. If you write those items down, you can forget about them until they become important or completion becomes a priority.

ADOPT A PLANNING SYSTEM

Because few people have the ability to remember everything, most people make notes to keep track of their tasks and appointments. There are a variety of good planning systems that you can use. The key to effective time management is finding a system that works for you and using it faithfully.

You have probably used a paper planner in school or at previous jobs. You may also have experience using an electronic planner such as *Microsoft Outlook*® messaging software. This software allows you to schedule meetings electronically and prepare a calendar and to-do list by day, week, and month. Others choose to use a smartphone or combination of planners. Regardless of

Photographer/Image Source

Professional POINTERS

Try these stress and time management techniques to help you work more productively:

- Do not allow yourself to lose sight of your vision and purpose in life. Take time to sit quietly and analyze whether you are living your values and being true to your purpose.
- Keep a journal of situations that make you feel stressed. Writing in a journal and reviewing your thoughts periodically can be like talking to a trusted friend.
- Identify the time of day when you are at your peak. Plan to tackle your most difficult jobs during your peak periods.
- Do not over-schedule yourself. Allow an hour or two of uncommitted time each day.
- Balance your professional life with a fulfilling personal life. Make time to pursue personal interests and to relax.

the type, a planner is a great tool for organizing your work and for tracking appointments and other commitments for yourself or your supervisor.

Your company or department may have a planning system that you are required to use. If not, think about your needs and choose the system that will work best for you. Take the time to become thoroughly familiar with the features of your planning system so you can optimize it to work best for you.

Use your planning system to record appointments, meetings, due dates, and reminders. Enter important dates and tasks as soon as you become aware of them so you will not forget to enter them later. Electronic systems allow you to prioritize tasks and set dates for their completion. You no longer have to remember dates and deadlines; instead, you can concentrate on the projects to be accomplished.

SET PRIORITIES

Many times you will not be able to do everything you are asked to do in one day. You must be able to distinguish the most important items, tasks that should be done first, from less important items, tasks that can wait until later. If you are new to a job, you may need help from your employer to determine which items are most important. But once you learn more about the job and your employer, you should be able to establish priorities on your own.

Making lists of things you need to do can be a very effective way of organizing your work. Each afternoon before you leave work, you should prepare a to-do list for the next day. List all the tasks, activities, and projects you need to accomplish in order of priority. A **priority** is something that merits your attention ahead of other tasks. Then review your list to determine how you will handle the items on it. Mark the items in this manner:

- Most important matters—A
- Less important items—B
- Remaining items—C

Tasks, activities, and projects that have a deadline of the following day will be in Category A. Examples of category A activities might be processing the weekly payroll information, getting rid of a computer virus, and preparing handouts for a meeting the next day. In addition, you may have a very large project due next week. To get the project done on time, you must break it into parts. One part might be given a Category A priority to be completed tomorrow. On the following day, another part might be given a Category A priority to be completed. By breaking the project into parts and assigning priorities to those parts, you make the project manageable. What once seemed overwhelming has been accomplished in an orderly and timely fashion.

Category B consists of those items that may be completed the next day, but no serious consequences will result if they are not. Examples of category B items would be planning the board meeting to be held in three months, preparing your presentation scheduled for next month, and handling routine information requests.

Category C consists of items that are fairly unimportant or that may be delegated. Examples include filing routine correspondence, copying handouts for a meeting next week, and transferring files from active to inactive storage.

If you are going to delegate an item, explain clearly to the individual who will be doing the task exactly what is expected of him or her. If the project is a complex one, you may want to give the person written instructions.

Reward yourself for priorities well set and goals achieved. Check off items as you finish them, and recognize each completed item as a success.

Avoid Procrastination

When you try to avoid a task by putting it aside with the intention of doing it later, that is called **procrastination**. The first step to getting something done is starting. Even if you know you cannot finish

Complete Work Correctly

One way to manage your tasks is to complete your work correctly the first time. Revising and redoing work because you failed to do it correctly is not an effective way to manage your time or tasks.

- Get appropriate instructions or procedures before beginning the work.
- Read any relevant files on similar tasks.
- Understand the scope of the task. What is the final product to be? What expectations does your supervisor have?
- If it is a new task for you, talk with the person who did it before you, if possible. Listen carefully to any pointers or suggestions.

Digital Vision/Getty Images

a project that you have been avoiding, promise yourself that you will tackle a small part of the project. Adding an activity to your to-do list should help you get started.

Perfectionism is defined as a propensity for setting extremely high standards and being displeased with anything else. For some people, perfectionism can cause procrastination. A perfectionist would rather put a task off than do the task incompletely. Certainly you should strive to achieve and perform well; however, no human being can be perfect. Rather than perfection, aim for progress by reminding yourself that any step toward completion is an accomplishment. Figure 4.3 gives suggestions for avoiding procrastination.

Handle Paper and E-Mail

Piles of letters, memos, and other documents can accumulate quickly. Handling paper over and over—putting it in piles on your desk, reshuffling, rehandling, rereading—can use up a lot of your time. The basic rule is to handle papers as few times as possible. Make sure to schedule time during non-peak hours to tackle paperwork so it doesn't accumulate. Handle routine requests or tasks immediately whenever you can. Do something with the paper as it reaches you, rather than adding it to a pile. Read it, route it, answer it, file it, or dispose of it—get it off your desk as quickly as possible without handling it repeatedly.

Tips for Avoiding Procrastination
■ Take the time each day to create a to-do list.
■ Start with the one thing you must get done today.
■ Avoid overplanning.
■ Limit your tasks to 30 minutes or less.
■ Do the most difficult or least desirable task early to get it out of the way.
■ Set a time limit.
■ Alternate unpleasant jobs with tasks you enjoy.
■ Review your progress at the end of each day.

FIGURE 4.3 Recognizing ways to avoid procrastination will help you be more productive.

E-mail programs allow you to set up folders to organize messages you really need to save. You can set up folders for messages that are related to a specific task or issue such as "Strategic Planning Committee" or "Staff Meetings." Store messages from any sender that relate to that project in the folder. You will learn about organizing and managing paper records in Chapter 11 and organizing electronic records, records retention, transfer, and disposal in Chapter 12.

Streamline Tasks

In most jobs there are tasks you do over and over again, sometimes daily, sometimes several times a day. Over time, you are likely to get faster at doing them and to find ways of performing them more efficiently. Think actively about ways to streamline this sort of work. Observe what your coworkers do, or ask their advice.

There are many ways to automate your work when using software. As you get to know various systems, you will learn how to automate certain steps to speed up procedures such as keying and entering data. There are dozens of shortcuts, automated commands, and time- and work-saving features in word processing software. For example, you can use predesigned templates to create and format documents. You can save commonly used text or specialized formatting so it can quickly be incorporated in future documents. You can use macros to record, save, and run automatic series or sets of commands or steps. In e-mail software, you can streamline tasks by creating group distribution lists so you don't have to enter individual e-mail addresses when sending a group message. You can use filters to sort incoming messages and store signatures. Take advantage of shortcuts, automated commands, and special features of your software to save yourself time and work.

Manage Large Projects

Most organizations have numerous large projects that must be managed. As an administrative professional, you may be responsible for assisting with the management of these projects. Generally, you will

PARTNERSHIP FOR 21ST CENTURY SKILLS

Productivity/ Accountability

Project Management

Effective administrative professionals are successful because they have the ability to manage their time, their work, and their responsibilities. In addition to handling daily activities, as an administrative professional you will be required to effectively manage other projects as they arise. The ability to manage projects from the simple to the complex is critical to your success.

Most people have experience managing projects as part of their daily activities. Completing your homework, writing an English paper, and doing your laundry are examples of projects you have already successfully completed. Creating a newsletter, completing an equipment inventory, and creating and giving a presentation are examples of projects an administrative professional may encounter. To manage a project, you must be able to:

- Set realistic goals.
- Plan your steps, including allocating the necessary resources such as money, time, and energy.
- Monitor your progress.
- Address and correct any problems.
- Achieve your goals.

Activity

Determine a project that you must accomplish sometime in the next week. Create a list of your goals for the project. List the steps you will take to successfully complete the project. As you move through the steps, monitor the progress you are making toward your goals. Were there obstacles you encountered along the way? How did you move forward toward your goals? Were you successful in achieving your goals?

Yuri Arcurs/Shutterstock.com

be working with a number of individuals. All team members need to understand not only the project but the intended outcomes. Here are several suggestions that will help you be successful:

- Establish clarity as to the scope of the project with your employer.
- Set clear goals or outcomes. This step is generally done in conjunction with the administrator who is responsible for the overall project.
- Determine what resources are needed; e.g., you may need to purchase software to help you with the management of the project.

- Establish who will be involved in the project with you.
- Have a group discussion with those individuals. As a group, determine the responsibilities and expectations of each person.
- Break the project down into manageable components.
- Set deadlines for the small tasks and steps to be completed.
- Follow through on tasks to completion.

You may be responsible for monitoring the completion of assignments. If so, you may choose to discuss assignments individually with team members. If a member has not completed a task on time, determine what the problem is and help solve it. Additionally, having regular group meetings to discuss overall progress can be helpful. If a portion of the project cannot be completed because someone has not performed a task on time, work as a group to identify the cause and ways to solve the problem.

AVAVA/Shutterstock.com

Socializing is most appropriate on breaks or at lunch.

Handle Time Wasters

Every day you waste time in a variety of ways. If you understand your own time wasters, you can become more effective at managing yourself in relation to your time. Listed here are several common time wasters.

CHATTER

If you presently have a job, do you go to work and get busy accomplishing the tasks of the day? Or do you report to work promptly and then spend the first 30 minutes of your workday talking to co-workers about what happened the night before? Certainly, it is important to have some time to talk about topics other than business, but socializing is more appropriate on breaks or at lunch. In most organizations, too much time is wasted in excessive socializing, when employees should be accomplishing the work of the organization.

INTERRUPTIONS

While some time wasters can be controlled or prevented, others cannot. Interruptions are the rule rather than the exception for administrative professionals. Not only do interruptions waste time, but it takes additional time to get back on track with what you were doing. To minimize the effects of interruptions, learn to take them in stride and to refocus quickly on your work after you address them. Something as simple as putting a check mark where you were in a document can help you get back on track after answering a question or the telephone.

E-mail, however, is an interruption you can have some control over. Don't allow yourself to be interrupted by responding instantly to the message signal from your computer. Allocate specific times throughout the day to read and answer messages. You may be able to check messages once in the morning and again right after lunch. You can determine how frequently you need to check messages by the role e-mail plays in your department or organization.

DISORGANIZATION

I had that letter just a few minutes ago, but now I can't find it. It couldn't have disappeared into thin air. Have you ever made such a statement and then proceeded to rummage through the clutter on your desk for 30 minutes in an attempt to find the paper you never should have misplaced? A disorganized and cluttered desk can be a major time waster for administrative professionals. You should know what goes into your desk, what stays on top of your desk, and what goes into your files. Do not clutter your desk with papers that should be filed electronically or manually.

Part of effective organization is organizing your day appropriately. For example, if you try to prepare a report, plan a meeting, and do a month's filing all at the most hectic part of the day (when the telephone is ringing constantly and clients are coming and going), the result will be wasted time, nothing accomplished, frayed nerves, and a stressed-out or angry feeling. When you have a detailed task to accomplish, plan to do it during a time when interruptions are minimal.

SUMMARY

To reinforce what you have learned in this chapter, study this summary.

- The successful administrative professional will set achievable goals that are aligned with the organization's and stay motivated to achieve them by measuring progress, rewarding accomplishments, and resisting interference.
- Maintaining your physical health and energy, managing your relationships, and finding an appropriate balance between work and home will help you be an efficient, productive worker.
- Manage stress by understanding the types, knowing what factors contribute to stress, and using appropriate strategies for coping with and preventing it.
- Manage your work through the adoption of systems, techniques, and habits that help you set priorities, avoid procrastination, manage your tasks, and handle time wasters.

KEY TERMS

incentive, 72
interference, 72
priority, 82
procrastination, 83
role ambiguity, 77
self-discipline, 70
stress, 77
visualization, 78

4

STUDY Tools

Located at www.cengagebrain.com

- Chapter Outlines
- Flashcards
- Interactive Quizzes
- Tech Tools
- Video Segments
- and More!

LET'S DISCUSS

1. Why is setting goals and priorities important?
2. What strategies can you employ to remain motivated to achieve your goals?
3. Name three benefits of a healthful diet and three benefits of exercise.
4. Define stress and identify at least five ways to cope with stress.
5. Discuss four strategies for managing your work.

PUT IT TO WORK

Handling stress You recently got a job as a part-time administrative assistant. You are attending college for the first time, taking 14 credit hours. Your classes require much more of your time than you anticipated. You work 20 hours per week and spend an average of 25 hours per week on classwork, but you are still not getting all your schoolwork completed. You have an apartment, which you share with two roommates; the three of you share the cooking and cleaning responsibilities. You have little time for fun and relaxation. The job is demanding, your classes are time-consuming, and you feel overwhelmed. You are finding yourself becoming stressed and irritable with your roommates.

How can you get the situation under control? Using the techniques suggested in this chapter, key a list of steps to take to prevent and cope with your stress. (Learning Objectives 1, 2, and 3)

COMMUNICATE SUCCESSFULLY

1. **Setting goals** List two long-term and two short-term goals that are related to your education or career and that are important to you. They can be goals you are currently working toward or goals you would like to achieve in the future. State each goal simply, specifically, and in positive terms. Make a timeline for reaching each goal with steps along the way. (Learning Objective 1)
2. **Manage yourself** Keep a log of how you spend your time for the next four days. At the end of the time, review the log. Analyze the way you spent your time by answering the following questions. What patterns and habits are apparent from your time log? What were your major time wasters? How can you control or minimize those time wasters? On which activities can you spend less time? Which activities need more of your time? Did you spend enough time on physical activity? Did you get enough sleep?

   Write a short essay in which you answer the questions in this activity and explain any changes you might make as a result of your analysis. (Learning Objectives 1 and 3)

3. **Manage stress** Add a new post to the blog you created in Chapter 1. In this entry, reflect on the following statement: **This chapter has helped me think about how I manage my stress in the following ways.** (Learning Objective 2)

Blog

DEVELOP WORKPLACE SKILLS

4. **Self-management** Analyze the following situations. Describe in detail how you would handle each situation, and explain your reasoning. (Learning Objectives 1, 2, and 3)

   - Although you go to bed early, you find it difficult to fall asleep and toss and turn until the early morning hours. You are extremely tired in the morning and are finding it takes you longer to get your work done.
   - You spent all day completing a rush job for your supervisor. When you took the completed job to your supervisor, you were told he did not need it until tomorrow.
   - Each day before leaving work, you carefully plan your work for the next day. However, the telephone rings continually, and you are having difficulty completing the items in your plan.
   - The weekly report is due every Friday at 9 a.m. Although you try to tackle the report earlier in the week, you never seem to get started until late Thursday afternoon, and then you have to work late on Thursday to get it done.
   - Your desk is next to the office copier. Your coworkers stand by your desk and chat while they wait for their documents to be copied. You don't want to be rude, but you are finding it hard to concentrate and are making mistakes with your work.

5. **Make appointments** You are working for Mrs. Carol Johnson, the vice president of marketing. She has asked that you update her calendar with the following appointments. Use *Microsoft Outlook* or another type of calendaring software to complete this activity. Enter the following appointments for Mrs. Johnson. Assume all the appointments should be scheduled during the first full week of next month. (Learning Objective 3)

   - Appointment with Maxwell Edwards from 2 p.m. to approximately 3:30 p.m. on Wednesday.
   - Appointment with Tomas Mendoza at 9 a.m. on Monday; Mrs. Johnson anticipates the appointment will last approximately an hour.
   - Luncheon meeting with Rodney Rodriguez at noon on Thursday; Mrs. Johnson will meet Mr. Rodriguez at the Palm Restaurant. It will take her 30 minutes to travel to the restaurant.

- Appointment with John O'Malley at 2 p.m. on Tuesday to discuss a new program your company will be launching. This appointment is extremely important, and the time cannot be changed.
- Every Monday Mrs. Johnson meets with her personal trainer during her lunch hour (from noon until 1 p.m.). It takes her 15 minutes to get to the Power Street Gym.
- Mrs. Johnson needs to complete employee evaluations for Rachel Harris, Gina Lombardini, and Jon Tiechman. Each evaluation meeting will take 30–45 minutes and must be completed by Thursday at noon.
- Every Tuesday there is a staff meeting at 9 a.m. The meeting typically lasts an hour but sometimes stretches to 1½ hours.
- Appointment with Raphael Simmons to review an employee grievance. The appointment will take one hour. Raphael is available anytime Tuesday or Wednesday morning.

BUILD RELATIONSHIPS

6. **Setting priorities** Yuan Chang works as a systems analyst and reports to Dianne Bradwell. He was given a major project two months ago; it is due next month. Recently Ms. Bradwell's workload increased dramatically as a result of the installation of a new computer system. She calls Yuan to troubleshoot problems with the system. Because these problems affect employees' work production, Yuan must handle them promptly.

   Yuan was planning to take a two-week vacation. However, he is behind on the project and has only four weeks left to finish it. Yuan feels burned out due to his heavy workload. He tries to work on the project every day, but Ms. Bradwell's calls keep him busy. Yuan has not told her that he is behind on the project. For the last two weeks, Yuan has been bringing a sandwich from home so he can work through lunch. He also stays late, working until at least 6 p.m. each day.

   Describe what may result if Yuan continues to handle his situation as he currently is. How can Yuan manage his time more effectively? Does Yuan need to talk to his supervisor about the situation? If so, what should he say? (Learning Objectives 2 and 3)

USE TECH TOOLS

TT

7. **Create a video** Choose a partner to work with for this assignment. Select one of the situations described in Activity 4 in the Develop Workplace Skills section. Use *Windows Live Movie Maker* to create a video to illustrate the situation. Include a section in the video that demonstrates how you would handle the situation. The digital story should include both pictures and sound.

PLAN AHEAD

Workplace stress Work with a classmate to complete this assignment. As a team, interview an administrator concerning stress in the workplace. Ask this person to respond to three of the following questions. Create two additional questions on your own.

- What factors contribute to stress in the workplace?
- What is the cost of negative stress to the organization?
- Does your organization offer workshops or other resources for employees on stress management?
- Does your organization offer resources for employees on effectively managing time?
- Does your organization offer opportunities to help employees maintain and improve their physical health?

Write a short report to summarize the interview. Make sure to include the name of the person interviewed, his or her title, and the name of the organization. Be prepared to make a short presentation to the class. (Learning Objectives 1, 2, and 3)

CHAPTER

5 Ethical Theories and Behaviors

LEARNING OBJECTIVES

1. Understand the basics of ethics and consider the importance of ethical behavior in the workplace.
2. Identify characteristics of an ethical organization.
3. Develop a framework for making ethical decisions.
4. Identify characteristics of an ethical administrative professional.

Ethics 101

Ethics are the standards that generally help people determine right from wrong or what they ought to do. They include widely accepted ideas such as the importance of loyalty, honesty, and kindness toward others as well as the wrongness of actions such as murder, theft, lying, and assault. **Business ethics** is the application of ethical standards in the workplace. This chapter will help you understand the role ethics plays in the workplace and how you can develop ethical habits as an administrative professional.

For individuals and businesses, ethics are important. For you as an administrative professional, your reputation as a trustworthy employee and your value in that respect are at stake with each decision you make. For example, will you repeat confidential or sensitive information that you are privy to as an administrative professional? Can your supervisor trust you to do your work diligently when he or she is away from the office? Can your coworkers trust you to act fairly?

Businesses must also face the issue of reputation. A business that consistently treats its employees fairly will tend to have satisfied and loyal employees. Businesses with questionable ethics may experience high turnover and may spend more time and effort finding and training employees. Reputation is also important when dealing with competitors and customers. Those who are treated fairly and honestly will respect and do business with an ethical organization.

Ethics are often confused with laws, character, and values, and they are also sometimes identified with feelings and religion. Laws are the rules established by governments, which may or may not be ethical (what people ought to do). You can probably think of some periods in history when certain laws were enacted that were later deemed unethical. The term **character** refers to your consistent personal standards of behavior. Character has been defined as the person you are when no one else is watching. **Values** are personal beliefs about what is right or wrong. Your values were, and still are, being shaped by parents, religion, culture, television, friends, social networking, and schools as well as various other influences. You rely most often on your personal values when making decisions about what is right or wrong.

Ethics are concrete standards that are not based on feelings. Feelings, when making an ethical decision, might be deceptive. For example, you promised a coworker that he is next on the list to get an outside cubicle, but your best friend has asked you for that workspace several times recently. Relying on feelings could lead you to choose pleasing your friend over keeping a promise to a coworker. Ethics are also not limited to religion. While most religions do advocate ethical behavior, and ethics certainly have roots in religion, ethics are not only for people with religious beliefs. They are standards for everyone, since they recognize obligations and benefits to society.

Characteristics of Ethical Organizations

When you begin looking for employment as an administrative professional, an important factor to consider is whether the organization is ethical. Many characteristics can demonstrate an organization's ethics. Here are a few to consider.

Environmental Responsibility

An environmentally responsible organization not only obeys environmental laws but shows a commitment to environmental concerns above and beyond what is legally required. A familiar example is a company recycling program. An environmentally responsible company might voluntarily upgrade its anti-pollution equipment, streamline its production processes to produce less waste, make corporate donations to support environmental causes, and adopt green building practices, such as using local materials and native landscaping.

Acting ethically regarding the environment benefits organizations in several ways. For instance, adopting environmentally friendly methods of waste disposal and water and energy conservation can help with public and employee perceptions and

SoulAD/Shutterstock.com

An ethical organization is environmentally responsible.

can motivate consumers to buy products and services. In contrast, skirting regulations could be detrimental. In addition to legal problems, there can be repercussions due to negative perceptions within the community.

Global Awareness

Directly or indirectly, many organizations do business with companies outside the United States. In deciding whom they will do business with and where, ethical organizations consider issues such as human rights, labor practices, and environmental policies. For example, a company that manufactures engines in the United States decides to purchase parts from one of two companies overseas. When it finds that one of the companies employs child labor in manufacturing the parts, the company chooses the other.

The drive to produce goods as inexpensively as possible can lead to ethical problems. For instance, in some foreign nations, a company might offer substantially lower labor costs because its employees work long hours for very low wages with few measures taken for safety. Globally aware organizations avoid countries or companies with poor ethical records or use their influence as customers to effect change.

Organizational Commitment to Ethical Behavior

As you learned in Chapter 1, every organization has its own particular culture, which may be ethically strong, ethically weak, or somewhere in between. The culture of the organization you work for will definitely impact your ethical behavior in the workplace. Employees who work for ethical companies generally act more ethically than employees who work for unethical companies. Peer pressure isn't just for teenagers and young adults; all age groups are susceptible.

The ethical culture of an organization is evident in the rewards and punishments given and the policies and procedures developed and adhered to within the organization. An organizational culture that is highly ethical is concerned about getting the job done in an ethical manner, as opposed to just getting the job done. Highly ethical organizational cultures in general experience less misconduct. Employees feel less pressure to do something unethical, are more likely to report misconduct seen in the workplace, and are less likely to be retaliated against if they do report wrongdoing. In contrast, organizations with a weak ethical culture have a higher incidence of employee-reported ethical violations—such as lying to employees or the public, falsifying time sheets, abusive behavior, abuse of company resources, safety violations, discrimination, and employee benefits violations—than do companies with a strong ethical culture.[1]

While mission statements and the like give some indication of an organization's culture, for it to be truly understood, you will need to discover it over time as you learned in Chapter 1 through observing how things work and what people say and do. A close acquaintance who works in an organization will also be able to tell you about the organization's culture. Is this the kind of company you want to be associated with? Is it a place where you would want to build a career?

Honesty

An ethical organization is honest when dealing with employees and other organizations and individuals. For example, the company makes its personnel policies, such as salary and promotion policies, clear to all employees. In a sales organization, product specifications and pricing structures are straightforward and easily understood by customers and business partners.

In an ethical organization, honesty, like other ethical behaviors, is demonstrated from the top down, with leadership at all levels setting an example. In turn, the organization holds employees accountable for honesty toward their fellow workers, supervisors, and customers.

---

[1] Ethics Resource Center, "The Importance of Ethical Culture: Increasing Trust and Driving Down Risks," 2010, http://www.ethics.org/files/u5/CultureSup4.pdf (accessed July 20, 2011), 1, 5, 7.

Corporate Philosophy Statements

Corporations usually have mission statements or corporate philosophies, which can help employees to know how to respond in certain situations. For example, due to an employee error, several workers at a paper mill were accidentally exposed to chlorine gas, a potentially fatal situation. It wasn't fatal in this circumstance, but the press immediately contacted the manager of the mill for information. The manager responded by explaining the mistake and subsequent accident. The company philosophy states that all employees should be honest in reporting information. In this case, the company philosophy served as a guide for the employee and allowed him to confidently report with honesty.

Here is Google's corporate philosophy:

As we keep looking towards the future, these core principles guide our actions.

1. Focus on the user and all else will follow.
2. It's best to do one thing really, really well.
3. Fast is better than slow.
4. Democracy on the web works.
5. You don't need to be at your desk to need an answer.
6. You can make money without doing evil.
7. There's always more information out there.
8. The need for information crosses all borders.
9. You can be serious without a suit.
10. Great just isn't good enough.

From Google, "Our Philosophy," http://www.google.com/about/corporate/company/tenthings.html (accessed July 20, 2011).

prodakszyn/Shutterstock.com

Commitment to Diversity and Nondiscrimination

Ethical organizations are committed to diversity, which they develop through affirmative action programs comprising recruitment, hiring, promotions, and other activities. As you learned in Chapter 3, a diverse workforce benefits companies in a number of ways. For instance, it offers different ideas and ways of thinking that can give companies a competitive edge, and it helps organizations attract and retain talented employees.

DISCRIMINATION

An ethical organization believes in treating all individuals equally. Federal laws prohibit employers from discriminating based on race or color, gender, religious beliefs, national origin, disability, age, or genetic information (Figure 5.1). Some states and cities, and a growing number of companies, go beyond federal regulations, banning, for example, discrimination based on sexual orientation.

Unfortunately, even with laws in place, discrimination continues to occur. The U.S. **Equal Employment**

Federal Laws Prohibiting Job Discrimination
■ The Equal Pay Act of 1963 (EPA), which makes it illegal to pay different wages to men and women if they perform equal work in the same workplace
■ Title VII of the Civil Rights Act of 1964 (Title VII), which prohibits discrimination based on race, color, religion, sex, or national origin
■ The Age Discrimination in Employment Act of 1967 (ADEA), which protects individuals age 40 or older from discrimination because of age
■ Sections 501 and 505 of the Rehabilitation Act of 1973, which prohibits discrimination against qualified individuals with disabilities who work in the federal government
■ The Pregnancy Discrimination Act of 1978, which makes it illegal to discriminate against a woman because of pregnancy, childbirth, or a related medical condition
■ Title I of the Americans with Disabilities Act of 1990 (ADA), which prohibits employment discrimination against qualified individuals with disabilities in the private sector and in state and local governments
■ The Civil Rights Act of 1991, which, among other things, allows monetary damages in cases of intentional discrimination
■ The Genetic Information Nondiscrimination Act of 2008 (GINA), which makes it illegal to discriminate against employees or job applicants on the basis of genetic information
All these laws also make it illegal to retaliate against someone who files a discrimination charge or otherwise complains about discrimination.

FIGURE 5.1 Many laws protect U.S. citizens against employment discrimination.

Source: U.S. Equal Employment Opportunity Commission, "Laws Enforced by EEOC," http://www.eeoc.gov/laws/statutes/index.cfm (accessed July 20, 2011).

Opportunity Commission (EEOC), the federal agency that enforces laws related to discrimination in the workplace, reports that in a recent year, 99,922 employees filed charges alleging workplace discrimination.[2]

SEXUAL HARASSMENT

A common form of workplace discrimination is **sexual harassment**, defined by the EEOC as "unwelcome sexual advances, requests for sexual favors, and other verbal or physical conduct of a sexual nature" that

- Explicitly or implicitly affects an individual's employment.
- Unreasonably interferes with an individual's work performance.
- Creates an intimidating, hostile, or offensive work environment.[3]

When sexual harassment is based on the first two criteria, it is referred to as *quid pro quo* (Latin meaning "this for that") sexual harassment. When sexual activity is presented as a prerequisite for getting a job, a promotion, or some type of benefit in the workplace, the behavior is illegal.

The third criterion is referred to as *hostile environment* sexual harassment. In this situation, the employer, supervisor, or coworker does or says things that make victims feel uncomfortable because of their gender. Hostile environment sexual harassment does not need to include a demand for sex. It can be the creation of an uncomfortable working environment.

[2]U.S. Equal Employment Opportunity Commission, "Charge Statistics, FY 1997 Through FY 2010," http://www.eeoc.gov/eeoc/statistics/enforcement/charges.cfm (accessed July 20, 2011).

[3]U.S. Equal Employment Opportunity Commission, "Facts About Sexual Harassment," http://www.eeoc.gov/facts/fs-sex.html (accessed Oct. 9, 2011).

The courts have found that suggestive comments, jokes, leering, unwanted requests for a date, and touching can be sexual harassment. Offensive comments about a person's sex that are not sexual in nature are still considered sexual harassment. Sexual harassment can occur between people of the same sex; it can be a woman harassing a man or a man harassing a woman. Victims can sue and recover for lost wages, future lost wages, emotional distress, punitive damages, and attorneys' fees.

Organizations have a legal duty to prevent and eliminate sexual harassment. An organization is liable for the behavior of its employees even if management is unaware that sexual harassment is taking place. Management is also responsible for the behavior of nonemployees on the company's premises. For example, if a visiting representative or salesperson harasses a company's receptionist, the receptionist's company is responsible. As a result of these responsibilities, many companies have published policy statements on sexual harassment (Figure 5.2).

Once the policy is established, it must be communicated to all supervisors and employees, along with a grievance procedure. If you are not made aware of the organization's sexual harassment policy and grievance procedure when you are employed, you should ask for a copy. A sample grievance procedure follows:

Any employee who believes he or she is being sexually harassed on the job shall file a written grievance with the director of human resources within 24 hours after the alleged sexual harassment has taken place. The grievance is reviewed by the supervisor, and appropriate action is taken. If the employee believes the grievance is not handled satisfactorily, he or she has the right to appeal to the next-level supervisor, with appeals going through the line of authority to the president.

To prevent sexual harassment in the workplace, management has the responsibility of educating its supervisors and employees concerning procedures. If you, as an employee, are faced with sexual harassment, you can seek help or handle the situation yourself, whichever you believe is more appropriate. If you are unsure whether a situation could be considered sexual harassment, talk with the human resources director of your company. Figure 5.3 gives several steps for handling sexual harassment in the workplace.

Sexual Harassment Policy Statement

It is against the policy of this company to discriminate against and/or exclude an employee from participation in any benefits or activities based on national origin, gender, age, sexual orientation, or disability. Harassment on the basis of sex is a violation of the law and a violation of company policy.

FIGURE 5.2 Many organizations have developed sexual harassment policy statements.

Steps for Handling Sexual Harassment

1. Know your rights. Know your organization's position on sexual harassment, what is legal under EEOC guidelines, and what your employer's responsibility is. Know what redress is provided by federal laws.
2. Keep a record of all harassment infractions, noting dates, incidents, and witnesses (if any).
3. File a formal grievance with your organization. Check your organization's policy and procedures manual, or talk with the director of human resources as to the grievance procedure. If no formal grievance procedure exists, file a formal complaint with your employer in the form of a memorandum describing the incidents, identifying the individuals involved in the harassment, and requesting disciplinary action.
4. If your employer isn't responsive to your complaint, file charges of sexual harassment with federal and state agencies that enforce civil rights laws, such as the EEOC.
5. Talk to friends, coworkers, and relatives. Avoid isolation and self-blame. You are not alone; sexual harassment does occur in the workplace.
6. Consult an attorney to investigate legal alternatives.

FIGURE 5.3 Be prepared ahead of time to help yourself or others if sexual harassment occurs.

Commitment to the Community

Ethical organizations understand they have a social responsibility to contribute to the community. In fact, it is in the organization's best interests to be involved in and committed to the community. For example, a company near a scenic river may recruit employee volunteers to help maintain a clean shoreline. This helps the community by improving the appearance of the local landscape at no cost to the community. It also helps the company recruit employees to the area and promote its public image. Activities like the following show an organization's commitment to the community:

- Contributing to charities
- Participating in the local chamber of commerce and other service organizations
- Working with youth groups
- Supporting an inner city in its crime reduction programs
- Assisting schools and colleges with internship programs
- Encouraging employees to participate in local communities by recognizing and rewarding their endeavors

Commitment to Employees

Another way to distinguish an ethical organization is by how it treats its employees. For example, an employee who has used up her vacation time needs several days off to help move her sister, who is a single mother, to another state. The employer agrees that family responsibilities are important and allows the employee to take unpaid leave.

It is in the best interests of an employer to treat employees well. Content employees are typically more productive and less expensive, and they are also a recruiting tool. A high turnover rate is very costly for organizations, since much time and money is spent hiring and training people. Here are some ways that organizations show their commitment to employees:

- Establish realistic job expectations
- Pay well and offer a good compensation plan
- Administer fair and useful employee evaluations
- Provide training for employees who want to learn new skills
- Ask for employee input regarding significant company issues
- Encourage cooperation and collaboration among employees

Identifying Ethical Organizations

It is much easier to join an organization whose values coincide with yours than to be placed in a difficult or unpleasant situation, and even to have to make a change, later. Here are a few suggestions on

Geoffrey Kuchera/Shutterstock.com

Organizations that give to the community help everyone.

how to evaluate an organization's ethics before you apply for a job or during the application process:

- Spend some time at the organization's website. Is there a mission statement or corporate philosophy? Does the company have a sexual harassment policy, an affirmative action policy, or other assurances regarding commitments to diversity and employee safety? Are there news releases that show a commitment to the community or global awareness? Does the organization have professional growth programs for employees?
- Use news reports to check the history of the organization. Has the company ever made headlines for behaving ethically or unethically?
- Talk with acquaintances who work for the organization. Ask them to describe the ethical environment of the company.

Beware of becoming complacent about ethical issues. Unless you are completely committed ethically, you may stay in an organization that becomes unethical and find yourself supporting unethical behaviors to the detriment of your own value system and career growth. Promise yourself that if your organization engages in unacceptable unethical behaviors, you will seek employment elsewhere. Commit now to making ethical behavior an important part of your professional life.

Brian A Jackson/Shutterstock.com

Know where you are going ethically.

Making Ethical Decisions

For some ethical decisions, the right answer is not obvious. In these instances, it is important to have a game plan. Be prepared and systematic in how you make ethical decisions. This will help you to be consistent, and although you may make mistakes, the bulk of your decisions will be characterized by ethical standards. This section of the chapter will give you some practical tools to use as you make ethical decisions.

Build an Ethical Road Map

A road map is a tool that helps people determine the right direction to go. An **ethical road map** helps individuals determine the right direction ethically. To build your own personal tool to help you make ethical decisions, it is important to develop yourself in several areas: integrity, responsibility, compassion, and forgiveness.

INTEGRITY

Integrity implies a commitment to a set of values. A person with integrity is firm in his or her dedication to a code of ethical and moral values. What are your core values? A person with integrity makes sound ethical decisions. Having integrity means engaging in activities that demonstrate truthfulness, sincerity, and an incorruptible attitude. As noted in Chapter 1, an employee with integrity doesn't engage in activities that will cause others to doubt his or her commitment to high ethical values.

PARTNERSHIP FOR 21ST CENTURY SKILLS

Leadership/ Responsibility

Responsibility

The word *responsible* is rooted in accountability and trustworthiness. A responsible person is accountable for her actions and trustworthy in her obligations. With responsibility, there is little cause for blame. A responsible person acts and reacts with this knowledge in mind. The responsible administrative professional

- Doesn't try to blame others when she makes a mistake.
- Always gets to work on time.
- Pays attention to commitments—makes them a priority, for example, and writes them down.
- Keeps her computer files secure, protecting sensitive information about clients, coworkers, her supervisor, and the company.
- Learns company guidelines so she can follow them—she doesn't hide behind an excuse of ignorance when a mistake is made.
- Answers questions honestly.
- Gives credit where credit is due.
- Doesn't leave jobs undone.
- Performs her duties rather than trying to give them to someone else.
- Takes responsibility for knowing how to perform her duties well. She asks or does research if she has a question.
- Understands she represents the organization even when she is off duty.
- Responds to all e-mail and telephone messages in a timely manner.
- Is aware that she is an example for new employees.
- Is helpful to new employees and other coworkers.

Activity

Use the list above to develop a "responsible student" list that demonstrates how a responsible student acts and reacts in a variety of circumstances.

Monkey Business Images/Shutterstock.com

RESPONSIBILITY

Developing your ethical road map in the area of responsibility means being willing to answer for your actions. A responsible person is trustworthy and willing to be held accountable. Can you be trusted with your obligations? Do you shift blame to others or admit mistakes and make amends? The 21st Century Skills feature, above, lists characteristics of a responsible administrative professional.

COMPASSION

Compassion means being aware of another person's problem and wanting to help. It isn't a term you hear often when talking about ethics, but it speaks to the core of ethical motives. Thinking of others—seeing from another person's perspective or putting someone else's needs above your own—helps bring ethical decisions into focus. Consider this example:

Jenny and Rick just heard that their coworker Deja is almost out of sick leave since she has been caring for her child, who is ill with leukemia. The company allows employees to donate sick days to others in times of need. Jenny gives Deja five days of her sick leave. Rick doesn't have many sick days, so he sends Deja a gift card for a local restaurant that has take-out food he knows she likes. He reasons Deja doesn't have time to cook. Both Jenny and Rick make ethical decisions as they demonstrate compassion by being aware of Deja's difficulty and trying to help.

FORGIVENESS

Forgiveness means not holding another person's offense against the person. Forgiveness can also be personal, meaning to forgive yourself for your own mistakes. Harboring resentment against those who have wronged you or dwelling too long on your own errors can hamper your ability to move forward with a positive attitude and make decisions based on ethics and not emotions. Using the tool of forgiveness will help you keep a clear, unemotional, and stable attitude.

AISPIX/Shutterstock.com

It is important to have all the facts before making a decision.

When Demetrius was working with Julie several months ago, he overheard her making some negative comments about him. He calmly confronted her about the comments, and she, realizing her mistake, apologized. Demetrius has forgiven Julie and does not hold her actions against her. He knows that he also makes mistakes and cannot expect forgiveness from others if he doesn't forgive as well.

Forgiveness is very hard and involves personal maturity. If you find yourself holding a grudge, try talking the situation over with a friend. Reflecting during a long walk or another quiet activity that allows you time to think can also help. Once you have thought through the situation and have reached a resolution, make a conscious decision to let it go.

Facts, Options, and Consequences

Train yourself not to act until you have all the facts. You cannot make a reliable decision based on incomplete information.

Your supervisor, Rhonda, doesn't like the proposal adopted by a committee, so she overrides it and then immediately goes around the office trying to find support for her decision. This causes mistrust and disunity in her department, and she is seen as unethical. Rhonda acted without talking with the committee, so she made her decision without having all the pertinent information.

The human resources department is considering three qualified candidates for a position. An HR officer calls the references on two of the three candidates and then offers the position to one of them. This is unethical, since the decision to hire was made without having all the information on all the candidates.

Once you have all the facts, you are in a position to examine your options. Look for several alternatives. Are there other options you haven't thought of yet? Consider similar situations. Ask others for their opinion. Your values plus the culture and expectations of the organization for which you work could make it difficult for you to determine what is right and wrong in a particular situation. Asking these questions can help you decide what is ethical:

- What are the facts of the situation?
- What are the ethical issues involved?
- Who are the **stakeholders** (people who have an interest in the outcome)?
- Who will be affected by my decision?
- Are there different ways of looking at this issue? If so, what are they?
- What are the practical constraints?
- What actions should I take?
- Are these actions practical?

If you are still unclear about what you should do, ask yourself these questions:

- If my actions appeared in the newspaper, would I feel comfortable knowing everyone was reading about what I did?
- Is what I anticipate doing legal?
- Could I proudly tell my spouse, parents, or children about my actions?
- Will I be proud of my actions one day, week, and year from now?
- Do my actions fit with the person I think I am?

Consider the consequences for all options. Be prepared to defend your decision. Can you? Do you have all the documentation you need? Is there a company policy for this?

Change Is Possible

Even though you may have established certain values early in life and held on to them into adulthood, you can change those values if you are open to honestly evaluating situations that suggest a need to change long-held beliefs. If you find yourself needing to change an unethical habit, you can form new habits in a matter of time. Do the right thing for several weeks, and you'll find it's now a habit.

Another way to change a bad habit is to concentrate on doing the opposite. In other words, you replace the unethical habit with an ethical habit. For example, suppose you are in the habit of coming back from lunch about ten minutes late most days. You decide you will break this unethical habit (since you are essentially stealing ten minutes from your employer every day) by returning five minutes early. You set a new habit of being at your desk early or on time from now on simply because you choose to make it a habit.

Some unethical practices are easier than others to change. For example, you may simply decide you aren't going to make personal copies anymore at work. However, leaving an employee's personal information file open on your computer screen when you are away from your desk may be an oversight and a habit you'll have to work harder to change. You make a plan to remember to lock your computer anytime you are away from your desk.

peepo/iStockphoto.com

Ask yourself questions when trying to make an ethical decision.

Characteristics of Ethical Administrative Professionals

If you are to be an ethical administrative professional, you need to understand the importance of ethics and corporate culture, and you need to have tools to help you make ethical decisions. You also need to address your own ethical behavior. An ethical administrative professional has integrity, responsibility, compassion, and the capacity to forgive. Pay careful attention to the following additional characteristics of ethical administrative professionals.

Committed to Ethical Behavior

Whenever you, as an administrative professional, encounter someone who is not acting ethically, take a stand. Be sensitive and direct. Let people who are cynical about ethics know you believe strongly in the concept. Let them know you believe honesty, concern for society, and respect for the rights of others are values that belong in the organization. Here is an example:

Michele comes back from lunch at 1:30. Luciana says to you, "Did you see Michele? She just waltzed in at 1:30. She did that yesterday also. She knows we're supposed to be back at 1, but she just does whatever she wants, apparently."

TECH TALK

Collaborative Websites

Collaboration is very important in business. Collaborative websites like wikis allow people to work together easily and securely. *Wiki* is the Hawaiian word for *quick*, and a **wiki** is a quick website that can be collaborative. One reason a wiki is considered quick is that it is easy to set up and use. By altering the membership settings, the owner can allow anyone from a single individual (such as a coworker) to the public at large (as on Wikipedia) to contribute material to the wiki or to edit what is already there. Here's a likely scenario for collaboration with a wiki:

Joe, Marquis, and Clara are putting together some information about benefits for new employees. Joe creates a wiki with pages for the categories of information they are collecting and enters a list of benefits information. He then invites Marquis and Clara to be members. Clara accepts membership, clicks the edit button on the benefits page, and adds some information Joe forgot. Marquis accepts membership and clicks the new page button to add a brainstorming page, since at their last meeting they discussed some ideas that might help new employees manage their benefits package. He enters those ideas on the page and then moves to the benefits page, where he adds one more item to the list that Joe and Clara worked on earlier.

Joe checks the wiki and sees Clara's and Marquis's contributions. He adds another page that will be the beginning of a handout. The information on this page might later be added to the company website or pasted into a Microsoft Word *document.*

In the above scenario, all members of the team own the document and contribute. Each can see the contributions of others, and each can take responsibility for the information.

There are many free wiki providers. Links to several are provided on the website for this text.

You don't know why Michele has been late, but you defend her by saying, "Well, she has been trying to sell her house, so maybe she had something to do related to that and had permission to come back late. I don't know all the facts, but I hate to accuse her without having all the information."

Later you discover that you were right. Michele had to sign some papers and so got permission to take her lunch 30 minutes later both days. You sent a subtle message to Luciana by defending someone who wasn't there to defend herself and set a good example of giving someone the benefit of the doubt when all the facts aren't known.

Refuse to Engage in Negative Workplace Politics

What does the term **workplace politics** mean? It means that the people you know within an organization can be important. It means that networks can exist in which favors are done for people based on the networks. Workplace politics can be good or bad. Consider this example of positive workplace politics:

You believe your department records management system is inadequate. You begin to talk with your supervisor and coworkers about a more effective system. You also talk with coworkers in other departments, express your concerns, and suggest possible solutions. You are able to garner support, and your supervisor goes to bat with upper management for the money to get the system. You have used your connections with other people in the workplace positively to get support for an idea that will benefit the organization.

Workplace politics become bad when they are used as a quid pro quo. That is, if you do something for me, I will do something for you, with no consideration of whether that something is good for the organization. It is merely good for you. Workplace politics are also bad when employees trade on their position or a powerful association in the company to get what they want. In other words, they are furthering their own personal interests.

Another unpleasant aspect of workplace politics is gossip. Do not gossip about people at work. If a conversation becomes negative about someone, turn it to another topic or withdraw from it.

In a perfect world, negative workplace politics do not exist. But the reality is that they do exist. So how do you handle them? First, you become aware of their existence. When you begin a new job, notice what is happening around you. Learn about the power bases, who knows whom, and what the relationships are. Next, hold on to your own value system. Don't ask for favors. Draw a clear line between being appropriately helpful and supporting and engaging in activities you know you shouldn't be part of. Use your awareness of workplace politics to help yourself do your job. Generally, if you live your values and do your job well, you will be recognized and respected for it.

Digital Vision/Getty Images

Be respectful and polite to everyone, regardless of position in the company.

Trustworthy with Confidential Information

Administrative professionals are often privy to information of a confidential nature. Working ethically means protecting the confidentiality of sensitive information. Protecting confidentiality is usually a legal requirement as well. In the heath care field, for example, the **Health Insurance Portability and Accountability Act of 1996 (HIPAA)** prohibits communication of a patient's medical and billing information, except for certain purposes, without the patient's written consent. In education, the **Family Educational Rights and Privacy Act of 1974 (FERPA)** prevents your college from providing your education records to anyone, including your parents, without your permission. Similar protections are afforded to client information in legal offices, as well as to company information and personal and financial data of employees and clients in many other types of businesses.

Other information isn't formally protected by law but has an assumption of privacy. Here are two examples:

A coworker sends you an e-mail asking for advice. You know another coworker will be able to advise her better. Before forwarding the writer's e-mail, you ask her permission. She has an assumption of privacy, and it would be unethical to forward her e-mail without her consent.

You and three coworkers are at a professional development conference to learn the new database software your company is adopting. At the end of a long day of training, the conference presenters host a two-hour architectural cruise down a local historic river. It's a great time to relax as well as talk with other attendees about how they use the software at their companies, not to mention you enjoy the fresh air and time with your coworkers. One of your coworkers is taking pictures with her smartphone, including a picture of you. Without asking you, she posts the picture on her social networking site. When you return to work on Monday, the whole office is talking about the "vacation" you took at company expense. It's never OK to post or pass along someone's picture without that person's permission.

It is very important that you be aware of your responsibilities in protecting private information. Make sure you know your company's policies and the law. Always ask questions when things are unclear. You should also know that while breaches of confidentiality are sometimes intentional, they can also occur through ignorance and carelessness. Figure 5.4 lists several common mistakes made with confidential information.

Honesty

Honest administrative professionals avoid hypocrisy. They do not tell white lies to supervisors or coworkers. Even a lie you consider small can cause major damage to your professional reputation. Honest employees do not blame someone else for their errors or break rules and then claim ignorance of the rules. Honest employees do not falsify expense reports, time reports, or personnel records.

Honesty includes actions as well as words. Would you be surprised to learn that employee theft costs employers billions of dollars each year, more than they lose to shoplifters? Honest employees do not take organizational supplies or equipment for personal use. Honest employees do not steal time from employers. For example, Bill checks his social

Violations of Confidential Information

- Leaving someone's personal information displayed on your computer when you step out of your office or when someone else comes in to talk with you
- Forwarding an e-mail without the writer's permission
- Posting or forwarding an image of someone without that person's permission
- Placing a note that contains personal information in an office mailbox
- Telling another person's age, which you know from personnel records you must occasionally access
- Discussing someone's illness, which you know about because you processed the sick-leave forms

FIGURE 5.4 Confidentiality is often breached through ignorance or carelessness.

Professional POINTERS

Here are some tips for helping you to behave ethically in the workplace:

- Critique ideas, not people.
- Do not publicly criticize your supervisor or coworkers.
- Do not listen to or pass along gossip about other individuals.
- Check out information you hear from the grapevine. If you know the information is false, say so without becoming emotional. Feed accurate information into the grapevine.
- Communicate in person when appropriate.
- Be a good listener, but do not pass on everything you hear. Remember that you must behave professionally; professionalism carries with it lack of pettiness and rumormongering.
- When you have a problem, go directly to the source of the problem in an attempt to correct the situation.
- Appreciate diversity. Understand that people have different values, abilities, and priorities.
- Practice empathy. Putting yourself in the situation of others (figuratively) allows you to relate more closely to the barriers they face or the feelings they have.

networking site throughout the day. Since he is paid for eight hours of work, this is not honest. He is essentially stealing time throughout the day. Joan doesn't use a social networking site, but she does occasionally take a ream of printer paper home from work for use in her personal printer.

Loyalty

The ethical employee is loyal to the organization. This is not a blind loyalty, in which mistakes are covered up and unethical or illegal behavior is tolerated. Instead, it is a commitment to directions that support the values of the company. Ethical organizations encourage employees to disagree constructively, to speak out on issues, and to be heard by management in the process. However, once a direction is decided on, employees must be loyal and productive members of the team. Ethical employees understand and live by this type of loyalty.

Loyalty involves speech and general attitude. A loyal employee doesn't complain behind the boss's back, deride company policy, or stir up strife within the department. A loyal employee goes directly to the source when there is a complaint. A loyal employee is a team player (see Chapter 3) and is committed to the goals of the team.

SUMMARY

To reinforce what you have learned in this chapter, study this summary.

- Ethics are standards that help people determine right from wrong. They represent obligations as well as benefits to society.
- Many characteristics distinguish an ethical organization. Examples are being environmentally responsible; globally aware; honest; and committed to ethical organizational behavior, diversity and nondiscrimination, the community, and employees.
- To make the right choice consistently in difficult ethical decisions, be prepared and systematic, build an ethical road map (integrity, responsibility, compassion, and forgiveness), and consider facts, options, and consequences.
- Additional ethical characteristics of administrative professionals are a commitment to ethical behavior, a refusal to engage in negative workplace politics, trustworthiness with confidential information, honesty, and loyalty.

KEY TERMS

business ethics, 93
character, 94
Equal Employment Opportunity Commission (EEOC), 96, 97
ethical road map, 100
ethics, 93
Family Educational Rights and Privacy Act of 1974 (FERPA), 106
Health Insurance Portability and Accountability Act of 1996 (HIPAA), 106
sexual harassment, 97
stakeholder, 103
values, 94
wiki, 104
workplace politics, 105

5

STUDY Tools

Located at www.cengagebrain.com

- Chapter Outlines
- Flashcards
- Interactive Quizzes
- Tech Tools
- Video Segments
- and More!

LET'S DISCUSS

1. In your own words, explain what you believe ethics is.
2. List and explain the characteristics of an ethical organization.
3. What is sexual harassment?
4. What groups are specifically protected by federal law from workplace discrimination?
5. Is discrimination ever ethical? Why or why not?
6. Explain what it means to have an ethical road map and why it is important to have one.
7. List and explain the characteristics of an ethical administrative professional.

PUT IT TO WORK

Unethical supervisor Isabella was recently hired in her first full-time position as an administrative professional. She has been working for the company for six months. She is not happy in her job. She does not like her supervisor because she believes he is unethical. He steals time from the company by surfing video-sharing websites throughout the day, almost always leaves 15 minutes early "to beat the traffic," never admits a mistake (he always finds someone to blame), and brags about "padding" his mileage when reporting travel expenses.

Recently Isabella talked with Dao, one of her friends in the company, and asked her advice about quitting her job. Yesterday Isabella's supervisor called her in and told her she was being disloyal to him. He explained that he was told she had been spreading vicious rumors about him throughout the company.

What is the problem? How should Isabella handle it? (Learning Objectives 3 and 4)

COMMUNICATE SUCCESSFULLY

1. **Corporate philosophy** Using the Internet, find the corporate philosophy or mission statement of a company, such as a company that produces common household products, automobiles, or technology or is in retail sales. In a group of two or three students, compare the statements and create a list of the ethics-related statements or principles from all the companies. (Learning Objective 2)
2. **Personal ethics** What are your personal ethics or core values as a student, an employee, or both? Write ten words that you believe describe your current life principles, and then write a one-paragraph statement of your

personal ethics. Start your paragraph with "I believe ethics is . . ." (Learning Objective 4)

3. **Research** Using the Internet, find a news article about a company that demonstrates ethical or unethical behavior. Write a one-paragraph summary and be prepared to share your information with the class. (Learning Objective 2)

4. **Ethical behavior at work** Add a new post to the blog you created in Chapter 1. In this entry, reflect on the following statement: **From this chapter I have learned about the importance of ethical behavior in the workplace in the following ways.** (Learning Objective 1)

Blog

DEVELOP WORKPLACE SKILLS

5. **Interview ethics** You have been asked to help interview candidates for an administrative professional opening at your company. After the team has reviewed all the resumes and completed the interviews, they begin to discuss the candidates. One team member says that she doesn't like one of the candidates because he has Tourette syndrome (TS). During the interview, the team learned that the candidate was subject to the following symptoms: involuntary blinking, shrugging, head jerks, grimaces, throat clearing, sniffing, tongue clicking, yelping, and other noises. The team member is concerned the candidate won't represent the company well when he greets clients.

   Would choosing not to hire the candidate on this basis be unethical? Would your decision be any different if the position did not include much client interaction? Look up TS on the Internet. What would your decision be if the candidate's symptoms were quite severe? (Learning Objective 2)

6. **Responsibility** Look again at the scenario in the previous question. Remember, you are a member of the team. What (if anything) should be your response to your team member's concerns? Consider what you learned about working in teams in Chapter 3 as well as what you have learned in this chapter. (Learning Objectives 3 and 4)

7. **Social network dilemma** You and a friend from work are on vacation. Your friend becomes intoxicated, and you take a short (and quite entertaining) video of her. Should you post the video on your social network page? Why or why not? (Learning Objective 3)

8. **Food for thought** You are the administrative professional responsible for ordering the food for the next "lunch and learn" seminar for your department. Your sister has just started a catering business, and you know she needs the work. Her prices are several dollars more per person than prices at the usual place. What should you do? Justify your actions. (Learning Objectives 3 and 4)

BUILD RELATIONSHIPS

9. **Office predicament** Inez Ramos has been working as an administrative professional at Kapor Pharmaceuticals for one year. Her supervisor has a friend from another company, Timothy Madeley, who visits the office three or four times a month. Inez has a pleasant relationship with him, and they usually chat for a few minutes each time he comes to the office. Mr. Madeley is married, and he frequently talks about his wife and their three children.

   On his last visit to the company, Mr. Madeley stopped by to chat with Inez. At the end of the conversation, he said, "Let's have lunch sometime." Inez, thinking she would enjoy a casual meal out, replied, "Sounds good to me." Today as he came to her office after his visit with her supervisor, he said, "I really want to have lunch with you. How about next Tuesday? I have the afternoon free. Maybe you can take the afternoon off so we can enjoy a pleasant outing."

   Inez was surprised and concerned when he suggested they spend the afternoon together. She did not know how to respond. She merely said, "Let me think about it." You are Inez's friend, and she has asked for your advice. How should Inez handle the situation? (Learning Objectives 2 and 4)

10. **Teamwork** You are supposed to be working with Todd on a short summary of a project your supervisor asked the two of you to review. Todd is very good at writing and has been an administrative professional two years longer than you have. He does the work and e-mails the finished summary to you, at the same time explaining that he is sick and has to miss the afternoon staff meeting. You give the summary to your supervisor but do not explain that Todd is sick or that he prepared it. Your supervisor assumes you worked on it together.

    Todd will probably never know that you didn't give him credit. Is this honest? What are the implications of what you've done or not done? Write one or two sentences describing how you could have responded when your supervisor said, "OK, let's hear from Todd and Marlena about the TGV summary." (Learning Objectives 1, 3, and 4)

USE TECH TOOLS

11. **Wiki** On a team of four to five students, create a wiki, with each person creating a page. The creator of the wiki should invite the other members or give them the URL so they can request to join. Each member is responsible for a page. On that page the member should put one element he or she considers important when building a personal ethical road map. Links to several free wiki creation sites are provided on the website for this text. (Learning Objectives 1 and 4)

PLAN AHEAD

Create an ethical road map With your team from the previous activity, create a team ethical road map on your wiki. Discuss your personal ethical road map, and then develop an ethics creed for your team. The creed could be for students or for administrative professionals. The home page should have a brief explanation and a visual of your creed. Use a concept mapping tool or drawing or chart tools in your word processing software to create the image. All the other pages should have explanations of the elements of your creed along with examples of each in the workplace (such as an explanation of responsibility and an example of getting enough rest so you can perform at 100 percent in your job). The creator of the wiki is responsible for the home page. Each other team member page must have a different element of the team ethics. Links to concept mapping tools are provided on the website for this text. (Learning Objectives 1 and 4)

CHAPTER

6 Leadership

LEARNING OBJECTIVES

1. Define leadership.
2. Discuss leadership theories.
3. Discuss leadership styles.
4. Discuss leadership traits.
5. Describe the qualities and strategies of an administrative professional who is an effective leader.

© Photographer/Image Source

What Is Leadership?

Leading is an important ability to develop as you progress in your career as an administrative professional. Regardless of the profession you choose, leadership skills will be very useful as you seek to gain promotions and earn more responsibility. Even if you do not become a manager or supervisor, you will still have opportunities to serve in leadership positions on teams, special projects, committees, and other groups.

As you learned in Chapter 1, expanding technology has allowed administrative professionals to get more work done in the same period of time, enabling them to take on responsibilities once held by managers. In Chapter 3, you learned about being a team leader—for example, leading a team to plan the company picnic or to find solutions to a departmental issue, such as a lack of standard procedures for filing records.

To lead means to go in advance as a guide to others. It implies providing direction and vision. In business, leaders inspire and motivate, and leaders keep the long run in mind. Leading is an attitude and a practice in the workplace. **Leadership** within an organization is the act of inspiring and motivating people to achieve organizational goals.

Management is the act of organizing and directing people to accomplish organizational goals. Managers plan, organize, coordinate, and provide purpose as they direct employees toward a specific goal. Managers focus more on the short term than leaders. The most effective managers are leaders, and conversely, effective leaders are also effective managers. While this chapter focuses on leadership, many of the skills, abilities, and methods associated with good leadership and good management overlap.

Developing your skills as an administrative professional involves learning from others. As you think about how to develop your leadership skills for any workplace, consider the leadership examples of Jack Welch, Howard Schultz, and Condoleezza Rice.

Jack Welch

Jack Welch was CEO of General Electric Company (GE) for 20 years. He did not like bureaucracy or old ways of doing things. General Electric expanded dramatically during Welch's tenure. He streamlined the company and purchased additional companies. Under his leadership, revenues increased from about $26.8 billion to almost $130 billion. He allowed managers to work quite independently as long as they followed the company ethic of always striving to do better and constantly change.[1] In 1999, Welch was named manager of the century by *Fortune* magazine. In 2004, the *Financial Times* of London reported a survey of chief executives who voted him one of the three most admired business leaders in the world. Welch has authored several books and, from 2005 to 2009, coauthored a syndicated business column.

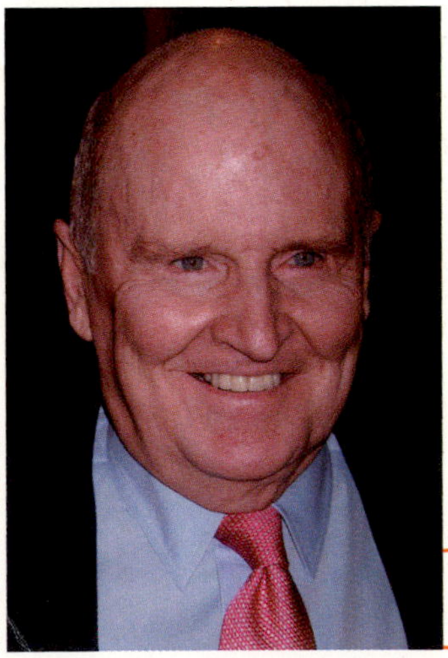
ROBERT PITTS/Landov

Jack Welch

Welch believes leaders must have certain qualities. Three basic characteristics are integrity, intelligence, and emotional maturity. Additionally, he says, leaders must have an upbeat attitude through good and bad, the ability to infect other people with this positive attitude, an aptitude for making tough decisions, the ability to get things done, and finally, passion or caring about work, life, and others.[2]

Howard Schultz

Howard Schultz is CEO of Starbucks Corporation. Since 1987, he has built his company from 17 shops in Chicago and Vancouver, Canada, to more than 16,000 around the globe.[3] Today, as economic difficulties cause people to think about every penny, Starbucks is adapting continually to compete with other companies and retain its appeal in the face of shifting customer priorities.

Schultz's leadership philosophy is anchored in caring. He holds monthly town hall meetings in which he is known for his truth-telling and casual, "what-you-see-is-what-you-get" style. The meetings are a useful forum because Schultz is genuinely interested in hearing what his managers and employees have to say. Schultz has won numerous awards for his leadership skills. He is committed to employees, and it shows: Starbucks was one of the first companies to give part-time employees health benefits. *U.S. News and World Report* has quoted Schultz as saying, "People aren't interested in how much you know. It's how much you care."[4]

Schultz is also concerned about growing a company in today's competitive market. He understands that sometimes hard choices have to be made, such as when considering outsourcing jobs. He keeps his

[1]General Electric, "GE Past Leaders: John F. Welch, Jr.," http://www.ge.com/company/history/bios/john_welch.html (accessed July 24, 2011).

[2]Jack and Suzy Welch, *Winning: The Answers* (New York: HarperCollins, 2006), 47.

[3]Starbucks, "Starbucks Company Timeline," http://assets.starbucks.com/assets/aboutustimelinefinal172811.pdf (accessed Oct. 9, 2011).

[4]William Meyers, "Conscience in a Cup of Coffee," *U.S. News and World Report,* Oct. 31, 2005, http://www.usnews.com/usnews/news/articles/051031/31schultz.htm (accessed July 24, 2011).

AP Photo/Kin Cheung

Howard Schultz

eye on the bottom line and is ready to embrace new ideas and new technologies if they can improve productivity and flavor.[5]

Condoleezza Rice

In 2001, Dr. Condoleezza Rice became the first woman to hold the position of national security advisor. In 2005, she became U.S. secretary of state. In her autobiography, Rice recalls working 14-hour days as part of the National Security Council—sometimes whispering information to the president of the United States and other times at the copy machine making copies. There was no job "below" her. Rice was committed to doing whatever was necessary. She provides a good illustration of a person with an attitude of leadership who sets an example for others.

Photo courtesy of the U.S. Department of State

Condoleezza Rice

Rice is an expert on Soviet studies and international security, and she speaks several languages, including Russian and Czech. She has won several distinguished teaching awards and has a caring attitude toward students. In her autobiography, Rice recalls struggling as a student, looking for a job, and tackling difficult tasks. She resolved to use those experiences to help others.[6]

Leadership Theories

Just as it is helpful to study the lives and careers of effective leaders, it is also helpful to consider what respected writers and researchers say about leadership.

Robert Greenleaf

Robert Greenleaf was a management consultant and director of management research for AT&T. He introduced the concept of **servant leadership**. According to Greenleaf, a servant-leader is a person who leads out of a desire to serve others.[7] Servant leaders:

- Ask questions and genuinely listen to the response.
- Listen, observe, and think to identify customer and employee needs.
- Recognize their own weaknesses and biases.
- Know how they impact those around them.
- Create teams of leaders to share information and challenge ideas (even those of the CEO).
- Help employees fulfill their potential by providing opportunities for them to learn, mentoring rather than controlling them, and allowing them to make decisions.
- Lead by using foresight rather than reacting to situations.[8]

[5]Ibid.

[6]Condoleezza Rice, *Extraordinary, Ordinary People* (New York: Random, 2010).

[7]Source: Kent M. Keith, "The Key Practices of Servant-Leaders," http://www.greenleaf.org/whatissl/TheKeyPracticesOfServant-Leaders.pdf (accessed July 24, 2011).

[8]Robert K. Greenleaf, *Servant Leadership: A Journey into the Nature and Legitimate Power of Greatness* (Mahway, NJ: Paulist Press, 2002), 27.

Many companies have adapted the concept of servant leadership with the idea that helping employees grow and succeed makes them better employees and improves their value to the company.

Peter Senge

Peter Senge is a senior lecturer at the Massachusetts Institute of Technology. His writing encourages leaders to build learning organizations—organizations in which a shared vision of the future allows the organization to move forward in the accomplishment of significant goals and objectives. He believes leaders play three important roles:

- Designer: Leaders create the guiding ideas for an organization, such as its purpose and mission, and they design the practical methods, such as policies and processes, for carrying them out.
- Teacher: Leaders are coaches and facilitators. They arrange means for people, including themselves, to learn from one another.
- Steward: Leaders care for the people they lead and the purpose or mission for which they are responsible.[9]

Stephen Covey

Stephen Covey is a well-known author on the topic of leadership and vice chairman of FranklinCovey, a company that provides consulting and training services in leadership and other topics. Like Senge, Covey has also developed a list of roles leaders play:

- Modeling: The effective leader sets a good example and inspires trust through character and competence.
- Pathfinding: The effective leader involves others in setting goals, which earns their commitment and ensures leaders and followers agree on what is important.
- Aligning: An effective leader makes sure an organization's structures, systems, and processes are consistent with its values and facilitate work rather than setting up roadblocks.
- Empowering: Leaders empower employees by setting commonly understood goals and agreed-on guidelines and then letting employees decide how to accomplish the goals, while being available to provide support as needed.[10]

Jim Collins

Jim Collins is the founder of a management laboratory, a teacher of executives, a university professor, and a leadership researcher. In his book *Good to Great*, he lists five levels of leadership, which build to the top level of being a great leader. He emphasizes that there are many good leaders but few great leaders. The levels of leadership shown in Figure 6.1 illustrate the evolution that is possible in an individual and that ends in being a great leader. The first level is being a strong individual contributor to a company. The second level is being a good team member. The third is being a competent manager. The fourth is being a driven executive. The fifth is becoming ambitious for the good of the company, rather than for power, prestige, or personal gain.

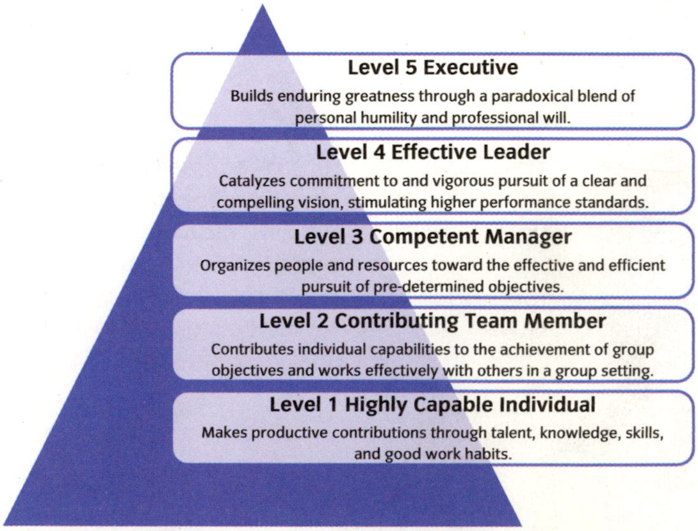

FIGURE 6.1 The five levels of leadership

Source: *Good to Great*. Copyright © 2001 by Jim Collins. Reprinted with permission from Jim Collins.

[9]Peter Senge, *The Fifth Discipline: The Art & Practice of the Learning Organization* (New York: Doubleday, 2006), 321–339.

[10]Stephen Covey, *The Eighth Habit: From Effectiveness to Greatness* (New York: Simon & Schuster, 2004), 98, 114, 233–234, 256–257.

Leadership Styles

Leaders have different styles, or patterns of behavior, associated with their leadership. You have been exposed to different **leadership styles** throughout life, from coaches, teachers, supervisors at work, and other types of leaders.

Leaders usually prefer a particular style of leadership, but they often adopt other styles in different situations. This is known as **situational leadership**. For example, a team leader may usually use a democratic leadership style and work with the team to reach decisions. But when a decision is needed immediately and there isn't time for the team process, the leader switches to an autocratic, or controlling, style and makes the decision alone. Autocratic and democratic are two common leadership styles. A third is laissez-faire, which is a more relaxed style.

Autocratic

An autocrat is a person who has complete control over others. The **autocratic leadership style** is one of control. The leader directs and closely supervises the work that is done. He or she has complete authority; subordinates have no input into decisions. The autocratic style is appropriate for some situations when close control is very important. It was once a common style in business, but for many years, it has been used less often. Organizations and leaders tend to favor other styles that do not involve such close control and that allow employees to make many decisions. As an administrative professional, you will likely be given varying degrees of freedom and opportunities to make decisions and accomplish tasks on your own. This is one reason why developing appropriate skills and work habits is so important.

TT TECH TALK

Online Surveys

Online surveys are an effective way to gather information. As an administrative professional, you are likely to find them useful on many occasions. For example, you may be asked to find out the needs or preferences of office staff with regard to holiday celebrations, vacations, or overtime scheduling. At an online survey site, you can quickly and easily design a form or survey to gather the information you need. You e-mail a link to staff members, who can complete the form or survey equally quickly and easily.

The site gathers the input and analyzes the data for you. Some sites, such as SurveyMonkey and QuestionPro, collect data and then allow the results to be downloaded as a spreadsheet or in another format. Other sites, such as Google Docs, automatically deposit the data as they are collected into a spreadsheet. So the spreadsheet is a constantly changing file that can be altered at any time, either directly or by using the form.

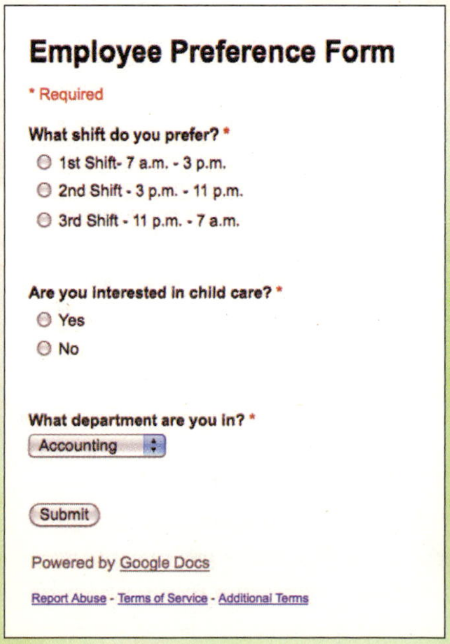

Employee Preference Form
* Required
What shift do you prefer? *
1st Shift- 7 a.m. - 3 p.m.
2nd Shift - 3 p.m. - 11 p.m.
3rd Shift - 11 p.m. - 7 a.m.
Are you interested in child care? *
Yes
No
What department are you in? *
Accounting
Submit
Powered by Google Docs
Report Abuse - Terms of Service - Additional Terms

© Google

Democratic

As the name implies, the **democratic leadership style** is one in which subordinates share in authority, decisions, and plans. It is a popular style in the workplace, one that both managers and employees often favor. In general, when the leadership style is more flexible, morale is better and attitudes are more positive. Employees enjoy being able to work with less supervision, and having a voice in plans and decisions makes them feel more valued. This leadership style is commonly used on teams.

As you learned in Chapter 3, you may sometimes be asked to lead a team as an administrative professional. Remember this leadership style for those situations. Leaders who value the input of other team members open the doors to efficiency and creativity. A team with all members working usually accomplishes more than just one person. A team typically generates more ideas, which means a higher probability of creative and effective results.

Laissez-Faire

When this French term (which means everyone doing as he or she chooses) is applied to leadership styles, it refers to a leader who allows subordinates to lead themselves. The leader who practices the **laissez-faire leadership style** does not direct or control tasks. He or she may monitor employees' progress in completing tasks and respond to requests for assistance. This leadership style is most appropriate when employees are skilled and responsible and have been assigned clearly defined tasks.

Leadership Traits

You have probably encountered people whom you consider good leaders. Think about what makes you put someone into that category. Is it respect for others? Is it the ability to motivate people and get a job done? Is it the capacity to guide others or the trust and rapport the person establishes? This section describes several important traits for leadership.

Integrity

In Chapter 5, you learned that integrity implies a commitment to a set of values. Leaders act with integrity by applying their personal ethical standards consistently. Integrity is considered the most important factor in leadership and is the cornerstone of good leadership. Leaders with integrity earn trust from others because they can always be relied on to "do the right thing."

Responsibility

Effective leaders take responsibility for their actions and decisions. They admit mistakes and reflect on past decisions. The trait of responsibility engenders trust in others.

The responsible leader also understands his or her responsibility to the organization. This leader exercises integrity, communicates vision, maintains a positive attitude, gathers diverse opinions, and considers the impact of his or her decisions. A responsible leader makes sure team members have the skills, supplies, and equipment to do their work well. A responsible leader also provides clear and concise directions so members know what is expected of them.

Lifelong Learner

An effective leader is eager to learn and continue learning. People with this leadership trait value continued personal and professional growth. In addition, they are willing to learn from others and value the opinions of others.

Today at work and in life, success requires keeping up with a constant stream of new information and

Leadership requires continued growth.

marylooo/Shutterstock.com

Leading With Integrity

General Ronald Fogleman, a former U.S. Air Force chief of staff and member of the Joint Chiefs of Staff, believes that leaders with integrity have four characteristics: they are sincere, they are consistent, they have substance, and they are good finishers.[11]

- Sincerity: Their actions match their words. People are loyal to leaders with sincerity.
- Consistency: Leaders with consistency always act with integrity. For example, they never discriminate based on friendship or positions. They always apply rules fairly.
- Substance: Integrity is more than appearance. Leaders with integrity have the internal strength to persevere even through difficult times.
- Good finishers: Good leaders persevere until a task is completed, and they always perform at their maximum in accomplishing a task.

General Ronald Fogleman

Photo Courtesy of the U.S. Navy

technology and taking what is useful from it. Leaders must read applicable information, recognize new ways of doing old tasks, keep up with technological innovations, and take professional development courses if necessary. No matter how intelligent and committed you are, you cannot, in the long term, lead others without committing to constantly developing yourself. If you are to be an outstanding leader, you must develop a plan for yourself that allows you to continually grow and learn.

[11]Ronald Fogleman, "The Leadership-Integrity Link," *Concepts for Air Force Leadership* (Maxwell AFB, AL: Air University Press, 1983).

Vision

Excellent leaders are **visionary**, which means that they are able to see what is possible. They know how to set goals and remain focused on those goals. Effective leaders picture what the future is for their team or organization. Without vision, there is no forethought or foresight about what the focus of the organization should be. Having vision does not necessarily mean the leader knows the exact path a team or organization will need to take, but it does mean the leader knows where the team or organization is going.

Other Traits of Leaders

Effective leaders have several other important qualities. They include self-understanding, self-management, and confidence.

SELF-UNDERSTANDING

Self-understanding involves knowing your values and goals as well as being aware of your attitudes, shortcomings, and strengths. Everyone should strive for it. For leaders, defining who you are is essential to guiding others effectively. Self-knowledge helps leaders understand others and keeps them focused in life. As you try to understand this concept better, ask yourself questions like these:

- What do I value?
- What are my life goals?
- How do I define success?

SELF-MANAGEMENT

As you learned in Chapter 4, self-management is important for every administrative professional, especially for those in leadership positions. Leaders should be able to set goals, measure progress, exercise self-discipline, manage stress, and solve problems.

Leslie is an administrative professional in a large organization. She serves on the Positive Action Committee, which organizes philanthropic activities for the organization, such as raising money for area schools and organizing campaigns for the Red Cross and United Way. She led a subcommittee tasked with raising money for a local school that had sustained extensive tornado damage. As a leader, Leslie had to formulate goals for the fund-raising activity (what is it we want to accomplish?) and then problem-solve as the activity unfolded.

Andresr/Shutterstock.com

Effective leaders set goals and solve problems.

CONFIDENCE

Effective leaders see themselves as competent and able to do the job. Good leaders have had successes, even small ones, and have gained confidence from those successes. Good leaders aren't overconfident—that is, they don't overrate their abilities or overlook their weaknesses. They understand their weaknesses but are not embarrassed or deterred by them. Good leaders plan and navigate around their weaknesses and use their strengths to achieve the goals of the team or organization.

The Administrative Professional as a Successful Leader

You will encounter numerous opportunities for leadership in your job as an administrative professional. They could be as simple as helping a new employee understand his or her duties or leading a small team to select new software. Leadership opportunities could also be more complex, such as leading a team to update the job description for administrative professionals at your organization. Make plans now for your success as a leader. Small successes will give you the confidence to move on to more challenging opportunities. Besides the traits described in the previous section, strive to develop these methods for successful leadership: plan well, communicate effectively, set a good example, invest in relationships, delegate tasks, and ask questions when necessary.

Plan Well

Planning is the process of thinking about the activities required to accomplish a goal—in the case of a team or organization, the desired future of the business or goal of the team. Planning involves setting goals and objectives and developing plans for accomplishing them.

DEVELOP STRATEGIES

The first part of planning when you are asked to lead should be to develop strategies. *Begin with the end in mind* is popular advice that says a lot. If you don't know your purpose and goals, developing effective strategies is difficult. Here are a few simple steps to get you started:

- Write down the purpose of the group you are leading. Why does it exist?
- Determine the goals of the group.
- Before your first meeting, develop initial strategies for accomplishing the goals.

TAKE OWNERSHIP

Taking ownership is just another way to say *taking responsibility*. "Own" the responsibility for the success or failure of the group. How will the work get done? Who will call the next meeting? Such decisions are yours as the leader. If you don't do it or delegate it, it won't get done. Ownership of responsibility is an important part of the planning process since it helps you define what you need to do and be motivated to do it. Consider this example:

You are asked to lead a team of administrative professionals to revamp mail delivery practices. Your first steps in owning responsibility for this assignment are to develop strategies and then to e-mail the team members, telling them what the team needs to do and giving several options of when you'd like to meet. At the first meeting, you remind everyone of the purpose and goals of the team. In a brainstorming session, the team identifies some additional strategies. You work with the group to make assignments, set deadlines, and schedule future meetings.

Communicate Effectively

When leading others, you must communicate your expectations clearly. Writing down your goals will help you make them more concrete and precise. Communicating goals and establishing deadlines at the very beginning is important. If you overlook communicating the goals, your group members will be left trying to ascertain what you want. Similarly, failing to communicate directions and information so they are understood can have serious consequences.

When you give information verbally, remember that it is not enough simply to speak clearly. You need to take steps to ensure your listeners actually understand. For instance, you can repeat what you have said in another way and ask if anyone has questions. Chapter 9 provides additional suggestions for making sure listeners understand.

Don't underestimate the power of face-to-face communication. While technology provides many modes of communicating, a face-to-face meeting is the most effective. It is also sometimes the easiest. Whether you are meeting with an individual or a group, being able to look people in the eye and to observe their body language helps you gauge their understanding and detect any resistance.

PARTNERSHIP FOR 21ST CENTURY SKILLS

Leadership/ Responsibility

Leadership

Leadership is a skill for the 21st century administrative professional. An attitude of leadership in all aspects of your life can reap powerful benefits. Part of good leadership is setting an example. Effective leaders do whatever it takes to complete a job and to do it well, and they expect the same of others.

Earlier in this chapter, former U.S. Secretary of State Condoleezza Rice was profiled as a leader. Her first understanding of an attitude of leadership came from the examples set by her family. Rice began life in the 1950s in the segregated South. Her grandfather had raised cotton. With the help of a scholarship, he managed to get a college education. He became a Presbyterian minister and raised money to begin a string of private K-12 schools with the goal of giving African Americans the same quality of education as Caucasian children. Despite occasional setbacks and the work involved in constant fund-raising, he remained focused on the goal: preparing African American youth to go to college.

Rice's parents were leaders of the African American community in Birmingham, Alabama, a center of struggle during the civil rights movement. At a time of ugliness and strife, they forged lasting relationships across racial boundaries. Rice's mother taught the baseball legend Willie Mays, who remembers her as a woman who recognized his abilities and encouraged him to pursue them.[12]

Activity

Whom do you know with a similar attitude of leadership? Describe several leaders in your family background or other leaders you have heard or read about. Explain what you believe an attitude of leadership means.

Stockbyte/Jupiter Images

Good written communication skills are equally important. Whenever possible, set messages aside before you send them. Allowing as little as 20 minutes between preparing and sending a message can help you identify unclear writing or missing information. You will learn more about writing effective messages in Chapter 8.

[12]Condoleezza Rice, *Extraordinary, Ordinary People* (New York: Random, 2010), 21.

Whether verbally or in writing, get information to your team quickly. They will feel supported and will be encouraged in their tasks related to the team.

Leaders must follow up on both verbal and written communication. For verbal communication, provide a written summary of what was said or reiterate information in a short e-mail. Send reminders of deadlines if appropriate. Arrange for periodic status reports on work that is delegated.

Good leaders listen actively and use effective listening skills. Truly listening means you value what other people say and seek to understand their point of view. You will learn more about active listening and effective listening skills in Chapter 9.

Photodisc/Getty Images

Effective leaders lead by example.

Set a Good Example

An effective leader is someone who sets an example. Do you want the people you lead to have a good work ethic, not complain, and work toward the common goal of the group? Do you have a good work ethic? Do you complain? Do you work toward the common goal of the group? The power of modeling the conduct you expect from others is often underestimated. Effective leaders approach the task of directing other people by holding themselves accountable and avoiding double standards.

Young adults in leadership positions may experience challenges due to their age and lack of experience, particularly when the group they are leading includes people who are older than they are. If you find yourself in such a situation, leading by example can be especially helpful. For what you lack in age, make up for in character. Convey the qualities of patience, compassion, integrity, modesty, and confidence. Be honest, do not talk about others in a derogatory manner, and do not use sarcasm. Be professional.

Invest in People

Many leaders demonstrate their investment in people and relationships by involving employees in the decision-making process as much as possible. Leaders who ask for input or pose a problem and ask for solutions and options are showing they value the opinions and abilities of their team members. Actually following through with employee suggestions is the key to this investment process. When employees feel they are trusted and valued, they are empowered and are encouraged to do an excellent job. They are also more likely to step up in confidence and themselves be leaders in other situations.

BUILD RELATIONSHIPS

Good leaders get to know the people with whom they work. They invest time in talking with their team members and are genuinely interested in them.

Strive to develop these behaviors of effective leaders:

- Effective leaders promote a spirit of cooperation.
- Effective leaders praise employees and work groups for their contributions and celebrate those successes.
- Effective leaders believe the basic human needs of employees are important. (Employees must believe an organization cares about them.)
- Effective leaders recognize the skills and potential of their employees and look for opportunities to help them grow.

Developing relationships with team members is a personal touch that isn't manipulative but rather is based in a selfless, friendly attitude. Having a good working relationship with those you may supervise in the future will make it easier if you need to correct some behavior or discuss a similarly difficult issue.

MOTIVATE

People are motivated to do work and do it well for a variety of reasons. As you learned in Chapter 1, motivation may be extrinsic or intrinsic. An extrinsic motivation might be a salary increase or promotion. An intrinsic motivation might be the desire for personal recognition or a feeling of satisfaction from a job well done.

Good leaders try to find out what motivates the people they are leading. Then they use that knowledge to encourage these individuals to have a positive attitude and to do their work well. For example, you may notice that Jessica frequently asks you if she's doing OK on a project you are working on together. You respond by giving her more personal and frequent feedback. This meets her need for additional assurance and motivates her in the task.

MANAGE CONFLICT

Effective leaders deal with conflicts that arise within the group they are leading. In investigating problems, an effective leader goes on a fact-finding tour. He or she observes activities and processes, listens objectively, reviews documents such as e-mail, and asks questions. This is not an easy process, and it requires a leader with a professional attitude, one who is willing to look at facts and put emotions and personal friendships aside. Chapter 9 provides additional advice for managing conflict.

Leaders not only act to solve problems when they arise but also look for situations and events that might create problems and try to prevent them. For example, if you are asked to form a team, you can avoid some problems by choosing hard-working and noncontentious people to be members.

Delegate Tasks

To **delegate** is to give the responsibility for a task to another person. A leader who delegates is able to get more accomplished. Delegating also helps cultivate future leaders by giving them responsibility, and it serves as a motivator as well.

Before you delegate, think carefully about the task so you can give clear instructions and communicate your expectations concisely. Try to anticipate questions. If appropriate, write down your directions so the person can refer to them later.

Give the delegated assignment in person, if possible, so you can answer any immediate questions.

Arrange for the person to check in with you periodically, and make yourself available for these exchanges. Make sure the person knows you are available for questions, and let him or her know the best way to contact you.

Delegating can be difficult because you have to relinquish control. You will need to trust the people to whom you delegate to complete tasks responsibly.

Orange Line Media/Shutterstock.com

Delegate in person when possible.

Ask Questions

Leading in any situation will be new at first, and you will naturally have questions. You may be given instructions that are not completely clear. There may be steps or terms that are unfamiliar to you, and the person giving you the task may not realize that. As you progress in your work, issues and situations may arise that you need help on. Don't be afraid to ask!

While you should try to avoid asking questions unnecessarily, always ask when you are unsure. Listen carefully to instructions. Train yourself to repeat them back so you get clarification. Whenever possible, pose questions at a time that is convenient for the other person, and give the person as much as time as possible to respond. For instance, if today is Monday and you need an answer by Friday, e-mail your question today, and include the Friday deadline. If a question is urgent, however, don't wait. Make sure you get a timely answer.

Never be concerned that a question is too simple or that you should have heard the answer the first time. It is always better to ask than to miss something or do it incorrectly. Asking questions shows you are conscientious, and it instills confidence in your ability to get the job done. Your supervisor can give you a leadership task knowing that if you are unsure about something, you will ask.

SUMMARY

To reinforce what you have learned in this chapter, study this summary.

- Leadership skills are important in all vocations. Administrative professionals have opportunities to lead others in a variety of ways.
- Leadership theories describe the attitudes, qualities, skills, and strategies of effective leaders. Robert Greenleaf, Peter Senge, Stephen Covey, and Jim Collins have devised popular leadership theories.
- Leadership styles are patterns of behavior associated with leadership. Three common leadership styles are autocratic, democratic, and laissez-faire.
- Several important traits for leadership are integrity, responsibility, lifelong learning, and vision.
- Methods for successful leadership are to plan well, communicate effectively, set a good example, invest in relationships, delegate tasks, and ask questions when necessary.

KEY TERMS

6

STUDY Tools

Located at www.cengagebrain.com

- Chapter Outlines
- Flashcards
- Interactive Quizzes
- Tech Tools
- Video Segments
- and More!

LET'S DISCUSS

1. How might an administrative professional use leadership skills on the job?
2. Describe some of the leadership traits or beliefs of Jack Welch, Howard Schultz, and Condoleezza Rice.
3. What is servant leadership?
4. What leadership styles have you experienced? Describe the positives and negatives.
5. As a leader, which leadership style would or do you prefer and why?
6. What is integrity and how does it relate to leadership?
7. How have you seen leaders display responsibility?
8. Why might it be important for an administrative professional to be prepared for leadership?

PUT IT TO WORK

Flexible hours You work for Cabrera Manufacturing, which has 1,400 employees in three locations. Several department heads have approached management about the possibility of offering flexible working hours for employees (hours are currently 8 a.m. to 5 p.m.). Management has formed a committee of employees from different areas of the company to gather information from all employees and particularly to consider what sort of flextime arrangement employees would like. You are the co-leader of this committee and represent mostly other administrative professionals. How will you gather information from the employees and department managers? What questions would you ask each group? How do other companies use flexible schedules?

Form a committee with two to four fellow students, do some research on flextime, and develop a plan for how your committee will complete this assignment. If you will use a survey, write sample questions. Your plan will be reviewed by the senior vice president for employee affairs (your instructor), so do a thorough job. (Learning Objective 5)

COMMUNICATE SUCCESSFULLY

1. **Leadership** Leadership has been defined as the act of inspiring and motivating people to achieve organizational goals. Think about three leaders you have had in the past (at school, at work, on an athletic team, etc.). What goals did each leader try to achieve? Did each leader inspire and motivate people? If so, how? If not, why not? (Learning Objective 1)
2. **Leadership styles** Form a team with one or two classmates, and come up with examples of the three common leadership styles (autocratic, democratic, and laissez-faire) that you have seen in the workplace, school, sports, or politics. Explain/justify your examples. (Learning Objective 3)

3. **Team e-mail** Upper-level managers of your organization have had multiple complaints from lower-level managers about employees using work time to do online shopping, banking, and social networking. You have been asked to lead a team that will examine possible solutions to this issue. After this morning's meeting, you drafted an e-mail to your team and set it aside to review later.

   Access the *Word* file *Ch06_Meeting_E-Mail* from the data files. Review the e-mail for unclear writing and missing information. Then revise it, inventing any details you feel are needed. (Learning Objective 5)

4. **Future leader** Add a new post to the blog you created in Chapter 1. In this entry, reflect on the following statement: **This chapter has made me think about my future role as a leader in the following ways.** (Learning Objective 5)

Blog

DEVELOP WORKPLACE SKILLS

5. **Professional development** Imagine you are a new administrative professional working in an organization for which you would really like to work. It could be a medical office, a law firm, or some other kind of setting. You want to continue to learn and grow both personally and professionally. Make a list of specific areas in which you need to keep current or improve on a professional level (for example, software skills). For each item, include one or more real resources you could use. Locate a professional development course you could take. (Learning Objective 4)

6. **Theory research** This activity will ask you to think deeply about your role as a leader and an administrative professional. Review the "Leadership Theories" section of the chapter, and choose the writer whose theory most interests you. Assume it interests your supervisor, too. She has asked you to research the theory further and to prepare a bulleted list of important factors. The list should include information in addition to that presented in the text. Provide your source(s), and recommend one good source your supervisor can read for further information. Hint: Being able to justify your ranking is more important than the actual ranking. (Learning Objective 2)

7. **Thinking skills** Rank in order of importance the successful leadership skills found in the chapter section "The Administrative Professional as a Successful Leader," and justify your ranking. Use a table format—one column for the skills and another for your reasoning. Form a team of two to three classmates, and discuss your rankings and justifications. Come to a consensus, and create one ranking on which your team agrees. (Learning Objective 5)

BUILD RELATIONSHIPS

8. **Servant leadership** You have just been promoted to office manager of another department within the organization. One of the first things you

notice is the poor office morale. You learn that the previous office manager, who recently retired, didn't invest much time in her staff and didn't appear to care about them. For example, she always stayed in her office with the door closed, and she never attended any of the Friday office lunches, commenting that she was too busy. She also didn't delegate much work, stating, "If you want something done right, you have to do it yourself." If she did delegate a job, she always changed trivial details, as if they were grievous errors. Those around her felt mistrusted and disliked.

You've decided that as the new office manager, you are going to adopt the idea of servant leadership and attempt to boost morale. Make a list of things you could do that would follow the idea of servant leadership and help restore morale. If time allows, consider using the Internet to find additional information about servant leadership. (Learning Objective 2)

9. **Morale booster** You have been the office manager (see Activity 8) for a few weeks, and you have noticed that several of the office staff are completely unmotivated. They arrive late, call in sick quite often, complete reports and other documents without proofreading them for errors, and generally drag around the office in an uninterested fashion. What could you do to motivate these employees to do better work? Make a list, and share it with a classmate if time allows. (Learning Objective 5)

USE TECH TOOLS

10. **Online survey** In the Put It to Work activity, you considered what information was needed from coworkers regarding a new flexible schedule. Individually, create an online survey or form that could be used to gather this information. Use one of the links provided on the textbook website. (Learning Objective 5)

PLAN AHEAD

Leader story Imagine you work for one of the following companies: General Motors, Procter & Gamble, Starbucks, Google, Intel, Apple, Coca-Cola, BP, Cisco, Dell, or Target. You have been asked to develop a profile of a leader in the company for an awards presentation at this year's annual luncheon. Using *Windows Live Movie Maker, iMovie*, or other video editing software, create a digital story about a successful leader in the company. Describe this person's leadership qualities and leadership style. Use pictures and copyright-free music if available. Add transitions, titles, and credits to give your movie a professional look. (Learning Objective 1)

CHAPTER

7 Customer Service

LEARNING OBJECTIVES

1. Define customer service and explain the importance of an organization's commitment to customer service.
2. Develop skills for providing effective customer service.
3. Describe strategies for delivering effective customer service.
4. Describe how to handle difficult customer service situations.

© Photographer/Image Source

Customer Service

Customer service is important to businesses and many other organizations. A *customer* is someone who buys or uses the products or services of a company or organization. Customers may also be called clients or buyers. **Customer service** is often defined as the ability of an organization to consistently give customers what they want and need.

Importance of Customer Service

Providing information to help people decide which products or services best meet their needs; offering options such as delivery, installation, or service plans; and answering questions about product use after a sale are all examples of customer service. This attitude and commitment is called **customer focus.** Organizations with a customer focus understand the importance of providing excellent customer service to attract and maintain customers. Customer service is not simply a job or a department; it is a way of thinking within an organization.

In your career you may work for a variety of organizations—businesses, nonprofit organizations, or government entities. Although different types of

Keep these points in mind to help you deliver effective customer service:

- Treat all customers with respect and courtesy, even when they are at fault or do not have a legitimate complaint.
- Never say "I don't know" without also saying "but I will find out." Find someone in the organization who knows the answer and get back to the customer.
- Avoid saying "We don't," "We can't," or "You'll have to . . ." Instead, tell customers what you can do for them.
- Do not say "That's our policy." Instead, be flexible and creative when attempting to solve customer problems.
- Do not say "It will be ready tomorrow" unless you are sure that will happen. Do not make promises you are not sure you can keep.

Source: Pattie Gibson-Odgers, *The World of Customer Service*, 2nd ed. (Cincinnati: South-Western, 2008), 57.

organizations may have different goals, many businesses and other organizations cannot fully achieve their goals without a focus on effective customer service to their external and internal customers.

External and Internal Customers

Everyone within an organization has a role to play in developing an environment that is focused on the customer. Most people are aware of the importance of providing service to external customers but must also remember the importance of internal customer service.

EXTERNAL CUSTOMERS

The most recognized customers of any business or organization are its external customers. **External customers** are the people or organizations that buy or use the products and services provided by your organization. For example, a consumer who buys a new car is an external customer of an automobile dealership. A student who visits a nonprofit public library is an external customer of the library.

BananaStock/JupiterImages

Providing effective customer service to external customers is vital to the success of a business.

A major goal of business is to make a profit. A focus on effective customer service is vital to achieving this goal. External customers who are not satisfied with the service they receive are likely to take their business elsewhere in the future and to share their frustrations and experiences with others. When many customers take these actions, lower sales may result in lower profits. However, customers who are pleased with the service they have received are more likely to buy from the company again, and they may also recommend you or your organization to others. If a customer's problem is handled quickly and effectively, the customer will continue to work with your organization.

Increased sales and profits can be a major benefit of providing effective customer service. Excellent external customer service can lead to customer satisfaction, customer loyalty, and customer retention.

INTERNAL CUSTOMERS

In addition to considering the needs of external customers, an organization must also recognize the importance of internal customers. **Internal customers** are departments or employees within an organization who use the products or services provided by others within the organization. Employees in the technical support department, for example, serve the needs of other company employees. These employees are the internal customers of the workers in the technical support department. Without the services this department provides, others in the company would not be able to do their work, and service to external customers would suffer. Employees who have no direct contact with external customers can make important contributions that help the organization provide quality customer service.

Effective internal customer service is essential for a business to provide good external customer service. The relationships among managers, employees, associates, and peers are all important when developing an internal customer focus. Developing strong relationships with those who depend on you to provide answers or services is essential to creating an environment that puts customers first. By developing positive relationships with internal customers, you are showing that you value their importance to the organization. Excellent internal customer service can lead to employee satisfaction, employee loyalty, and employee retention as well as a higher level of external customer service.

Future Customers

You have already learned about the impact of diversity in the workforce in Chapters 1 and 3. The population of the United States as a whole is more diverse than it has ever been in race and ethnicity. Thus, the future customers of any organization, both internal and external, will be diverse as well. You may deal with people who are very different from you. These individuals may come from various cultures and be of various ages, yet you will still be expected to meet their needs and desires by providing excellent customer service.

With the increased globalization of business, customers may live in the United States or outside the country. You may encounter language and cultural issues that are very different than when working with customers from the United States. In many cases, you may never talk with the customer. Business is increasingly being conducted through electronic means. When you cannot see or sometimes even hear your customers, communicating effectively is more difficult. The information and skills you will learn in Chapters 8 and 9 on written and verbal communication will help you communicate effectively with many different customers in different situations and establish good customer relationships.

Customer Service Skills

Your role as an administrative professional will often include the first contact a customer has with your organization. If so, you play an extremely important part in customer service. Whether you are dealing with customers in a face-to-face situation or by telephone, e-mail, or websites, you can develop skills that will help you have successful interactions. Several skills you will need when working with customers are discussed in this section.

Serving Internal Customers

Administrative professionals should be committed to serving internal customers effectively. Demonstrate your commitment to internal customers by following these guidelines:

- Come to work on time. Arriving at work on time demonstrates your commitment to the company and fellow employees.
- Be polite and courteous. Say "please" when asking for assistance and "thank you" when someone has helped you. Whether your interactions are face-to-face or by e-mail or telephone, politeness goes a long way toward maintaining a successful relationship.
- Answer questions or calls quickly. Get back to your colleagues with answers to their questions in a timely manner. Do not wait for them to contact you again.
- Be professional at all times. Offer to help someone if you see he or she needs assistance and you have time to provide it.
- Go the extra mile and exceed the expectations of others. When you go out of your way to help others, they will often do the same for you when you are in a similar situation.

AVAVA/iStockphoto.com

Problem-Solving Skills

Regardless of your effectiveness as an administrative professional, problems will arise. What is important, however, is how you choose to handle the problems that occur. Although there are some customers who are difficult to please, most of them are not interested in making your job more stressful. Most customers simply want you to provide information or help them solve a problem.

Terryl/iStockphoto.com

Most customers want you to help them solve a problem.

Make sure to meet the needs of your customers and handle any issues that occurs promptly and with a smile. If a problem occurs, follow a systematic method to solve it. Steps for solving problems, which were introduced in Chapter 4, are discussed in more detail in this section.

DEFINE THE PROBLEM

Attempt to identify and understand the problem. This is often the most difficult step in the process. When defining the problem, ask yourself these questions: What problem am I trying to solve? What will be the outcome of this problem? Sometimes the true problem will be difficult to identify. You may need to complete part of the next step, collecting information, before you can correctly identify the problem.

Megan is an administrative professional in the IT Department. When employees have problems with their computer hardware or software, they contact her office. Megan's first task is to determine the employee's problem. Today Raymond, an employee in the Accounting Department, brings in his notebook computer, saying it doesn't turn on.

COLLECT AND ANALYZE INFORMATION

Collect and analyze information related to the problem. To do this, you must ask a series of questions related to the problem you have identified. The more information you can collect that is related to the problem, the more likely you can solve the problem in a timely manner. Look for patterns, trends, or relationships in the data you have collected. Your goal is to develop a clear understanding of the problem and related issues before trying to determine a solution.

Part of Megan's job is to determine whether the problem is related to the hardware or software. She asks Raymond several questions: "Does the monitor turn on? Does the battery indicator light display? What happens when you plug in the unit?" She also checks that the power cord is correctly connected. From his answers and her check of the cord, Megan determines that the problem relates to the power source.

GENERATE ALTERNATIVES

The next step in solving a problem is to generate options or possible solutions. Sometimes the problem will be unique, and it will be challenging to develop a solution. Other times, it will be a problem you have seen before, and you may rely on past solutions when determining your course of action. If a problem has occurred frequently, your company may have collected information or developed specific policies related to the problem. This information can be helpful in finding a solution.

Because this is a common problem with notebook computers in her organization, Megan consults the procedures manual and reviews some possible solutions: taking the battery out and reinserting it, trying a different power cord, and trying a battery that she knows is working.

ASSESS AND IMPLEMENT

Effective problem solving requires that you evaluate each of the options you have defined as possible solutions. Sometimes the best alternatives will be obvious, and other times, it will be difficult to make that determination. The positive and negative results of a particular solution should be considered from both the company's and the customer's perspective. Once your evaluation is complete, implement the best option.

Megan tests all the suggested solutions, but the computer still does not turn on. According to company policy, at this point, she should pass the computer to an IT technician, preferably someone who has expertise with the problem. For this problem, that would be Josefa. Megan takes the computer to her.

EVALUATE THE SOLUTION

After a solution has been implemented, it should be evaluated. Evaluation helps you decide whether you have made the right decision for the immediate situation. It also helps you improve your problem-solving skills for the future.

Josefa finds a loose connection between the power supply and the battery and repairs it. Because this is an internal computer problem, there was no way for Megan to correctly identify the source of the problem. If the same situation arose again, sending the computer to a technician would still be the right decision.

Effective Listening Skills

Listening cannot be overemphasized when you are dealing with customers. Listening says to the customer that you believe he or she is important. Listening shows you care about the customer and respect his or her questions and concerns.

Let the customer tell you the story. Even though it is time-consuming to hear a customer's entire story when you think you understood all that was necessary to solve the problem at the beginning of the conversation, it is important to let the customer finish his or her statement. You may be wrong; you may not have understood the real problem. Let the customer talk freely without your interruption.

Listening is more than hearing what the speaker is saying. Effective listening requires that you be focused on what the other person is saying and not on what is happening around you. Learn to use the listening strategies given in Chapter 9, "Verbal Communication and Presentations." Also read carefully the listening tips provided in Figure 7.1.

Verbal Communication Skills

Verbal communication is extremely important in effective internal and external customer service. When talking to customers, coworkers, or your supervisors, adopt a pleasant and professional manner. Strive to speak clearly, directly, and simply so you are understood. Remember that you should remain calm and courteous even when talking with customers who are not. You will learn more about effective verbal communication in Chapter 9.

Nonverbal Communication Skills

Nonverbal communication consists of messages you convey without words. These messages can be as important as the words you speak. Nonverbal communication can occur through eye contact,

Listening Tips

- Listen actively, focusing all your attention on the customer.
- Listen for facts. Mentally register the key words the speaker is using, and mentally repeat key ideas or related points.
- Notice the body language of the speaker for clues to the real meaning of what is being said.
- Let the customer finish the entire complaint or description of the problem. Do not interrupt.
- Repeat in concise terms the problem as you understand it. Ask the customer to verify that you have understood.
- Listen carefully to the customer's responses as you ask questions to further clarify the issues.

FIGURE 7.1 Effective listening will help you build and maintain relationships.

Both verbal and nonverbal communication skills are vital components of effective customer service.

facial expressions, gestures, body language, and voice qualities such as tone and pitch. Work to develop effective nonverbal communication skills to help you in dealing with customers.

Eye contact is a powerful form of nonverbal communication. It lets customers know that you are interested in and attentive to what they are saying. It may also convey compassion and caring. Avoiding eye contact may suggest a lack of concern or honesty. When dealing with customers, you should make eye contact frequently. Customers may perceive you are not interested in what they are saying if you do not periodically make eye contact with them.

Facial expressions, such as a warm smile, can be valuable in communicating with customers. A smile signals that you care about the customer and are eager to help. Typically a smile shows the emotion of happiness. However, if the customer is extremely upset, a smile can signal that you are laughing at the individual, suggesting to the customer that you are not taking his or her issue seriously.

Strive to keep strong emotions such as anger from showing in your voice. The tone of your voice can be as important as your words when talking with customers. You can convey friendliness and empathy or anger and disbelief simply by the tone of voice you use.

Speak at a normal volume—not too loud or soft. Pay attention to the rate of speech you use. Speaking too quickly may make it difficult for a customer to understand what you are saying or make the customer think you do not want to take time to talk about a problem or answer a question.

Human Relations Skills

Human relations skills are abilities that allow one to interact with others effectively. These abilities are sometimes called people skills. Showing respect for others, having empathy for others, and showing support for the skills and ideas of others are demonstrations of human relations skills.

Customer service is more than saying the words the customer wants to hear. It involves both the words you say and the way you say them. As mentioned above, when you are talking with internal or external customers, your tone of voice is very important. Your tone can convey concern, respect, and compassion. Most importantly, your words must sound sincere.

Empathy is understanding or concern for someone's feelings or position. It is the ability to imagine yourself in the other person's situation. Showing empathy is a skill that must be practiced. You must listen to what the person is saying without evaluation. Empathy does not involve agreeing or disagreeing; it involves attempting to understand the other person's point of view.

Being able to show genuine empathy for a customer who is describing a problem will help you gain and keep the customer's trust. An empathy statement such as "I can imagine it is frustrating

Make a Connection

When someone you have just met immediately calls you by name, how do you feel? Do you feel as if the person is interested in you and your concerns? Most of us would answer yes. When someone takes the time to actually hear your name and then uses it, you tend to think that person cares about you. This is especially important in business. Calling customers by name is a first step in establishing a positive relationship and shows customers you care about them and their business.

JHDT Stock Images LLC/Shutterstock.com

when equipment doesn't operate as expected" acknowledges how the customer is feeling without admitting or denying fault. These are some additional examples of empathy statements:

- I see.
- Interesting.
- Tell me more about . . .

Using empathy statements can help defuse feelings of anger or frustration. These statements let the customer know you are interested in what he or she has to say.

E-Mail Customer Service Skills

As an administrative professional, you will probably communicate with internal and external customers through e-mail. Steps for writing effective e-mail messages are presented in Chapter 8, "Written Communication."

The large volume of e-mail sent and received daily continues to be a major issue in business. Handling e-mail effectively is an important part of developing a customer focus for many organizations. Even if your only job responsibility is to answer e-mail, it is not realistic to assume you can answer each e-mail message within minutes of receiving it. Still, messages should not sit in your inbox for long periods of time before you answer them.

One way to handle e-mail effectively and still be productive at work is to designate specific times during the day to check and answer your e-mail messages. Determine the scheduled times based on the proportion of your job devoted to serving e-mail customers and the volume of messages you receive. For example, if most of your job requires handling e-mail customers, you will need to check your messages every hour or half hour (depending on the volume of e-mail). However, if only a small portion of your job requires handling e-mail customers, you may want to check your messages only three or four times a day. Keep in mind that the customer should be served in a timely, caring, and efficient manner.

Telephone Customer Service Skills

Although the use of e-mail in business continues to rise, the telephone remains an important business tool. As an administrative professional, you must be effective in your telephone communications. Without appropriate telephone customer service skills, you may make customers angry or lose customers for your organization.

Blend Images/Jupiter Images

Greet callers professionally and courteously.

It is important that all your telephone conversations be conducted professionally. Answer the phone courteously and identify yourself and the organization. Put a "smile" in your voice by using a friendly tone. Speak at an appropriate volume, pitch, and speed. Ask questions tactfully and respond calmly even when the caller is loud or angry. Use good listening skills:

- Listen for facts.
- Search for subtle meanings.
- Be patient.
- Practice active listening and repeat back important points to make sure you have understood correctly.
- Act to handle the problem or issue.

Always assist the customer to the best of your ability. Ask questions about anything that is not clear to you. Let the customer know what will happen next, especially if you cannot solve the problem or answer the questions right away. Figure 7.2 suggests phrases to avoid and phrases to use in dealing with customers.

Conclude every telephone call in a positive manner. At the end of the conversation, thank the caller and ask if there is anything else you can do to help. Effective telephone communication skills are discussed in Chapter 9.

Web Customer Service Skills

In the past when customers had questions, they contacted an organization's customer service representatives by telephone. Today, more and more companies are offering customers the option of searching for answers to common questions on the company website. This option, called web self-service, may be in addition to or an alternative to contacting representatives by telephone. Often this service allows customers to use the same tools and knowledge databases that customer service agents

Trigger and Calming Phrases	
Avoid Trigger Phrases	**Use Calming Phrases**
"It's our policy."	"Here's what we can do." "Here's how we can handle this." (Quote the policy; don't call it "policy.")
"I can't." "We don't."	"I can." "We do."
"What seems to be the problem?"	"How can I help?"
"I don't know."	"I can find out."
"You should have . . ."	"Let's do this." (Move to the future, not the past.)
"Why didn't you . . . ?"	"I can see why . . ."
"The only thing we can do . . ."	"The best option, I think, is . . ."
"I don't handle that; it's not my job."	"Let's find the right person to handle your concern."

FIGURE 7.2 Trigger and Calming Phrases

Adapted from Pattie Gibson, *The World of Customer Service*, 3rd ed. (Cincinnati: Cengage, 2012), 111.

within the organization use to locate answers to customer questions.

As an administrative professional, your work may not directly involve customer service via the web. However, the organization for which you work may offer web self-service or live chat as an option for customers. Familiarize yourself with web self-service if your organization offers this option. It is important for you to be knowledgeable about it when talking with customers. You may also use the database to find answers to questions you have.

Customer Service Strategies

To be successful as an administrative professional, you must understand the importance of customer service in all your relationships. You should practice the same high standards of service with both internal and external customers. Strategies for developing a customer service focus are discussed in this section.

Show Respect for Customers

You may have heard the statement "The customer is always right." The intent of this statement is to show the importance of customers and that customers should be valued and their concerns should be taken seriously. However, the statement should not be taken literally. Customers are people, and people are not always right. If a customer comes to you with a concern, you should give it serious attention. Consider this simple but realistic situation.

Assume you have recently taken a test. When you get your test back, you have received no credit for a question you think you answered correctly. You talk with your instructor. She explains that your answer is not correct and refers you to a source for the correct answer.

In this situation, you are the customer—you receive the services of your school and instructor. If the instructor had agreed that you were right when you were not, you would have gone away with incorrect information.

Even when customers are not right, they deserve to be treated with respect and to have their complaint or question heard. Show the customer you are sincere and serious about providing assistance. In the example above, the instructor listened to your question. She then referred you to a source where you could get the correct answer, which helps you learn. Perhaps the best principle to follow is that the customer should always be treated fairly and with respect. Customers should be given an explanation if there is a question about a product or service.

Go the Extra Mile

Have you ever been disappointed in a product or service you purchased? When you brought your concerns to the attention of a customer service representative, did he or she listen intently? Were you offered a solution to your problem? Did he or she give you something extra for your trouble? Assume you ordered an item from an online store, and when you received it, it was the wrong size. When you called the customer service line, the representative explained how to return the merchandise and gave you a coupon for free shipping on your next order or 15 percent off of a future order. By going the extra mile, the company has maintained a valued customer for a small cost.

Doing something special or extra that is not required of you as part of your job or obligations to the customer is often beneficial. This action can help maintain a valued external customer or help build a good relationship with an internal customer.

Although keeping customers happy is important, never do anything that violates company ethics or standards to keep a customer happy. A good question to ask yourself is, Would I be comfortable explaining what I did to my supervisor the next day? Talk to your supervisor ahead of time so you will know the scope of actions you can take to maintain customers. Sometimes these actions will include giving discounts on orders or reducing fees.

Take Responsibility

Everyone occasionally makes an error. When you make a mistake, do you admit it or try to hide it? If you answered honestly, you probably had to say

TECH TALK

Screen Capture

The ability to capture the image displayed on your computer screen is called screen capture. This capability is a standard feature of the *Microsoft Windows* operating system. The print screen (PrtSc or PrtScn) function enables users to share the exact content of their computer display with others. Many different terms are used to describe the screen capture process, including *screen cap, screenshot, screen grab*, and *screen dump*.

With screen capture software, users can do more than simple screen shots. For example, they can create short videos, add narration, and crop and edit captured images. Some software also allows you to import photos and video.

The ability to pictorially represent the information on your computer screen is useful when you want to share a particular screen, or series of screens, with coworkers. The captured images can be included as part of an e-mail message, pasted in a word processing document, or shared as part of a presentation. Screen capture is especially useful for sharing error messages with information technology (IT) personnel when you experience software or hardware malfunctions.

As an administrative professional, you may need to answer questions from external customers or coworkers about how to complete a task on the computer, such as how to find a link on the company website or complete an online form. Your response could include a screen capture with the link circled or a short video demonstrating form completion. Links to several screen capture programs are provided on the website for this text.

there were times when you did not admit you made a mistake. However, the mature individual willingly takes responsibility for his or her mistakes and learns from them.

Admitting you made a mistake is difficult for anyone. However, refusing to admit to being wrong can damage your reputation and can label you as dishonest. When you or your company makes a mistake, the key is to apologize quickly for the error and then solve the problem. When a mistake is made, take the time to determine what went wrong and how you can prevent the same mistake in the future. If you skip this step, it's possible you will repeat the mistake in the future.

inkastudio/iStockphoto.com

Doing something special or extra is a simple way to maintain customers.

Positive experiences can also be learning experiences. At the end of the day, take time to review your positive experiences. Note strategies or procedures that worked particularly well so you can use them again in the future.

Maintain Effective Relationships

Maintaining effective relationships strengthens your ability to provide excellent customer service. Working with others allows you to build on the synergy that working with another person creates. When you are working with an external customer, you may find that you encounter problems or issues you have not experienced before. If that happens, take the time to ask one of your colleagues for assistance. Use the experience and expertise of others to solve the customer's problem and put your best foot forward.

When you are helpful and provide exceptional assistance to your internal customers, they are likely to return the favor by providing you with excellent service as well. For example, have you ever been working with a colleague who has exhausted his knowledge of the situation, but then says, "I know someone here who has experience with this situation. Let me see if she can help us." It is likely that these individuals have worked together in the past, providing each other with assistance. These two-way relationships continue to build as each person helps the other and eventually develop into solid working relationships built on internal customer service practices.

Explain the Situation

When dealing with customers, explain issues or points clearly and with complete details. Do not assume the customer already has all the information related to the issue or problem.

Have you ever been in a situation in which you spoke clearly, articulated well, and gave details and yet the individual to whom you were talking still did not understand you? For most people, the answer is yes. Why? Perhaps the person is not using the same frame of reference you are. Consider this story. You are talking with your friend and say, "My new car is a lemon." Your friend responds, "I didn't know you bought a yellow car." You almost laugh

PARTNERSHIP FOR 21ST CENTURY SKILLS

Flexibility and Adaptability

Adapt to Change

Change in the workplace is inevitable; it will happen whether we want it to or not. As an administrative professional, you will face change on a daily basis: in technology, routine, your surroundings. The effective administrative professional not only copes with change but adapts to change and embraces it.

Be proactive. Staying current with technology and keeping up-to-date with changes in your business is imperative. Anticipate change; try to predict the changes you will face and prepare for them. Read the strategic directions for your organization; discuss them with your employer. Read books or journal articles that relate to your position and business. Align yourself with people in the organization who possess skills you believe are key to helping you perform your job to the best of your abilities. Take a class or workshop to learn a new skill or increase your knowledge in a new area.

Accept change. Adaptability is the trait that allows people to change their way of thinking, change the way they do their work, and embrace and learn new ways of completing tasks and conducting business. To adapt to change, you must be optimistic and keep a positive attitude. Recognize the need for change, and understand how it will benefit both the customer and the organization.

Activity

Purposefully make a change to your daily routine. Take a different mode of transportation, park in a different location, or sit in a different place in class or the cafeteria. The change should be one that is outside your normal comfort zone. Think about how this change made you feel. Write a list of the feelings you encountered. How long would you feel this way before the new behavior becomes comfortable? What can you do to make yourself more adaptable to change?

shapecharge/iStockphoto.com

out loud because you are so surprised. However, you restrain yourself and explain that you have had one mechanical problem after another with the car. That is why you call it a lemon.

What you thought was a simple statement turned into a communication problem. However, at least the person let you know how the message was interpreted. Often, you do not know; thus, it is important to explain clearly what you mean. Then give the person a chance to let you know if he or she understands by asking, "Does this make sense to you?" With such a statement, you are giving the individual a chance to tell you whether you have been clear in your communication.

Seek Customer Input

Seeking input from customers is an important component of effective customer service. Take the time to ask questions. Give customers the opportunity to express their opinions (both positive and negative) about the quality of products and services the business provides. After asking questions, take the time to listen to the information you receive.

Take advantage of problem situations by using them as learning opportunities for you or your organization. Use problem situations to obtain information from customers. A customer concern or complaint is really just a request for action. If you listen to the customer, he or she will often have ideas about how to solve the problem.

Customers may also give you ideas about how a problem can be avoided in the future. Asking for a customer's feedback gives him or her an opportunity to participate in the process of improving a situation. Sometimes a customer will recognize issues you may not see. Allowing the customer to participate in solving a problem is a positive step toward reestablishing goodwill.

Follow Up on the Issue

Once a problem has been solved, make sure to follow up with the customer. Follow-up is checking back to determine whether the solution has been implemented. The most effective problem solving has little or no value if the solution was never put in place.

A customer remembers the end result. Customers who have had excellent service throughout the process do not remember that if their problem does not get resolved. Phone a customer to let him or her know if you need more time to find or implement a solution. Keeping the customer informed will go a long way toward maintaining customer satisfaction.

Keep a Positive Attitude

A positive customer service encounter starts and ends with a positive attitude. The attitude you display is often as important as the answers you give and the actions you take. Show your positive attitude by attempting to help customers even when you do not have all the answers. People will come to you for help and will be more eager to help you with issues or problems if you have a positive attitude.

Handling Difficult Situations

As you work in administrative support positions, you will find success when you treat each customer with respect and follow the suggestions given in this chapter for providing excellent customer service. However, there will be times when you will encounter individuals who behave inappropriately. You need to understand how to respond when difficult situations arise.

Monkey Business Images/Shutterstock.com

A positive attitude is an important part of a positive experience.

Handling Conflict

One of the best customer service techniques is learning how to avoid problems. This can be accomplished by being proactive with customers. Learn to anticipate customers' needs and provide solutions to their concerns before they ask. Sometimes, however, it's not possible to anticipate concerns or avoid problems. When that happens, conflict may occur.

Effective customer service includes learning how to handle conflict. When dealing with conflict, listen carefully to customers' concerns or problems. Work hard to make your customers happy even if it means making changes to something you do not think is a major concern. When possible, offer several resolutions for the client to choose from to give him or her the feeling of being in control of the situation.

Accept the blame for a mistake or problem if it is your fault. At times you will also need to accept the blame for a problem or mistake that is not your fault. In these situations, you accept the blame on behalf of your company or department. Then take the necessary steps to correct the mistake or problem.

Handling Difficult Customers

Although you can control your own behavior, you cannot control the actions of others. Sometimes a customer will get angry. It may be because someone in the organization was rude or indifferent or did not listen to a concern. A customer may also get angry if he or she did not get what was promised. Sometimes issues arise when a customer does not have adequate information about you or your products or services.

When a customer gets angry, don't take it personally. Usually the customer is not angry at you, but rather at something that has happened. Try to defuse the anger as quickly as possible by listening to the customer's concerns. Take a deep breath and tell yourself you have done the best you can. Use positive self-talk. Here are some statements you can make to yourself:

- I will not get angry.
- I have been successful in situations like this one in the past, and I will be successful again.
- I know this anger is not directed against me personally. I will use calming phrases to describe what can be done to help solve the problem.

Acknowledge the situation, and ask what you can do to solve the problem or make the situation better. Sometimes just asking the question will get the situation back under control. Other times, an apology is the best approach. If you or your organization has made a mistake, apologize for the error and then correct it.

At times difficult customers are extremely knowledgeable about your products and services. It's best to understand that some people are going to be difficult no matter how helpful and professional you are. They are not angry at you; they just want solutions. Handling difficult customers helps you improve your responses and ultimately helps you or your company provide the best product or business possible.

Dealing With Abusive Customers

Usually, you cannot help an abusive customer until he or she calms down. Do not let yourself become angry; this behavior merely escalates the situation. Look for points of agreement with the customer and voice those points. These techniques generally work well, and you can then begin to help solve the problem with the customer. If the exchange is over the phone and the customer continues to be abusive, you may have to ask the customer to call back later when he or she can discuss the issue calmly.

Many organizations have a policy concerning difficult or abusive telephone situations. Find out what the policy is and observe it. Some companies have a recorded announcement telling customers a call may be recorded for customer service quality or training purposes. Customers may be less likely to make threats or inappropriate comments if they know the call might be recorded.

SUMMARY

To reinforce what you have learned in this chapter, study this summary.

- Effective customer service is a way of thinking within a company and is vital to its future success.
- It is important to develop skills that will help you have successful interactions with customers including skills in problem solving; listening; verbal and nonverbal communication; human relations; and e-mail, telephone, and web customer service.
- Strategies for delivering effective customer service include showing respect for customers, going the extra mile, taking responsibility, maintaining effective relationships, explaining the situation, seeking customer input, following up on the issue, and keeping a positive attitude.
- To provide effective customer service in difficult situations, make sure to understand how to handle conflict, handle difficult customers, and deal with abusive customers.

KEY TERMS

customer focus, 130
customer service, 130
empathy, 136
external customers, 131
human relations skills, 136
internal customers, 132

7

STUDY Tools

Located at www.cengagebrain.com

- Chapter Outlines
- Flashcards
- Interactive Quizzes
- Tech Tools
- Video Segments
- and More!

LET'S DISCUSS

1. How can you contribute to effective customer service in an organization?
2. Describe the difference between internal and external customers and give an example of each.
3. Explain the steps you should follow to solve a customer service problem.
4. Give an example of going the extra mile to resolve a customer problem.
5. How should you handle an abusive customer?

PUT IT TO WORK

Customer contact Susie Chang works as an administrative assistant in the Human Resources Department. This morning she received this call, which she answered promptly on the second ring.

Susie:	This is Susie Chang in HR. How may I help you?
Customer:	Hello, is this the Albrinck Corporation? I'm trying to reach Tom Cushner.
Susie:	Yes, this is the Albrinck Corporation, but as I said, I'm Susie Chang. You must have dialed the wrong number. I think someone named Tom works in the accounting department, but I'm not sure. Please hang up and try your call again.
Customer:	Well, could you transfer me to Mr. Cushner?
Susie:	Sorry, I don't have that number. Goodbye.

Did Susie handle this customer contact effectively? What did Susie do that was positive? What could she have done differently to improve customer service? (Learning Objectives 2 and 3)

COMMUNICATE SUCCESSFULLY

1. **Role play** Use the scenario above in the Put It to Work section. Work with a partner to create a simulation of how the situation could have been handled using effective customer service techniques. Be prepared to present your suggestions to the class. (Learning Objectives 2 and 3)
2. **Customer service workshop** You are an administrative assistant in the printing services department of a large organization. Your department provides copying and professional printing services for all other departments. Your supervisor, Mr. Lopez, has heard that some departments are considering moving their business outside the organization because they are not pleased with the way they are being treated by the printing services staff.

   You have recently returned from customer service training. Mr. Lopez has asked you to prepare a short presentation (10–15 minutes) for the other printing services employees about the importance of customer service within your department. He has asked that you include specific tips and strategies to help the other employees maintain effective relationships within the organization. He has also asked that you include brief information on how to handle difficult customer service situations. (Learning Objectives 1, 2, 3, and 4)

3. **Customer value** Pay attention to positive customer service situations you encounter in the next few days. Write a short reflection that includes specific examples from these situations, and explain why they made you feel valued as a customer. (Learning Objectives 1, 2, and 3)
4. **Customer service questionnaire** After discussing effective customer service skills with the staff (Activity 2), Mr. Lopez wants to determine whether employees are putting these skills into practice. He has asked that you create a short survey so customers can provide feedback on their experiences. The survey should include 15 questions related to the customer service skills and strategies discussed in the chapter. (Learning Objectives 2 and 3)
5. **Importance of customer service** Add a new post to the blog you created in Chapter 1. In this entry, reflect on the following statement: **I believe customer service skills are important for me to have as an administrative professional for the following reasons, and here is how I can demonstrate this importance to customers.** (Learning Objectives 1 and 2)

Blog

DEVELOP WORKPLACE SKILLS

6. **Excellent customer service** Write a description of a situation in which you received excellent customer service. Indicate whether you were an internal or external customer. Evaluate your experience according to the customer service skills described in the chapter and/or discussed in class. Give at least four examples of why the experience was positive. Explain why you continue to do business with this company. (Learning Objectives 1, 2, and 3)
7. **Poor customer service** Write a description of a situation in which you received poor customer service. Indicate whether you were an internal or external customer. Evaluate your experience according to the customer service skills described in the chapter and/or discussed in class. Give at least four suggestions for ways the situation could have been handled better. Discuss whether you will continue to do business with this company. (Learning Objectives 1, 2, and 3)
8. **Handling an angry customer** Annette Osterhout purchased a new notebook computer from Warren Hutchinson at Welbright Electronics. Because the notebook was last year's model, it was the last one of its kind in the store. Two days later when Annette tried to start the computer, the notebook had no power. Annette connected the power cord and waited for the battery to charge. When she attempted to start the computer three

hours later, the computer still was not charged. Annette called Warren, and he asked Annette to bring the notebook back to the store.

Warren did some troubleshooting and believes the power cord connection on the notebook is defective. Because he has no other notebooks of that type in stock, Warren tells Annette he will send the notebook for repairs, which will take 7–10 days. Annette is furious and wants her notebook today. She is threatening to take her business to another store. What strategies can you give Warren for handling this angry customer? (Learning Objectives 3 and 4)

BUILD RELATIONSHIPS

9. **Difficult situation** You have been dealing with a customer over the telephone for several months. Over the years he has been an important customer, and he continues to buy communications equipment from your organization. At this point, he has spent more than $1 million with your organization. You have never had any problems with him; he has always been very professional in his conduct with you, as you have with him. When he calls, he always asks for you by name. He has been extremely polite and businesslike. However, on two recent occasions he has told you that you sound so nice over the telephone that he would like to meet you. You have made statements such as, "Thanks for the compliments; I do care about customers." You have evaded the suggestion that you meet him, thinking he would not insist.

   The last time the customer called to place an order, he repeated his interest in meeting you, making a threatening statement (you believe) that he will stop ordering from the company unless you are willing to meet him. He did laugh after he made the statement, but you believe he is serious. You know your employer values his business. He has mentioned to you that he appreciates your help with this valuable customer. You are single, but you do not think it would be wise to meet the customer. How should you handle this situation? (Learning Objectives 1, 2, and 3)

10. **Unhappy customer** Access the *Word* file *Ch07_Customer_Service* from the data files. Read the case and answer the questions that follow it. (Learning Objectives 1, 2, 3, and 4)

USE TECH TOOLS

11. **Screen capture** Using the print screen button on your computer or screen capture software, make a one-page instruction sheet for a simple software function or command. For example, explain how to set tabs, insert a graphic, or create a table in a word processing program or create a chart, an *if* function, or conditional text in a spreadsheet program. Links to screen capture software are provided on the website for this text.

12. **Create a video** Create a short video demonstrating a simple software function or command. Links to screen capture software with a video function are provided on the website for this text.

PLAN AHEAD

Create a web page Your company is launching a program to improve customer service. As part of this effort, you have been asked to create a web page to be posted on the new section of the company website devoted to improving customer service. (Learning Objectives 2 and 3)

1. Review the tips for improving customer service given in this chapter. Using the Internet or other sources, find and read at least three articles about improving customer service. Note the source information for these articles.
2. Create a web page to be posted on the company website. Only employees (not customers) will have access to this page.
   - Use "Customer Service" as the main heading for the page.
   - Use "Tips for Improving Customer Service" as the subheading for the page.
   - Under the subheading, include a bulleted list of ten tips for improving customer service.
   - Place footnotes at the bottom of the page for any material that is quoted or paraphrased from the articles you read.
   - Use an attractive design and color scheme for the page. Add appropriate artwork if desired.
3. Save the document as a single file web page using an appropriate name. View the page in a browser. Make changes or corrections as needed so you have a page that is attractive and easy to read.

PART

3

Communication Essentials

CAREER PROFILE

Visit www.cengagebrain.com to listen to the complete interview.

Medical Assistant

Kyra Nance is a medical assistant at South Carolina OB-GYN Associates in Columbia, South Carolina.

What are your biggest challenges on the job?
Remembering a schedule of 40 patients, trying to make sure the providers get to their destinations, handling phone calls, triaging patients, and trying to get everybody's needs met.

What are your major responsibilities besides scheduling?
Getting the patients back, working them up, vital signs, getting their history, and getting the information as to why they're in the office for that day.

How important are computer skills?
Computer skills are a must. You have to know *Word, Excel,* even sometimes *PowerPoint*. Everybody has a different EMR [electronic medical records] system, but if you know the basics, you can learn the rest of it.

What about written communication skills?
If a patient is telling you they have this problem, they're saying it in layman's terms. You have to translate and put that on a piece of paper to hand to the provider, into the EMR system, into your computer system. Then you need to be able to relate to the patient, This is what this means. You have to know both sides.

What about verbal communication skills?
Verbal communication is key. You have to know how to deliver a message. You have to be able to get your point across for people to understand exactly what you want them to know.

What are some of the most important qualities a person would need to do your job?
You need to be organized. You have to use your critical thinking skills. You have to be able to think on your toes, assess whatever may be going on, be able to direct that attention to wherever it is needed, and have a caring manner.

How did you prepare for your job?
With my medical assisting classes and externship. And then getting my associate's degree gave me an extra boost.

PictureMe Portrait Studio

CHAPTER

8 Written Communication

LEARNING OBJECTIVES

1. Prepare effective written communications using the "C" characteristics.
2. Use a writing process to create effective written messages.
3. Apply appropriate guidelines for writing e-mail, memos, letters, and reports.

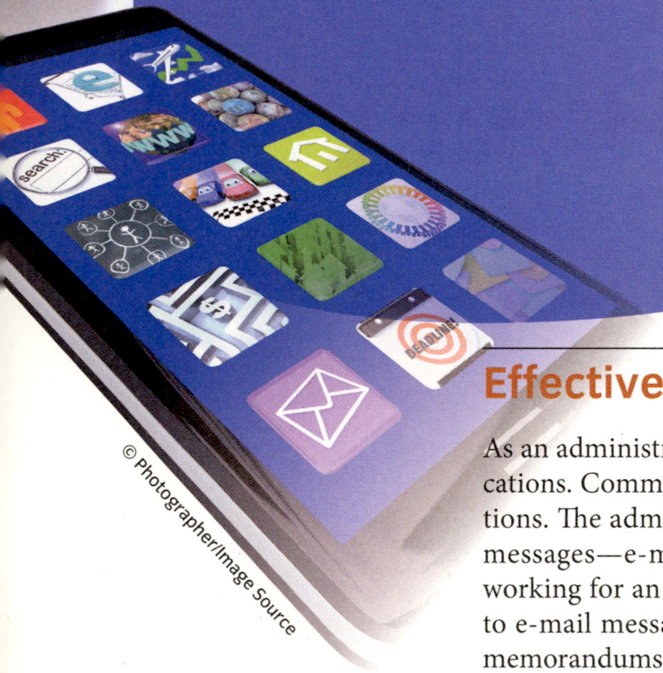

Effective Written Communication

As an administrative professional, you will produce many written communications. Communicating effectively is essential to successful business operations. The administrative professional produces four basic types of written messages—e-mail, memorandums, letters, and reports. When you begin working for an organization, you will be expected to compose and respond to e-mail messages. You may compose draft copies of correspondence and memorandums. You may conduct research and prepare informal and formal reports. As you learn your position and the needs of the organization, you may send out written messages under your own signature or write final copy for your employer to sign.

Being a competent and careful writer is important to your success. This chapter will help you develop techniques for writing effectively.

Importance of Effective Communication

Businesspeople today are writing more than ever before. The ability to transmit messages faster, farther, and more easily than in the past has increased the reliance on written communication.

Your communication skills are vital to your success in the workplace. In fact, the ability to communicate effectively with others is often listed by employers as a top attribute of the successful businessperson. Excellent written communication skills may help you find and keep a job. A quick look at classified advertisements and job descriptions will show you that the majority of companies believe excellent communication skills, both oral and written, are necessary qualities of a successful applicant. The ability to communicate effectively with customers, coworkers, subordinates, and supervisors may be the determining factor in your career success or job advancement.

REFLECTION ON YOU

Whether you like it or not, how you communicate with others plays a part in their opinion of your overall competence. The messages you write demonstrate your ability to communicate. People form opinions about your abilities and intelligence based on the quality of your writing, which includes the accuracy of your spelling, punctuation, and grammar. You may be an extremely intelligent, talented, and knowledgeable individual. If your communication skills are poor, however, others will tend to question your abilities.

In addition to judging your competence by your writing, individuals may also be judging your integrity. Being ethical in your written communications is very important. If you make promises you do not keep, if you make statements that are not factual, if you make untruthful comments about others, or if you are careless in your writing, others will question your integrity.

REFLECTION ON YOUR COMPANY

Customers also form opinions and draw conclusions about your organization based on the appearance and content of the written communications they receive. As discussed in Chapter 7, customers will form an opinion about your company based on their interaction with you. The same is true for written communications. As an employee, you can help customers develop a positive opinion of your organization by creating accurate, ethical, and professional-looking written communications.

"C" Characteristics of Effective Communication

Certain characteristics of effective written communication are common to letters, e-mails, memorandums, and reports. As you write, you must pay careful attention to each of the "C" characteristics described here.

COMPLETE

Written communication is complete when it gives the reader all the information he or she needs to

AVAVA/Shutterstock.com

Effective written communication is vital to the success of a business.

accomplish the results the writer intended. To help you achieve completeness, answer the *W questions*:

- *Why* is the message being written?
- *What* information is needed for the message?
- *Who* needs to receive the message?
- *When* is the action taking place?
- *Where* is the action taking place?

In Figure 8.1, compare the ineffective statements on the left with the effective statements on the right in which the W questions were applied.

CLEAR

After reading a message, the reader should be able to determine (without a doubt) the purpose of the correspondence. Writing clearly requires good organization and simple expression. Each sentence should have one thought; each paragraph, one purpose. Clear messages are more likely to be understood as they were intended.

Business correspondence is not the place to impress a person with your vocabulary. Your aim is to get your purpose across in a simple, concise manner. Use the same words you would use when talking to that person face-to-face. If a short, easily understood word is appropriate, use it. Your words should *express* rather than *impress*.

CORRECT

Communication should be correct in every way. Get the facts before you write, and check your information carefully. Even a minor error in a date or an amount of money may result in loss of time, money, or customer goodwill. If you are quoting prices, be certain you have the correct price list. If you are presenting dates, confirm them. Proofread your documents carefully. Use a dictionary, thesaurus, or other reference to select appropriate language.

When you are writing, keep your biases out of the correspondence as much as possible. Your task is to write objectively. Do not slant the information or overstate its significance. Deal with the facts—simply and accurately.

Writing Ethics

- Do not take credit for something you did not write.
- Do not make negative comments about people or events.
- Do use positive or neutral statements when writing.
- Use appropriate language; do not use clichés.
- When writing to an international audience, recognize and respect their culture.

Asking the W Questions

Ineffective	Effective
The Residential Housing Office will be open Saturday. (*WHEN on Saturday?*)	The Residential Housing Office will be open Saturday from 8 a.m. to 4 p.m.
The meeting will be held on November 5 at 2 p.m. (*WHAT meeting and WHERE will it be held?*)	The Action Committee meeting will be held on November 5 at 2 p.m. in Conference Room B.
The meeting was canceled. (*WHAT meeting and WHY was it canceled?*)	The planning meeting scheduled for November 5 at 2 p.m. has been canceled due to a time conflict. It has been rescheduled for November 15 at 2 p.m. in the Executive Conference Room.

FIGURE 8.1 Ask the W questions to make your writing more complete.

CONCISE

Strive for conciseness in your writing—use only as many well-chosen words as you need to convey your message. To make your message more concise, eliminate unnecessary words or repetitious ideas. A concise message does not waste the reader's time. It has impact because it is easier to read and understand. As a checklist for conciseness, ask yourself these questions:

- Are my sentences and paragraphs short?
- Have I used simple, easy-to-understand words?
- Have I used bullets or numbered lists whenever possible?
- Have I avoided unnecessary repetition?
- Have I eliminated excessive information?
- Have I avoided wordy phrases?

Concise doesn't mean short or rude. It means saying what you need to say without cluttering your communication with irrelevant information or needless words. Figure 8.2 lists several wordy expressions and gives examples of more concise writing.

Concise Writing

Many wordy expressions can be shortened to one or two words. Notice how the words and phrases in the right column have greater impact than those in the left column.

Wordy	**Concise**
at the present time	now
come to the conclusion	conclude
each and every	each, every (do not use both)
feel free to	please
as a general rule	generally
due to the fact that	because
for the period of	for
in the near future	soon, on (exact date)
free gift	gift
consensus of opinion	consensus
in the event that	if
until such time as	until

FIGURE 8.2 Shorten wordy expressions to make your writing more concise.

COURTEOUS

Courteousness in correspondence means the use of good human relations skills as you write. Treat the reader with respect, and demonstrate that you care about the reader. Keep in mind that writing is similar to talking. When you are talking with people face-to-face, courtesy and consideration are necessary in order to develop and maintain goodwill. The same or perhaps even greater concern must be evident in written correspondence since only the written word conveys the message; a smile or friendly gesture cannot be observed.

Do not show your anger in a communication. You may be extremely unhappy about a situation, but showing your anger merely compounds the problem. Angry words make angry readers. Both parties may end up yelling at each other through the written word, accomplishing little. Remember, anger and courtesy are not logical partners. Courtesy also means being considerate. If a person is asking you something, respond. If you are unable to give a positive response, explain why. Explanations let others know you are sincere.

CONSIDERATE

Consideration for the reader is demonstrated by creating a positive message. People hear the word *yes* easier than the word *no*. Certainly you will not always be able to say yes to someone or something. However, if you use a positive tone when saying no, the reader will respond in a more favorable manner. You set a positive tone by the words you choose and the way you use them. Figure 8.3 on page 156 lists some negative expressions and their positive equivalents.

Yuri Arcurs/Shutterstock.com

Anger has no place in business correspondence.

Writing Effective Messages

Good writing is almost always the result of a process. It rarely results when a person simply jots down ideas without planning or sends a message without checking it for errors. An effective writing process consists of determining the goal or purpose, analyzing the audience, considering the tone, gathering the appropriate information, organizing the content, drafting and editing the message, and preparing the final product. Additionally, you must be able to organize your time so you can produce your messages in a timely manner.

Determine the Goal or Purpose

Planning is important for all types of written messages, from a simple e-mail to a long report. Many times people start the writing process before they clearly understand their purpose or goal. As you begin, ask yourself these questions:

- What is my purpose in writing?
- What do I hope to accomplish?

You may want to inform the reader, request information, provide information, establish a record of facts, promote goodwill, or persuade the reader to take or forego some action. Once you have identified the purpose, make a few notes about the information you will need to include. List the main ideas, and identify any specific details you will need to include to explain or reinforce them.

Analyze the Reader/Audience

An important consideration in the writing process is understanding the reader or audience. The strongest communications focus on readers and their needs and wants. When writing, identify the needs and interests of the reader as they relate to the message. State your message in a way that addresses these needs and interests.

Positive Expressions

Negative	Positive
sorry	glad
whenever I can	immediately
unsatisfactory	satisfactory
You failed to let us know.	Please let us know.
I hate to inform you that your order has not been shipped.	Your order will be shipped on February 24.
The difficulties are . . .	To help you avoid further problems . . .
You will not be able to . . .	You can . . .
Do not throw trash on the grounds.	Please put your trash in the receptacles.

FIGURE 8.3 Positive expressions have more impact on the reader.

You should also think about the reader when determining the level of formality of your communication. You can understand this more clearly if you think about your own personal communications. For example, your language would be more formal when writing a letter to a business client than to your 80-year-old grandmother. These two people are quite different in what they need, want, and understand. Ask yourself some basic questions about your readers:

- What are the ages, genders, backgrounds, and biases of my readers?
- What are their values and beliefs?
- What attitudes do readers have? Will they be receptive or resistant to the message?
- What knowledge or experience related to the message topic do readers have?
- What will readers do with the document? Will they read only a portion of it? Study it carefully? Skim it?
- Will readers consider the message to be positive, neutral, or negative news?

If you are writing for a general audience, you need to use simple vocabulary and explain any concepts that may be confusing. Additionally, if a concept is complex, you may want to use examples. You should concentrate on what your communication will mean to the reader and what you expect the reader to do with the information.

If you are writing for a professional audience (engineers, lawyers, physicists, etc.), you can use technical vocabulary common in that particular field without defining the terms. Additionally, you can deal with the subject immediately, without spending time explaining the background of the material.

Remember, words do not have the same meaning for all audiences. This statement is particularly true for international audiences. When writing for an international audience, make certain that words do not offend or translate into incorrect meanings. Figure 8.4 lists a number of general principles to keep in mind when writing for international audiences.

General Principles for International Correspondence

- Use relatively formal language. Informality often means disrespect in other countries.
- Be certain you understand the order of first and last names. In many Asian countries, the last name appears first.
- Do not use humor; it may be misunderstood.
- Do not use expressions unique to the United States or refer to events that are common only to the United States.
- Use the dictionary meanings of words; do not use slang.
- Be courteous; use *thank you* and *please* often.
- Be complimentary when appropriate, but do not be excessive in your comments. Such outpourings may be seen as insincere.
- Avoid asking questions that can be answered yes or no. For a number of other countries, these two words do not have the same meaning as in the United States.
- Ask questions tactfully.
- Respect all customs of the country (social, religious, etc.).
- Learn all you can about countries your organization interacts with; read extensively.

FIGURE 8.4 Writing for an international audience requires special consideration.

Consider the Tone

Project an attitude that focuses on the reader. Your **tone** (the attitude your words express to the reader) should show your sincerity and desire to be of service. Show the reader you understand and are genuinely interested in communicating. Consider that individual's background, knowledge, interests, needs, and emotions.

As you write, keep the reader uppermost in your mind, and attempt to put yourself in the place of the reader. This approach, called the *you* approach, demands empathy on the part of the writer. You must place yourself in the reader's shoes and try to understand the situation from the reader's perspective. If you are trying to sell a product or service, you must look at the benefits it offers the reader. If you are trying to persuade someone to speak at a conference, you must highlight the contributions the proposed speaker can make—his or her unique gifts and skills.

When carrying out the *you* approach, adhere to two words of caution: Be sincere. Your goal is not to flatter the reader but to see the situation from the reader's point of view.

Remember that most written communications replace conversation. The tone of your writing should be conversational but must remain professional. To project a professional image, you must sound educated and mature. Use the C's of communication presented at the beginning of this chapter to help you prepare professional written documents.

Gather the Appropriate Information

Next, gather the information you need to include in your message. The information you collect will help shape the message. In gathering information, you may do the following:

- Review any files your organization has on the subject.
- Talk with your employer or colleague (if he or she has any background information).
- Research the topic through the Internet, periodicals, or books.

Particularly for reports, you may need to do research to find the information you need. Conducting research is discussed later in this chapter, in the "Reports" section.

Organize the Content

Did you ever read a document and, once you finished, realize you did not understand what the writer was trying to convey? Why? This could happen for a number of reasons:

- The text was unnecessarily long and wordy.
- The writer failed to clarify the message; the purpose was not discernible.
- The content jumped from one topic to another with no apparent pattern.

You have already put some thought into the content of the document. For most simple messages, you may have written down notes as you thought about the purpose. You may have taken additional notes when you were gathering information. When organizing the content, read through your notes and group like ideas together. Determine which ideas are related and should be in the same paragraph. If you are creating a complex document, you might make an outline to help organize your ideas. Select an order for your message that will help you achieve your objectives. Messages can be organized using the direct, indirect, or persuasive approach.

iofoto/Shutterstock.com

Because most written communications replace conversation, the tone should always be professional.

DIRECT APPROACH

The direct approach is appropriate for positive or neutral messages that deliver good news or make a routine request. The **direct approach** begins with the reason for the message, followed by supporting details if needed. If you are making a request or an inquiry, state it. Continue with whatever explanation is necessary so the reader will understand the message. Close with a courteous thank-you for an action taken or a request for action by a specific time. The letter in Figure 8.8 on page 167 is written using the direct approach.

INDIRECT APPROACH

The **indirect approach** is used for messages that give negative news. Supporting details are presented first to prepare the reader for the main idea that comes later in the message. An example is a letter that refuses a request. When writing indirect messages, use this format:

- Begin with an opening statement that is pleasant but neutral.
- Review the circumstances and give the negative information.
- Close the message on a pleasant and positive note.

Figure 8.9 on page 168 is an example of a letter using the indirect approach.

PERSUASIVE APPROACH

Use the **persuasive approach** when you want to convince someone to do something or change an indifferent or negative reader's reaction. Your goal is to turn a negative or indifferent attitude into a positive one. The *you* approach is essential in the persuasive approach. When writing a persuasive message, use this format:

- Get the reader's attention quickly; open with the *you* approach.
- Continue by creating interest and desire.
- Close by asking for the desired action.

Figure 8.10 on page 169 illustrates a letter written using the persuasive approach.

At this stage, you should also decide on the message format. Most organizations have a preferred format for letters, and many have a preferred format for memorandums and reports. If your organization does not have a preferred format, you can use one of the standard formats described later in the chapter.

Compose and Edit the Document

The first step in writing is to create a draft of the correspondence. Your goal should be to write down everything you want to say in rough-draft form. Do not spend time agonizing over each word and punctuation mark. Get your ideas down. A complete business message typically has an opening, one or more developmental paragraphs, and a closing.

- The opening paragraph identifies the subject of the message. If the message uses the direct approach, this paragraph also gives the main idea of the message.
- The developmental paragraphs supply supporting details and the main idea if the message uses the indirect approach.
- The closing paragraph ends the message. This paragraph may summarize earlier points of the message, ask the reader to take or forego some action, or build goodwill.

While it is a good idea to draft your message in the format you plan to use for it, do not be too concerned about format while you are writing. Leave the details of formatting for later.

Once you have completed the draft document, the next step is to edit it. Remember, effective messages are complete, clear, correct, concise, courteous, and considerate. Review your messages with these characteristics in mind. Make sure the document is factually and grammatically correct, the language is clear, and the sentence structure is appropriate. During the editing process, you are precise—you address the writing mechanics.

ENSURE EFFECTIVE PARAGRAPHS

Effective paragraphs possess unity, coherence, and parallel structure.

Promptness

A conscientious business correspondent is prompt. Prompt answers to messages say to readers that the writer or organization cares about them. Conversely, late messages may give the following impressions:

- The writer or organization is indifferent to the needs of the reader.
- The writer is grossly inefficient.

The basic promptness rule is this:

- Reply to e-mail the day you receive it.
- Reply to memorandums within one day.
- Reply to letters within three to five days.
- Respond to reports within the timeline established by the cover letter or memorandum.

LuckyBusiness/iStockphoto.com

Unity A paragraph has **unity** when its sentences clarify or support the main idea. The sentence that contains the main idea of a paragraph is the **topic sentence**. For example, in this paragraph, the topic sentence is at the beginning. However, it may also be at the end of the paragraph. The point to remember is that the topic sentence helps the reader focus on the main idea of the paragraph.

Coherence A paragraph has **coherence** when its sentences relate to each other in content, grammatical construction, and choice of words. When the paragraphs in a message fit together, the reader will be led naturally from the opening paragraph to the closing paragraph without having to reread.

Parallel Structure **Parallel structure** helps you achieve coherence. Words, phrases, or clauses within a sentence that are related in meaning should be written in the same form. Using the same form makes related ideas easier to see and compare. Writers should balance a word with a word, a phrase with a phrase, a clause with a clause, and a sentence with a sentence, making parallel parts grammatically the same. Consider the following examples of nonparallel and parallel construction:

Nonparallel: *The position is prestigious, challenging, and also the money is not bad.*

Parallel: *The position is prestigious, challenging, and financially rewarding.*

Nonparallel: *We voted and we were discussing marketing during our last staff meeting.*

Parallel: *We voted and discussed marketing during our last staff meeting.*

Nonparallel: *Our primary goals are to increase retention, reduce costs, and the improvement of learning outcomes.*

Parallel: *Our primary goals are to increase retention, to reduce costs, and to improve learning outcomes.*

For more information and examples, see the "Parallelism" section of the Reference Guide at the end of the text.

USE APPROPRIATE SENTENCE STRUCTURE

Sentences should be simple but varied. Use a combination of sentence structures to hold your reader's attention. There is no formula for determining sentence length, but shorter sentences help keep the reader's interest. Generally, shorter sentences are also easier to understand. Consider this sentence:

January reports indicate that sales in the pharmaceutical market increased by more than 40 percent, which serves to support the proposed plan presented at last week's board meeting for 20 additional positions.

Did you get lost? The sentence has 32 words. A reader generally loses interest when a sentence is more than 20 words long. You do not need to count the words in each sentence or limit sentences needlessly. However, you should be aware that messages are generally more readable when sentences are short.

January reports indicate that sales in the pharmaceutical market increased by more than 40 percent. This supports the proposed plan presented at last week's board meeting for 20 additional positions.

ELIMINATE THE PASSIVE VOICE

Voice is the form of a verb indicating whether the subject is engaging in the action or receiving the action. A verb is in the **active voice** when the subject performs the action. Here are two examples of the active voice:

Mylien drove to the hospital.

Dustin enrolled in the company dental plan.

A verb is in the **passive voice** when the subject receives the action. Here are the same examples written in the passive voice:

Mylien was driven to the hospital.

Dustin was enrolled in the company dental plan.

The active voice is more direct and concise, so you should use it most of the time. The passive voice is appropriate for these uses:

- When you do not know, or when it does not matter, who or what performed the action. *Your order was shipped today.*
- When you want to emphasize the receiver of the action. *Gina was selected to represent the company.*
- To avoid sounding as if you are assigning blame. *The payment was received after the due date.*

Although the passive voice is sometimes appropriate, if it is overused, it can result in wordy, dull writing. Use the passive voice when it is the best choice, but do not overuse it.

Prepare the Final Document

The last step is to prepare the final document. At this stage, you make any needed adjustments to the format. You also review the document for errors, consistency, and overall appearance. Many people rush through this final stage. Plan enough time to check your documents so you can be sure they represent your best work: well-written, professional in appearance, and error-free.

Check the format of your document to be certain it is correct. For example, if the document is a letter, does the return address appear in the correct place? If it is a report, have you sized the headings appropriately?

Check for consistency in formatting, style, and facts. For example, is the body text 11-point at the beginning of a report and 12-point later? Does the verb tense shift unnecessarily from present to past? Does the subject line of an e-mail say the conference is on May 13, while the body says it is on May 31?

Use the grammar and spelling features of your software to help you locate errors. Be aware, however, that the software will not catch all errors. Always proofread a document after running the grammar and spelling features to help ensure all errors are detected. First, proofread the document on the computer screen. Then print a copy and proofread again. You also might ask someone else to proofread the document. Commonly used proofreaders' marks are shown in the Reference Guide. Figure 8.5 lists several proofreading tips.

Guides for E-Mail, Letters, Memos, and Reports

The "C" characteristics and writing process steps should be used for all business communications. In addition, when writing e-mail, memorandums, letters, and reports, you must adhere to a number of guidelines specific to that type of document.

E-Mail

Throughout the United States, individuals send billions of e-mails each day. Due to its speed and ease of use, e-mail is a major form of communication for both businesses and individuals. For business writers, e-mail offers a number of advantages, including the ability to:

- Compose and send messages all over the world in a matter of minutes.
- Send messages at the convenience of the sender that can be read at the convenience of the recipient.
- Save messages as permanent records of business activity.
- Provide quick answers for questions.
- Transfer files from one organization to another or within organizations as e-mail attachments.
- Make appointments quickly and efficiently.

In many cases, messages are delivered almost instantly. Users may send a message in haste or anger

PROOFREADING TIPS

- If possible, do not proofread a document right after keying it. Let the document sit while you perform another task.
- Proofread the document in three steps:
  - General appearance and format
  - Spelling and keyboarding errors
  - Grammar, punctuation, usage, and content
- When proofreading on screen, use the top of the screen as a guide in reading each line.
- Pay attention to dates. Do not assume they are correct. For example, check to be sure that Thursday, November 15, is actually a Thursday. Check that the year has been keyed correctly.
- Do not overlook proofreading the subject line, enclosure notation, and names and addresses of the recipients.
- Use the thesaurus if you are not certain a word is appropriate.
- Watch closely for omissions of *-ed*, *-ing*, or *-s* at the ends of words.
- Be consistent in the use of commas, capital letters, and format.
- Check numerals.
- Keep a current reference manual at your desk to look up grammar or punctuation rules.

FIGURE 8.5 Proofread your documents carefully.

and wish they could take back the message a few minutes later. Some individuals seem to assume that there are no inappropriate messages—whatever one wants to say at that particular time is appropriate to say. However, even though you can say anything at any time through e-mail, it is not always a good idea to do so. You must consider the person to whom you are writing and the message you want the individual to receive.

GUIDELINES

Because your e-mail messages represent you and your company, think about the impressions they make. Though e-mail is a less formal means of communicating than letters or memos, the basic characteristics of effective written communication still apply. Be sure to use complete sentences, capitalize and punctuate properly, and proofread and correct all errors. Follow these additional guidelines when writing e-mail:

- Be appropriately formal. The rule of thumb is to be almost as formal as you are in standard memorandums. For example, avoid using abbreviations or all uppercase or lowercase letters.
- Write a descriptive subject line for all messages. The subject line should be concise yet give enough information so the receiver knows the purpose of the message at a glance.
- Limit your message to one screen. If you are writing a longer message, send a traditional hard-copy memorandum. People become frustrated when they must scroll from screen to screen and then scroll back to reread something.
- Edit and proofread carefully. Most e-mail programs have a spelling feature.
- Include your name and title (if appropriate) when replying to an e-mail. Often you can add a signature in your preferences, which will automatically include this information at the end of every e-mail you send.
- Be wary of humor or sarcasm. Electronic communication is devoid of body language; thus, the slightest hint of sarcasm could be badly misinterpreted.
- When forwarding messages, key your comments at the top.

Figure 8.6 shows an appropriate format for e-mail.

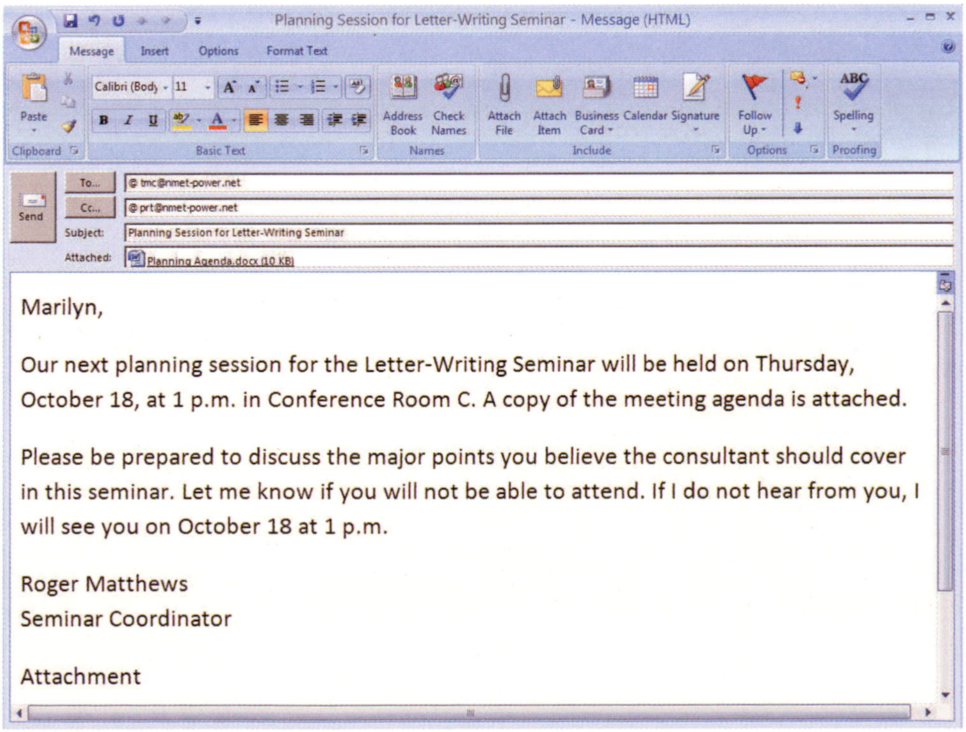

FIGURE 8.6 E-Mail Message

E-mail messages are often used to transmit memos or reports as attachments. If you plan to send a large file as an e-mail attachment, contact the receiver and ask whether sending a large attachment is acceptable. Some e-mail systems do not handle large file attachments.

ETHICS

When you are corresponding through e-mail, ethical behavior is important. Ethics with respect to e-mail means you do not misuse the organization's e-mail system.

- Do not send personal e-mail from your office computer.
- Do not use e-mail to berate or reprimand an employee or colleague. Be professional when speaking of others and to others.
- Do not use e-mail to send information that might involve legal action.
- Assume any message you send is permanent.
- Do not forward junk mail or chain letters.
- Do not forward an e-mail message unless you know the message is true.
- Do not forward a message without permission from the sender.
- Do not include personal information, such as credit card numbers, Social Security numbers, or passwords, in e-mail messages. It is possible to intercept e-mail in transit; thus, an unscrupulous individual can steal and inappropriately use this information.

Remember that in most cases e-mail is not as private as you might hope. Even if you and the receiver delete the message, it may not be deleted everywhere it was stored. Many companies have software that can read all e-mails, even those that have been deleted. The receiver can also forward your e-mail to others. Think carefully about what you say when you write an e-mail. Numerous court cases have determined that company e-mail messages belong to the company, not the individual. If a subpoena is issued to your Internet service provider, everything you have done or said can be traced.

Make ethical decisions when sending e-mail messages.

Memorandums

Although e-mail is widely used in most organizations, memorandums continue to have a place in the work environment. A memorandum (memo for short) is generally written when the message is longer than one computer screen or a hard copy with a signature is necessary. Memos are also preferred when the message is confidential or sensitive.

Memos are slightly more formal in style than e-mail, but less formal than letters. A memorandum is usually written in the same format throughout the organization, with a common format including these elements: *To, From, Date,* and *Subject* lines. The word *memorandum* or an organizational name or logo may also be included. A copy notation,

Professional POINTERS

In written communication, the message is affected by the way it is presented. As you strive to prepare professional messages, keep these points in mind:

- Be critical of the documents you prepare. Make certain your work is accurate and has a professional appearance.
- Use reference guides for punctuation, grammar, and usage.
- Use technology tools such as the spelling, grammar, and thesaurus features.
- Continually strive to improve your writing skills. Take a writing seminar if possible.
- Develop a manual of preferred document styles and formats for your office if one does not exist.
- Use technology to create interesting and professionally prepared documents. Today's readers are accustomed to documents that are visually appealing and that include graphics.

indicated by the letter *c*, may follow the body of the memorandum.

General guidelines for writing memorandums include the following:

- Use the first name (or initial) and last name of the individual to whom you are sending the memo.
- Use the job title of the individual if company policy dictates doing so; many organizations do not use titles in memorandums.
- Do not include courtesy titles (such as *Ms.* or *Mr.*).
- If you are sending a memorandum to more than one individual, list the names in alphabetical order or by hierarchical order within the company.
- List *c* recipients alphabetically or hierarchically.
- If you are addressing a memo to ten or more people, use a generic classification, such as *Strategic Planning Team*.
- If the memorandum is more than one page, key the additional pages on plain paper with an appropriate heading. A typical heading is shown in the Reference Guide.

Figure 8.7 on page 166 presents an appropriate format for a memorandum.

Letters

Letters represent the company to the public—customers, clients, and prospective customers and clients. Well-written letters can win or maintain clients and customers. Conversely, poorly written letters can lose them. Organizations communicate extensively with their external customers by phone, e-mail, and occasionally memo. Still, letters are more formal and are the preferred document when writing to current and prospective clients and customers.

Figure 8.8 on page 167 shows a letter that uses the direct approach. This approach is appropriate because the reader's reaction to the message is anticipated to be favorable or neutral. The letter is formatted in block style with open punctuation. In block style, all text is aligned at the left margin. Open punctuation means no punctuation is used after the salutation or complimentary close.

Figure 8.9 on page 168 is an example of a letter using the indirect approach. This approach is

GRAND VISTA PROFESSIONAL SERVICES

TO: Madelyn Ice
Liam Nelson
Rico Osbourne

FROM: Ruth Shank

DATE: November 15, 201-

SUBJECT: Budget Session

The next budget session will be held in my office on November 23, 201-, from 1 to 3 p.m. The final budget will be presented to the Board of Directors at their December meeting.

Please be prepared to discuss your budget actuals for the past three months and any changes to your proposed budget (with justification) for the next six months. I have attached last year's actual expenses to assist you in this process.

mos

Attachment

c Darius Hamilton
Miguel Quinones

FIGURE 8.7 Memorandum

Kapor Pharmaceuticals
1211 East Eighth Street ◆ Fort Worth, TX 76104-5201
(412) 555-0137 ◆ http://www.kaporpharmaceuticals.com

October 9, 201-

Dr. Leonard Montgomery
700 Melrose Court SE
Grand Rapids, MI 49508-3415

Dear Dr. Montgomery

Thank you for talking with me last Monday concerning our new cancer drug. At your request I am enclosing a copy of the research data.

You will notice that Kapor Pharmaceuticals conducted these studies over a five-year period, using a sample group of 1,500 people. The results were excellent, and we are pleased to offer a drug that has such potential for significantly dropping the cancer mortality rate.

I will call your administrative assistant within the next few days to schedule a follow-up meeting after you have had a chance to review the studies. I look forward to discussing any questions you may have.

Sincerely

Kataline Komanie

Kataline Komanie
Sales Representative

ks

Enclosure

FIGURE 8.8 Letter Using the Direct Approach

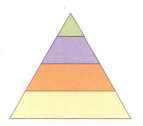

Palm Atlantic Airlines

1720 East Higgins Road
Schaumburg, IL 60173-5114
(847) 555-0197
http://www.palmatlanticair.com

November 14, 201-

Ms. Grace Edwardson
Maximum Media Production
243 High Street
Marquette, MI 49855-2345

Dear Ms. Edwardson:

Thank you for asking me to speak at your conference in December. I greatly enjoy my association with your group; you truly provide an excellent growth opportunity for managers.

The demands on my time for the next several months are extremely heavy. In addition to a new planning process that I must implement, we have recently employed two managers who are looking to me for assistance in learning their jobs. As you might expect, I am extremely busy. I must say no to your request at this time. However, if you need a speaker in the future, please contact me again. I always enjoy talking with your group.

I look forward to working with you in the future. Best wishes for success with the conference.

Sincerely,

Rachel Portales

Rachel Portales
Chief Operating Officer

es

FIGURE 8.9 Letter Using the Indirect Approach

Shell Cove Enterprises, Inc.

12500 Coastal Highway
Ocean City, MD 21842-4711
Tel: (410) 555-0100
Fax: (410) 555-0110

www.shellcove.com

December 10, 201-

Dr. Consuelo Soto
Soto and Sayer
508 Light Street
Baltimore, MD 20202-5121

Dear Dr. Soto

Your expertise is needed! Our administrative professionals need your assistance in developing their letter-writing skills. Some of them have several years of writing experience, yet they have not perfected their skills to the level we require. Others are relatively new employees with little experience writing letters.

Your work with our employees in the past helped tremendously. They not only learned from your presentation but also enjoyed the experience. We would like to offer the workshop in February. Our preferred dates are February 5–6 or February 25–26.

I will call your office next week to talk with you further. I hope your answer will be yes. We know you can make a difference in the quality of letters sent out by our company.

Sincerely

Wanda Foster

Wanda Foster
Human Resources Manager

ws

FIGURE 8.10 Letter Using the Persuasive Approach

appropriate because the writer must refuse a request. The letter is formatted in modified block style with mixed punctuation. In modified block style, the date and complimentary close begin at the center point. Body paragraphs may be blocked or indented to the first tab stop. Mixed punctuation means using a colon after the salutation and a comma after the complimentary close.

Figure 8.10 on page 169 illustrates a letter using the persuasive approach. This approach is appropriate because the writer's purpose is to persuade the reader to present a workshop. The letter is formatted in block style with open punctuation.

Letters share many formatting features with memos, such as a heading on subsequent pages for long letters. A sample heading is shown in the Reference Guide. The envelope should match the stationery used for the letter and should be free of errors and smudges. The format for business envelopes is presented in Chapter 16, along with other information about mailing correspondence. Additional information on letter formatting is provided in the Reference Guide.

Reports

Many types of reports are prepared in the workplace. Business reports are used to provide information or to describe a problem and suggest a solution. Some reports are informal and contain only two or three pages. An informal report is frequently used for internal communications. Some examples of informal reports are progress reports, monthly sales reports, and team or task force reports. Informal reports may be prepared using a formal report style or may be created as memo reports.

Other business reports are more formal in content and structure. Reports sent outside an organization are always formal. When the report topic is important or the information is detailed, internal reports are prepared formally as well. Formal reports usually take the form of business proposals or research reports. Proposals are used to solve problems or to make a request for something such as new equipment, additional personnel, or a change in procedures. Other formal reports investigate an issue and present organized information and data to assist individuals in making informed business decisions.

The administrative professional's role in preparing reports varies. You may have the responsibility of keying the report, producing the final copies, and distributing the report to the appropriate individuals. Or you may assist with the creation of visuals for the report (charts, graphs, etc.), do research, and draft some or all portions of the report.

Since formal or long reports often require a lot of time and effort to prepare, it is especially important that the writer clearly identify the objective of the report. For a long or complicated report, a timeline should be developed to set deadlines for completing stages of research and composing the report.

CONDUCTING RESEARCH

Most reports involve some type of research. The research may be **primary research**—collecting data through surveys, observations, or data review and analysis. If you are conducting primary research, you must decide how you are going to gather the information. For example, suppose your manager asks you to create a report on use of company sick days. You might need to review the attendance records for all employees for the past five years to determine whether use of sick days has been increasing or decreasing. Your report might include a graph that shows total sick days used for each of the last five years. It might also include other information that you calculate, such as the percent of increase or decrease in the use of sick days and the time of year when most sick days are used.

The research may also be **secondary research**—finding data or material that other people have discovered and reported via the Internet, books, periodicals, and various other publications. You may go to a brick-and-mortar library to do research. Certainly these libraries have advantages:

- Libraries have materials that may not be on the Internet, including historical, highly specialized, and rare materials.
- Libraries are increasing their reliance on the Internet. Many periodicals, journals, or

newspapers are no longer physically stored in a brick-and-mortar building. Instead, the library website provides access to these materials for registered users.

- Libraries employ librarians to assist you in finding what you need. These people have specialized degrees and can help you locate information in their own collections as well as in collections in other locations or on the Internet.

When you are searching for information on the Internet, using the appropriate search terms will help you find the information you need. This is sometimes the most difficult part of searching for information. If you do not sufficiently clarify your search, you may find yourself looking at hundreds of articles that do not match what you need.

Suppose you want to find information related to injuries resulting from improper keyboard-

TECH TALK

Concept Mapping

Concept mapping is a common business tool. It's the creation of a visual image (or map) of concepts—for an upcoming project, for example, or a plan that has to be written. This technique is also used to gather ideas during team problem-solving sessions. Seeing a plan or problem represented visually can give clarity to thought, encourages creativity, and lets you see patterns and relationships. Concept mapping also helps you spot gaps in information, generate new ideas, and recognize the importance of certain items or concepts.

For example, Joan is an administrative professional who needs to prepare a summary of the notes from the weekly section meeting for district supervisors. Many items were discussed in the meeting, and Joan knows it will be difficult to organize and summarize them. To help collect her thoughts, she starts by mapping out the concepts. That way, she is able to see which concepts are the most important and which ones are similar:

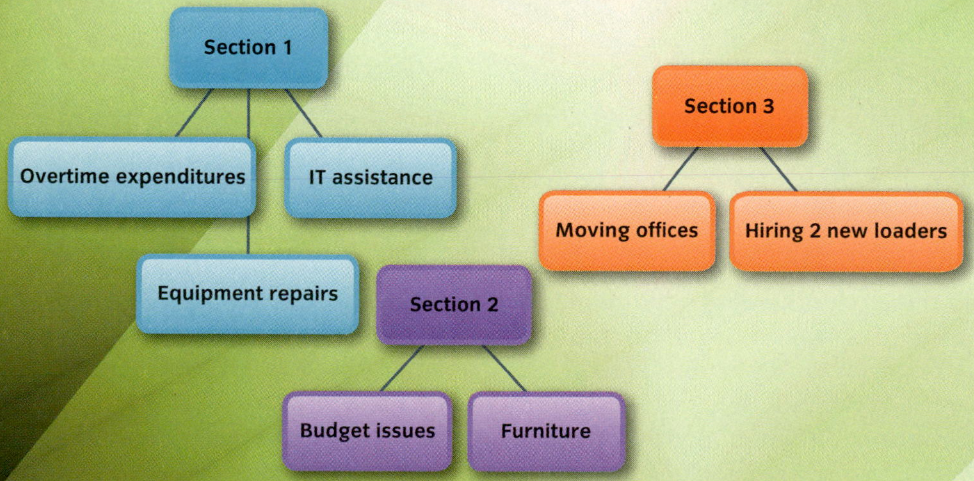

Concept mapping can be done with pencil and paper; however, software and online tools are often more efficient. You can use the shapes and SmartArt features in *Microsoft Office* or free online tools, some with apps for mobile devices such as the iPhone or iPad devices. Links to several popular free concept mapping sites are provided on the website for this text.

Diego Cervo/Shutterstock.com

Support the information in a report with the appropriate research.

ing. If your search term is too broad (*ergonomics*, for instance), the search will return thousands of results that do not relate to the specific research topic. If your search term is too narrow (*carpal tunnel syndrome*), the results may exclude articles that would be relevant to your research topic. The search term *healthy keyboarding* or *keyboarding ailments* would be more effective in returning results that meet your needs. When conducting a search for an exact word or phrase, put the words in quotation marks.

EVALUATING INFORMATION

Determining the credibility of the companies or individuals providing the information you find when doing research is important. Noting the dates of any articles or studies you use is also important. All information found in print or on the Internet is not necessarily reliable or current. Ask yourself these questions to help you evaluate the credibility of sources. Who wrote the information? What education or expertise does the person have? Is the person representing a respected organization? Is the information current? Is the information biased toward a particular viewpoint?

DOCUMENTING SOURCES

You must credit the sources used in a report. This is true when you are using a reference from a textbook or periodical or a reference you found on the Internet. If you quote a source directly, use quotation marks around the quote within the body of the report. If you paraphrase your source, no quotation marks are necessary, but you should credit the source. Documentation may follow several different styles using footnotes, endnotes, or internal citations and a reference page. Additional information about documentation styles is provided in the report formatting section of this chapter and in the "Business Reports" section of the Reference Guide.

Some Internet sites spell out their copyright policies; others do not. Other websites invite you to distribute freely the information on the site. However, the general rule is to give credit for all information you obtain from another source. Do not reprint copyrighted material without the consent of the copyright holder.

REPORT PARTS AND FORMATTING

An informal report may have only one or two parts—the body and sometimes an executive summary. Other informal reports are formatted as a memo. The name of the person requesting the report appears in the *To* line. The name of the report writer appears in the *From* line. The title of the report appears in the *Subject* line. Side headings similar to those used in a formal report may be used to identify sections of the report if the report contains more than one page.

PARTNERSHIP FOR 21ST CENTURY SKILLS

Communication/ Collaboration

Writing in Teams

Workplace teams produce reports and other written communications. To be an effective member of a writing team, you need excellent teamwork skills. You must possess the ability to work well with others and be respectful when working with diverse team members.

Collaborative writing projects require that team members follow excellent written communication strategies. In addition, the team must assume shared responsibility for collaborative work. Your team can produce a better written document by following these suggestions:

- Select a leader. The leader is responsible for setting procedures for meetings, facilitating meetings, helping the group meet deadlines, solving problems, and seeing that the group produces the document in a timely manner.
- Set a work schedule. Decide when and where the team will meet. Set timelines and stick to them.
- Allocate the work. Define the tasks of each team member. Determine each member's writing strengths, and use these strengths when assigning tasks.
- Monitor progress. The group must stay focused and produce the document by the deadline established.
- Reduce the chance of conflict. Actively listen to each team member, pay attention to cultural differences, and acknowledge the worth of other members and their points of view.

Activity

Hold a mock team report-writing meeting. With three or four classmates, choose a topic of interest to the group. For this activity you will not actually create a report. Instead, go through the steps you would take to work collaboratively to create the document. As you implement the suggestions in the bulleted list above, monitor how the team works together. At the end of the activity, write a group memo reflecting on the collaborative writing process.

Konstantin Chagin/Shutterstock.com

Formal reports are typically formatted in manuscript style. If you are asked to prepare a report that will be submitted for publication, you may need to use a particular report format. Modern Language Association (MLA) style is often used for reports related to the liberal arts and humanities. American Psychological Association (APA) style is commonly used for reports related to the social sciences. You should refer to a style guide published by the particular organization if you are asked to prepare a report in a special format.

Your company may use one of those styles for its formal reports, or it may have another format that you will be expected to use. Refer to the company's style guide for documents if one is available. If a style guide is not available, look through the company files to see how other recent reports have been formatted, or ask a colleague.

Formal business reports usually contain several parts. These parts may include an executive summary, a title page, a table of contents, the body, a bibliography or reference section, and one or more appendices. Not all reports will contain all these parts. Review the "Business Reports" section of the Reference Guide to learn more about report parts and formatting and to view a sample business report.

The **executive summary** is a one- or two-page summary of the document. It is written for business executives who wish to preview the report to determine whether to read it in full or who need essential information from the report but not a detailed understanding of all its aspects. The executive summary contains the following information:

- Background—establishes why the report was written; identifies the problem or issues
- Major findings—explains what was discovered
- Recommendations

The body of a report should present information in a logical order. For example, a report dealing with a business problem or issue might be organized into the following sections:

- Introduction
- Research
- Findings
- Conclusions and Recommendations

Lists, used effectively in a report, call attention to important information and contribute positively to readability. Word processing software contains a variety of bullet styles. Choose an appropriate bullet style, and use it consistently throughout the report.

Tables and graphics can sometimes be used in reports to convey information more effectively than text. For example, a table could be used to list sales figures by region by year (Figure 8.11). A pie chart could be used to show the sales contributed by one sales region (Figure 8.12). Use consistent formatting for all tables within a report. Introduce the table or chart in the paragraph above where it is placed in the report (or on the page before if the graphic requires a full page). Include titles and other labels in tables and charts so the data are easy to understand.

Shaw's Machines
Regional Sales Report

	2012	2013	Total
Region 1	$14,250	$15,215	$29,465
Region 2	$13,125	$14,250	$27,375
Region 3	$15,715	$17,210	$32,925
Region 4	$12,245	$13,390	$25,635
Total	$55,335	$60,065	$115,400

FIGURE 8.11 Table in Report

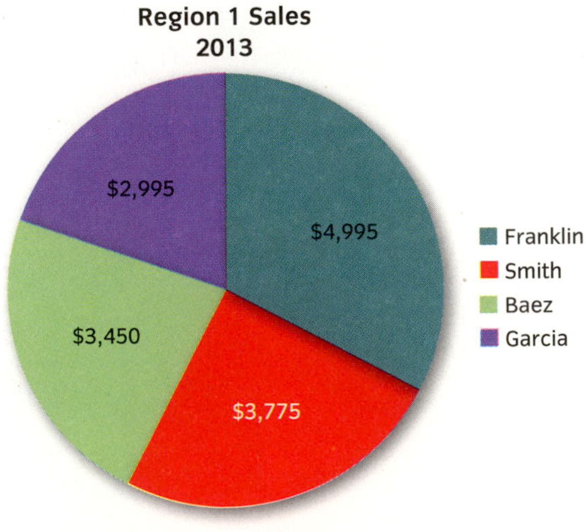

FIGURE 8.12 Graphic in Report

SUMMARY

To reinforce what you have learned in this chapter, study this summary.

- Prepare effective written communications using the "C" characteristics to create a positive impression of you and your company.
- Follow the steps in the writing process to create effective messages: determine the goal or purpose, analyze the reader, consider the tone, gather the appropriate information, organize the content, draft and edit the message, and prepare the final product.
- Apply appropriate guidelines to produce effective e-mails, memorandums, letters, and reports.

KEY TERMS

active voice, 161
coherence, 160
direct approach, 159
executive summary, 174
indirect approach, 159
parallel structure, 160
passive voice, 161
persuasive approach, 159
primary research, 170
secondary research, 170
tone, 157
topic sentence, 160
unity, 160

8

STUDY Tools

Located at www.cengagebrain.com

- Chapter Outlines
- Flashcards
- Interactive Quizzes
- Tech Tools
- Video Segments
- and More!

LET'S DISCUSS

1. List and describe the "C" characteristics of effective writing.
2. Explain why concise writing is important. Create or find three examples of wordy expressions and rewrite them into more concise statements.
3. How can a writer demonstrate consideration in written communications?
4. List and explain the different types of approaches that may be used in business writing.
5. List six principles you should keep in mind when writing for international audiences.
6. Explain what is meant by effective paragraphs.
7. List six guidelines you should follow when preparing e-mail.
8. Why might a writer use tables, charts, or other graphics in a report?

PUT IT TO WORK

Writing assistance Eduardo Mendez began his career five years ago as an administrative professional with Southwest Directives. He has excellent administrative skills. He writes well—so well, in fact, that he composed most of the correspondence for his previous supervisor, the vice president of research. He also has outstanding computer skills and superior human relations skills.

Two months ago, Eduardo's supervisor left Southwest Directives for another position, and Janelle Duderstadt was promoted to take her place. Ms. Duderstadt seems to be a nice person and capable; however, she almost totally ignores Eduardo. He rarely sees her; she is out of the office about half the time. When she is in, she stays busy in her office. She does give Eduardo rough drafts of correspondence she has written on the computer to format.

Eduardo believes he can help his new employer with her writing. If she would verbally tell him what the correspondence should include, he believes he can write it satisfactorily. Also, Ms. Duderstadt spends a considerable amount of time preparing internal reports. Again, Eduardo believes he could help her in at least writing a rough draft of certain reports.

What advice would you give Eduardo? Should he suggest to Ms. Duderstadt that he can assist her? If so, should he ask for a meeting with her? Should he inform her that he did most of the written correspondence for his previous supervisor?

COMMUNICATE SUCCESSFULLY

1. **Edit and proofread a memo** Your supervisor, Carol Vroman, has drafted a memo to the company's department heads regarding annual performance appraisals. She has asked you to edit the memo, paying special attention to clarity and conciseness. She would also like you to format the memo for distribution and proofread it. Open the *Word* file *Ch08_Performance_Memo* from the data files and complete these tasks. For this and all other writing activities, you can use the Reference Guide at the end of the textbook for questions on grammar, formatting, and style. (Learning Objectives 2 and 3)
2. **Write an e-mail** Open the *Word* file *Ch08_Meeting_E-Mail* from the data files. Write an e-mail to Fujio Komuro, Ray Edwards, and Rita Wilson. Inform the recipients of a meeting next Wednesday to discuss progress on the goals for their department. The meeting will be in Room A304 beginning at 10 a.m. and will last approximately one hour. The meeting is being called by Dominique Lindquist, vice president of marketing. (Learning Objectives 1, 2, and 3)
3. **Write a memo** Shelby Cobb and Alexis Hinojosa, the two supervisors to whom you report, have asked you to compose a draft memorandum for their joint signatures. Recently there has been a flurry of negative e-mails in the company. Many are very negative and even use inappropriate language. Ms. Cobb and Mr. Hinojosa are creating an ethics policy that will be distributed with the memo.

   Before you begin to write, think through what should be said and how the message should be worded. What should you consider as you draft the memorandum? What should the tone be? (Learning Objectives 1, 2, and 3)
4. **Strengthen written communications** Add a new post to the blog you created in Chapter 1. In this entry, reflect on the following statement: **This chapter has helped me recognize that I can strengthen my written communication in the following ways.** (Learning Objectives 1, 2, and 3)

Blog

DEVELOP WORKPLACE SKILLS

5. **Direct letter** Write a letter to Mr. Roger Edwards, 945 Fourth Street, Detroit, MI 48202-9451, inviting him to speak to a group of medical assistants from Danby Medical Associates about management theory and practices. The event will be held on the first Thursday of next month at the Danby Medical Associates office at 7:30 p.m. You are to sign the letter. Your title is Administrative Medical Assistant. Use block format and open punctuation. (Learning Objectives 1, 2, and 3)

6. **Persuasive letter** You work in the public affairs office of a hospital. Write a letter to Dr. David VanderFleet, Director of Research at Kapor Pharmaceuticals, at the address in Figure 8.8 on page 167, asking him to serve on a panel with Natalie Heinlein, Public Affairs Director, to discuss future directions of cancer research. The panel will address the Southlake Chamber of Commerce one month from today; the session will begin with lunch and conclude at approximately 2 p.m. Dr. VanderFleet is to prepare and deliver a presentation explaining the direction that Kapor Pharmaceuticals is taking on cancer research. His presentation should be no longer than 30 minutes, with a 10-minute question-and-answer session. Ms. Heinlein will sign the letter. Save the closing lines using the *Word* Quick Parts feature. Use block format and open punctuation. (Learning Objectives 1, 2, and 3)
7. **Direct letter** Assume Dr. VanderFleet has said yes to the request in the activity above. Write a second letter to him acknowledging his positive response. Tell him Ms. Heinlein will meet him at the Southlake Chamber of Commerce, 100 Windsor Drive, Southlake, at 11:50 a.m. on the meeting date. Also tell him she will call him next Thursday at 9 a.m. to discuss the presentation. Ask him to suggest another time if he will not be available. Ms. Heinlein will sign the letter. Date the letter one week from the current date. Use your saved Quick Part from the previous activity. Use block format and open punctuation. (Learning Objectives 1, 2, and 3)
8. **Indirect letter** You are employed as an administrative assistant for a local company. Write a letter declining an invitation to speak to the local chapter of IAAP a month from today. The letter should be sent to Anna Garcia, the IAAP program chairperson. Make up an address for her from your city. Acknowledge Ms. Garcia's request, thank her for the invitation, and explain you will not be able to speak due to the press of work. Include some details regarding your current commitments. Offer to speak the following month. Include other details you think are appropriate. Use modified block format and mixed punctuation. (Learning Objectives 1, 2, and 3)
9. **Report** Open the *Word* file *Ch08_Meeting_Documentation_Report* from the data files. Format the report using the report formatting guidelines in the Reference Guide. Use styles, and add a title page. The report is being prepared for Moss Springs Company by Kathy Everitt, project director. Create a table of contents using the *Word* table of contents feature.

BUILD RELATIONSHIPS

10. **Provide and accept feedback** Choose one of your writing assignments for this chapter. Before you submit it, ask a classmate to critique and proofread the document you have created. Critique and proofread one of that person's assignments as well. Make corrections as needed and submit the assignment. (Learning Objectives 2 and 3)

11. **Improve written communication** Access the *Word* file *Ch08_Improve_Written_Communication* from the data files. Read the case and answer the questions that follow it. (Learning Objectives 1, 2, and 3)

USE TECH TOOLS

12. **Use concept mapping** Work with three or four students on this activity. Assume the group is going to prepare a report. Select a report topic related to one of the chapters in the textbook. As a group, discuss the information that will be included and make a list of the suggestions for the report content. Use content mapping to create a visual representation of your ideas. Links to several concept mapping tools are provided on the website for this text.
13. **Create a letterhead** Create a letterhead for a business of your choosing that you can use when writing letters or memorandums for this class. Use block format and open punctuation. Save the letterhead using the *Word* Quick Parts feature. Include all necessary information and an appropriate graphic.
14. **Portfolio** Add one of your written communication activities from this chapter to your online portfolio.

e-Portfolio

PLAN AHEAD

Conduct research and write a report Work with two classmates for this project. You will conduct primary research and write a report on time management. (Learning Objectives 1, 2, and 3)

1. Conduct primary research by surveying eight to ten students on your campus. Ask the following three questions, and determine three other questions you will ask:
   - What time management strategies do you use?
   - What are your major time wasters?
   - Which activities need more of your time?

   Review one periodical and three Internet sources on time management.
2. Write a report of your findings. Include the following parts in the report: title page, table of contents, body, and a references page. Use side headings to divide the body into sections, and include a list or chart. Use footnotes or internal citations in the body for any material quoted or paraphrased from the articles you read. Use styles and report formatting features to save time and work in creating your report.

CHAPTER 9

Verbal Communication and Presentations

LEARNING OBJECTIVES

1. Identify elements of effective verbal communication.
2. Examine elements of nonverbal communication.
3. Describe effective techniques for telephone communication.
4. Prepare and demonstrate an effective presentation.

Verbal Communication

To be an effective administrative professional, you must develop your verbal communication skills. You will use these skills daily as you communicate with your employer, colleagues, customers, and clients, both face-to-face and on the telephone. You may have to deal with a person who is frustrated about a problem. Such a situation will test your communication skills.

Just as you've read books that were more interesting than others, you've also heard speakers and had conversations that were more captivating than others. Why are certain speakers easier to listen to and some conversations more interesting? It's because verbal communication is a skill that needs to be developed, just as writing is a skill that you work on in order to improve.

Verbal communication is the process of exchanging information through the use of words. This chapter deals primarily with two forms of verbal communication: serious conversations, such as a discussion with a coworker, client, or manager, and formal presentations, such as a presentation to a group of coworkers. Regardless of the form it takes, verbal communication involves a sender, a receiver, and a message. Successful communication occurs when a listener (receiver) has heard and understood the message of the speaker (sender).

Essentially, all speech is, to some degree, persuasive since you are trying to persuade others to listen to what you have to say. If they do not understand you or have some interest in your topic, you will not succeed.

Initially, the concept of verbal communication seems simple. Everyone understands words and knows what they mean. In actuality, verbal communication is not simple at all. Words can have different meanings for different people. In a diverse workforce, communication can be complex and challenging.

Dennis Owusu-Ansah/Shutterstock.com

Verbal communication involves a sender, a receiver, and a message.

In most forms of written communication, which you studied in Chapter 8, a person can go back over the message to correct errors and reword confusing sentences before sending it, but when speaking a person cannot take anything back or make corrections before the remarks are heard. This makes speaking effectively more difficult to control and emphasizes the importance of continual improvement of your verbal communication skills.

Listen and Understand

An important step in effective verbal communication is to listen. Hearing and listening are similar to seeing and reading. You may *see* a newspaper article and not *read* it. You may *hear* someone talking but not be *listening* to that person. A large portion of your day is spent communicating, and the majority of that time is spent listening. Still, listening is a skill that most people need to improve.

LISTEN ACTIVELY

Listening actively means making a conscious effort to hear and understand. Listening is an activity of the mind, not the ear. To use a sports analogy, the catcher in a baseball game is just as active as the pitcher. She watches the ball, adjusts her position, and uses her muscles, balance, and thought processes in an effort to catch the ball and participate in the unfolding play. Similarly, the listener reaches out to catch the meaning of the speaker. This is true whether you are having a serious conversation with a coworker, listening to a teacher, or listening to a speaker at the annual employee assembly.

Here are some tips to help you be a more active listener in almost any situation:

- If possible, maintain eye contact with the speaker, and respond occasionally. Remarks such as "yes" and "I see" will help you stay focused on the speaker's message.
- Do not think about what you are going to say next or what you would say if you were the speaker.
- Do not interrupt. Interrupting is a clear sign that you want to be the speaker, not the listener.

dcdebs/iStockphoto.com

Listening requires a conscious effort.

- Try to discover the speaker's main point(s).
- Be attentive to nonverbal communication, and listen for feelings as well as for words.
- Be aware of distractions. The speaker's mannerisms, your emotions, or vocabulary you don't understand can cause you to lose focus or stop listening.
- When possible, minimize distractions in the environment by shutting a door, turning off a phone, etc.
- Take notes on what the speaker is saying. Do not write about your thoughts but about what the speaker actually says.
- When possible, ask for clarification if you do not understand.
- Change your body position if you find yourself getting distracted or bored.
- Practice the habit of listening. Make situations at home, school, clubs, etc., opportunities to practice.

ASK THE RIGHT QUESTIONS

It's already been noted that listening effectively can involve asking questions. Obviously, there will be situations when questions are not appropriate, such as during formal presentations or speeches. In conversations, however, you have more freedom to ask questions, and you can often ask questions during less formal presentations and after presentations or speeches.

Specific questions, such as *how* or *why* questions, will invite positive interactions. Less specific, open-ended questions (as suggested in Chapter 3) are easy for the responder to answer and can lead to more specific questions. Closed questions, which require only a simple yes or no answer, yield little information. Here are some examples:

Specific question:	*Which HR form do we use for overtime?*
Closed question:	*Is there an HR form we use for overtime?*
Open-ended question:	*What happened after yesterday's HR meeting?*
Closed question:	*Did something happen after yesterday's HR meeting?*

Asking the right questions is important in the skill of listening since questions help with understanding. Usually the best strategy is to paraphrase what you believe the speaker said and then ask if that is correct. To **paraphrase** is to restate a concept in different terms. You do not state your opinion, but rather try to understand the speaker's point by restating it. For example, you might say, "If I understand correctly, we will be using the new overtime form starting January 1." Don't be afraid to say, "I don't understand the reason for that" or "I don't understand what you mean."

Speak to Be Understood

In addition to listening and attempting to understand what others are saying, good verbal communicators seek to speak so they are understood. They concentrate on thinking before they speak and using language appropriately to get their point across. Effective speakers also understand that good communication can help prevent or resolve conflict.

THINK BEFORE YOU SPEAK

It is easy to simply start talking when asked a question or to enter a conversation without being prepared. Try to develop the habit of pausing to think and prepare what you will say before you talk. This will help you make your remarks to the point and not overly lengthy. It will also help you clearly convey information to others or ask questions effectively.

In addition, taking time to plan what you will say gives you the opportunity to assess the situation. It is helpful to consider your audience. This is a common strategy used in public speaking, but it is also very useful for serious conversations.

USE LANGUAGE APPROPRIATELY

The language people use often prevents clear communication. Cultural differences impact the meaning certain words have for individuals. For

Rules for Serious Conversations

- Pick the right place and time for the conversation.
- Know in advance the substance of the conversation you want to have. This will help you have a productive, serious conversation.
- Have the conversation with the right people or person. Don't start a serious conversation when some of the people present are not appropriate for the discussion.
- Listen to the other person.
- Answer the question that was asked. Make sure you understand the question before you start talking, and then stick to answering the question. When someone asks you a question, that isn't your cue to start speaking about whatever is on your mind.
- Ask questions clearly. Be ready to phrase your question another way if the person doesn't understand it.
- Interrogating someone, that is, asking question after question without commenting on the responses, is not conversation.
- Don't interrupt when another person is speaking. If you interrupt, you are showing you are impatient to say what is on your mind and can't wait for the other person to finish.
- Don't have side conversations. Give your full attention to the person with whom you are speaking.
- Every serious conversation should have a beginning, middle, and end. Ramblings that have no purpose, do not explore the problem, or fail to come to a conclusion make serious conversations tedious.

Blend Images/Shutterstock.com

Source: Mortimer J. Adler, *How to Speak, How to Listen* (New York: Touchstone, 1983), 140–146.

example, even though British and American people speak the same language, they use words in different ways. In England, a Band-Aid is called a *plaster,* and an elevator is called a *lift*. If you are waiting for a taxi, you are not in a line; you are in a *queue*.

Using language appropriately means choosing your words carefully. Make sure any terminology specific to your job is clarified if you are speaking with someone outside your area. However, you should not talk down to people—assuming they know nothing is inappropriate. If you don't know your audience, risk talking over their heads because if you talk down to people, they may feel patronized.

Here are some tips for using language appropriately:

- Pay attention to the different meanings words can have. Clarify your meaning when necessary.
- Use an appropriate tone and the proper degree of formality for the situation and the message you want to share.
- Be sensitive to whether the individual or group seems to understand what you are saying. Paraphrase when appropriate.

EXAMINE YOUR LANGUAGE PATTERNS

You will have a difficult time communicating verbally and being respected in the business community if you use language patterns that are not the norm. Record yourself in a conversation and then listen to the recording critically. Do you use filler words (known as **verbal pauses**) such as *umm*, *well*, or *like*? Do you frequently use words such as *always* and *never*? Those words can invite an argument. Do you use slang terms or poor grammar, mumble, or use nonstandard English? These habits affect how others perceive you in the workplace. You want to be perceived as a competent professional who can communicate well, so you need to make sure your speech sets you up for success.

Resolve Conflict

As you learned in Chapter 3, **conflict** is a state of opposition or disagreement between persons, ideas, or interests. Effective communication can help resolve conflicts.

When a conflict arises at work, listen and talk with your coworkers or others involved in the situation. Although the situation may seem straightforward to you, you may find that different people have different ideas about it. In attempting to understand another person's perception of a situation, you should withhold judgment while you attempt to think from that person's point of view. Attempting to understand another person's point of view is not the same as agreeing with it. In fact, you may never agree with the person. However, attempting to understand allows you to consider another perspective and gives you a chance to learn from it.

StockLite/Shutterstock.com

Communication can resolve conflict before it starts.

After listening and talking with others, analyze the situation and try to determine the real cause of the conflict. Once the issues are clearly understood, work with the others involved to determine what is needed to resolve the conflict. Concentrate on solving the problem, not on assigning blame. Be tactful in expressing ideas, and show concern for the feelings of others. Do not react to an emotional outburst with an outburst of your own. If the discussion becomes too emotional, stop for a while. Resume the discussion later in the day, or wait until the next workday.

Compromises are often required to resolve conflicts. Remember to examine your role in the situation. Is your position reasonable and appropriate? What can you do to help resolve the conflict? Be willing to compromise when appropriate. Figure 9.1 lists suggestions for resolving conflicts.

Understand Factors That Affect Verbal Communication

The way people understand messages is influenced by their backgrounds and experiences. Based on their backgrounds and experiences, they interpret the meaning of information they receive. They may make assumptions based on their interpretation of the information. They may also draw conclusions, adopt beliefs, or take action.

Assumptions can help or hinder communication. For example, suppose you attend a professional development seminar. The presenter is a speaker you heard in the past. This person was easy to listen to and gave practical and accurate suggestions. You may assume that the information presented today will also be practical and helpful. Because of this past experience, you are likely to listen actively during the presentation, and your assumption will make communicating the message easier for the speaker.

Being aware that many factors can affect your ability (and someone else's) to speak and listen effectively will help you develop an understanding for others and work to hone your own communication skills. Factors such as level and quality of education, self-esteem, experiences with different cultures and nationalities, family concerns, and emotional maturity level impact to some degree your ability to communicate. The best way to contend with them is to develop a tenacity for understanding. Rephrase, ask questions, listen actively, and summarize, all with an attitude of perseverance to understand and be understood.

Resolving Conflicts
■ Identify the issue causing the conflict. Is it an injustice or the need for power, resources, recognition, or acceptance? Many times one or more of these items is at the heart of the conflict.
■ Be willing to listen to the other person. By understanding the needs of the other person, you may be able to find ways to resolve the conflict.
■ Identify points of agreement. Work from these points first, and then identify points of disagreement.
■ Create a safe environment for discussion. Meet in a neutral location.
■ Share your feelings with the other person, and keep your emotions under control.
■ Be objective. Don't act too quickly. Take time to collect your thoughts and see the situation from the outside.
■ Do not seek to win. Examine yourself in case pride and stubbornness creep in.
■ Listen actively. Watch the individual's eyes and body language.

FIGURE 9.1 These suggestions can help in resolving conflicts.

Professional POINTERS

Practice these tips when communicating with others:

- Respect cultures and traditions that are different from your own.
- Avoid stereotyping or generalizing.
- Assume people can always be trusted until proven otherwise.
- Always seek to understand others and their behaviors.
- Encourage cooperation rather than competition.
- Be willing to compromise.
- Listen to an associate's point of view without interrupting.
- Respond calmly to a loud or angry voice. An angry response only generates anger.
- If you disagree with someone's ideas, deal with the disagreement calmly and rationally—not angrily and emotionally.

Nonverbal Communication

Nonverbal communication is the sharing of information through body language, gestures, voice quality, or proximity rather than words. The nonverbal elements of a message can enhance or even change its meaning. For example, smiling and stepping forward to shake someone's hand when you first meet communicates beyond the verbal greeting. You are expressing genuine pleasure in meeting that person when you accompany the words with these gestures.

Vadym Drobot/Shutterstock.com

A smile is recognized in all cultures.

As has been discussed in Chapters 2 and 7, nonverbal communication is important for you as an administrative professional. Your body language, voice tone and quality, demeanor, and mannerisms communicate your attitude and interests. To make good impressions in almost all situations, have a warm and confident smile, stand tall, make eye contact, and greet people with a firm handshake. Avoid fidgeting gestures such as playing with your hair or the loose change in your pocket. A smile is probably the gesture most recognized and favorably received in all cultures.

Body language and gestures can have different meanings to people of different backgrounds or cultures. For example, in the United States it is acceptable to point at someone, use your finger or hand to beckon a person to come, and use the "OK" sign made by placing the forefinger and thumb in a circle. However, in some cultures, these gestures are considered offensive.

Another example of cultural differences in nonverbal communication is eye contact. In the United States, eye contact is seen as a sign of respect, sincerity, and interest. However, in many other cultures, the absence of eye contact is appropriate and acceptable between a manager and a subordinate. To understand nonverbal communication of a different culture, you must study that culture.

Pitch is an attribute of sound that can be described as high or low. The pitch of your voice affects how well you communicate. A lower-pitched voice projects calm, control, and confidence. Listeners are more likely to value what you say if you use a lower pitch. When you are nervous, you are more likely to speak with a higher pitch.

The pace and volume of your speech is also important for effective communication. Speaking too quickly may mean the listener misses all or part of your message. Speaking too slowly or loudly can frustrate and irritate the listener. Be conscious of the pace and volume of your speech patterns, and speak with medium pace and volume so your message will be understood.

Being too close to or far from others can adversely affect communication. If you think someone is too close, you may be uncomfortable or distracted and unable to concentrate on the message. Be considerate and aware of the personal space boundaries of others, and be flexible with your own.

While being aware of your own nonverbal communication, you should also be aware of that of others. You are probably familiar with many types of nonverbal communication, and you should use that familiarity to help you understand what customers, coworkers, and supervisors are thinking and feeling. For example, slouching in a chair and looking at the floor, sitting with arms crossed, or leaning forward and nodding send different messages about a person's degree of interest in a conversation. Figure 9.2 lists ways body language may be interpreted.

Body Language	
listening	Tilts head, makes eye contact, nods
evaluating	Chews on pencil/glasses, strokes chin, looks up and right
eager	Leans forward with feet under chair
bored	Stares into space, doodles
aggressive	Leans forward with fists clenched
rejecting	Moves back with arms folded and head down, walks with hands in pocket
defensive	Clenches hands, stands, crosses arms on chest
lying	Looks down, shifts in seat, glances at you
disbelief, doubt	Rubs eye
sincerity, openness	Offers open palm
confidence	Walks briskly with upright posture
authoritative	Steeples fingers
indecisive	Pulls or tugs at ear

FIGURE 9.2 Body language may be interpreted in different ways.

Telephone Communication

As an administrative professional, you will communicate by phone daily with many people. You may be the first and only contact a person will have with your organization, and that first impression will stay with the caller long after the call is completed. Professionalism and good human relations skills are crucial to making a positive impression of you and your company.

Answering the Telephone

When your telephone rings, answer promptly—on the second ring if possible. You may lose a potential customer if you are slow in answering the telephone.

Most business and supervisors have specific procedures for answering the telephone. Many large organizations have voice messaging systems that identify the organization and give callers the available options. Other large companies have individuals who personally answer the phone with the name of the organization and route the incoming call to the appropriate party, who may be a supervisor's administrative professional. For example, if the call is for Ms. Diaz, you might answer her line as "Ms. Diaz's office, Dana Wilson speaking." If the call is for you, you might answer, "Good morning, Dana Wilson. How may I help you?" If you are answering the phone for your department, you might say, "Administrative Services, Julaine speaking." If you are answering an outside call directly, you might say, "Thank you for calling Kapor Pharmaceuticals; this is Terrill Grant."

Your voice carries clearly when you speak directly into the mouthpiece with your lips about an inch away from the transmitter. You cannot speak distinctly with something in your mouth. Do not have gum or food in your mouth when you answer the telephone. Speak in a normal tone of voice; do not mumble or speak too fast or loud. Callers may become irritated if they must ask you continually to repeat what you said or if they need to hold the telephone one or two inches from their ear.

Elena Elisseeva/Shutterstock.com

Answering the telephone is a responsibility that should be taken seriously.

Managing Incoming Calls

As an administrative professional, you will need skills to effectively screen calls, place and handle calls on hold, transfer calls, take messages, and terminate calls.

SCREEN CALLS AS INSTRUCTED

Many executives have two telephone numbers, one that is published and one that is not. The executive uses the unpublished number to make calls and may also give it to colleagues, close friends, and family members.

The administrative professional is often expected to screen calls from the published number. When the executive receives a call, the administrative professional determines who is calling and why and then either handles or routes to others those calls the supervisor will not take. If someone else in your company can handle the call, transfer it to that person after requesting permission from the caller. If the call is not of interest to your supervisor or anyone else, such as an unsolicited phone call, let the person know courteously. For

An Effective Voice Message

If you use a voice mail system when you are away from your desk, make sure your message provides the appropriate information. For example, your message might say, "This is Lauren Recker. I am away from my desk now. Please leave your name, your number, and a brief message. I will return your call as soon as possible. Thank you." If you will be out of the office or away from your desk for some time, include instructions on whom to contact if the call is urgent. Keep your message up-to-date. For example, record a new message if you will be out for the day or away for several days.

Make your voice message concise, pleasant, and professional. Your message is very important, as it can create either a favorable or an unfavorable impression on the caller.

wavebreakmedia ltd/Shutterstock.com

example, you might say, "I appreciate the information; however, Ms. Winwright is not interested in pursuing the matter."

It is your responsibility to learn the caller's name. Usually a caller identifies herself or himself. If not, ask for a name tactfully. Do not say, "Who is this?" Say, "May I tell Ms. Winwright who is calling, please?" Try to put yourself in the other person's place, and ask questions the way you would want to be asked.

MANAGE HOLDS EFFICIENTLY

You may be responsible for answering your supervisor's phone when he or she is not available to take a call. A call may come in when you are on another line. A caller may request information you do not have at hand. You may need to check with someone else or look through your records for it. In instances like these, you will need to put the caller on hold.

Before putting a caller on hold, ask permission. For example, you may say, "Ms. Hoover is on another call. Would you like to hold?" or "May I place you on hold for a moment? I must answer another line" or "I need to locate the information in my files. Would you like to hold for a minute while I get it, or shall I call you back?" If you need to get information for the caller, consider how long it will take. If you know it will take an hour, say so. Tell the caller you will phone back with the information.

If the caller agrees to hold, get back to him or her as soon as possible. For longer holds, check back about every 30 seconds. Ask if the person would like to continue holding. For example, you may say, "Ms. Hoover is still on another call. May I take a message, or would you like to continue to hold?"

Once you can put through the call or have the information, thank the caller. You may say, "Thank you for waiting. Ms. Hoover is available now" or "Thank you for waiting. Here are the dates you needed."

Office Telephone Equipment

You will find a variety of telephone equipment in the workplace, including standard phone sets, cordless sets, conference call speakers, and headsets to use with computers and software. Common features on business phone sets include the following:

- Multiple phone lines
- Built-in speaker phones
- Caller identification information
- Programmable buttons
- Call forwarding and call waiting
- Conference calling
- Call transfer and hold features

Jo Lomark/Shutterstock.com

TRANSFER CALLS PROPERLY

Before you transfer a call, explain why, and make sure the caller is willing to be transferred. You may say, "Ms. Winwright is out of the office now, but I believe Mr. Sanchez can help you. May I transfer you to Mr. Sanchez?" Do not automatically transfer clients or customers to a voice mail system. Instead, ask, "Would you like me to transfer you to Mr. Sanchez's voice mail?"

If it is not against company policy, consider giving the caller the complete number or extension of the person to whom you are transferring the call in case you are disconnected. Stay on the line until the person picks up the phone, and announce the transfer. If the person is not in, ask if the caller would like to leave a voice message. If the caller does not want to, take the caller's number and have someone return the call.

Make certain you know how to transfer calls on your telephone system. Callers dislike being told they are going to be transferred and then getting disconnected.

RECORD MESSAGES CAREFULLY

When taking messages, you are responsible for getting the necessary information from the caller and recording it accurately. Be prepared with a pen and message slip or paper when you answer the phone. Record the following information:

- Caller's name (spelled correctly). If you are not sure how to spell the name, ask the caller to spell it. If necessary, repeat the spelling to the caller to be certain you recorded it correctly.
- Caller's organization. If you are unfamiliar with the business name, ask the caller for the correct spelling.
- Telephone number, including the area code. Repeat the number to be certain you heard it correctly.
- Message. If the person leaves a message, get the necessary details. For example, if the caller says he will call your employer tomorrow, you might respond, "May I tell him when to expect the call?"

- Date and time. This gives the recipient a point of reference for the message. The message "Mr. Wong will call you tomorrow" has no meaning if you do not know the date of the original call.
- Your initials or name. The recipient will then know to contact you with any questions.

Organizations usually have a procedure for recording and delivering messages. They may provide message pads or a form that can be completed on the computer. E-mailing the message is another possibility. Figure 9.3 shows a properly filled-out message form.

TERMINATE CALLS COURTEOUSLY

Have you ever noticed that characters in movies and television sitcoms don't ever seem to say good-bye when they finish a telephone call? That's a producer's way to save valuable seconds of airtime; it isn't the model for telephone etiquette in the real world. When closing a call, thank the person with whom you are speaking when appropriate. Don't make promises you can't keep. For example, don't promise your supervisor will call someone back. Instead, let the caller know you will give your supervisor the message. Say good-bye pleasantly. Let the caller hang up first.

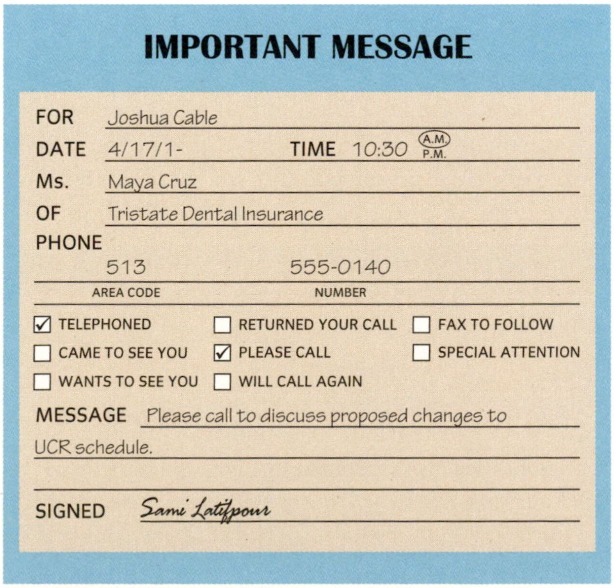
IMPORTANT MESSAGE

FOR Joshua Cable
DATE 4/17/1- TIME 10:30 A.M. P.M.
Ms. Maya Cruz
OF Tristate Dental Insurance
PHONE 513 555-0140
AREA CODE NUMBER

☑ TELEPHONED ☐ RETURNED YOUR CALL ☐ FAX TO FOLLOW
☐ CAME TO SEE YOU ☑ PLEASE CALL ☐ SPECIAL ATTENTION
☐ WANTS TO SEE YOU ☐ WILL CALL AGAIN

MESSAGE Please call to discuss proposed changes to UCR schedule.

SIGNED Sami Latifpour

FIGURE 9.3 Recording messages correctly is important.

Placing Calls

As an administrative professional, you may be responsible for making business calls or placing calls for your supervisor. Professional handling of outgoing calls is just as important as for incoming calls. A good strategy is to treat the call as if it were a meeting. Take a few minutes to plan your call before you make it. Know the purpose of your call, and plan what you intend to say. Always identify yourself and your company as soon as the call is answered. For example, you may say, "This is Susan Wilson of Kapor Pharmaceuticals. I'm calling to confirm your appointment with Ms. Winwright on June 13 at 3:30 p.m." If you have sensitive or confidential information to convey, do not leave it in a voice message.

If your business will take several minutes, be sure to state that, and ask if you are calling at a convenient time. This allows the person an opportunity to call you back, or to have you call back, at a more appropriate time. If you arrange to call back at a certain time, be sure to call when promised.

Remember time zone differences when placing calls. There are four standard time zones in the continental United States: Eastern, Central, Mountain, and Pacific. Most of Alaska is in the Alaska Time Zone. A portion of the Aleutian Islands and St. Lawrence Island are in the Hawaii-Aleutian Time Zone, as is Hawaii.

There is a one-hour difference between neighboring zones. For example, when it is 10 a.m. in New York City (Eastern Standard Time), it is 9 a.m. in Dallas (Central Standard Time). If you need to place a call from New York to Los Angeles, you do not want to call at 9 a.m. Eastern Standard Time; it would be only 6 a.m. in Los Angeles (Pacific Standard Time). It is a good idea to note on your telephone list time differences for frequent callers. Websites that provide time zone information are available (Figure 9.4). There are also mobile apps for smartphones, such as *TimeZoner*, which give quick access to time zone information.

Be aware of international time zones as well. For example, the person who places a call from New York to London must remember that when it

FIGURE 9.4 The Official U.S. Time Website

Source: National Institute of Standards and Technology/U.S. Naval Observatory, http://www.time.gov (accessed June 10, 2011).

is 11 a.m. in New York, it is 4 p.m. in London. If you place many international calls, you should become familiar with international time zones.

Develop Your Telephone Personality

The way you speak on the telephone with customers and clients goes a long way toward creating a positive impression of you and your organization. You will project a positive telephone personality when you use a pleasant voice, use the caller's name, use language effectively, are helpful and discreet, and are attentive to the caller.

USE A PLEASANT VOICE

Always answer the telephone with a smile. If you are smiling, the caller can hear your friendly attitude reflected in your voice. Treat the caller the same as you would a person sitting across from you requesting information or assistance. Make your voice positive and full of energy and enthusiasm. Let all callers know you want to help with whatever needs they have.

USE THE CALLER'S NAME

Remember that individuals like to be recognized and called by name. Use the person's name frequently. For example, say, "Yes, Mr. Jordan. I will be happy to get the information." End the conversation with a comment such as "It was nice to talk with you, Mr. Jordan."

Use titles, such as *Ms.* or *Mr.*, even when communicating with administrative professionals from other organizations. This is a way to show respect and prevent you from offending someone unknowingly. Once another employee at your level has addressed you by first name, you can use his or her first name as well. For higher-level employees and customers, even if they call you by first name, wait until they expressly say you can use their first name before doing so.

Be aware of other titles as appropriate for the type of job you have. For example, a job in state government will require that you use titles for state senators and representatives: "Good afternoon, Senator Lewis. Congresswoman Beauregard is in a committee meeting . . . ." Similarly, in a college or university setting, address faculty members and administrators who have doctoral degrees as *doctor.*

USE LANGUAGE EFFECTIVELY

Use correct English and pronunciation. People who have a good grasp of the English language develop a negative impression of your organization if they hear you use a grammatically incorrect statement. Slang is not appropriate in business calls. Figure 9.5

Common Slang Expressions

Avoid	Say
Yeah.	Certainly.
OK.	Yes.
Uh-huh.	Of course.
Bye-bye.	Good-bye.
Huh? What?	I'm sorry; I didn't understand you.

FIGURE 9.5 Avoid slang and speak professionally on the phone.

lists several slang expressions, followed by more appropriate expressions.

BE HELPFUL, YET DISCREET

When someone calls and your employer is not available, tell the caller about how long your employer will be gone, or ask if someone else can help. Let the person know you are trying to help. Here are two examples of how to handle such a call—the wrong way and the right way.

Incorrect Handling of Call

Caller: *This is Pablo Rodriguez. May I speak with Shareen Edwards?*

Felicia: *Ms. Edwards is out of the office.*

Caller: *When will she be back?*

Felicia: *I expect her back sometime this afternoon.*

Caller: *Will she be back in an hour?*

Felicia: *She might be.*

Caller: *Ask her to call me when she comes in.*

Felicia *OK.*

What is wrong with the conversation? Perhaps you do not see any glaring errors. Felicia answered Mr. Rodriguez's questions—which is precisely the point. Mr. Rodriguez had to ask all the questions; he probably thought Felicia was uncooperative. The closing "OK" was too informal. Additionally, Felicia did not get a phone number. Notice the improvement in the next example.

Correct Handling of Call

Caller: *This is Pablo Rodriguez. May I speak with Shareen Edwards?*

Felicia: *Ms. Edwards is out of the office; I expect her back in about two hours. If you'd like to give me your number, I'll ask her to call you when she returns.*

Caller: *That would be fine. My number is 555-0129.*

Felicia: *Thank you, Mr. Rodriguez. I'll give her the message.*

Felicia has saved time for Mr. Rodriguez and Ms. Edwards and has probably left a positive impression with Mr. Rodriguez.

Another important point to remember in such a situation is to be discreet. In other words, do not give the caller unnecessary information.

Incorrect Handling of Call

Caller: *This is Pablo Rodriguez. May I speak with Shareen Edwards?*

Felicia: *Ms. Edwards went to see Bill Chung at Frost & Nabors about an advertising matter. I expect her back in about two hours. If you'd like to give me your number, I'll ask her to call you when she returns.*

Felicia gave out too much information. It was not necessary to tell Mr. Rodriguez where Ms. Edwards was, whom she went to see, and why. Felicia could be revealing information that is confidential or that would hurt the business relationship. A good rule to remember is to be helpful about when your supervisor is returning without specifying where the supervisor is or what he or she may be doing. Figure 9.6 provides examples of appropriate telephone responses.

Appropriate Telephone Responses

Avoid	Say
She's out.	She's not in the office at the moment. Would you like to leave a message?
I don't know where he is.	He's stepped out of the office. Would you like to leave a message?
She's busy.	She's unavailable right now. Would you like to leave a message?
He hasn't come in yet.	I expect him shortly. Would you like to leave a message?
She took the day off *or* She's out sick.	She's out of the office for the day. Can someone else help you, or would you like to leave a message?
He's in the men's room.	He's stepped out of the office. Would you like to leave a message?

FIGURE 9.6 An appropriate response is courteous but does not reveal too much information.

BE ATTENTIVE

As you are talking with the caller, visualize the person. Speak *with* the person, not *at* the phone. Listen politely to what the person is saying. Do not interrupt or do other work. If the caller is unhappy about an experience with the company, listen to the person's complaint. You will have an easier time dealing with a disgruntled caller after you hear what the caller has to say. Follow the suggestions in the "Telephone Customer Service Skills" section of Chapter 7 on page 138.

Take notes during a long or involved conversation so you will remember all the information. Courtesy is always important. Use words like *please* and *thank you* often. Let the caller know you care about him or her and the situation.

Business Presentations

In the workplace, information is often presented verbally to a small or large group of people. With the team approach commonly used in organizations today, administrative professionals sometimes give presentations. These presentations may be informal ones to a small group or formal ones to a large group. You also may have occasion to speak at professional organization meetings. In addition to presenting yourself, you may be asked to develop slides for someone else to use in a presentation. Because presenting can be an important part of your professional life, the remainder of this chapter focuses on proper presentation techniques.

Many people fear presenting to even small groups of people. For most people, becoming an effective presenter is a learned skill, so don't be discouraged if presenting isn't something you currently enjoy or do well. This skill is so important to individuals and organizations that some businesses develop training programs to help people become effective verbal presenters. As with all skill development, you must practice the skill. The next sections will help you develop your presentation skills. The Plan Ahead activity at the end of the chapter will give you the opportunity to practice these skills by preparing a brief presentation and delivering it to your instructor and classmates.

Plan the Presentation

Preparing a good presentation takes time. A good presentation is carefully written and thoroughly practiced. It often requires research and the development of visual aids such as *PowerPoint* presentations, as well as paper or electronic handouts. But the first step is to plan. In the planning stage, you define the purpose of the presentation, consider the audience, and give some attention to the time and setting. Beginning preparation several weeks before the presentation is not too soon.

DETERMINE THE PURPOSE

The first step in planning a presentation is to define the purpose clearly. Ask yourself these questions as you begin to plan your presentation:

- Why am I giving this presentation?
- What do I want the audience to know as a result of my presentation?
- What, if anything, do I want the audience to do as a result of my presentation?

KNOW YOUR AUDIENCE

Consider the characteristics of the people who will hear the presentation. Try to determine areas of common interest to which you can relate points of information. For example, if your audience is a group of administrative professionals, you know some of their interests. You can use anecdotes or stories that have meaning for them. If you are speaking to a group of colleagues from your workplace, again you know some of their interests. You can tailor your message to meet their needs. If you are speaking to a general audience, keep the following questions in mind as you begin to plan your remarks:

- What are the **demographics** of the audience (characteristics such as age, gender, and educational level)?
- What does the audience know about the subject?
- What preconceived ideas or biases may audience members have?
- What will be the size of the audience?

A small audience allows greater interaction. With a large audience, there is little chance for interaction other than a question-and-answer period at the end of the presentation. The event organizer is a good resource for this and other information.

Digital Vision/Getty Images

Consider your audience when planning a presentation.

CONSIDER THE TIME AND SETTING

Ask the meeting organizer when you will present and how long the presentation should be. Plan a presentation that you can give effectively within the allotted time. The time of day when you will present may affect how you cover your topic. For example, at mid-morning listeners are typically alert. Right after lunch, listeners may become drowsy if you show slides that require the lights to be low.

Find out whether any other activities are scheduled immediately before or after your presentation. That way, you will know when the room can be set up and how quickly you need to remove any materials or equipment.

Consider where the presentation will be given. Is it in the workplace, a hotel, a conference center, or a school? What is the size of the room, and what are the seating arrangements? If the audience is small, will they be sitting around a table? Are the chairs to be set up in a circle?

If you have an opportunity to influence the setting, do so. Be certain the size of the room is appropriate. You do not want to give a presentation to 12 people in a room designed for 100 people. It will look as though you gave a party and no one came. Nor do you want to give a presentation to 50 people in a room designed for 25. People are not comfortable when they are crowded. As far as possible, be sure the chairs are comfortable, the temperature is pleasant, the room is clean, the lighting is appropriate, and the acoustics are good.

Research and Write the Presentation

Research the topic, if necessary, using resources from your company, a library, or the Internet. If you are researching on the Web, take special care to be sure your sources are credible. In Chapter 8 you learned about evaluating online information. Anyone can have a website about anything, and all or none of it may be factual or appropriate. As the speaker, it is up to you to determine if the information you present is correct. Public wikis, such as Wikipedia, are not generally considered a credible source when giving a business presentation. These sites may afford you a place to start but should never be relied upon for valid information.

Conduct original research if needed. For example, you may be developing a presentation for the local chapter of the IAAP on e-mail ethics. Therefore, you decide to do primary research with IAAP members on ethical and unethical e-mail practices they have observed in their organizations.

Research your topic, taking care to use credible sources.

can decide on the best order in which to present the main points.

Do not attempt to cover too many points. If you do, you will lose your audience quickly. Three or four is usually enough. If your audience is knowledgeable about the topic, you may be able to cover as many as ten main points; however, that number is too many for most audiences. Generally, with fewer points that are more developed, you will retain the audience's attention to a greater degree.

If your talk will include a question-and-answer session, identify questions listeners are likely to have and prepare answers. Learn as much as you can about the topic of the presentation so you will be better able to answer questions you did not anticipate.

Individuals usually gather more information during research than they can use in a presentation. An audience can absorb only so much information. You do not want to burden your audience by giving them more information than they can comprehend and remember. Your next step is to select the most relevant material appropriate to the subject and audience for the presentation.

ORGANIZE THE MATERIAL

Organize the main points of the material by first reading thoroughly the information you collected, underlining, highlighting, and making notes as you come across potential information for your presentation. Go back to the purpose of the presentation, which you established earlier, and then develop several main points. Make an outline or numbered list of the main points you want to include. Then work on each item to develop it individually. Later you can decide on the best order in which to present the main points.

DEVELOP AN OPENING

The opening for a presentation should get the audience's attention immediately. For example, you may do one of the following:

- Tell a story.
- Use a quotation.
- Ask a question.
- Refer to a current event.

Starting with a brief story that has a connection to your topic is an effective way to get your audience interested. For example, suppose you are speaking to an eighth-grade class about your work, specifically proper etiquette at a business dinner. You start with a story about how, when you were growing up, your mother made you use proper table manners. She thought it was so important that she devised a game for the dinner table that encouraged proper etiquette. Relating this story would be a good way to get the audience interested and to make the topic relevant to their age and experience.

Knowing what *you* do best is important. If you can never remember the punch line of a joke, do not try to tell a joke. Nothing is worse than an opening that flops. If you do tell jokes well and decide to tell one, make sure the joke is in good taste. Jokes based on ethnicity, race, gender, or religion are never appropriate. Anything crude is not acceptable for any audience.

Speak With Credibility

Credibility (being perceived as reliable or believable) is important for a successful presentation. When your audience thinks you are credible, they will be more likely to accept your message or take the action you want them to take. One obvious way to appear credible is to be very knowledgeable about the topic of your presentation. Use examples from your own experience. Be able to answer questions or provide more details about the topic when asked. If you make contradictory statements or give incorrect information, the audience will not find you credible. State the source of facts and figures you present. These steps will lend credibility to your presentation.

jacomstephens/iStockphoto.com

WRITE THE BODY

Look at the main points for the presentation that you identified earlier. Expand on each point, including appropriate details. Make notes about visuals you could use to emphasize various points. Use language creatively to help keep listeners' attention and convey your points. The following techniques can help you write the body of the presentation:

- Establish a link with your audience. For example, if your audience is a group of administrative professionals, what concerns do audience members have in common? Relate your major points to experiences common to both you and the audience.
- Use interesting facts, figures, and quotations. If you are giving a motivational talk on the importance of service, for example, you might cite facts about Mother Teresa's work and use a quote from her. Relate the quote to a point in your presentation.
- Use direct language. Do not use long words when simpler words would be just as powerful, but at the same time, do not talk down to your audience.
- Personalize your talk. Address your audience directly; use *you* frequently.
- Talk in a conversational tone.
- Use the active rather than the passive voice. For example, say "I believe . . ." rather than "It is believed . . ."
- Use analogies (comparisons of different things that stress their similarities) to help explain your ideas. For example: *Stress is like a roller-coaster ride; it has numerous highs and lows.* Tie the analogy directly to the presentation subject matter.

DEVELOP A STRONG CLOSING

The closing must tie together the opening and the overall purpose of your presentation. The conclusion is your destination. It is the part of your presentation that should take your audience where you want them to be—to what you want them to learn or do. A good conclusion gets the audience's attention. It helps them see the relationship between each part of your presentation—between the opening and the body and the body and the conclusion. The closing puts the pieces of your presentation together in a creative and interesting way so the audience leaves thinking you have helped them learn and/or have motivated them to take some action.

Let the audience know you are ready to conclude by stating simply, "In conclusion" or "My final point is . . ." Make the conclusion short (about 5 to 10 percent of your talk) and powerful. The conclusion can be a moving statement, story, call to action, or challenge. For example, if you are delivering a presentation on human potential, you might end by saying, "I leave you with three challenges—to do your best always, to reach beyond yourself, and to continue to grow and learn." The last few lines of your conclusion should be memorable. They should help you connect with the audience for one final moment—to make them laugh or think.

Prepare Visuals

A **visual aid** is an object or image used to help an audience understand a spoken or written message. A *PowerPoint* presentation is one of the most common computer-based visual aids used today. Computer-based visual aids are generally easy to use. With presentation software or a web presentation tool, a speaker can create slides with text, images, video clips, web links, and other elements and navigate through them with ease. Flip charts and whiteboards are also common visual aids. According to research by Edward Dale, an educator at Ohio State University, on average people retain about 20 percent of what they hear, about 30 percent of what they see, and about 50 percent of what they see and hear. If you want your audience to remember what you say, show them effective visuals during your presentation.

The medium you choose will depend on the equipment you will have available during the presentation and the size of the audience. **Flip charts** are tablets of large paper for drawing pictures or recording notes during a presentation. They are effective for small, informal group meetings. Some presentation venues may have electronic or interactive whiteboards. An **electronic whiteboard** scans whatever is drawn on it so the drawing can be printed or delivered electronically. An **interactive whiteboard** displays a computer desktop by a connection with a digital projector; the user can interact with the computer by touching the board. Do not be afraid to try these devices if you have the opportunity, but make sure you practice on one beforehand or arrive early so you can see how it will work with your presentation.

An interactive whiteboard is an effective visual aid.

Slide shows are effective for small or large groups and formal or informal presentations. They can be created easily with *PowerPoint* or other presentation software or web presentation tools. Figure 9.7 is an example of a slide created in *PowerPoint* software. Here are a few points to consider as you prepare electronic presentations:

- It is typically very easy to choose a theme or color scheme that will make your slides look professional and appropriate for the topic.

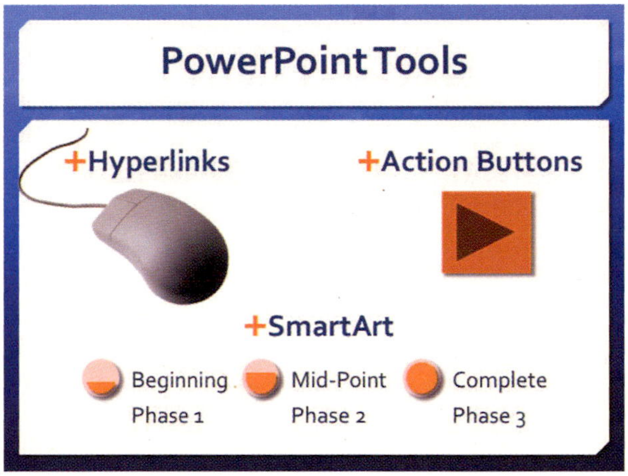

FIGURE 9.7 Images add interest and illustrate points.

- Images can be used to add interest or illustrate points. They also help break up the text on a slide. Be sure to follow any copyright restrictions on Internet images.
- Videos embedded in a presentation can illustrate points, help the audience understand the topic, and help retain their interest.
- Sound can be used effectively to build excitement or emphasize transitions. Use it only for a specific purpose, and do not overuse it.
- Graphs can be used to illustrate data visually.
- Transitions between slides and slide animations provide an interesting way to reveal points as you make them. Both, especially animations, are easy to overuse.
- Don't plan to read your slides to the audience. Make short bullet points, not full sentences. Generally, use no more than six lines per slide and six words per line.
- Do not crowd the text or images on the slides.
- Know your equipment. Will you use your own laptop or is one provided? Do you have videos that need to be buffered? Is there sound, and will you need external speakers?
- Make sure visuals can be read easily. Text should be 28 to 32 points in a sans serif font such as Arial or Calibri.
- Use only one or two fonts (one for the title and another for the bullet points).
- Use a contrasting font color, such as yellow on a dark blue background. Do not use a red font.

Although visual aids can be effective, they can also detract from your presentation if you do not use them well. Visuals must be clear and large enough to be read easily. Every visual must relate to the presentation, and there should not be too many (Figure 9.8). One slide for every two or three minutes of your presentation is a good rule. Visuals should be proofread carefully so they are error-free.

Handouts are not necessary but can be helpful if you are presenting a lot of information that is instructional or that the audience may need later. For example, if you are doing a presentation about the new human resources forms for new hires, you may wish to prepare a handout of screen shots or links for your audience to use when they return to their desks. The simplest handouts are copies of the slides. Other handouts list the main points to be discussed and provide space for notes. Some presenters like to

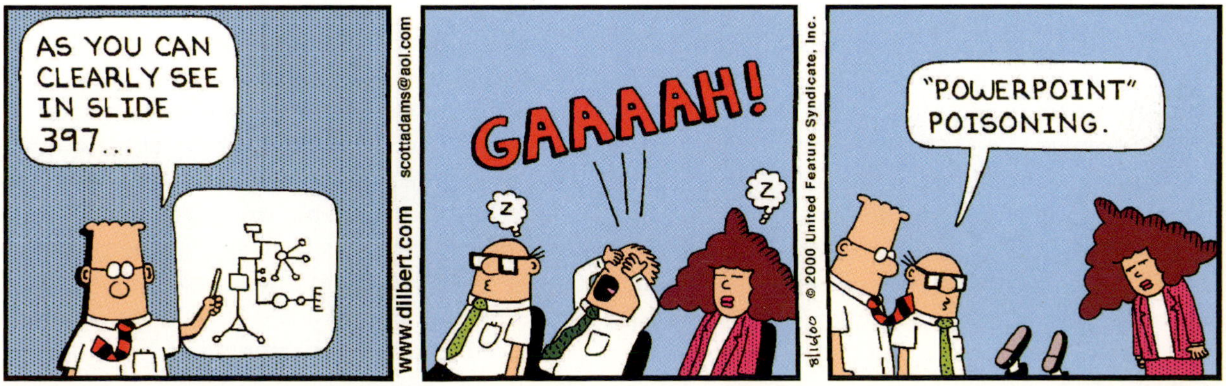

FIGURE 9.8 Avoid using too many slides in your presentation.

offer a **green handout**—information provided on a website. The presenter tells the audience the URL or provides a small slip of paper or card with the URL on it. Handouts should be attractive, easy to read, and free of errors.

Practice and Prepare to Present

Rehearse the presentation exactly as you plan to give it. If you will stand at a lectern during the presentation, stand at one during the rehearsal. If you will use a microphone during the presentation, use one during the rehearsal. If you plan to use visuals during the presentation, use them in the rehearsal. Practice facing the audience during your presentation. Do not turn around and look at the slides.

You might ask a trusted colleague to listen to and critique your rehearsal presentation. Ask the person to be totally honest with you. You want to be able to correct your errors before you make your presentation.

MANAGE FEAR AND ANXIETY

Remember that it is normal to be nervous and have some fear of speaking in public. Even professionals experience it. Practicing helps you become confident in yourself and thus less nervous. You know who your audience is, what you intend to say, and how you will say it. A well-prepared and well-rehearsed presentation can eliminate many of your fears. Try not to push yourself to the limit with work responsibilities in the last few days before a presentation. When you are overly tired, you increase your chances of being nervous.

CHECK THE ROOM AND EQUIPMENT

Visit the room where you will make your presentation. Know how the room will be set up. Find out where the lectern is going to be if you are using one. If you have a slide presentation, check it on the actual equipment if possible, especially if you have links and videos embedded. Be certain the equipment is in good working order and you know how to use it. How will you advance your slides? If you are at all uncomfortable using the equipment, ask a colleague to assist you by operating it. Stand in different parts of the room to make sure visuals can be seen and read.

CONSIDER YOUR APPEARANCE

Decide what you will wear several days before the presentation. The usual attire for women is a suit or dress; for men, a suit and tie. Wear something that is comfortable and looks good on you. Bright colors are perfectly acceptable. Avoid necklaces and earrings that are large and showy. Rings and bracelets are appropriate, but avoid large, noisy bracelets. Hair should be well groomed and away from the face.

WRITE YOUR INTRODUCTION

One way to build credibility with your audience is to tell them your credentials. Write a succinct statement (that will take no more than two minutes to deliver) highlighting your major accomplishments. If you will be introduced by someone, send it to that person. Do not send a packet with pages of information about you and leave it up to the introducer to determine the important points to make. Take a copy of the introduction with you on the day of the presentation in case the introducer has misplaced the copy you sent. If your presentation will include a question-and-answer session, prepare a short closing statement to deliver after the questions.

Deliver the Presentation

Arrive early enough to check out the microphone, the equipment, and the layout of the room. Confirm that the temperature is comfortable, the room is clean, and the lighting is appropriate. If changes need to be made, find someone who can assist you. In the 10 or 15 minutes before your presentation begins, find a private place (maybe a small room away from the gathering audience) and sit quietly to relax.

Pay attention to your body language as you are being introduced. Use nonverbal cues to help establish your credibility. Look at the person who is speaking, and then look slowly at the audience. As you approach the lectern, walk with confidence. Place your notes (paper or electronic) where you can refer to them easily. Respond briefly to the introduction. You might say, "Thank you very much" and exchange a handshake. If you are not being introduced by another person, introduce yourself as you begin.

CONNECT WITH THE AUDIENCE

Pause for a moment before beginning your presentation. Let your eyes sweep the room. Do not think about being nervous. Focus on sharing your message with the audience. Remember these points to help you deliver a successful presentation:

- Maintain eye contact with the audience. As you speak, focus on one side of the room and then (after a period of time) the other. Make eye contact with as many people as you can.
- Watch for nonverbal feedback. For example, puzzled looks or blank stares are obvious cues that the audience does not understand. You may need to speak more slowly and give examples.
- Use natural gestures. It's fine to use your arms and hands to emphasize points, but too many gestures can distract the audience.
- Be natural; do not perform. Speak in a normal tone of voice and at an appropriate rate—not too fast and not too slow.
- Speak loudly enough so everyone can hear you.

ANSWER QUESTIONS

Your presentation may include a question-and-answer session. Unless the audience is a very small group in which everyone can be heard easily, repeat each question before answering it. This helps ensure that everyone will know what was asked and gives

TECH TALK

Advanced *PowerPoint* Features

Several often-overlooked features of *PowerPoint* presentation software are particularly valuable. They include SmartArt, Outline, hyperlinks, and action buttons.

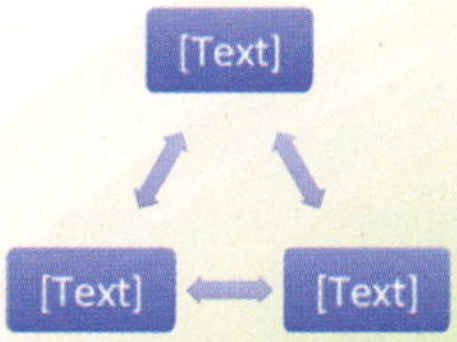

SmartArt SmartArt allows you to make visual representations of processes, relationships, cycles, lists, and hierarchies, as well as custom visuals, easily. You can use it, for example, to illustrate steps in a series or an organizational chart. SmartArt is located on the Insert tab.

Outline Some presenters find it easier to key their slide text into the presentation before selecting fonts, backgrounds, images, etc. With the Outline tab, available in Normal view, you can easily insert all the text for your presentation. You can also see the organization of your presentation at a glance, which may help you spot connections or organizational issues before you begin the visual design.

Hyperlinks A **hyperlink** is a piece of text or graphic that links to another place in a file, a website, or another file. In *PowerPoint* software, you can use hyperlinks to move around in your presentation and to access examples on the Internet. To create a hyperlink, simply select the text or object and choose Hyperlink from the Insert tab.

Action buttons An action button is a type of hyperlink that allows you to jump from one slide to another by using a graphic that looks like a button, rather than text or a picture. Action buttons help you keep focused, show the organization of your presentation, and remind the audience of where you have been and where you are going. They are located in Shapes on the Home tab.

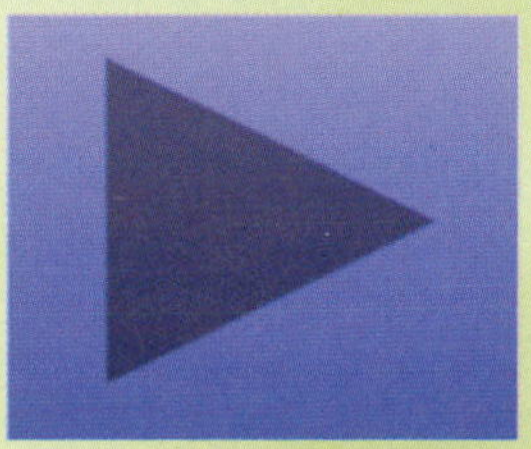

PARTNERSHIP FOR 21ST CENTURY SKILLS

Communication/ Collaboration

Prepare

Fear of speaking in public is a common fear. While you may never be totally free from this fear when speaking to large groups, you can take some steps to minimize it. Preparation is the best way to alleviate many fears. The following acronym will help you think about your preparations and reduce anxiety.

- Package—you are preparing a package to present to a group of people. As you prepare, consider the big picture and how one section flows into another.
- Relax—intentionally remind yourself to relax.
- Expectations—what are the expectations for what your audience will take away from your talk? Make sure you have established in your own mind the objectives for the talk you are giving.
- Panic isn't an option, so plan panic out of your talk. Do you have an outline? Are your notes large enough and well organized? Could they get out of order? Think about what could go wrong, and then plan it out of the picture as much as possible.
- Audience—when preparing, keep your audience in mind. Consider their skills and interests. For example, if you will be speaking to a group of administrative professionals about how to use the newest travel form, consider what might be most helpful to them. This will help you have confidence in the value of what you are presenting.
- Race—it isn't a race. The point is not to get it done, but rather to relay information to your audience. Focus on the objectives of the speech and how you can best fulfill them. Remind yourself to slow down.
- Enthusiasm—get excited about your topic, and your audience will follow suit. In addition, you will relax and enjoy it more.

Activity

Consider a talk or speech you gave in the past, such as a report in class or information in a meeting for work or a club. Share with the class how you did or did not prepare properly, considering just one of the concepts above.

you a minute to think about the answer. If you do not know the answer to a question, admit it. Offer to find the answer and provide it later, if appropriate, or suggest another source for the information. End the session with the short closing statement you prepared.

Evaluate Your Presentation

Within a day after the presentation, critique your performance. Think objectively about it. List what you did well, and identify one or two items you need to improve. Make notes on these items. Repeat the process each time you give a presentation. Evaluation is an ongoing process. Give yourself credit for the improvements you make.

Additionally, get feedback from other people. You can ask a respected colleague to evaluate you. You or the individuals who asked you to speak may provide evaluation forms for the audience. Review the evaluations carefully. Do not let yourself become upset over a few negative comments. Know that there will always be some negative feedback. Take valid points seriously, and strive to address them in your next presentation.

Team Presentations

You learned in Chapter 3 that teams are used extensively in business today. They often report on their activities or findings in a team verbal presentation. Team members work together to prepare and deliver the presentation. The techniques presented in the previous section also apply to team presentations. Some additional suggestions for team planning are given below.

- Discuss as a team the goal or purpose of the presentation, the main points it will include, and how best to present the information.
- Decide who will deliver each part of the presentation.
- Determine how you will make the transition from one speaker to another. One way is for the speaker who is finishing to introduce the next speaker.
- Practice your presentation as a group. If visual aids or handouts are part of the presentation, decide who will prepare them.
- Determine appropriate dress. Speakers should dress in a similar fashion. For example, they may all wear suits.
- Determine how the group will be seated before and after each person's part of the presentation. Will the speakers be on a stage? In what order will they be seated? The first speaker should be closest to the podium.

SUMMARY

To reinforce what you have learned in this chapter, study this summary.

- It is important for administrative professionals to develop skills in verbal communication so they can listen well, speak in a professional manner, resolve conflict, and understand factors that affect communication.
- Nonverbal communication differs for each culture. Considering body language, voice quality, and personal space will help the administrative professional be a more effective communicator.
- Using good human relations skills in handling telephone calls leaves the caller with a positive impression of the administrative professional and the organization.
- To give a successful business presentation, the administrative professional must plan, research, write, prepare visuals, practice, deliver, and then evaluate the presentation.

KEY TERMS

9

STUDY Tools

Located at www.cengagebrain.com

- Chapter Outlines
- Flashcards
- Interactive Quizzes
- Tech Tools
- Video Segments
- and More!

LET'S DISCUSS

1. How can you be an active listener?
2. How is listening different from hearing?
3. Are speaking and listening of equal value? Why or why not?
4. Describe some of the messages body language sends.
5. Describe how an administrative professional should respond when someone phones and asks to speak with an absent supervisor.
6. Describe the elements of a telephone personality.
7. What activities should be completed when planning a presentation?
8. What activities should be completed when researching and writing a presentation?
9. What are some general rules to consider when creating a *PowerPoint* show for use in a presentation?
10. What strategies can you use to help you connect with the audience during a presentation?

PUT IT TO WORK

Presentation adjustment Gloria Delgado is an administrative professional in the human resources department of her company. Gloria's supervisor asked her to give a presentation to 20 employees regarding changes to employee benefits that will take effect in the following year. Gloria reviewed a report that summarized the changes and prepared her comments using information from the report. Gloria assumed the audience for her presentation would be other administrative professionals, so she prepared opening comments and examples to which other administrative professionals would relate.

On the day of the presentation, Gloria was surprised to see that the audience included people from several different departments and job positions. During the question-and-answer session, several people asked about aspects of the benefit plan other than the changes. Some listeners seem annoyed when Gloria was not prepared to answer these questions.

What went wrong? What should Gloria have done differently in preparing for the presentation? What could she have done during the presentation when she realized that some of her assumptions were incorrect? (Learning Objective 4)

COMMUNICATE SUCCESSFULLY

1. **Voice mail** You are about to call Mr. Adrian Tarniceriu of Rom National Timber Company regarding a pulp and paper grant his company applied for last month. You work for Laramie Paper Company as an administrative professional. You need to know if he is still interested in the grant, and if so, what rate he would consider equitable. You know that Mr. Tarniceriu is away at a conference but that he will be checking voice mail. With a partner, simulate the voice mail you will leave. Critique each other's work. (Learning Objectives 1 and 3)
2. **Telephone responses** You work as an administrative assistant for Teresa Winwright, vice president of marketing at Kapor Pharmaceuticals. One of your responsibilities is to screen calls for her. Analyze the following situations and determine an appropriate response. (Learning Objective 3)
   a. Ms. Winwright leaves the office at 11:30 a.m. for a luncheon with the Fort Worth mayor. She tells you she will return at approximately 2:30 p.m. The luncheon is at the Hammersmith Country Club. David Anderson, president of Kapor Pharmaceuticals, calls at 1:30. He says he needs to speak with Ms. Winwright immediately.
   b. At 2:30, Ms. Winwright leaves for a meeting in David Anderson's office. She says she does not know exactly when she will be back. Maurice Templeton, Kapor's senior vice president and general counsel, calls and asks to see her at 8 the following morning. He says the meeting is urgent and will take approximately 30 minutes. He informs you he cannot meet after 8:30. You see that Ms. Winwright already has a meeting scheduled for 8 to 8:30 on her calendar. However, you know she will not want to miss the 8 a.m. meeting with Mr. Templeton.
   c. At 3, a man calls for Ms. Winwright. He refuses to give his name or the purpose of his call. He says he must talk with her. Ms. Winwright has not returned from her meeting with Mr. Anderson.
   d. At 3:30, a reporter from a local television news station calls and asks to speak with Ms. Winwright. (She has not returned from her meeting with Mr. Anderson. She also has a 4 p.m. meeting scheduled.) The reporter tells you he is working on a story about a drug being developed by Kapor. The story will air on tomorrow's early morning show.
   e. At 4, Ms. Winwright is in a conference call with two managers who report to her. Before going into the meeting, she asked that she not be disturbed. She told you the meeting would last approximately an hour and a half. At 4:30, Alexander Espinosa, chairperson of the Fort Worth Arts Committee, of which Ms. Winwright is a member, calls and ask to speak with her.
3. **Importance of verbal communication** Add a new post to the blog you created in Chapter 1. In this entry, reflect on the following statement: **Verbal communication skills are important for me to have as an administrative professional for the following reasons.** (Learning Objective 1)

Blog

DEVELOP WORKPLACE SKILLS

4. **Listening skills** You are the executive secretary to Linda Jones. She will be in a meeting this morning, but she has left you a voice mail with some assignments. Access the sound file *Ch09_Assignments* from the data files. Play the file, taking notes as you listen. Do not pause the recording or replay the file. Working from memory and your notes, list everything you can remember. Now play the file again. Were you able to list all the assignments? Fill in any tasks you missed. (Learning Objective 1)
5. **Nonverbal communication** Connie is a senior administrative associate for a company that trains entrepreneurs. She is in Japan, assisting her supervisor with a conference the company is conducting with business students in that country. After a few days, one of the students tells her that the students are a little frustrated because she bows too low. Connie decides she needs to research cultural and business customs in Japan. Using the Internet, make a short list of tips for business travelers to Japan that you think will be useful. Include advice on how Connie should bow. (Learning Objective 2)
6. **Telephone etiquette practice** Access the *Word* file *Ch09_Telephone_Rating_Form* from the data files. Choose a class member to work with. Call each other, recreating the five situations in Activity 2. One of you should be the caller; the other should be the administrative professional. Then switch roles and replay each situation. Use the form to rate each other and the handling of each situation. Individually, prepare an action plan for improvement. (Learning Objective 3)

BUILD RELATIONSHIPS

7. **Evaluation** With one or two classmates, prepare an evaluation form for *PowerPoint* presentations in the college classroom using the information in the "Business Presentations" section of the chapter. The form can be a rubric, checklist, or any other type of evaluation your team believes will help in effectively judging the quality of presentations. (Learning Objective 4)
8. **Resolving conflict** Think of a situation that involved a conflict. The situation could be one in which you were involved personally, read about or viewed on television or the Internet, or witnessed at work. Answer the following questions. (Learning Objective 1)
   a. Who were the people involved in the conflict?
   b. Describe the conflict situation. What was the cause, or what were the underlying issues?
   c. Did you or someone else listen and attempt to understand the conflict? If so, describe how.
   d. Was the conflict resolved? If it was, explain how. If it was not, explain why you think no resolution was reached.
   e. What could you have done differently (if you were involved) to improve communication and help resolve the conflict?

USE TECH TOOLS

9. **Advanced features** Access the *PowerPoint* file *Ch09_Presentation* from the data files. This presentation has prepared slides, which need some additions. Open the file and do the following: (Learning Objective 4)
   a. On Slide 2, select the text **Point 1**. Make it a hyperlink to Slide 3.
   b. On Slide 2, select the text **Point 2**. Make it a hyperlink to Slide 4. Do the same for **Point 3**, linking it to the appropriate slide.
   c. On Slides 3, 4, and 5, add an action button that links to Slide 2. You can create the button on one slide and copy and paste it onto the other two.
   d. Add a professional theme or choose a professional background so all slides are uniform in appearance.
10. **Outside the box** Prezi is an example of web-based presentation tool. With Prezi, you can create presentations on a single digital canvas, rather than slide by slide, and show them on a whiteboard, for example. Explore Prezi (link found on the textbook website). Watch some sample presentations. Pair up with a classmate and share at least one presentation you enjoyed. Compare Prezi to the *PowerPoint* software. What are some advantages and disadvantages of Prezi? (Learning Objective 4)
11. **Recording** Record the voice mail you practiced with a partner in Activity 1. Computers have recorders as standard software, or you can download free recording software such as Audacity (link found on the textbook website). Listen to yourself, noting improvements you could make, and then record the voice mail again. (Learning Objectives 1 and 3)

PLAN AHEAD

Presentation Choose one of the following topics, and prepare a five- to ten-minute presentation for your class. Follow the steps in this chapter to plan, prepare, and deliver your presentation. Plan for two to three main points, each developed through research. Create slides for the title, table of contents/main points, body, and credits. Use action buttons linked to points in the presentation, smart art, hyperlinks, backgrounds, and multiple images. Add a copy of your computer-based visual aids and notes to your online portfolio. (Learning Objective 4)

e-Portfolio

Topics

- Time management
- Stress management
- Conflict resolution
- Public speaking tips
- Overcoming fear on stage
- Telephone etiquette
- Dress for success
- Developing a professional portfolio
- Leadership tips
- Plagiarism in workplace writing
- Ethics of social networking at work
- Another topic your instructor approves

CHAPTER

10 Global Communication—Technology and Etiquette

LEARNING OBJECTIVES

1. Understand how people communicate globally.
2. Identify technology issues that impact the business environment.
3. Examine technology etiquette for the administrative professional.

Global Communication

Businesses are expanding globally, and communications technologies are adjusting to keep pace. **Telecommunications** (the transmission of text, data, voice, video, and images electronically from one location to another) makes global communication possible as well as fast and affordable. Whether your company does business across the city or across the globe, these rapidly changing technologies will enable you to communicate and accomplish other work-related tasks more efficiently and effectively. They will also allow you to collaborate in new and interesting ways. Increased global communications and new technologies also bring increased security concerns. The etiquette developing around these technologies is important to know so you can communicate professionally when using them.

Computers

Computer technology is constantly progressing. It enables people to stay connected and to work faster and with great portability. Desktop and laptop computers continue to be common hardware for businesses. With increasing speed and computing power, they remain useful, convenient, powerful, and affordable for almost any industry or organization. While the *Windows* operating system is used the most in businesses around the world, Apple computers are used more frequently in certain industries, such as those involving graphic design.

Mobile Devices

Mobile devices such as smartphones, tablet computers, and intelligent mobile hotspots offer the administrative professional portability and productivity options. Mobile applications can be used to enhance and customize these devices.

TABLET COMPUTERS

Portability in the world of computers is changing rapidly. With the release of tablet computers, such as the Apple iPad tablet or comparable systems from Blackberry, Dell, and Acer, information can be distributed to and received from almost anywhere and in almost any form. These computers are small, with screens usually no larger than 10 inches.

Tablet computers can help you be more productive and mobile. For example, a recent iPad tablet connects to a digital projector or TV for quick and convenient presentations using apps installed on the device or presentation software such as the *Keynote®* or *PowerPoint* application programs.

Some tablet computers may need to be synced with a laptop or desktop computer to update operating system software or to add programs and information. Maintaining a tablet may be one of your duties as an administrative professional.

SMARTPHONES

A **smartphone** is a full-featured cellular phone with many of the functions of a handheld computer. It combines a cell phone with functions that were once available only on a personal digital assistant (a handheld device), such as Internet access, e-mail, and file storage. In addition to typical telephone features, smartphones may include a camera, a video camera, and a variety of mobile applications, such as contact management and scheduling software, e-mail, and Internet access. Smartphone operating systems (such as the *Apple* and *Android* operating systems) enable touch-screen technology.

The administrative professional with a smartphone can be readily accessible and productive away from the office. However, constant connectivity has both advantages and disadvantages, and it should be intentionally managed for maximum productivity.

PRNewsFoto/Verizon Wireless/AP Photo

An intelligent mobile hotspot is a traveling Internet connection.

INTELLIGENT MOBILE HOTSPOTS

An **intelligent mobile hotspot** is essentially a traveling Internet connection. Available through a mobile telecommunications company, the intelligent mobile hotspot is a small wireless router that gives mobile broadband Internet access through a cellular network. Some smartphones are equipped with a personal intelligent mobile hotspot feature, which can allow up to five other devices (such as a laptop, tablet computer, or other device that can access the Internet wirelessly) to share the phone's Internet connection.

Smartphone Safety

Paying bills by phone (also referred to as mobile payments), banking by phone, checking in for a flight, posting on a social network, maintaining blogs, and accessing files remotely are all examples of actions possible on a smartphone. The availability and use of these types of activities is increasing. This means smartphones are more at risk than ever before from hackers or thieves who attempt to defraud people. Take these precautions if you have a smartphone:

- Create a password for access to your phone, and keep your phone locked.
- Have good, reliable antivirus protection.
- Consult your bank for any antitheft protection features you can enable.
- If possible, use a remote wipeout service (such as MobileMe®) so you can delete the contents of your phone if it is stolen.
- Always log out of banking apps or websites.
- Treat your smartphone as if it were a wallet or purse—don't leave it lying around on your desk or on the seat of your unoccupied car. Keep it locked in a drawer or on your person.

Supri Suharjoto/Shutterstock.com

MOBILE APPLICATIONS

A **mobile application** (app) is software that runs on a handheld device or computer. Mobile apps abound for smartphones and tablet computers, and they are also available for desktop and laptop computers running *Lion* or *Snow Leopard*® operating system software. With mobile apps, an administrative professional always has up-to-date yellow pages, weather, and directions available. Common applications for administrative professionals include scheduling, file storage, maps, note-taking, presentation, spreadsheet, and word processing applications.

Social Networking Sites

Social networking sites allow people with common interests to connect to one another. Used personally, they provide the opportunity to stay in touch with friends and family and to share photos, videos, and thoughts. Social networks are truly global since anyone with an Internet connection and access to a social networking site can connect with others around the world.

Some social networking sites, such as LinkedIn and BranchOut, have professional rather than personal uses. Chapter 2 suggested ways that you as an administrative professional might use a professional networking site: for instance, to develop and maintain a network of professional contacts and to look for additional business opportunities.

The lines between personal and professional networking frequently overlap. For example, you may have "friends" on Facebook who are colleagues or clients, and you may have contacts on LinkedIn who are neighbors or friends from a social club or church. Your business may use Facebook to advertise, send out notices, or inform clients about new products. You might be asked to work with both types of sites to monitor or maintain the company's social network presence, find candidates for a job opening, maintain advertising, or report on industry or business news.

Since social and professional identities intersect, it is an individual responsibility to recognize the permanency of all social media as well its comprehensive nature. Remember that, in your online presence, you should always consider the professional image you portray. For example, you would not want to post anything on your personal Facebook page that would reflect negatively on you or your employer or reveal confidential information such as the post, They've cut the year-end bonuses–I wonder if we're going under. Similarly, keep in mind that too much personal information posted on a professional network such as LinkedIn is not appropriate.

VoIP

Voice over Internet Protocol (VoIP), sometimes called Internet phone service, is the transmitting of voice over the Internet. Basically, a traditional phone shares an Internet connection with a computer by use of a converter that translates analog phone signals to digital signals that can travel over the Internet. While using traditional phones is one option, there is also the option to use VoIP without a telephone. Software and services such as Skype make it possible to call another computer and chat with audio, video, and/or text.

Businesses use VoIP instead of or in conjunction with traditional land telephone lines. VoIP is a way to save money on long-distance calls but isn't considered quite as reliable as a landline. With VoIP you are also susceptible to computer viruses, worms, and voice-messaging spam attacks.

VoIP with video gives businesses a way to see clients or collaborators and to have face-to-face meetings or conferences. This option is very inexpensive and easy to set up. It requires the use of a computer with high-speed Internet access, a webcam, and a microphone.

Web Conferencing

Holding a conference via the Internet is known as **web conferencing**. The technology often includes VoIP for the synchronous audio portion. High-speed Internet is required, and a microphone and webcam must be installed on the computer. Web conferencing allows people to share application files (such as a *Word* document or *PowerPoint* presentation), poll participants, and interact using audio, video, and text.

Web conferencing is often an attractive option for companies since it eliminates the need for travel in many situations, saving travel costs as well as time. Web conferencing is also frequently used for training employees or holding meetings with individuals who are off-site. Some organizations do not maintain offices but have employees work from home and meet using web conferencing software or VoIP technology such as Skype.

Instant Messaging and Text Messaging

Instant messaging (IM) is the sending and receiving of messages over a network instantly in real time. In addition to text messaging, IM features

Virtual Office Professional

A **virtual office professional** (VOP), also known as a virtual assistant, provides administrative assistance to one or more clients on a contractual basis from a remote location. For example, John, an independent real estate agent, uses a VOP (Sheila) to help manage the details of his business. She creates publications, places orders, prepares contracts, and performs other duties as they arise. Sheila works out of her home and does not live in the area.

VOP is a rapidly growing field that offers many exciting and desirable opportunities. VOPs are independent business owners, and they enjoy the flexibility this status provides. For instance, VOPs can work from home, choose their assignments, and set their own schedules. They can serve clients globally and work in a range of different fields. Many VOPs work as author's assistants, handle social media for a client, and arrange meetings. Others specialize in areas such as real estate, legal services, receptionist duties, and transcription. Several professional organizations support and promote VOPs, such as the International Virtual Assistants Association (IVAA).

VOPs must be proficient in basic computer technology and willing to learn new technology as needed. They must also have excellent communication skills, especially in communicating by e-mail and preparing written documents. An effective VOP needs to be well organized, be a self-starter, have an excellent work ethic, be able to plan work effectively, and be proficient in determining expectations and monitoring progress and performance on tasks.

Photodisc/Jupiter Images

To be successful as an administrative professional, you must stay current with technological advances. Follow these pointers to learn about new technology:

- Read articles in computer journals and magazines.
- Enroll in technology-related continuing education courses or workshops.
- Learn from others about the software they use.
- Visit computer retail stores to observe hardware and software demonstrations.
- Take online software tutorials.

include voice chat, video, and file sharing. Typically, IM is used when the response time of e-mail is not fast enough or when a quick exchange of technical or specific information is needed. While there are many types of IM clients, they all function in a similar manner.

Many businesses have adopted IM because it:

- Allows them to communicate both internally and externally with clients around the world.
- Encourages people to work together as delays associated with e-mail and voice mail are eliminated.
- Facilitates group communication and messaging since it allows you to broadcast messages to groups of people.
- Enables quicker and often more complete answers to customer queries (since writing allows you to think longer about a topic than speaking).
- Allows others to join a dialog if needed.
- Eases communication with off-site employees or consultants because it is considered more personal than e-mail and less intrusive than the telephone.

Short message service (SMS), also known as text messaging, is the ability to send and receive short text messages through telecommunications channels. Most messages are limited to 160 alphabetic and numeric characters and, depending on the account and equipment, can contain images or graphics.

Although the most common application of SMS is personal messaging from one individual to another, SMS is used in business as well. Text messages are often used to interact with automated business systems, as when ordering products and services or responding to a survey or poll. Salespeople may use SMS to contact clients, or businesses may use it to remind clients of appointments. An administrative professional could use text messaging to remind attendees of an upcoming meeting and list what they should bring.

Cloud Computing

Cloud computing is the use of computer services from virtual servers available on demand over the Internet. This growing trend allows consumers to purchase only the computer services they need or actually use, similar to paying for only the electricity you use from the power company. Cloud computing is a broad term that can encompass many different aspects of computing for the IT department at an organization—such as software applications, hardware infrastructure, e-mail systems, and file storage. For administrative professionals, one of the primary uses of cloud computing is file storage.

PARTNERSHIP FOR 21ST CENTURY SKILLS

Information, Communications, and Technology Literacy

Apply Technology Effectively

Because technology is such an important tool for administrative professionals, you need skills not only in using it but in discerning which technologies will work best for the tasks you do.

1. **Know what is available.** Use your company IT department as a resource. For example, Susan edits PDF documents frequently. She learns from her IT department that the professional version of the *Adobe® Acrobat®* software makes editing quicker and easier. Visit news websites for daily technology updates. Read blogs and visit other websites that report on new business technologies.
2. **Compare what you do to what is available.** Just because a new technology is out there doesn't mean you need to use it. First, examine what you do, and then consider what technology accomplishes that task. It isn't "How can I use this new technology in my job?" but "What do I currently do, and is there a technology that could help me do it better?" For example, accounting software was introduced as a tool to accomplish an already-established task.
3. **Be eager and willing to learn new technologies.** Keep an open mind, and be ready when change comes.
4. **Be a problem solver.** Susan does several on-site inventory reviews each month. Through the technology news source she reads weekly, she learns about an iPad app that will enable her to fill out inventory forms in PDF format while on-site—eliminating her doing the work twice when she has to transfer written notes to PDF. The app will also allow her to attach pictures and audio explanations to an inventory in case of discrepancies or needed reminders.

Activity

Susan's supervisor has asked her to take notes at off-site meetings and e-mail them to him. He doesn't want an audio recording, just an outline of what was discussed and decided. He wants it almost immediately. What technology do you recommend that Susan use to accomplish this task? Discuss your ideas in a small group.

File storage "in the cloud" through services such as Dropbox or SugarSync eliminates the need for constantly backing up, copying, and transferring files with flash drives. With smartphones and a mobile device such as the iPad, you always have all your files available to you. These files can also be shared with others easily. For example, suppose you are assisting with registration at a conference away from work. Your supervisor e-mails you that she cannot find the latest copy of the departmental budget. You receive the e-mail on your smartphone. Using your smartphone, you access your file storage app and e-mail her the link to the budget. It takes you less than five minutes.

Web 2.0

Web 2.0 simply means web resources that are interactive. For example, consider a simple web page that gives you information, and then consider a web page that gives you information along with the ability to comment (such as a blog), add information (like Wikipedia), or give opinions in a poll or vote. These last examples are Web 2.0 applications.

As you learned in Chapter 5, the term *wiki* is the Hawaiian word for *quick*, and a wiki is a quick web page that can be collaborative. Wikis are an excellent way for businesses to provide information quickly, inexpensively, and easily. For example, an administrative professional may create a wiki to disseminate information to other administrative professionals about how to process new claims information. The wiki could be made private so that only the administrative professionals in that company would have access to it, and it could also be shared so certain people would be able to edit and add information.

Blogs (Chapter 1 Tech Talk) are another example of a Web 2.0 tool. Information is presented, and others can interact through comments. You may wish to subscribe to blogs to stay current in technology or learn about software updates, office procedures, time management skills, or other areas that pertain to your job.

Technology Issues

Individuals and organizations rely on computers to create, store, and manage critical information. Keeping that information secure yet accessible is a continual challenge. All employees are responsible for taking steps to prevent the loss or misuse of company information. The administrative professional often has special responsibility for certain confidential and sensitive information, such as personnel, client, or financial data. Protecting oneself from identity theft is another technology issue.

Security

It is important to make the information on your computer and network secure. There are a variety of ways you can accomplish this. The first step is to recognize the security threats that exist. Then you can take the steps necessary to protect your hardware and software.

SECURITY THREATS

A **computer virus** is a program that attaches itself to files or software so it can spread to other files or programs and destroy or interfere with computer operations. It cannot be spread to a computer unless a user opens a file or runs a program that has the virus attached. Viruses are often transmitted when you open a file you receive through e-mail or when you open a file on a flash drive.

A **worm** is a malicious, self-replicating program similar to a computer virus in design, but unlike a virus, it does not need human interaction to propagate. For example, a worm could send an infected e-mail to everyone in your e-mail address book. Worms are not limited to e-mail programs. They can also be acquired though instant messaging programs, chat rooms, and shared network folders. Worms can delete files, transmit data, or create a secret electronic entrance into a network.

Another computer threat is the Trojan horse. A **Trojan horse** is malicious software designed to look like something interesting or useful. Unlike worms and viruses, a Trojan horse does not self-replicate or reproduce by attaching to other files. Trojan horses may appear harmless, such as a free game or a movie or song file, but they are harmful when executed. Like viruses, Trojan horses are most often spread through e-mail attachments. Be wary of opening any attachment sent via e-mail, especially if it is from someone you do not know. Trojan horses can erase, corrupt, or overwrite data on a computer, upload and download files, log keystrokes to steal information such as passwords, or allow remote access to a computer.

An additional computer security threat is unauthorized access. Although unauthorized access can take place in several ways, it is most often perpetrated by a hacker. A *hacker* is an individual who uses his or her computer knowledge to break into computer systems and delete, steal, or alter files. The motivation for hacking is to steal information, sabotage a computer, or perform some other illegal act.

Advertising-supported software (adware) is software that displays advertising. It can be installed on your computer without your knowledge, when you click a pop-up advertisement, for example. Most adware can also be considered **spyware** because, once installed on your computer, it tracks

TECH TALK

VoiceThread

VoiceThread is a web resource useful in business for training, collaborative presentations, and asynchronous meetings. It is a multimedia tool that allows conversations around different types of media, such as images, documents, or video.

Because VoiceThread allows comments to be added "around" media, it offers a warm and personal option for relaying information for training purposes or for any situation in which material needs to be presented asynchronously. Comments can be in the form of audio, video (webcam), and text. It is also possible to annotate (write or mark on an image) while making a comment. Sharing options allow presentations to be public or private. Presentations can be shared among team members, with different members adding media and making comments.

Businesses use VoiceThread for just-in-time training (training just when it's needed) for employees, advertising, collaborating with colleagues, and getting feedback from clients or staff. The figure below shows a medium (in this case, an image) and, on the left, an icon that represents a comment. Presentations can be started and stopped at the viewer's discretion.

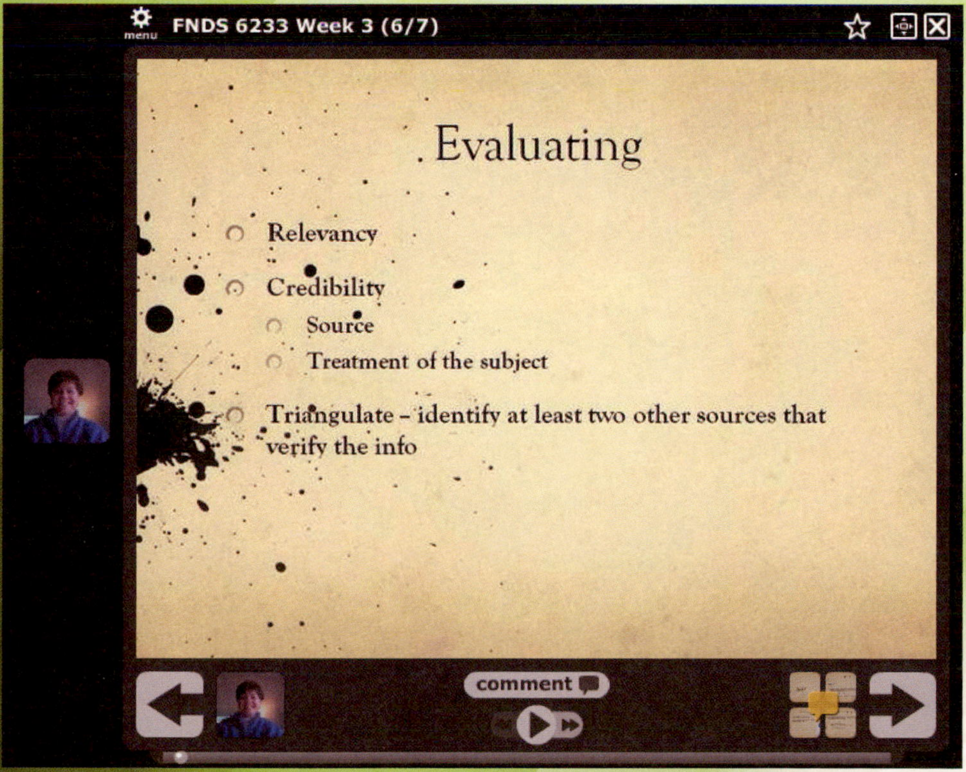

the websites you view and possibly other information about you. Besides invading your privacy, spyware slows down your computer, sometimes to the point where it can barely function, because it is constantly sending data to the originator. Common sources of spyware are free programs you may download and peer-to-peer file-sharing programs.

Peer-to-peer (P2P) file sharing is a system of sharing files on an informal network with other users who have the same software (a common use of P2P file sharing is downloading music). Files are directly transferred from one computer to another without using a server. This practice is not without risks. You could share files with others that you never intended to share, and you could inadvertently download computer viruses, spyware, copyrighted material, and pornography. The Digital Millennium Copyright Act (DMCA) prohibits the distribution of copyrighted materials (music, games, videos, etc.) from your computer without the owner's permission.

Do not install P2P file-sharing software on your work computer unless authorized to do so by your organization's IT person or department. Since businesses store sensitive and confidential information on company networks, the Federal Trade Commission offers guidelines and security information for businesses that wish to either use or ban P2P networks.

SECURITY SOLUTIONS

You can protect your computer in a number of ways. Having reputable software that provides virus and spyware protection is essential. You must also be cautious and make wise decisions when maintaining your computer, storing information, and sharing information with others.

Antivirus software, such as *McAfee AntiVirus Plus* or *Norton AntiVirus*, can be used to combat the threats and annoyances caused by computer viruses. *Antivirus software* is a utility program that protects against, detects, and removes viruses from a computer's memory or storage devices. Typically, antivirus software scans incoming e-mail for hidden threats and alerts users to attempts to infect the computer when they are surfing the web. Many programs also provide protection against spyware and spam. Some programs test websites for security and display the ratings next to each result of an Internet search. Figure 10.1 shows a window from McAfee SecurityCenter.

Because new viruses and other computer threats are continually being developed, it is important to

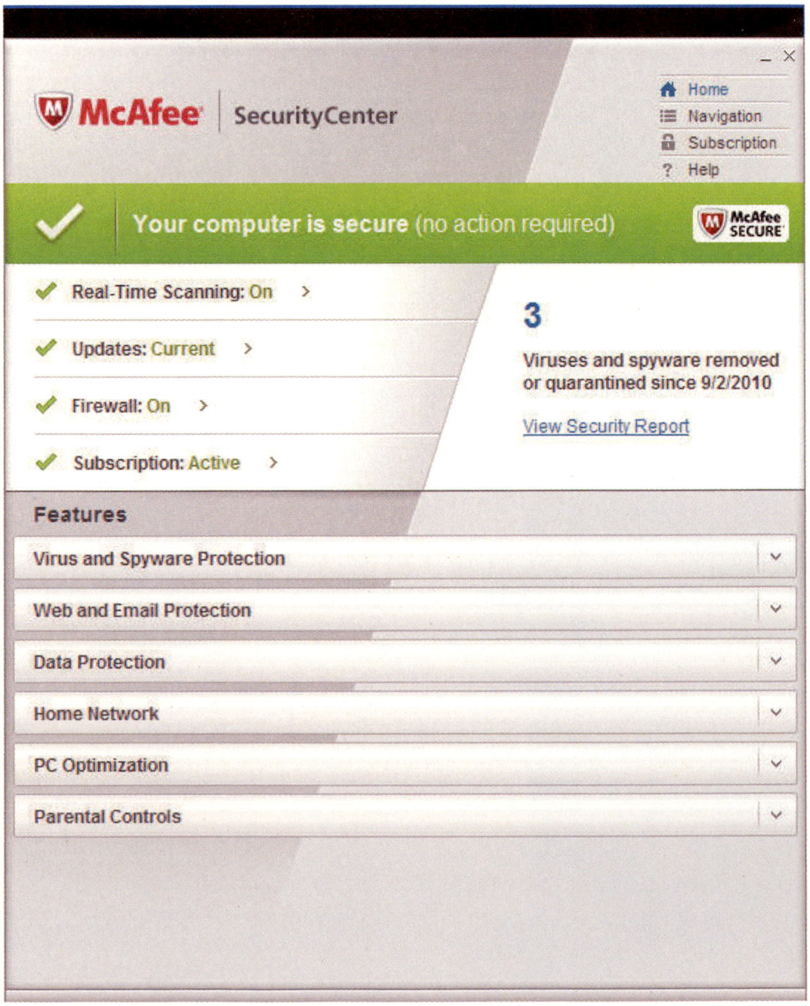

FIGURE 10.1 Antivirus programs provide essential computer protection.

keep your antivirus software up-to-date. Most antivirus software checks for and installs updates automatically and automatically scans your entire computer system, both at intervals of your choosing. Take advantage of these automatic features to protect your computer and save yourself time and work.

To protect your computer against spyware and other unauthorized uses, make sure you are using a **firewall** (software that monitors information as it enters and leaves the computer). A firewall may come with your operating system, and antivirus software usually includes a firewall as well.

It is important to back up important information regularly and to carefully store the backup copy in case the data on your computer are lost or corrupted. If your organization does not have a system for backing up files automatically, you can back up files manually in a number of ways, such as copying them to a CD or flash drive. Take these additional practical steps to protect your computer and keep your data secure:

- Make sure your e-mail program is not set to open attachments automatically.
- Only click links or open attachments in e-mail from people you know.
- Never respond to an e-mail that asks for your password or user ID. Report it to your network administrator.
- Don't save e-mail that contains sensitive information. If your account is hacked, you don't want others to have access to that information. Empty your trash and sent folders periodically.
- Be very selective about what you download.
- Use effective passwords.
- Log off your computer or network, or lock your computer before leaving your desk, to prevent unauthorized users from accessing information.

Creating Effective Passwords

- Create passwords that are at least eight characters long.
- Do not use words that can be found in the dictionary.
- Use a combination of uppercase and lowercase letters, numbers, and special characters when possible.
- Do not use the same password for everything.
- Do not use personal information, such as a name, nickname, or pet's name.

Identity Theft

In addition to safeguarding information for your company, you must also take steps to protect your own personal information. *Identity theft* is the act of stealing personal information. Spyware is one means of stealing personal information through computers. Another common method of attempting to steal personal information is **phishing**. In a phishing scam, online criminals send spam that looks as though it is from a legitimate financial institution or business, such as a bank, requesting credit card numbers, Social Security numbers, or other personal information. The e-mail may be dressed up with company logos and contact information to make it look legitimate. It may contain a link that appears to be to the institution's website.

These steps can help protect your identity online:

- Never respond to e-mails requesting personal information.
- Do not click a link in a suspect message.
- Use effective passwords.
- Obtain a personal credit check periodically. Consumers are entitled to one free copy of their credit report annually from each of the three nationwide credit bureaus: Equifax, Experian, and TransUnion. Reports may be requested from AnnualCreditReport.com.

If you believe your identity has been stolen, file a fraud alert with one of the three credit bureaus, file a police report so you can provide proof to your creditors, and report the theft to the Federal Trade Commission. If access to your financial information has been compromised, report the theft to your bank immediately.

Technology Etiquette

It is important to be aware of society's expectations for how to behave when using technology. New and evolving technologies often change the way we operate in the workplace or in our personal lives. For example, almost everyone has a cell phone and is continually connected with friends, relatives, and work colleagues. This fact has changed the way people view connectivity and how we function on a day-to-day basis. People have their phones with them at all times—talking while waiting at the post office or setting an appointment while walking back to work from lunch. Because the lines of business and personal use are often blurred, you must make an intentional effort to ensure your use of technology is always professional.

StockLite/Shutterstock.com

Always be aware of your surroundings and respect the rights of others when using your cell phone in public.

Mobile Phone Etiquette

When using a mobile phone for business, you should follow the telephone etiquette guidelines discussed in Chapter 9, such as always being polite and professional, using a pleasant voice, and being attentive. However, because mobile phones may be used in many different places and situations, some additional considerations apply:

- Maintain ringer settings that are as low as possible.
- Turn your cell phone off or use vibrate or silent settings when attending a meeting, seminar, class, or other event.
- When in a meeting, do not use your cell phone to read or send e-mail, text, or play games.
- Make calls only when absolutely necessary when in public places such as restaurants or elevators.
- If an expected call cannot be avoided, alert your companions ahead of time and excuse yourself when the call comes. If you are in a meeting, set the phone to vibrate, and sit near the door so you can leave quietly.
- Keep your phone voice as low as possible.
- Keep calls short if you are with someone else.
- Do not discuss private matters or sensitive topics unless you are in private.
- If you walk and talk on your mobile phone, be aware of your surroundings, and respect the rights of others.

Instant Messaging Etiquette

To present a professional image, you must follow some basic rules of etiquette when using IM for business purposes:

- Pay attention to status indicators (busy and away indicators), and allow the individual to answer before posing another question. Update your status indicators as appropriate.
- Make your message concise.

- Do not write anything in an IM that you would not write in an e-mail or a printed letter. Do not use instant messages to be confrontational, criticize a colleague, or reprimand an employee.
- Use professional writing conventions such as correct capitalization and spelling. Avoid jargon, abbreviations, acronyms, and emoticons.
- Consider cultural differences. Reflect on what you are saying as well as how it might impact the other person. If you do not understand something that has been said, politely ask the sender to repeat it.
- Be courteous. In an effort to be concise, do not be curt or rude. Review the "C" characteristics of effective communication in Chapter 8.

E-Mail Etiquette

E-mail was discussed in detail in Chapter 8, "Written Communication." Here are some etiquette tips for using e-mail to communicate:

- Do not forward a message if you are not certain the original sender would want it forwarded.
- Always use a subject line that is brief and that clearly indicates the topic of the e-mail.
- Answer e-mail on the day sent if possible.
- Contact the receiver before sending a large attachment. Not all e-mail servers can handle them.
- When forwarding, place your comments at the top of the message.
- Before you begin to write, consider if the message is really necessary.
- Make messages clear and concise to minimize the time required to read and understand.
- Take a last look before sending to ensure your message is courteous and considerate.

SUMMARY

To reinforce what you have learned in this chapter, study this summary.

- Telecommunications makes global communications fast and affordable. With new and evolving technologies, administrative professionals can communicate more efficiently and effectively.
- Security threats to an organization's computers and network are inevitable, and identity theft is also a concern. You can reduce risks by using antivirus software, being cautious, and making wise decisions on maintaining your computer and handling information.
- Be aware of what is considered proper behavior when using communications technologies. Understand and use appropriate etiquette for cell phones, instant messaging, and e-mail.

KEY TERMS

advertising-supported software (adware), 216
cloud computing, 214
computer virus, 216
firewall, 219
intelligent mobile hotspot, 210
mobile application, 211
peer-to-peer (P2P) file sharing, 218
phishing, 219
smartphone, 210
spyware, 216
telecommunications, 209
Trojan horse, 216
virtual office professional, 213
Voice over Internet Protocol, 212
Web 2.0, 215
web conferencing, 212
worm, 216

10

STUDY Tools

Located at www.cengagebrain.com

- Chapter Outlines
- Flashcards
- Interactive Quizzes
- Tech Tools
- Video Segments
- and More!

LET'S DISCUSS

1. What global communications devices do you see used most in the workplace?
2. Explain how portability in computer technology could be helpful in business.
3. How will you keep your smartphone safe while at work?
4. What are mobile applications?
5. Can social networks be used for business? Explain your answer.
6. Describe some instances when you might use or have used web conferencing.
7. What is cloud computing?
8. What is the difference between a computer virus and a worm? What is the difference between adware and spyware?
9. Identify ways you can protect your files and identity.
10. Describe the proper etiquette to follow when using a mobile phone in public.

PUT IT TO WORK

Password chaos Recently your company hired five new administrative professionals. As you assist with some of the training on the organization's database and e-mail systems, you are aware of their passwords. So far these new employees have used a phone number, street address, street name, pet's name, and child's name as their passwords. At your next training session, you plan to have a short discussion about password security. What should you tell these naive employees? (Learning Objective 2)

COMMUNICATE SUCCESSFULLY

1. **Web conferencing** Using the Internet, research different web conferencing options for a small company. Find out the equipment and software requirements as well as the price. Be prepared to give a short report of your findings to the class. Some possible options are listed in the chapter links on the textbook website. (Learning Objective 1)
2. **Etiquette** Briefly explain the proper etiquette in the following situations: (a) You are standing in line at the post office when your supervisor calls you on your cell phone. It is important that you talk with him. (b) You expect an important personal phone call, but you need to attend a meeting with three colleagues. (c) You are having lunch with a friend from work, and your cell phone rings. You may offer multiple solutions if appropriate. (Learning Objective 3)

3. **Global communication skills** Add a new post to the blog you created in Chapter 1. In this entry, reflect on the following question: **How do I currently use my global communication skills, and what skills can I improve?** (Learning Objective 1)

Blog

DEVELOP WORKPLACE SKILLS

4. **Mobile apps** From your own experience or by researching them on the Internet, explore free mobile apps that would be helpful for the administrative professional. Which mobile apps do you see or hear of others using? Make a list. (Learning Objective 1)
5. **Memo** Using the information you found in the previous activity, write a memo to your supervisor, Robert Valido, about a mobile app you believe would be helpful in the workplace (you select the type of workplace). Explain the purpose of the app, its advantages, and how it can be used at work. Option: Instead of a memo, create a flyer about the mobile app. (Learning Objective 1)
6. **Cloud computing** Lilly Watkins is an administrative professional who works from home as well as at several other locations besides her company office. She uses laptop and desktop computers, an iPad, and a smartphone. Several times Lilly has inadvertently left an important file on her desktop computer and later discovered she needed it when she was at home. Research file storage options for Lilly in the cloud. In *Word*, make a table of at least three options with information about storage limits and pricing for each option. Choose one of *Word's* preformatted tables for the design. (Learning Objective 1)

BUILD RELATIONSHIPS

7. **Virtual office professional** You and two or three of your classmates have decided you want to be virtual office professionals and form a business together. As a team, develop a plan to use technology to connect with your clients. Describe the equipment and software you might need for a variety of communication methods. (Learning Objectives 1 and 2)

USE TECH TOOLS

8. **Brochure** Create a brochure to distribute to all employees at your company that stresses the importance of professional behavior when using a cell phone, instant messaging, and e-mail. Use a *Word* template if possible, and ensure the formatting is attractive. Use bulleted lists and graphics. Add this document to your online portfolio. (Learning Objective 3)

e-Portfolio

9. **VoiceThread introduction** With a classmate, watch one of the VoiceThread tutorials linked on the textbook website. Next, create a VoiceThread together with one slide contributed by each team member that introduces the other member. Each slide will contain media chosen by the team member who created it (such as an image, a video, or a *PowerPoint* slide) along with a comment (using any method of commenting) introducing the partner. (Learning Objective 1)

PLAN AHEAD

VoiceThread project Choose one of the following options:

- You are an administrative professional in a small law firm. You have been assigned to help train a new administrative professional who will join the office team next month. It's important that he know proper technology etiquette, since this law firm is highly visible in a small community. Working with a classmate, create a VoiceThread for training purposes. (Learning Objectives 1 and 3)
- Form a team with several classmates and create a VoiceThread about smartphones (including a picture, advantages/disadvantages, features, and costs). One person should create the VoiceThread, and then all members should contribute media (such as images or files) and comments. You should have one smartphone example per teammate; each teammate should upload the media and make comments for his or her smartphone. Suggestion: Each person makes one *PowerPoint* slide with all the information and then uploads it to the group VoiceThread. (Learning Objectives 1 and 2)
- Form a team and create an informative VoiceThread presentation on any instructor-approved topic from this chapter.

PART
4

Records and Financial Management

Purestock/Jupiter Images

CAREER PROFILE

Visit www.cengagebrain.com to listen to the complete interview.

Executive Assistant

Stacey Brewer is an executive assistant at Redstone Federal Credit Union in Huntsville, Alabama, and a Certified Administrative Professional (IAAP).

What do you do in your job?
I provide administrative support to four vice presidents, their managers, and departments.

What are your biggest challenges?
I support many people—different personalities, responsibilities—it's difficult sometimes juggling those and determining priority. I do things that aren't as traditional in the administrative role—travel, project management, budgeting, strategic planning.

What are your major responsibilities?
I'm responsible for schedule management. I handle correspondence. I do reporting for branches on sales, financials, that sort of thing. I also do event planning and customer/member relations.

How have previous administrative professional positions helped you advance in your career?
Prior to being an executive assistant, I was an administrative assistant. It helped me understand more about the administrative profession, what it meant to support an executive.

How important are computer skills?
Computer skills are essential. I use *Outlook*, *Word*, *Excel*, *PowerPoint*. It's very important that I have a fast typing speed as well as good verbal and written communication skills. I need to ensure I'm using proper grammar, spelling, and punctuation, especially since I'm writing on behalf of executives.

What is the benefit of membership in a professional organization?
It provides a networking opportunity. You can share experiences, best practices. It also provides professional development in the form of training, leadership opportunities—it helps you stay up-to-date on trends, skill sets, and what's going on in the profession.

Glenn W Campbell Photography

What is the value of professional certification?
Professional certification sets you apart. It shows you are a trained professional and have the skills necessary to do your job.

CHAPTER

11 Managing Records

LEARNING OBJECTIVES

1. Understand the importance of managing records.
2. Describe the considerations in managing paper records.
3. Apply the alphabetic filing rules.
4. Describe the types of records storage systems.

© Photographer/Image Source

Importance of Records Management

To be successful, businesses and organizations rely on current, accurate, and accessible information so appropriate decisions can be made. In business, information is received in many ways. Letters, memorandums, and e-mails are sent and received from clients and customers. Meeting minutes, reports, accounting records, and inventories are created within an organization. Newspaper articles, journal articles, and marketing materials are also part of business records. The amount of information a business handles can be overwhelming unless it is managed effectively. Managing information is an important part of an administrative professional's duties.

Business Records

A **record** is information that is evidence of an event, activity, or business transaction, created or received by an organization and stored on any medium. For example, information may be:

- Written and recorded on paper such as a printed document.
- Written and recorded in electronic form such as an e-mail message or spreadsheet or database file.

- Produced and stored on electronic media or microfilm, such as images, photographs, sound records, or movies.

Records are assets to a business just as products and services, management expertise, and a good reputation are assets. Some records are important because they provide a history of the business. Other records document current events and trends. Successful organizations use the information contained in records to make decisions and plans. Records have value in four areas:

- Legal value by providing evidence of business transactions
- Financial value by supplying information needed in audits and for tax purposes
- Historical value by documenting specific business activities and events
- Day-to-day operational value by providing information necessary to conduct business

Figure 11.1 lists examples of records in each of these areas.

Records Life Cycle

Because records are valuable to an organization, they must be properly managed. **Records management** is the systematic control of records from creation or receipt to final disposition. Receipt of the record to final disposition is considered the records life cycle. This life cycle has five distinct phases:

1. Creation or receipt of the record
2. Distribution of the record to internal or external users
3. Use of the record (for making decisions, determining directions, and so on)
4. Maintenance of the record (filing and retrieving)
5. Disposition (retaining or destroying the record after a period of time)

A major error in managing records is to assume every piece of paper is a record worth keeping. To be classified as a record, an item must have value to the organization. Documents that have no continuing value to the organization are not considered records and should not be kept. These documents should be discarded after they are read or the information is no longer needed. For example, an e-mail message that states the time for a meeting will have no value after the meeting has taken place. After the event the message can be discarded. Records retention, transfer, and disposal are discussed in Chapter 12, "Managing Electronic Records."

Value of Records	
Area	**Examples**
Legal	Articles of incorporation, contracts, deeds
Financial	Budgets, balance sheets, income statements, receipts for travel and equipment purchases, bank statements
Historical	Employee evaluations, payroll records, job termination records, patient histories
Daily Operations	Policy and procedures manuals, organizational charts, meeting minutes, sales reports, production reports

FIGURE 11.1 Importance of Records in Organizations

Effective Systems

The administrative assistant may be responsible not only for maintaining existing files but for designing and installing records systems. In planning an effective records system, three factors must always be considered: findability, confidentiality, and safety.

FINDABILITY

The most important criterion for judging a records management system is findability. If a record cannot be located when needed, it has no value. Think of file folders as places to find materials, not just places to put materials. Before determining where to file an item, consider these questions:

- How will this information be requested?
- How can I most efficiently locate the information when it is needed later?

The ability to find electronic and paper records quickly is the most important criterion of any records system.

The system must allow any user to locate a record quickly. Regardless of whether the records are in paper or electronic form, the ability to find records in a timely manner is crucial.

CONFIDENTIALITY

Confidentiality is an important aspect of a records management system. Great care must be exercised to maintain the security of highly confidential information. Reasonable protection must also be exercised over less sensitive materials. When working with highly sensitive records, users are required to follow company policies designed specifically for handling confidential information. In some offices, a written request bearing the signature of a designated officer of the organization is required for release of certain classified or confidential records. In an electronic system, access is limited to those users who know the password or have been given access through a security system. In other instances, confidentiality of records may preclude users from removing them from the storage area.

SAFETY

The administrative professional is often responsible for the safety of records in the workplace. Many records are irreplaceable, and their loss would be extremely costly. Identity theft and privacy are also extremely important issues when discussing records safety. For these reasons, administrative professionals should pay careful attention to security.

Security measures protect records from improper access, accidental loss, theft, damage, and unwanted destruction. Detectors that can perceive changes in levels of light, heat, and air conditioning may be installed. These units can send electronic messages to notify staff when changes in the environment occur. Other sensors can recognize heat from fire and activate sprinkler systems as needed.

Many organizations improve the safety of their paper and electronic files by installing security systems. Traditional key-and-lock systems may be installed on important file cabinets, file shelves, or records storage rooms. Electronic keys, magnetic cards, or other electronic access devices may be installed to control and monitor access to storage areas. Biometric devices such as fingerprint or retinal scanners may also be used. Many of these devices also record an employee's name and the date and time of access.

Organizations frequently keep backup copies of their most important records in an off-site, secure location. These copies will be available if the original records are lost due to flood, fire, or some other cause.

Managing Physical Records

The selection and arrangement of records storage supplies and equipment depend on whether the organization's records management systems contain

PARTNERSHIP FOR 21ST CENTURY SKILLS

Information Literacy

Use and Manage Information

Most organizations have records that must be kept confidential. If you are working for an organization that develops or designs products, any research or new product innovation information must be kept from competitors. If you are working for a social service organization, client information must be kept private. If you work in the payroll department of your organization, you may have access to employee information that would not be appropriate to share. Although you may have access to confidential records to make decisions, do not abuse your rights and privileges by sharing that information inappropriately.

Some organizations' records are protected by federal laws. For example, if you accept a position in a health-related organization, it is likely that you will be expected to complete training on the HIPAA regulations. If you are employed in an educational institution, you must understand the FERPA guidelines. Similar laws protect the privacy of client information in legal offices, as well as company information and personal and financial data of employees and clients in many other types of businesses. In addition to federal guidelines, organizations have their own rules that govern the release and distribution of information to outside constituencies. Make sure you understand and implement appropriate records procedures to conform to applicable laws and to your organization's standards.

Activity

Contact a business or organization in your area or the records department at your school and ask about the records policies. How is the confidentiality of records protected? Are there laws or regulations that employees must follow? Write a short report that describes your findings.

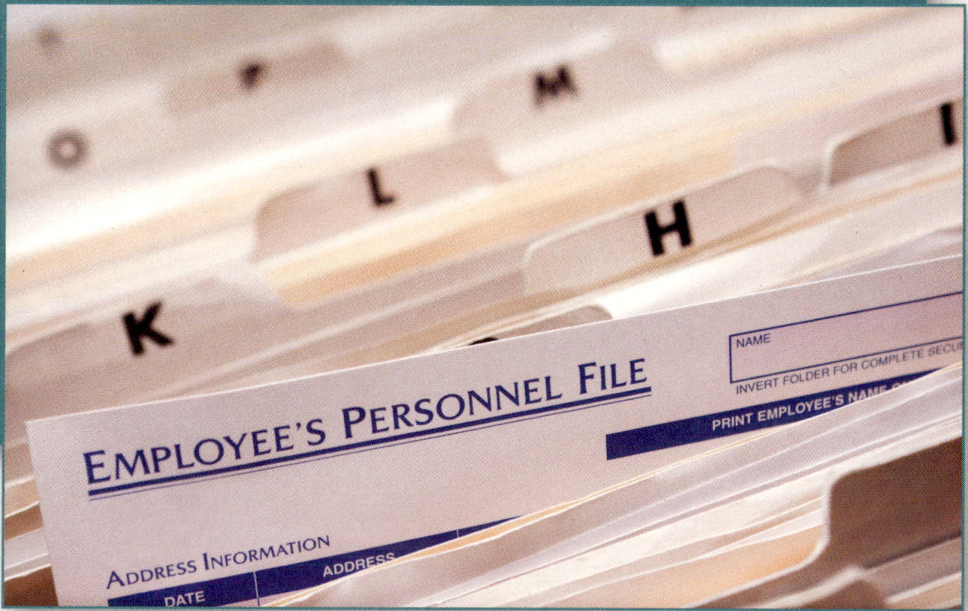

youngvet/iStockphoto.com

physical records, electronic records, or both. Physical records include items such as traditional paper documents including forms, correspondence, contracts, reports, and printouts of e-mail or web pages. Physical records also include microfilm rolls or sheets, films, videos, recordings, and photographs. Managing electronic records will be discussed in Chapter 12.

Basic Equipment and Supplies

Basic equipment and supplies for managing physical records include storage cabinets, file folders, file guides, and file folder labels.

STORAGE CABINETS

The conventional storage cabinet for physical records is a vertical file cabinet. In a vertical file system, the arrangement of folders in the file drawers is from front to back because the cabinet is deeper than it is wide. Vertical cabinets are available in one- to five-drawer designs; the most common vertical file has four drawers. Although they are most commonly found in standard letter size (8½ by 11 inches), they are also available in sizes to accommodate legal-sized records (8½ by 14 inches). Lateral files are similar to vertical files except the drawer rolls out sideways, exposing the entire contents of the file drawer at once. Less aisle space is needed for a lateral file than a vertical file because the drawers extend sideways.

Open shelf filing systems are used in many organizations because they can store many records in a minimal amount of space. In fact, open shelf files typically occupy 50 percent less floor space than drawer files having the same capacity. Open shelf files are simple shelving equipped with dividers. File folders are shelved like books; therefore records can be accessed quickly and easily. However, open shelf files are exposed to potential fire and water damage and should be kept in a fireproof room.

Many open shelf systems utilize moveable-aisle systems. Mobile systems consist of a series of shelving units that move on tracks attached to the floor or wheels attached to the bottom of the unit. Mobile systems are popular in instances where floor space is scarce or expensive.

Comstock Images/Jupiter Images

Open shelf files typically occupy 50 percent less floor space than drawer files having the same file capacity.

FILE FOLDERS

A file folder is a container used to hold and protect the records in a file. The most popular types of folders are manila folders and hanging folders. File folders are typically made of heavy cardstock or manila and are available in a variety of colors. Most folders have a tab, used for a caption that identifies the folder's contents. The tab is at the top of a folder used in filing cabinets and at the side of a folder used for open shelf filing.

The width of the tab is referred to as its cut. Folders are available in a variety of cuts including straight cut, one-half cut, one-third cut, and one-fifth cut. If the tab is one-fifth as wide as the folder, it is called a one-fifth cut tab. If the tab is half as wide as the folder, it is called a one-half cut tab.

Suspension folders are often used to hold several interior file folders to subdivide a file, and they provide additional support for holding records in a neat, upright position. Also called hanging folders, suspension folders have metal extensions that allow them to hang on file drawer frames. The

Professional POINTERS

You may have the opportunity to be involved in recommending, implementing, or expanding a records management system. If so, keep these steps in mind:

1. Define the filing needs. Know the types of records used, how long they are to be retained, who can have access, and the capacity needed for storage.
2. Conduct research. Based on your identified needs, collect recommendations from representatives of records supplies and systems firms. Solicit input on systems used in similar organizations.
3. Ensure everyone has adequate training on the system that is chosen.
4. Provide a list of the filing procedures/rules as a reference source for all individuals who have access to the files.
5. Evaluate the system periodically for efficiency and cost-effectiveness.

frame serves to support both the front and back of the folder with hooks on the drawer rails. Suspension folders are available in an assortment of colors. They have up to ten slots across the upper edge for placement of plastic tabs with insertable labels to identify the folder contents.

FILE GUIDES

A file guide is a rigid divider used to separate a file drawer into sections. Guides are usually made of heavy materials such as pressboard, manila, or plastic. A guide typically has a tab with a caption that contains a name, number, or letter representing a section in the file drawer. Depending on the storage system used, the tab may appear at the top or side edge of the guide. A guide may also contain one or more pockets suitable for holding small slips of paper or full-sized documents. Guides are always placed in front of the file folders. Guides for Sections A and B of an alphabetic file are shown in Figure 11.5 on page 248.

FILE FOLDER LABELS

Guides and folders must be labeled to draw the eye to the appropriate storage location. The label, usually paper or plastic, has a caption with the name, subject, number, or letter assigned to the file folder or section contents. The caption is a title, heading, short explanation, or description of a document or record. A label may also be color-coded or have a bar code to denote its place in an overall filing system.

Labels can be purchased as pressure-sensitive adhesive paper in continuous folded strips or on sheets. They can be white, colored, or white with a colored stripe across the top. Labels also can be prepared with computer software. Some computer programs have features to format standard label sizes. Using the software features makes creating and printing labels easy.

Be consistent when you key labels for files. Key captions in all capital letters with no punctuation as shown in Figure 11.5. In an alphabetic filing system, the section of the file (A, B, etc.) is keyed at the left of the folder label followed by the filing segment (name). Always key the name on the label in the correct indexing order. Indexing order is covered later in the chapter.

Paper Storage Procedures

Storing records is an important job that must be taken seriously. Replacing or locating a missing record can be costly to an organization in both time and money. Therefore, certain procedures should be followed before placing a record in the file. These steps include inspecting, indexing, coding, cross-referencing, and sorting documents.

INSPECTING

Incoming records must not be stored until they have been reviewed and acted upon. The process of checking a record to determine whether it is ready to be filed is called **inspecting**. The copy of an outgoing document is usually ready to be stored when it is received by the filer. However, before storing any incoming record, the filer should check for a release mark. A release mark is an agreed-upon mark such as initials, a stamp, or another symbol to show the record is ready for storage. The person who handled the document (prepared the reply or made a calendar notation) usually puts the release mark on the document. On the letter shown in Figure 11.2, the initials GM serve as the release mark. Sometimes records will be placed in the filing area by mistake. If there is no release mark, check to make sure the record is ready to be stored.

INDEXING

Indexing is the process of determining the filing segment to be used in storing. The **filing segment** is the name, subject, number, or geographic location by which a record is stored and requested. An alphabetic filing system uses names—Alma Foods or Boston Steel, for example. Other systems are discussed later in the chapter.

Although the rules for indexing may vary slightly from one business to another, most organizations use the indexing rules established by ARMA International, an association for information management professionals. Those rules are described in detail later in this chapter. Indexing is extremely important. Accurate indexing is essential for quick retrieval of information.

When selecting a name as a filing segment, choose the name most likely to be used in asking for the record. Use the following guidelines when indexing incoming correspondence in an alphabetic system:

- The name for storage purposes is usually on the letterhead.
- If a letterhead has no relationship with the contents of the letter, the writer's name or business connection is used. In this instance, the letterhead is disregarded for filing purposes. An example is a letter written on hotel stationery or plain paper when an executive is traveling.

2 3

Morency/Advertising/Agency

1240 Second Avenue | New York, NY 10065-1421 | 212-555-0146 | www.morencyad.com

September 24, 201-

SEPT 25, 201- 11:03 A.M.

Ms. Graciella Melena
Melena & Daughters, Inc.
600 E 52nd Street
New York, NY 10019-0185

GM

Dear Ms. Melena

1 2 3

Your ad with Kirkman/Products/Inc. is well underway. Executives at Kirkman are more than a little excited about the advertising tie-in with your company. We have a two-page ad for spring distribution we would like to share with you and Juan Ramos, the advertising director at Kirkman. X

FIGURE 11.2 This letter has a release mark and is coded for filing.

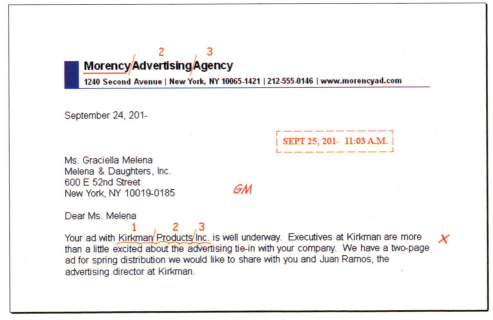

- Incoming correspondence on plain paper (paper without a letterhead) is usually personal and will be called for by the name in the signature line.
- When both the company name and the name of the writer seem to be of equal importance, the company name is used.

When indexing outgoing correspondence in an alphabetic system, follow these guidelines:

- The most important name on a file copy of an outgoing letter is usually the one in the letter address.
- When the letter address contains both a company name and the name of an individual, the company name is used for filing unless the letter is personal or unless a name in the body is the correct name to index.
- On a copy of a personal letter, the writer's name is usually the most important and should be used for storage.

CODING

For paper records, **coding** is the process of marking a record to indicate the filing segment and indexing units. The first step in coding paper records usually consists of placing diagonals (/) between the parts of the filing segment. The next step is to underline the first filing unit, or **key unit**. The key unit is the part of the segment considered first when determining where the record will be stored. The last step is to number each succeeding unit you identified in the indexing process. For example, the coded personal name *Raymond Thomas Johnson* would appear as follows:

2	3	
Raymond /	Thomas /	<u>Johnson</u>

The company name, Morency Advertising Agency, is coded on the letter shown in Figure 11.2. A name to be used as a cross-reference, Kirkman Products Inc., is also coded. You will learn about cross-references later in this chapter. Coding is important because it saves time in the filing and refiling process. When a document has been removed from the files and must be refiled, the user does not need to reread the document if it has been coded.

SORTING

Sorting is arranging records in the order in which they are to be stored (placed in filing cabinets or other storage containers). The records should be sorted as soon as possible after coding, especially if storage must be delayed. Typically records are sorted into a few groups and then into the final arrangement. The records are often sorted more than once. For example, in an alphabetic system, items may be arranged into groups of A to C, D to H, I to M, N to S, and T to Z. The last sorting consists of arranging the items in exact alphabetical order. When the last sort is complete, the materials are ready to be filed.

STORING

Storing is the process of placing the records into storage containers. Storing records correctly is very important. The time at which records are actually stored depends on the workload during the day. In some offices, storing is the job performed first in the morning; in others, storing is done when a lull in other work occurs. As you are accumulating documents for storage, keep them in order at your desk in case someone needs to refer to a record.

Before placing a document in a storage location, remove any paper clips used to keep pages together. Staple the pages together in the upper left corner. Paper clips often fall off in the files; if records that need to be kept together are not stapled, other records may be inserted between them by mistake. Steps in storing records will vary somewhat depending on the type of records storage system used. Follow these general steps to store records in an alphabetic filing system:

1. Locate the proper file drawer by reading the drawer labels.
2. Search through the guides in the drawer to find the needed alphabetic section of the file.
3. If an individual folder has been prepared for records with this name, place the record in the individual folder. Individual folders are used when several records with the same name are

placed in the file. Place records in the folder by date, with the most recent date in front. Place the front of the record facing the front of the folder and the top of the record at the left side.

4. If no individual folder has been prepared for this name, file the record in the general folder for that section. For example, if a coded name begins with *A* and there is no individual folder for the name, file the record in the A general folder. Arrange records in a general folder alphabetically by name. If two or more records have the same name, they are arranged by date with the most recent date in front. Place the front of the record facing the front of the folder and the top of the record at the left side.

Records Retrieval

In all records management systems, it is important to be able to retrieve records, retain them for their useful life, and transfer them to other locations in order to reduce the size of the active files. Retrieval of physical records is discussed here. Retrieval of electronic records and records retention are discussed in Chapter 12.

If a record is taken from a file, it is necessary to indicate what was taken, who has possession of the record, and when it was removed. It may also be helpful to indicate when the record will be returned. Procedures using requisition forms, OUT guides, and OUT folders provide a system for tracking records when they are taken from the files.

A requisition form includes a space for identifying the record borrowed, the name and location of the borrower, data about the borrowed record, and the date the record is to be returned to the files. This form may be prepared on a computer or handwritten in duplicate. One copy is typically kept in a tickler file (a file used to tickle your memory and remind you to take certain actions). The other copy is inserted in the pocket of an OUT guide or in an OUT folder.

An *OUT guide* is used to replace an individual record or entire folder that has been removed from the files; an *OUT folder* is used to replace a folder. The guide or folder has the word *OUT* printed on the tab. An OUT guide is usually made of pressboard or plastic. It may have a small pocket suitable for a requisition slip and a larger pocket for records that will be filed in the folder when it is returned. It may also have a requisition form printed on it. An OUT folder holds records that will need to be placed in the file when it is returned to the

An OUT guide or OUT folder indicates the location of a file.

file drawer. The OUT guide or folder remains in the file until the borrowed record or folder is returned. An OUT guide within a file drawer is illustrated in Figure 11.5 on page 248.

Alphabetic Indexing Rules

Alphabetic filing rules are used for indexing and coding physical records. Following a systematic set of rules for storing and retrieving records helps to maintain an accurate, efficient records management system. The rules for filing may vary slightly from business to business based on the specific needs of the organization. However, most organizations base their systems on the rules generated by ARMA International. The rules presented in this chapter are compatible with ARMA International filing rules.

Rule 1: Indexing Order of Units

A. PERSONAL NAMES

A personal name is indexed in this order: (1) the surname (last name) is the key unit, (2) the given name (first name) or initial is the second unit, and (3) the middle name or initial is the third unit. If it is difficult to determine the surname, consider the last name written as the surname. An initial precedes a complete name beginning with the same letter—nothing before something. Note that punctuation is omitted.

Rule 1: Personal Names

Filing Segment	Indexing Order of Units		
Name	**Key Unit**	**Unit 2**	**Unit 3**
Francine Sanderson	Sanderson	Francine	
Martha J. Sanderson	Sanderson	Martha	J
F. Joseph Severson	Severson	F	Joseph
Franklin J. Severson	Severson	Franklin	J
Frederick L. Severson	Severson	Frederick	L
Frederick Leonard Severson	Severson	Frederick	Leonard

B. BUSINESS NAMES

Business names are indexed and written using letterheads or trademarks as guides. Each word in a business name is considered a separate unit. Business names containing personal names are indexed as written.

Rule 1: Business Names

Filing Segment	Indexing Order of Units		
Name	**Key Unit**	**Unit 2**	**Unit 3**
Herman Franklin Paving	Herman	Franklin	Paving
Herman Franks Photography	Herman	Franks	Photography
Howard Ogea Excavating	Howard	Ogea	Excavating

Rule 1: Business Names *(continued)*

Filing Segment	Indexing Order of Units		
Name	Key Unit	Unit 2	Unit 3
Howard Oil Company	Howard	Oil	Company
Huron Mountain Bread	Huron	Mountain	Bread
Huron Waters Realty	Huron	Waters	Realty

Rule 2: Minor Words and Symbols in Business Names

Articles, prepositions, conjunctions, and symbols are considered separate indexing units. Symbols are considered as spelled in full. When the word *The* appears as the first word of a business name, it is considered the last indexing unit.

Examples

Articles: a, an, the

Prepositions: at, in, out, on, off, by, to, with, for, of, over

Conjunctions: and, but, or, nor

Symbols: &, ¢, $, #, % *(and, cent* or *cents, dollar* or *dollars, number* or *pound, percent)*

Rule 2: Minor Words and Symbols

Filing Segment	Indexing Order of Units			
Name	Key Unit	Unit 2	Unit 3	Unit 4
A & A Drilling	A	and	A	Drilling
Dollar and Cents Store	Dollar	and	Cents	Store
The $ Shop	Dollar	Shop	The	
The Gingerbread House	Gingerbread	House	The	
Lawton & Lawton Shoes	Lawton	and	Lawton	Shoes
Lawton Interiors by Design	Lawton	Interiors	by	Design

Rule 3: Punctuation and Possessives

All punctuation is disregarded when indexing personal and business names. Commas, periods, hyphens, apostrophes, dashes, exclamation points, question marks, quotation marks, underscores, and diagonals (/) are disregarded.

Rule 3: Punctuation and Possessives

Filing Segment	Indexing Order of Units		
Name	**Key Unit**	**Unit 2**	**Unit 3**
Alger-Marquette Community Foundation	AlgerMarquette	Community	Foundation
Bob's Septic Service	Bobs	Septic	Service
E-Z Storage Co.	EZ	Storage	Co
North/South Collection Agency	NorthSouth	Collection	Agency
Irene B. Oakley-Peters	OakleyPeters	Irene	B

Rule 4: Single Letters and Abbreviations

A. PERSONAL NAMES

Initials in personal names are considered separate indexing units. Abbreviations of personal names (*Wm., Jas., Jos., Thos.*) and nicknames (*Liz, Bill*) are indexed as written.

Rule 4: Single Letters and Abbreviations, Personal Names

Filing Segment	Indexing Order of Units		
Name	**Key Unit**	**Unit 2**	**Unit 3**
J. T. Hung	Hung	J	T
Jas. T. Hung	Hung	Jas	T
L. Pauline Hung	Hung	L	Pauline
Liz P. Hung	Hung	Liz	P

B. BUSINESS NAMES

Single letters in business and organization names are indexed as written. If single letters are separated by spaces, index each letter as a separate unit. Index acronyms (words formed from the first few letters of several words, such as *ARCO* and *NASDAQ*) as one unit regardless of punctuation or spacing. Abbreviated words (*Corp., Inc.*) and names (*IBM, GE*) are indexed as one unit regardless of punctuation or spacing. Radio and television station call letters are indexed as one unit.

Rule 4: Single Letters and Abbreviations, Business Names

Filing Segment	Indexing Order of Units			
Name	**Key Unit**	**Unit 2**	**Unit 3**	**Unit 4**
E C I Inc.	E	C	I	Inc
EG Environmental	EG	Environmental		

Rule 4: Single Letters and Abbreviations, Business Names *(continued)*

Filing Segment	Indexing Order of Units			
Name	**Key Unit**	**Unit 2**	**Unit 3**	**Unit 4**
F A D Mfgs.	F	A	D	Mfgs
K & L Enterprises	K	and	L	Enterprises
KBER Radio	KBER	Radio		

Rule 5: Titles and Suffixes

A. PERSONAL NAMES

A title before a name (*Dr., Miss, Mr., Mrs., Ms., Professor, Sir, Sister*), a seniority suffix (*II, III, Jr., Sr.*), or a professional suffix (*CRM, D.D.S., M.D., Ph.D.*) after a name is the last indexing unit. Numeric suffixes (*II, III*) are filed before alphabetic suffixes (*Jr., CPA*). If a name contains a title and a suffix (*Ms. Emily Pagel, Ph.D.*), the title (*Ms.*) is the last unit. Royal and religious titles followed by either a given name or a surname only (*Princess Anne, Father Mark*) are indexed and filed as written.

Rule 5: Titles and Suffixes, Personal Names

Filing Segment	Indexing Order of Units			
Name	**Key Unit**	**Unit 2**	**Unit 3**	**Unit 4**
Gary J. Estevant	Estevant	Gary	J	
Gary J. Estevant, II	Estevant	Gary	J	II
Gary J. Estevant, Jr.	Estevant	Gary	J	Jr
Mr. Gary J. Estevant	Estevant	Gary	J	Mr
Father Paul	Father	Paul		
Gaynelle D. Hawkins, M.D.	Hawkins	Gaynelle	D	MD
Miss Gaynelle D. Hawkins	Hawkins	Gaynelle	D	Miss
Sister Gaynelle Hawkins	Hawkins	Gaynelle	Sister	
Sister Gaynelle	Sister	Gaynelle		

B. BUSINESS NAMES

Titles in business names are indexed as written. Exception: The word *The* that begins a business name is considered the last indexing unit.

Rule 5: Titles and Suffixes, Business Names

Filing Segment	Indexing Order of Units			
Name	**Key Unit**	**Unit 2**	**Unit 3**	**Unit 4**
Aunt Joan's Fudge	Aunt	Joans	Fudge	
Doctor Frank's Greenhouse	Doctor	Franks	Greenhouse	
Dr. Kim's Counseling	Dr	Kims	Counseling	
The Dr. Store	Dr	Store	The	
Mr. Tom's Bait Shop	Mr	Toms	Bait	Shop
Sister Suzy's Shrimp Shack	Sister	Suzys	Shrimp	Shack

Rule 6: Prefixes, Articles, and Particles

A foreign article or particle in a personal or business name is combined with the part of the name following it to form a single indexing unit. The indexing order is not affected by a space between a prefix and the rest of the name (Amber La Cruz), and the space is disregarded when indexing.

Examples of articles and particles are *a la, D', Da, De, Del, De La, Della, Den, Des, Di, Dos, Du, E', El, Fitz, Il, L', La, Las, Le, Les, Lo, Los, M', Mac, Mc, O', Per, Saint, San, Santa, Santo, St., Ste., Te, Ten, Ter, Van, Van de, Van der, Von,* and *Von der.*

Rule 6: Prefixes, Articles, and Particles

Filing Segment	Indexing Order of Units			
Name	**Key Unit**	**Unit 2**	**Unit 3**	**Unit 4**
Mrs. Francis R. De Gabriele	DeGabriele	Francis	R	Mrs
Le May's Fine Foods	LeMays	Fine	Foods	
Dr. Marsha P. O'Connell	OConnell	Marsha	P	Dr
St. Germain and McDougal, CPAs	StGermain	and	McDougal	CPAs
Mr. Alexis P. Von der Grieff	VonderGrieff	Alexis	P	Mr

Rule 7: Numbers in Business Names

Numbers spelled out in business names (*Sixth Street Grocery*) are considered as written and filed alphabetically. Numbers written in digits are filed before alphabetic letters or words (*3 Day Cleaners* is filed before *Adams Cleaners*).

Names with numbers written in digits in the first units are filed in ascending order (lowest to highest number) before alphabetic names (*229 Boutique, 534 Grocers, First National Bank of Marquette*). Arabic numerals (*2, 3*) are filed before Roman numerals (*II, III*).

Names with inclusive numbers (*33–37 Fence Court*) are arranged by the first digit(s) only (*33*). Names with numbers appearing in places other than the first position (*Pier 36 Cafe*) are filed immediately before a similar name without a number (*Pier 36 Cafe* comes before *Pier and Port Cafe*).

When indexing names with numbers written in digit form that contain *st*, *d*, and *th* (*1st Mortgage Co., 2d Avenue Cinemas*), ignore the letter endings and consider only the digits (*1, 2, 3*).

When indexing names with a number (in figures or words) linked by a hyphen to a letter or word (*A-1 Laundry, Fifty-Eight Auto Body, 10-Minute Photo*), ignore the hyphen and treat the term as a single unit (*A1, FiftyEight, 10Minute*).

When indexing names with a number plus a symbol (*55+ Social Center*), treat the number and symbol as a single unit (*55Plus*).

Rule 7: Numbers in Business Names

Filing Segment	Indexing Order of Units			
Name	**Key Unit**	**Unit 2**	**Unit 3**	**Unit 4**
5 Step Cleaners	5	Step	Cleaners	
5th Street Bakery	5	Street	Bakery	
50% Discounters	50Percent	Discounters		
65 Ice Cream Treats	65	Ice	Cream	Treats
65+ Senior Center	65Plus	Senior	Center	
400-700 Rustic Way	400	Rustic	Way	
The 500 Princess Shop	500	Princess	Shop	The
XXI Club	XXI	Club		
Fifth Street News Shoppe	Fifth	Street	News	Shoppe
Finally 21 Club	Finally	21	Club	
Finally Free Club	Finally	Free	Club	
I-275 Garage	I275	Garage		
#1 TV Deals	Number1	TV	Deals	
Sixty-Six Highway Deli	SixtySix	Highway	Deli	

Rule 8: Organizations and Institutions

The names of banks and other financial institutions, clubs, colleges, hospitals, hotels, lodges, magazines, motels, museums, newspapers, religious institutions, schools, unions, universities, and other organizations and institutions are indexed as written on their letterheads. Exception: The word *The* that begins an organization name is considered the last indexing unit.

Rule 8: Organizations and Institutions

Filing Segment	Indexing Order of Units			
Name	**Key Unit**	**Unit 2**	**Unit 3**	**Unit 4**
1st National Bank	1	National	Bank	
Assembly of God Church	Assembly	of	God	Church
Bay de Noc High School	BaydeNoc	High	School	
Disabled American Veterans	Disabled	American	Veterans	
Grace United Christian Church	Grace	United	Christian	Church
The Marquette Exchange Club	Marquette	Exchange	Club	The
Northern Michigan University	Northern	Michigan	University	
University of Michigan	University	of	Michigan	

Rule 9: Identical Names

When personal names and names of businesses, institutions, and organizations are identical, the filing order is determined by the addresses. Compare the addresses in the following order:

1. City names
2. State or province names (if city names are identical)
3. Street names, including *Avenue*, *Boulevard*, *Drive*, and *Street* (if city and state names are identical)
4. House or building numbers (if city, state, and street names are identical)

Rule 9: Identical Names

Filing Segment	Indexing Order of Units					
Name	**Key Unit**	**Unit 2**	**Unit 3**	**Unit 4**	**Unit 5**	**Unit 6**
Take-N-Bake 101 University Ave. Grand Forks, North Dakota	TakeNBake	Grand Forks				
Take-N-Bake 6490 Hwy. 192 Greenville, Michigan	TakeNBake	Greenville	Michigan			
Take-N-Bake 1493 28th St. Greenville, Ohio	TakeNBake	Greenville	Ohio	28	St	
Take-N-Bake 1692 Birch Ave. Greenville, Ohio	TakeNBake	Greenville	Ohio	Birch	Ave	

Rule 9: Identical Names *(continued)*

Filing Segment	Indexing Order of Units					
Name	**Key Unit**	**Unit 2**	**Unit 3**	**Unit 4**	**Unit 5**	**Unit 6**
Take-N-Bake 21500 Birch St. Greenville, Ohio	TakeNBake	Greenville	Ohio	Birch	St	21500
Take-N-Bake 32890 Birch St. Greenville, Ohio	TakeNBake	Greenville	Ohio	Birch	St	32890
Take-N-Bake 255 SW 15th St. Greenville, Ohio	TakeNBake	Greenville	Ohio	SW	15	St
Take-N-Bake 572 SW Eighth St. Greenville, Ohio	TakeNBake	Greenville	Ohio	SW	Eighth	St
Take-N-Bake 159 Tamarack Way Greenville, Ohio	TakeNBake	Greenville	Ohio	Tamarack	Way	159
Take-N-Bake 253 Tamarack Way Greenville, Ohio	TakeNBake	Greenville	Ohio	Tamarack	Way	253

Rule 10: Government Names

Government names are indexed first by the name of the governmental unit—city, county, state, or country. Next, index the distinctive name of the department, bureau, office, or board.

A. STATE AND LOCAL GOVERNMENT NAMES

The first indexing unit is the name of the state, province, county, city, town, township, or village. The next unit is the most distinctive name of the department, board, bureau, office, or government/political division. The words *State of, Province of, Department of*, etc., are retained for clarity and are considered separate indexing units. If *of* is not part of the official name as written, it is not added as an indexing unit.

Rule 10: State and Local Government Names

Filing Segment	Indexing Order of Units				
Name	**Key Unit**	**Unit 2**	**Unit 3**	**Unit 4**	**Unit 5**
Alabama Department of Education	Alabama	Education	Department	of	
Alabama State Attorney General	Alabama	State	Attorney	General	

Rule 10: State and Local Government Names *(continued)*

Filing Segment	Indexing Order of Units				
Name	**Key Unit**	**Unit 2**	**Unit 3**	**Unit 4**	**Unit 5**
City of Arlington Public Library	Arlington	City	of	Public	Library
City of Arlington Senior Center	Arlington	City	of	Senior	Center
Arlington County Highway Patrol	Arlington	County	Highway	Patrol	
Ashley County Department of Elections	Ashley	County	Elections	Department	of
Augusta City Water Works	Augusta	City	Water	Works	
Baker County Bureau of Licenses	Baker	County	Licenses	Bureau	of
Barstow Municipal Court	Barstow	Municipal	Court		
Benton City Hall	Benton	City	Hall		
Benton Mayor's Office	Benton	Mayors	Office		

B. FEDERAL GOVERNMENT NAMES

Use three indexing "levels" (rather than units) for United States federal government names. Use *United States Government* as the first level. The second level is the name of a department; for example, *Department of Agriculture*. Level 3 is the next most distinctive name; for example, *Forest Service*. If necessary, invert the names to file by the distinctive name. (Change *Department of Commerce* to *Commerce Department*.) The words *of* and *of the* are extraneous and should not be considered when indexing. They may be placed in parentheses for clarity.

Rule 10: Federal Government Names

Filing Segment			
Name	**Level 1**	**Level 2**	**Level 3**
National Weather Service, Department of Commerce	United States Government	Commerce Department (of)	National Weather Service
Office of Civil Rights, Department of Education	United States Government	Education Department (of)	Civil Rights Office (of)
Department of Health and Human Services	United States Government	Health and Human Services Department (of)	
Federal Emergency Management Agency, Department of Homeland Security	United States Government	Homeland Security Department (of)	Federal Emergency Management Agency

Rule 10: Federal Government Names *(continued)*

Filing Segment			
Name	**Level 1**	**Level 2**	**Level 3**
Bureau of Reclamation, Department of the Interior	United States Government	Interior Department (of the)	Reclamation Bureau (of)
Federal Bureau of Investigation, Department of Justice	United States Government	Justice Department (of)	Investigation Federal Bureau (of)
Federal Bureau of Prisons, Department of Justice	United States Government	Justice Department (of)	Prisons Federal Bureau (of)

C. FOREIGN GOVERNMENT NAMES

The names of a foreign government and its agencies are often written in a foreign language. When indexing foreign names, begin by writing the English translation of the government name on the document. The English translation is used for indexing. The most distinctive part of the English name is the first indexing unit. Then index the balance of the formal name of the government, if needed, or if it is in the official name (*China Republic of*). Branches, departments, and divisions follow in order by their distinctive names. States, colonies, provinces, cities, and other divisions of foreign governments are followed by their distinctive or official names as spelled in English.

Rule 10: Foreign Government Names

Filing Segment	English Translation in Indexed Order			
Name	**Unit 1**	**Unit 2**	**Unit 3**	**Unit 4**
Govern d'Andorra	Andorra	Government		
Republik Osterreich	Austria	Republic	of	
Druk Yul	Bhutan	Kingdom	of	
Bundesrepublik Deutschland	Germany	Federal	Republic	of
Jamhuri ya Kenya	Kenya	Republic	of	

Cross-Referencing Records

Some records of persons and businesses may be requested by a name that is different from the one by which the record was stored. This is particularly true if the key unit is difficult to determine. For example, the name *Andrew Scott* should be filed under *Scott* but may be misfiled under *Andrew*. When a record is likely to be requested by more than one name, a cross-reference is prepared. For instance, a business that includes several last names like Smith, Barker, and Jones, Inc., should be filed under *Smith* with cross-references for *Barker* and *Jones*. A **cross-reference** shows an alternate name or subject by which the record might be requested and indicates the storage location of the original record.

Cross-referencing will save time when there may be confusion about where a record is stored.

On the original document, the name for the cross-reference should be underlined with a wavy line and the filing segments numbered. An *X* should be placed in the margin of the document near the cross-reference name as shown in Figure 11.2 on page 234. The cross-reference may be prepared using a cross-reference sheet (Figure 11.3). The cross-reference sheet shows the name under which the item is cross-referenced, and the sheet is filed under that name. The sheet also shows the name under which the record is filed. As an alternative to preparing a cross-reference sheet, a copy of the document may be made and filed under the cross-reference name.

CROSS-REFERENCE SHEET

Name or Subject: Kirkman | 2 Products | 3 Inc.

Date of Item: September 24, 201-

Regarding: Two-page ad for spring distribution

SEE

Name or Subject: Morency | 2 Advertising | 3 Agency

Authorized by: G. Melena   Date: September 29, 201-

FIGURE 11.3 This cross-reference sheet was prepared for the letter shown in Figure 11.2.

Use cross-referencing for personal names and business or organization names that may be requested under a different name. Similar names that sound the same but have different spellings should also be cross-referenced. Figure 11.4 shows examples of names that should be cross-referenced.

Name Type	Original	Cross-Reference
Easily confused name	Thomas / Joseph	Joseph / Thomas SEE Thomas / Joseph
Hyphenated personal name	Francine / Haslitt-Higgins	Francine / Higgins SEE Francine / HaslittHiggins
Hyphenated business name	Trenton-Harding / Excavating	HardingTrenton / Excavating SEE TrentonHarding / Excavating
Compound name	Kendricks / and / Adamini / Cleaners	Adamini / and / Kendricks / Cleaners SEE Kendricks / and / Adamini / Cleaners
Alternate name	Isabel / Rodriguez	Isabel / Perez SEE Isabel / Rodriguez
Popular or coined name	Tom / Chung's / Asian / Garden	Tommys SEE Tom / Chungs / Asian / Garden
Name with acronym	MADD	Mothers / Against / Drunk / Driving SEE MADD
Changed name	Harris / Distribution / Inc.	Harris / Supply SEE Harris / Distribution / Inc
Similar name	Allstate / Insurance / Co.	All / State / Insurance / Co SEE Allstate / Insurance / Co

FIGURE 11.4 Examples of Cross-References

Records Storage Systems

Records may be organized in a variety of ways. Four methods commonly used in organizations are alphabetical order, subject order, numerical order, and geographic order. Records in a physical or electronic system may be stored by any of these methods.

Alphabetic Storage Systems

An alphabetic storage system uses letters of the alphabet to determine the order in which the names of individuals, businesses, and organizations are filed. This method is the most commonly used storage method and is found in one form or another in almost every organization. With an alphabetic storage system, records placement is based on the alphabetic indexing rules described previously in this chapter.

Figure 11.5 illustrates an alphabetic file for physical records. In this figure, the primary guides are placed in the first position. A primary guide is a divider that identifies a main division or section of a file. It always precedes all other material in a section. Special guides, used to lead the eye quickly to a specific area of the file, are in the second position. A general folder holds records for names that do not have enough records to warrant an individual

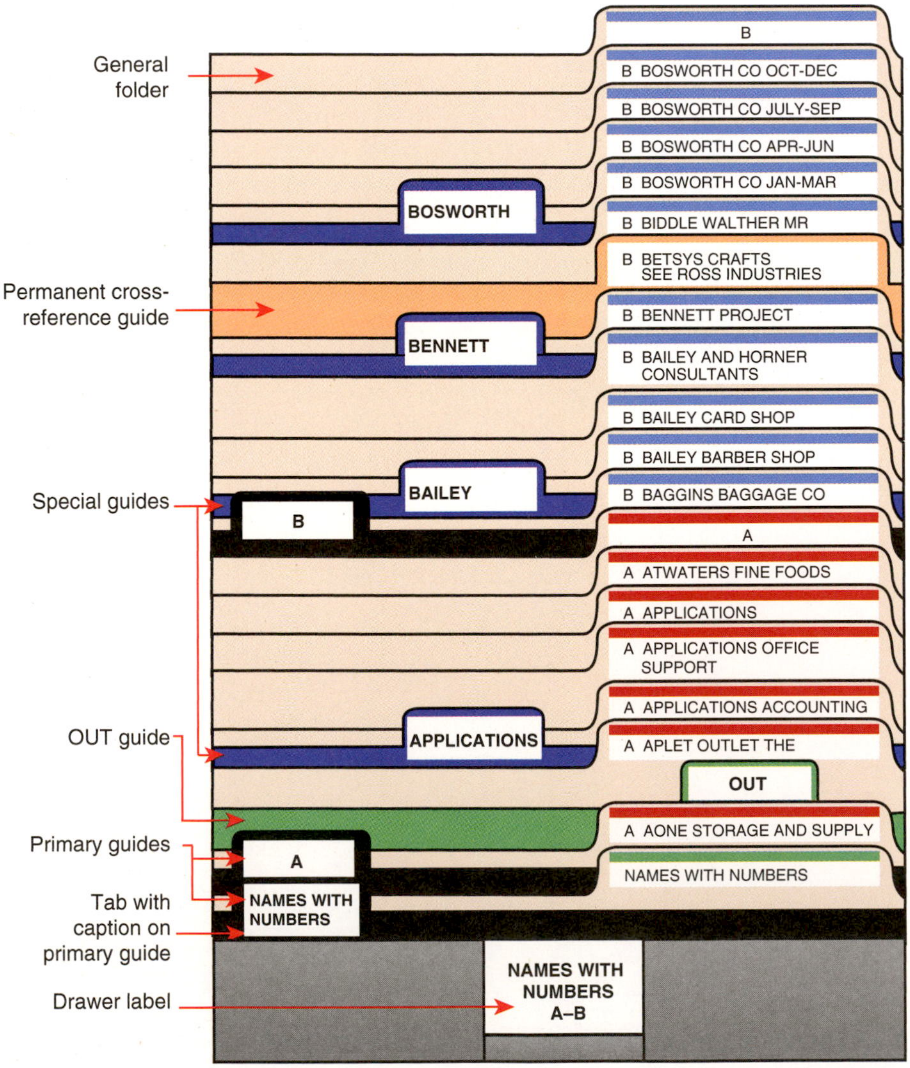

FIGURE 11.5 Section of an Alphabetic File

folder. Typically an individual folder is made when three to five records have been gathered.

Records in the general folder are arranged alphabetically. If there are two or more records for the same name, the records are arranged by date with the most recent date in front. Individual folders, such as APPLICATIONS ACCOUNTING in Figure 11.5, hold only records related to that company. Records in the folder are arranged by date with the most recent record in front.

An alphabetic system has several advantages over other systems. It is a direct access system. There is no need to refer to anything except the file to find the name, which saves time. In addition, the dictionary arrangement is simple to understand. Misfiling is easily checked by the alphabetic sequence.

An alphabetic system also has some disadvantages. For example, misfiling can easily occur if rules for alphabetic storage are not followed. Confidential records are not secure since names are indicated directly on the file. Related records with different correspondent names are filed in more than one place.

Subject Storage Systems

The subject storage method is widely used in organizations. In a subject storage system, records are coded, stored, and retrieved by their subject or topic. Filing by subject requires that each record be read completely to determine the subject—a time-consuming process. Subject filing is recommended when the range of topics used within an organization is broad and the records may include a variety of materials including correspondence, reports, news clippings, and other items.

Figure 11.6 shows a subject file. The main subjects are indicated by the primary guides in first position. Secondary guides indicate subdivisions of the main subjects. A subject folder holds records for each secondary guide. When there are not enough records to make a specific subject folder, those records go into a general folder. For example, records for customer services that are not related to discount cards would be in the Customers Services general folder. A permanent cross-reference guide directs filers to look for records related to *advertising* under *sales promotions*. Preparing cross-references was discussed previously in this chapter.

A subject system can be a direct or indirect access system. When the system is direct, the subject file is a simple one (with only a few subjects), and access can be obtained directly through its alphabetic title. Keeping the subjects in alphabetical order is necessary.

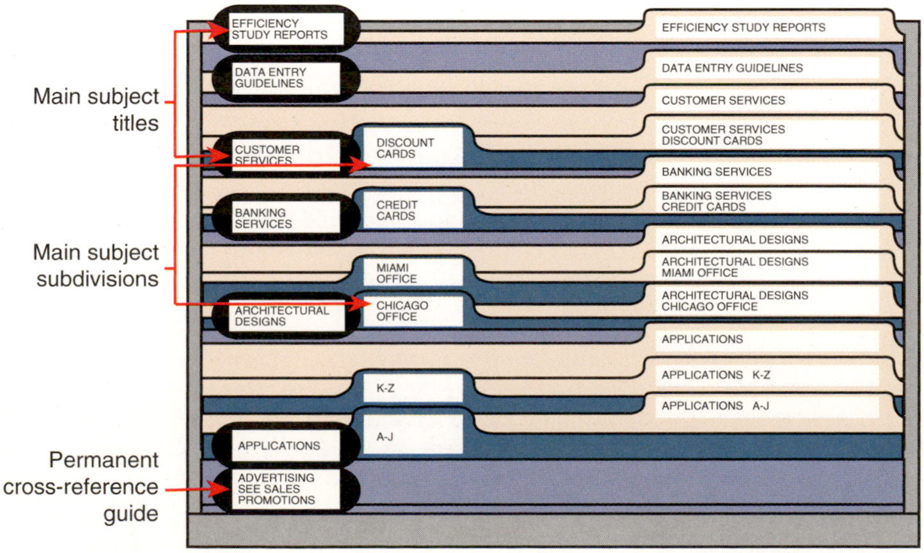

FIGURE 11.6 Subject File

Most subject systems are more complex and require some type of index. The **index** is a list of all the names or titles used in a filing system. Without an index, it is almost impossible for the subject storage method to work well. The index should be kept up-to-date as new subjects are added and obsolete subjects are eliminated. When new subjects are added, the index provides guidance to avoid the duplication of subjects.

Subject filing systems have some advantages over other types of systems. Subjects are easier to remember than names. Related records are stored in the same location, and files can be expanded easily by adding subdivisions of topics.

Subject filing systems have several disadvantages as well. One, already mentioned, is the time required to read records completely. Users must be careful to file records under established topics and subtopics; otherwise, finding records will be difficult. This method is difficult to control because one person may read a record and determine the subject to be one thing, and another person may read the record and decide the subject is something entirely different. For example, one person who classifies records about advertising promotions may determine that the subject is advertising while another person may decide that it is promotions. The following suggestions will help users avoid some of the disadvantages associated with subject filing systems:

- Select subject titles that best reflect stored records, are meaningful to users, and are easy to remember.
- Use one-word subject titles whenever possible.
- Designate one person to select the subjects and add new categories as needed.

TECH TALK

Social Bookmarking

Social bookmarking is the practice of saving bookmarks to a public website so they are organized and easy to access. You can save links to web pages you want to remember for yourself or links you want to share with others. Social bookmarking is not file sharing because the resources themselves aren't shared, just the bookmarks that reference them. Since the bookmarks aren't saved on your computer, you can access them anytime from any Internet connection.

Social bookmarking sites were started as a way to share bookmarks with family, friends, and colleagues. From a business perspective, social bookmarking is used to grow a business by providing a link-building strategy. Social bookmarking sites have grown into social search engines where individuals can share bookmarks with people they've never met who have similar research interests. Links to several popular social bookmarking sites are provided on the website for the text.

The sites have a number of useful features. Sharers can categorize their links quickly, adding keyword "tags" when a link is saved. The tags group websites by topic, so other users don't have to scroll through a list of saved favorites but can simply enter a keyword to search for links. Searching by keyword tags also allows users to see what others have found and tagged and to add their own tags to these sites. For instance, if you find an interesting website about records storage in Pennsylvania, you might tag it "records storage" and "Pennsylvania." You can locate the bookmark by keying either tag in the search box. Other users searching for "records storage" will also find the link you bookmarked.

- Combine filing methods when subdividing records in a large subject filing system. For example, records should be sorted alphabetically within a subject category.

Numeric Storage Systems

Under the numeric storage method, records are given numbers and are arranged in a numeric sequence when stored. The numeric system is particularly useful to organizations that must maintain confidentiality of their records. The use of numbers adds security to the records, making it difficult to locate personal or private records. Examples of organizations that might use a numeric system include the following:

- Insurance companies that keep records according to policy numbers
- Social welfare agencies or law firms that assign numbers to cases and/or clients
- Real estate agencies that list properties by code numbers
- Physician offices that maintain patient records by medical record numbers

A physical numeric file has four basic parts:

- Numeric file
- Alphabetic general file
- Alphabetic index (a file containing the names of individuals, organizations, and companies with the number that has been assigned to each one)
- **Accession log** (a file containing a list of the numbers that have been used)

The basic procedures to file records in a numeric filing system are as follows:

1. When a document is ready to be filed, the alphabetic index is consulted to get the number that corresponds to the name by which the record is to be filed.
2. The number is placed on the document; the document is placed in the numeric file.
3. If the filing name is new and no number is established, the document may be placed in the alphabetic general file until there are enough records for this name to open an individual numeric file.
4. If it is necessary to establish a new numeric file, the accession log is consulted to determine the next number to be used.

Although the records are filed in numeric sequence, the alphabetic rules are still a major part of a numeric system. Individual or company names in the alphabetic index are organized according to the ARMA filing rules.

Numeric systems have several advantages. Expansion is easy and unlimited. In addition, confidentiality is maintained because names do not appear on the guides or folders. All records for one name are located in the same place. Finally,

andreiorlov/iStockphoto.com

Many organizations use a numeric storage system.

accuracy is enhanced because numbers are easier to recognize and sequence than alphabetic characters.

Numeric systems also have disadvantages. Because more supplies are necessary, the system usually costs more than other systems. Filing is more time-consuming because records must be sorted first alphabetically and then numerically. The accession log and alphabetic index must be consulted often.

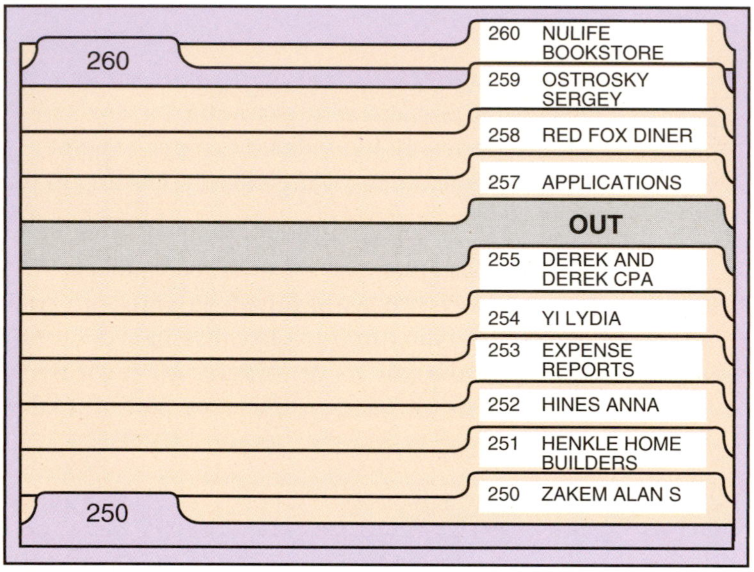

FIGURE 11.7 Numeric File With Consecutive Numbers

Most businesses that use a numeric filing system rely on either the consecutive storage method or the terminal-digit storage method.

CONSECUTIVE STORAGE METHOD

In the consecutive storage method, numbered records are arranged in ascending order (lowest number to highest number). This method is also called serial, sequential, or straight-number filing. In this system, the numbers are compared to determine filing order and filed in numeric order. The number used may be part of the record itself, such as a number on an invoice, or the number may be written on the record.

Figure 11.7 illustrates a numeric file in which consecutive number are used. Primary guides in first position divide the file drawer into sections. Folder labels show individual numbers and names of the correspondents to the right of the number (names can be included if privacy or security is not a factor).

In the consecutive method, the number assigned becomes higher as each new record is added to the system. Each new file is placed behind all

Chronological Filing

Chronological filing is a variation of numeric filing. The physical records are arranged by reverse date order within a file folder. This arrangement places the oldest records at the back of the file and the newest records at the front. The files may be divided by year or month, depending on the number of records.

Chronological filing is also used for tickler files. For example, in a manual tickler file the items are arranged by the date the item should be completed. You may have a folder that is subdivided by months. Items that need to be completed are placed in the folder. Each day you would review the materials in the folder and add them to the list of tasks you plan to accomplish each day.

the lower-numbered files, which means the file arrangement expands at the back. This also means the newer records are often located in the back of the file cabinet. Consecutive numeric filing is a simple system to use because numbers are easier to put in order than letters.

TERMINAL-DIGIT STORAGE METHOD

The terminal-digit storage method is another variation of numeric filing. Numbers in a terminal-digit system may be assigned sequentially, or they may mean something specific. For example, the first group of numbers may be a customer identification number; the second group may indicate a sales district or department; and the third group may indicate a date or salesperson. If the digits in the number are not separated into groups by a space or a hyphen, the assigned number is divided into three groups of digits. For example, 125784 becomes 12-57-84 or 125784773 becomes 125-784-773. Zeroes are added to the left of a smaller number to create three groups. For example, the number 58293 becomes 05-82-93. The purpose is to create three indexing units that will tell the location of the record. The primary (first) unit indicates the file drawer, section, or shelf number; the secondary unit indicates the guide number; and the tertiary (third) unit indicates the folder number. The following numbers are in proper order for terminal-digit filing. Reading from the front of the file drawer:

Tertiary (Folder)	Secondary (Guide)	Primary (File Drawer, Section, or Shelf)
268	449	105
268	982	105
557	233	166
558	233	166
115	449	289
782	482	289

Terminal-digit filing is an arrangement of numeric files that groups together all file numbers that end in the same last two digits. Although file numbers are written in straight numeric sequence, location is determined by reading them in reverse order (right to left) in groups of two or three digits. This system is often used in organizations with large file areas such as hospitals, insurance companies, banks, and government agencies.

Figure 11.8 illustrates a terminal-digit file in which consecutive numbers are used. The example is for Shelf 32. Primary guides divide the file drawer into sections. Folder labels show individual numbers.

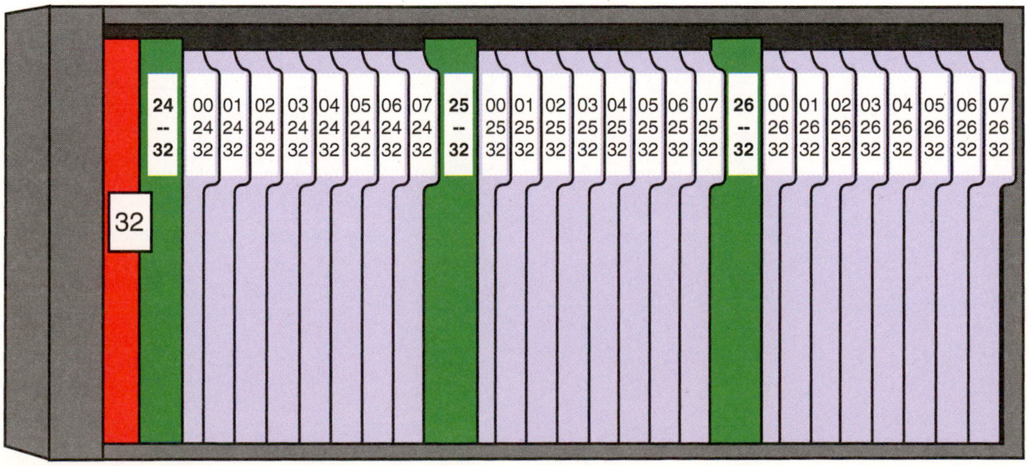

FIGURE 11.8 Terminal-Digit Arrangement

MIDDLE-DIGIT STORAGE METHOD

In a middle-digit storage system, the assigned numbers are once again divided into groups. The groups are read from middle to left to right. For example, in the number 125784773, 784 is the first indexing unit, 125 is the second indexing unit, and 773 is the third indexing unit. The primary unit indicates the file drawer, section, or shelf number; the secondary unit indicates the guide number; and the tertiary unit indicates the folder number. This system is often used in organizations such as health care facilities and libraries. The following numbers are in proper order for middle-digit filing. Reading from the front of the file drawer:

Secondary (Guide)	Primary (File Drawer, Section, or Shelf)	Tertiary (Folder)
557	223	166
558	223	166
115	449	289
268	449	105
782	482	289
268	982	105

Geographic Storage Systems

Another variation of an alphabetic system is the geographic storage method, in which related records are grouped by location. This method is used when records are requested by location rather than by name. Geographic filing is considered a direct method if you know the geographic location (city or state) of the file needed. If you do not, it is an indirect system and requires a separate geographic index file in a physical storage system. Figure 11.9 shows a geographic file.

Geographic filing is particularly useful for these types of organizations:

- Utility companies, for which street names and numbers are of primary importance in troubleshooting
- Real estate firms that track listings by area
- Sales organizations that are concerned with the geographic location of their customers
- Government agencies that file records by state, county, or other geographic division

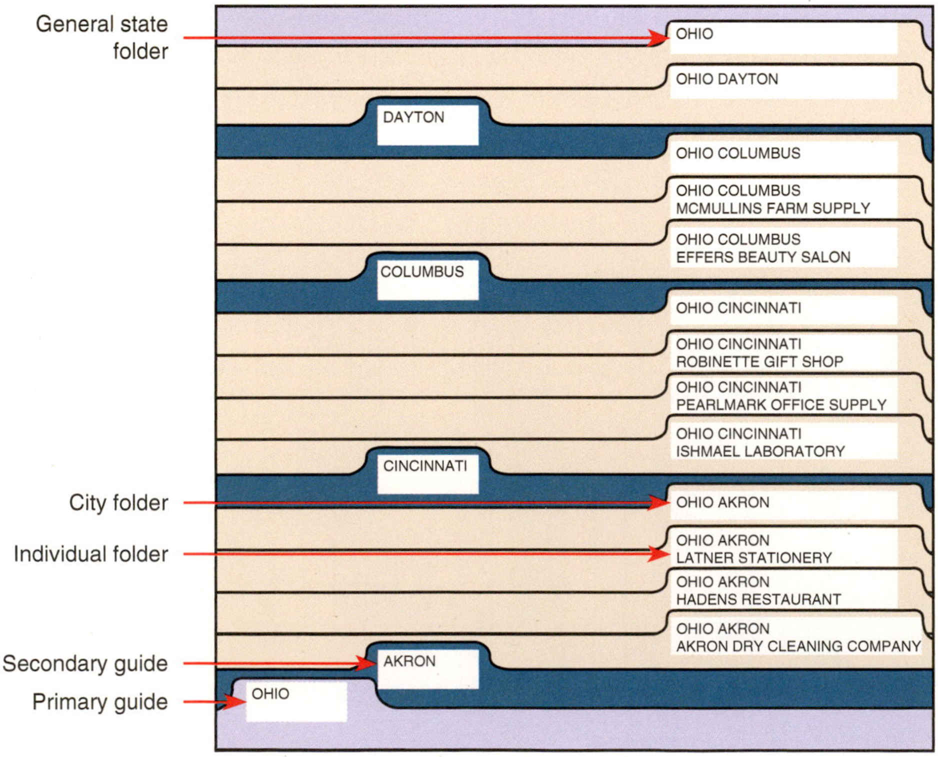

FIGURE 11.9 Geographic File

In Figure 11.9, the primary guide in first position shows the main division of the file, state names. The secondary guides in second position show city names. Folder captions are in last position. There are three types of folders: individual folders, city folders, and general state folders. Individual folders hold records for one person or company. City folders hold other records for that city. General state folders hold records for that state that do not relate to one of the individual or city folders.

For a geographic system to function correctly, the breakdown into geographic divisions must fit the type of business, its organization, and its need for specific kinds of information. Also, an alphabetic index is required for a geographic system. This index lists all correspondents or subjects in geographic storage. The index can be a computer database index or a list printed from a word processing program. However the index is kept, it must be easy to update and a copy should be stored in the first file drawer.

The main advantage of a geographic system is that records relating to a specific location are filed together. This can be very important for some businesses. Because each geographic area is a unit or group, moving records is easily accomplished.

A disadvantage of geographic storage is that several cross-references may be necessary for organizations having more than one address or more than one business in the same location. Because this is an indirect filing method, the user must check the alphabetic index often to ensure accurate placement of files.

SUMMARY

To reinforce what you have learned in this chapter, study this summary.

- Records are business assets that must be properly managed from creation or receipt to final disposition. Findability, confidentiality, and safety are the three criteria of an effective records management system.
- Basic equipment and supplies for managing physical records include storage cabinets, file folders, file guides, and file folder labels. Procedures for filing physical records include inspecting, indexing, coding, sorting, storing, and preparing cross-references as needed.
- ARMA International has developed alphabetic indexing rules designed to assist the administrative professional in indexing and coding records for filing.
- Records may be organized in alphabetical order, subject order, numerical order, or geographical order.

KEY TERMS

accession log, 251
coding, 235
cross-reference, 246
filing segment, 234
index, 250
indexing, 234
inspecting, 234
key unit, 235
record, 228
records management, 229
social bookmarking, 250
suspension folder, 232

11

STUDY Tools

Located at www.cengagebrain.com

- Chapter Outlines
- Flashcards
- Interactive Quizzes
- Tech Tools
- Video Segments
- and More!

LET'S DISCUSS

1. In what ways may a record have value for an organization?
2. Describe the three factors that must be considered when planning an effective records system, and explain the importance of each factor.
3. What is the difference between the indexing and coding filing procedures?
4. What is the purpose of a cross-reference?
5. Describe three instances in which a name should be cross-referenced, and provide an example of each instance.
6. What is the purpose of a general folder in an alphabetic filing system?
7. When is it advantageous for an organization to use a numeric filing system?

PUT IT TO WORK

Filing fiasco Dawon Abrego's work space is filled with stacks of papers. He has three neatly piled stacks on his desk and at least eight stacks on the floor. Although Dawon has two vertical filing cabinets, it appears most of the documents do not make it from the stacks to the cabinets. Many of Dawon's coworkers tease him about his unique filing system, but they are impressed that he can locate information in a short period of time. In fact, Dawon's system seems to work quite well for him. He has never had a problem locating information in a timely manner.

Two weeks ago Dawon requested an extended leave from work to take care of personal matters. In his absence, several projects were reassigned to other employees. The majority of these projects could not progress because the employees were unable to locate the necessary information in Dawon's stacks. One employee contacted Dawon, but Dawon could not guide him in locating the information. Although Dawon's supervisor did not approve of his filing methods, it was never an issue previously because Dawon was able to find information quickly. Now, however, the supervisor can see how Dawon's method has an impact on the workplace. Dawon will not be back in the office for at least three months.

How can the supervisor handle this situation so the work gets done? What suggestions could you make to the supervisor to prevent this type of problem from happening again?

COMMUNICATE SUCCESSFULLY

1. **Organize personal records** Three factors must be considered in planning effective records systems: findability, confidentiality, and safety. Write a paragraph that describes how you take these three factors into

consideration in the organization of your personal records. Provide examples of how you label and protect your personal records. If you have ever had issues with findability, how did you resolve the problem? (Learning Objectives 1, 2, 3, and 4)

2. **Update personal records** Write a paragraph or list that describes how you will update your personal recordkeeping habits and storage systems after reading this chapter. (Learning Objectives 2, 3, and 4)
3. **Understand records management** Add a new post to the blog you created in Chapter 1. In this entry, reflect on the following statement: **This chapter has helped me better understand the importance of managing records in the following ways.** (Learning Objectives 1, 2, 3, and 4)

Blog

DEVELOP WORKPLACE SKILLS

4. **Practice alphabetic filing** Correspondence has been received from a number of individuals, companies, and government agencies. Their names are stored in a data file. The correspondence must be indexed and coded for the alphabetic file.
   a. Access the *Word* file *Ch11_Names* from the data files.
   b. Use the alphabetic indexing rules found in this chapter to determine the indexing order for each name. Key each name in indexing order under the name that already appears in the file. Do not key punctuation in the indexed name. Code the name by underlining the key unit and keying diagonals (/) between the units.
   c. In the same file, copy and paste the coded names to create a list of names in alphabetic filing order.
5. **Prepare cross-references** Your supervisor, Alexis Kooperman, has asked that you review a number of files to determine if cross-references are necessary. Access the *Word* file *Ch11_Cross-References* from the data files. Follow the instructions in the file to prepare any necessary cross-references. (Learning Objective 3)
6. **Create a subject file** Mr. Kooperman has gathered a large number of articles related to communications, management, and telecommunications. He has asked for your help in organizing the documents into a subject filing system. Access the *Word* file *Ch11_Subject_Filing* from the data files. Follow the instructions in the file to organize the records for subject filing. (Learning Objectives 3 and 4)
7. **Organize records for numeric filing** Access the *Word* file *Ch11_Numeric_Filing* from the data files. Follow the instructions in the file to organize records for consecutive, terminal-digit, and middle-digit filing. (Learning Objectives 3 and 4)

BUILD RELATIONSHIPS

8. **Missing file** Mr. Atkins has asked his administrative assistant, Kimberly, for a file so he can complete an important report by the end of the week. When Kimberly looks for the file, she finds that it is signed out to her colleague Melissa. Melissa has stacks of files on her desk and is known for her poor file management habits. When Kimberly asks Melissa for the file, Melissa says she returned it the previous week.

   Kimberly reports to Mr. Atkins that she cannot find the file. He tells her to "drop everything until you find it." Kimberly asks Melissa again, but Melissa just shrugs and goes back to work. Kimberly returns to her desk frustrated. She has a sneaking suspicion that the file is still on Melissa's desk.

   What suggestions would you give Kimberly to help her locate the file? Are there other places in the files that Kimberly can look? Should Kimberly approach Melissa again? If so, what should she say? (Learning Objectives 1, 2, and 3)

9. **Checkout procedures** Alice Dao is a clerk in the medical records department at a large hospital. Solomon Keyes, a patient services advocate, routinely uses patient files to update billing information for patients and insurance companies as new tests and procedures are completed. Alice and Solomon have been working together for several years, and they have become somewhat informal in their handling of patient records. Rather than fill out the paperwork to request a file, Solomon has become accustomed to going directly to the file room and retrieving the files as he needs them. He is so familiar with the system that he also puts the files back when he is done. John, who works with Solomon, has also started retrieving and refiling records without paperwork.

   Recently other employees have been unable to locate several patient files. Alice and Solomon have come under scrutiny because of the way they handle files. Although they know they are not responsible for the missing files, they are facing serious questions from other department managers.

   What could Alice and Solomon have done differently to avoid their present situation? What should they say to John? What should they say to the department managers about how they will handle files in the future? (Learning Objectives 1 and 2)

USE TECH TOOLS

10. **Create an account** Create a social bookmarking account. Locate three or more articles or websites related to the chapter content that you can tag and save to your account. Find two websites that sell filing supplies or products. Tag and save those sites to your account as well. Share your account with a friend in this class. Use a site provided by your instructor or one of the social bookmarking sites provided on the website for this text.

11. **Teach social bookmarking** You have been asked to make a short presentation about social bookmarking at the next staff meeting. Locate a free social bookmarking program. You can access the links to social bookmarking sites on the website for this text or complete a web search using the search term *social bookmarking*. Read the information presented about the system, and prepare a one-page summary of how to use the program. Create a handout to distribute to your colleagues with simple instructions. Select an appropriate document theme to create a professional-looking handout. If you completed Activity 10, you may use the social bookmarking site you chose for that activity and include comments on your experience using the site.

PLAN AHEAD

Recommend filing supplies Your supervisor, Mark Constance, has determined that your department needs to expand its paper filing system. Mark has asked that you research two office supply companies for information on filing supplies and equipment. Mark anticipates the following needs:

- An additional file cabinet. The cabinet will hold confidential records and needs to be secure.
- Suspension (hanging) folders. You need at least 500 hanging folders, tabs, and insertable labels. The current folders use one-third cut tabs.
- File folders. You need at least 1,500 colored file folders. The current system includes an assortment of primary colors with one-third cut tabs.
- OUT guides or folders. You will need at least 200 OUT guides or folders.
- Mark also asks that you include at least one new, innovative supply that would be helpful in this system.

1. Work with two classmates to complete this assignment.
2. Research vertical and lateral file cabinets, hanging folders, file folders, and OUT folders or guides on the Internet or at office supply stores. Identify and research a new, innovative supply as Mark suggested. Links to the websites for two companies, TAB and Smead Manufacturing, that sell filing supplies and equipment are provided on the website for this textbook. Find other companies by searching for *filing systems*, *filing equipment*, or *filing supplies*.
3. Prepare a spreadsheet that shows individual and total costs for each item from at least two different companies. Prepare a memo to Mark recommending the supplies you think the company should purchase and why. Discuss prices and include the spreadsheet with the memo. (Learning Objectives 1 and 2)

CHAPTER

12 Managing Electronic Records

LEARNING OBJECTIVES

1. Understand systems to manage electronic, microfilm, and image files.
2. Describe records categories and the processes for records retention, transfer, and disposal.

Managing Electronic and Microfilm Records

Management of paper records has always been important; however, with the increased use of electronic records in business, management of electronic records has become an important priority. An **electronic record** is a record stored on electronic storage media that can be accessed or changed. An **image record** is a digital or photographic representation of a record. Image records can be stored on computer networks, hard drives, or external media including flash drives, DVDs, and microforms.

The computer has become a major electronic records management component. In many instances, records move from computer to computer and are never printed. Therefore, administrative professionals must be able to name, organize, file, distribute, and otherwise manage electronic records.

Types of Electronic Records

Electronic records may be part of an electronic database or automated system. For example, customer names, addresses, and telephone numbers may be recorded in a database. Electronic records may also consist of individual files. Letters, reports, and contracts may be stored as word processing files. Budgets and cost analysis reports may be stored as spreadsheet files.

AUTOMATED RECORDS

Electronic records are often created automatically. For example, when a customer enters an order online using an automated order system, a record of the order is created and stored electronically. The customer's contact and payment information is added to a customer database. When the customer orders from the company again, that information can be accessed by the order system so the customer does not have to reenter it. Often, an e-mail is automatically sent to the customer confirming the order. The order information is automatically sent to the warehouse. Once the items have been shipped, tracking information may be available from the company's records or the delivery company's records.

Although these types of records are created and distributed automatically, they are used and maintained by employees within an organization. Knowing how to access the records is important. For example, an electronic order record might be retrieved by entering the order number, the customer's name, or the customer's phone number. Once the record has been retrieved, it can be used, for example, to answer a customer's question about the order. Although your position may not require involvement with the disposition of these kinds of records, someone in the company will be responsible for this aspect. Disposition may involve transferring the records to off-line storage and eventually destroying them or placing them in permanent storage as company policy dictates.

INDIVIDUAL RECORDS

Creation and receipt of electronic records is a routine process for you when you work in an office. For example, you will receive many e-mails. You will key memorandums, letters, and reports. You may prepare other documents including flyers, budgets, and presentations. However, it is important to remember that not all electronic information you create or receive should be treated as a record. Only those items that have continuing value for the organization should be considered records. An e-mail from a coworker reminding you about tomorrow's monthly birthday celebration does not have continuing value and is not considered a record.

DATABASE RECORDS

A **database** is a collection of records about one topic or related topics. The records can be updated, copied, or deleted as needed. You can use database queries and filters to find particular subsets of information and to create reports using the information. An electronic database (Figure 12.1) may

Clients

Title	First Name	Last Name	Address	City	State	Zip	Home Phone
Mr.	David	Morad	100 Bent Tree	Fairfield	OH	45221	(513) 555-0105
Ms.	Sue	Coates	691 Meadow Lane	Cincinnati	OH	45228	(513) 555-0110
Mr.	Alfredo	Morales	5773 Beech Rd.	Covington	KY	41011	(606) 555-0104
Mr.	Mike	Goldstein	321 Asbury Dr.	Cincinnati	OH	45230	(513) 555-0112
Mr.	Chris	Wong	3115 Dunne Rd.	Alexandria	KY	41032	(606) 555-0111
Mr.	Carlos	Moretz	1128 Eighth Ave.	Lawrenceburg	IN	47025	(812) 555-0106
Mr.	Stephen	Joyner	4563 Findley Ave.	Lawrenceburg	IN	47025	(812) 555-0108
Mr.	Al	Skirvin	1005 Dayton Ave.	Dayton	KY	41201	(606) 555-0104
Ms.	Anna	Tipton	54 Dumfries Ave.	Ft. Thomas	KY	41075	(606) 555-0102
Ms.	Betty	Jung	1589 East St.	Dayton	OH	45410	(513) 555-0108
Mr.	Kwaishan	Sneed	5100 Burlington Pike	Florence	KY	41042	(606) 555-0198
Mr.	Bang Van	Phan	1831 Pleasant Run	Cincinnati	OH	45281	(513) 555-0109
Mr.	Chris	Wones	412 Terwilleger's Run	Cincinnati	OH	45227	(513) 555-0103
Mr.	Scott	Barkley	4100 North Bend	Cincinnati	OH	45251	(513) 555-0101
Ms.	Margaret	Balli	224 Grandview Dr.	Newport	KY	41071	(606) 555-0107
Mr.	Don	Sujak	4050 El Paso Drive	Naperville	IL	62263	(630) 555-0242
Ms.	Linda	Hartley	2570 Foxfield	Naperville	IL	62263	(630) 555-4548
Mrs.	Dineen	Ebert	27 Main	Indianapolis	IN	46201	(317) 555-3999
Ms.	Dorothy	Wiese	28 South Water	Elgin	IL	60123	(847) 555-2997
Mrs.	Betsy	Wascher	2270 Homer	Elgin	IL	60123	(847) 555-2901
Ms.	Jenna	Ericksen	34 Emerson	Covington	KY	41011	(606) 555-3201
Mr.	Randall	Ramey	40 Hydraulic	Yorkville	IL	60560	(630) 555-8212
Mrs.	Petrina	Jackson	120 Western	Naperville	IL	62263	(630) 555-4576

Record: 1 of 37 No Filter Search

FIGURE 12.1 Example of an *Access* Client Database

be available to many users in an organization via a network or intranet, or it may be stored on a single computer for use by a few people. *Microsoft® Access®* is an example of a popular database program.

Managing Electronic Records

Many electronic records are stored on a computer network or hard drive. They may also be stored on a variety of external storage media including external hard drives, CDs, DVDs, and flash drives. Cloud computing, as discussed in Chapter 10, is an additional mechanism for file storage. Electronic files are created using programs such as word processing, spreadsheet, presentation, and e-mail software. They can also be created automatically through the use of an automated order system or database. To know how to organize electronic files, users must understand the phases of the life cycle for an electronic record:

- Creation and storage
- Use and distribution
- Maintenance
- Disposition

CREATION AND STORAGE

Electronic records contain data that are created, distributed to, or received from others using computer software or through an automated system. Electronic files are created in specific software applications such as *Word*, *Excel*, and *Access*. Creating and storing (saving) a document is the first step in the electronic records life cycle.

Just like paper files, electronic records must be managed properly to ensure that only information that is useful or required is maintained and all other information is deleted. As electronic information is created or received, it is stored as a file on a network, a hard drive, or another storage device. Whatever type of storage device is used, the data should be stored using meaningful filenames and in a logical structure of folders or directories to facilitate retrieving the information.

A saved document is any stored information that requires a user to give it a filename. A filename is a unique name given to a computer file that must follow the company's operating system rules. For example, the operating system may limit the filename to a certain number of characters. Using meaningful filenames is an important part of managing electronic files. An organization may have procedures in place for naming files. If no procedures or guidelines exist, think about how the data might be requested when you need to retrieve it.

Because computers can store millions of files, organization is essential. Users should store their electronic files in folders. A folder (also called a directory) is a subdivision of storage space created by the operating system of a computer. Users can create new folders as needed. Each folder is given a name. Also, just like a folder in a file drawer, a computer folder can contain files and other folders, sometimes called subfolders.

Files on computer storage devices are organized using the operating system's filing system. The electronic filing system maintains a list of all files and their location. Information that shows the location of a computer file is called a file path. A typical path contains the computer drive designation, the folders and subfolders in which the file is located, and the filename. For example, in the path *C:\Documents\Applications\JWGreen.docx*, *C* is the drive designation. *Documents* is the main folder. *Applications* is a subfolder within the main folder. *JWGreen.docx* is the filename. Depending on the settings that were selected for the operating system, the filename extension *.docx* may or may not display. By understanding how these filing systems work, you can manage the files stored on a computer logically and consistently.

The folders and subfolders where documents are saved should be structured in a manner that is similar to the filing system created for paper documents. This is true regardless of whether you create the documents or receive them. For example, if you would file a paper memo, note, or letter relating to the advertising budget in the administrative section of your file cabinet designated for budget

Use a systematic process when naming electronic files. Filenames must follow company specifications and make sense to others who may need to access them in the creator's absence. The following guidelines will help you name files effectively:

- Avoid special characters (\ / : * ? “ < > | [ ] & $, .), which are frequently used for specific tasks in an electronic environment. For example, a forward slash is used to identify folder levels in Microsoft products, while *Mac® OS®* operating systems use the colon.
- Use underscores instead of periods. Periods before filename extensions denote file formats such as .jpg and .docx; using them in a filename could result in lost files or errors.
- Use underscores instead of spaces, which are often translated in a web environment as the percent sign. For example, the filename *e-mail procedures* would be translated as *e-mail%procedures*.
- Make each filename unique and independent from its location so that, if the file is moved, the name will not conflict with names of files already in the new location. For example, don't create a document named *Memo1* in a Budget folder and use the same name for a memo in the Personnel folder.
- Indicate versions when appropriate. For example, if you have several drafts of committee bylaws and must retain them all, include information about the version in each filename.
- If you use dates as part of a filename, format them consistently for all your documents.
- Rename files you receive from others to fit your naming conventions.

records, an electronic memo, note, or letter relating to the advertising budget might be filed in a folder structure similar to the example shown in Figure 12.2. If your organization files paper records using a geographic filing system, then the electronic folders should be set up using a geographic system. If the organization typically files information according to subjects, the electronic folders should be set up using a subject system.

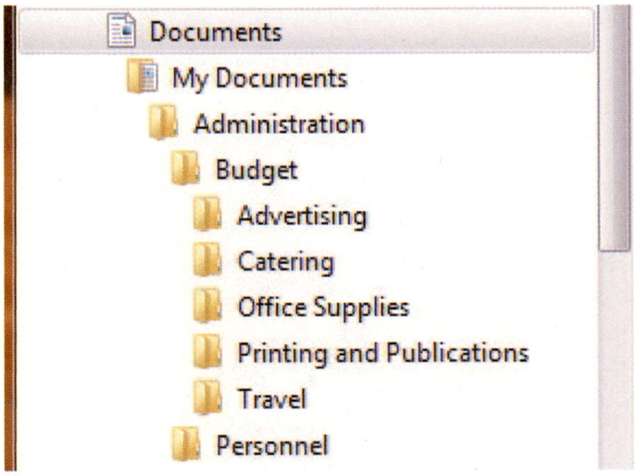

FIGURE 12.2 Folder Structure in *Windows 7*

Once a logical structure for storing files has been established, all members of an organization will be able to save or retrieve documents efficiently. The most important rule to remember in organizing electronic files is that the same methods that work with paper also apply to computers.

USE AND DISTRIBUTION

The next phase of the cycle is using and distributing the information in the electronic files. Use of the information contained in electronic records is as varied as for physical records. You or the recipients of a record may use the information it contains to answer questions, make decisions, compile data, or complete other activities. Automated records might be used to track inventory levels.

Distribution can take place through electronic channels such as e-mail or shared folders on a network. Files can be copied and distributed on removable storage devices such as DVDs or flash drives. Electronic files can also be printed and sent by regular mail or fax. When e-mail systems are used to distribute electronic files, an additional records management opportunity exists. Most e-mail programs allow the user to create and manage folders to store and organize messages.

As with paper records, electronic records can sometimes be difficult to locate. The record may have been saved in or accidently moved to an incorrect folder. The filename may be inconsistent with the naming scheme used for similar records. The search feature of an operating system such as *Microsoft Windows* can help you locate electronic records. In *Windows*, for example, users can search by filename, date, or specific text within a file on any drive on the computer or any drive to which the computer connects. For example, the search feature can help you locate a document with the name *FallBudget14.docx*. If you don't remember the document name, you can search by the creation date or text contained within the document.

MAINTENANCE

Files and folders can be moved from one location to another as part of managing records. Moving electronic files that are more than a year old to an external hard drive or DVD, for example, can free storage space on a computer's internal hard drive. Moving older files that are accessed infrequently can make finding active files easier as there will be fewer files to look through in a folder.

As with paper records, copies of electronic records can be useful. For example, an employee can copy a file to a removable storage device and then edit the file using another computer while away from the office. When the employee returns to the office, the updated file is copied to the office computer. The earlier version of the file may be retained or deleted, depending upon its usefulness.

A **backup** is a copy of electronic files or folders made as a precaution against loss or damage of the original data. Users should follow a regular schedule to back up vital and important electronic records. If data are lost or damaged, they can be restored using backup copies. Many networks use software that automatically makes copies of some or all the data on the network on a regular schedule.

DISPOSITION

Disposition is the act of retaining or destroying a record after a period of time. Several disposition methods are available for electronic records.

Data Migration *Data migration* is the process of copying electronic files and folders onto new media and in new formats as they become available. Users must be aware of hardware and software upgrades that may affect the ability to retrieve and read electronic records. Also, the available storage media continue to change. In addition, the medium on which the information is stored has a useful life span that may depend on how many times it is accessed. Cloud computing storage eliminates these concerns.

Users must anticipate and follow through with the migration of electronic records to new media as they are developed. Hardware and software upgrades must be monitored to ensure electronic records will continue to be available and readable as long as they are needed. When using cloud space, an organization can purchase migration services to avoid hardware or software upgrade issues.

Deleting Files When electronic records are no longer needed, they should be deleted or the storage medium, such as a DVD, should be destroyed. Procedures for deleting confidential files and a discussion of how long records should be retained are presented later in this chapter.

Managing Database Files

Although many electronic records are stored as files created with other software, much of the information used in business today is stored in electronic

PARTNERSHIP FOR 21ST CENTURY SKILLS

Information, Communications, and Technology Literacy

Identify Files With Document Properties

Using a consistent naming procedure is extremely helpful when trying to locate saved files. Sometimes, however, it can still be difficult to remember an exact filename. Other times you may wish to locate several files with related content. One way to organize documents effectively is to update document properties when creating *Microsoft* files.

When you create an application file, certain information is automatically added to it as part of the document properties. This includes the author name (if defined by the user) and creation date. If you do not remember a filename but know the date the document was created, you can use this information to search for a file. Other system properties, such as the date a document was last modified and file size, are also automatically generated.

Microsoft Office programs allow you to add information to the document properties of files you create. For example, in *Word*, you can add a title, subject, and keywords. Updating document properties helps users to:

- Find documents more efficiently when a document name or creation date is unknown.
- Locate several documents on a particular subject by searching for keywords or subjects.
- Save time locating a file because they can view document properties without opening documents.
- Better organize their files by creating consistent properties for files with similar content.

Activity

Open several files you have created for this class or other classes. If possible, open more than one type of file (word processing, spreadsheet, presentation, or database). Add subjects, keywords, or other information that describes the file content in the document properties. Use the search feature of your operating system to locate the files by date, keywords, subject, or category.

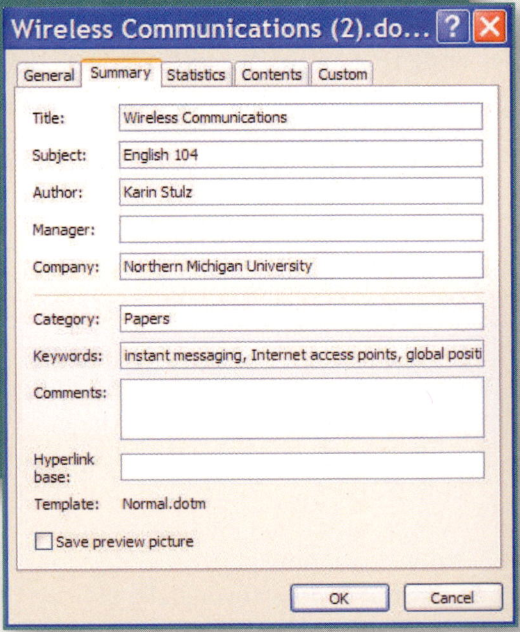

databases. With database software, data can be created, modified, reorganized, sorted, selected, and accessed in a variety of ways to carry out administrative tasks and to help solve business problems. Businesses use databases to store information about customers, inventory, products, and employees. Many organizations use a database to create an index of their paper and other records. For example, all personnel information for a company could be stored in a database rather than in paper files. In this way, it is easy to locate information as well as to create letters and mailing labels from the data.

UNDERSTANDING DATABASE FILES

The data stored in a database are organized into tables. When creating a database to store records, group data into tables of related information. For example, an automobile dealership might place customer contact information (name, address, e-mail address, and telephone number) in one table. The brand, model, year, and date of purchase of vehicles bought by each customer might be placed in another table. The tables can be related using a common field in each table, such as a customer name or customer number. Storing data in related tables eliminates redundant data (information stored in more than one place) and allows you to create queries and reports that show data from several related tables at once.

Data in a table is organized into fields and records. A field contains a single piece of information or fact (for example, an employee's last name or ID number). When deciding which fields to use in a database table, consider the smallest unit of information you might use separately from the other information. For example, when creating personalized letters using mail merge, you might want to include a person's last name in the salutation. This field would not be available if you create only one field in the database for the customer name. If you create separate fields for the customer title, first name, and last name, you can easily create personalized salutations that include the customer's title and last name. Other fields might include phone number, address, date of birth, or other facts related to the individual.

A field has a unique name and contains a defined type of information. The most common field type is a text field, which can contain text or combinations of text and numbers such as a customer's last name or address. Text fields may also be used for numbers that do not require calculations such as phone numbers or patient account numbers.

In addition to text fields, a database may contain memo, number, currency, date, and logical fields. Memo fields are similar to text fields except that they can hold much more information such as notes, comments, and product descriptions. Number fields store numeric data that may be used for mathematical calculations such as the number of bedrooms or bathrooms in a house or the number of passengers in a car. Currency fields have the same purpose as numeric fields, but they are designed to store monetary values such as a purchase price or an amount due. Date fields are used for date or time information such as a date of hire or a birth date. Logical fields contain one of two values such as yes/no, true/false, or preapproved/not approved.

A database record includes all the fields (or facts) related to one entity. This could be a customer, employee, vendor, client, company, organization, product, or other entity. Records related to one subject or topic (customers, students, orders) are usually stored in one or more related tables (Figure 12.3). Each table must have a primary key, which is a unique record identifier chosen by the user. For example, if you are working in a human resources department and are entering employee information, the primary key might be the employee number.

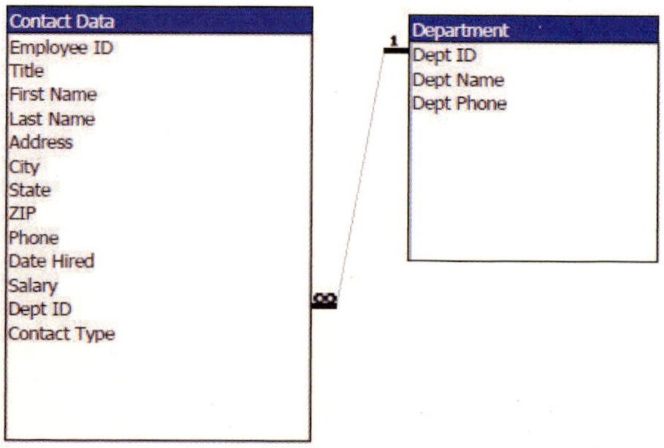

FIGURE 12.3 Establishing relationships helps eliminate duplicate information in a database.

Besides tables, a database can contain several other objects. Objects are the parts of a database that will help a user edit, manage, and analyze the data. Tables, forms, reports, and queries are all database objects.

WORKING WITH DATABASE INFORMATION

Locating a specific piece of information in a database is relatively easy using the search or find feature. A database query can be used to retrieve data that meet specific criteria set by the user. For example, you can search a database for employees who are making less than $75,000 or for all females in the accounting department. The design of the database allows the user to ask for information efficiently and retrieve it in a useful format.

A database is often used to create an index or an accession log for the physical records system. If you want records in the database and the physical system to be sorted in the same way, experiment or read the program documentation to see how text and numbers are sorted in the program. You might need to make adjustments to the way you enter data or file records so both systems work the same way. For example, some programs require the use

TECH TALK

Designing a Database

Most often, you will work with existing databases rather than designing and creating your own. Your job may require that you add, delete, or edit records. You may also use the data to answer questions or create reports. At times, however, you may be expected to design and create a database. These guidelines will help:

- Identify the tables. Examine the requirements for the database in order to define the main subjects involved. There will be a table for each subject you identify.
- Determine the primary key. Remember that the primary key is the unique identifier for records in the table. For example, in an employee database the unique identifier might be the employee ID number. Each table must have a primary key.
- Determine the additional fields. A table will typically contain many other fields besides the primary key. Examine the project requirements to determine these additional fields. For example, in an employee table, the additional fields might include First Name, Last Name, Street Address, City, State, ZIP Code, Date Hired, Salary, and so on.
- Determine relationships among the tables. Examine the list of tables you have created to see how the tables are related. A one-to-many relationship indicates that one record in one table will match many records in a related table (one department might have many employees). When you determine two tables are related, make sure you include matching fields. You must include the same field in both tables to establish relationships.
- Determine data types for the fields. For each field, determine the type of data the field can contain. Most fields will be text fields containing text or a combination of text and numbers. Others might be date fields (Date Hired) or currency fields (Salary).
- Eliminate redundancy. Remember, redundancy is the storing of a piece of data in more than one place. Redundancy can cause problems such as wasted space, difficulties with updating information, and data inconsistency. Check each table for redundancy and eliminate it.

of leading zeros to make all the numbers that need to be sorted the same length.

Managing Image Files

Document imaging is the process of scanning paper documents and converting them to digital images. Imaged documents can be stored using the same media as electronic files. Image files come in a variety of formats such as .gif, .jpg, .tif, or .pdf. Some formats require specialized software to retrieve or work with the images.

Sometimes images are stored in photographic format on microform media. **Microform** is a general term for several types of microimage media such as microfilm, microfiche, and aperture cards. The prefix *micro* is used because the images are so small that magnification is required to read them. To view microfilm images, for example, you must use a machine called a reader or viewer, which magnifies the images and displays them on a screen. A reader/printer both displays the images and prints full-size documents on paper.

Not all microforms are created from printed documents. **Computer output to microfilm (COM)** is the process of converting computer data to a microform without first printing the records. This process saves money because microforms are less expensive to produce. It also conserves paper and saves on storage space. COM is particularly useful when multiple copies of output from the computer are needed. COM output can be in either roll or flat form.

Microforms

A few common types of microforms are used in business:

- Microfilm is a roll of film that contains a series of frames or images much like a movie film. This is the most widely used and least expensive microform to create.
- Microfiche is a rectangular sheet of film that contains a series of images arranged in a grid pattern. Microfiche sheets are easy to use, handle, and identify.
- A microfilm jacket is a flat, transparent plastic carrier with a single or multiple film channels created to hold single or multiple film strips. Jackets are often used for medical records because they can be updated by inserting new records into a channel and because they keep related records together. The jacket also protects the microfilm from surface abrasion.
- An aperture card is a data processing card with a rectangular holder (or aperture) into which a piece of microfilm can be inserted. These cards are typically used to store engineering and architectural drawings or blueprints.

thyme/iStockphoto.com

To produce images and use imaging storage media, you should have a system that includes the following phases:

- Document preparation
- Processing and duplicating
- Document indexing
- Inspecting
- Storage

DOCUMENT PREPARATION

Preparing source documents for imaging is the most time-consuming and expensive process associated with document imaging or micrographics (conversion to microforms). Whether the output is image files, magnetic media (hard drives), or microforms, specific guidelines and instructions should be developed to make sure the information is prepared in a consistent manner. Preparing documents for imaging can involve many of the following steps:

- Remove the documents from file cabinets or other storage areas and organize them in the correct sequence.
- Review the records and remove all duplicate and obsolete information.
- Check all documents carefully. Unfold and flatten all papers. Remove paper clips, staples, and rubber bands. Mend torn pages. Remove unnecessary envelopes, sticky notes, and routing slips.
- Replace taped, brittle, or thin sheets of paper with copies so a jam does not occur when scanning.

Regardless of the system used, document preparation is typically completed by an individual within the organization. Once the records have been prepared, they are ready to be filmed.

PROCESSING AND DUPLICATING

Sometimes the imaging will take place within an organization. An organization may invest in an image scanner to convert paper documents to digitized images. Many types of scanners are available. Automatic document feed scanners are typically capable of converting large volumes of standard-size documents into digital forms. Flatbed scanners can be used for delicate or hard-to-handle documents but are typically slower. Film scanners convert paper documents to microfilm, microfiche, and jackets. They are available at a variety of prices and processing speeds.

Image documents can also be created by saving computer-generated documents in a specialized format. For example, documents created in *Word* or *Excel* can be saved as .pdf files through the save option.

Because equipment costs for in-house processing can be quite high, many organizations hire commercial service bureaus or independent contractors to assist in the conversion of paper documents to images. Commercial organizations may offer imaging, processing, duplicating, and inspecting services.

DOCUMENT INDEXING

Once the documents have been scanned, they must be indexed. An index attaches identification data, called an address, to microforms or image records. The process of adding indexing information to serve as a location directory for microforms or image records is an important step in managing image records.

In many imaging systems, document indexing is the process of adding "tags" or search terms to the document. This procedure provides a path to locating a document quickly and efficiently. For example, if an organization converts its paper purchase orders to document images, indexing would be very important. There are a number of ways employees might wish to search for an invoice including purchase order number, vendor name, invoice number, or maybe even date of purchase. If all these items are added as part of the document index, a user could search for the purchase order by any of them. Indexing is crucial for retrieving scanned documents or digital images.

INSPECTION

The next step in imaging is to conduct technical and content inspections. The user should conduct technical inspections to verify that the images are of high quality and can be quickly and easily accessed and used. Technical inspection also verifies that the equipment is working properly. Content inspection checks ensure all images are included, are complete, and are not obscured or distorted. Inspection is particularly important if the original records will be destroyed after microfilming or scanning. For legal purposes it is important to have a documented inspection procedure that indicates the records have been filmed in the normal course of business and have been verified for completeness before they are destroyed.

STORAGE

As noted earlier, image records should be organized and filed using the same system (alphabetic, numeric, subject, or geographic) as the organization's other types of records. Image files may be stored in folders on your computer's hard drive. If other electronic storage media or microforms are used, they are organized and stored in cabinets or other containers designed for each type of media.

For microform records, typically the original will be stored and a duplicate working copy will be prepared for reference and use. Although microfilm has a life expectancy of up to 500 years, it is highly susceptible to physical and environmental damage. Many organizations choose to store their microform records at a commercial storage facility or off-site location. If your organization will store its records on-site, make sure to research the environment requirements associated with microform storage.

The greatest concern for storing digital images is the changes that continue to occur in the computer environment. The system must be capable of displaying digital images for as long as possible, which often requires frequent updates of equipment and software.

Advantages of Imaging

Document imaging has advantages and limitations that must be considered before making a decision to adopt this storage option. Document imaging will not change poor records management into good records management. Advantages of an effective imaging system include the following:

- Space savings. The media that store images can store more records in a much smaller space than paper files.
- Quick retrieval. Image files can typically be accessed much more quickly than paper records when they are imaged correctly. This quicker retrieval time saves personnel costs and improves customer assistance.
- Multiple users. Two or more users can access image files at the same time.
- Image enhancement. Poor-quality originals can be enhanced by software.

Records Retention, Transfer, and Disposal

As you learned in Chapter 11, records are documents that have value to the organization. Records may be valuable for legal, financial, or historical reference or for use in daily operations. A major mistake in handling records is to assume every paper or electronic record is worth keeping. To be classified as a record, a document must have value to the organization. Many documents do not meet this requirement. Much incoming paperwork should be kept only temporarily or discarded immediately. Many e-mail messages or electronic documents should be read, handled, and deleted. You must recognize the difference between information that is of no value to the organization (and is discarded) and information that is of value (and is kept as a record to be managed).

Records Categories

Records can be classified as to their importance or usefulness to the organization as vital records, important records, useful records, or nonessential records. The record classification will determine, in part, how long the records should be retained. Figure 12.4 lists examples for each classification.

VITAL RECORDS

Records that cannot be replaced and should never be destroyed are called **vital records**. These records are essential to the effective continued operation of the organization and/or are required by law to be retained.

IMPORTANT RECORDS

Records that are necessary to an orderly continuation of the business and are replaceable only at considerable cost of time and money are known as **important records**. Such records may be transferred to inactive storage but are not destroyed.

USEFUL RECORDS

Useful records are those needed for the smooth, effective operation of the organization. Such records are replaceable, but their loss involves delay or inconvenience to the organization. These records may be transferred to inactive files or destroyed after a certain period of time.

Records Classifications

Category	Examples
Vital records	Corporate charters, deeds, tax returns, constitutions and bylaws, insurance policies, procedures manuals, audited financial statements, patents, and copyrights
Important records	Financial statements, operating and statistical records, physical inventories, electronic business records, and board minutes
Useful records	Letters, memorandums, reports, and bank records
Nonessential records	Newsletters, employee announcements, periodicals, and routine e-mail and phone messages

FIGURE 12.4 Examples of Records Classifications

Limitations of Imaging

Although imaging offers some advantages, it also has limitations, such as the following:

- Expense. The costs of hardware, software, system maintenance, and administration must be considered, as well as conversion costs for document preparation, indexing, and quality control.
- Reliance on equipment. Digital images are not readable without computers or specialized equipment or software.
- Quicker obsolescence. System hardware and software change frequently. Users must be willing to continue to upgrade their equipment and knowledge as advances are made.
- Difficulty of use. Although some systems use common business equipment (scanners, hard drives, and computers), a certain amount of technical skill and experience is often necessary.

NONESSENTIAL RECORDS

Documents that have no future value to the organization are considered **nonessential records**. Once the purpose for which they were created has been fulfilled, they may be destroyed.

Records Retention

A **retention period** is the time that records must be kept according to operational, legal, regulatory, and fiscal requirements. The cost of maintaining documents that are no longer of any use can be significant, particularly in manual systems because of the floor space necessary for the files. Even though electronic storage takes up less space, there is some cost to maintaining unneeded documents.

To avoid keeping records longer than necessary, organizations use a records retention schedule. A records retention schedule lists the types of records and how long they should be kept. Retention times for some records vary by state because they are based on state laws. The retention schedule may also identify how long records are needed in the active storage area and how long records should be retained in inactive storage.

Benefits of using a records retention schedule include the following:

- Vital legal, financial, compliance, regulatory, and administrative records will not be disposed of prematurely.
- Valuable historical records will be preserved.
- Records that are no longer needed can be disposed of systematically.
- Clear procedures for when to transfer records from active to inactive storage and whether to convert to microform or digital format will be established.

As an administrative professional, you will be responsible for making decisions about the files you use or maintain. If you work for a large organization, you may not make decisions about how long important documents should be kept. Instead, you will adhere to retention schedules that were developed by someone else. Typically, company managers will consult with legal counsel and then prepare appropriate retention schedules. Large organizations may employ a records manager to make decisions regarding records retention. If the company does not have a records retention schedule, check with your supervisor before making any decisions about transferring or destroying documents.

When a retention schedule is developed, the following issues should be considered:

- Use. How long does the organization require the use of the records?
- Inactivity. At what point should records be declared inactive? Should inactive records be transferred to low-cost storage, or should they be destroyed?

R-J-Seymour/iStockphoto.com

A records retention schedule determines when records should be sent to a storage facility.

- Laws and regulations. What federal, state, and local requirements for keeping records must be followed?
- Cost. What is the cost of keeping records versus the cost of not keeping them?
- Off-site storage. Which records should be transferred to a less expensive or more secure storage location away from the central offices?
- Integrity and security. Will transferred records maintain their integrity so specific records can be located when needed? Will transferred records be protected properly from destruction and unauthorized use?

Records retention schedules are based on the value of the information in the records. By closely following an approved records retention schedule, an organization can reduce the costs associated with the storage of unnecessary records.

Records Transfer

At some point in the life cycle of a record, the decision is made to destroy the record, retain it permanently, or transfer it to inactive storage. Records transfer is the act of changing the physical location of records. Two common methods of records transfer are perpetual transfer and periodic transfer.

PERPETUAL TRANSFER

With **perpetual transfer**, materials are continuously transferred from active to inactive storage when they are no longer needed for frequent reference. The advantage of this method is that all files are kept current because inactive files are immediately transferred to storage. The perpetual transfer method works well in organizations where jobs are completed by units. Examples include legal cases that no longer need attention, student records after graduation, construction jobs that are complete, and research projects when results are finalized.

When distinguishing between active and inactive records, use the following categories:

- Active records used 3 or more times a month should be kept in an accessible area.
- Inactive records used fewer than 15 times a year may be stored in less accessible areas than active records.
- **Archive records** (records with historical value to the organization) are preserved permanently.

The perpetual transfer method should be applied to electronic as well as paper records. Remember, not all electronic records need to be retained. Electronic documents can remain on the local or network hard drive until they are scheduled to be deleted or are no longer active. Electronic documents can be transferred to storage media described previously in this chapter.

PERIODIC TRANSFER

With **periodic transfer**, active records are transferred to inactive status at the end of a stated time. For example, you may transfer records that are more than six months old to the inactive file and maintain records that are less than six months old in the active file. Every six months you would repeat the procedure. This method of transfer works well and is used by many businesses. Periodic transfer should be used for electronic as well as paper files. For example, electronic records that no longer need to be retained should be deleted; electronic records that need to be kept can be transferred to permanent storage.

Records are transferred to either inactive or archive storage. Inactive storage indicates the record will be referenced infrequently. At the end of the retention period, inactive records are destroyed. Archive records must be kept permanently.

Records Disposal

Records that are no longer of use should be destroyed. Paper records that are not confidential can be disposed of by simply dropping the paper in a bin for recycling. Electronic records that are not confidential are simply deleted or erased from the storage medium.

Confidential information should be destroyed beyond reconstruction. Confidential paper records should be destroyed by shredding, burning, or pulping. Some organizations contract with an outside service for destruction of paper records. Electronic files can be deleted from the computer or storage media. Next, the user must clean the unused portions of the media. This can be accomplished with special software that will overwrite those areas of the disk that are no longer in use. The cleaning process prohibits sophisticated users from restoring deleted files whose space has not been overwritten. It also helps ensure that electronic information that is no longer useful or required is not inadvertently retained.

SUMMARY

To reinforce what you have learned in this chapter, study this summary.

- Electronic records may be created as part of an electronic database, generated by an automated system, or created individually. They are managed through the four phases of the records life cycle.
- Because electronic databases are widely used in business, the ability to manage and use them is essential.
- An effective system for managing digital image records consists of document preparation, processing and duplicating, document indexing, inspecting, and storage.
- Records retention, transfer, and disposal procedures that take into account the records classifications should be implemented and followed.

KEY TERMS

12

STUDY Tools

Located at www.cengagebrain.com

- Chapter Outlines
- Flashcards
- Interactive Quizzes
- Tech Tools
- Video Segments
- and More!

LET'S DISCUSS

1. Describe three types of electronic records you may encounter in business, and give an example of each type.
2. List and define the four phases of the life cycle for an electronic record.
3. List six suggestions for creating effective filenames.
4. How are documents prepared for storage in an image system?
5. How can a database help an organization manage employee information?
6. Describe the issues that should be considered when developing a retention schedule. Describe the four record categories, and explain how these categories impact retention.
7. Explain the difference between perpetual and periodic transfer.

PUT IT TO WORK

Imaging training The organization you work for recently purchased a new document imaging system. Although the system won't be up and running for several months and many training seminars must still be conducted, the staff has been instructed to get an early start on this program. All paper files from the last fiscal year need to be pulled and prepared for scanning. This processing includes batching all work orders by company or client name. (The current paper filing system was organized by subject.) The records need to be batched in groups of 50 files, and each batch must include a cover sheet listing the client names included in the batch.

The employees who must prepare the files for imaging are not happy with this change. They believe the old system worked fine. They have no idea how the new document imaging system works and do not like the fact that they had no input into the purchase of the system.

What needs to be done to prepare the files for imaging? How could the department managers have made this transition less intimidating? What steps can be taken to give employees an understanding of how the new system will affect their work and the company's overall operations? (Learning Objective 1)

COMMUNICATE SUCCESSFULLY

1. **Proofread and format** Your supervisor, Martha Moore, has drafted a memo to all employees discussing appropriate records disposal. She has asked you to edit the memo for clarity and correctness. She would also like you to proofread the memo and format it for distribution. Access the *Word* file *Ch12_Disposition* from the data files and complete these tasks. (Learning Objective 2)

2. **Electronic records** Create an electronic slide presentation about managing electronic records. Include examples of the types of electronic records. Identify and describe the phases in the electronic records life cycle. Select an appropriate theme to produce a professional-looking presentation. Include graphics and speaker notes. (Learning Objective 1)
3. **Organize e-mail messages** Write a paragraph that describes how you currently organize your e-mail messages. Write a second paragraph that describes how you will better organize your e-mail messages after reading this chapter. (Learning Objectives 1 and 2)
4. **Manage electronic records** Add a new post to the blog you created in Chapter 1. In this entry, reflect on the following statement: **This chapter has helped me better understand how to manage my electronic records in the following ways.** (Learning Objectives 1 and 2)

Blog

DEVELOP WORKPLACE SKILLS

5. **Create an accession log** Your department has been filing records using an alphabetic records system. Recently your supervisor, Estelle Lombardini, decided that a more confidential records system is needed. Estelle has asked that you help convert the records to a consecutive number system. Client numbers will be assigned in ascending order starting with 100. (Learning Objective 1)
   a. Access the *Word* file *Ch12_Log* from the data files. Numbers have been assigned to five names as shown in the file.
   b. Create a database to serve as an accession log. Name the database appropriately. Create a table named *Accession Log* to include the fields shown in the following table. Establish the appropriate primary key.

FIELD NAME	DATA TYPE	DESCRIPTION
File Number	Number	Unique number assigned to a name
Indexing Order	Text	Name or subject in indexing order in all capitals with no punctuation
As Written	Text	Name as written
Date Assigned	Date	Date the number is assigned

   c. Enter the data for the five names for which numbers have already been assigned. Use the current date in the Date Assigned field.
   d. Index and code the correspondence that has been received. Assign a number and create a database record for new names.
6. **Organize electronic files** Use the files you have created for this course or the files you plan to place in your electronic portfolio to complete this activity. (Learning Objective 1)
   a. Organize the files according to the skills demonstrated. For example, create a folder for those activities that demonstrate communication

skills; create a second folder for those activities that demonstrate teamwork skills. Follow this procedure to create other folders and organize all your electronic files for this class.

b. Rename the files using a system that describes the content of the file.

c. Create a one-page handout that describes your naming and storage procedures so others could easily retrieve files if necessary. Include a list of the folders you created and the names of the files you placed in each folder. Select an appropriate document theme to create a professional-looking handout.

7. **Work with a database** Access the *Word* file *Ch12_Database* from the data files. Follow the instructions in the document to update a database, perform filters or queries, and create reports. (Learning Objective 1)

BUILD RELATIONSHIPS

8. **Confidential information** Sally works in the human resources department of a large organization. Every day she eats lunch with Albert, who works in the shipping department. Last week Franklin was hired in the receiving department in a position similar to Albert's. Although Albert has been with the company for more than five years, he heard yesterday that Franklin is receiving a higher salary.

   Sally has access to the personnel records, but she has not seen Franklin's hiring information. However, yesterday she heard her supervisor discussing Franklin's salary with another manager. Is it OK for Sally to tell Albert what she knows? How should she respond if he asks if the rumor is true? Is it unethical for Sally to share information she didn't see in the files but overheard? In the future, how could Sally respond to questions and maintain her professionalism when asked about confidential information? (Learning Objective 2)

9. **File ethics** Your supervisor has asked you to destroy a file containing design documents and research related to one of your company's products. You know the product was quickly removed from the market six months ago. You believe customers have taken legal action against your company because the product is considered unsafe. How will you respond to this situation? What will you say to your supervisor? (Learning Objective 2)

USE TECH TOOLS

10. **Design and create a database** Your organization is hoping to increase the physical activity of its employees. Your supervisor has asked for your help in preparing a database of fitness centers in your local area. At a minimum, she would like you to include the following information: the types of membership offered (annual, monthly, daily), fees, street

address, telephone number, and opening and closing times and days. Since many employees may be interested in group fitness activities, include a section that will indicate whether fitness classes are offered. Design and create a database that will meet your supervisor's needs. Create the necessary tables, determine the necessary fields, enter some sample data, and prepare a sample report to show your supervisor. Add the database to your online portfolio. (Learning Objective 1)

e-Portfolio

PLAN AHEAD

Investigate electronic file management Work with a classmate to complete this assignment. Identify someone from a local government office, hospital, bank, or insurance company who works with the organization's records. Interview this person, asking him or her to respond to three of the following questions. Create two additional questions on your own.

- How are the company's electronic records protected from loss?
- How are the records protected from unauthorized access?
- Are there laws that govern records management activities?
- How does the organization dispose of records that are no longer needed?

Write a short report describing your findings, and be prepared to present them to the class. (Learning Objectives 1 and 2)

CHAPTER

13 Personal Finance and Investment Strategies

LEARNING OBJECTIVES

1. Identify the purpose and steps for financial planning and budgeting.
2. Understand investing for retirement and future wealth.
3. Identify payroll taxes and optional payroll deductions.
4. Describe the costs and benefits of credit.
5. Understand and prepare organizational financial statements.

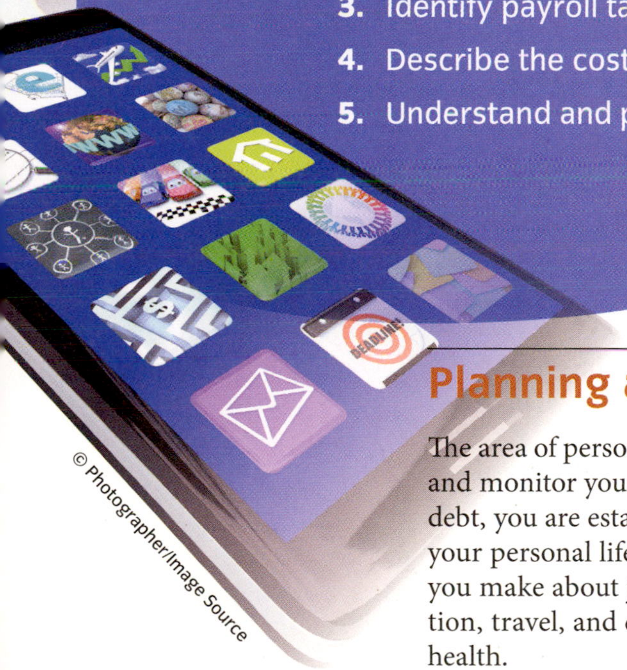

Planning and Budgeting

The area of personal finance is important to everyone. By learning to evaluate and monitor your spending, plan for the future, and recognize the impact of debt, you are establishing direction for your future. The choices you make in your personal life affect your performance at work. They affect the decisions you make about jobs, education, and expenses such as housing, transportation, travel, and clothing. They can also influence stress levels and personal health.

When dealing with your personal finances, one of the first things you must do is develop a plan. Additionally, you have to be wise in planning your future investments through retirement and having a good understanding of debt.

The Planning Process

In making a **financial plan**, you consider your financial goals and then determine the steps needed to meet those goals. A plan in any situation serves as a guide to point you in a set direction. In the case of your personal finances, a plan can serve as your guide to financial security and obtaining the things you need and want. Figure 13.1 shows part of a financial plan.

Financial Plan (One Goal)			
Personal Goal	**Financial Goal**	**Steps**	**Timeline**
Have a car I can rely on	Own a newer car	1. Take care of my current car so I can sell it for the maximum amount	Now
		2. Save money for a newer car	3 years
		• $200 per month	each month
		• Open separate savings account for car fund	next week
		3. Have a job that provides enough so I can save	6 months
		4. Start researching cars	2 years

FIGURE 13.1 A financial plan lists personal and financial goals as well as steps and a timeline for reaching them.

To start a financial plan, you need to consider your current financial situation. Note the amounts you have in your checking and savings accounts and the value of any stocks or other assets you own. You should also consider debt (how much you owe on a car, furniture, a home, etc.). Finally, include your current income and other expenses, either exact or estimated.

If you are just starting your career, you may not be considering financial issues in the distant future, such as retirement, long-term care insurance, Medicare, and Social Security. However, planning for your financial future will involve some thought about those items. Consider how you will plan your spending and saving now so you can meet your personal financial goals in the future.

CREATE A BUDGET

A budget (Figure 13.2) is essential both for managing your monthly expenses and for longer-range financial planning. A **budget** is a spending and saving plan based on anticipated income and expenses. A budget should list all your sources of income for a certain length of time, such as a year, and all the expenses you anticipate. *Microsoft Excel* is an excellent program to use for a personal budget. You can easily adjust planned savings and discretionary spending to stay within your means.

Figure 13.2 shows a budget that Mariana, a student, prepared in *Excel.* The figure shows the first four months of the year. The current month (April) is highlighted. The Total column at the right tracks total income, savings, and expenses. As the month progresses, Mariana updates the amounts as necessary. For instance, she spent $5 extra on entertainment in February and $10 less on gas in March. The Net row shows how much she is over or under budget for the month.

SET GOALS

Make a list of your personal and financial goals. Ask yourself what you would like to achieve and how you will pay for it. Owning a newer car may be one of your personal goals; a **financial goal** describes how you will pay for that car. Making a list of your personal and financial goals will help you keep focused on those goals for the future.

Setting goals usually involves timelines. Personal and financial goals are often categorized as short-term, intermediate, or long-term. A long-term goal might be to own your own home—five or ten years in the future, possibly, but you are still saving money each year toward one day achieving that goal. An example of an intermediate goal would be to become a virtual office professional in three years. A short-term goal is more immediate, within the year. For example, you know you need a new computer, so you set aside some money each month so you can purchase it later in the year.

MAKE REALISTIC CHOICES

Administrative professionals work in a practical environment and must make practical and realistic

	A	B	C	D	E	F
1		Jan.	Feb.	March	April	TOTAL
2	INCOME					
3	Work	$900.00	$900.00	$900.00	$900.00	$3,600.00
4	Financial aid	$900.00	$900.00	$900.00	$900.00	$3,600.00
5	TOTAL INCOME	$1,800.00	$1,800.00	$1,800.00	$1,800.00	$7,200.00
6						
7	SAVINGS					
8	Direct deposit	$100.00	$100.00	$100.00	$100.00	$400.00
9						
10	EXPENSES					
11	Books	$75.00	$75.00	$75.00	$75.00	$300.00
12	Tuition	$775.00	$775.00	$775.00	$775.00	$3,100.00
13	Gas	$60.00	$60.00	$50.00	$60.00	$230.00
14	Groceries	$200.00	$200.00	$200.00	$200.00	$800.00
15	Rent	$325.00	$325.00	$325.00	$325.00	$1,300.00
16	Auto insurance	$100.00	$100.00	$100.00	$100.00	$400.00
17	Entertainment	$40.00	$45.00	$40.00	$40.00	$165.00
18	Eating out	$35.00	$35.00	$35.00	$35.00	$140.00
19	Charity	$90.00	$90.00	$90.00	$90.00	$360.00
20	TOTAL EXPENSES	$1,700.00	$1,705.00	$1,690.00	$1,700.00	$6,795.00
21						
22	NET	$0.00	-$5.00	$10.00	$0.00	$5.00

FIGURE 13.2 Budget in *Microsoft Excel*

choices each day on the job. The same is true when planning personal finances. Making payments on an expensive car isn't realistic if you're working a part-time job and make minimum wage. As you develop a personal financial plan and consider your goals, be realistic in your short-term, intermediate, and long-term goals. That expensive car will be a more realistic purchase several years in the future.

SEEK ADVICE

Many books and magazines, as well as websites and blogs on the Internet, can give you insight, help, and encouragement in this process of planning (Figure 13.3 on page 284). Also, there are probably people in your life who can offer useful advice. For example, Roberto is starting out as an administrative professional and wants to begin his career by getting control of his finances. He is just out of school, so he doesn't have much money. Roberto asks his aunt for advice. He chooses his aunt because she has always managed her money very well. His aunt shares some of her own financial successes and failures from that time in her life, and she offers some suggestions. The information is very helpful to Roberto. Most importantly, Roberto is willing to listen and to learn, and he has someone he can discuss his finances with who will consider his best interests.

MONEY MANAGEMENT 101

If you have an opportunity to take a personal financial course, do it. Such courses teach good habits and encourage a lifelong pattern of being organized and responsible financially. As a rule, you will do well if you remember several basics: live on less than you earn, control your debt, save money each month, have money set aside for emergencies, keep track of what you are spending, and have financial goals and plans.

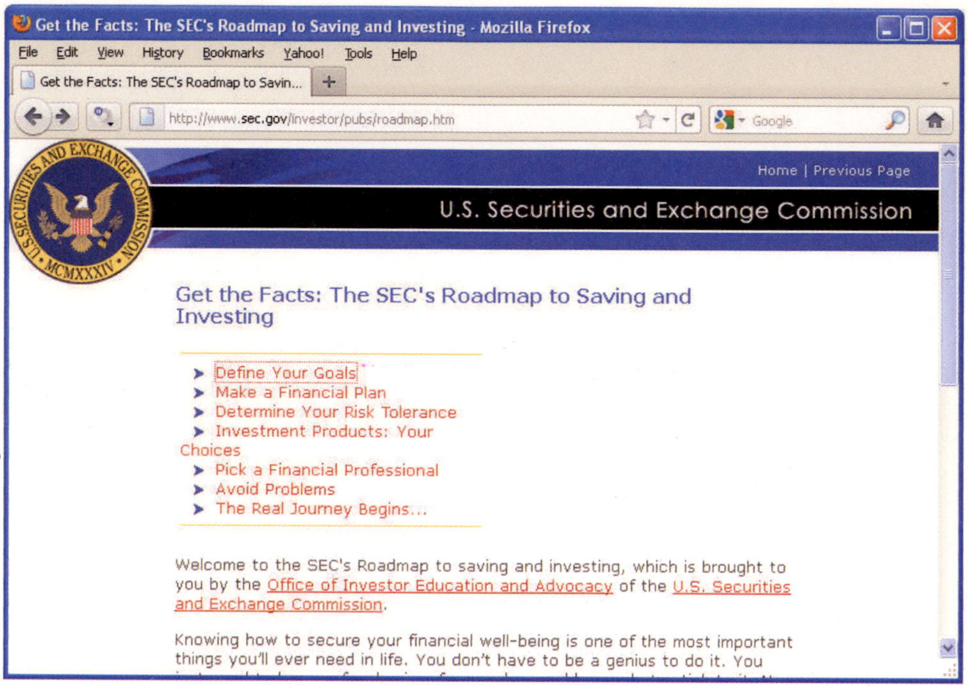

U.S. Securities and Exchange Commission

FIGURE 13.3 Many government websites provide financial advice.

CHECKING

Your checking account is probably the account that gets the most activity in your household each month. Most people keep track of account transactions with a checkbook register, whether by hand, on the computer, or on a mobile device. Tracking your income and expenditures is necessary so you can verify your bank statements, do not spend more than you have, and can keep your budget updated.

Computer programs such as *Quicken* financial software are useful for managing a personal or small-business checking account. Such programs will print checks, track expenditures, assist in reconciling bank statements, and communicate information to tax preparation software for tax returns. Mobile applications offer options such as viewing account and loan balances and tracking spending.

SAVINGS

Savings help you plan for future needs or wants. A savings account is also a way to plan for emergencies or unplanned spending (like replacing a tire on your car). You should not have to borrow money to fix a tire. It is your responsibility to plan for contingencies. Having savings minimizes interruption to your daily life when something unplanned occurs. For example, if you have money in savings, you can have your car repaired quickly and not have to depend on others to give you a ride, risk being late to work or class, or miss work due to transportation issues.

Vacations are also a popular reason for saving money. Start out by saving money for inexpensive vacations such as going camping or traveling within your state or region. Longer, more expensive

MidwestWilderness/iStockphoto.com

Camping or visiting state parks are vacation options that can save you money.

TT TECH TALK

Spreadsheet Templates for Personal Finance

An often-overlooked feature of *Microsoft Excel* is the collection of templates provided with the software and at Microsoft Office Online. Excellent templates are available for use in personal finance, such as the personal monthly budget and loan amortization schedule.

Personal monthly budget This template has detailed listings for income, expenditures, investments, savings, and donations. It is easy to plan a personal budget using this form.

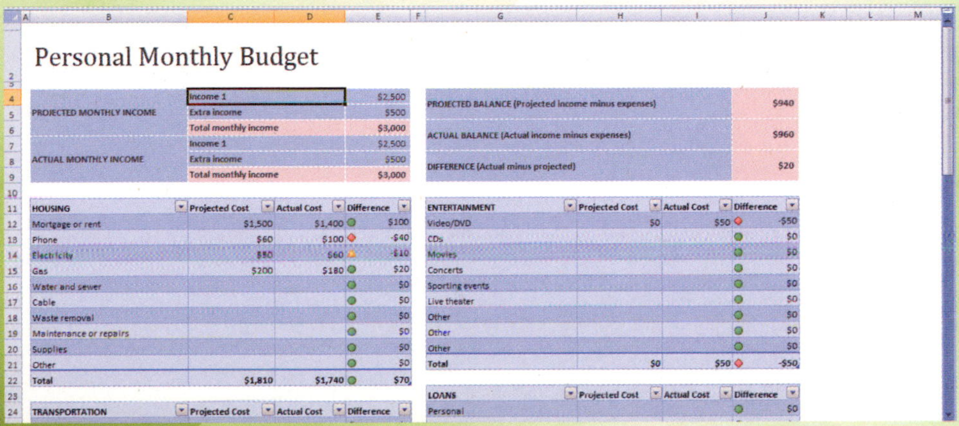

Personal Monthly Budget

PROJECTED MONTHLY INCOME	Income 1	$2,500
	Extra income	$500
	Total monthly income	$3,000
ACTUAL MONTHLY INCOME	Income 1	$2,500
	Extra income	$500
	Total monthly income	$3,000

PROJECTED BALANCE (Projected income minus expenses)	$940
ACTUAL BALANCE (Actual income minus expenses)	$960
DIFFERENCE (Actual minus projected)	$20

HOUSING	Projected Cost	Actual Cost	Difference
Mortgage or rent	$1,500	$1,400	$100
Phone	$60	$100	-$40
Electricity	$50	$60	-$10
Gas	$200	$180	$20
Water and sewer			$0
Cable			$0
Waste removal			$0
Maintenance or repairs			$0
Supplies			$0
Other			$0
Total	$1,810	$1,740	$70

ENTERTAINMENT	Projected Cost	Actual Cost	Difference
Video/DVD	$0	$50	-$50
CDs			$0
Movies			$0
Concerts			$0
Sporting events			$0
Live theater			$0
Other			$0
Other			$0
Other			$0
Total	$0	$50	-$50

TRANSPORTATION	Projected Cost	Actual Cost	Difference

LOANS	Projected Cost	Actual Cost	Difference
Personal			$0

Loan amortization schedule This template is very practical for comparing terms and predicting monthly payments for loans you are considering, such as a home or auto loan. You must know the loan amount, annual interest rate, number of years for the loan, number of payments per year, and start date.

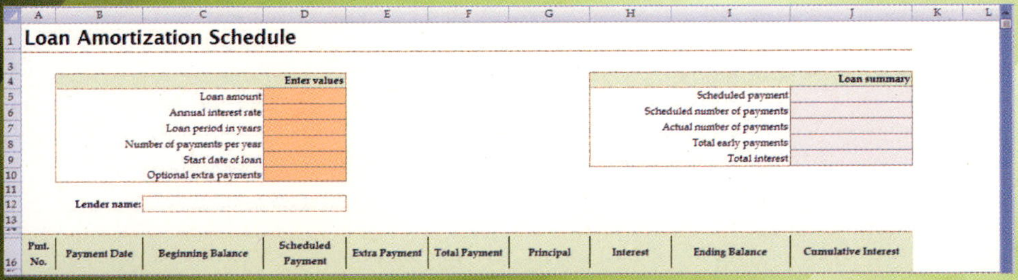

Loan Amortization Schedule

Enter values	
Loan amount	
Annual interest rate	
Loan period in years	
Number of payments per year	
Start date of loan	
Optional extra payments	

Lender name:

Loan summary	
Scheduled payment	
Scheduled number of payments	
Actual number of payments	
Total early payments	
Total interest	

Pmt. No.	Payment Date	Beginning Balance	Scheduled Payment	Extra Payment	Total Payment	Principal	Interest	Ending Balance	Cumulative Interest

Other templates are worth investigating. For example, with a stock investment performance template, you can track current investments or follow stocks that interest you before investing. Specialized budgets include a wedding budget or an event budget for a company. Balance sheets and income statements might be customized for your use in business.

vacations (such as to Europe) will probably require saving for several years.

Savings accounts earn interest usually at a very low rate. Banks offer many ways to save money, such as traditional savings accounts, certificates of deposit (CDs), money market accounts, U.S. savings bonds, and retirement accounts. When you are saving money, the emphasis is on putting it in a safe place where you can get access to it fairly quickly. Typically, you sacrifice a higher rate of return for greater security.

ONLINE BANKING

Since online banking is popular and most companies deposit employee paychecks electronically, many people have little need to physically visit a bank. Online banking makes paying bills and managing your bank accounts easy and convenient. With online banking you can enter your account number or swipe your debit card at a store and then view your account balances online. You can also have bills paid automatically or pay them manually online without ever writing a check. You can transfer funds between accounts or have money automatically transferred from checking to savings at specified times. This is helpful in saving since it removes money from the line of spending. All these features make it easier to keep your personal finances in order.

Investments

The essence of investing is to earn a sufficiently high rate of return on your money so it can grow. While savings provide security (keeping your money safe), investments provide wealth (using money to make

Reconciling Your Bank Statement

Every month, you should reconcile your check register with your bank statement. You can do this manually or use software such as *Excel*. Follow these steps:

1. Record the ending balance from the bank statement.
2. Verify that all transactions in your check register are correct on the bank statement (checks, ATM or debit card withdrawals, and deposits).
3. List any checks and other withdrawals since the statement date, and total the amount.
4. Repeat Step 3 for deposits.
5. Add the total from Step 4 to the statement balance, and then subtract the total from Step 3.
6. Subtract bank fees or charges and add account interest or other credits (if any) to your checkbook register total.
7. The new statement balance from Step 5 should be the same as your checkbook register total from Step 6. If they are not the same, complete the steps again and check your calculations.
8. Make any adjustments necessary to your check register if you find errors. Contact the bank if you conclude it has made an error. Clearly explain adjustments in your register, and make a note of the date your account is balanced.

more money). Once you have saved enough money for short- and medium-term goals and emergency needs, you can turn your attention to investing.

Retirement Plans

An important investment goal is to have enough money for retirement. In an era when individuals cannot expect to be employed by one organization for their entire career and when organizations are continuing to limit **fringe benefits** (employment benefits given in addition to wages), individuals must be concerned about their financial security when they are no longer working.

Several types of employer-sponsored retirement plans exist. Some are *tax-deferred* plans, meaning you do not pay taxes on the money when you put it into the plan. You do pay taxes on the money when you start withdrawing it for retirement. You can also supplement your income and retirement funds by investing in stocks, bonds, or mutual funds on your own or through a financial planner or stockbroker.

INDIVIDUAL RETIREMENT ARRANGEMENTS (IRAs)

An **individual retirement arrangement (IRA)** is a plan that permits individuals to invest for retirement (as opposed to an employer-sponsored plan). You decide how to invest the funds; however, the types of investments that can be purchased through an IRA are restricted. Money can be invested in items such as stocks, bonds, mutual funds, and certificates of deposit. Money cannot be invested in collectibles such as artwork, antiques, gems, and coins. The following are three common types of IRAs:

- Traditional IRA. Money set aside in a traditional IRA can be deducted from gross income if you meet certain requirements. This lowers your taxable income. You will not pay taxes on the account's earnings until the money is withdrawn during retirement.
- Roth IRA. With a Roth IRA, your contributions are taxed at the time you make them. However, if you meet certain requirements, the earnings on a Roth IRA are tax-free. Thus, when you withdraw money at retirement, you do not have to pay taxes on it.
- Spousal IRA. A spousal IRA is set up to benefit a spouse who does not work outside the home. To qualify, the couple must file a joint tax return. Spousal IRAs may be traditional or Roth IRAs.

With all types of IRAs, there may be limits on the amount that can be invested and restrictions on when the money can be withdrawn. If you are interested in opening an IRA, research all the requirements and restrictions first. Details about contribution amounts can be found on the Internal Revenue Service (IRS) website.

DEFINED BENEFIT PLANS

Some employers offer retirement accounts that are paid for by the employer. These accounts are called **defined benefit plans** or simply pensions. In some plans, the employee can also contribute money to the account. Defined benefit plans usually require that you work a minimum number of years (typically five) before you qualify for the plan. The amount contributed to the plan on your behalf increases as you continue to work for the organization. The benefit amount you receive when you retire depends on the number of years worked, your salary, and other factors. When retired employees receive payments, they must pay taxes on the money. Defined benefit plans are offered by fewer companies now than in the past.

401(K) AND 403(B) ACCOUNTS

Many companies and organizations offer employees an option to enroll in a 401(k) or 403(b) plan. A **401(k) account** is a tax-deferred retirement plan for employees of private companies and corporations. Employees pay taxes on the money only when it is withdrawn. The employee sets aside money each month through a pretax payroll deduction. The employer may also contribute money to the account. Sometimes employers match a certain percentage of employee contributions. Employees choose investments for their 401(k) accounts based on their willingness to take risks. Some investments carry a higher risk of economic loss than others.

Planning for Retirement

Begin planning for your retirement early in life. Saving and investing money now will help ensure you have the resources you need to live comfortably after you retire. Follow these suggestions:

1. Examine your present finances. Determine how much you can save or invest toward retirement at the present time.
2. Think about the lifestyle you want to have in retirement. For example, do you want to live in a house that you own? Do you want to travel?
3. Look at your current living expenses, and estimate an amount for living expenses after retirement. Books, magazines, and online resources are available to help you do this.
4. Establish an investment plan for your working years to generate the income you will need in retirement. Write your plan down and live by it.
5. Evaluate your plan every year to determine if it is still financially sound. Revise it as your circumstances and goals change.

Blend Images/Shutterstock.com

If your organization matches 401(k) contributions, you should contribute at least as much money as the employer will match. This is a "no-brainer" in financial management since your employer is giving you something for free. The money you contribute is pretax, which means you won't feel the full amount of your contribution in your paycheck, and you will double your money with the employer contribution. For example, suppose your employer will match up to $40 per month for your 401(k). If you contribute $40 before taxes, you may only miss $25 to $30 from your paycheck (depending on your other deductions) because you will pay less tax, and you will gain an additional $40 from your employer for your 401(k). This amounts to an extra $480 that you did not have to work for each year.

A **403(b) account** is a tax-deferred retirement plan for employees of nonprofit organizations or educational institutions. Teachers, nurses, professors, and ministers are examples of people who might qualify for a 403(b) account. If you work as an administrative professional at a nonprofit organization, such as a charity, you might also qualify for a 403(b) account.

A 403(b) account is very similar to a 401(k), the main difference being who is eligible to contribute—public versus private. There are three other key differences between a 401(k) and a 403(b):

- With a 403(b) plan, money can be withdrawn early with no tax penalty if it is put in an annuity fund.
- Individuals with a 403(b) plan can leave the account with an employer if they change jobs.
- 401(k) plans traditionally have more investment options.

SIMPLIFIED EMPLOYEE PENSION PLANS (SEP)

A **simplified employee pension plan** (SEP) is a retirement plan for small business owners and their employees. It is similar to an IRA. A SEP may be an option for you if you become a virtual office professional. The amount of money that can be set aside for a SEP is higher than for an IRA. Contributions are tax-deductible, and you do not need to contribute every year.

Stocks, Bonds, and Mutual Funds

Investments vary by the amount of risk involved, the rate of return on your investment, and the **liquidity** (how easily the investment is converted into cash). In deciding whether to purchase stocks, bonds, or mutual funds, you should consider all these factors as well as your long-term investment goals.

STOCKS

Stocks are shares of ownership in a company. Stockholders become partial owners of a company through buying stock. If the price of stock you own increases due to its growth and profitability, your personal assets increase. You may also be entitled to a share of the company's profits that may be paid as **dividends**. However, if the stock goes down in

Maintaining Retirement Benefits

You may be employed by several different organizations during your working years. You may have a 401(k) account or a defined benefit plan at one or more of these organizations. Keep careful records of your benefits at each organization. When you leave an organization, determine whether your retirement investments can be rolled over into another account or will stay in the current plan. You should receive statements about your retirement accounts periodically. Review them, and keep them for future reference.

price due to the company's poor performance or poor economic conditions in the world, your personal assets also go down. As a stock owner, you are vulnerable to the volatility of stocks.

Most stocks are *common stocks*; however, some companies also sell *preferred stocks*. As an investor, you need to understand the major differences between common and preferred stocks:

- Owners of common stock have voting rights in decisions made by shareholders.
- In many companies, owners of preferred stock have a guaranteed dividend rate.
- When dividends are declared, preferred stockholders are paid in full before common stockholders are paid any dividends.
- The market value of common stock may fluctuate more than the market value of preferred stock.

Historically stocks as a whole increase in value over time. However, the price for an individual stock may rise or fall regardless of how the stock market is doing overall. The smart investor carefully researches a company before buying its stock. Look at how the company has performed over a period of time. You can use a smartphone app (such as *Bloomberg*) to follow a stock.

You can also compare an individual company to an index of stocks. The Dow Jones Industrial Average (often called *the Dow*) is the best-known U.S. index of stocks. It contains 30 stocks that trade on the New York Stock Exchange. The Dow is considered an indicator of what is happening in the stock market. Even though the Dow represents only 30 stocks, these stocks have been a mainstay in the U.S. economy for years. If they are down as a group, it is likely that the majority of stocks are down. The Standard & Poor's 500 (S&P 500) index is derived from the price of common stocks of 500 publicly traded companies. The S&P 500, like the Dow, is an indicator of stock market trends.

Investing in the stock market demands time on your part in tracking your investments, researching potential purchases, and modifying your portfolio when needed. Stockbrokers are professionals who can help you make investment decisions; however, you will pay for their services.

BONDS

A **bond** is basically a loan that a buyer makes to a bond issuer. The bond issuer may be a government or a corporation. Bonds are designed to be long-term investments. They represent a bond issuer's promise to pay a definite sum of money to the holder of the bond at a specified time. Thus, bonds do not represent a share of ownership in a company (as stocks do), but are evidence of a debt owed by the issuer. When the stock market is down, bonds generally yield a greater return for the investor than stocks. However, when the stock market is doing well, stocks may yield a greater return for the investor than bonds.

Types of bonds include corporate, government, and municipal bonds. Corporate bonds are issued by corporations to raise money. The interest from corporate bonds is taxable. Some corporate bonds

Track stocks that interest you before purchasing.

akinbostanci/iStockphoto.com

are considered low-risk investments; others are not. The risk depends on the issuing company's ability to make interest payments and repay the bond. Investment-grade bonds are considered fairly low-risk investments. Speculative-grade bonds (also called junk bonds) are considered medium- to high-risk.

Government bonds are issued by the U.S. Treasury and other federal government agencies. These bonds are low-risk when held to maturity. You do not have to pay state and local taxes on the income from some government bonds. Municipal bonds are issued by states, counties, cities, and towns. You do not have to pay federal, state, or local taxes on the income from many municipal bonds. Municipal bonds are relatively safe investments.

MUTUAL FUNDS

A **mutual fund** is an investment fund that consists of stocks, bonds, and other investments focused on an investment strategy such as balance (good earnings with acceptable risk) or growth (high earnings with greater risk). It is operated by a professional investment company that selects, buys, and sells investments based on the fund's investment objective. The company sells shares in the mutual fund and uses the money to purchase the investments.

Mutual funds provide one of the simplest ways for the small investor to buy stocks and bonds. The individual investor in a mutual fund owns a small fraction of each share of stock or bond that is purchased. Mutual funds are *diversified*, which means they contain a variety of investments. Diversification reduces the investor's risk because losses in one type of investment are offset by gains in others. In addition, the investor benefits from the expertise of a professional manager who is buying and selling the investments.

Employee Stock Purchase Plans

Some companies offer their employees an opportunity to buy stock in the company through payroll deduction. Such a plan allows employees to have a stake in the company's financial growth. The benefits of buying stock in this manner are the following:

- You can save money to purchase stock through automatic deduction from your paycheck.
- The company may provide a discount on the price compared to what you would pay on the open market. It may also give bonuses in the form of stock.
- You do not have to pay for the services of a stockbroker.

Payroll Deductions

Whether you are working for an organization or are self-employed, a portion of your salary goes to the federal government in the form of payroll taxes. These taxes include federal income, Social Security, and Medicare taxes. Some states and cities tax personal income. If so, this tax is also withheld from your check. You may have optional deductions taken from your check for items such as health insurance, a retirement plan, and charitable contributions (such as deductions through a corporation's United Way campaign).

Figure 13.4 on page 292 shows the taxes and deductions section of a payroll check stub. In this example, deductions are made for Social Security, Medicare, and federal, state, and city income taxes. Pretax deductions are made for an optional 401(k) retirement plan and medical insurance. Notice the deductions on your next pay stub. When you begin a new job or make changes to your deductions, double-check your subsequent pay stub to ensure all the appropriate deductions are listed and are correct.

Taxes and Deductions		
Description	**Current Amount**	**Year-to-Date Amount**
Taxes Withheld		
Social Security tax	217.00	1,953.00
Medicare tax	50.75	456.75
Federal income tax	420.00	3,730.00
State tax	122.50	1,102.50
City tax	87.50	787.50
Total Taxes	897.75	8,029.75
Pretax Deductions		
401(k)	350.00	3,150.00
Medical insurance	125.00	1,125.00
Total Pretax Deductions	475.00	4,275.00

FIGURE 13.4 Payroll Check Deductions

Federal Income Tax

Federal income tax is a mandatory deduction under federal law. Taxes are withheld from each payroll check on the basis of information furnished by the employee on a Form W-4 (Employee's Withholding Allowance Certificate). The number of exemptions claimed on the Form W-4, in addition to the amount of money you earn and current tax rates, determines the amount to be withheld. Taxes from the federal government are determined for each of the following categories of people:

- Single
- Married Filing Jointly
- Married Filing Separately
- Head of Household
- Qualifying Widow(er) With Dependent Child

Figure 13.5 shows how the amount of federal income tax to be withheld is determined for single taxpayers. Though tax rates change periodically, the procedure is the same. Separate schedules are available for each of the other four categories.

Income Tax Withholdings For Annual Wages in 2011—Single Taxpayers		
If taxable income is over—	**But not over—**	**The tax is:**
	$2,100	$0
$2,100	$10,600	$0 plus 10% of the amount over $2,100
$10,600	$36,600	$850 plus 15% of the amount over $10,600
$36,600	$85,700	$4,750 plus 25% of the amount over $36,600
$85,700	$176,500	$17,025 plus 28% of the amount over $85,700
$176,500	$381,250	$42,449 plus 33% of the amount over $176,500
$381,250		$110,016.50 plus 35% of the amount over $381,250

Adapted from Internal Revenue Service, "Publication 15, (Circular E), Employer's Tax Guide for Use in 2011," July 28, 2011, http://www.irs.gov/pub/irs-pdf/p15.pdf (accessed October 26, 2011), 37.

FIGURE 13.5 Tax rates vary according to income and other factors.

State, City, and Local Income Tax

Most states have mandatory state income taxes. At the time of this writing, the following states had no state income tax: Alaska, Florida, Nevada, South Dakota, Texas, Washington, and Wyoming. Two others, New Hampshire and Tennessee, limited their state income tax to dividends and interest income only. State income tax rates vary but are lower than federal rates. Like federal rates, state tax rates can change.

A number of cities in the United States have a city income tax. Some counties also have income taxes. The deduction on a payroll check may say *local* instead of *city* or *county*. Cities and counties often levy taxes to improve parks, fund schools, pay for police and fire departments, build and repair local roads, and pay for other services. Tax rates may vary depending on whether you are a resident or a nonresident. Nonresidents are people who earn income in the area but do not live there.

Social Security and Medicare

Social Security is a social insurance program with its beneficiaries being retired individuals, survivors (of a deceased spouse or parent), and people with disabilities. Social Security benefits are paid when a person retires or becomes disabled. The program may also pay benefits to survivors and/or dependents of an insured person in the event of the person's death.

Medicare is a health insurance program for people age 65 or older. Certain people younger than age 65 can qualify for Medicare, such as those who have disabilities and certain other medical conditions. The program helps with the cost of health care, but it does not cover all medical expenses or the cost of most long-term care (such as a nursing home).

Social Security's Old-Age, Survivors, and Disability Insurance (OASDI) program and Medicare's Hospital Insurance (HI) program are financed primarily by employment taxes. Tax rates for Social Security apply to earnings up to a maximum amount per year. In 2011 the maximum amount was $106,800. Medicare is also financed in part by monthly premiums deducted from Social Security checks. The 2011 Social Security tax rate was 4.2 percent for an individual employee and 10.4 percent for a self-employed individual. The 2011 Medicare tax rate was 1.45 percent for an individual employee and 2.9 percent for a self-employed individual. For self-employed individuals, both Social Security and Medicare taxes can be offset by income tax provisions.[1] Social Security taxes are sometimes called FICA taxes because they are collected under the authority of the Federal Insurance Contributions Act (FICA).

The earliest age at which benefits are payable through Social Security is 62. However, if an individual elects to take early retirement, Social Security benefits are reduced. Individuals receive full benefits at varying ages depending on date of birth. However, the retirement age is gradually increasing to 67. A worker under 70 and eligible for retirement can delay receiving benefits past full retirement age. The worker's eventual retirement benefit and the surviving spouse's benefit are increased due to a credit that is applied to the account for each month's delay in receiving retirement benefits, up to age 70.

Since the money supplied through Social Security is usually not enough to provide you with adequate retirement income, you need to understand and engage in retirement investment strategies that will give you a solid financial future. Sound investment strategies require that you understand the types of investment opportunities available to you and the importance of saving for your retirement.

Credit

Understanding credit is a large part of managing your personal finances. You incur debt when you secure credit from an individual, a bank, or another company. Understanding the costs and benefits of credit will help you balance your personal spending and make good decisions in debt management. It is

[1]Social Security Administration, "Update 2011," http://www.ssa.gov/pubs/10003.pdf (accessed October 26, 2011).

important to understand how to manage credit and to know your rights as a consumer.

Benefits and Costs of Credit

Credit increases your spending power, allows you to keep a certain standard of living, and can save you time and money. For example, suppose you have just moved into your first apartment, and you decide to buy a washing machine and dryer. You make the purchase using credit and then repay the amount with interest over a period of time. Buying these appliances on credit saves you the time and expense of driving to a Laundromat. Credit also allows people to purchase expensive items they might never be able to save enough money for, such as a house.

Health Insurance Deductions

One of the most valuable benefits of employment is group health insurance. Many people have group health insurance through an employer. Usually the employer and employee share in paying for coverage; the employee's portion is deducted automatically from the paycheck. *Basic* coverage includes medical, hospital, and surgery services, such as doctor fees, office visits, and lab work. Elective or cosmetic services (such as laser eye surgery) are usually not covered. *Major medical* covers very serious injuries or illnesses, such as those that would require an organ transplant. *Dental* and *vision* coverage is frequently offered for an additional fee and includes services such as eye exams or dental x-rays. For most health coverage of any type, employees pay part of the cost each time they use a service, such as a copayment (*copay*) of $15 to $30.

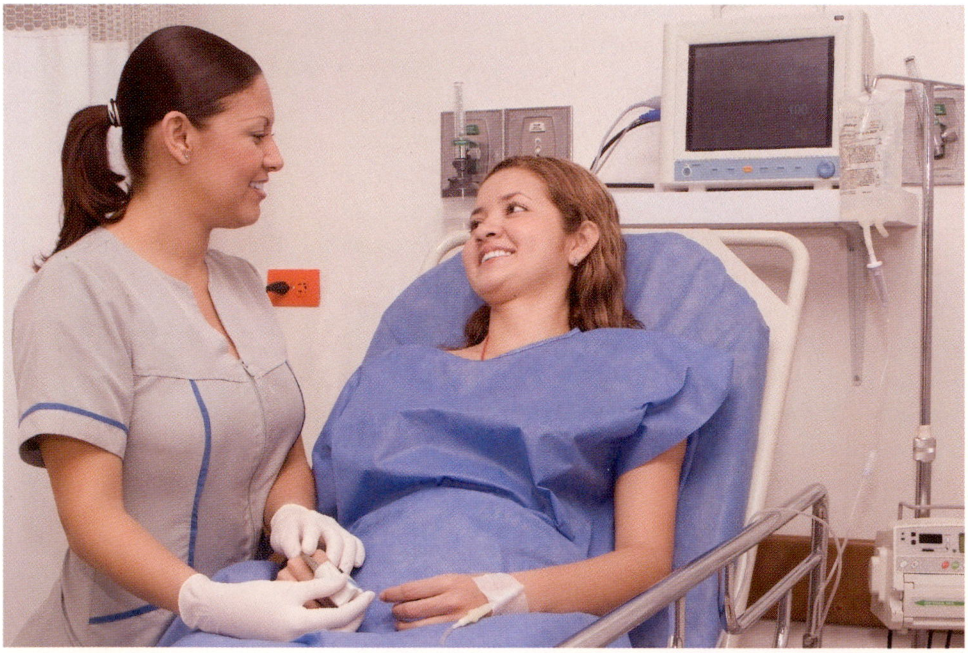

Reflekta/Shutterstock.com

Credit cards are a convenient option for consumers. They make online shopping possible and easy. With a credit card, you do not need to carry large amounts of cash. You can pay for many purchases through a single credit card bill instead of individually. With credit card receipts and your monthly statement, you have a record of your purchases.

Buying with a credit card also gives you certain kinds of purchase protection. For example, you can contact your credit card company and have it dispute a charge if there is a question.

Purchasing with credit—whether with credit cards, store accounts, bank loans, or other types—isn't without risks. Your credit rating will suffer if you do not make payments on time. Using credit often leads to overspending. It can also mean interest fees or finance charges, which add to the cost of the item purchased.

Managing Credit

Whether you borrow from relatives, have a loan with a bank, or owe money on a credit card, the management of that debt is important. Here are several suggestions for managing debt:

Set personal limits for debt. A good rule is to limit the amount you owe to less than 20 percent of your take-home pay (not including a home mortgage). Less than 10 percent is even better. The advantages of having less debt include greater spending power in the future. Before incurring additional debt, have money set aside in reserve for emergencies.

Pay bills on time or early. By doing so, you will establish a good credit record and a good relationship with creditors. A finance charge for a late payment is money wasted, and a poor credit score because of late payments means higher interest rates on future loans.

If you pay off loans early, you save money. With a loan amortization calculator (page 285), you can see how additional or early payments will reduce the amount of interest you will pay and the life of a loan.

Ask good questions. Comparison-shop when you need a loan, credit card, or bank. Create a table in *Word* or *Excel* to compare features. Find out specifics about late fees and finance charges. Determine how much you will actually pay in interest. Read all credit offers thoroughly, and make sure you understand the fine print.

Credit Cards

Credit cards are one of the easiest forms of credit to obtain and use. You can take advantage of their benefits and avoid their pitfalls by evaluating credit card offers carefully and using credit cards wisely.

CHOOSING A CREDIT CARD

It's a good idea to start out with just one card. As with other forms of credit, you can save money by shopping wisely. Figure 13.6 lists items to look for when evaluating a credit card offer.

Look first at the **annual percentage rate,** or **APR,** which is the interest rate for the card expressed as an

Credit Card Terms	
0% interest	Usually only 0% for a short time. Find out what the interest rate will be after the introductory offer expires. It could be much higher than the rates for other offers.
Default interest rate	Some cards will default to a much higher rate, such as 28% or 35%, if you miss a payment or if certain situations apply.
Late fees	Know what they are.
Cash advance and balance transfer fees	Know what they are. The interest rates for cash advances and balance transfers are usually higher than the rates for other purchases.

FIGURE 13.6 Check credit card terms carefully.

Partnership for 21st Century Skills

Financial, Economic, Business, and Entrepreneurial Literacy

Make Appropriate Credit Choices

Being financially literate means knowing how to manage your money, in good times and bad. You are the person responsible for your financial status, and you have the capacity to make excellent decisions that affect your current and future financial security. The following hints can help you make good credit choices:

- Take time to plan for a loan. Don't make snap decisions to purchase large items on credit. For example, if you need a car, begin looking months in advance. This will help you choose the right vehicle, find the loan with the best terms and interest rate, save for a down payment, and plan for repayment. Shop around for your loan and compare offers.
- Check your credit score months before getting a loan. This will give you time to address any items that are incorrect or negative and to increase your credit score. The higher your score, the better interest rate you will get on your loan.
- Contact your creditors as soon as possible if you have trouble making a payment.
- Avoid payday and title loans. Payday loans are essentially a cash advance on your next paycheck. This is a very expensive type of credit. Consider having to pay $60 to borrow $100 for only 14 days. That's what could happen if you need $100 and it takes you a month and a half to pay it back. Title loans (secured by the title on your car) are also poor choices. Interest rates could exceed 300 percent, and you could lose your automobile. Consider banks or credit unions for small loans.

Activity

If you had to make one rule for yourself regarding credit, what would it be? Be prepared to defend your rule to the class.

Goodluz/Shutterstock.com

annual rate. Generally, unless you are sure you will pay your balance in full each month, you should look for the lowest APR. If you anticipate carrying a balance from month to month on a card, the APR is very important since it determines how much you will pay in interest. Check the offer carefully to make sure a low APR is not simply an introductory rate that will move to a higher rate later. Also consider whether the card has an annual fee and a rewards feature that will be useful to you.

USING CREDIT CARDS WISELY

The key to using credit cards wisely is to plan your spending. Some people put into their budget a maximum amount they can charge each month, an amount they know they will be able to pay in full. If you pay your balance in full, you will not have to pay any interest charges. Do not use a credit card for consumable items, such as food or vacations, unless you are able to pay off the balance within one or two months. It is very easy to accumulate a large amount of debt on credit cards, and it is also easy to fall into a pattern of paying heavy interest charges. If you want to make a large purchase, such as for a new flat-panel television, a good plan is to set aside money each month in savings so you can buy it outright.

If you carry a balance, always try to pay more each month than the minimum payment. The minimum payment is a small percentage of your actual debt. If you make only the minimum payment, you will be paying for your purchase for a long time, and you will pay a large amount of interest. For example, suppose you have a balance of $3,000, and your APR is 14.4 percent. If you make only the minimum payment of $90, and you make no additional purchases on your card, it will take you about 11 years to pay off the $3,000, and you will pay about $4,745 in interest.[2] This type of payoff information appears on your credit card statement. The bottom line is that the faster you pay off your balance, the more money you will have to spend, and the less money you will give the credit organization for its profit.

Check your credit card statement as soon as you receive it. Compare your receipts to the charges. If you find an error, call the credit card company, and then follow up with a detailed letter. Include your name, contact information, account number, and details of the disputed charge. Use the address for billing inquiries, which is often not the same as the

[2]U.S. Federal Reserve Board, "What You Need to Know: New Credit Card Rules," January 2010, http://www.federalreserve.gov/consumerinfo/files/wyntk_ccrules.pdf (accessed October 26, 2011).

Purchasing Cards

Both small and large companies now generally use purchasing cards rather than petty cash funds. This makes tracking and establishing accountability for individual spending easier. Companies use purchasing cards for expenditures related to items such as health care benefits, fleet (company automobile) costs, customer rebates, and event expenses.

Temych/Shutterstock.com

address to which you send your payment. Send the letter by certified mail, return receipt requested, within 60 days of receiving the inaccurate statement. Enclose copies of your receipt and any other documents that support your position. Keep the originals for yourself, along with a copy of your letter. For any telephone contacts, make notes of the date, the person's name, and what was said.

Consumer Protection

The Federal Trade Commission (FTC) is the federal consumer protection agency for the United States. The FTC's Bureau of Consumer Protection (BCP, Figure 13.7) enforces laws that protect consumer rights. It also keeps the public informed of their

Credit Card Safety Tips

- Report lost or stolen cards immediately. Keep a record of telephone numbers for reporting lost or stolen cards.
- Don't lend a credit card to anyone.
- Shred unwanted card offers you receive in the mail and cards you are canceling.
- Shred credit card receipts before throwing them away (which you can do as soon as you have verified them against your monthly statement).
- If you receive cash advance checks in the mail, shred those before discarding them.
- Carry only one or two cards with you at a time. If you have additional cards, store them in a safe place in your home.
- Exercise your right to obtain up to three free credit reports each year (see page 219).
- Never respond to e-mail asking for your credit card information or passwords.
- Access online account information frequently so you can report fraudulent charges quickly and will always be aware of what you are spending.

silabob/Shutterstock.com

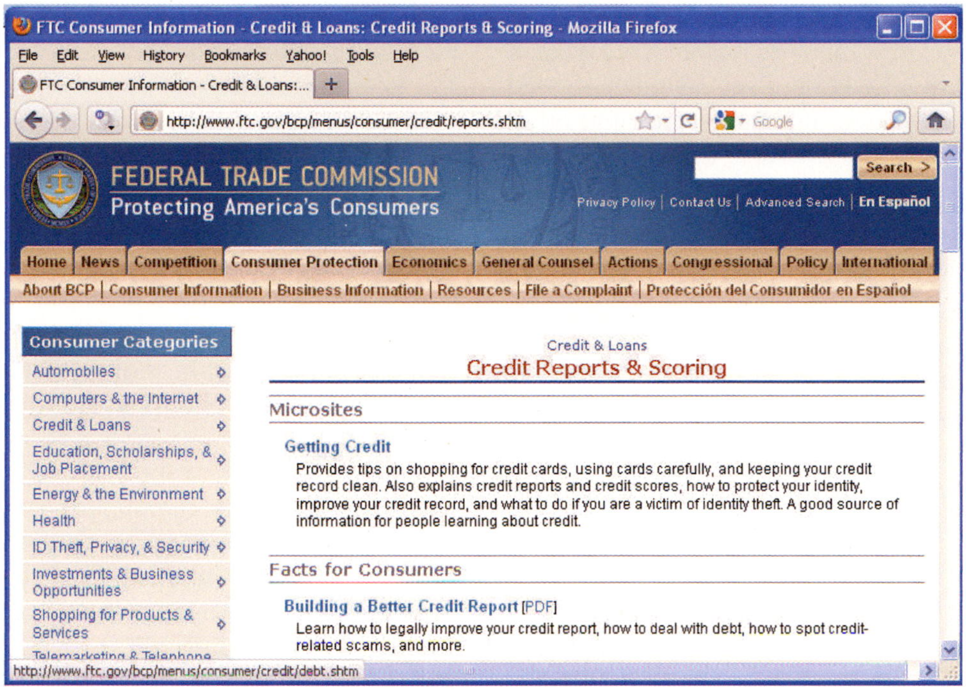

www.ftc.gov

FIGURE 13.7 The BCP is charged with the duty of protecting your rights as a consumer.

rights as consumers. The following are some consumer rights with respect to credit:

- Not to be denied credit due to race, sex, marital status, religion, age, national origin, or receipt of public assistance
- To know the contents of your credit report
- To know the APR on loans and credit cards
- To be free of harassment by creditors. Federal law governs the steps creditors may take in seeking payment.
- To know why you were denied credit
- To file a dispute with a credit reporting company if you believe its report is in error
- To get an additional copy of your credit report if a company takes action against you
- To know who has requested your credit report

Problems with credit can be stressful. Beware of offers for instant solutions to debt problems. In the event that you have problems with credit, remember that you have options, one of which is consumer credit counseling. Some employers and housing authorities offer free or low-price counseling, and the Federal Trade Commission has information about counseling agencies. You should consider counseling if you have a lot of high-interest debt and find it hard to make ends meet. You may just need a little advice and a sound budget to get you back on the right track. You should seek counseling if you have a large amount of debt or your credit score is bad. Solving debt problems or just getting out of debt requires persistence, but the effort is worth it. Poor credit prevents you from becoming financially independent.

Organizational Financial Statements

As an administrative professional, you may be required to prepare financial statements. Therefore, you need to know the purpose of different types of statements and how they are organized. A basic knowledge of these documents will also help you understand the financial condition of an organization.

Who uses financial statements? Internal users consist of owners, managers, and employees of the organization. External users include potential investors, banks, government agencies, and other individuals who need financial information concerning the business.

Balance Sheet

A **balance sheet** (Figure 13.8) shows the assets, liabilities, and owner's equity of an organization as of a given date—how much the company owns and how much it owes. Assets are resources owned by the company. Current assets consist of cash and other items of material value that are expected to be turned into cash or consumed within a year. Liabilities are debts that must be paid. Current or short-term liabilities must be paid within one year. Long-term liabilities are not due for a longer time (more than one year). Owner's equity is the financial claims to the assets of the organization by the owner or stockholders after all debts have been paid. If the company is a corporation, this part of the balance sheet may be called *stockholders' equity* or *capital*. The stockholders' equity section reports the amount of each of the two sources of stockholders' equity. The first source is capital contributed to the company by stockholders, which is called paid-in capital. The second source is the accumulated, undistributed net income of the company, which is called retained earnings. These two sources equal the total stockholders' equity.

Income Statement

An **income statement** (Figure 13.9 on page 302) shows the total amount of money earned and the total amount of expenses incurred in earning the money for a given period of time. Typically, an income statement is prepared to show income and expenses for the month, and a yearly income statement is prepared to show income and expenses for the fiscal year. A fiscal year is a 12-month period used for accounting purposes. It might be from January 1 through December 31, from July 1 through June 30, or any other continuous 12-month period. The excess of revenue over expenses is called net income or net profit. If expenses exceed revenue, the results are a net loss.

Cash Flow Statement

A **cash flow statement** (Figure 13.10 on page 303) shows incoming and outgoing cash for a given period. Keeping track of cash flow is important so the company has enough cash on hand to fund its payroll and pay other bills. Cash flow statements are typically created monthly or on an as-needed basis.

Follow these tips to help you work with financial records and information:

- Review statements from the files to find acceptable formats for financial statements.
- Double-check figures on all reports or statements you prepare.
- Proofread figures by having someone read them to you and by checking all calculations.
- Read the financial section of a newspaper, business magazine, or website regularly.
- Watch television programs dealing with the economy and investments.
- Read at least one book about investing each year.

Kapor Pharmaceuticals
Balance Sheet
As of December 31, 201-
(Dollars in Thousands)

Assets	
Current Assets	
Cash and Cash Equivalents	$200,012
Accounts Receivable	276,282
Inventories	399,026
Prepaid Expenses	52,380
Total Current Assets	927,700
Property and Equipment, Net	1,354,151
Investments in Affiliates	55,000
Total Assets	$2,336,851
Liabilities and Stockholders' Equity	
Current Liabilities	
Current Portion of Notes Payable	$9,559
Accounts Payable	246,920
Accrued Expenses	225,009
Total Current Liabilities	481,488
Notes Payable	658,697
Total Liabilities	$1,140,185
Stockholders' Equity	
Common Stock ($1 Par Value, Authorized Shares 100,000,000, Issued Shares 56,587,129)	$56,587
Additional Paid-in Capital	520,989
Retained Earnings	619,090
Total Stockholders' Equity	1,196,666
Total Liabilities and Stockholders' Equity	$2,336,851

FIGURE 13.8 Balance Sheet

Ramineni Company

Income Statement

For the Month Ended March 31, 201-

			% of Sales
Sales		$200,000	
Cost of Goods Sold	$100,000		
Gross Profit on Sales		100,000	50%
Operating Expenses			
Advertising Expense	3,500		
Insurance Expense	5,600		
Miscellaneous Expense	459		
Salaries Expense	35,000		
Payroll Taxes Expense	2,800		
Utilities Expense	4,560		
Total Operating Expenses		51,919	
Net Income From Operations		48,081	24%
Other Income and Expenses			
Interest Income		2,000	
Net Income Before Income Tax		50,081	25%
Less Income Tax		14,023	
Net Income After Tax		$36,058	18%

FIGURE 13.9 Income Statement

Maycomb Company
Cash Flow Statement
For the Month Ended May 31, 201-

Cash Inflows		
Cash Collections	$6,000	
Credit Collections	78,000	
Investment Income	2,500	
Sale of Equipment	6,500	
Total Cash Inflows	$93,000	
Cash Outflows		
Advertising Expense	$4,000	
Insurance Expense	6,000	
Miscellaneous Expense	945	
Salaries Expense	35,000	
Payroll Taxes Expense	2,800	
Utilities Expense	5,230	
Total Cash Outflows	$53,975	
Net Cash Flow		$39,025
Beginning Cash Balance		$150,000
Ending Cash Balance		$189,025

FIGURE 13.10 Cash Flow Statement

SUMMARY

To reinforce what you have learned in this chapter, study this summary.

- Managing personal finances is important for any professional. It is important to budget and plan for the future.
- By careful investment in retirement plan options, stocks, bonds, and mutual funds, you can meet long-term financial goals.
- Employers may deduct money from your pay for items such as taxes, insurance, retirement plans, or stock purchase plans.
- To manage your finances effectively, you need to understand the benefits and costs of credit, how to manage credit, and how to choose and use credit cards wisely. You should also know your consumer rights.
- Organizational financial statements help people understand the financial condition of an organization. Three common types of statements you may be required to prepare are balance sheets, income statements, and cash flow statements.

KEY TERMS

401(k) account, 287
403(b) account, 289
annual percentage rate (APR), 295
balance sheet, 300
bond, 290
budget, 282
cash flow statement, 300
defined benefit plan, 287
dividend, 289
financial goal, 282
financial plan, 281
fringe benefit, 287
income statement, 300
individual retirement arrangement (IRA), 287
liquidity, 289
mutual fund, 291
simplified employee pension plan (SEP), 289
stock, 289

13

STUDY Tools

Located at www.cengagebrain.com

- Chapter Outlines
- Flashcards
- Interactive Quizzes
- Tech Tools
- Video Segments
- and More!

LET'S DISCUSS

1. What factors should be considered in preparing a financial plan?
2. Name some ways to begin planning for retirement.
3. How does a 401(k) plan differ from a 403(b) plan?
4. What is the difference between a stock and a bond?
5. What is a mutual fund?
6. Explain some of the deductions you may see on your pay stub.
7. Why is the APR important to consider when choosing a credit card?
8. What should you do if you find an error on your credit card statement?
9. List at least three ways you can avoid getting into financial trouble.
10. What is the purpose of an income statement, balance sheet, and cash flow statement?

PUT IT TO WORK

Payroll When Joe Chin went to work for his company, he filled out a Form W-4 and listed no dependents. Several months ago, Joe married Alice. She is going to school full-time and does not have a job. Joe asked the HR department for a new Form W-4 and changed the dependent status from zero to one. Joe's check is automatically deposited by his employer each month. Four months have passed, and Joe is attempting to reconcile his bank statements. Joe notices that the amount of money deposited to his account for his pay is considerably more than he expected. Joe thinks an error has been made; however, he is embarrassed that he did not report it earlier. He is tempted to just forget about it. After all, isn't it the responsibility of the company or the federal government to find such an error?

What is the problem? How should Joe handle this problem? (Learning Objective 3)

COMMUNICATE SUCCESSFULLY

1. **Purchasing cards** You work for a small company. Your supervisor wants to eliminate the office petty cash fund and switch to purchasing cards instead. He asks you to research purchasing card options. Research three purchasing card offers and select the one you think is best. Be prepared to report the costs and benefits of your first choice to your supervisor. (Learning Objective 4)
2. **Balance sheet** Your supervisor has asked you to proofread a balance sheet prepared by a new administrative professional at your company. Access the *Word* file *Ch13_Balance_Sheet* from the data files. Proofread the balance sheet and check all the figures. (Learning Objective 5)

3. **Blog** Add a new post to the blog you created in Chapter 1. In this entry, reflect on the following question: **In what ways do you believe your personal finances may have an impact on your success in the workplace?** (Learning Objective 1)

Blog

DEVELOP WORKPLACE SKILLS

4. **Retirement savings** Find an online savings or retirement calculator, or use an *Excel* template. Assume you are planning to start saving for retirement today. If you are not currently employed, pretend you are, and estimate your annual starting salary. Select a realistic retirement age and a realistic amount you could contribute regularly to a 401(k) or other retirement plan. You may need to fill in other options depending on the calculator you choose. Invent details as needed.

   With a classmate or in class, discuss the amount you invested and the interest earned. Links to several online calculators are provided on the website for this text. (Learning Objectives 1 and 2)

5. **Financial plan** Using the table feature in *Word*, create a financial plan modeled on Figure 13.1. Consider your short-term, intermediate, and long-term goals as you enter information into the table. Include at least one investment in your plan—stocks, bonds, or mutual funds. Add the financial plan to your online portfolio. (Learning Objectives 1 and 2)

e-Portfolio

6. **Payroll deductions** Interview someone who is presently employed full-time. Ask this person to explain the mandatory and optional payroll deductions taken from his or her pay and other optional deductions that could be requested. (Do not ask the individual to be specific about the deduction amounts, and do not ask the individual's salary.) Your objective is to understand more concerning mandatory and optional payroll deductions. Write an e-mail to your instructor explaining what you learned. (Learning Objective 3)

7. **Vacation** Complete one of the following activities. Share your ideas with the class or a classmate. (Learning Objective 1)

   - You and your coworkers are discussing vacation plans during lunch one day. Make a list that includes two inexpensive vacation ideas—state parks, historic locations, etc. Estimate costs in transportation, food, entrance fees, and lodging for three days.
   - Graduation is approaching, and a group of your friends want to celebrate their accomplishments by taking a trip to Cancun. You have been saving money for a car, but you have not budgeted for this trip. You think you may be receiving some gift money for graduation. What will you do?

8. **Credit report** Request a free copy of your credit report. You can request a copy online at AnnualCreditReport.com, by phone at 1-877-322-8228, or by regular mail by printing and completing an Annual Credit Report Request Form, available at the FTC website. Links to the AnnualCreditReport.com website and the appropriate page of the FTC website are provided on the website for this text. (Learning Objective 4)

BUILD RELATIONSHIPS

9. **Bonus** Justin is getting a bonus at work this year. His company had record earnings, and all employees will receive $500 at the end of the year. Justin plans to use part of his bonus to pay off the last $275 on his car loan. He would like to use the remainder to start a savings account. A coworker asks him for a loan. What should he do? (Learning Objectives 1 and 2)

10. **Lunch expenses** You are a dental assistant in a busy practice. You are often asked to join the office manager and other dental assistants and hygienists for lunch. You want to be friendly and certainly enjoy their company; however, dining out frequently is expensive, and you haven't budgeted for it. What can you say or do to keep the goodwill of your fellow employees and stay within your lunch budget? (Learning Objective 1)

USE TECH TOOLS

11. **Budget** Use *Microsoft Excel* to prepare a personal budget for three months. As closely as possible, estimate your income and expenses. Use formulas to compute totals and do other calculations. If you have a suitable *Excel* template, use it. Add the budget to your online portfolio. (Learning Objective 1)

e-Portfolio

12. **Cars** Research a car you would like to own. Assume you plan to get a loan to buy it and have $1,000 for a down payment. Determine a reasonable current interest rate for a three-, four-, and five-year loan. Use the loan amortization schedule template in *Excel* to compare the loans. Assume you will make monthly payments, and obtain the following information. (Learning Objective 4)

	Three-Year	Four-Year	Five-Year
Interest Rate			
Monthly Payment			
Total Interest Paid			

PLAN AHEAD

Stocks Use the Internet to research five Fortune 500 companies. Investigate the industry sector of each company and the products or services it provides. Track the stock price for the five companies each day for ten days. Develop a one-page report of your findings. Include at least one graphic or figure in your report, such as an *Excel* chart illustrating the stock prices over the ten-day period or a *Word* table of the prices. At the end of your report, answer this question in a short paragraph: If you could purchase stock from any of the five companies, which would you choose and why? (Learning Objective 2)

PART

5 Professional Responsibilities and Growth

Neustockimages/iStockphoto.com

CAREER PROFILE

Visit www.cengagebrain.com to listen to the complete interview.

Executive Assistant

Linda Tunney is executive director of the AT&T Pebble Beach Junior Golf Association in Carmel, California.

What do you do in your job?
I administer a nonprofit junior golf program for 1,500 juniors ages 6 to 17.

What are your biggest challenges?
Recruiting board members who possess a passion for junior golf and raising funds to support programs for lessons, clinics, and tournaments.

How important are project planning skills?
Project planning skills are vital to make our organization run smoothly.

How about budgeting, utilizing resources, time management?
I have to organize a proposed budget for the board to vote on. Scheduling is vital because I have to arrange schedules for lessons and tournaments, and I recruit new golf professionals as others leave our program.

What would you see as your major responsibilities?
Tournaments. For example, next Monday we have a tournament for our silver and bronze divisions. We have 50 players. I arrange the courses, supervise the volunteers, provide the awards, provide tee times, and make sure each child has a lunch.

Could you speak about computer skills?
They're very important. I communicate with the golf pros, e-mail parents. I write newsletters, grants. I spend about four to five hours every day responding to inquiries, sending e-mails and letters.

How did you prepare for your job?
I depended on my experience with other nonprofit organizations. My work with the American Lung Association—I was assistant to the executive director and program manager with Meals on Wheels and on the ombudsman program and other volunteer programs—helped.

So your previous administrative professional jobs helped you advance in your career?
Absolutely.

Katalina Photography

CHAPTER

14 Meeting and Event Planning

LEARNING OBJECTIVES

1. Describe the variety of meeting types and delivery formats.
2. Describe meeting roles and responsibilities of executives, leaders, administrative professionals, and participants.
3. Identify considerations for an effective conference or convention.

Effective Meetings

Meetings are more important than ever. Businesses rely on teamwork, sharing of ideas, and effective project coordination to be successful. Although e-mail, telephones, and text messaging allow quick communication for business professionals, they have not replaced the need for meetings. In fact, the use of face-to-face and electronic meetings continues to increase in the business world. Effective meetings make you and your organization function more efficiently. An effective meeting has the following qualities:

- There is a definite need for the meeting.
- The purpose is stated clearly and understood by all participants.
- The appropriate people attend.
- An agenda is prepared and followed.
- All members participate.
- Productive outcomes result.

With the continued emphasis on teams to solve problems and make decisions, meetings will continue to be an important component of conducting business. Although effective teams communicate frequently through e-mail, they also meet frequently, either face-to-face or electronically. Because organizations invest a great deal of time and money in meetings, the expectation is that they will be effective and productive. This chapter will help you develop the knowledge and skills you need to assist your supervisor in holding meetings that are productive for all participants. It will also help you continue to develop the skills to be a productive team member and to lead an effective meeting.

Meeting Types

A wide variety of meetings are conducted in businesses. As an effective administrative professional, you should understand the types of meetings that are held.

STAFF MEETINGS

Staff meetings are very common within organizations. Staff meetings occur when an executive meets with members of his or her staff. They may be scheduled on a regular basis or arranged when needed. For example, an executive may meet weekly with the six people that report directly to him or her. The purpose of staff meetings is to review directions, plans, and assignments and to handle routine problems.

COMMITTEE MEETINGS

Most organizations schedule committee meetings regularly. You were introduced to the function of committees in Chapter 3. Committees are established to solve a problem, monitor an issue, or complete a task. They may be ongoing or may have a definitive end. An example of an ongoing committee is a wellness committee that meets every month to identify and address wellness issues in the workplace. It is ongoing because wellness is a continuing concern. An example of a committee with a definitive end is a search committee appointed by a nonprofit organization to find a new director. Once the new director has been chosen, the committee is no longer needed.

PROJECT TEAM MEETINGS

As you learned in Chapter 3, project teams are established to accomplish a specific project. For example, a project team may be organized to determine the type of document imaging software that will be used in an organization or to implement quality control procedures within a company. Once the project has been completed, the team is disbanded or takes on another project. A task force is a common type of project team set up to deal with a specific issue or problem. Your organization may establish a task force to look at increasing wellness opportunities in the workplace.

CUSTOMER/CLIENT MEETINGS

Most employers hold meetings with customers, clients, or special visitors. These meetings are generally small, including only two or three people.

Stockbyte /Getty Images

Board meetings usually follow strict procedures.

For example, a lawyer may meet with a client to discuss the evidence in a case. An engineer may meet with a customer to discuss the design of a product.

BOARD OF DIRECTORS MEETINGS

Most large corporations and organizations operate with a board of directors. Board meetings are run with **bylaws**, written policies and procedures that clearly define how the meetings are to be conducted. A board may meet every two to three months. The chairperson of the board conducts the meetings, and strict procedures are usually followed. An agenda is distributed before the meeting indicating the items to be discussed. If the organization is a public entity required by law to hold open meetings, notice of the meeting is posted according to legal procedures. Participants generally follow parliamentary procedures as set forth in *Robert's Rules of Order*. These guidelines help a leader run a meeting effectively and fairly.

CONFERENCES AND CONVENTIONS

A conference or convention involves a large number of participants. It can take the form of a formal annual meeting of the members of a professional group or a meeting in which discussion on certain issues or topics takes place. For example, a conference or seminar may be held on topics such as conflict management, written communications, and union negotiations. A convention or conference can involve hundreds or thousands of people. Planning and executing these types of meetings is so complicated that meeting planners are often hired to assist in carrying out the details.

Face-to-Face Meetings

The traditional meeting, where people gather for face-to-face discussion of an issue or problem, is an important means of conducting business. Even with increased use of web conferencing and other types of remote meetings, face-to-face meetings continue to be an essential component of a successful organization. Advantages of face-to-face meetings include the following:

- A creative, interactive group discussion is more likely to take place when people are together in the same room.
- People can observe and respond to body language of participants.
- People generally feel more relaxed with this type of format because it is familiar and comfortable.

Meetings can be an effective business tool if used correctly. A meeting with no purpose can result in wasted time, frustration for participants, and unnecessary costs for the organization. Meetings should not be held if there is insufficient time to prepare or inadequate data. Calling a meeting is appropriate when:

- A group needs to be involved in solving a problem or making a decision.
- An issue arises that needs clarification.
- Complex information needs to be shared with a group.
- Communication needs to occur quickly with a large number of people.
- Coworkers or teams need to see the progress of what they are doing or what others are doing in terms of daily work or projects.

Meetings should not be held when the same information could be covered in a memo, an e-mail, or a brief report.

- The atmosphere generally allows people to deal more effectively with difficult items.
- More group members are likely to participate.

Although face-to-face meetings can be effective, they have some disadvantages:

- Travel to and from the meeting can be costly, particularly when traveling to another city, state, or country.
- Productive work time is lost during travel time.
- Excessive socializing can consume some of the meeting time if not properly controlled by the leader.

Electronic Meetings

The growing emphasis on teamwork and the global nature of business have contributed to the increased need to communicate with individuals across the globe. Although some of these meetings take place in the traditional format, time and money make it impossible to conduct all meetings in person. Widespread access to technology and a wide variety of applications have made electronic meetings an economical alternative to meeting face-to-face. Audio conferences, video conferences, and web conferences are effective alternatives to meeting in person.

AUDIO CONFERENCES

An **audio conference** is a meeting in which a number of people can participate via telephone or some other device. An audio conference differs from a telephone conversation in that it involves more than two people in at least two locations. The communication device may be as simple as a speakerphone or as elaborate as a meeting room with microphones, speakers, and bridging technology. Bridging services, supplied by telephone and communication service companies, allow participants in multiple locations to dial in to a single phone number to talk with each other. One important advantage of an audio conference can be the ability to assemble individuals on short notice. Additional advantages include the following:

- The ability to connect individuals at any location, nationally or internationally
- The use of inexpensive technology that is readily available to almost everyone
- Decreased time and expense associated with travel

Although audio conferences can be effective, they also have some disadvantages. The primary disadvantage is the lack of visual input. Participants cannot see others' body language and may misinterpret something that is said. Also, without visual cues it's difficult to identify the speaker or to manage turn-taking. Successful audio conferencing requires participants to follow protocols such as announcing who is speaking and asking if anyone else has something to say. Figure 14.1 provides tips for effective audio conferences.

VIDEO CONFERENCES

A **video conference** is a meeting in which two or more people at different locations use equipment such as computers, video cameras, and microphones

Audio Conference Tips
■ If there are materials everyone needs to use during the conference, distribute them ahead of time.
■ Take turns speaking.
■ Identify yourself whenever you speak.
■ Move the microphone as close as possible to the speaker.
■ Avoid side conversations; they compete with the speaker and distract other participants.
■ Mute the phone or microphone when your site is not actively participating.

FIGURE 14.1 Tips for Effective Audio Conferences

Video Conference Tips
■ Designate a central contact person who is responsible for organizing the video conference.
■ Research video conference providers and vendors. Compare prices, accommodations, and technical expertise.
■ Prepare and distribute an agenda prior to the conference.
■ Develop a plan to handle technical issues if they arise.
■ Practice appropriate meeting etiquette; for instance, be on time and avoid side conversations.

FIGURE 14.2 Tips for Effective Video Conferences

to see and hear each other. A web camera, a microphone, and speakers may be connected to computers and used to transmit video and audio to other computers. On a larger scale, a videoconferencing room may be used to provide audio and video communication for several people in different locations. Smartphone applications are available that allow users to include a video component in their conversations. Software is also available for notebook and tablet computers to incorporate video features in web conferencing.

Video conferences have advantages and disadvantages similar to those of an audio conference. Figure 14.2 provides tips for effective video conferences.

WEB CONFERENCES

Web conferencing, described briefly in Chapter 10, allows events to be shared with remote locations using a computer and a network connection. Web conferences typically allow information to be shared simultaneously across geographically dispersed locations. Web conferences can take several forms including the web meeting, webinar, and webcast.

A **web meeting** is a meeting in which two or more people at different locations communicate and share information via computers and a network connection, such as the Internet or a local area network. Some web meetings are fully interactive, allowing participants to see video of one another, talk in real time, and exchange information via computers. *Microsoft Live Meeting* can be used for such a web meeting. For other web meetings, participants may speak with one another via a traditional telephone conference while using meeting software to share information. *Windows Meeting Space* is a program that allows you to set up a meeting and share documents, programs, or your computer desktop with several other people who have the same program. Microsoft Lync™ Online is a cloud communication service that allows participants to meet online and to move quickly from online chat to an online meeting.

A **webinar** is a seminar presented over the World Wide Web. It enables the presenter to share information with participants but does not provide the same degree of interaction as a web meeting. Interaction is limited to question-and-answer sessions with participants. A webinar does not allow full participation between the audience and the presenter.

A **webcast** is a type of broadcast that is similar to a television broadcast, except it takes place over the World Wide Web. Because of its one-way nature, this type of conferencing provides little opportunity for the presenter and audience members to interact. A webcast is primarily a presenting tool that can be broadcast simultaneously to hundreds of recipients.

ADVANTAGES AND DISADVANTAGES OF REMOTE MEETINGS

Remote meetings (audio, video, and web conferences) have both advantages and disadvantages. Advantages include:

- Savings in travel time and costs, including meals and hotel rooms.
- Bringing people together who have expertise in a number of different areas.

Remote conferencing continues to be an important way to conduct business.

Disadvantages include:

- Less chance for effective brainstorming on issues.
- Less spontaneity among individuals because of a structured environment.
- No chance for the types of interaction before or after the meeting that are so effective in face-to-face meetings.
- A more formal nature because not all individuals are comfortable with the technology.

International Meetings

For international organizations, meetings with staff or clients outside the United States are common for upper-level managers. Also, as organizations within the United States continue to broaden their international scope, meetings to pursue international opportunities are held with business leaders in many other countries.

You may help set up and/or participate in face-to-face or electronic meetings with individuals from other countries. International meetings are typically more formal in nature than local meetings, and being prepared for cultural differences is crucial. For example, in Japan, it is appropriate to give a gift at the end of a business meeting. In Malaysia, however, gift giving might be considered a form of bribery. The success of a meeting often depends on differences being understood and respected.

You and your employer should do your homework before the meeting. Find out how meetings are typically conducted, and learn about the culture or cultures that will be represented. Both face-to-face and electronic meetings should reflect the customs and traditions of the people involved. Be sensitive to the needs of the individuals in the meeting. Also remember to consider differences in time zones. For example, when it is noon in Chicago, it is the following day in Tokyo. Time zone calculators are available on the Internet.

International Meeting Considerations

Consider these suggestions when conducting or participating in international meetings:

- Learn and use proper greetings.
- Do not use first names of participants. Even though using first names is common in U.S. meetings, it can be considered too forward in other cultures.
- Disagree agreeably; in some cultures, it is considered offensive to be contradictory.
- Avoid gesturing with your hands. A hand gesture may mean something you do not intend in another culture. Also, some people are offended by gestures.
- In general, watch your body language; remember that body language has different meanings in different cultures.
- Understand that time in some cultures is precise, while in others it is more fluid.
- Research the appropriate way to exchange business cards.
- Show respect for everyone but especially for people in positions of authority.

Photodisc/Getty Images

Meeting Roles and Responsibilities

As you plan and organize a meeting, remember that several people play an important part in ensuring that the meeting is effective. These people include the executive who calls the meeting, the person who makes the arrangements for the meeting, the leader who facilitates the meeting, the meeting participants, and the administrative professional who assists in planning and preparing materials for the meeting. Each individual or group has specific roles and responsibilities to help ensure an effective and productive meeting.

Executive's Responsibilities

The executive has a variety of responsibilities when planning a meeting. He or she must determine the purpose of the meeting, set the objectives, select participants, and plan the agenda. The executive may work closely with the administrative professional in accomplishing these tasks.

DETERMINE THE PURPOSE AND OBJECTIVES

Every meeting must have a purpose; without it, there is no need for a meeting. Generally, the executive calls the meeting, so it is his or her role to state the purpose. Although the administrative professional is not responsible for determining the purpose, he or she must understand it so appropriate materials can be created and arrangements can be made.

Every meeting should also have specific written objectives. Objectives clearly define the purpose and describe what is to be accomplished. For example, if the purpose is to determine the training needs of the organization, the meeting objectives might be as follows:

- Establish training needs for each department
- Determine whether these needs will be met by internal staff or an outside consultant
- Determine the amount of time necessary for training
- Determine the budget for training

The meeting notice should include the purpose and the objectives. The purpose should be clearly stated so all participants understand why the meeting is occurring. Understanding the purpose and objectives beforehand will allow participants to prepare. It will also allow them to ask questions before the meeting.

SELECT PARTICIPANTS

The person who is calling the meeting is generally the one who will determine who should be included. Attendees are often selected based on the meeting topic and type. The people invited to the meeting should include those who:

- Have knowledge that can contribute to meeting the objectives.
- Will be responsible for implementing the decisions.
- Represent a group that will be affected by the decisions.

In determining who should attend a meeting, the executive should always consider the purpose of the meeting and who is most affected by the issue or problem to be discussed. Consideration should also be given to the background of each individual

Digital Vision/Getty Images

Every meeting must have a purpose.

being asked to attend. For example, a **heterogeneous group** (a group with dissimilar backgrounds and experiences) can often solve problems more satisfactorily than a **homogeneous group** (a group with similar backgrounds and experience). A heterogeneous group will usually bring varying views to the problem, so creative thinking is more likely to occur than in a homogeneous group.

The ideal number of participants is based on the purpose of the meeting and the number of people who can best achieve the purpose. A good size for a problem-solving and decision-making group is from seven to ten people. This size group allows for creative synergy. It provides enough members to generate divergent points of view and to challenge each other's thinking.

Small groups of seven or fewer may be necessary at times. For example, if the purpose of a meeting is to discuss a personnel issue, the employee, supervisor, and human resources director may be the only ones in attendance. If the purpose is to discuss a faulty product design, the product engineer, the department manager, and a technician may attend.

PLAN THE AGENDA

The executive plans the agenda. The **agenda**, which should be distributed before the meeting, is a document that lists the topics to be discussed at the meeting. The agenda should also include the following information:

- Name of the group, department, or committee
- Date and time of the meeting
- Location of the meeting
- Items to be discussed, in order of presentation
- Names of individuals responsible for presenting each agenda item
- Background materials (if needed)

A well-planned agenda saves time and increases productivity in a meeting. Participants should receive a detailed agenda at least two days before the meeting. Sometimes an agenda will list the amount of time allocated for each item on the agenda. Although this is not essential, it does remind people of the importance of time and of adhering to a schedule.

All agenda items should be directly related to the purpose and objectives of the meeting. The order of agenda items can vary. Some people believe the most difficult items should be presented first; others believe they should be presented last. If your group follows formal parliamentary rules, the agenda may need to follow a specific format. Figure 14.3 shows a sample agenda.

Agenda—Board of Directors

Conference Room C | *10:30 AM* | *11/20/201-*

10:30	Call to Order	Juan Chen
10:35	Approval of Minutes	Juan Chen
10:40	CEO Report	Juan Chen
10:50	Financial Review	Benjamin Johnson
11:15	Sales and Business Development Update	W. Kevin Young
11:40	Operating Plan	Ruth Bishop
12:00	Adjournment	Juan Chen

FIGURE 14.3 Meeting Agenda

Leader's Responsibilities

The leader is the individual who is in charge of the meeting. Sometimes the meeting leader will be your supervisor. At other times, particularly in team meetings, other employees may have this responsibility. In such instances, you as an administrative professional may be the team leader or co-leader. If that is the case, you will be in charge of the meeting. You have learned about the qualities, skills, and general responsibilities of leaders in Chapters 3 and 6. This chapter discusses the responsibilities of leaders during and after a meeting.

FOLLOW THE AGENDA

When the meeting begins, the leader should state the purpose. The leader should also review the objectives, specifying what must be accomplished at the meeting and what must be completed after it. The leader may also want to tactfully remind participants to turn off cell phones. If attendees stray from the agenda, the leader must sensitively but firmly bring them back to it. The leader might say, "Thank you for your comments about that issue. We can put it on the agenda for a future meeting. Now let's continue with the agenda for today."

MANAGE THE MEETING

Meetings should begin on time, even if several people are not present. Waiting for others to arrive is not fair to the individuals who have made an effort to be on time. Just as important as starting on time is ending on time. The leader must be sensitive to other commitments of participants. Time frames, both beginning and ending, should be established before the meeting notice is sent out.

The leader is responsible for seeing that everyone participates. The leader can use well-placed questions to draw out less talkative participants with questions such as "Roberto, what direction do you think we should take?" The leader is also responsible for making sure one or two participants do not dominate the discussion to the exclusion of others, even if their contributions are beneficial. The leader might say, "Alexa, that's an excellent suggestion. Warren, how could it be implemented in your area?" to shift the focus to another participant. The leader can guide a balanced and controlled discussion by following these suggestions:

- Keep the participants focused on the agenda.
- Positively reinforce all individuals for their contributions.
- Keep the discussions moving toward accomplishing the identified objectives and outcomes.

The leader is responsible for helping the participants reach a decision about the issue, problem, or direction. The leader should carefully assess all alternatives that have been discussed. If further discussion is necessary, the leader might ask, "Does anyone else have anything to add? Are there problems we haven't addressed?" If the group seems comfortable with the alternatives that have been discussed, the leader can move to resolution by saying, "Now, of the solutions that have been proposed, let's determine which will work best for our organization." After additional discussion, the leader may summarize the discussion and ask the group for consensus.

EVALUATE THE MEETING

Generally, for informal meetings within an organization, no formal evaluation is necessary. However, an informal evaluation by the leader (and possibly the participants) should be done. The participants are usually very forthright. They may even tell the leader they found the meeting a waste of time. If participants make this type of statement, the leader should seek clarification on exactly what was meant. The leader should also consider the following questions to help evaluate the meeting:

- Did everyone take part?
- Was the nonverbal behavior positive?
- Were the participants creative problem solvers?
- Did the participants exhibit a high energy level?
- Was the purpose of the meeting satisfied?
- Were the objectives met?
- Were appropriate decisions made?
- Can I improve the ways I handled the issues, the people, or the meeting?

Meeting Evaluation Form	Yes	No
1. Were the purpose and objectives of the meeting accomplished?	❑	❑
2. Was the agenda received in time to prepare for the meeting?	❑	❑
3. Did the leader adhere to the agenda?	❑	❑
4. Were the appropriate people included in the meeting?	❑	❑
5. Did the leader encourage participation by all members?	❑	❑
6. Did the participants listen to one another?	❑	❑
7. Did the meeting start on time?	❑	❑
8. Did the meeting end on time?	❑	❑
9. Did the leader help bring closure to the objectives?	❑	❑
10. Were decisions consistent with the purpose and objectives of the meeting?	❑	❑
Comments:		

FIGURE 14.4 Meeting Evaluation Form

If the meeting is relatively formal, the leader may ask participants to fill out an evaluation form as shown in Figure 14.4.

Administrative Professional's Responsibilities

As an administrative professional, you have a number of responsibilities before, during, and after a meeting. You must communicate with your supervisor to clarify the meeting's purpose and the duties you are expected to perform. When you first join an organization or begin to work with a supervisor, take time before each meeting to understand his or her needs and preferences. Once you understand the supervisor's preferences, you will have less need to discuss details. However, you should continue to discuss the purpose of the meeting, the objectives, and the general expectations. Otherwise, you may make decisions about details that cause problems.

CONFIRM THE MEETING

At times, the executive will require a meeting on a specific date and at a specific time. In these cases, it will be your responsibility to confirm the meeting date and time with the expected participants. On other occasions, only a general time frame will be given. If you are responsible for selecting a date and time, you will need to consider the expected participants' other commitments. Avoid scheduling meetings on Monday mornings and Friday afternoons. Employees often use Monday mornings to get an overview of the week and to handle any pressing items that occurred over the weekend. Friday afternoons are often used to complete projects.

The time of the meeting is also an important consideration. Avoid scheduling meetings immediately after lunch or near the end of the day. Meetings generally should last no longer than two hours. When people must sit longer than two hours, they can get restless. If a meeting will last longer than two hours, schedule five- or ten-minute breaks.

Regardless of who sets the date and time, a meeting notice must be prepared. If the meeting is scheduled within the organization, you can notify participants by e-mail or memorandum. If you have access to employees' individual online calendars, you can check the schedules of any employees who have been invited to attend to determine whether they will be free. The meeting notice should include the following information:

- Purpose and objectives of the meeting
- Location, date, and time
- A request to let you know whether they can attend
- Driving and parking directions if the meeting will be held off-site or if an attendee has not been to your offices previously
- Agenda
- Background information
- Assigned materials for preparation

You may also be responsible for following up on meeting notices. E-mail or telephone the people who have not responded to determine if they will be present. Let your supervisor know who will be attending the meeting and who will be late. If a number of people are unable to attend, your supervisor (or you, if you scheduled the meeting) may choose to change the time and/or date.

Room arrangements should be made as soon as you have confirmed the date and time of the meeting and the number of attendees. Most organizations have a limited number of conference rooms, and they are often booked far ahead. If conference rooms of varying sizes are available, select a room that is appropriate for the size of the group. If you choose a room that is too large, participants may feel "lost" in the room. Conversely, if you choose a room that is too small, participants may feel crowded.

MAKE OTHER ARRANGEMENTS

Other preparations must also be made for an effective meeting to occur. As an administrative professional,

TT TECH TALK

Electronic Invitations

Face-to-face and electronic meetings can be quickly organized using electronic invitations. With scheduling software such as *Microsoft Outlook®* or *IBM Lotus Notes®* software, an administrative professional can check the availability of the facilities, review the calendars of those who are to attend the meeting, and find a time when all participants are available. Online meeting schedulers allow you to propose times for a meeting. Recipients can respond to a meeting invitation using their computer or smartphone. Once availability has been established, the meeting information can be automatically added to participants' calendars.

Typically, electronic invitations allow the sender to include a subject and location and to confirm the start and end dates and times. Some programs also include a function that will send an automated reminder message or e-mail to all attendees prior to the event. The message space of the invitation can be used to provide details such as the meeting purpose and objectives, background reading links, and other useful information to help attendees prepare. Electronic invitations also allow the sender to attach an agenda and any other documents that might be needed before the meeting.

Electronic invitations have several business advantages. They eliminate postage and printing costs as well as time delays associated with regular mail. Also, an electronic invitation documents the event and lists all invitees, which makes it less likely that individuals will be forgotten. Sending additional invitations, if necessary, is quick and easy.

you may be responsible for making seating arrangements, ordering equipment, and ordering food and beverages.

Seating Arrangements The seating arrangement of the room depends on the objectives of the meeting and number of participants. The five basic seating arrangements are rectangular, circular, oval, u-shaped, and semicircular. Figure 14.5 depicts these seating arrangements.

The rectangular arrangement allows the leader to maintain control since he or she sits at the head of the table. This arrangement is most effective in formal meetings and is also effective when participants will be talking in groups of two or three. Individuals seated next to or opposite each other have a chance to discuss issues as they arise.

If discussion is important, the table should not be too long. A long table may make communication difficult because people may not be able to observe the nonverbal behavior of other participants. A long table may also prevent the leader from taking part in discussions if he or she is seated away from other participants.

The circular and oval arrangements work best when the purpose of the meeting is to generate ideas and discussion and the meeting is relatively informal. These arrangements encourage collaboration, shared communication, and participation. Attendees can make eye contact with everyone else in the group. Communication channels are considered equal since no one person is in a dominant position.

The u-shaped and semicircular arrangements work well for groups of six to eight people. The leader retains moderate control since he or she is in a dominant position. Both arrangements are also good for showing visuals because the visuals can be positioned at the front of the configuration.

Make certain you have enough chairs for the number of participants scheduled to attend. Too many extra chairs will get in the way, and it will appear as though some people failed to attend. You also do not want to have too few chairs.

Equipment Determine what equipment, if any, is needed, and follow through to make sure it will be available. It is a good idea to make a list of the necessary equipment and the arrangements that have been made. List the person responsible (including yourself) for obtaining each item.

Food and Beverages For a morning meeting, coffee, tea, and juice can be provided for

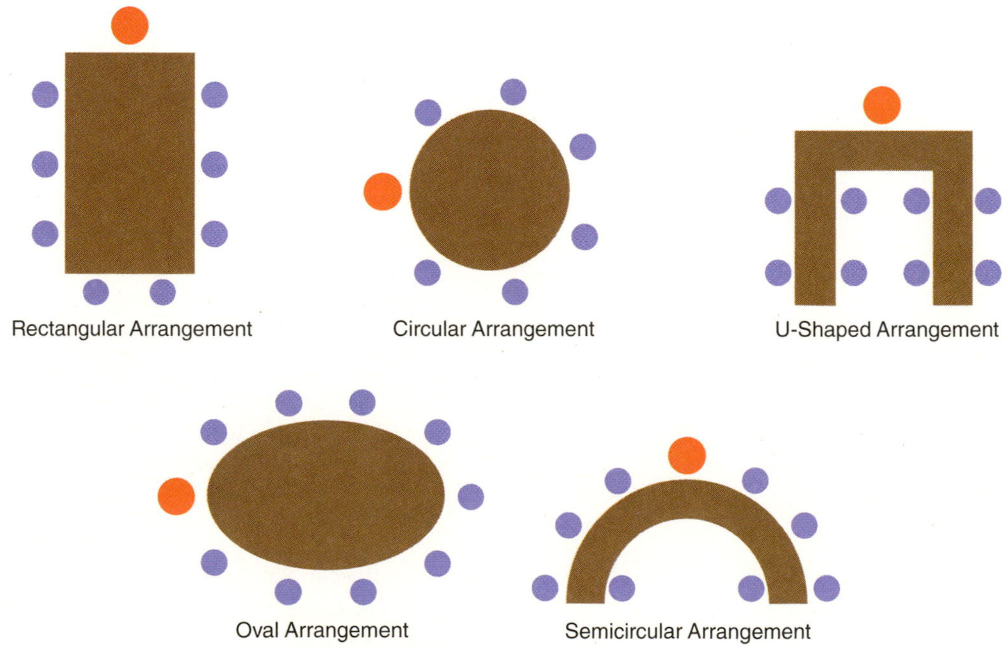

FIGURE 14.5 Seating Arrangements for Meetings

participants. Water should also be available. For an afternoon meeting, you may want to provide coffee, tea, water, and soft drinks. Supplying beverages is not absolutely necessary, however. Check with your supervisor to see what he or she prefers.

For a breakfast or luncheon meeting, you may have the responsibility of selecting the menu, calling the caterer, and arranging for the meal to be delivered. Depending on the formality of the meeting, you may choose a light plated breakfast or a less formal continental-style breakfast. A continental breakfast is easy to serve because it includes a variety of items that can be served at room temperature. The lunch should be a salad or light entrée if you expect the participants to work afterward; a heavy meal often makes people sleepy. For a dinner meeting, you may work with an outside caterer. If you are aware of participants who have special dietary needs, make special accommodations for them. If you know the attendees, consider their preferences when selecting the food. If you do not know the participants, ask the caterer what dishes other clients order in this circumstance (vegetarian, nondairy, etc.). Be certain to ask your supervisor what the budget allocation is for the meal.

For a dinner meeting at a hotel, you can expect assistance from the hotel staff. You will usually be responsible for selecting the menu. If the event is formal, you might wish to have table decorations and place cards. You should consider the group when selecting the seating arrangement; your supervisor can advise you.

PREPARE MATERIALS

Often the administrative professional is responsible for preparing materials for the meeting leader. If the meeting is scheduled for an off-site location, you may need to include directions to the meeting location and instructions or suggestions on where to park. A variety of Internet sites provide maps, driving directions, and traffic reports. A facility website or phone contact will provide parking guidelines. Materials for the leader should include:

- The meeting notice with a list of the people who will attend.
- Materials that were sent out before the meeting.
- Notes that are needed at the meeting.
- Visuals or handouts.

Materials also need to be prepared for the attendees. If handouts are to be distributed during the meeting, prepare them well in advance. Use a template or the theme feature of your software to create professional-looking handouts. If the handouts are made up of several documents, place them in individual folders. Sometimes attendees are expected to take notes. If so, you might provide a pad of paper and pen in the folder. Plan to make extra pens and pencils available.

MAKE FINAL PREPARATIONS

Shortly before the meeting begins, you should visit the meeting room. Check to be sure the furniture is arranged as requested. Verify that any necessary

Anyka/Shutterstock.com

Final preparations for a meeting include checking the meeting room.

equipment has been delivered and set up and is in working order. For example, if you have ordered a computer display, connect your laptop to make sure it is working correctly.

Check that the lighting is adequate and the room temperature is appropriate. A hot, stuffy room or a room that is icy cold can be a distraction for people who are trying to make important decisions. If you ordered food and/or beverages, make sure they have arrived and have been set up appropriately. Check details such as whether napkins and coffee stirrers are available and have been placed where they are most likely to be needed. Set out agendas, folders, and any other necessary materials so participants will have them at the start of the meeting.

HANDLE DUTIES DURING THE MEETING

The administrative professional's responsibilities during the meeting are varied. For example, you may be expected to greet guests and introduce them to other participants. Your courteousness, warmth, and friendliness can go a long way toward making people feel comfortable and getting the meeting off to a good start.

Your main responsibility during the meeting will probably be to take notes for the **minutes** (a written record of a meeting). Sit near the leader so you can clearly hear what he or she says. A notebook computer can be an efficient tool for taking notes. Minutes should contain a record of the important matters that were presented in the meeting. A **motion** is a proposal presented for discussion and voting in a meeting. You do not need to record the meeting discussions **verbatim** (word for word) with the exception of motions. For motions, include the name of the person who made the motion, the name of the person who seconded it, the exact wording of the motion, and whether it passed or failed. For discussions, summarize and record all pertinent information.

HANDLE DUTIES AFTER THE MEETING

Your duties after the meeting include seeing that the meeting room is left in order, preparing the minutes, and handling other details. These routine tasks should be performed after a meeting:

- Return all equipment.
- See that additional chairs or tables are removed and returned to their proper location.
- Clean up any papers and materials left in the room. Notify the cleaning staff if the room needs additional care.
- Send out any necessary follow-up messages.
- Note on your calendar any items that need future attention by you or your supervisor.
- Evaluate the meeting. Review what happened; consider how you might improve the arrangements for the next meeting.
- Keep notes on meetings long enough to refer to them when planning the next similar meeting. You might also keep names and telephone numbers of contact people. Your notes will help ensure future success.

Sometimes brief committee or project team meetings are held to answer a question or discuss progress on a task. For these types of meetings, minutes are often not required. If minutes are necessary, they should be prepared in a timely manner, usually 24 to 48 hours after the meeting. Prompt preparation and distribution of minutes reminds participants of what they must do before the next meeting. Figure 14.6 shows sample minutes from a meeting. Items included in the minutes are as follows:

- The title *Minutes* and name of the group
- Date, time, and place of the meeting
- Names of the presiding officer and members present and absent
- Reports of committees, officers, or individuals
- Motions made, including the exact wording of the motion, the names of the people who made and seconded it, and whether it passed or failed
- Items on which action needs to be taken and the name of the person responsible for taking the action

Minutes—Board of Directors

Conference Room C *10:30 AM* *11/20/201-*

The Board of Directors meeting of Kapor Pharmaceuticals was held on November 20, 201-, at 10:30 a.m. in Conference Room C at the Midtown Hotel. Board members present were Juan Chen (chair), Arnold M. Beckman, Ella R. Bronson, Ruth Bishop, Leroy T. Carroll (via telephone), Benjamin Johnson, Christine L. Ostwald, Michelle Stine, Emily C. Thompson, and W. Kevin Young.

Call to Order

Juan Chen called the meeting to order at 10:30 a.m. Eastern Standard Time, and Christine Ostwald recorded the minutes. A quorum of directors was present.

Minutes

The minutes of the August meeting were read and approved.

CEO Report

Juan Chen reviewed the agenda and welcomed everyone to the meeting. Next, Mr. Chen discussed the current status of the company and its progress toward annual goals. A number of questions were asked, and extensive discussion followed.

Financial Review

Benjamin Johnson provided a comprehensive update on the financial plan and forecast. Mr. Johnson also reviewed the financial transactions for the past month and the ending cash balance.

New Business

Sales and Business Development Update: W. Kevin Young provided an update on the overall sales progress and sales pipeline of the company. He also explained the status of business development discussions.

Operating Plan: Ruth Bishop described the timing and creation of the annual operating plan. It was moved and supported that an ad hoc committee be established to create a draft of the operating plan. Ella R. Bronson, Ruth Bishop, and Leroy T. Carroll agreed to serve on the committee and to write the draft. They will present the draft at the February meeting.

Adjournment

The meeting was adjourned at 11:55 a.m.

FIGURE 14.6 Meeting Minutes

- A concise summary of the important points of discussion
- The date and time of the next meeting (if one is scheduled)
- The name and title of the person who will be signing the minutes (the secretary) along with a signature line (included if that is the practice at your organization).

Ask your supervisor if any nonparticipants should get copies of the minutes. For example, minutes of a company board meeting may be made available to all executives within a company. Minutes should be stored for future reference. In addition to keeping a copy of the electronic file, you will probably want to store the minutes in hard-copy form in a notebook. The agenda and all pertinent materials presented in the meeting should be stored with the minutes.

Participants' Responsibilities

Just as a leader has responsibilities, so do the participants. Their role is much broader than attending the meeting. Their responsibilities begin before the meeting and continue after it.

BEFORE THE MEETING

Participants are responsible for reading the meeting notice and responding to it promptly. They are also responsible for reading the agenda and any related materials received before the meeting. Participants should make sure they understand the purpose of the meeting and their responsibilities in relation to the purpose. Each participant must take his or her role seriously and arrive at the meeting prepared to contribute in a positive way.

DURING THE MEETING

Participants are responsible for arriving on time and contributing thoughtful, well-considered, and well-researched comments. Other responsibilities include:

- Respecting the leader's role.
- Listening to others without judging.
- Participating responsibly without dominating the discussion.
- Demonstrating courteous behavior to all other participants.
- Taking notes.

Although making these types of contributions sounds simple, it is not always so. Participants should give their full attention to the meeting and not answer text messages, e-mails, or cell phone calls. All electronic devices should be turned off so full attention can be directed toward the meeting. At times during a meeting, your mind may wander or focus on other work-related tasks. However, participants can help the leader keep the meeting on track and focused on the agenda with appropriate comments. It is the obligation of all participants to always contribute in a positive manner to the success of a meeting.

AFTER THE MEETING

Once the meeting is over, a participant's responsibilities do not end. The participant may be responsible for research, study, or action. He or she may be asked to work with a small group to prepare a recommendation for the next meeting. Whatever follow-up is necessary, the participant must be committed to carrying it out in a timely manner.

Conferences and Conventions

A conference or convention is much larger in scope and has many more participants than a meeting. For example, a company or companies may hold a national sales conference each year to introduce and market new products. Executives may belong to a professional organization in their field of expertise such as accounting, financial management, or human resources. Many professional organizations hold at least one convention a year, and executives are encouraged to participate as a means of broadening their knowledge and staying current in their field. Your role as an administrative professional may be to work with a meeting planner or event coordinator to set up a conference for your supervisor. If you are a member of a professional organization such as IAAP, you may attend and help plan some of the organization's conventions. Though the term *conference* is used in the remainder of this discussion, tasks and responsibilities for a convention will be similar.

Before the Event

Preparing for a regional or national conference takes months of work, and planning is extremely important. Good planning will ensure a smooth, successful conference; poor planning will result in a disorganized, ineffective conference. Two of the most important considerations are to determine the location and to arrange for meeting facilities. You may wish to contact the chamber of commerce in

PARTNERSHIP FOR 21ST CENTURY SKILLS

Communication and Collaboration

Collaborate With Others

The successful administrative professional must collaborate effectively with clients and colleagues in everyday activities and especially team meetings. *Collaboration* means working together toward a common goal. It is often better than individual effort when solving problems, generating ideas, or planning for the future. Collaboration helps participants build on each other's ideas and challenge each other to identify and correct omissions and weaknesses in suggestions or potential solutions.

Although group members should have a shared goal, they often have different views on how to achieve it. Everyone must be flexible in ideas and approaches to find the most appropriate, creative, and workable solution. Sometimes flexibility requires compromises. Do not compromise your ethics and values, and never compromise the final outcome. Instead, recognize that a goal may be accomplished in more than one way and that your way might not be the best. Listen to other members, and consider their ideas. Be flexible enough to accept someone else's thinking and to use that person's ideas toward achieving the common goal.

Collaboration is most effective when group members share in the process, responsibility, and rewards. Although successful collaboration is based in part on individual proficiencies, at its heart is the ability to work together to achieve a common goal. When the assignment is complete, assume shared responsibility for the effort. Value and recognize the group's accomplishments, and recognize the outcome as a group success. When we develop and implement our collaboration skills, all of us are smarter together than any of us is alone.

Activity

Think of an activity in which you were asked to collaborate with others (perhaps a team activity from this class or a task at work). How did your team or group work together? Were participants flexible? Were there compromises? How was the success of the group recognized? Write a short paper reflecting on the collaborative experience.

MarcusPhoto1/iStockphoto.com

any cities being considered to ask for information about the city and appropriate conference facilities. You may also request conference planning guides from hotels and conference centers you are considering. These guides usually provide floor plans of the facilities, descriptions of dining and catering services, price lists for rooms and services, and the layout of meeting rooms.

Your tasks will not include inviting someone to speak unless you are a member of the planning committee. However, you may contact presenters to make travel and lodging arrangements. Make sure to consider a presenter's preferences and needs as well as the budget. If you are making flight reservations, you need to know the person's desired arrival and departure times and rental car needs. You may also make arrangements for someone from the organization or a limo service to pick up the guest at the airport.

A preregistration period usually takes place during which people can register for the conference (sometimes at a reduced rate). Most registration is completed online. You might be responsible for designing the online registration process. Often the system creates a database of registrations, which you may use to create name tags, folders, and tickets for meals or special events. You may also be involved in preparing packets of information for registrants. A registration packet generally includes program information, a list of participants, and a small gift or two.

During the Event

Your responsibilities during the conference may include running errands, delivering messages to participants, and solving problems that arise. Other duties may include checking on room and meal arrangements and equipment needs, as well as handling many other last-minute details. Remember, you are a representative of the company or organization for which you work. You must present a positive image at all times. You must keep a smile on your face and handle even the most difficult situations with poise and confidence.

After the Event

After the conference, your basic duties involve cleaning up and following up. You must see that all equipment is returned, presenters are assisted with transportation to the airport, letters of appreciation are sent to presenters and others as appropriate, expense reports are filled out, and bills are paid.

You may also be responsible for seeing that the proceedings of the conference are published and mailed to participants. Some conference proceedings are a compilation of written documents such as papers presented at the conference. Others may include recordings of conference presentations. Your assignment may include working with a vendor to compile the information for the proceedings.

All individuals who worked on the conference should participate in a post-conference evaluation session. At this meeting, you will review what was successful and what was not. If participants in the conference filled out a formal evaluation, the evaluation forms should be tallied before the session and then presented and discussed. Take notes on any issues or problems, and share them with the appropriate organization or company personnel so that people involved in the next conference will have the benefit of your experiences.

Meeting or Event Planner

Meeting or event planners coordinate the details of a meeting or conference as requested by a client. The client may be a business, an organization, or an individual. A meeting planner typically handles tasks such as these:

- Determine and arrange for the meeting location.
- Handle lodging arrangements.
- Coordinate transportation to the meeting site for participants.
- Plan meals and other food and beverage distribution.
- Arrange all forms of electronic communication, such as e-mail, voice mail, video, and online communication.
- Arrange presentation technology and audiovisual equipment.
- Select and hire entertainment or speakers.
- Assign exhibit space and work with exhibitors to resolve any issues.

A more recent option for planners is to decide whether the goals of the meeting or conference can be achieved in a virtual format versus the traditional meeting format.

Your company or professional organization may hire a meeting planner to coordinate the details of a large meeting or conference. You may work with the planner to explore ways to meet your company's needs and stay within your budget.

Neustockimages/iStockphoto.com

SUMMARY

To reinforce what you have learned in this chapter, study this summary.

- Typical business meetings include staff meetings, committee meetings, project team meetings, customer/client meetings, board of directors meetings, and conferences and conventions.
- Meetings can occur in a variety of formats including face-to-face meetings and electronic meetings, which include audio conferences, video conferences, and web conferences.
- Understanding meeting roles and responsibilities is vital to the success of a meeting.
- The administrative professional will have a variety of responsibilities before, during, and after a conference or convention.

KEY TERMS

agenda, 318
audio conference, 313
bylaws, 312
heterogeneous group, 318
homogeneous group, 318
minutes, 324
motion, 324
verbatim, 324
video conference, 313
web meeting, 314
webcast, 314
webinar, 314

14

STUDY Tools

Located at www.cengagebrain.com

- Chapter Outlines
- Flashcards
- Interactive Quizzes
- Tech Tools
- Video Segments
- and More!

LET'S DISCUSS

1. What are the characteristics of an effective meeting?
2. What items should be considered when deciding on a meeting delivery format?
3. What are the meeting responsibilities of the executive?
4. Why is an agenda so important?
5. What are the components of an effective agenda?
6. What are the meeting responsibilities of the administrative professional?
7. Why are seating arrangements so important in meeting preparations?
8. What is the purpose of meeting minutes?
9. How do meeting participants play a role in the success of a meeting? Explain their responsibilities.
10. What are typical responsibilities of an administrative professional when planning a conference?
11. When would it be appropriate to hire event planners, and what types of responsibilities would they handle?

PUT IT TO WORK

Meeting mayhem Carol has been in charge of the monthly staff meeting for the past six months. Although Carol has participated in these meetings for the last three years, her recent promotion has put her in charge. For as long as Carol can remember, the meetings have been held on the first Tuesday of the month from 10 a.m. to noon. All sales representatives assigned to Carol (about twenty) are expected to attend.

Carol believes that, in the past, the meetings were boring, and she decided to take a new approach. She thought the meetings were too scheduled and determined to allow her staff time to chat informally before they began. She also believed the agendas were too restrictive and decided to let her staff use this meeting time to "blow off steam."

Carol thinks the first meeting went well. All sales representatives were there at 10. Carol started the meeting at 10:15 after giving everyone a few minutes to chat. Several employees had questions about the health insurance policy, and Carol answered them to the best of her ability. Without the policy information in front of her, however, she found a few questions difficult to answer. Carol promised to get the answers and share them at the next meeting.

Carol believes the second meeting was productive as well. Several employees had questions about the recycling program, and Carol was able to answer them. Staff members were also interested in the upcoming holiday party, and the details of that event were discussed as well. There were a few questions about the sexual harassment policy that Carol could not answer, but she said she would ask the company attorney to make a presentation at the next meeting.

The next few meetings were conducted in a similar open manner. Employees asked questions, and Carol attempted to answer them. Unanswered questions that were asked in previous meetings were asked again, and Carol still did not have the answers.

By the sixth meeting, there was an obvious change in the tone. Most participants did not arrive until 10:20, and Carol could not get the meeting going until after 10:30. Staff members did not participate in the topic discussions, but chatted with coworkers instead. Carol listened to complaint after complaint, becoming frustrated because so little was accomplished.

What is Carol doing wrong? How can she structure future staff meetings so they are more productive? (Learning Objectives 1 and 2)

COMMUNICATE SUCCESSFULLY

1. **Meeting research** Your supervisor, Lincoln Tyler, has asked that you investigate the costs of holding a one-day staff retreat at a local hotel. There will be 15 participants, and Mr. Tyler would like to have a continental breakfast and lunch. Contact or visit the websites of three hotels, and investigate the costs for the retreat. Prepare a memo that details the costs for Mr. Tyler. Include your recommendation. (Learning Objective 2)
2. **Meeting planning** Mr. Tyler has asked that you brainstorm and identify what needs to be done to plan the one-day retreat described in the previous activity. Mr. Tyler would like to start the retreat with a team bonding activity. Next, he would like to make a short *PowerPoint* presentation to review the current mission statement. Mr. Tyler would like participants to break into small groups and discuss the company's strategic plan and its fit with the mission statement. The retreat will end with a large group discussion. Work with a partner to prepare a list of what needs to be done to ensure a successful event. (Learning Objectives 1 and 2)
3. **Evaluate a meeting** Attend a business meeting for a local club, governmental body, or civic organization. Write a short report that describes the behavior and comments of the meeting leader and participants. Evaluate the effectiveness of the meeting. (Learning Objective 2)
4. **Effective participant** Add a new post to the blog you created in Chapter 1. In this entry, reflect on the following statement: **I can be a better face-to-face and electronic meeting participant in the following ways.** (Learning Objectives 1 and 2)

Blog

DEVELOP WORKPLACE SKILLS

5. **Prepare a meeting notice** Your supervisor, Lincoln Tyler, chairs a research task force that includes individuals from several local organizations. He has asked you to prepare a meeting notice for the next meeting. The meeting is scheduled from 9 a.m. to 3:30 p.m. on the second Wednesday of next month and will be held in Conference Room B of the Adams Building. The purpose is to implement several quality measures for the Research Committee. The objectives are to discuss the creation of a Quality Control Board and to present information from the Annual Research Conference. Include an attachment notation. You will prepare an attachment in the next activity. (Learning Objectives 1 and 2)

6. **Prepare an agenda** Mr. Tyler has asked that you prepare an agenda for the meeting in the previous activity. Use the information in Activity 5 and the additional information below to prepare the agenda. Format it as in Figure 14.3. (Learning Objective 2)

    - The meeting will start at 9:30; the continental breakfast is scheduled from 9 to 9:30.
    - Mr. Tyler will need about ten minutes at the beginning of the meeting to introduce the individuals in attendance.
    - Leonardo French will outline how to be an effective board member from 9:40 until 10:30.
    - There will be a 15-minute break starting at 10:30.
    - Mariah Beckman will lead the discussion of the creation of a Quality Control Board from 10:45 until 11:45.
    - Lunch will be served from noon until 1:15 p.m. Allow participants a few minutes to freshen up before lunch.
    - Bruce Walton will review information from the Annual Research Conference from 1:15 until 2.
    - Elizabeth Chen will introduce a Review Board assessment instrument from 2 until 2:40.
    - Mr. Tyler will answer questions and conclude the meeting from 2:40 until 3.

7. **Prepare minutes** Attend a club or business meeting at your school or in the local community. Take notes at the meeting and prepare minutes. Format the minutes as in Figure 14.6. (Learning Objectives 1 and 2)

BUILD RELATIONSHIPS

8. **Meeting etiquette** Lucille, one of the assistants in another department, has come to you for advice. She was recently put in charge of the weekly team meetings. Although the meetings have run fairly smoothly, two

staff members are texting and checking e-mail. They are not contributing to the discussions and, twice last week, asked questions that had been clearly answered during the meeting. Lucille is frustrated. What advice can you give to help her make the meetings effective? (Learning Objective 2)

9. **Sticking to the agenda** You are in charge of the one-hour monthly recycling committee meeting. The meeting is scheduled to start at 10 a.m. Brittany Pearce, who is supposed to present the first item on the agenda, just called and said she will be 15 minutes late. You know that at least two committee members have meetings immediately following this meeting. What steps should you take to handle the situation? (Learning Objective 2)

10. **Meeting planning** Access the *Word* file *Ch14_Meeting* from the data files. Read the case and answer the questions that follow it. (Learning Objectives 1 and 2)

USE TECH TOOLS

11. **Create an account** Use *Microsoft Outlook* or search the Internet to locate a free electronic invitation or meeting scheduling service. If you are using an Internet service, create an account. Learn how to use the software to send an electronic invitation. Links to several electronic invitation sites are available on the website for this text.

12. **Teach electronic invitations** You have been asked to make a short presentation about electronic invitations at the next staff meeting. Use *Microsoft Outlook*, or locate a free electronic invitation site. Links to several sites are available on the website for this text. Read the information provided. If you completed Activity 11, you may use what you learned in that activity.

    Prepare a one-page handout that you could distribute to your colleagues with instructions on how to use the software. Select an appropriate document theme to create a professional-looking handout.

13. **Create a flyer** Your supervisor is in charge of his research group's annual conference next year. He has asked that you create a one-page flyer announcing the conference that can be distributed to prospective participants. Include the following information:

    - The event title is Annual Research Conference.
    - The conference will be held on the first Tuesday, Wednesday, and Thursday in April of next year.
    - It will be held in Minneapolis, Minnesota, at the Minneapolis Convention Center.
    - Several product vendors will be present on Tuesday and Wednesday.
    - A recognition banquet will be held Wednesday evening.
    - A motivational keynote speaker will open the conference on Tuesday.

- The opening conference session is at 3 p.m. on Tuesday.
- Participants will be able to choose from over 30 breakout sessions.
- Several hands-on computer workshops will be available.

PLAN AHEAD

Prepare and conduct a meeting Work with five or six classmates to complete this assignment. Your task is to prepare for and conduct or participate in an effective 20- to 30-minute informational meeting. The purpose of the meeting is to increase the group's knowledge about a topic related to the material covered in this chapter. Examples include audio conferencing, video conferencing, web conferencing, agenda preparation, meeting types, and international meetings. Each group must select a different topic. Conduct research on your topic. Incorporate information from at least two resources in your meeting (give credit to the sources). As a group, prepare a meeting notice, an agenda, and any handouts that are necessary. Decide which team member will lead the meeting. Conduct or participate in the meeting with your team. Prepare minutes for the meeting. (Learning Objectives 1 and 2)

CHAPTER

15 Travel Arrangements

LEARNING OBJECTIVES

1. Understand how to make domestic travel arrangements.
2. Understand how to make international travel arrangements.
3. Implement organizational travel procedures.

© Photographer/Image Source

Domestic Travel

Many companies and organizations in the United States have locations in a number of different cities across the country. Although a great deal of business is now effectively and efficiently conducted using VoIP, teleconferencing, or other technologies as discussed in Chapter 10, many times only a face-to-face meeting will do. Conferences, conventions, speaking engagements, and other commitments also require travel.

As an administrative professional, your job is likely to include making travel arrangements for others and in some cases for yourself. To do this effectively, you must become familiar with the types of services available. You also need to understand your responsibilities while the executive is out of the office.

Air Travel

Because time is a valuable resource for business executives, they often travel by air. The business traveler is a major part of the airline industry's clientele, and airlines offer a variety of schedules and services to accommodate these customers.

FLIGHT CLASSIFICATIONS

The three common classes of flight accommodations are first class, business class, and economy class. While different airlines may use slightly different names, the classes are basically the same. Some airlines offer all three classes, while other airlines do not.

First-Class Accommodations First-class accommodations are the most expensive and luxurious. Seats are more comfortable, are larger, and offer more legroom than those in economy class. A higher level of services is provided. For example, first-class passengers are usually allowed to board and exit the flight before other passengers. Free beverages and snacks are typically offered, and meals are served on long flights. Headsets for listening to music or movies and personal media players may be provided at no additional cost. First class offers more flight attendants per customer than other flight classifications, which means greater attention and service for each flyer.

Business-Class Accommodations Business-class travel is a level that falls between first class and economy class. Designed specifically for passengers traveling for business purposes, this flight classification is not available on all commercial airlines or flights. Typically, business class is offered on long-distance flights such as those between New York and cities on the West Coast. Business-class passengers generally board the plane before economy-class passengers. This class offers wider and more comfortable seats, which usually recline more fully than those in economy class and provide more lateral space as well. Business services such as laptop power ports and wireless Internet access may be available. Complimentary beverages and snacks are provided, and meals may be served on long flights.

Economy-Class Accommodations Economy-class accommodations are typically the lowest-priced seats on the airplane. This classification is also called coach or tourist class. Economy-class seats are located in the main cabin area. They are closer together than in first class and generally than in business class. Fewer flight attendants are available to serve the needs of passengers. Some airlines offer complimentary soft drinks, juice, tea, coffee, and light snacks, with other food and beverage options available for purchase. In-flight entertainment may be offered, but customers may be required to buy or rent headsets if they have not brought their own.

With increased emphasis on reducing the expense of air travel, several low-fare airlines offer only economy-class accommodations. Low-fare airlines can typically charge less because they have eliminated many traditional passenger services. In addition, low-fare airlines may offer limited flight schedules, fly into secondary airports, and serve fewer destinations.

TICKETING

An **e-ticket** is an electronic ticket that represents the purchase of a seat on a specific flight, usually through a website or by telephone. This type of

A printed boarding pass is not necessary at most airports if you have a smartphone.

ticket has essentially replaced paper tickets. The buyer receives a ticket confirmation or receipt number, usually by e-mail or fax. To obtain a boarding pass, passengers may present their e-ticket information at an airport ticket counter; enter it at a self-serve kiosk near the ticket counter; check in online, printing the boarding pass themselves; or go paperless with a smartphone app that displays the boarding pass (this option is not available at all airports worldwide). A boarding pass is required to go through airport security. Travelers can save time by securing a boarding pass beforehand and having only a carry-on bag so they can bypass the ticket counter.

Occasionally it is necessary to change or cancel flight reservations. In either case, travelers may be charged a fee. The policy for changes or cancellations is described at the airline's website. The policy or fee may be different for different classes of flights. Some airlines will apply the refunded ticket cost toward a future flight, charging a small penalty. Passengers are not charged when a flight is canceled or changed because of mechanical problems or other issues. Since passengers are usually inconvenienced by such changes, airlines attempt to make them as painless as possible. If the change results in an overnight stay or long delays, the airline may provide vouchers for food or pay for a hotel room.

SECURITY

Everyone who travels by air must go through airport security checkpoints, and their baggage must go through security checkpoints as well. These checkpoints were developed to help prevent passengers from bringing anything on a plane that would enable them to take over or damage the plane. A variety of security precautions are taken at airports across the United States.

Business travelers should be aware of security procedures as well as what can and cannot be carried on a flight. The U.S. Transportation Security Administration (TSA) provides up-to-date information on its website and a free app, *My TSA*, for smartphone users. The app offers information on airport delays, wait times in airport security lines, items that can be taken through airport security checkpoints, weather, acceptable forms of identification, and advanced imaging technology (AIT), a form of passenger imaging technology used to scan the entire body. Figure 15.1 lists security measures that should be observed when traveling.

The following suggestions will help business travelers cope with airport security procedures:

- Make sure nothing you pack or plan to carry is prohibited. Unacceptable items for carry-on and for checked baggage differ. Examples of prohibited carry-on items are some kinds of sporting equipment and certain types and quantities of chemicals. Figure 15.2 shows limits for carry-on items such as shampoo and toothpaste. Lists of prohibited items are available on most airline websites and at the TSA website.
- Wear shoes that can be removed easily.
- Bring proper identification. An acceptable government-issued photo identification is required, such as a state-issued driver's license, state ID card, military ID card, or passport.
- Arrive early. Airlines advise arriving at the airport from one to two hours before your scheduled departure. The recommended time varies

Airport Security
Watch your bags and personal belongings at all times.
Do not accept packages from strangers.
Report unattended bags or packages to airport security.
Report suspicious activities and individuals to airport security.
Know and be ready to comply with screening procedures.

FIGURE 15.1 Air travel requires observing certain security measures.

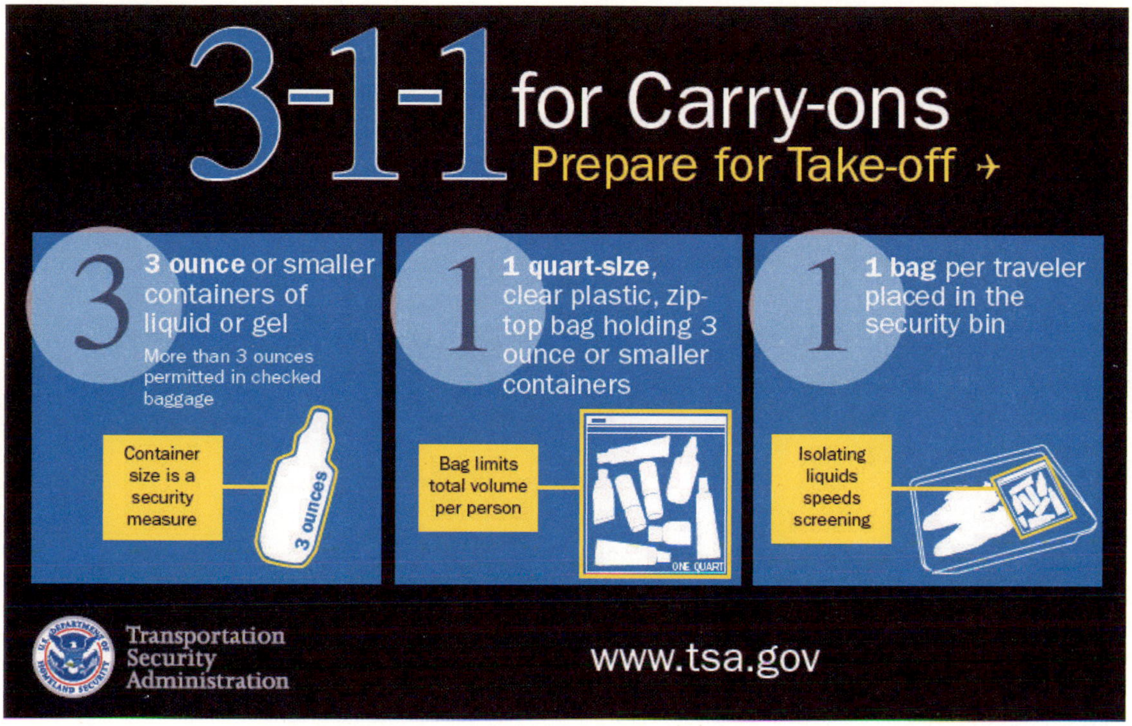

U.S. Transportation Security Administration

FIGURE 15.2 The TSA limits carry-on liquids and gels.

depending on the airline, departure city, and other factors.

- Keep your identification and boarding pass in a convenient location.
- Follow the screening guidelines. Take your laptop and other electronic devices from their cases and 3-1-1 plastic bags out of carry-on luggage. Remove jackets, coats, sweaters, belts, and shoes.
- Check to be certain you have all your belongings before you leave the security area—wallet, keys, jewelry, cell phones, and so on.

AIRLINE CLUBS

For the frequent business traveler, membership in an airline club may be a worthwhile investment. Major airlines provide private rooms for club members in large airports. Membership is available through individual airlines; fees vary. Some airlines offer daily passes that allow entry into any of their clubs during a 24-hour period and one-time admittance passes that allow entry into a single club. Membership may also include privileges at some other airlines' club facilities. Airline clubs offer a variety of travel perks, including the following:

- Computer equipment, fax, and copy machines
- Conference rooms and lounge space
- Reading material
- Complimentary soft drinks, juice, and coffee
- Alcoholic beverages
- Pastries and snacks
- Assistance with airline reservations
- VIP transportation to a departure terminal

PARKING SERVICES

Large airports generally provide free shuttle service from airport locations; however, you are charged for parking your car. The fee is based on the location of your car, with parking lots closer to the airport being more expensive, and the time your car is in the lot.

Private shuttle services are available in many large cities. Shuttle buses take you to and from the airport. They run frequently, with generally no more than a ten-minute wait between runs. Taking the shuttle may be cheaper than parking at the airport for an extended time.

COMPANY-OWNED AND CHARTERED PLANES

Large organizations may have their own plane or fleet of planes if the amount of travel by company employees makes doing so advantageous. Some small airlines specialize in privately chartered jet service. In this instance, a business would rent an entire airplane rather than purchase seats on a commercial flight. Chartered planes are generally small, since most private chartering is for small groups of people. Sometimes called air taxis, chartered planes may be housed at locations adjacent to regular airports and use the same runways as major airlines. Food is often available on these jets for an additional cost; flight attendants are generally not available.

Laptop Security

When traveling with a laptop computer, treat the computer as if it were cash. For example, put it on your lap or position it close to your body while you repack a bag in the airport. Some travelers secure laptops with a security cable when leaving their hotel room. Others leave the television playing and the "do not disturb" sign on the door. Never leave your laptop behind in the car, and never pack it in checked luggage.

DallasEventsInc/iStockphoto.com

Ground Transportation

Once executives arrive at their destination, they may need some type of ground transportation to their hotel. That transportation may be a taxi or shuttle bus. When making arrangements, you should check taxi costs and the availability of shuttle services. Some hotels provide free shuttle services to and from the airport. Shuttle services from private vendors are less expensive than taxi service. Check the hotel's website for directions and information about getting from the airport to the hotel.

If executives must attend meetings at several locations during their stay, renting a car may be the most economical and convenient method of ground transportation. Car rental agencies are available at most airports. Cars may also be rented through airlines or travel agencies or on the Internet. When renting a car, specify the make and model preferred, along with the date and time the car will be picked up and returned. Both states and car rental agencies impose age restrictions on renters. Generally, drivers must be 25, but younger drivers may be allowed to rent for an additional daily fee. Age may also affect the class of vehicle that can be rented. Since franchises for national companies may have their own rules, check with a local rental agency.

Hotel Reservations

Hotel reservations are easily made online or by telephone. They can also be made through travel agents or airlines. Most hotels offer special corporate rates for business travelers. Always check for booking fees or cancellation restrictions when making reservations. The lowest room rate may require immediate payment and may not be refundable if the reservation must be canceled.

Many hotels have business centers with computers, copiers, fax machines, and other equipment for use by business travelers. However, smartphones and laptop computers are standard equipment for most traveling executives. Hotels provide wired or wireless Internet access for a fee or sometimes at no cost. Meeting rooms are also available in many hotels. If you are making hotel reservations directly with the hotel, arrange with the reservations clerk for any equipment and/or meeting rooms that will be needed. If the executive will be arriving late, it is important to give that information to the clerk. Rooms can be released at a certain hour if reservations have not been confirmed for late arrival. With notice, early check-in can often be accommodated.

Car Travel

An executive traveling only a few hundred miles may prefer to travel by car. Some executives use cars furnished by the company. Others are reimbursed on a per-mile basis for business-related car travel. Your responsibilities for a trip by car may include determining the best route to follow, making hotel reservations, and identifying restaurants along the way. You can obtain this information from the American Automobile Association (AAA) if the company is a member. You can also use websites such as MapQuest or Google Maps (see Figure 15.3, page 342). Many cars have built-in GPS devices, but portable options, such as Garmin or TomTom devices, are also available. Free smartphone apps also provide GPS services with turn-by-turn directions.

Rail Travel

Rail travel is seldom used for business travel in the United States because it takes more time than traveling by air. Rail travel is available between many major cities in the United States, including high-speed, express rail service between Northeast cities such as Washington, Philadelphia, New York, and Boston. Few rural locations are served. First-class and sleeping accommodations are available, as well as coach accommodations for more economical travel. Routes, schedules, and rates can be checked, and reservations made, at the Amtrak website.

International Travel

Because of the increasingly global nature of business, executives often must make trips abroad. As an administrative professional, you need to know how to make arrangements for an international trip. You should also know something about the business culture of the country the traveler is visiting.

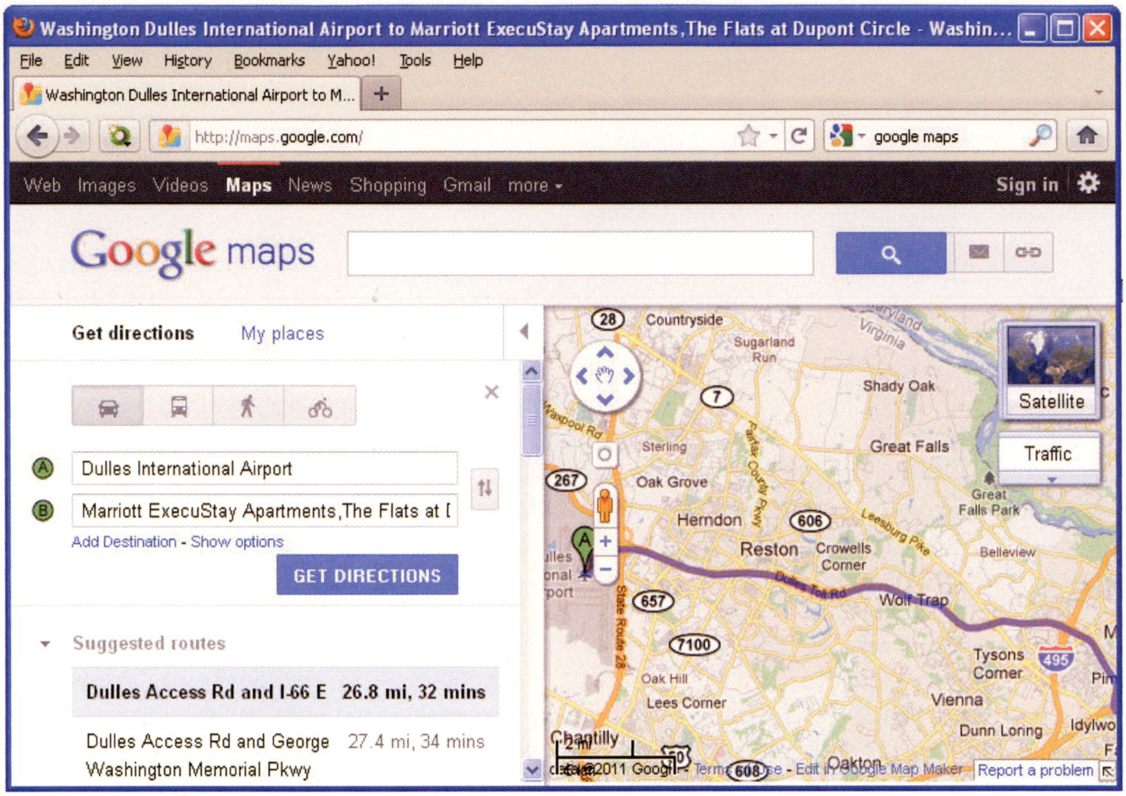

FIGURE 15.3 Websites and GPS devices make driving directions simple.

Cultural Differences

A basic understanding of the culture and business customs of the country the executive will be visiting will help you make appropriate travel arrangements. Chapter 2 provides general information on international business customs and etiquette, including dining etiquette, business dress, and other topics. Figure 15.4 gives additional guidelines. Remember that business practices can differ greatly from country to country. Information about countries can be obtained from a variety of sources, including:

- Consulates of the country to be visited. A **consulate** is an office of a government in a foreign city that acts to assist and protect citizens of the represented country. Check the consulate website of the country.
- Travel books. Travel books with information about local customs and business practices are available in bookstores and libraries.
- Seminars and short courses. Colleges and universities often provide short courses or one-day seminars on the culture of various countries and tips on conducting business in specific countries. Online courses may also be available.
- The Internet. Many websites and articles discuss international cultural differences and business etiquette.

International Flights

International flight classifications are the same as those for domestic air travel. Classes of flights are first class and economy or coach, with business class available on many international flights. Weight and size restrictions for luggage may vary slightly from one airline to another, so the administrative professional or executive should check with the airline. International travelers must arrive at the airport earlier than domestic travelers, generally two hours before flight time.

Guidelines for International Travel
■ Learn the appropriate greeting for the country you will be visiting.
■ Learn how to say "please" and "thank you" in the language of the country.
■ Do not criticize the people or customs of the country you are visiting. Show appreciation for the music, art, and culture of the country.
■ Remember that for the most part business is conducted more formally in other countries than in the United States.
■ Have business cards printed with your name and your company name in both English and the language of the country you are visiting.
■ Dress appropriately—generally, business suits for men and conservative dresses or suits for women. Although dress in the United States has become more casual, you cannot assume this is true in other countries.
■ Eat the food offered to you. Do not ask what you are being served. Show appreciation to the host.
■ Be courteous and respectful at all times.

FIGURE 15.4 Follow these guides to interact effectively with others on international trips.

Passports and Visas

A **passport** is an official government document that certifies the identity and citizenship of an individual and grants the person permission to travel abroad. In almost all instances, a passport is required to travel outside the United States. Some exceptions exist that were designed for frequent travel by land or sea between the United States and Mexico, Canada, the Bahamas, and some other Caribbean destinations. In those cases, one or more of the following alternatives may be acceptable:

- A passport card issued by the U.S. State Department
- An enhanced driver's license issued by several states bordering Canada (at the time of this writing, Michigan, New York, Vermont, and Washington)
- A Trusted Traveler Program card issued by U.S. Customs Border Protection for travel to Canada or Mexico

You can obtain information about passports and check current exit and entry requirements for specific countries at Travel.State.Gov, a U.S. Department of State website (Figure 15.5, page 344). Keep in mind that requirements can change at any time.

Passports are granted by the Department of State. First-time applicants must apply in person. You can apply at many post offices, public libraries, clerk of court offices, and other state, county, township, and municipal government offices. Application forms may also be downloaded from Travel.State.Gov.

A passport is valid for ten years from the date of issue. (Passports issued to children 15 and younger are valid for five years.) As soon as the passport is received, it should be signed. Also, the information in the front pages should be completed, including the address of the bearer and the name and contact information for an emergency contact. The State Department recommends packing an extra set of passport photos and a copy of the front pages of your passport to facilitate replacement if your passport is lost or stolen. Travelers should always carry passports with them while abroad; they should never be left in hotel rooms unless secured in a room safe.

A **visa** is an approval granted by a government that permits a traveler to enter and in some cases to travel within that particular country. A visa usually appears as a stamped notation on a passport indicating the bearer may enter the country for a certain time. Rules and restrictions for visas vary from country to country; check the Travel.State.Gov website.

Bureau of Consular Affairs/U.S. Department of State

FIGURE 15.5 The Travel.State.Gov website provides helpful information on passports and other travel topics.

Health Documents and Precautions

Some countries require visitors to have specific vaccinations or health tests, such as testing for contagious diseases. Records documenting these vaccinations or tests may be required for travel to the country. The entry requirements for a particular country should be checked before every trip in case of changes. The U.S. Centers for Disease Control and Prevention (CDC) website provides this information.

Travelers should check on whether their health insurance covers them while abroad. For the most part, medical insurance is not accepted outside the United States, and medical care can be expensive. Short-term health insurance policies designed specifically for travel are available.

Because environmental factors may be different from those in the United States, there is a possibility of developing an illness related to the food, water, or climate of another country. Plan for this possibility by visiting a physician before your trip or taking over-the-counter medicines with you, such as medications for pain, allergies, and stomach disorders.

If you are staying with a host family in a country where there are health precautions that must be taken or you personally have some health issues that do not allow you to eat certain foods, you should politely explain these issues to your host. For example, if you have an allergy to fruits such as mangos that your host is likely to serve, explain this as soon as you arrive.

Tap water in another country may be safe for local residents; however, it may contain different microbes than water in the United States and may cause digestive problems for travelers. To be safe, use purified water at all times, even when brushing your teeth, washing your hands, or rinsing raw foods. For the same reasons, you may want to avoid having ice served in drinks. Most restaurants and markets serve and sell purified water.

Travelers who take prescription medicine should pack enough to cover their needs while they are away. It is a good idea to take extra medicine in case some is lost or the trip lasts longer than planned. Do not pack prescription medicine in a bag that will be checked. You should take written prescriptions for the medication as well as the names and contact information for the doctors and pharmacist at home.

The CDC website is a good source of information about current health issues in specific countries. The Travel.State.Gov website describes medical facilities.

Foreign Currency

Before leaving the United States, executives can exchange money at certain banks and currency exchange offices for the currency of the country being visited. Many travelers prefer to exchange a small amount of money in the United States and then exchange more money when arriving at the destination. Any currency left over at the end of a trip can be exchanged for U.S. currency.

It is always a good idea to be aware of exchange rates before and during travel to another country. They can vary daily and are not always the same at every location. For example, the exchange rate at a bank may be more favorable than the rate at an airport. Many business travelers prefer to withdraw spending cash from ATMs during their visit and to use credit cards for most purchases. Besides the convenience, the exchange rate for ATM withdrawals and credit card purchases is typically a little better than the rate for exchanging cash or travelers' checks for local currency. Travelers planning to use an ATM should check that their access code will work in the country and check fees. They should also notify their bank and credit card company of their travel plans so that overseas transactions do not trigger theft concerns.

Travelers may wish to carry a currency exchange "cheat sheet" or index card with rates for common amounts such as $1 and $20. Rates of exchange and currency converters are easy to find on the Internet. Free smartphone apps provide currency calculators and exchange rates.

TECH TALK

Travel Apps

Mobile technologies fit best in mobile environments, and travel is just such an environment. Travel apps make flight and confirmation numbers, addresses, directions, airport delays, traffic patterns, etc., accessible in seconds. Travelers with smartphones are not searching for file folders or having to manage papers. Here are four helpful apps for travelers:

Airline apps Most airlines have apps that allow you to check in and retain boarding pass information on a mobile device. These apps also provide flight itineraries, information about airport delays, and changes in flight information.

XE Currency This app provides exchange rate information, a currency calculator, and historical data about exchange rates between selected currencies.

Smart Traveler The U.S. Department of State provides this app, which features information about countries, travel alerts, embassy locations, and more.

Expensify With this app, travelers can take pictures of receipts that can be used later to create an expense report online or accessed by an administrative professional via the web.

International Car Rental and Driving

Cars are readily available for rent at most international destinations. Arrangements can be made online by the executive or assistant, through a travel agent, or by the executive after arriving. In some countries, a U.S. driver's license is sufficient; however, most countries accept an International Driving Permit (IDP), which provides your license information in ten languages. Travelers may obtain an IDP from AAA or the National Automobile Club. Travelers should secure appropriate insurance and become familiar with the driving regulations of the country they are visiting.

Driving conditions and customs are sometimes quite different from those in the United States. For example, in some countries you must drive on the left-hand side of the road and pass on the right-hand side. Steering wheels are mounted on the right-hand side of the car. Travel.State.Gov provides general and country-specific information on road safety, including road conditions and driving regulations.

International Rail Transportation

Many countries have excellent rail service, particularly in Europe. A traveler can get from one city in Europe to another in a short period of time. Trains are generally clean, and the accommodations are comfortable. Underground rail is available in a number of European cities.

Organizational Travel Procedures

Procedures for travel arrangements vary from organization to organization. Some companies use a travel agency to schedule all travel. This agency becomes knowledgeable about the needs of the organization and is able to provide services the executives need with limited assistance. Other organizations ask that individual executives or their assistants make travel arrangements.

Arrangements by Travel Agencies

Travel agencies can make all travel arrangements for the executive. They are especially helpful when the executive is traveling internationally. An agency can schedule the flights, make hotel reservations, and arrange car rental. The agency will also provide an **itinerary**, a document that gives travel information such as flight numbers, arrival and departure times, hotel reservations, and car rental arrangements.

Travel agencies receive commissions from airlines, hotels, and other service industries when they sell services. However, they may also charge the customer a minimum fee or service charge for some of the arrangements they make.

Arrangements by the Administrative Professional

Regardless of how travel arrangements are made, you as an administrative professional will be involved. The first time you help plan a trip for an executive, talk with the person about general travel preferences. Set up a folder when you learn about an upcoming trip, and place all notes and information relating to the trip in the folder. The folder is then available for instant referral when needed.

Although you may telephone some airlines or hotels that you use frequently, typically the most efficient method of making reservations is to use the Internet. You can make flight reservations at airline websites or through independent travel websites that give prices for several airlines at the same time. Hotel and car reservations can be made at some of these sites or at individual hotel and car rental websites.

If an executive is traveling by air, you need to know:

- The name of the preferred airline (if the executive has a preference) as well as his or her frequent flyer program number. A **frequent flyer program** is an incentive program that provides a variety of awards after the accumulation of a certain number of mileage points. Awards may include upgrades from coach to first class and free airline tickets.

- Whether the flight is to be direct (if possible) or whether the executive is willing to change planes. Less expensive flights are often available if the executive is willing to change planes.
- The class of flight preferred—first class, business, or economy.
- Seating preference—aisle or window and section of plane.

If you are making arrangements for more than one top-level executive to travel to the same location at the same time, company policy may dictate that the executives fly on separate flights. With both executives on the same plane, both might be injured or killed if there were a serious accident.

EdBockStock/Shutterstock.com

You will handle many responsibilities for business trips.

You may assist executives with travel arrangements by determining passport and visa requirements, checking on currency needs, researching health issues and business etiquette in the country to be visited, making flight and hotel reservations, arranging car rental, and arranging rail transportation. You will also prepare an itinerary. In addition, you may have the following responsibilities:

- Scheduling appointments and meetings
- Obtaining travel funds
- Preparing and organizing materials for the trip
- Determining procedures to follow in the executive's absence

SCHEDULE APPOINTMENTS AND MEETINGS

If you will set up appointments or meetings for the trip, be sure to consider any time zone differences. **Jet lag** is a feeling of exhaustion following a flight through several time zones. It causes prolonged periods of fatigue and disrupts eating and sleeping cycles. As a result, jet lag can greatly restrict an executive's effectiveness. Try to give the traveler an extra day to recover from the trip before scheduling the most important meetings.

If executives do not have the luxury of a full day before appointments or meetings, they can apply certain techniques to help with jet lag. For example, if they will be traveling west, they can postpone bedtime by two or three hours for two or three days before the flight. If they will be traveling east, they can retire a couple of hours earlier than normal. Travelers can also shift mealtimes nearer to those at their destination. Although their body clock will still have to adapt, they will experience less jet lag if they use these techniques.

Avoid scheduling appointments the day before the executive leaves on a trip and the day the traveler returns. The day before a trip is usually needed for final preparations. When executives return from a trip, they may need to contend with time zone changes and handle business issues that arose while they were away.

PARTNERSHIP FOR 21ST CENTURY SKILLS

Information, Media, and Technology Skills

Media Development

Administrative professionals must be able to work with not only traditional media development tools such as office software but also emerging forms of media used in business. QR code generators are an example.

A **QR** (quick response) **code** is a two-dimensional bar code that can be scanned and quickly decoded with a smartphone camera and a mobile reader app. The code provides information such as a text message, directions, contact information, or the URL for an organization website. The QR code for the State Department's *Smart Traveler* mobile app appears at the lower right.

QR codes are used by businesses for marketing and organizations for dispensing information. Some cities have them on street signs so people can obtain information about their location. Museums and libraries use the codes to connect users with a phone number for assistance or to direct them to a website or text about an artifact or exhibit.

Two common uses of QR codes for the administrative professional are business cards and marketing materials. On a business card, a QR code can yield the individual's contact information in a format that can be saved directly to a smartphone contact list. Administrative professionals may also be asked to generate QR codes for marketing materials, such as brochures, flyers, or information sheets.

Codes can be created easily with a free online QR code generator. Simply copy and paste the code into the appropriate document, or save it as an image (right-click the code, or use the online generator's option to download it).

Activity

Using an online QR code generator, create a code for the home page of your school website or a code that could be used for contact information on a business card. (For contact information, choose the vCard format.) Links to several QR code generators are provided on the website for this text.

QR code: U.S. Department of State

Check the executive's calendar to see if any appointments have been scheduled for the period when the executive will be away. If so, find out whether they should be canceled or if someone else in the company will handle them. Notify the people involved as needed.

Before preparing the itinerary, write, e-mail, or call the people your employer plans to see during the trip to confirm the appointments. Verify addresses and directions from the hotel to meeting locations. Include this information on the itinerary

When preparing an itinerary, include the following information:

- Flights. Include flight numbers and times as well as the name of the airport and airline.
- Hotel. Include the name and address, telephone number, and confirmation number. It may also be helpful to include the type of room reserved, hotel amenities, and nearby restaurants.
- Rental car. Include the company name, telephone number, type of car, and confirmation number. Give directions on where the rental office is located.
- Transportation. If the executive will use a transportation service, include the company name, telephone number, and confirmation number.
- Meetings or appointments. Include a contact name or number the traveler can call if he or she has questions or is delayed. Include driving directions if needed.

or on a separate appointment schedule as the executive prefers.

PREPARE AN ITINERARY

The itinerary is a must for you and your employer. If you are working with a travel agency, the agency will prepare an itinerary that includes flight numbers, departure and arrival times, car rentals, and hotel reservations. However, this itinerary will not include information about appointments and other special events. Because the executive needs an itinerary that includes all activities of the trip, you should prepare a complete itinerary. Copies should be distributed to the executive and the person who will be in charge while the executive is away. The executive may request a copy to leave with family members. A file copy should also be retained at the office. Figure 15.6 on page 350 shows a sample itinerary. Executives with smartphones may wish you to put all the information directly on their calendar or to provide it in a format recognized by their calendar (such as *Microsoft Outlook*).

Some executives prefer to have their trip appointments separate from the rest of their itinerary. When this is the case, an appointment schedule is prepared. Figure 15.7 on page 351 shows a sample appointment schedule. An appointment schedule may be prepared on paper or printed from calendar software. It should include the following information:

- City, date, and time of the appointment
- Individual or group involved in the appointment
- Location (including room, building name, and street address if it is an unfamiliar location)
- Telephone number of location
- Special instructions or remarks

OBTAIN TRAVEL FUNDS

Organizations differ in how they handle funds for trips. Airline tickets may be charged directly to the organization, or the traveler may pay and be reimbursed by the company. Hotels, meals, and car rentals may be charged on a credit card provided by the organization. Another practice is for individuals to get a cash advance to cover all expenses for a trip. To do so, the individual fills out a travel form before leaving, indicating how much money he or she will need for lodging, meals, and other expenses. The company advances the money to the employee before the person leaves on the trip. Another practice is for the executive to pay the expenses; he or she is then reimbursed by the company upon returning. Company policies generally

Itinerary for Daniel Mullee

Fort Worth to Grand Rapids *March 5–7, 201-*

Monday, March 5	**Fort Worth to Grand Rapids**
9:30 a.m. CST	Leave Dallas Fort Worth International Airport (DFW) on Delta Flight 57 and arrive at Gerald R. Ford International Airport (GFIA) at 2 p.m. EST (e-ticket confirmation in briefcase); take Esteban's Transport to the Amway Grand Plaza Hotel, telephone 616-555-0124 (Confirmation 44038). Pickup at Entrance 11-B on the lower level by baggage claim.
	Hotel reservations at the Amway Grand Plaza, 187 Monroe Avenue NW, telephone 616-555-0156 (Confirmation 828382).
3:30 p.m. EST	Meeting with Isabelle Marin, Room 212, Ranier Building, telephone 616-555-0129. Blue folder contains papers for meeting.
Tuesday, March 6	**Grand Rapids**
10 a.m. EST	Meeting with Joel Wang, Conference Room A, Temple Building, telephone 616-555-0165. Manila folder contains papers for meeting. Lunch with Joel follows the meeting; he is making arrangements for lunch.
3:30 p.m. EST	Meeting with Julia Wilcots, Conference Room C, Temple Building, telephone 616-555-0166. Red folder contains meeting notes.
Wednesday, March 7	**Grand Rapids to Fort Worth**
9:30 a.m. EST	Meeting with Arjun Haryana, Room 220, Thurston Building, telephone 616-555-0138. Yellow folder contains proposed contract.
1:30 p.m. EST	Leave GFIA on Delta Flight 70 (e-ticket confirmation in briefcase) and arrive in Fort Worth at 5 p.m.

FIGURE 15.6 Travel Itinerary

require employees to provide receipts for expenses over a certain amount.

PREPARE AND ORGANIZE MATERIALS

Several items may be needed for a trip. If it is an international trip, items such as passports, medications, business cards, and small gifts may be necessary. Whether the trip is domestic or international, several items usually must be prepared, such as proposals, reports for meetings, and presentation materials. Once the materials have been prepared, the administrative assistant assembles the appropriate number of copies and gives them to the executive. The traveler needs items such as these:

- Itinerary
- E-ticket confirmations
- Passport and visas

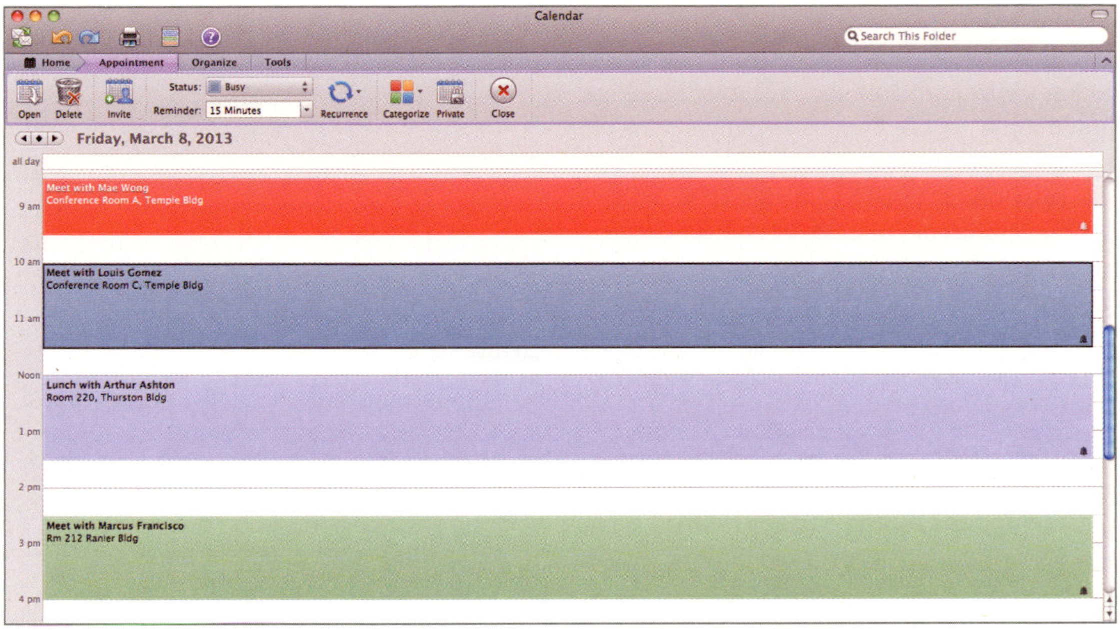

FIGURE 15.7 Appointment Schedule

- Calendar or appointment schedule
- Credit cards and currency
- Hotel and rental car confirmation numbers
- GPS device and appropriate addresses
- Special materials, reports, or presentation materials
- Business cards
- Cell phone or smartphone and tablet or laptop
- Information on organizations to be visited
- Reading materials

You may be asked to select business gifts for the executive. In some countries business gifts are expected; in others they are not appropriate. If a business gift is given, it should be a small item, such as a nice pen or memento representative of the United States. Be certain the gift is made in the United States. Appropriate gifts include pens or pen-and-pencil sets, items from your home state, and books about historical areas of your state. Photo albums containing pictures of people the executive met on the trip are also appropriate gifts. However, both you and the executive should be aware of the gift-giving etiquette of the particular country to avoid offending someone without knowing it. The Internet is a good source of information on gift-giving etiquette.

DETERMINE PROCEDURES

Find out who will be in charge during the executive's absence. Check to see if the executive is expecting important papers that should be forwarded. Be sure you understand how to handle all incoming mail, both e-mail and traditional mail. The executive may want you to refer all mail that has a deadline to another executive within the organization, answer routine mail, and retain other mail until he or she returns.

Duties During the Executive's Absence

Your pace may be somewhat slower while the executive is out of the office, or it may accelerate. Your responsibility is to handle the workflow smoothly and efficiently during the traveler's absence.

MAKE DECISIONS

You must make wise decisions within the scope of your responsibilities during the executive's absence. You should know which matters to handle yourself, which to refer to someone else in the company, and which to refer directly to the executive through an e-mail, a telephone call, or a fax. Make sure you understand your responsibilities and make appropriate decisions when necessary.

HANDLE CORRESPONDENCE, MESSAGES, AND APPOINTMENTS

The executive will probably have specific preferences for the handling of correspondence, messages, and appointments while he or she is away. For example, the executive may direct you to forward all correspondence or e-mail a PDF of a report as soon as it is done, or he or she may wish to attend to those items upon returning. This depends partly on how connected the executive wishes to be while traveling. Chapter 16 provides general guidelines on handling mail during the executive's absence.

Executives may e-mail or call the office daily while away. If the executive prefers to call, determine the approximate time of day of the call so you can have all messages and items reviewed and be ready to discuss them. Keep urgent messages and correspondence in a place where you can find them quickly. You may find it helpful to keep a list of all items that need to be discussed in the call.

While the executive is away, you may need to set appointments for individuals who wish to meet with him or her after the trip. Your employer will probably have a full day of work to handle on the first day back, so avoid scheduling appointments for that day. If the trip was abroad, the executive probably will have some jet lag. If an appointment is absolutely necessary on the first day, schedule it in the afternoon. Avoiding morning appointments is also a good idea in case of delayed return flights.

Post-Trip Activities

When the executive returns, you should brief him or her on any important activities that occurred at the office during the trip. You should also inform the executive of the appointments you set up and the telephone calls, e-mail, and other correspondence you received.

EXPENSE REPORTS

Following a trip, many organizations require employees to prepare an expense report and turn in receipts for expenses above a certain amount. The following information is often included on an expense report:

- Employee name and department
- Date of expense
- Category of expense (meals, lodging, airfare)
- Description of entertainment expenses (lunch with client Tom Chung)
- Expense amount (converted to U.S. dollars if the expense is from international travel)
- Receipts if required (some organizations do not require receipts if a corporate credit card is used or if the expense is below a certain dollar amount)
- Employee signature and date
- Supervisor signature and date

The executive will usually provide you with a list of receipts from the trip, including flight, hotel, and meal receipts. Your task is to complete the expense report carefully, double-checking all individual figures and totals. Copies of the receipts are usually attached to the expense report. Figure 15.8 shows a sample expense report prepared in *Microsoft Excel.*

Smartphone apps are available that help travelers track expenses. With this type of resource, an administrative professional can track an executive's expenses from a distance and can create reports with copies of receipts. *Expensify,* described in the Tech Talk on page 345, is an example of this type of app.

FOLLOW-UP CORRESPONDENCE

The executive may need to write several follow-up letters after the trip. For example, he or she may want to send thank-you letters to the executives or clients contacted on the trip. Customers or potential customers may be sent information on products or services. Contracts may be written and mailed. The executive may also need to answer correspondence that accumulated during the trip or ask you to respond to certain items.

For Office Use Only

Expense Report

PURPOSE: Sales | STATEMENT NUMBER: 1412875 | PAY PERIOD: From 2/1/2012 To 2/15/2012

EMPLOYEE INFORMATION:

Name: Roger Milston | Position: Sales Director | Date: 2/10/2012

Department: Pharmaceutics | Manager: Alexis Dubois | Employee ID: 14927

Date	Account	Description	Hotel	Transport	Fuel	Meals	Phone	Entertainment	Misc.	Total
2/6/2012	103	Airfare: Atlanta-San Diego-Atl		$ 486.34						$ 486.34
2/6/2012	67	Marriott Marquis	$ 299.00							$ 299.00
2/6/2012	85	Meals				$ 34.00				$ 34.00
2/6/2012	103	Excess Baggage							$ 25.00	$ 25.00
2/7/2012	67	Marriott Marquis	$ 299.00							$ 299.00
2/7/2012	85	Meals				$ 105.32				$ 105.32
2/7/2012	103	Taxis		$ 53.00						$ 53.00
2/8/2012	85	Meals				$ 76.85				$ 76.85
2/8/2012	15	Airport Parking							$ 30.00	$ 30.00
										$ -
										$ -
										$ -
										$ -
										$ -
										$ -
			$ 598.00	$ 539.34	$ -	$ 216.17	$ -	$ -	$ 55.00	
									Subtotal	$ 1,408.51
									Advances	
									Total	$ 1,408.51

APPROVED: *Alexis Dubois* NOTES:

FIGURE 15.8 Expense Report

SUMMARY

To reinforce what you have learned in this chapter, study this summary.

- Domestic travel arrangements handled by administrative professionals include air travel, hotel reservations, car rentals, and other types of transportation.
- International travel arrangements handled by administrative professionals include air travel, travel documents, research on topics such as cultural differences and health precautions, foreign currency, and other types of transportation.
- As an administrative professional, you will have a role in making travel arrangements, preparing materials for the trip, handling issues while the executive is away, and completing follow-up activities after the trip.

KEY TERMS

consulate, 342
e-ticket, 337
frequent flyer program, 346
itinerary, 346
jet lag, 347
passport, 343
QR code, 348
visa, 343

15

STUDY Tools

Located at www.cengagebrain.com

- Chapter Outlines
- Flashcards
- Interactive Quizzes
- Tech Tools
- Video Segments
- and More!

LET'S DISCUSS

1. List and describe the three flight classifications most commonly used for domestic travel.
2. Explain ways to obtain a boarding pass.
3. List three security measures that passengers are requested to follow in an airport.
4. List three ways to obtain driving directions to a domestic address.
5. Describe two guides for business etiquette in foreign countries.
6. What is the difference between a passport and a visa?
7. How may an administrative professional assist executives with travel arrangements?
8. Describe some of the items that should be included on an itinerary. Why is an itinerary important?
9. What are the responsibilities of the administrative professional when the executive is traveling?
10. What types of post-trip activities might the administrative professional be asked to perform?

PUT IT TO WORK

Travel arrangement problems Angelina Morganhouse is an administrative professional for a telecommunications company. Last week her supervisor, Elena Perez, asked her to make arrangements for Ms. Perez to go to Orlando for a meeting. Angelina obtained the necessary travel information from Ms. Perez and made the flight reservations. Ms. Perez requested a rental car for three days while in Florida and indicated she had three appointments scheduled. She gave Angelina the names and appointment times.

Angelina wrote out the meeting contact and flight information on a sheet of paper and gave it to Ms. Perez. Ms. Perez was not impressed with the itinerary's lack of detail: it didn't include the appointments, hotel, or rental car information. The itinerary was also barely legible.

When Ms. Perez arrived at the rental car office, she learned there was no record of her reservation. In fact, Angelina had forgotten to make rental car arrangements. Upon her return, Ms. Perez found her mail unsorted, unopened, and piled on her desk. There were also multiple voice messages on her office phone (which had not been forwarded to Angelina) making simple requests.

What should Angelina have done to ensure smooth and uneventful travel for Ms. Perez? What should Angelina have done while Ms. Perez was gone? (Learning Objective 3)

COMMUNICATE SUCCESSFULLY

1. **Business customs** You work part-time for a small business, and your boss has just secured a number of accounts in an Asian country. He will visit his clients in this country next month. Working with a classmate, research business etiquette in an Asian country of your choice. Look particularly for information about meetings, gifts, professional attire, and dining. Prepare an e-mail to your boss with helpful information for the visit. (Learning Objective 2)
2. **Blog** Add a new post to the blog you created in Chapter 1. In this entry, reflect on the following question: **What do you believe is the most challenging part of traveling internationally and why?** (Learning Objective 2)

Blog

3. **Follow-up correspondence** Your supervisor, Ralph Oxbridge, just returned from a sales meeting with a potential client, Dr. Frederick March. Compose a letter to Dr. March from Mr. Oxbridge. Thank Dr. March for his time, and tell him the specifications he requested are on the product spec sheets that are enclosed. Also, inform him that a local company representative will be contacting him to arrange a demonstration of the heart-rate monitoring device that particularly interested him. Indicate that Mr. Oxbridge will contact him in two weeks to further discuss how this and other company products can benefit him in his practice. Dr. March's address is Kensington Medical Associates, 1240 Beacon Street, Boston, MA 02116-3048. (Learning Objective 3)

DEVELOP WORKPLACE SKILLS

4. **Itinerary** Access the *Word* file *Ch15_Trip_Plans* from the data files. Use the information in this file to prepare an itinerary for your supervisor, Melody Hoover. Format the itinerary as in Figure 15.6 on page 350. (Learning Objectives 1 and 3)
5. **Expense report** Ms. Hoover has returned from a trip and asks you to prepare an expense report. Access the *Word* file *Ch15_Expenses* and the *Excel* file *Ch15_Expense_Report* from the data files. Prepare the report using the spreadsheet file and the information provided by Ms. Hoover. (Learning Objective 3)
6. **Directions** Using an online site or a mobile app, obtain a map and turn-by-turn directions from your college to a local business. (Learning Objective 1)
7. **International travel** With a partner, use the Travel.State.Gov website to research a foreign country. Prepare a one-page information sheet for the executive you work for, who is traveling to that country next week. Include embassy or consulate telephone numbers, entry and exit requirements for U.S. citizens, primary languages spoken, a map of the country, a short description (in your own words) of the country, and any current security concerns or threats for

the country. Assume the executive will travel within the country and may stay a few extra days as a tourist. Put this information sheet in the online portfolio you created earlier in the semester. (Learning Objective 2)

e-Portfolio

BUILD RELATIONSHIPS

8. **Away from the office** You are Angelina from the Put It to Work activity on page 355. Plan what you will say to Ms. Perez to repair the damage that has been done to your working relationship. Include specifics about how you will improve your performance for her next trip. (Learning Objective 3)

USE TECH TOOLS

9. **Scanning QR codes** In groups of three or four, be the first to find out what this QR code means. At least one person in your group needs a smartphone, and you will need to download a free QR scanner app. Links to several apps are provided on the website for this text.
10. **Airline apps** Work in the same group as in the previous activity. Suppose you are employed in an office where executives fly most often on a particular airline for business trips within the United States. Choose an airline, and download a free app for it. Explore features of the app that would be useful for an executive when traveling. Be prepared to explain to a group of executives (your class) how the app works and what features they would find helpful. (Learning Objective 1)
11. **Calendar** Using *Microsoft Outlook* or a free online calendar program such as *Google Calendar*, create an appointment schedule for Daniel Mullee, the executive for whom the itinerary in Figure 15.6 on page 350 was prepared. Include the appointments in Figure 15.6. (Learning Objective 3)

PLAN AHEAD

International travel arrangements Your supervisor, David Anderson, will travel to Frankfurt, Germany, in April to meet with several clients. He has asked you to make all travel arrangements for the trip.

- The trip will be during the first full week of April. Mr. Anderson will leave Saturday and return the following Sunday. If the current date is before April of the current year, use the current year for the travel dates. If the current date is after April of the current year, change the month to two months after the current month. This will be necessary because many reservation systems will not provide information for dates more than 6 to 11 months in the future.

- Choose flights using the Web. Select the flight class, note flight numbers and times, and make sure seats are available.
- Mr. Anderson will leave his car at Logan International Airport. He will take a taxi from Frankfurt Airport to his hotel. All his meetings will be at his hotel.
- Plan reservations for him at the Steigenberger Frankfurter Hof for a nonsmoking room with a queen-size bed for his entire stay except Thursday and Friday. Check availability.
- Mr. Anderson wants to travel by train to Munich on Thursday for a meeting. Find a five-star hotel in downtown Munich for him. He will return to Frankfurt Saturday.

Create an itinerary for Mr. Anderson. Include the travel arrangements you made and the following appointments. Use the itinerary format in Figure 15.6 on page 350. Invent details such as confirmation numbers as needed.

- Monday—meeting with George Muller and Stefan Bonhoeffer from 10 a.m. until 2 p.m., Conference Room A
- Tuesday—continuation of meeting with George Muller and Stefan Bonhoeffer from 11 a.m. until 3 p.m., Conference Room A
- Wednesday—meeting with Dietrich Zwingli and Katharina von Bora from 9 a.m. until 1 p.m., Conference Room C
- Friday—meeting in Munich with Hildagard Rheinstein from 11 a.m. until 2 p.m., Conference Room C

Write a memo to Mr. Anderson providing the costs of the arrangements for his travel and any other necessary information that was not included in the itinerary. Be sure to include rail costs, and estimate meals and taxi costs based on your research. All amounts should be in U.S. currency. (Learning Objective 3)

CHAPTER

16 Workplace Mail and Copying

LEARNING OBJECTIVES

1. Process incoming and outgoing mail.
2. Understand appropriate use and features of copiers, shredders, and fax machines.

© Photographer/Image Source

Handling Mail

Although many large organizations outsource the handling of mail, small companies generally do not. It is important that you as an administrative professional understand how mail should be handled. You cannot assume that all mail will be outsourced or automated. Mail is delivered by a variety of methods including the United States Postal Service (USPS), private delivery companies, and e-mail.

Preparing Outgoing Mail

Your duties as an administrative professional will vary depending on the organization where you work. You will prepare and mail items such as individual letters, contracts, reports, and packages. You may also prepare bulk mailings, such as advertising brochures, flyers, or letters going to dozens or hundreds of recipients. Important suggestions that will help you effectively handle outgoing mail are listed below:

- Place all interoffice correspondence in appropriate envelopes with the name and department of the addressee listed on the envelope.
- Use the notations *Attachment* and *Enclosure* appropriately. Use *Attachment* when an item is attached to the document. Use *Enclosure* when the

item is placed behind the document without being attached.

- Key the address on the envelope carefully; check the letter address against the envelope address. You may want to keep a list of frequently used addresses.
- Seal and stamp the envelope. If you work in a large organization, the mail may be sent to a mail room or outsourced. If you work in a small office, you may seal and stamp envelopes using a postage meter or purchase postage online.

The address on an envelope should be located in an area that can be read by the U.S. Postal Service's automated equipment, such as an optical character reader. An optical character reader (OCR) is a machine that scans printed text, converting it to a form that can be used by a computer to sort mail or for other purposes. The Postal Service's website provides specific instructions for preparing envelopes. Follow these guidelines to ensure quick and accurate delivery.

With many software programs, envelopes can be created automatically for letters that contain a recipient's address. Creating an envelope automatically saves time and ensures that exactly the same name and address appear on the letter and envelope. Envelopes are formatted according to USPS guidelines. Figure 16.1 shows a correctly addressed envelope. Follow the specific steps for your word processing program to create an envelope. Many word processing programs allow you to include a return address for your organization. The software may also allow you to omit the return address if you will be using envelopes with a printed return address.

In many word processing programs, similar procedures can be followed to create a mailing label. You will be given options to select the label size and to print a full page of the same label or a single label. When you use the program's default settings, the address will be positioned correctly on the label. When you place a label on an envelope or create an envelope address manually, be sure the address is placed properly so it can be read by the OCR. Other products for generating labels include desktop label makers that may connect to the computer and may also print postage.

Most organizations have correspondence they send to certain groups of individuals on a regular basis. **Mail merge** is a feature of word processing programs that allows you to create personalized letters. Mail merge can also be used to prepare labels or envelopes for large mailings. The standard text of the letter or other document is stored in the main file. A list of recipients (names, addresses, and other needed information) is stored in a data file. A data file may be saved as a word processing table,

FIGURE 16.1 Correctly Addressed Envelope

spreadsheet file, or database table or query. Codes are placed in the main document at places where personalized data should appear. Personalized data include the name and address of the recipient, which can be used to create the letter address and salutation, and any other information needed to individualize the letter that person receives. The codes in the main document match the names of columns or fields in the data file.

The mail-merge operation creates new documents that combine the text of the main file and data from the data file. Using mail merge is an efficient way to create letters for several recipients when only a small amount of data specific to each recipient changes with each letter. *Microsoft Word* includes a Mailings tab that helps users create customized letters, e-mail messages, envelopes, labels, and a directory. *Word* also provides a mail-merge wizard you can use to create personalized letters or other merged documents.

Sending Outgoing Mail

Outgoing mail may be picked up and delivered by the USPS or by a private mail carrier or delivery company. You can schedule a mail pickup and pay for shipments for private mail carriers or the USPS online or by phone. Scheduling and purchasing services online often results in cost savings and complimentary services. When deciding which service to use, consider when the envelope or package should reach its destination, the cost of sending (and sometimes of insuring) the item, possible safety precautions for the contents, proof of delivery, and any other services needed.

USPS DOMESTIC MAIL CLASSIFICATIONS

The U.S. Postal Service continues to be a cost-effective choice for mailing business documents and packages. You should be familiar with USPS recommendations and restrictions for items you mail. The Postal Service identifies a letter or postcard as machinable if it has a correct address and can be processed by Postal Service equipment. Prepare your envelopes and labels correctly to help ensure items are machinable.

If your letter or package has clasps, buttons, or strings, does not meet size or weight requirements, or exceeds size or weight requirements, it may be considered nonmachinable. In most cases you should make sure individual envelopes you mail are in the machinable category to avoid additional fees. If your letter or package is nonmachinable, be prepared to pay an extra fee.

For large mailings, you may be able to save money by meeting the requirements for items in the automation category. Mail in the automation

Follow these suggestions to handle outgoing mail effectively:

- Always double-check addresses on letters and envelopes to be certain they are correct.
- Check the spelling of names of organizations and individuals.
- Check ZIP Codes for accuracy.
- Before placing a letter in an envelope, check that it is signed.
- Make sure all necessary enclosures are included.
- Maintain updated mailing lists for individuals within the organization and external clients or customers.

category contains bar codes and can be processed by high-speed equipment. Other requirements, such as a minimum number of pieces, may apply. Consult the U.S. Postal Service website to learn about current requirements and costs for mailing items in the automation category. The USPS offers discounted mailing rates for companies that choose to do some of the work that typically would have to be done by the Post Office.

The USPS offers several standard classifications for mailing business materials. Choosing the appropriate mail classification helps ensure that the materials are delivered in a timely manner and at the most cost-effective rate. Commonly used classifications are the following:

- Express Mail is the fastest delivery service available from the USPS, offering guaranteed overnight delivery to most U.S. locations 365 days a year. The maximum weight is 70 pounds. A flat rate or set fee (regardless of weight) is charged when the USPS's own Express Mail envelopes are used.
- Priority Mail is a cost-effective choice for envelopes and packages with delivery usually within two days. The maximum weight is 70 pounds. Flat rates apply with use of USPS Priority Mail envelopes and boxes.
- First-Class Mail is an economical choice for letters, large envelopes, postcards, and small packages, with delivery usually within three days. The maximum weight is 13 ounces.
- Parcel Post is an option for envelopes and packages with a maximum weight of 70 pounds and a maximum combined length and width of 130 inches. It is frequently less expensive than Priority Mail, but delivery may take longer, from two to eight days.

Mail Considerations

When mailing business documents, consider the following items:

- Type of mail. The USPS has several mail classifications with different features, service levels, sorting requirements, and prices.
- Weight and size. Both the weight and the size of the item are taken into consideration when determining postage.
- Distance. For some mail classifications, price is determined by how far the item will travel.
- Number of pieces. A minimum number of pieces are required for commercial postage classifications.

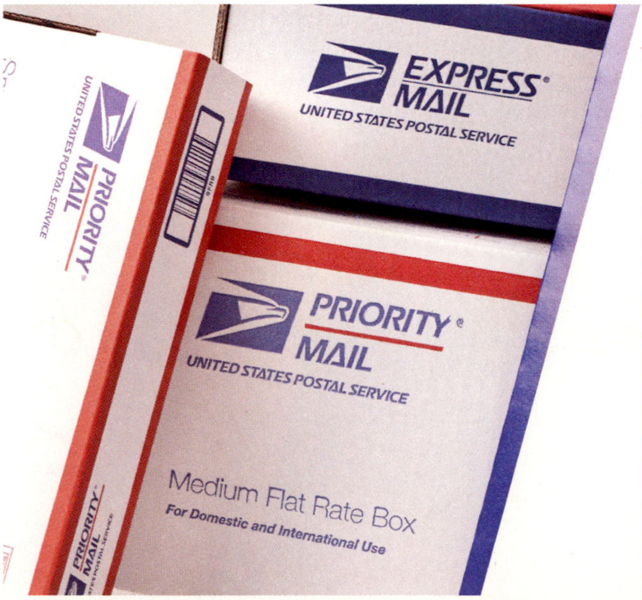

asiseeit/iStockphoto.com

USPS INTERNATIONAL MAIL CLASSIFICATIONS

The USPS offers several delivery options for sending letters and packages to international destinations, with delivery to more than 190 countries. You can receive discounted rates on most international mail if you purchase the postage online. The principal categories of international delivery services are described below:

- Global Express Guaranteed is the fastest international mailing service offered by the USPS. This service provides delivery usually in 1–3 days. Items must be at least 9.5 inches long by 5.5 inches wide, and the maximum weight is 70 pounds.
- Express Mail International is a less expensive option with delivery typically in 3–5 days. Weight limits vary by country; items can have a maximum length of 36 inches and a maximum combined length and width of 79 inches. A flat rate is charged when using USPS Express Mail International envelopes.
- Priority Mail International is a cost-effective choice for delivery generally in 6–10 business days. The maximum weight is 70 pounds, and the maximum combined length and width is 108 inches. Flat-rate packaging is available for this mailing category as well.
- First-Class Mail International is the most affordable international service for letters, large envelopes, and small packages weighing up to 4 pounds. Delivery time varies by location. Size and thickness standards are available at the USPS website.

When sending packages to other countries, be sure to check the Postal Service website for general instructions as well as specific rules and restrictions, which vary by country. You should also review the information related to the customs forms that need to accompany international packages. Without the correct form, the package may not clear customs in the country in question.

USPS SPECIAL SERVICES

The Postal Service offers several special services for mail delivery. Some commonly used services are described in the following list:

- Certified Mail allows you to verify the date and time of delivery either through an online tracking system or by phone. You also receive a receipt for the mailing.
- A Certificate of Mailing is a receipt that shows the date your item was mailed. It provides evidence of when you sent the item.
- Delivery Confirmation allows you to verify the date and time of delivery either online or by phone.
- Return Receipt provides proof of delivery in the form of a postcard or electronic notification that

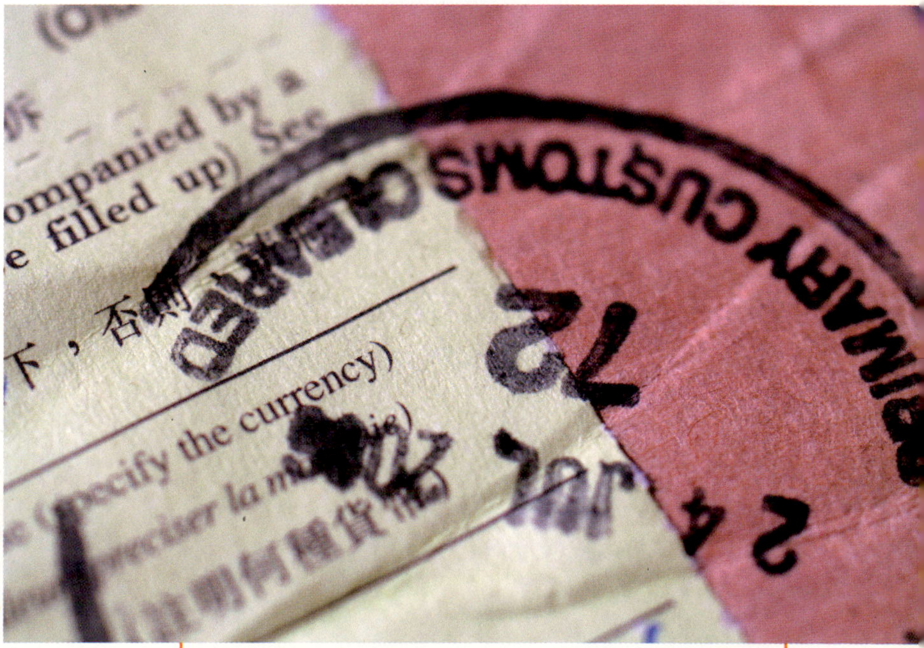

imagemonkey/iStockphoto.com

Check instructions and rules to ensure smooth processing of international mail.

shows the signature or stamp of the receiver, delivery date, and recipient address information.

- Signature Confirmation provides the date, time, and location of delivery and the name of the person accepting the item. This information is available online or by phone. You can request a printed copy of the signature.
- Restricted Delivery limits the individuals who can sign for and receive mail to only those listed.
- Insurance against loss or damage is available for mailed items. Items can be insured for their actual value up to $5,000.
- Registered Mail is the most secure service the USPS offers. It provides a mailing receipt and proof of the date and time of delivery, either online or by phone. Items can be insured for the actual value up to $25,000.

Special services can be purchased for both domestic and international mail classifications. Some mail classifications include special services as part of the purchase price. For example, $100 worth of insurance is included in Express Mail service. Check the USPS website for rates and restrictions.

PRIVATE DELIVERY COMPANIES

Private delivery companies such as FedEx and United Parcel Service (UPS) offer fast and effective mail services to recipients locally, around the country, or worldwide. The cost of services from private companies can be lower or higher than from the U.S. Postal Service, depending on the delivery time, distance to the recipient, and size or weight of the envelope or package. Private companies also offer guaranteed overnight or second-day delivery of items.

Detailed information about the services offered by private mail companies is available on their websites. Users can also access detailed price and delivery information. Websites allow users to track packages from mailing to delivery. Some private carriers make scheduled daily pickups and deliveries to businesses. Some organizations have contracts with private delivery companies or routinely use their services. Drop-off locations are also available where packages can be mailed.

Handling Incoming Mail

Responsibilities for handling incoming mail depend on the size of the company. One of your responsibilities in a small firm may be to receive and process mail. In large companies, many mail services may be outsourced to independent companies. If mail is not outsourced, however, large companies have a centralized mail department that receives and distributes mail.

When a company has a centralized mail department, mail is generally delivered by mail department employees at set times during the day. In small organizations, a Postal Service carrier may deliver the mail directly to the organization. If the small organization maintains a post office box, you may be responsible for picking up the mail.

SORT MAIL

Once you receive the mail in your office or department, you must do a preliminary mail sort. If several individuals work in the department, sort the mail according to the addressee. An alphabetical sorter is handy if you are sorting mail for a number of individuals. Once the mail is sorted, place the mail for each individual into separate stacks. When the preliminary sort is complete, sort each person's mail in the following order:

1. Personal and confidential items. Do not open mail marked "Personal" or "Confidential." Place this mail to one side so you do not inadvertently open it.
2. Special Delivery, Registered, or Certified Mail. This mail is important and should be placed so the individual to whom it is addressed sees it first.
3. Regular business mail (First-Class Mail) from customers, clients, and suppliers. This mail is also considered important and should be sorted so it receives priority.
4. Interoffice communications. Although many interoffice messages are sent by e-mail, there are times when a memorandum is more appropriate, particularly when the correspondence is long or the information is confidential. Reports

Partnership for 21st Century Skills

Communication and Collaboration

Give Effective Instructions

Being able to give effective instructions to another person or group of people is an important component of the administrative professional's responsibilities. Some instructions will be oral, and others will be written. For example, you may be asked to teach a coworker how to use the new copy machine or to prepare written instructions for handling the mail in your absence.

Regardless of the format, instructions must be complete in order to be effective. Take time to think through the process and generate a plan of what you need to include. Write down some notes about what you will say or what your document will include. Take the time to organize your ideas in a way that is logical for the user. Here are some tips to help you communicate effective instructions:

- Be clear and specific about what you want. Use direct and concise language.
- Break the task into step-by-step procedures whenever possible.
- Demonstrate or provide illustrations to clarify the instructions.
- Provide complete information, but be careful not to overwhelm by providing too much unnecessary detail.
- Make sure your message is understood. If you are giving oral instructions, have the learner repeat your message in his or her own words. If the instructions are written, ask a colleague to test them and give you feedback.

Make yourself available to answer questions, or let the person know the best way to contact you. Remember, your effectiveness in providing instructions will impact the user's ability to complete the task correctly and in a timely manner. The few extra minutes it takes to plan your instructions can save a great deal of time and frustration for a user.

Activity

Write down step-by-step instructions about how to make a peanut-butter sandwich. Make sure someone can complete the task without asking questions. Give your instructions to a friend or classmate, and ask the person to follow the instructions exactly. Were your instructions clear?

iofoto/Shutterstock.com

of various kinds are also often sent through interoffice mail. Interoffice mail is generally sent in a distinctive interoffice envelope that can be readdressed and reused.

5. Advertisements and circulars. Advertisements and circulars are considered relatively unimportant and can be handled after other mail is answered.
6. Newspapers, magazines, and catalogs. These materials should be placed at the bottom of the correspondence stack since they may be read at the recipient's convenience.

OPEN MAIL

Mail may be opened in the mail room using a machine to slit the envelope or at your desk. When opening

Mail should be sorted and then opened.

mail at your desk, you will usually use an envelope opener. Follow these procedures when opening mail:

- Have necessary supplies readily available such as an envelope opener, a date and time stamp, routing and action slips, sticky notes, a stapler, paper clips, and a pen or pencil.
- Before opening an envelope, tap the lower edge on the desk so the contents fall to the bottom and will not be cut when the envelope is opened.
- Empty each envelope. Carefully check to see that everything has been removed.
- Your organization may require that you stamp each item to show the date and time received. You may use a machine that automatically dates and time-stamps or a manual stamp.
- Fasten any enclosures to the correspondence. Attach small enclosures to the front of the correspondence. Attach enclosures the same size as or larger than the correspondence to the back.
- Mend any torn paper with tape.
- If a personal or confidential letter is opened by mistake, do not remove it from the envelope. Write "Opened by Mistake" on the front of the envelope, add your initials, and reseal the envelope with tape.

Stack the envelopes on the desk in the same order as the opened mail in case it is necessary to refer to the envelopes. A good practice is to save all envelopes for at least one day in case they are needed for reference. Then they may be thrown away. Envelopes should be retained when one or more of the following situations exist:

- An envelope has an incorrect address. You or your supervisor may want to call attention to this fact when answering the correspondence.
- A letter has no return address. The envelope usually will have the return address.
- An envelope has a postmark that differs significantly from the date on the document. The document date can be compared with the postmark date to determine how much of a delay there was in receiving the document.
- A letter specifies an enclosure that is not enclosed. Write "No Enclosure" on the letter and attach the envelope. You may contact the sender to obtain a copy of the missing item.
- A letter contains a bid, an offer, or an acceptance of a contract. The postmark date may be needed as legal evidence.

In many organizations, all incoming mail is stamped with the date and time of receipt. This procedure provides a record of when the correspondence was received. It is useful when correspondence is not dated or documents are received after a deadline. For example, a contract may arrive after a deadline date. The stamped date of receipt on the document or envelope is a record showing it arrived too late. The date and time stamp may appear on the front or back of the correspondence depending on the organization's or executive's preference.

REVIEW MAIL

Busy executives need help with the large amount of mail that crosses their desks each day. As an administrative professional, you can help by reviewing the mail and noting important parts of the correspondence. To **annotate** the document, you might underline or highlight important words and phrases. You may check calculations and dates that appear in the correspondence. Follow the executive's preferences.

You may also annotate by placing sticky notes on the correspondence to bring attention to or clarify information. Notes can be used in a variety of circumstances but are especially helpful in the following situations:

- An enclosure is missing from the letter.
- A bill is received. Check the computations, and indicate any discrepancies in a note.
- The correspondence refers to a previous piece of correspondence. Locate a copy of the correspondence, and attach it to the reply letter with a note indicating the original correspondence is attached.
- A meeting is suggested at a time when the executive is already committed.

PRESENT MAIL

After the mail has been opened, dated, time-stamped, and reviewed, you should do a final sort before presenting it to the executive. You may use these categories:

- Immediate action. This category consists of mail that must be handled on the day of receipt or shortly thereafter.
- Routine correspondence. This category includes memorandums and other types of non-urgent mail.
- Informational mail. This category includes magazines, journals, newspapers, advertisements, and other types of mail that do not require a response but merely provide information for the executive.

TECH TALK

Communications Software

A variety of communications software enables users to make voice calls through the Internet. Software applications for computers and smartphones offer typical telephone features including voice mail, caller ID, call forwarding, call transfer, and conference calling. There is no cost for the software, and regardless of distance, computer calls are often free. Because most of these software applications cannot be used for emergency calling, Internet phone service is not recommended as a replacement for a landline or cell phone.

One of the most widely known software applications is Skype™. Skype software may be downloaded to all types of computers including desktops, laptops, and tablets. It is also available as a smartphone application and can be accessed on some brands of televisions and Blu-ray players. Besides Internet calling, Skype software permits text messaging and real-time chat. Additional features include file transfer, screen sharing, and videoconferencing. Users can purchase a subscription that allows them to access some of the additional features, or they can pay for these services through a debit system. Calls to both landline and mobile-phone numbers may be made for a small fee.

In smaller organizations you may receive external mail only one time a day. If external mail is received in the morning and afternoon, the executive may ask that you distribute and present the mail two times a day. If you have been with the company and the executive for a period of time, he or she may not want to see all mail. You may be authorized to handle routine requests, distribute magazines or advertisements, and file some types of routine information.

At times, more than one person may need to read a piece of correspondence. In those cases, send a copy of the correspondence to each individual, or route the correspondence to everyone using a routing slip. When determining whether to make copies, ask yourself if it is urgent that all individuals receive the information contained in the correspondence immediately. If the answer is yes, make the copies. If the answer is no, use a routing slip, particularly if the correspondence is lengthy.

A routing slip provides a reference so you know when and to whom you sent the correspondence if there are questions. When each person on the routing slip receives and reads the copy, the person initials next to his or her name before sending the copy to the next individual on the list. The last person to receive the correspondence generally returns it to the individual who sent it.

HANDLE E-MAIL

Because e-mail is quick and easy to use, businesses and individuals use it to send billions of messages each day. Reading and responding to e-mail messages can consume a great deal of your workday. Allocate specific times throughout the day to read and answer messages. Review the suggestions provided in Chapter 4 to manage your e-mail messages and to organize your inbox.

Your supervisor may expect that you assist with his or her e-mail. You may also be in charge of a general e-mail account for the organization. If so, be certain you understand how you are expected to handle them. Remember, when possible, e-mail should be answered the day it is received. Here are some suggestions for handling e-mail for your company or supervisor:

- Check e-mail regularly, depending on your employer's instructions.
- Do not open e-mail marked "Confidential" unless your employer instructs you to do so.
- Read the e-mail and reply to it or forward it to the appropriate individuals.
- If the correspondent does not know you handle your employer's e-mail, indicate that in your e-mail when you respond.
- If you cannot handle the e-mail, notify your employer so he or she can respond.

PaulPaladin/Shutterstock.com

Check e-mail regularly.

Proofread your e-mail and correct all errors. Make sure your messages convey a positive impression of you and your company. Review and apply the guidelines provided in Chapter 8 to ensure your e-mail messages are effective.

HANDLE MAIL DURING THE EXECUTIVE'S ABSENCE

You may be expected to handle the executive's mail while he or she is away from the office. Before the executive leaves, discuss your responsibilities in handling the mail. Ask specific questions so you have a clear understanding of what to do. Mistakes in handling mail can be costly or embarrassing to the company. When the executive is away, follow these general guidelines:

- When urgent mail or e-mail comes in, handle it immediately. If possible, respond to the correspondence the same day. If you cannot answer the mail, send it to the appropriate person in your organization. Usually your employer will have designated someone who is in charge in his or her absence. See that this person receives the urgent correspondence quickly.
- Answer mail that falls within your area of responsibility in a timely manner.
- Keep a copy of mail you've answered (attached to the original document) in a folder. Your employer may want to review it when he or she returns.
- Maintain mail that can wait for the executive's return in a separate folder. Retrieve any previously written correspondence that the executive will need when reviewing the mail, and place it in the folder.

Office Equipment and Green Practices

Most offices have copiers, and many have shredders and fax machines. You will need to learn how to use office equipment properly. Your organization may purchase standalone copiers or fax machines or a multifunction machine that combines printing, faxing, copying, and scanning capabilities. Multifunction machines are often cost-effective and take up less space than separate machines.

Keeping information confidential and secure is an important consideration with copies and faxes. Chapter 14 describes methods of disposing of confidential information. Documents that are not confidential can simply be recycled.

Office Copiers

As an administrative professional, you will use office copiers extensively. You will make file copies of outgoing mail. You will make copies of some incoming mail to route to others or to use as working copies. You will make copies of documents such as reports for meetings or to share with others in the organization. It is important that you know the capabilities of copiers and also that you avoid wasting resources by making unnecessary copies.

COPIER FEATURES

You could be involved in selecting a copier for your business or home office. If you work for a small company, you may be asked to research and recommend a copier for purchase by the company. To make the best decision, you must understand the copier needs of the organization. Figure 16.2 on page 370 provides questions you should consider when discussing copier needs.

Copiers are generally categorized according to the volume of copies that can be produced and the features they provide. For example, high-volume and multifunctional machines typically have the ability to:

- Produce 50 to 140 or more copies per minute (cpm) and 500,000 ppm (pages per month).
- Print, scan, and fax.
- Sort, fold, staple, punch holes, and saddle-stitch pages (staple through the centerfold).

Mid-volume copiers produce approximately 25 to 60 cpm and 80,000 ppm, and low-volume copiers produce approximately 18 to 30 cpm and 5,000 to 10,000 ppm. Copy/duplicators are typically high-performance machines found in specialized copy/duplication centers or print shops. As copy technology becomes more advanced, copiers will continue to improve in speed and features offered.

Office copiers have several features that can be helpful in your work. Learn to use the features of your particular copier by reading the manual, viewing videos provided by the manufacturer, or attending training sessions. Common copier features include the following:

- Reduction and enlargement. This feature allows users to increase or decrease the size of the copy. For example, reduced copies can be made of large documents so all filed copies are uniform in size. The enlargement feature allows a copy of a document to be magnified. Fine details can be made more legible by using the enlargement feature.
- Duplex. Copying on both sides of a sheet of paper is called **duplexing**. On this setting, the copier automatically prints on both sides of the paper.
- Automatic document feeder (ADF). This device feeds a stack of original documents without your having to lift and lower the platen cover for every sheet. A recirculating ADF flips pages inside the machine and can be used to copy batches of double-sided pages.
- Editing features. A number of copiers have built-in editing features. These features include border erasing, centering, color adjusting, marker editing, and masking. Marker editing lets you change the color of specific sections of a document to highlight these areas. Masking allows you to block out areas of sensitive or confidential information.
- Finishing features. Finishing features such as automatic staplers, three-hole punchers, saddle-stitch binders, and folders can save a great deal of time in finishing the project after you copy.

Other features to consider when purchasing a copier include the following:

- Wireless capabilities. Wireless functionality allows you to copy a document simply by sending a file to the copier from your computer.
- Energy-saving capabilities. Energy-saving copiers often offer a sleep mode that conserves energy when the machine is not in use.
- Multifunction capabilities. A machine that can scan, fax, and print will save office space and money.

COST CONTROL

Many organizations monitor the use of copiers. Keeping track of the number of copies produced by individuals helps an organization monitor use and avoid the waste created by making more copies than needed. For example, when the number of copies is being monitored, employees will think twice about making ten copies of a document when only six are required. The additional copies are made "just in case," and the extra copies are often thrown away.

Some organizations use copy control devices. For example, the user may enter an access code or account number on a keypad or swipe a card through a card reader to activate the copier.

Considering Copier Needs
■ How many people will use the copier?
■ How many copies will be made per month?
■ Is there a projected increase or decrease in copy volume during the next three years?
■ What features are necessary?
■ Will color copying be needed?
■ What space limitations exist for the copier?
■ Should a maintenance contract be purchased?
■ How much money is available for purchasing the copier?

FIGURE 16.2 Questions to Be Considered When Selecting a Copier

Although originally created to prevent unauthorized use, control devices allow the organization to track use of the machine by department or even by user. At the end of the billing period, a manager can print an access report to view the total pages copied or printed by each access code.

Copy control devices can also make copies more secure. When documents are sent directly from a computer for copying, some machines with control devices can hold the documents in memory until a code is provided by a user. This prevents users from sending materials to the copier and then leaving confidential documents accessible in the output bins. This type of security feature is more common on larger, more expensive machines.

Tommounsey/iStockphoto.com

Copy control devices can help reduce copier costs.

Selecting the proper supplies for the copying job and recycling used paper are additional ways to control costs. In-house documents such as a department meeting agenda can be printed on less expensive paper, while documents that will be sent outside the organization may require higher-quality paper. Specialty papers, such as colored paper, cardstock, or glossy stock, may be used to copy documents such as advertising brochures and flyers. These papers are more expensive than standard copy paper and should be used only when needed.

COPIER MAINTENANCE

As an administrative professional, you will certainly use the office copiers. In addition, you may be responsible for some copier maintenance. Keep the following suggestions in mind so maintenance costs are minimal:

- Store paper properly. It should be stored in a dry area, away from extreme hot or cold temperatures. Keep paper flat, wrapped, and boxed until needed.
- Check the paper before you load it into the machine. Paper that is wrinkled, curled, or damp can cause repeated paper jams.
- Fan packaged paper before loading it. This increases the amount of air between the sheets, helping to ensure the paper feeds through the copier one sheet at a time. Fanning also helps eliminate static in the paper and lessens the possibility of a paper jam.
- When a particular problem appears consistently, inform the key operator or technician of the malfunction.

Be cautious in copier maintenance. Some copier areas become hot during operation. If you attempt to make a minor repair or adjustment, such as clearing a paper jam or adding toner or ink, be very careful.

Sometimes an organization will designate a **key operator**, a person who is responsible for copier maintenance and simple repairs. Often, a person whose work area is located near the copier is responsible for clearing paper jams, fixing malfunctions, replenishing supplies, and determining when a repair call is justified. Consistent care adds to the operating life of the equipment.

Ethical Considerations

Unfortunately, some employees use office copiers to copy materials for personal use without the approval of the company. Others make copies of documents that are needed for an outside professional group without approval from the organization. Such behavior is clearly an ethical violation. Behave ethically by using office copiers for approved uses only.

There are legal restrictions on the copying of certain documents. Employees should not copy materials such as portions of books or magazines that are protected by copyright laws without the permission of the copyright holder. You should not copy certain documents such as paper money, passports, and postage stamps. If you have questions about what is legal to copy, check with your organization's attorney, or review regulations on the U.S. Copyright Office website. A link to this site is provided on the website for this textbook. The FAQs section shown in Figure 16.3 will answer many of your questions about copyright.

Etiquette Considerations

As with all shared equipment, observing basic courtesies is important. No one enjoys trying to use equipment and finding that the copier is not working, no copy paper is available, or the room is disorganized. Be considerate of others' time. Observe the courtesies listed here:

- If you have an extensive copying job, try to plan it for a time when the copier is generally not in use, or notify your colleagues beforehand.
- Let them interrupt if they have only a few pages to copy.
- When the toner or ink runs out, refill it.
- When paper gets low, add more.
- When a paper jam or another problem occurs, fix it, or call the key operator or a service repairperson.
- If you are using additional supplies such as paper clips or scissors, put them back where they belong before leaving the copier.
- If you make copies that are not usable, destroy them. Put them in a shredder or recycle bin.

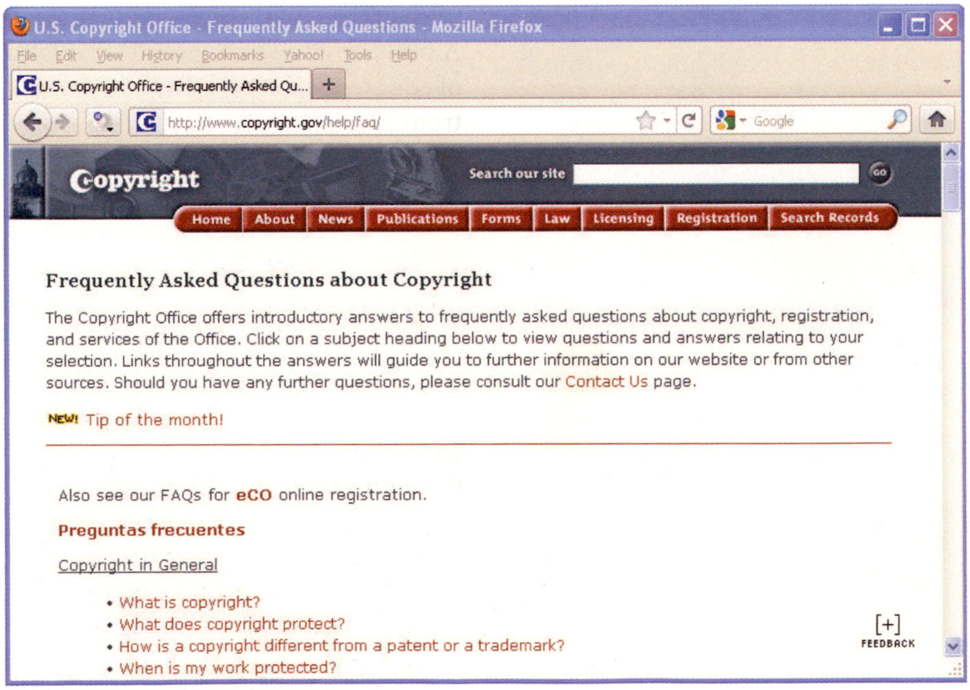

U.S. Copyright Office

FIGURE 16.3 Frequently Asked Questions About Copyright

Do not leave a messy work area for the next person to clean up.

- When you finish your project, return the copier to its standard settings.

Shredders

For those times when a machine malfunctions and copies must be destroyed, businesses often place a shredder in proximity to the copier. The type of shredder used depends on the level of confidentiality required. Government organizations, businesses, and private individuals use shredders to destroy private, confidential, or otherwise sensitive documents. A shredder can be used to cut paper into strips or small confetti-like pieces.

Shredders are being used more extensively by individuals due to increased identify theft. To prevent fraud and identity theft, experts recommend that individuals shred bills, tax documents, credit card and bank account statements, and other personal items. Shredder features have been developed to increase user convenience and to improve efficiency and safety. Users can purchase shredders with some or all of the following features:

- Safety sensors. Sensors will automatically disable the shredder when a hand or finger is too close to the paper entry.
- Low noise operation. Because shredders are often used in shared spaces, machines have been designed that are less noisy when operating.
- Jam reductions. Shredders have more powerful motors to handle more sheets at a time or jumbled or misfed papers. Built-in sensors can detect paper thickness and reject paper when too many pages have been fed.
- Energy savings. Some shredders enter a power-saving mode similar to a copier's when idle.

If the shredder doesn't cut paper small enough, confidential documents could be removed from the trash, reassembled, and read. Several new shredders have been developed that cut paper into pieces significantly smaller than the length of a staple. Some government agencies and businesses have improved their shredding techniques by adding pulverizing, pulping, and chemical decomposition as part of their document disposition.

Brad Wynnyk/Shutterstock.com

A shredder can help protect confidential information.

Fax Machines

A fax machine continues to be an important piece of equipment in the workplace. A fax machine electronically sends a facsimile (images and text) of an original document from one location to another via a communications network. It usually consists of an image scanner, modem, and printer. Some fax machines can be connected to a computer, with the scanner and printer used independently.

In the business world, many stand-alone fax machines have been replaced by systems capable of receiving and storing incoming faxes electronically and routing them to their destination on paper or through secure e-mail. Services are available that allow the use of the Internet to send and receive faxes. Some of these services are free, and some are pay services. You can send and receive faxes via e-mail or a website.

Fax messages are usually automatically printed at their destination. Because many faxes contain sensitive or confidential information, it is important to protect fax messages when they are received. Follow these guidelines to secure fax messages:

- Limit access to the fax machine by placing it in a private location.
- Use a fax cover sheet that includes the recipient's and sender's names, fax numbers, and phone numbers. Indicate the date and number of pages in the fax on the cover sheet.
- Check the page count on incoming fax messages to ensure no pages are missing.
- Request a confirmation that a fax has been received when sending a fax with urgent or sensitive information.

Recycling

Recycling and other green practices are very important to businesses and organizations. Many companies keep bins for used paper near the copier area. Pages that have smudges or do not copy properly can be put in the bins for recycling. Documents that are no longer needed can also be recycled. This paper may be sent to a recycling center or shredded to use as packaging material for shipping items.

jonya/iStockphoto.com

Recycling provides many benefits for organizations.

Recycling of paper and other materials is one way an office can "go green." Recycling has many benefits. A number of these benefits are listed here:

- Save money. Recycling services can be cheaper than trash disposal services.
- Divert material from disposal. Keeping paper out of the waste stream saves landfill space and reduces pollution by avoiding incineration.
- Conserve natural resources. When recycled paper is used, fewer trees are cut down.
- Save energy. Less energy is used in recycling products than in processing virgin materials.
- Reduce greenhouse gas emissions. Recycling reduces greenhouse gas emissions that may lead to global warming.

In addition to recycling, organizations can take other steps to reduce the amount of paper used. Some suggestions are provided in the following list:

- Increase the use of e-mail to save paper used for printed memos.
- Use recycled paper.
- Convert scratch paper into memo pads and telephone answering slips.
- Print or copy only the number of copies needed.
- Shred used paper to use as packing materials instead of plastic pellets or Styrofoam.
- Ask employees to write or print on both sides of the page.
- Use a single-space format for the text of a document.

If your company does not have a recycling program, you can see suggestions for how to start a program by visiting the paperrecycles.org website hosted by the Paper Industry Association Council.

SUMMARY

To reinforce what you have learned in this chapter, study this summary.

- The administrative professional is often responsible for handling incoming and outgoing mail.
- Mail is delivered in a variety of ways including the USPS, private delivery companies, and e-mail. Special services and international delivery options are also available.
- The administrative professional will use office copiers extensively and must understand copier features, cost control, maintenance, and ethics and etiquette considerations.
- Recycling and other green practices are very important to businesses and organizations.

KEY TERMS

annotate, 367
duplexing, 370
key operator, 371
mail merge, 360

16

STUDY Tools

Located at www.cengagebrain.com

- Chapter Outlines
- Flashcards
- Interactive Quizzes
- Tech Tools
- Video Segments
- and More!

LET'S DISCUSS

1. List three items you should consider when mailing business documents, and describe why they are important considerations.
2. Why might you select Parcel Post for mailing a package with the U.S. Postal Service rather than Priority Mail?
3. When would you send a document by Certified Mail? Give an example of when you would purchase Delivery Confirmation.
4. Why might you choose to use a private delivery company to mail an item rather than the U.S. Postal Service?
5. Describe how incoming mail should be sorted. Why should you sort mail before presenting it to the executive?
6. What items should be considered when investigating copier needs?
7. What are two strategies a company might use to reduce copying costs?
8. What are four features you should investigate when purchasing a shredder?
9. List three benefits to recycling, and explain why it is an important consideration for an organization.

PUT IT TO WORK

Mail handling Joseph Mendoza is frustrated. He has been working for Kapor Pharmaceuticals for one year, and he prides himself on doing good work on each job he is given. He also thinks he has significantly improved his human relations and technical skills during his time with Kapor. Because the company is growing, Joseph recently asked his supervisor, Rebecca Masterson, if it would be possible to employ a student from one of the local community colleges for 20 hours a week. She agreed, and Gloria Romero was hired. Joseph has spent numerous hours helping Gloria learn her job including working with mail.

Ms. Masterson was out of the office for two weeks, and Joseph gave Gloria the task of opening, sorting, and annotating her mail. Ms. Masterson returned this morning. In the afternoon, Ms. Masterson asks Joseph to come to her office. She has been going through her mail and is furious. She tells Joseph that she can't find the enclosures for several letters. The mail was not arranged for her in a logical order. One piece of correspondence has no date, and there is no envelope with the document. Another letter contains an urgent request for material. Ms. Masterson asks Joseph if the material was sent, and he can only reply that he does not know. Ms. Masterson asks Joseph, "What in the world happened here?"

How should Joseph respond? What steps can he take to prevent problems with handling mail in the future? (Learning Objective 1)

COMMUNICATE SUCCESSFULLY

1. **Prepare instructions** Your supervisor has recently seen several items in the outgoing mail in envelopes that are handwritten. She has asked you to create simple instructions for preparing envelopes and labels using your word processing program that she can distribute at the next staff meeting. (Learning Objective 1)
2. **Research ethical and legal considerations** Work with a partner for this activity. Locate an article about ethical or legal considerations related to copying or shredding documents. Prepare a memo that summarizes the main points of the article. Include source information for the article. (Learning Objective 2)
3. **Handling mail** Add a new post to the blog you created in Chapter 1. In this entry, reflect on the following statement: **This chapter has helped me better understand the importance of properly handling mail in the following ways.** (Learning Objective 1)

Blog

DEVELOP WORKPLACE SKILLS

4. **Process incoming mail** Your supervisor, Amanda Hinojosa, has asked you to open and sort (by importance) all incoming mail. The incoming mail listed below was received today. Indicate the order in which the items should be sorted, items for which you should attach the envelope, and items to which you would add a note or attach related materials. (Learning Objective 1)
   - An equipment catalog
   - A letter requesting information about a new service your company is offering
   - A letter that indicates a contract is enclosed but has no enclosure
   - A letter from a client about a proposal Ms. Hinojosa sent last month
   - A newspaper
   - A proposal sent by Certified Mail
   - A flyer announcing a one-day sale at an office supply store
   - An interoffice memo about a meeting held last week
   - A letter marked "Confidential"
5. **Handle outgoing mail** Ms. Hinojosa has given you several pieces of outgoing mail and has asked that you research the cost to mail the items through the USPS and at least one private mail service. Create a table of the items, identifying the costs and mailing services. Recommend a shipper for each item, and explain your choice. Choose an attractive table format. (Learning Objective 1)
   - A 1-ounce letter to Sunil Vettickal in Bhopal, India. It must be received within one week.

- A 3-ounce letter to Eduardo Sanchez at Kapor Pharmaceuticals in New York, New York. His address is 123 Fifth Avenue. The letter is not urgent.
- A 2-pound package for John Hamilton in Grand Rapids, Michigan. He needs it tomorrow, and signature confirmation is required.
- A book (over 15 ounces) for Yao Chen in Guangzhou, China. It must reach him within two weeks.

BUILD RELATIONSHIPS

6. **Confidential letter** You have recently become responsible for opening Ms. Patel's mail. Ms. Patel is out of the office, but she will return early this evening to review the mail. Several items are in the afternoon mail. You complete the preliminary mail sort, open the items, and date and time-stamp them.

   Now you begin to read and annotate the mail. The first letter requests that Ms. Patel attend a meeting the following Monday. You underline the date in the letter and mark it on her calendar. As you continue to read the letter, you realize it is about her child and the meeting is scheduled with the school counselor and principal. Clearly the letter is not business-related. You check the envelope and notice it is marked "Personal and Confidential."

   What should you have done to avoid this problem? How should you handle the situation? Explain what you should do to correct the problem and maintain a good working relationship with Ms. Patel. (Learning Objective 1)

7. **Copier etiquette** Eight months ago you were designated the key operator for the copying room. Several employees have come to you with concerns about one of the new administrative assistants, Tomas Alvarez. Apparently Tomas frequently leaves the copier jammed and a huge mess after using the copying room. Additionally, he seems to be copying a number of items for his personal use. You have not confronted Tomas about his behavior because you had no proof of the violations. However, your coworkers are becoming more and more agitated about his behavior.

   Last week you found several copies of a flyer announcing a car wash for a local little-league team on the copy-room counter. You know it belongs to Tomas because his phone number was listed at the bottom. Also, when you were unjamming the machine, you found a copy of the same flyer stuck inside.

   Yesterday Alice Wong complained to you about a mess left in the copying room by Thomas. The copier was jammed, copies were scattered all over the room, and paper supplies were not put back in the appropriate places. Alice remarked that Tomas had used the copy machine immediately before she did. She is furious and is threatening to go to your supervisor.

   How should you handle this situation? With whom should you discuss the problem first? What should you say to Tomas? What should you say to the other employees? (Learning Objective 2)

USE TECH TOOLS

8. **Create an account** If you do not have one already, create a communications software account for your computer or smartphone. Use the software to conduct a voice chat and/or a video chat with a classmate. Be prepared to discuss your experience with the class.
9. **Create instructions** Prepare a one-page handout that you could distribute to your colleagues with instructions on how to use your communications software from Activity 8. Select an appropriate document theme to create a professional-looking handout.

PLAN AHEAD

Purchase a copier Your department needs to replace its aging copier with a newer model. The copier will serve you and 19 other employees. It should print color as well as black-and-white copies. It should have basic features such as reduction/enlargement, duplexing, and automatic document feeding. The copier should print at least 20 pages per minute and handle a volume of at least 25,000 pages per month. Find two copiers that would work in your organization. Prepare a memo to your supervisor that includes all relevant copier details including the cost and vendor information. Recommend which of the two copiers you would purchase, and provide supporting information for your recommendation. (Learning Objective 2)

CHAPTER

17 Job Search and Advancement

LEARNING OBJECTIVES

1. Analyze your skills, abilities, and interests.
2. Determine your job search plan.
3. Prepare employment documents.
4. Interview successfully.
5. Develop skills for job advancement and job changes.

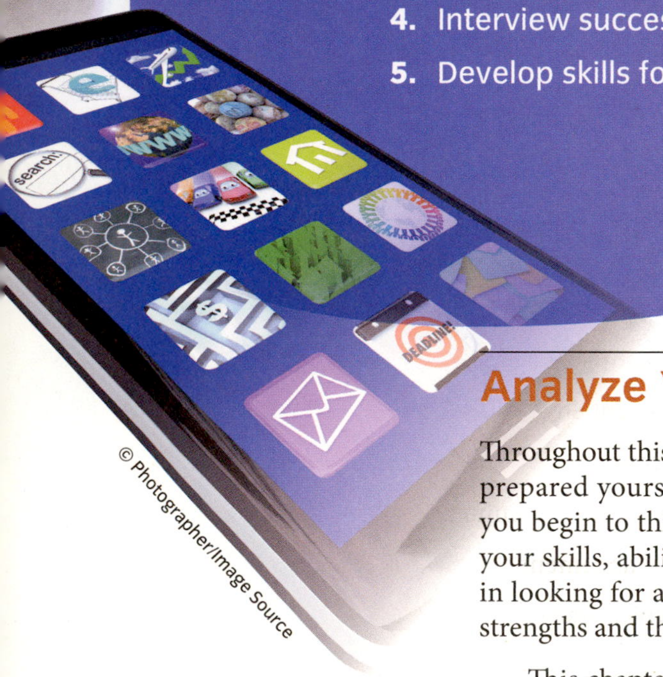

Analyze Your Skills, Abilities, and Interests

Throughout this course, you have improved your skills and abilities and have prepared yourself to seek a position as an administrative professional. As you begin to think about jobs you would like to hold, you must understand your skills, abilities, and interests. You need to develop proficiency not only in looking for a job, but also in finding one that will make the most of your strengths and the directions you wish your career to go.

This chapter can be one of the most important chapters you study, one that helps you find the right position so you can be happy and confident in your work. When you consider that you are likely to spend 8 hours per day, 5 days per week, and 50 weeks each year (allowing two weeks for vacation) on a job, you can quickly understand the importance of finding a job in which you can succeed and that you will enjoy.

Evaluate Your Skills

Figure 17.1 lists skills you will need as an administrative professional. They were discussed initially in Chapter 1, and you have learned about these and other skills in subsequent chapters.

Essential Skills for Administrative Professionals
■ Communication (listening, reading, verbal presentation, and writing)
■ Interpersonal relations
■ Time management
■ Critical thinking
■ Decision making
■ Creative thinking
■ Teamwork
■ Technology
■ Leadership
■ Stress management
■ Problem solving
■ Customer focus

FIGURE 17.1 An administrative professional career requires these skills.

A prospective employer will want you to be able to answer the question *What skills do you bring to our organization?* Identify the skills you have that would be valuable to an employer, both those described in this text and others. Also consider which skills are your strengths. For instance, do you excel at doing research? Do you have excellent math skills? Do you speak another language proficiently?

Identify Your Abilities

Ask yourself this question: *What personal qualities do I have that employers want?* Figure 17.2 lists qualities that are essential to success as an administrative professional. These qualities were introduced in Chapter 1 and have been discussed in the text.

In answering the question, consider the qualities listed in Figure 17.2, others you have learned about in the text, and still other personal qualities of your own. Identify qualities that are your strengths. For instance, are you self-confident? Do you exercise good judgment? Do you conduct yourself professionally? Are you always open to improving your job performance?

Determine Your Interests

What interests do you have? If you have trouble identifying your interests, try asking yourself this question: *If I had the opportunity to do something all day long, what would it be?* In other words, what are your passions? Are you interested in health care? If so, you might want to work in a hospital, a doctor's or dentist's office, or a pharmaceutical organization that researches new drugs. Are you interested in the legal profession and the court systems? If so, you might want to work in an attorney's office or the local or state judicial system. Perhaps you may be interested in an insurance company or the technology, airline, or telecommunications industry.

Many resources are available to help you identify fields and types of businesses and organizations where you might like to work. A useful starting resource is the *Career Guide to Industries* (CGI), produced every two years by the U.S. Bureau of Labor Statistics (BLS). You can access the CGI on the web at http://www.bls.gov/oco/cg/. For dozens of industries from construction to social services, the CGI describes:

- The nature of the industry.
- Working conditions.
- Current employment and job outlook.
- Occupations in the industry.
- Education, training, and other requirements.
- Advancement opportunities.
- Typical earnings.

Success Qualities
■ Openness to change
■ Initiative and motivation
■ Integrity and honesty
■ Dependability
■ Confidentiality
■ Commitment to observing and learning

FIGURE 17.2 An administrative professional career requires these qualities.

Other useful resources for this type of information include the web, school and public libraries, school career counseling and placement offices, and people you know or can meet through your personal network. For instance, if you wanted to work in a large company, you could do a web search for "Fortune 500 company information" to find out the rankings of America's largest corporations. (**Fortune 500 companies** are identified by *Fortune* magazine as the top 500 American public corporations as measured by gross revenue.) If you wanted to find out what working at an automobile dealership was like, you could talk with a relative or neighbor who works at a dealership or arrange a job-shadow or internship through your school.

Set Goals

As you begin applying for jobs, you should think through your long-term and short-term goals. For example, a short-term goal may be to obtain a job in an organization where you can use your skills and abilities effectively. A long-term goal might be to find an organization where you can build a successful career.

Very few individuals start out in an organization where they will stay for the remainder of their work life. You may want to set a short-term goal of focusing on getting work experience in two or three types of organizations. Once you have broadened your work experience, you should be ready to satisfy your long-term goal of building a successful career.

Look for Mentors

Is there someone who can give you good advice as you search for a job? This person could serve as your mentor. He or she should be familiar with your skills and abilities and know about the job search path you are navigating. Don't be afraid to ask for advice from one or more mentors. People enjoy helping others, especially when those others are eager to learn and can benefit from a mentor's experiences and counsel. A mentor can also help you keep your perspective if, for example, you are not hired for a job you especially wanted. They can offer additional advice and encouragement.

Adopt a Job Search Plan

As you begin to look for a job, you must establish an effective search plan—one that will provide focus for you as you begin the very important task of finding a position that matches your skills and abilities. You may decide to do a **traditional job search** or a **targeted job search**. You may choose to use both these avenues as you look for a position in which you can grow, learn, and feel secure.

With a traditional job search, you apply for job openings that match your career goals in many organizations. These openings may be listed in newspapers, available from employment agencies, or given to you by friends, professional acquaintances, or family members. With this approach, you know the company is hiring, and you submit your resume. You apply for a specific job, one that matches your skills and abilities. Because the job is usually advertised widely, you may be competing with dozens of individuals. Organizations commonly receive numerous applications for one opening, particularly when the economy is in a downturn and fewer jobs are available.

A targeted job search focuses on particular companies rather than a position. These companies may have no position currently available, but they are ones for which you would like to work. They may be companies that are growing and replete with good job opportunities for the future, are known to treat their employees well, are interesting and pleasant places to work, or have other qualities that appeal to you. You have researched these companies. You believe your skills and abilities would be an asset for them. Your task with a targeted approach is to sell yourself and your capabilities so well that the companies want to hire you.

With the targeted approach, you have the responsibility of finding companies where you want to work, regardless of whether there is an announced opening. You may find these companies through friends or family members, reading the business section of local newspapers or national publications such as *Fortune*, or using the web to identify top companies to work for, in the United States or in your local area. You may look for companies that

PARTNERSHIP FOR 21ST CENTURY SKILLS

Initiative and Self-Direction

Be a Self-Directed Learner

Twenty-first century learners need to be self-directed in the personal process of learning. It is important to be aware of what you know and don't know and to learn from failures and successes. In the job search process, you are constantly gathering information, and what you do with that information matters. For example, suppose that during an interview, the interviewer describes the benefits package. This is the first full-time job with benefits you have applied for, so much of the information is new to you. For your next interview, you will know some questions to ask regarding benefits.

As you search for jobs, you are gathering information not just about the job you are applying for but also about higher-level jobs. This process, again, is very useful. Learning about higher-level jobs can help you set goals for the future. You can identify the skills and training needed for a management position that could be within your reach in the next five years. This might mean continuing your education so that you finish a four-year degree in business administration or attending training seminars at your workplace on supervising workers. These examples show that thinking ahead, planning, and being observant can all have meaning for you and your future.

Being self-directed in your personal learning is also about self-assessment. Analyze strengths and weaknesses related to how you might interview for a job. For example, do you communicate well in new situations? Do you ask questions? Do you know how to shake hands properly and with confidence?

Activity

In your own words, define what being self-directed is, and then give an example of being self-directed in the workplace and in school.

matzaball/iStockphoto.com

are expanding multinationally if you would like to live and work outside the United States.

With a struggling economy, searching for a job becomes even more challenging. You must be willing to consider different options or scenarios, such as taking a part-time or temporary job to get your foot in the door or to gain experience that will make you more marketable later. You may wish to work for an insurance company but decide to work for an engineering firm because a job is available. Several sources of information about job opportunities are presented here.

Develop Networks

Identifying and establishing a network of individuals who can assist you in the job search is one of the best strategies for finding a job. Look for individuals (such as friends, relatives, teachers, coworkers, or fellow students) who are willing to help you. Networking online, through professional networks such as BranchOut or LinkedIn, is another good way to connect with people and companies worldwide. Building relationships with people who have different interests and career goals than you will provide a greater opportunity for different job connections.

When you talk with someone in your network about your job search, ask questions such as these:

- What companies in the area are known for being great places to work? Do you have any suggestions as to how I can obtain more information about these companies?
- Do you know of any companies that have openings for administrative professionals? If so, whom should I contact? May I mention your name?
- Are there other people you know whom I should be contacting about job openings? Who are they?

When contacting people you do not know personally, be sure to mention the name of the person who suggested the contact. For example, you might say, "Rebecca Edwards suggested I contact you. I have known Rebecca for several years, and I called her recently to ask for suggestions on where to apply for a job."

Keep in touch with your network throughout the job search process. For example, if one of your network members suggested you contact someone at a particular company, and you did so but have heard nothing back, let your contact know. He or she may be able to offer another source or may call the individual to discuss your strengths.

Image Source/Getty Image

Networking is one of the best strategies for finding a job.

Search Online

Through the Internet, you can identify companies and organizations where you may wish to apply. Many organizations allow you to post your resume directly on their website. The Internet has a variety of other resources for job seekers, including examples and tips for resume and cover letter preparation and interviewing.

Many sites on the web contain job listings. Online recruitment sites such as Monster offer various services to employers and those seeking employment. These sites, which are also called **job boards,** allow you to browse job listings by job title, company, industry, location (country, state, city), and pay. On some of these sites, you may also post your resume, and employers can list job openings and review resumes posted by job seekers. Many online recruitment sites are free to job seekers. Employers may be required to pay a fee to post job openings or search resumes on a job board.

USAJOBS (Figure 17.3) is the official website for federal government online recruitment, offering listings for jobs within the federal government. Many states and some cities have similar websites with information about their job listings. Some online recruitment sites allow users to create **job agents**, programs that automatically search job listings and retrieve jobs matching criteria you set. For example, you might request jobs in a certain geographic area. The results will be sent to you by e-mail at an interval you select, such as daily or weekly.

Read Newspapers

Although the Internet is an important information source for most people, newspapers are also a useful resource for employment ads, especially for local employers. Scan newspaper advertisements periodically during your job search, particularly the Sunday newspaper, which generally carries the most ads. For local newspapers that have a website, you can often search job ads at the site. You need to follow every avenue possible to find a job you like that fits your skills and abilities.

Visit Employment Agencies

You can find employment agencies in your area on the Internet or in the yellow pages. These agencies may be state-sponsored or private agencies. Typically, they work with entry-level to mid-level positions. Private agencies charge a fee; state agencies do not charge. The fee may be paid by the company that is seeking personnel, paid by the applicant, or split between the applicant and the company. If you are considering working with a private employment agency, ask who pays the fee and the amount.

Be professional. Treat employment agency contacts as you would a potential employer. If you

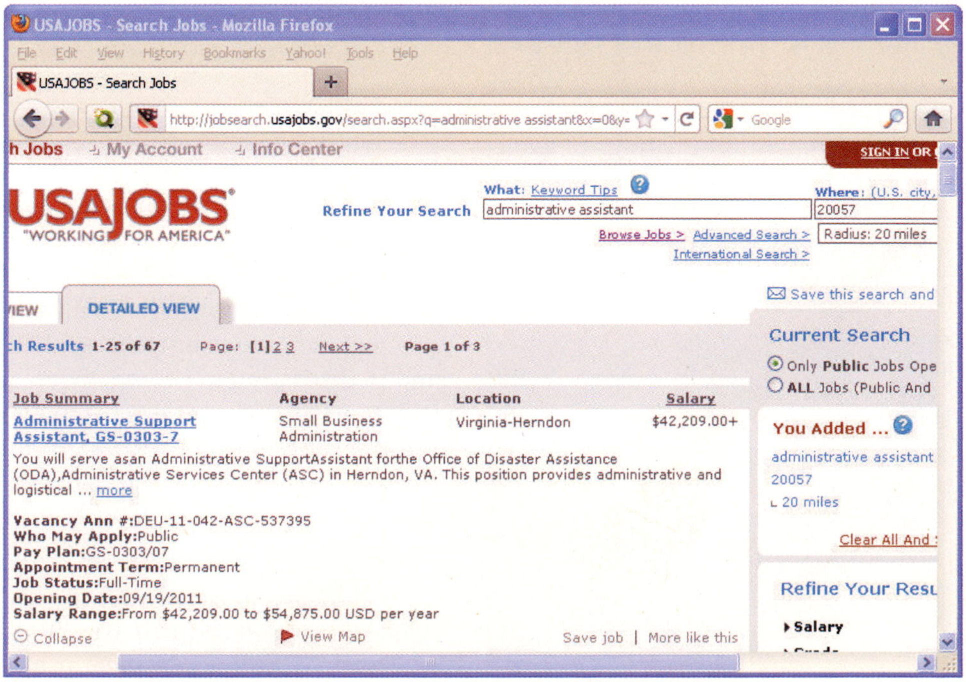

FIGURE 17.3 You can search for federal government jobs at the USAJOBS website.

decide to apply for a position with an agency, dress professionally when you visit the office. Even though the representatives you deal with at the agency will not be hiring you, they are your contacts with the companies where you will have your interviews.

Some agencies handle temporary work assignments. If you are uncertain about the type or size of organization where you want to work, you might want to take temporary assignments for a period of time. Temporary work is also useful in a tough economy as a springboard to permanent employment. Tell the agency about your long-term employment goals. If you are required to sign a contract, check the terms carefully so that you understand any rules regarding moving from temporary work for the agency to full-time work for a private employer. Also make sure any fee is clearly stated and explained.

Work With Your College or University

Most colleges and universities have a placement office or career center staffed with counselors who help students with career planning and job placement. These offices can help you prepare for job interviews, show you how to write a resume and application letter, offer testing to help you determine your career interests, and provide counseling about potential careers and job opportunities. They also maintain listings of available jobs, sometimes through alumni who are hiring or are willing to assist fellow graduates in securing a job at their organization.

Mobile Apps

Online recruitment tools often offer mobile apps to help you manage your job search. Sites such as USAJOBS and Monster have apps that allow you to post a resume and search job postings using mobile phones or tablet computers such as the iPhone or iPad mobile digital devices.

Take full advantage of any placement or career services at your school. In most cases your tuition money will cover the costs. Start visiting this office during your first year of college.

Many colleges and universities have job fairs where corporate recruiters set up recruiting booths on campus for students to visit. If you want to learn more about a company, it is a good idea to talk with the recruiter. If you know you want to interview with a particular company, come prepared as you would for an interview—professionally dressed, equipped with a resume, knowledgeable about the company, and ready to talk about what you can offer it.

Your college or university may also have opportunities for internships with local companies. These are excellent chances to apply what you've learned in school to the workplace, determine whether you would like a certain type of job or would like to work at a particular company, and possibly secure a job there. In many cases you must apply and interview for the position, and this experience prepares you for your job search in the future. If you secure an internship, remember that each day you are essentially interviewing for a full-time position, so you must always act and dress professionally.

Research Organizations

You should do some preliminary research on companies that interest you to help you decide whether you want to apply there. Once you have made that decision, you should do additional research on a company, with the goal of using the information you gain in preparing your application materials and in discussing the company on a job interview. What interviewers most want to know is what you can offer their particular organization. To answer that question in a way that will convince them to hire you, you need to know about their particular organization.

Read periodicals or websites that profile organizations. For example, *Fortune* provides a list of the 100 best companies to work for in the United States. *Working Mother* lists the 100 best companies for working mothers. Similar lists are available for other groups from other organizations.

When doing research on a company, look for answers to questions such as these:

- What are the organization's services or products?
- Is the organization multinational? Does it have branches in other states?
- What has been the profit picture of the organization for the past several years?
- Is the organization financially secure?
- Is it growing? What is the reputation of its chief executive officer?
- Does the organization have a good reputation in the community?
- Is there a good relationship between the employer and the employees?
- Is the organization an equal opportunity employer?
- Are there opportunities for advancement?

Ambient Ideas/Shutterstock.com

Research will help you decide which companies are right for you.

Company websites have a wealth of information that will be useful to you. Large companies often post their annual reports on their websites. From an annual report, you can obtain answers to many of these questions.

Besides visiting the company website, gather information on the organization from other sources. Search online using a search engine such as Google, or visit a library. Investors are extremely interested in corporate America. Therefore, news stories concerning company performance, activities, and practices appear often on the Internet and in newspapers and magazines. Information about the organization may be available from your local chamber of commerce or college placement office.

If the company is a small one, you may be able to learn about it from friends, relatives, and acquaintances. If you know a person or people employed at the company whose judgment you trust, talk with them. Positive information that you uncover will give you something to talk about or reference in job interviews or application letters. Negative information will help you decide whether the company is one where you would like to work.

Prepare Employment Documents

As you begin your job search, you will need to create resumes and letters of application specific to each company where you wish to apply for a job.

Prepare a Resume

A **resume** is a concise statement of your background, education, skills, and work experience. Its purpose is to communicate your qualifications to prospective employers. A resume is your personal marketing document. A well-prepared resume markets you and your credentials so effectively that it sets you apart from other candidates for the job. Both the content and the format of a resume are critical to its effectiveness. Two commonly used types of resumes are presented here: the chronological resume and the functional resume.

CHRONOLOGICAL RESUME

A **chronological resume** gives an applicant's work experience in order with the most recent experience listed first. This type of resume is the most common and most preferred. It works well for showing progress and growth if the jobs listed reflect increasing responsibility. Figure 17.4 shows a resume in chronological order.

FUNCTIONAL RESUME

A **functional resume** focuses on the skills and qualifications of an applicant for a particular job rather than on work experience. In this type of resume, the same information is included as in a chronological resume; however, the organization is different. Your education, experience, and activities are clustered into categories that support your career goals.

A functional resume is appropriate for someone who is entering a new field, just completing his or her education and beginning to seek full-time employment, or returning to work after a period

Wyatt Isburgh

Permanent Address: 114 Woods Street | Camp Verde, AZ 86322-7143 | Telephone: 928-555-0148

Temporary Address: (May 20, 201-): 451 Bridge Street, Apt. A | Prescott, AZ 86303-9445 | Telephone: 928-555-0198 | wgi@web.com

CAREER OBJECTIVE	To obtain an office management position.
SUMMARY OF ACHIEVEMENTS	Associate's degree with Administrative Professional major; key software applications. Relevant work experience in two organizations.
EDUCATION	A.A.S. Administrative Professional, Mount Vernon Community College, Prescott, Arizona. August 201-. GPA: 3.6/4.0.
COMPUTER SKILLS	Proficient in *Microsoft Word, Excel, PowerPoint, Access, Outlook, Dental Star Plus*, Internet research, and web page design. Keyboarding skills: 100 wpm.
EMPLOYMENT HISTORY	Whipple Park Dental Associates. Prescott, Arizona. Office Administrator, April 201- to present. • Manage dental insurance claims. • Send weekly statements and reconcile account balances. • Communicate with patients verbally and in writing. • Manage patient and business records. • Handle confidential and secure information. Whipple Park Dental Associates. Office Assistant, June 201- to April 201-. • Input patient insurance data and new patient information. • Scheduled and billed for appointments. • Filed and pulled dental records. • Answered patient phone calls and questions. • Handled confidential and secure information. English Department, Mount Vernon Community College. Prescott, Arizona. Administrative Associate, September 200- to May 201-. • Prepared class scheduling information. • Set up files for incoming students. • Maintained filing system for department. • Handled confidential and secure information.
HONORS AND ACTIVITIES	Dean's List; executive board positions in numerous student organizations; volunteer, Prescott Community Health Fair.
REFERENCES	References available on request.

FIGURE 17.4 Chronological Resume

of absence. It de-emphasizes gaps and emphasizes skill sets. Figure 17.5 shows a functional resume for someone who is graduating from a two-year college program and has little job experience.

Follow these guidelines when preparing a chronological or functional resume:

- Be accurate and honest when listing information.
- Keep the resume short—preferably a page and not more than two.
- Tailor your resume to each job. Highlight those areas of your background or work experience that fit the position.
- If you are a recent graduate and have held only part-time jobs, list them.

Patricia LaFaver

Permanent Address: 212 Ann Street | Savannah, GA 31401-0583 | Telephone: 912-555-0119

Temporary Address: (June 14, 201-): 340 Ross Avenue, Apt. 3G | Euless, TX 76040-0743 | Telephone: 817-555-0189 | plf@adm.net

CAREER OBJECTIVE To obtain a position as an administrative professional with the opportunity to use my technology, communication, and human relations skills.

SUMMARY OF ACHIEVEMENTS Associate's degree in Administrative Professional and Office Technology; major software applications. Relevant work experience.

PROFESSIONAL EXPERIENCE While employed in the Business Division of Oakwood Community College, I performed the following duties:

- Communicated in writing and verbally with students, faculty, administrators, and the public.
- Used *Microsoft Office* to prepare and work with documents, spreadsheets, databases, and electronic presentations.
- Employed human relations skills while working with 15 faculty and 50 students.
- Assisted students with schedules and degree plans.
- Keyed syllabi, tests, and general correspondence for faculty.
- Set up computer and paper filing systems and maintained files.
- Researched curriculums at other colleges.
- Handled confidential and secure information.

EDUCATION A.A.S. Administrative Professional and Office Technology, Oakwood Community College, Fort Worth, Texas. August 201-. GPA: 3.4/4.0.

EMPLOYMENT HISTORY Business Division of Oakwood Community College. Fort Worth, Texas. Intern, September 201- to August 201-.
Brandon Bookstore. Fort Worth, Texas. Salesclerk, October 200- to August 201-.

HONORS AND ACTIVITIES Member, International Association of Administrative Professionals; volunteer, Volunteer Center of North Texas.

REFERENCES References available on request.

FIGURE 17.5 Functional Resume

- If you have not had any paid work experience, list volunteer jobs or leadership positions you have held.
- Do not use personal pronouns (*I, me, you*).
- Describe your qualifications and skills in specific terms using action verbs; avoid vague language.
- Read the resume several times. Check spelling, grammar, and factual information such as phone numbers. Ask someone else who is good at spelling and grammar to read your resume, too.
- Take advantage of professional help in writing your resume.
- Print your resume on quality paper, on a good printer and at a high-quality print setting.

ELECTRONIC RESUME

An **electronic resume,** or e-resume, is a resume in electronic (rather than print) format. Some prospective employers will ask that you e-mail them an electronic resume. You may also want to prepare an e-resume to post on a job board.

Although the information presented in an electronic resume should not differ from that in a printed resume, the format should be different. Because it is being transmitted electronically, the resume should have a simple format. Because it may be scanned for keywords that match the keywords in a job description, it should contain keywords that relate to the job listing. Follow these suggestions when preparing an electronic resume:

- Use a single-column format that does not exceed 65 characters per line.
- Left-justify all text, and do not use tabs, tables, italics, bold, underlining, or graphics.
- Use asterisks or other symbols from the keyboard to replace bullets.
- Do not use abbreviations. For example, using *A.A.S.* will not be acceptable. Spell out the degree (associate of applied sciences).
- Use a sans serif font such as Arial or Calibri and a font size of 11 or 12 points.
- Put your name, address, phone number, and e-mail address each on a separate line.
- Work keywords or keyword phrases into the resume text. Look to the job description for examples, such as *experience*, *word processing skills*, *writing skills*, and *human relations skills*.
- Use only keywords and keyword phrases that apply to you.

Figure 17.6 shows an electronic resume. Notice that it does not have bullets, bold, lines, or italicized words. Also, notice that all lines begin at the left margin.

Show/Hide

The Show/Hide button in *Microsoft Word*, which looks like this ¶ on the Home toolbar, shows additional characters that are on your page but won't print, such as the spaces you key between words or the end-of-paragraph marks that are inserted when you press Enter. Show/Hide is useful for self-assessing your productivity skills. Open your resume and click the ¶ button. Do you see any places where you could have used the TAB key instead of the Space Bar?

You can use Show/Hide to confirm you have the correct spacing between letter parts. It can also help you troubleshoot formatting problems—to find and delete unwanted section breaks, manual page breaks, or hard returns. Other word processing software has a similar feature.

PATRICIA LAFAVER

PERMANENT ADDRESS
212 Ann Street
Savannah, GA 31401-0583
Telephone: 912-555-0119

TEMPORARY ADDRESS
340 Ross Avenue, Apartment 3G
Euless, TX 76060-0743
Telephone: 817-555-0189
E-mail: plf@adm.net

CAREER OBJECTIVE
To obtain a position as an administrative assistant with the opportunity to use my technology skills, communication skills, and human relations skills.

SUMMARY OF ACHIEVEMENTS
Associate's degree in Administrative Professional and Office Technology; Microsoft Office applications. Relevant work experience.

PROFESSIONAL EXPERIENCE
While employed in the Business Division of Oakwood Community College, I performed these duties:
* Communicated in writing and verbally with students, faculty, administrators, and the public.
* Used Microsoft Office to prepare and work with documents, spreadsheets, databases, and electronic presentations.
* Employed human relations skills while working with 15 faculty and 50 students.
* Assisted students with schedules and degree plans.
* Keyed syllabi, tests, and general correspondence for faculty.
* Set up computer and paper filing systems and maintained files.
* Researched curriculums at other colleges.
* Handled confidential and secure information.

EDUCATION
Associate of Applied Sciences, Administrative Professional and Office Technology, Oakwood Community College, Fort Worth, Texas. August 201-. GPA: 3.4/4.0.

EMPLOYMENT HISTORY
Business Division of Oakwood Community College. Fort Worth, Texas. Intern, September 201- to August 201-.
Brandon Bookstore. Fort Worth, Texas. Salesclerk, October 200- to August 201-.

HONORS AND ACTIVITIES
Member, International Association of Administrative Professionals; volunteer, Volunteer Center of North Texas.

REFERENCES
References available on request.

FIGURE 17.6 Electronic Resume

REFERENCES

A resume reference is a person who knows your academic ability and/or work skills and habits and is willing to recommend you to employers. A reference should be able to verify part of the information on your resume. Do not use relatives or personal friends for references. Consider using supervisors, teachers, or other professionals who bring credibility to your resume.

References are generally not listed on a resume. Instead, the phrase *References available on request* is used. Prepare a list of references, and take it with you to all your job interviews. You may need to list references on an application, or the interviewer may ask you for them.

Ask a person's permission before providing his or her name as a job reference. Three references are generally sufficient. Confirm each reference's address and telephone number, as well as current employment and job title/duties. Include this information in your reference list.

Portfolios

A **portfolio** is a compilation of samples of your work and other career-related information. It is a way to showcase for potential employers what you are capable of producing. In Chapter 2, you began an online portfolio, and you have added documents to it in subsequent chapters. For a hard-copy portfolio, the information and work samples should be arranged attractively in a binder. A portfolio might include the following items:

- Your resume
- A skills list
- Education, training, or certifications
- Awards or honors received
- Employee evaluations and recommendations
- Volunteer work in the community
- Letters you have written and keyed that demonstrate your writing style
- Reports you have produced that demonstrate your ability to conduct research and present it in an attractive format
- Spreadsheets, graphics, and electronic slides you have created that demonstrate your knowledge of software
- Other samples of work you have created, such as a newsletter or brochure
- A streaming audio or video clip (of a presentation or as an introduction)

Include only your highest-quality work. Have someone who is knowledgeable in your field review your portfolio, and make any necessary changes. Page 32 of Chapter 2 provides guidelines for preparing an online portfolio.

Prepare a Letter of Application

A **letter of application** is generally the first contact you have with a potential employer and is key, along with the resume, to obtaining an interview.

TECH TALK

Personal Websites

A personal website can be an asset in a job search. Many applicants use an online portfolio, such as the one you created in Chapter 2. Others create a website. Either option demonstrates your ability to use technology, specifically tools on the Internet.

You can create a free personal website at Google Sites, Weebly, or similar sites. They provide basic directions, templates, and formatting tools. The sites permit you to upload files and to add pages with different elements (text, images, videos, forms, etc.) and designs.

You do not need to know any programming languages or have specialized skills to design a personal website, but you do need to consider how items are displayed on the Internet. Website designers pay attention to the quality of graphics; the size, type, and consistency of fonts; and the credibility of written material (e.g., grammar and spelling). You become a website designer when you create your own personal web presence and unleash the creative "you" that sets you apart by showing your skills in creating quality web materials.

Think of it as a sales letter—one in which your purpose is to sell your abilities. The person reading your letter gets a favorable or unfavorable impression of you from the content, your writing skills, and the letter's appearance. The letter must be correctly formatted and free of keying and spelling errors. If you make mistakes in the letter, you have little chance of getting an interview. The basic goals of the letter are to:

- State your interest in the position.
- Provide general information about your skills (specific information appears in your resume).
- Sell your skills (let the reader know you have something to offer the organization).
- Transmit your resume.
- Request an interview, providing your contact information.

If possible, address the letter to a specific person. If the name is not given in the job notice, call the company or check with the placement office, agency, or person who told you about the job. If you cannot find a name, use the organization name and address with "Ladies and Gentlemen" as the salutation. Check the address you have keyed against the position advertisement. You do not want to key the wrong title, misspell the recipient's name, or even send the letter to the wrong person.

Figure 17.7 on page 394 is a sample of the type of letter you might write. Notice how it addresses the five basic goals of an application letter. The opening paragraph provides a brief statement of the applicant's interest. The middle paragraph describes and sells her skills. The closing paragraph requests an interview, providing her contact information; it also mentions the enclosed resume. Three or four paragraphs are generally sufficient for an application letter. The letter should be short; details belong in the resume.

Print your letter on high-quality bond paper, on a good printer and at a high-quality print setting. If possible, use the same paper and printer you used for your resume. Send an original letter for each application—do not send photocopies. If you are asked to submit a letter of application electronically, follow the same formatting guidelines you would use for an electronic resume. Keep the format simple so the letter can be transmitted and scanned easily.

Interview Successfully

A job interview is a meeting between a job applicant and an employer to discuss a job and the applicant's qualifications. It is an opportunity for a prospective employer to get to know you and for you to learn more about the organization. Your performance during the interview process is critical. You must present your strengths in a way that shows you can perform the job well and can contribute to the organization. Now is the time to focus on developing excellent interviewing skills. Skills for making the interview a success are presented in the following sections.

Online Prescreening

A growing number of organizations prescreen applicants online. **Prescreening** is the process of gathering information about an applicant prior to a formal in-person interview. If you apply to a company that prescreens, be prepared to answer questions on the following topics:

- Salary requirements
- Present employment
- Education
- Experience in the type of job for which you are applying
- Current employment status
- Whether you have ever been fired

Additionally, you may be asked several questions about skills and personal qualities, such as these:

- Are you able to work well under pressure?
- Can you multitask?
- Do you finish tasks in the time frames established?

Have your resume with you as you answer the questions. It will help you remember dates of employment and similar information.

Patricia LaFaver

340 Ross Avenue, Apt. 3G ▪ Euless, TX 76040-0743 ▪ 817-555-0189 ▪ plf@adm.net

July 7, 201-

Mr. Alberto Rodriguez
Trimart Industries, Inc.
1001 East Eighth Street
Fort Worth, TX 76102-5201

Dear Mr. Rodriguez

Your job announcement for an administrative assistant came to my attention through your posting on the Employment Opportunities page of your website. I am eager to talk with you about joining Trimart Industries in this capacity.

I believe my skills and experience make me a strong candidate for this position. My qualifications include the following:

- An associate's degree in the Administrative Professional and Office Technology program at Oakwood Community College
- One year of work experience in the field
- Excellent human relations and communication skills
- Proficiency in *Microsoft Office*

The enclosed resume gives further details about my experience and skills. Also, please feel free to examine my online portfolio (www.plafaver.pro-portfolio.com), which provides evidence of the quality of work of which I am capable. May I have the opportunity to discuss the position and my qualifications with you? Please call me at the number above to arrange a time when we can meet.

Sincerely

Patricia LaFaver

Patricia LaFaver

Enclosure

FIGURE 17.7 Letter of Application

Write a thank-you letter to the person(s) involved in the online prescreening. An example letter is provided later in this chapter.

Telephone Prescreening

Some employers use telephone prescreening to conduct initial interviews. If you are invited to engage in a telephone interview, here are several suggestions for handling it smoothly and effectively:

- Prepare for the interview by anticipating questions and preparing your responses.
- Ask friends for an honest appraisal of how you sound on the telephone. Make changes as needed.
- Have your resume with you for the call. Be prepared to talk about any items on your resume.

Your Online Profile

As you begin the job interview process, check your social presence. If you use a social networking site such as Myspace or Facebook, look over what you have put on that site. If a stranger can find you online, so can a prospective employer. If you have personal information online that you feel will embarrass you, is unprofessional, or will present you in a negative light, remove it. Consider making your profile private. Search for your name online, using a search engine such as Google, to see what potential employers will find when they research you.

iofoto/Shutterstock.com

- Standing while being interviewed may help. Some research indicates you sound more self-confident and dynamic when you stand while talking on the phone.
- Remember that the tone of your voice carries a lot of weight over the telephone.
- Smiling as you speak can make you sound more pleasant.
- Speak clearly and loudly enough so the person can hear you.
- Write a thank-you letter after the interview.

In-Person Interview

The in-person interview is often the most important factor in deciding whether an applicant will be hired. You should prepare for an in-person interview by learning about the organization, preparing answers to likely questions, and practicing. Since first impressions are powerful, attention to your personal appearance is also essential. In addition, you must assemble the appropriate materials to bring with you to the interview and be sure you can get to the interview location on time.

Stephen Coburn/Shutterstock.com

Preparation is essential to a successful job interview.

LEARN ABOUT THE ORGANIZATION

Review the information you found when researching the organization earlier. Do additional research if needed. You should be well enough informed about the company to discuss it intelligently and to ask a few pertinent questions. If you had an online or telephone screening, review what you learned from this process.

Develop a list of questions that you might ask given the opportunity. Asking questions shows your interest in the organization and indicates you have taken the initiative to find out a little about the company prior to the interview. Here are several good questions you might ask:

- What does the person in this position do in a typical workday?
- Could you tell me about the people I would work with? To whom would I report?
- How would you describe your company culture?
- I read on your website that your organization has grown over the last ten years. To what do you attribute the growth? Do you expect it to continue?
- What opportunities do you have for training and advancement?
- What is the next step in the interview process? When will you make a decision about hiring?

PRACTICE FOR THE INTERVIEW

Preparation is the key to a successful job interview. A human resources executive remarked that the biggest problem among the many job applicants she interviews is lack of preparation. They don't know what they want to say to her about why they'd be a good candidate for the organization, or they haven't thought about how they're going to say it. They're not ready to provide examples of what they've contributed to other organizations and of their leadership skills.[1] Practicing can also minimize nervousness and can prepare you to go into the interview with more confidence.

For each interview, make a list of likely questions. Spend some time thinking about how to respond to each question in a way that shows strongly that you are a good match for the position. Choose solid, specific examples of what you've contributed to past employers or what you've done in school or extracurricular activities. Think about your goals and objectives and what you could say to show they are a good fit for the organization's goals and objectives.

Then practice. Practice by yourself, and ask a counselor in your school's career planning office, mentor, or friend to do one or more mock interviews with you. Keep practicing until you are satisfied that you are prepared. Figure 17.8 lists common interview questions.

[1] *Interviewing in Business*, video (Cincinnati: South-Western, 2001).

Frequently Asked Interview Questions
Questions Relating to Your Interest in the Company and the Job
■ How did you learn about this position?
■ Are you familiar with our company?
■ Why are you interested in our company?
■ Why do you think you are qualified for this position?
■ Why do you want this job?
■ What is the ideal job for you?
■ What are your career goals?
■ Where do you see yourself in five years?
Questions Regarding Your Ability to Do the Job
■ Tell me about yourself.
■ What are your greatest strengths?
■ What is your greatest weakness?
■ What is the biggest work-related mistake you have made?
■ Why should I hire you?
■ What in your last job did you enjoy the most? Why?
■ What in your last job did you enjoy the least? Why?
Questions Regarding Your Education
■ Why did you choose your major area of study?
■ What was your academic average in school?
■ What honors did you earn?
■ In what extracurricular activities were you involved?
■ What courses did you like best? Least? Why?
■ How have the classes you completed as part of your major helped you prepare for your career?
Questions Regarding Your Ability to Fit Into the Organization
■ If your supervisor asked you to engage in an activity that did not fit your values, what would you do?
■ What type of work atmosphere do you prefer?
■ Is a sense of humor important in your work? Why or why not?
■ Tell me about a conflict you have had with someone. How did you handle it?
■ What is your definition of diversity?
■ How do you handle pressure?
■ How would your previous employers and coworkers describe you?
Questions Regarding Experience
■ Have you ever been fired or asked to resign from a position?
■ You have moved frequently from one job to another. Why?
■ Why did you leave your previous job?
■ Have you had any problems with previous supervisors?

FIGURE 17.8 Be prepared to answer these common interview questions.

One of the most popular questions to start an interview is "tell me about yourself." The interviewer does not want your life history, such as where you were born. He or she wants to know how well you express yourself, the impression you will give to customers or clients, and how you will fit into the organization. Prepare a brief, polished speech in which you highlight your educational background, relevant work experience, professional goals and strengths, and important accomplishments.

Interviewers will sometimes ask difficult questions, often referred to as *stress questions*, to determine how you perform under pressure. Several questions in Figure 17.8 fall into this category, such as *What is the biggest work-related mistake you have made? Why should I hire you?* and *Have you ever been fired or asked to resign from a position?* Certain items in a resume, such as employment gaps or the appearance of being overqualified for the job, may also prompt such questions. Give some thought to them and to any questions you think might be asked based on your particular background or experiences. Although answering such questions is not easy, these suggestions may be helpful:

- Attempt to answer any potentially negative question in a way that positively showcases your abilities. For example, if asked what your greatest weakness is, you could respond, "My greatest weakness is getting nervous when speaking in public, so last semester I took a public speaking course as one of my electives. It really helped me so that I'm now more at ease in those situations." This answer addresses a real weakness and shows what has been done to improve on it.
- Answer truthfully and steer your answer to something positive. For example, if asked why you stayed only two months at one job, you could answer, "I realized I could not work 40 hours a week and still be a full-time college student. I gave three weeks' notice and found a part-time job on campus requiring fewer hours. While I regret having to leave that job, it was a good learning experience. I got my priorities in order and learned excellent time management skills. You can see from my resume that I stayed in my next position for two years."
- Do not say more than you need to say in answering the question. In such a situation, brevity is more important than thoroughness.

It is illegal for employers to ask certain questions that might lead to discrimination. Ethical organizations go to great lengths to train interviewers properly and prevent illegal questions from being asked. Figure 17.9 lists several questions that are not legal for employers to ask.

While these questions are sometimes asked intentionally, other times, the interviewer does not know the questions are inappropriate. In either case, you should have a plan for how you will respond. An effective approach is not to answer the question directly but to reply in a way that reflects positively on your ability to do the job, as in the examples below. If you believe an illegal question was asked intentionally, you may want to reconsider whether you would like to work for the organization.

- If asked, "How old are you?" you might respond, "As you can see from my resume, I've just finished my degree. I am eager and energetic and ready to apply the skills I've learned. I'm also willing to learn from the more experienced administrative professionals as well as set a good example for others."
- If asked, "Are you married?" you might respond, "I'm ready to give my full attention to this job. I am free to travel and work late to learn what is necessary to do excellent work."

Illegal Questions
■ How old are you?
■ Are you married?
■ How many children do you have?
■ What child-care arrangements do you have for them?
■ Have you had any operations or illnesses recently?
■ How is your health?
■ Do you have a disability?

FIGURE 17.9 Some questions on age, marital status, children, and health are illegal.

WHAT TO TAKE WITH YOU

Plan to take several copies of your resume with you to the interview as well as a list of references. You may wish to take a briefcase. Some interviewees take a small notebook portfolio with samples of their work, such as a newsletter, brochure, report, or business letter they have prepared. If you choose to do this, make sure your portfolio is brief, neat, and professional-looking. A thin portfolio is a good choice. Take a pad, pen, and pencil in case you need to take notes or fill out an application.

gehringj/iStockphoto.com

Dress is extremely important when interviewing.

Don't take too many items with you. You don't want to be distracted or made nervous by having to keep track of items or not being able to find them. Turn off your cell phone. Do not take a media player, food, drink, or gum. Arrange your items in an orderly way so you will not have to shuffle through papers or hunt to find something during the interview. Go alone; do not take another person with you.

MAP THE ROUTE

If you do not know how to get to the job interview site, map the route you will take. GPS systems, mobile GPS apps, and websites such as Google Maps or MapQuest are easy-to-use resources that can assist you in determining the best route and sometimes parking options. Organization websites are another good resource. Choose your route several days in advance; do not leave it to the last minute. Allow plenty of travel time in case traffic is heavy. It is a good idea to drive to the location the day before to check the route, travel time, and parking availability.

DRESS APPROPRIATELY

Dress is extremely important when interviewing. Someone who is not appropriately dressed for the interview begins the session with a negative impression that is often difficult to overcome. For both men and women, a conservative two-piece business suit is appropriate. Women may also wear a conservative dress. A short skirt or plunging neckline that shows cleavage is not appropriate. Review the "Professional Business Attire" section of Chapter 2 (page 33).

Choose your clothing a few days before your interview so you have time to have it dry-cleaned if needed. Check it carefully to be sure it is clean and lint-free. Clothes should be pressed and shoes shined. Tattoos should be covered up during the interview. For both men and women, a minimum of jewelry is appropriate—no noisy bracelets or dangly earrings. If you have multiple piercings, it's a good idea to only have earrings visible and only one per ear.

Attention to personal hygiene is also important. Avoid excessive makeup and strong cologne, body wash, or other fragrances. The checklist on page 35 of Chapter 2 will help you remember the important points about grooming.

ARRIVE EARLY

Plan to arrive 15 minutes before the interview time. This shows you are eager and prepared and makes

Professional POINTERS

Strive to avoid these common interview mistakes:

- Being late
- Not making eye contact
- Criticizing past employers
- Asking questions about salary and benefits immediately
- Not answering questions concisely
- Not asking questions
- Providing a resume with grammar and typographical errors
- Not having references available
- Not articulating interest in the position

an excellent first impression. Be pleasant with everyone you see— receptionists, administrative assistants, and other employees you may encounter. Keep a smile on your face and say "thank you" often. Do not underestimate the impression you make on receptionists and others waiting in the reception area. Anyone at the job site may be evaluating you, even as you wait for the interview to begin.

DURING THE INTERVIEW

Stand to greet the interviewer. Smile, establish eye contact, and give a firm handshake. Wait to sit down until invited.

Show genuine interest in what the interviewer is saying. Try to learn more about the prospective employer's needs, and shape your replies and other remarks to show strongly that you can fill them. Describe relevant skills, abilities, and accomplishments, and provide good, solid examples from previous jobs, school, or extracurricular activities. Follow these suggestions:

- Listen carefully, and be sure to answer the question that was asked.
- Answer questions thoroughly but concisely; do not talk too much.
- Be enthusiastic; demonstrate pride in your skills and abilities.
- Do not criticize past employers, supervisors, instructors, or fellow students or colleagues.
- Do not argue with the interviewer, tell jokes, or brag.

Employment Applications

You may fill out an employment application form before or after an interview. Follow these suggestions when completing employment applications:

- Read the entire application before starting to complete it.
- Print neatly or key your answers.
- Answer questions completely.
- If a question does not apply to you, put NA for "not applicable."
- Be honest. Describe your skills and experiences accurately. Try to state any negative information in a positive manner.
- Check your work carefully.

- Be aware of your body language. Sit slightly forward, make frequent eye contact, and avoid fidgeting. Review the "First Impressions" section of Chapter 2 (pages 26–27).
- Use the interviewer's name from time to time.

CLOSE PROFESSIONALLY

End the interview in a professional manner, even if you feel it didn't go well. Smile warmly, and shake hands again. Express your interest in the position, and thank the interviewer for his or her time. For example, when the interview is over, you could say, "Thank you so much for your time. I appreciate the opportunity and am excited about the possibility of working at your company." Ask when you may expect to hear from the company regarding the job. Thank the receptionist as you leave.

FOLLOW UP

Write a follow-up letter immediately after the interview. The letter should (1) thank the person for the opportunity to interview, (2) recap your skills and experience, (3) restate your interest in the job (if you are still interested), and (4) remind the interviewer of the next steps discussed in the interview, such as when the decision will be made. You should also provide any important details that you did not mention during the interview. A sample letter appears in Figure 17.10 on page 402.

DO A SELF-ASSESSMENT

After each interview, go over the experience in your mind. Note the questions you had trouble answering, any questionable reactions from the interviewer, and any errors you believe you made. Review your impressions with a trusted adviser, and ask this person how you may improve. Job rejections are common since many people may apply for the same job and you cannot be the best fit for all positions. Do not be discouraged. Each interview provides you with experience and information that will help you do better in the next interview.

Prepare for a Job Offer

You need to ask yourself some questions before you decide whether you will accept a job offer. Answer them truthfully considering the interview, the people you met, and the research you have done on the company.

- Is the work environment comfortable, challenging, and exciting?
- Will I have a chance to work with people I believe I can respect and admire?
- Will the work be interesting?
- Are the values of the organization consistent with my own?
- Are the benefits and compensation packages acceptable?
- Are there opportunities for advancement?
- Did the people I met seem to be pleased with the organization?
- Do there seem to be ongoing planning and goals that meet the long-term needs of the organization?

Making the right job decision is extremely important. Remember that your goal is to find the right position for you—one in which you can grow and learn.

Job Advancement and Changes

Once you have accepted a position, you will begin the process of learning and growing in your job. Your task will be to apply your skills and knowledge in performing the job well. Start strong by following these suggestions:

- Maintain the same enthusiasm you had when you applied for the position.
- Listen to what coworkers and supervisors tell you.
- Learn from them and your experiences.
- Ask questions when you do not understand.
- Accept feedback gracefully.

Patricia LaFaver

340 Ross Avenue, Apt. 3G ▪ Euless, TX 76040-0743 ▪ 817-555-0189 ▪ plf@adm.net

July 15, 201-

Mr. Alberto Rodriguez
Trimart Industries, Inc.
1001 East Eighth Street
Fort Worth, TX 76102-5201

Dear Mr. Rodriguez

Thank you for interviewing me this morning for the administrative assistant position in your Human Relations Department.

I believe that my associate's degree and my experience at Oakwood Community College have prepared me well for this position and that I would be a good fit for your company. My written and oral communication skills, along with my computer skills, are strong. Additionally, my problem-solving and people skills will be assets to the Human Relations Department. I am pleased and excited about the possibility of being a part of your team at Trimart Industries, Inc., and remain very interested in this position.

You may reach me by calling 817-555-0189 or e-mailing me at plf@adm.net. As we discussed, I look forward to hearing from you within the next two weeks.

Sincerely

Patricia LaFaver

Patricia LaFaver

FIGURE 17.10 Follow-Up Letter

- Observe and learn what is expected and accepted in your workplace.
- Pay attention to what is happening in the organization.

Ask your boss regularly for feedback on your performance. Do not wait for a formal six-month or yearly evaluation. Listen carefully to any suggestions your supervisor makes. Realize that criticism is not directed at you as an individual. Typically, it focuses on skills you need to improve to perform your work the way the company needs it done.

Handling Job Change

You may decide to leave a job voluntarily, or you may be given no choice. Whatever your reasons for leaving, you must be professional in handling your departure.

EXIT INTERVIEW

Many organizations ask employees who are leaving the company to complete an exit interview. An **exit interview** is a meeting between an employee who is leaving the company and a company representative. The purpose of the interview

Office Building Blocks

Use *Word's* building blocks feature in the job search process to make yourself more productive. With this feature you can create a personal letterhead for application and thank-you letters. You can also create a building block for the closing lines of a letter. Here's how you would create your own letterhead and save it as a building block:

1. Create the letterhead.
2. Select it.
3. On the Insert ribbon, click Quick Parts.
4. Choose the Save Selection to Quick Part Gallery option.
5. Assign a name and click OK.

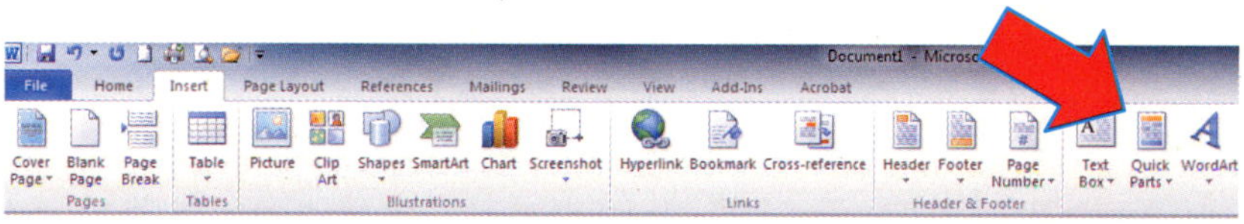

is to gain insights from the employee about what the company is doing well and how it could improve. Generally an impartial person, such as a staff member in the human resources department, conducts the interview.

An exit interview is not a time to get even, to make derogatory remarks about a supervisor or coworkers, or to unduly criticize the company. Keep in mind the old adage about not burning your bridges. If you are leaving voluntarily, you may wish to return to the company someday. Regardless of your reason for leaving, you will probably need a reference from the organization.

LAYOFF OR TERMINATION

With companies downsizing, layoffs are common. If you are laid off, keep in mind that you did not cause the situation. Even though the situation is difficult, the skills, abilities, and experience you gained from your job will help you find another one. Consider what you want to do next, and mobilize your resources to help you find a position.

Assume your job is terminated. Even though you will probably feel a sense of rejection and insecurity, it is not a time to blame yourself or feel sorry for yourself. It is a time to analyze why you lost your job. Listen carefully to what your employer tells you about your performance. Then determine that you will learn and grow from it. For example, if the firing is due to your lack of skills, determine what skills you need to develop as you continue to pursue your career goals.

Windows 8

Windows 8 is a new operating system for PCs that will work not only on desktop and laptop computers but also on tablets or touch-screen handheld computers. It will have the feel of a touch-screen user interface experience. For example, a picture password option to unlock the screen requires you to click or touch certain parts of a picture in the correct order.

Windows 8 will offer two interface options: Metro, which has a start screen with customizable tiles instead of icons, and Desktop, which has the traditional look of *Windows 7*. Some applications may also have the Metro or Desktop options. Tiles represent different applications (such as a web browser or blog you read regularly). Users will swipe left or right to navigate between screens of tiles. Tiles can be easily moved, added, deleted, or grouped (such as games or productivity tools) to create a customized screen. Note that *Windows 8* was still in the building stage at the time of this writing, so final features may be different.

SUMMARY

To reinforce what you have learned in this chapter, study this summary.

- When seeking employment you should first consider your skills, abilities, and interests; set personal goals; and find one or more mentors.
- You may decide to do a traditional job search, a targeted search, or both. Use every means available to you of finding job leads, and take the time to research organizations that interest you.
- Employment documents, such as the resume and letter of application, will help you market your abilities and skills.
- The interview process potentially involves many steps: online prescreening, telephone interviews, and face-to-face interviews. The details of the interview process are very important for a successful job search.
- To advance in your job, it's important to start well and to ask regularly for feedback. Whatever your reasons for leaving a job, you should be professional in handling your exit.

KEY TERMS

chronological resume, 387
electronic resume, 390
exit interview, 402
Fortune 500 company, 382
functional resume, 388
job agent, 385
job board, 384
letter of application, 392
portfolio, 392
prescreening, 393
resume, 387
targeted job search, 382
traditional job search, 382

17

STUDY Tools

Located at www.cengagebrain.com

- Chapter Outlines
- Flashcards
- Interactive Quizzes
- Tech Tools
- Video Segments
- and More!

LET'S DISCUSS

1. Why should you have a job search plan when starting to look for a job?
2. What are some important considerations when you begin the job search?
3. Explain why networking is important, and describe the process.
4. What services do online recruitment sites provide?
5. Why should you research an employer, and what are some examples of information you should try to obtain?
6. Describe the difference between a functional resume and a chronological resume.
7. Name some advantages of having an online portfolio.
8. What key elements are needed for success in the face-to-face interview?
9. What are some questions a potential employer might ask?
10. How should you answer if an interviewer asks you a stress question?
11. What are some common interview mistakes?
12. Why should you assess your performance after a job interview?
13. When you begin a job, what are some things you can do to help ensure success?

PUT IT TO WORK

Unemployed Alice Chang graduated with an A.A.S. degree a year ago. She was an A student; however, she was extremely shy. She did not take part in any extracurricular activities. After graduation, Alice decided that she would work in a variety of part-time positions through a temporary agency before applying for a full-time, permanent job. She thought this approach would help her determine where she would like to work. She held three part-time positions—one in an accounting firm, one in a legal office, and one in a college. She was offered full-time employment at each organization, but declined because she was still deciding which work environment she preferred. Alice believes she has learned a great deal from these jobs and is ready to pursue a position in a legal office.

Alice has applied for six jobs recently; however, she has not been offered any of the jobs. Alice had these experiences during the interviews:

- When asked about her present job, Alice said that she worked part-time through a temporary agency.
- When asked about her college experiences, Alice said she made good grades but did not do anything outside her classes.
- When asked by the interviewers if she had any questions, Alice said no.
- Alice was very nervous in all the interviews.

Alice knows she is capable; she has proven that in her performance at three different companies during the last year. However, she is still not very confident. What advice would you give Alice? (Learning Objective 4)

COMMUNICATE SUCCESSFULLY

1. **Company research** Using the Internet, research a large company in your state. With a partner, develop a list of questions you might ask if you interviewed for a job as an administrative professional at that company. Answer the following questions: How long has the company been in business? What types of products or services does the company provide? Is it growing, and if so, in what ways? (Learning Objective 4)
2. **Practice questions** Access the *Word* file *Ch17_Practice_Interview_Questions* from the data files. Key brief answers to the questions. Share your answers with a classmate, and ask for constructive feedback. If time allows, do a mock interview with your partner using the same questions, and see if your responses improve. (Learning Objective 4)
3. **Blog** Add a new post to the blog you created in Chapter 1. In this entry, reflect on the following statement: **Visualize yourself in a job interview for an administrative professional position. Describe the interview.** (Learning Objective 4)

   Blog

4. **Employment documents** Using the job description below or one related to a job posting in your area of interest, prepare your resume and a letter of application requesting an interview. Be sure to tailor your resume to the job description. (Learning Objective 3)

   Local health care company seeks an administrative assistant to support management personnel. This person must be extremely organized, detail-focused, flexible, and able to manage several projects at one time. The ability to communicate effectively with a wide audience orally and in writing is also required. The successful applicant will do data entry, prepare reports, coordinate events, manage a calendar, do basic bookkeeping, answer the phone, and distribute mail.
5. **Follow-up letter** Assume you have been interviewed for the position in Activity 4. Compose a thank-you letter to the interviewer. Invent details as necessary. (Learning Objective 4)

DEVELOP WORKPLACE SKILLS

6. **Skills** Access the *Word* file *Ch17_Skills_Form* from the data files. Rate yourself on the skills and abilities listed. Be honest with yourself. Next, make a job skills plan by listing the skills you need to improve and including some steps you can take to develop them. (Learning Objective 1)

7. **Strengths** In Activity 5 of Chapter 1, you were asked to assess some of your personal qualities and character traits in the *Word* file *Ch01_Self-Evaluation* from the data files. Retrieve the file you completed, and rate yourself again in Column 2. Now, list two areas of strength and explain how you would describe them in a job interview. (Learning Objectives 1 and 4)
8. **New job** You have just been hired for the position in Activity 4. Write a paragraph describing what you will do to adjust to your new job and prepare yourself for a long-term career with this company, where you want to advance to a supervisory position. (Learning Objective 5)

BUILD RELATIONSHIPS

9. **Networking** Think about your own personal network. Make a list of people you know who might have suggestions, advice, or contacts if you were beginning a job search today. (Learning Objective 2)
10. **Practice interviews** In groups of two or three, exchange resumes and then take turns interviewing each other. Draw your questions from Figure 17.8. Limit questions and answers to one minute each; then switch roles. Repeat until your instructor calls time. Include one or two stress questions. (Learning Objective 4)

USE TECH TOOLS

11. **Portfolio update** Add your resume to your online portfolio. Also, add other items from this course, such as letters or presentations, that you believe would best showcase your abilities to an employer. (Learning Objective 3)

e-Portfolio

12. **Letterhead** Using *Microsoft Word*, create a personal letterhead you could use if you were searching for a job currently. Save it using the Quick Parts feature. (Learning Objective 3)
13. **Website creation** Using a free online website service, start a personal website. Choose an appropriate template, and then add a picture of yourself and an introductory page. Links to several online website services are provided on the website for this text. (Learning Objective 3)
14. **Online professional network** Research and join an online professional network, such as BranchOut or LinkedIn. (Learning Objective 2)

PLAN AHEAD

Website development In this activity, you will finish the personal website you started in Activity 13. (Learning Objective 3)

1. Add your website address to your resume.
2. Write a letter of introduction on personal letterhead. If you completed Activity 12, use the personal letterhead you created in that activity. Add your website to the heading.
3. Attach your resume and letter to the introductory page of your website.
4. Add pages to your website that correspond to the main sections of your resume. For example, have a page for education and a page for skills and abilities or work experience (depending on the amount of work experience you've had).

   As you add pages, make sure they are consistently formatted. For example, if one title is Verdana 18 point, make equivalent titles on all the pages Verdana 18 point.
5. Add a page that contains two or three examples of your work that demonstrate your abilities as an administrative professional. Provide a brief explanation of each example, and then attach the appropriate files.
6. Review your website for correctness, consistency in formatting, and general attractiveness. Grammar and spelling should be perfect.
7. Exchange website addresses (URLs) with at least two classmates. Review each other's site for errors and ideas for improvement.
8. Make corrections and changes to your site.

Ergonomics

A Safe and Healthy Environment

Everyone prefers to work in a safe and healthy physical environment. If an environment is unsafe and unhealthy, productivity is affected. Employees are often sick and absent. Morale is low. For the employer, an unsafe and unhealthy environment results not only in lost productivity, but also in increased costs in the form of greater medical expenses and disability payments. The impact of the physical environment is great and affects the workplace team either positively or negatively.

As an administrative professional, what would you do if you developed these health problems?

- **Your wrists hurt so badly that you could not key material.**
- **You had so much back pain that you could not sit at the computer for any length of time.**
- **You developed vision problems so serious that you could not read small print.**

Health problems can result if you do not use proper techniques while working at your computer.

Ergonomics—A Definition

Ergonomics, according to the U.S. Occupational Safety & Health Administration, "is the science of fitting workplace conditions and job demands to the capabilities of the working population."[1] Ergonomics comes from the Greek words *ergos* (work) and *nomos* (natural laws). Simply stated, ergonomics is the fit between people, the tools they use, and the physical setting in which they work. The health problems that can occur due to inattention to ergonomic factors demand that you take ergonomics seriously. You should adopt an ergonomic approach to the design of your work site.

Common Injuries

Due to the amount of time people sit at their computers, several common injuries can occur. The generic name given to these injuries is repetitive stress injuries (**RSIs**) or cumulative trauma disorders (**CTDs**). Thousands of workers annually have ergonomic-related injuries, and many of these workers miss some work as a result. Thus, RSIs impact workers' health and cost organizations dollars in lost work and insurance claims. The RSIs discussed here include the following:

- Carpal tunnel syndrome (CTS)
- Computer vision syndrome

[1]U.S. Occupational Health and Safety Administration, "Ergonomics," http://www.osha.gov/SLTC/ergonomics (accessed November 21, 2011).

- Back pain
- Headaches

CARPAL TUNNEL SYNDROME (CTS)

CTS is a condition that occurs due to the compression of a large nerve, the median nerve, as it passes through a tunnel composed of bone and ligaments in the wrist. Symptoms include a gradual onset of numbness, a tingling or burning in the thumb and fingers, pain that travels up the arm and shoulder, and weakness of the hand causing difficulty in pinching or grasping objects.

COMPUTER VISION SYNDROME

Computer vision syndrome is a term coined by the American Optometric Association for eye complaints related to computer work. The symptoms of computer vision syndrome may include these:

- Inability to focus on distant objects after using the computer for several hours
- Dry or watery eyes
- Blurred vision
- Heaviness of the eyelids or forehead

A person's eyes can get extremely dry after using a computer for a long time. Individuals tend to blink less frequently when using a computer. Glare from a computer screen can also cause eye stress—as can glare from sunlight or from lighting in the workplace.

BACK PAIN

People who sit for long periods of time are at risk for back disorders. The two greatest problems are sitting upright or forward and not changing position.

HEADACHES

Headaches are frequently the body's way of saying something is wrong. Poor head and neck posture, as well as eyestrain, can be causes of headaches. Stress is another cause.

Digital Vision/Getty Images

People who sit for long periods of time or with poor posture are at risk for back disorders.

Prevention—The Key

To avoid common injuries such as repetitive stress injuries, vision problems, back pain, and headaches, you must take certain precautions. Having the right equipment and furniture (keyboards, mouses, chairs, footrests, and so on), as well as maintaining proper posture and taking frequent breaks, are preventative measures that help you avoid serious work injuries.

KEYBOARDS

Using keyboards that are placed too high or low or that are not centered in front of the body can cause the user to bend the wrists sideways or upward while inputting data. Failure to use proper keying techniques and good posture can force the hands into awkward positions when keying. In addition, using the smaller keyboards on laptop computers for long periods of time can increase stresses on the hands and arms. Placing the keyboard in the proper position and using good posture and keying techniques can help prevent stress injuries related to keying. Taking regular breaks from keying is also important.

Some users prefer alternative keyboards that have been designed in an attempt to change the user's hand and body position when keying. These alternative keyboards may help users maintain more natural hand and arm positions. Some of the most common alternatives include split keyboards, tented keyboards, supportive keyboards, and negative-slope keyboards.

- Split keyboards allow a natural separation of the hands. The keyboard can be split into two separate pieces, or the keys of the board may be separated by a neutral space.
- Tented keyboards arrange the keys into two separate keyboarding areas and tilt them upward and toward the middle. This creates a two-sided tent, with half the keyboard on each side. The purpose of this design is to eliminate bent wrist (inward and upward) positions.
- Supportive keyboards have built-in wrist or palm rests that help prevent bending the hands up by providing support that straightens the wrists. Wrist supports are also sold separately.
- Negative-slope keyboards allow the user to raise the front edge of the keyboard, which helps to straighten out the wrist.

Although alternative keyboards are popular with some users, available research does not provide conclusive evidence that these keyboard designs prevent discomfort or injury with long-term use.[2]

Voice recognition software is becoming an increasingly popular alternative. While the software does not replace a keyboard, it allows the user to be productive with limited keyboard interaction.

MOUSE ALTERNATIVES

Mouse alternatives include trackballs, mouse pens, mouses that use one finger, and touch tablets, plus a wide variety of mouse shapes and sizes. Additionally, a cordless mouse is available that allows much greater freedom of movement than the traditional corded mouse. When choosing an alternative to a mouse, evaluate whether the alternative really uses different muscles.

HEIGHT-ADJUSTABLE WORK SURFACES

Desks should be at a height where you can easily key with straight wrists and read or write without slumping forward or hunching your shoulders. One drawback to height-adjustable work surfaces is that they are more expensive than standard desks.

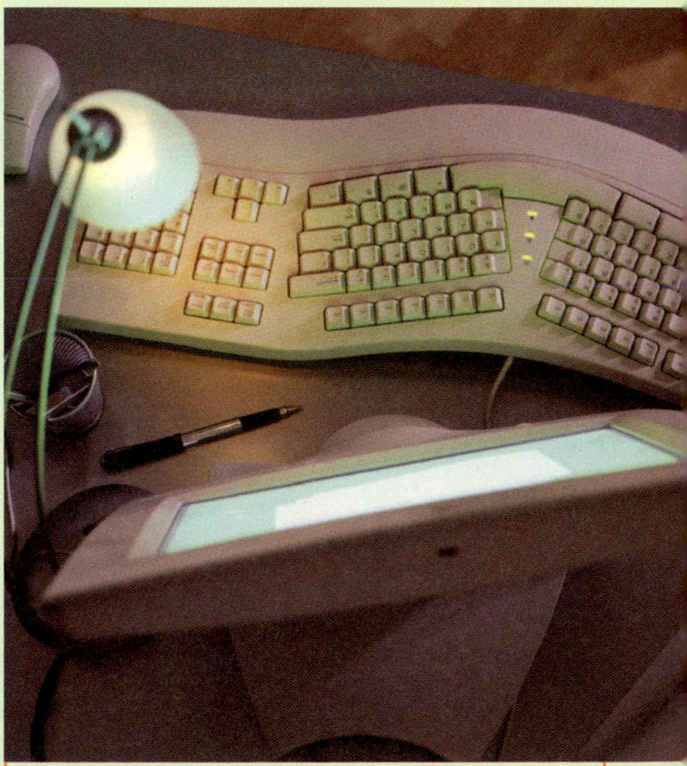

Ryan McVay/Photolibrary

Some users prefer alternative keyboards to the traditional computer keyboard.

[2]U.S. Department of Labor, Occupational Safety & Health Administration, "Computer Workstations, Keyboards," http://www.osha.gov/SLTC/etools/computerworkstations/components_keyboards.html (accessed November 17, 2011).

BananaStock/Jupiter Images

Mouse alternatives are preferred by some users.

MONITOR ARMS

Monitor arms allow forward, back, or up-and-down movement of the monitor to accompany posture changes. They can be useful for people with neck, shoulder, or upper back discomfort.

DOCUMENT STANDS

Stands reduce distortion of print that occurs when a document is slanted away from the eyes. Stands also reduce neck twisting by bringing the document close to the monitor at a readable angle. Since they allow you to put the paper in front of you, document stands can be useful if most of your work involves looking at paper rather than the screen.

FOOTRESTS

Footrests allow different positions for the legs and feet. When using a footrest, you should change foot positions often. An adjustable footrest is a good choice. Some footrests also exercise and massage the feet.

TASK LIGHTS

Task lights are used to reduce eyestrain by illuminating paperwork and reducing the need for bright light. Documents should be illuminated enough to be readable. However, too much light can cause a strong contrast between the brightness of the screen and the document, producing eyestrain rather than alleviating it.

CHAIRS

Adjustable chairs can help you avoid back pain by supporting multiple postures. The adjustable features on these chairs are typically the backrest, armrest, seat angle, and seat height.

Ergonomic Research

Ergonomic research has produced techniques for working at the keyboard that minimize the potential for injury. The following suggestions are from the Office-Ergo website posted by Workplace Ergo Inc.

- Sit as far away from the monitor as you can while still being able to read it clearly.
- Place the mouse close to you and next to the keyboard.
- The chair should be low enough for your feet to be on the floor even when the legs are extended. You should move your legs often; they should not stay in a fixed position.
- Posture research shows a hip width of 130 degrees or so as optimal. This position reduces and evens out pressure on the intervertebral discs.
- Take very short breaks of 30 seconds every 10 minutes or so in addition to normal 15-minute rest breaks.[3]

[3]"'Office-Ergo, Conventional Wisdom' vs. Current Ergonomics Thinking," http://office-ergo.com/current-ergo-thinking/#wisdom (accessed November 17, 2011).

Figure 1 provides a checklist of ergonomic problems with possible solutions.

Problem	Possible Solutions
Elbows splayed out from body	Lower work surface Lower chair armrests
Twisting the head side to the side	Bring viewed item closer to centerline of view
Elbow or forearm resting for long periods on hard or sharp work surface	Pad surfaces, corners, and armrests
Rapid, sustained keying	Greater work variety Aggressive break schedule
Significant amounts of hand stapling, punching, lifting, opening mail	Mechanical aids, such as electric stapler or punch Reduce size of lifted load
Prolonged sitting, especially in only one position	Greater work variety Chair that supports posture change through easy adjustability
Feet dangling, not well supported	Lower chair Lower work surface Footrest
Twisted torso	Rearrange work Provide more knee space
Frequent or prolonged leaning or reaching	Rearrange work Bring mouse and keyboard closer to body
Light sources that can be seen by the worker	Cover or shield light sources Rearrange work area
Reflected glare on computer screen	Shield light sources Glare screen Move monitor so light comes from side angle, not back
Monitor image dim, fuzzy, small, or otherwise difficult to read	Upgrade monitor Use software to enlarge image
Eyestrain complaints	Check all aspects of visual environment Suggest consultation with vision specialist

FIGURE 1 Ergonomic Problems – Possible Solutions

Source: Adapted from Chris Grant, "The Office-Ergo Checklist," Office-Ergo, http://office-ergo.com/checklists-tools/#checklist (accessed November 17, 2011).

Reference Guide

This Reference Guide is a handy and easy-to-use reference to a variety of rules you will use frequently in preparing documents. You can use it to check and review rules for grammar, usage, and punctuation. In addition, the guide includes basic formats for letters, envelopes, memos, and business reports.

Contents

Abbreviations

1. Use standard abbreviations for courtesy and personal titles, academic degrees, and professional designations.

Mr. Michael Khirallah	Dr. Cindy Bos
Ms. Shania Cole	Thomas Jones, Jr.
Mrs. Helene Chen	Nathan Portello, Ph.D.
Brian Edwards, CPA	

- Do not use a period after *Miss*. *Miss* is not an abbreviation.
- Use *Ms.* if you know a woman prefers that title or if you don't know her preference.
- Within the health care field, medical degrees are often written without periods.
- Professional designations such as CPA are written without periods when used alone but with periods when used with academic degrees.
- Do not use a courtesy title with an academic degree or with *Esq.* (*Esquire*).

  Incorrect Mr. Thomas McIntyre, M.B.A.

  Correct Thomas McIntyre, M.B.A.
- Do not "double" titles. A degree such as *M.D., J.D., Ph.D.,* or *D.D.S.* is a doctoral degree. Do not use *Dr.* and a doctoral degree together.

  Incorrect Dr. Elena Alonso, D.D.S.

  Correct Elena Alonso, D.D.S.

2. Most professional titles are spelled out. A professional title may be abbreviated if a person's fill name is used.

   Professor Helen Vendler

   R. Adm. Grace Hopper

3. Use periods following initials and a space between first and middle initials.

   Dwight D. Eisenhower   T. S. Eliot

4. Familiar abbreviations for companies, professional organizations, and government agencies may be used in most professional writing.

   GMC   NYSE   IRS

   Abbreviations are sometimes part of a company's official name. Abbreviations that people have used for some companies' names have become official names.

   FAO Schwarz   AAA   FedEx

   Abbreviated names of companies and professional organizations are usually keyed in capital letters with no periods and no spaces between the letters. Always follow an organization's preference, however, in abbreviating names.

   AFL-CIO   P.F. Chang's

5. Use abbreviated expressions that are commonly employed in professional writing.

e.g.	*exempli gratia* (for example)
etc.	*et cetera* (and so forth)
i.e.	*id est* (that is)

   Other abbreviations, while not appropriate for business writing, may be used in forms, tables, and charts.

   acct.   dept.   pd.

6. Geographic names, such as the names of countries, should be abbreviated only in tables, business forms, and the like.

   Spell out *United States* as a noun, and abbreviate it as an adjective.

   Dominic immigrated to the United States in 2011.

   The U.S. coastline is 19,924 kilometers.

   Do not abbreviate compass directions when they are part of an address; use *North,* etc. After a street name, however, you may use *NW, NE, SE,* and *SW.*

7. Use U.S. Postal Service abbreviations (two capital letters, no periods) in letter addresses.

   Dr. Alan Mossavi
   State College
   1800 College Street
   Somerset, KY 42501-1800

   Avenue, Boulevard, etc., are usually spelled out but should be abbreviated to avoid having a single long line in a letter address.

8. Use periods with *a.m.* and *p.m.* to designate time.

   6 a.m. 4:30 p.m.

9. When an abbreviation that ends with a period falls at the end of a sentence, use only one period. If the sentence ends with a question mark or an exclamation point, place the question mark or exclamation point after the period.

   The next speaker will be Hannah Tierney, R.N.

   Does that flight leave at 8:15 a.m. or 8:15 p.m.?

10. Do not abbreviate days of the week or months of the year.

- Abbreviations that are common within a company, an organization, or a profession are often used in its internal correspondence.
- Do not use an abbreviation if you are not sure your reader will understand it.
- Sometimes introducing an abbreviation makes sense. If you are preparing a report that refers repeatedly to the Agency for Healthcare Research and Quality, for example, using the agency's abbreviation, AHRQ, will be easier for your reader. Spell out the term the first time you use it, with the abbreviation in parentheses. After that, use the abbreviation.

  The Agency for Healthcare Research and Quality (AHRQ) has issued a report on patient safety.

Active and Passive Voice

Voice is the form of a verb indicating whether the subject is acting or is receiving the action. A verb is in the *active voice* when the subject performs the action.

Mylien drove to the hospital.

Dustin enrolled in the company dental plan.

A verb is in the *passive voice* when the subject receives the action.

Mylien was driven to the hospital.

Dustin was enrolled in the company dental plan.

The active voice is more direct and concise, so you should use it most of the time. The passive voice is appropriate:

- When you do not know, or when it does not matter, who or what performed the action.

  The package was delivered this afternoon.

- When you want to emphasize the receiver of the action.

  Gina was selected to represent the company.

- To avoid sounding as if you are assigning blame.

  The payment was received after the due date.

Capitalization

1. Capitalize the first word of a sentence, including a quoted sentence.

   Kyung-soon said, "Those prices are not a good indicator."

   Do not capitalize a quotation preceded by *that* or woven into the sentence in another way.

   Maya observed that "the board needs to refocus on retention."

2. Capitalize the days of the week, months of the year, and holidays.

   Monday May Labor Day

3. Capitalize *proper nouns*—the names of specific people, places, and things.

John G. Hammitt	Beacon Street
Kazakhstan	the Boston Marathon
the East Building	Honda Civic
the Business Club	History 101
the Renaissance	the Civil War

   Do not capitalize *common nouns*—names that do not refer to a particular person, place, or thing.

supervisor	street
country	race
building	sedan
club	history class

The is not usually capitalized before a proper noun, but it is capitalized if the company or organization does it that way.

The New York Times The Walt Disney Company

4. Capitalize proper adjectives.

Hispanic population English translation

5. Capitalize courtesy titles and professional titles that precede a name.

Ms. Giacomini

Deputy Chair Rex Schuman

Professor Victor Jones

But My psychology professor, Victor Jones, has written a book on personality theory.

Do not capitalize official titles that follow or take the place of a personal name.

Skylar Blum, vice president of sales

The president will address the nation tomorrow night.

Do not capitalize titles used as a general term of classification or occupational titles.

A U.S. senator is elected to a six-year term.

Isabelle is an administrative professional.

6. Capitalize directional words like *north* when they are part of names for regions or localities but not when they simply show direction.

the Midwest	northeast of the city
the South	the southern United States
the West Coast	He lives on the east side of town.

7. In a letter, capitalize the salutation and the first word of the complimentary close.

Dear Ms. Riviera Sincerely yours

8. Capitalize nouns used before numbers, except for such common words as *line, page, paragraph, sentence,* and *size.*

We are on Flight 1683.

You will find the material on page 15.

9. Capitalize the first and last words and all main words in headings and the titles of literary and artistic works. Do not capitalize articles (*a, an, the*), coordinating conjunctions (*and, but,* etc.), and prepositions of three or fewer letters unless they are the first or last word.

Effective Business Communication

The Grapes of Wrath

10. The names of specific departments within the writer's company or organization are sometimes capitalized.

our Customer Service Department

Collective Nouns

A collective noun is a word that is singular in form but represents a group of persons or things, such as *board, class, committee, company, department,* and *public.* A collective noun is singular when the group acts as a unit but plural when members of the group act separately as individuals.

The board has decided to hire a new CEO.

The audience took their seats.

If using a plural collective noun results in an unclear or awkward sentence, try inserting the words *members* before the noun and using a plural verb.

The committee members typically talk informally before a meeting.

Misused and Easily Confused Words and Phrases

A or *an* before the letter *h*

Use *a* when the *h* has a hard sound and *an* when the *h* is silent.

a historic event

an honor

A while, awhile

A while (two words) is a noun. *Awhile* (one word) is an adverb.

We plan to go home in a while.

She wrote the poem awhile ago.

Accept, except, expect

To *accept* an assignment is to agree to undertake it. *Except* is seldom used as a verb; it is usually a preposition.

Everyone except Ralph attended the meeting.

To *expect* someone is to believe that person will come.

Advice, advise

Advice is a noun meaning a recommendation; *advise* is a verb meaning to counsel.

She did not follow my advice.

The counselor will advise you.

Affect, effect

The verb *affect* means to influence or to change. *Effect* is usually used as a noun and means a result.

The new law will affect many large corporations.

The effect will be widespread.

All right, alright

All right is the only correct usage. *Alright* is incorrect.

Among, between

Use *among* when referring to three or more persons or things; use *between* when referring to two persons or things.

The inheritance was divided among the four of us.

The choice is between you and me.

Appraise, apprise

Appraise means to set a value on; *apprise* means to inform.

The house was appraised at $300,000.

Jack apprised me of the situation.

Bad, badly

Bad is an adjective; *badly* is an adverb.

He feels bad about losing.

The football team played badly tonight.

Can, may

Can means to be able to; *may* means to have permission.

Elise can repair almost anything.

You may leave when you finish your work.

Capital, capitol

Use *capital* unless you are referring to a building that houses a government.

The capital of China is Beijing.

We toured the U.S. Capitol in Washington.

Cite, sight, site

Cite means to quote, *sight* means vision, and *site* means location.

She cited the correct reference.

That is a pleasant sight.

The site for the new building will be selected soon.

Collage, college

A collage is a work of art made up of different items. A college is an institution of higher learning.

That collage of '60s photographs is interesting.

Kyle worked part-time while attending college.

Complement, compliment

Complement means to complete, fill, or make perfect; *compliment* means to praise.

His handouts complemented the presentation.

The manager complimented Apurva on his attention to detail.

Conscience, conscious

Conscience is a noun that refers to people's sense of what is right and wrong for them to do. *Conscious* is an adjective that means alert, awake, or aware.

Sylvia's conscience would not allow her to ignore the company's ethical problems.

Jordi was conscious during the procedure.

Farther, further

Farther refers to distance; *further* refers to a greater degree or extent.

The store is a mile farther down the road.

We will discuss the matter further on Saturday.

Fewer, less

Use *fewer* to refer to items that can be counted. Use *less* to refer to items that cannot be counted.

They had fewer speakers than last year.

Payroll takes less time with the new software.

Good, well

Good is an adjective. *Well* is typically used as an adverb but may be used as an adjective when referring to the state of a person's health.

You did a good job on that project.

The team did well in the playoffs.

I feel well today.

In, into

In means located inside an area or limits. *Into* means in the direction of the interior or toward something.

She is sitting in the room.

She went into the room.

Its, it's

Its is the possessive form of *it*; *it's* is the contraction of *it is*.

The company posted its quarterly earnings.

It's probably going to rain.

Lead, led

As a verb, *lead* means to be first or in charge, to take to, or to carry on. As a noun, it means an element. *Led* is the past tense and past participle of *lead*.

Emma leads the committee now.

Tendo led it last year.

That paint has lead in it.

Like, as

The conjunction *as* introduces a clause (a sentence part with a subject and a verb). In business writing, *like* is used only as a preposition.

Sales were up as we expected.

I want a car like Sam's.

Lose, loose

Lose is a verb that means to misplace. *Loose* is most often an adjective. It means free or not restrained.

Did you lose your cell phone?

Percent, per cent, percentage

Percent is always written as one word; *per cent* is incorrect. *Percentage* is preferred when a number is not used.

He received 56 percent of the vote.

Our team earned the highest percentage of "Excellent" ratings.

Perform, perform

To perform is to do something; *preform* is a rarely used word that means to mold or form something beforehand.

Jiao performed well during his internship.

Principal, principle

Principal as an adjective means *main*; as a noun, *principal* is the main person or a capital sum. *Principle* is a noun meaning a rule, guide, or truth; *principle* never refers to a person directly.

The principal character in the play is Geoff.

The principals in the case are present.

The company's principles of conduct are posted on its website.

Than, then

Than is a conjunction that compares two or more people or things. *Then* is usually an adverb and means at that time. It answers the question *when* of the verb.

Conor has more experience than Naima.

Then we will go to dinner.

That, which

That and *which* are relative pronouns (pronouns that relate or refer to nouns or other pronouns in a sentence) that introduce dependent clauses (clauses that have a subject and verb but cannot stand on their own).

That is used to refer to things or people. It introduces a clause that is essential to the meaning of the sentence.

Which is used to refer to things. It introduces a clause that contains nonessential information. A comma is used before *which* but not before *that*.

The seminar that was held last week focused on time management.

The first seminar, which was held last week, focused on time management.

There, their, they're

There is almost always used as an adverb. *Their* is a possessive adjective. *They're* is the contraction for *they are*.

We went there after lunch.

Their flight was delayed two hours.

They're bringing the guests to the meeting.

To, too, two

To is most often a preposition, so it is followed by a noun or pronoun in the objective case.

Alaina is going to the conference.

Too is an adverb. It means also, besides, very, or excessively.

That presentation was too long.

Two is a number. It is usually an adjective that tells how many.

You have two assignments this morning.

Who, whom

Who is used as the subject of a verb or as a predicate pronoun (a pronoun used to complete the meaning of the verb *be*, as in *Who is she?*). *Whom* is used as an object of a verb or a preposition.

Quick check If you can substitute *he* or *she, who* is correct. If you can substitute *him* or *her, whom* is correct. You may need to rearrange the sentence a little.

Marita is a manager who gets things done.
(*She* gets things done).

Who is calling?
(*He* is calling.)

Whom should I contact for more information?
(You should contact *her*.)

To whom should I send this report?
(You should send it to *him*.)

Who's, whose

Who's is the contraction for *who is* or *who has*. *Whose* is an adjective that shows ownership or possession.

Leona, who's been taking accounting classes, got the position.

Whose smartphone is this?

Would have, would of

Would have is the only correct usage. *Would of* is incorrect.

Your, you're

Your is a possessive adjective. *You're* is the contraction of *you are*.

Your supervisor called.

You're going to be late if you don't hurry.

Spelling Feature Errors Sometimes words aren't misused but simply missed—a person runs the spelling feature but doesn't proofread afterward. Two examples of such "wrong-word" errors that appear often in student papers: *defiantly* for *definitely* and *mangers* for *managers*.

Numbers

1. Spell out numbers one through ten; use figures for numbers above ten.

   We ordered nine memory sticks and four flash drives.

   Rita sent out 60 letters.

2. If a sentence contains related numbers any of which is over ten, use figures for all the related numbers.

   Please order 12 memo pads, 2 reams of paper, and 11 boxes of envelopes.

   (The numbers are related; they all refer to office supplies.)

   But The company offers 15 wellness seminars, each of which lasts two hours.

   (The numbers are not related. *Fifteen* refers to seminars, and *two* refers to time.)

3. Express numbers in the millions or higher with a figure and a word for easy comprehension.

   3 billion (rather than 3,000,000,000)

4. Spell out a number that begins a sentence.

   Five hundred customers completed the survey.

   For larger numbers, rearrange the sentence so the number doesn't come first.

   Instead of Two thousand nine was the year of the restructuring.

   Use The restructuring took place in 2009.

5. Spell out indefinite numbers.

   A few hundred voters made the difference.

6. Spell out ordinals that can be expressed in one or two words. See Rules 7 and 11 for exceptions.

   The store's twenty-fifth anniversary was this week.

7. Use figures to express dates written in normal month-day-year order. Do not use *st, nd, rd,* or *th* after the day.

   March 8, 2012

   Not March 8th, 2012

   If the date stands alone or comes before the month, use *st, nd, rd,* or *th* after the day.

The meeting is on the 8th.

The plans will be completed by the 1st of October.

8. In times of day, use figures with *a.m.* and *p.m.*; spell out numbers with the word *o'clock*. In formal usage (formal written invitations, for example), spell out all times.

   9 a.m.

   10 p.m.

   eight o'clock in the evening

   Do not use zeros with on-the-hour times, even if they appear with times expressed in hours and minutes.

   The nonstop flights are at 9 a.m., 1:30 p.m., and 4 p.m.

   Use the words *noon* and *midnight* alone, without the number *12.*

   noon **Not** 12 noon

9. Amounts of money over a dollar are usually expressed in figures.

   $1,000 $3.27

   Amounts of money under a dollar are expressed in figures with the word *cents*, except when used together with related amounts over a dollar.

   79 cents

   The receipts are for $15.70, $8.09, and $.95.

10. Express percentages in figures; spell out the word *percent.*

    10 percent

11. Use words for street names from First through Tenth and figures or ordinals for street names above Tenth.

    Third Street 14th Street

    Write house numbers in figures, except for the number *one.*

    One Main Place 13 Brook Avenue

    When figures are used for both the house number and the street name, separate them with a dash.

    122—33rd Street

12. Use figures for the larger of two adjacent numbers.

    Please order three 8-gallon sharps containers.

13. Spell out isolated simple fractions in words. Write mixed fractions and decimals in figures.

    one-half cut 5 3/4 hours 0.125 inch

Parallelism

Parts of a sentence that are parallel in meaning should be parallel in structure. Writers should balance a word with a word, a phrase with a phrase, a clause with a clause, and a sentence with a sentence. Parallel parts of a sentence should be grammatically the same.

Your goals should be *clear, realistic,* and *they should be attainable.*
(adjective, adjective, and clause—not parallel)

Your goals should be *clear, realistic,* and *attainable.*
(adjective, adjective, and adjective—parallel)

Tyne interviews the applicants, and they are tested by Oren.
(active voice and passive voice—not parallel)

Tyne interviews the applicants, and Oren tests them.
(active voice and active voice—parallel)

A common mistake in parallelism occurs with the use of **correlative conjunctions**, such as *both-and, either-or, neither-nor, not only-but also,* and *whether-or.* The text that follows the two conjunctions should be parallel in structure.

Priya not only *handles administrative tasks* but also *some clinical duties.*
(verb plus object and noun phrase—not parallel)

Priya handles not only *administrative tasks* but also *some clinical duties.*
(noun phrase and noun phrase—parallel)

Plurals

1. To form the plural of most nouns, add *s.*
2. For nouns ending in *s, x, z, sh,* or *ch,* add *es* to form the plural.

   address addresses

box boxes
waltz waltzes
dash dashes
speech speeches

Quiz/quizzes is an exception.

3. When a noun ends in *y* preceded by a vowel, form the plural by adding *s*.

   attorney attorneys

   When a noun ends in *y* preceded by a consonant, change the *y* to *i* and add *es* to form the plural.

   company companies

4. When a noun ends in *o* preceded by a vowel, form the plural by adding *s*.

   video videos

   For nouns ending in *o* preceded by a consonant, the plural is formed in different ways (*s* is added, *es* is added, or either is acceptable). Consult a dictionary if you are not sure of the correct form.

5. For compound nouns consisting of separate or hyphenated words that include a noun, make the main or base part plural.

   cross-examination cross-examinations
   runner-up runners-up

   If no part of a hyphenated compound is itself a noun, make the last element plural.

   trade-in trade-ins

6. Add *s* to make numbers expressed in figures plural.

   1900s 1099s

Possessives

1. To form the possessive of most singular nouns, add an apostrophe plus *s* ('s).

   My sister's name is Sheila.

   Thomas's office is down the hall.

   If a singular noun ends in a silent *s*, or if adding an apostrophe plus *s* would make the word difficult to pronounce, add just an apostrophe.

   What is the Peace Corps' mission?

   What is Ms. Luebbers' address?

2. To form the possessive of a plural noun ending in *s*, add just an apostrophe.

   The managers' decision was unanimous.

   The Garcias' house sold for $575,000.

3. To form the possessive of a plural noun not ending in *s*, add an apostrophe plus *s* ('s).

   The children's play area is on the lower level.

4. Rules 1–3 apply to compound nouns as well.

   The mayor-elect's plans are impressive.

   The copy editors' hours have been cut.

5. To show joint possession, make the last element possessive.

   We are near Jan and Keith's store.

   To show individual possession, make each element possessive.

   Mantero's and Ria's job descriptions overlap.

6. Write the possessive form of personal pronouns without an apostrophe.

   This book is hers.

   She will deliver yours tomorrow.

Pronouns

1. A pronoun agrees with its *antecedent* (the word or words to which the pronoun refers) in number (singular or plural), gender, and person (first, second, or third).

   Carlos wants to know if *his* new computer has been delivered.

   Marty and Tomie are bringing *their* cameras.

   The company issued *its* annual report. (not *their* annual report)

   See also "Collective Nouns."

2. When a pronoun has an indefinite pronoun, such as *everybody*, as its antecedent, make sure the two pronouns agree in number.

   Everyone should bring *his or her* company ID. (not *their* company IDs)

   For lists of singular and plural indefinite pronouns, see "Subject-Verb Agreement."

3. A singular pronoun is used when the antecedent consists of two singular nouns joined by *or* or *nor*. A plural pronoun is used when the antecedent consists of two plural nouns joined by *or* or *nor*.

   Either *Elizabeth* or *Olivia* will need to bring *her* tablet.

   Neither the *medical assistants* nor the *nurses* have received *their* benefits packets.

4. When the antecedent consists of a singular and a plural noun connected by *or* or *nor*, the pronoun agrees with the noun that is closer to it.

   When *Jamie* or *the managers* give *their* opinions, you should listen.

5. Use *who*, *whom*, and their compounds (such as *whoever*) when referring to persons. Use *that* when referring to people or things. *Who* refers to an individual person or group; *that* refers to a class or type.

   Shoko, who heads the recycling committee, will present the new program.

   He is the type of candidate that we like to employ.

   The building that I work in is LEED-certified.

   Use *which* and *whichever* when referring to things.

   The reservation, which was made two weeks ago, was for a smoke-free room.

   Use *which* to introduce a clause that is not essential to the meaning of the sentence. Use *that* to introduce a clause that is essential to the meaning of the sentence. A comma is used before *which* but not before *that*.

   See also the *That, which* entry in "Misused and Easily Confused Words and Phrases."

6. Nominative case pronouns (*I, you, he, she, it, we, you, they, who,* and *whoever*) are used as subjects.

   He maintains the company's website. (subject of the sentence)

   Alécia, *who* lives in Salem, commutes to Boston by train. (subject of a dependent clause)

   Use a nominative case pronoun after a linking verb (a form of the verb *be*).

   It was she who got the promotion. (not *It was her*)

7. Objective case pronouns function as direct objects, indirect objects, or objects of prepositions. These pronouns include *me, you, him, her, it, us, you, them, whom,* and *whomever.*

   Kyle asked *him* for a list of clients. (pronoun as direct object)

   Mr. Komnick gave Elizabeth and *me* a new assignment. (pronoun as indirect object)

   Look for *them* near the registration desk. (pronoun as the object of a preposition)

8. Possessive case pronouns show ownership. These pronouns include *my, mine, your, yours, his, her, hers, its, our, ours, your, yours, their, theirs,* and *whose.*

   Whose cell phone is this?

9. Two pronouns that are often confused are *who* and *whom.*

   - *Who* is used as the subject of a verb or as a predicate pronoun (after the verb *be*, to complete its meaning).

     Who is making the arrangements for the conference?

     The keynote speaker was *who*?

   - *Whom* is used as an object of a verb or preposition.

     Whom can we expect to give the welcoming address? (direct object of the verb *expect*)

     To *whom* does Grant report? (object of the preposition *to*)

   For a quick check on using *who* or *whom*, see the *Who, Whom* entry in "Misused and Easily Confused Words and Phrases."

10. Reflexive pronouns serve to emphasize that the subject receives the action of the verb. Reflexive pronouns include *myself, herself, himself, themselves,* and other *-self* or *-selves* words.

    I intend to do the painting *myself.*

    Be careful not to use a reflexive pronoun as a subject.

    Incorrect Roberto and *myself* will attend the webinar.

    Correct Roberto and *I* will attend the webinar.

Punctuation

Punctuation is important if the reader is to interpret the writer's thoughts accurately. Correct punctuation is based on accepted rules and principles.

Period

1. Use a period at the end of a declarative or imperative sentence.

   Jake works for the prosecutor's office.
   (declarative sentence)

   Please send me a copy of the report.
   (imperative sentence)

2. Use a period after an initial and after the courtesy titles *Mr., Mrs.,* and *Ms.*

   J. D. Salinger   Ms. Tabitha Todd

3. Use periods in academic degrees that follow a person's name.

   Yichen Tan, M.D., has joined the medical staff of Metropolitan Hospital.

   Within the health care field, medical degrees are often written without periods. Professional designations such as *CPA* (*certified public accountant*) are written without periods when used alone but with periods when used with academic degrees.

   Kirsten Brownstein, M.B.A., C.L.U., will speak on personal financial planning.

4. Use periods with *a.m.* and *p.m.* to designate time.

   10 a.m.   4:30 p.m.

5. Use a period between dollars and cents. A period is not required when an amount in even dollars is expressed in figures.

   $42.65 $25

6. Use a period to indicate a decimal.

   3.5 bushels   12.65 percent

   See also "Abbreviations."

Question Mark

Use a question mark after a direct question.

When do you expect to arrive in Philadelphia?

An exception to this rule is a sentence phrased in the form of a question when it is actually a courteous request.

Will you please send us an up-to-date statement of our account.

Exclamation Point

The exclamation point is used to express sudden or strong emotion and to give urgent warnings or commands. Use it rarely.

Congratulations!
I can't believe it!
Stop!

Comma

1. Use a comma before a coordinating conjunction (such as *and, but, or, for, nor,* and *yet*) that links independent clauses. The comma may be omitted in a compound sentence if the clauses are short and closely connected.

   We have a dozen boxes, but I think we should order a dozen more.

   He sent a proposal and they accepted it.

2. Use a comma to set off an introductory phrase from the rest of the sentence, except for short prepositional phrases that do not contain a verb form.

   To finish the project, Joel worked late several evenings.

After planning the orientation, Len organized the training.

At noon I have my first appointment.

3. Use a comma to set off a dependent clause that precedes a main clause.

Assuming no changes are needed, let's implement the plan.

4. Use a comma to set off nonessential elements—words, phrases, and clauses that could be left out of the sentence without affecting its structure (it would still be a sentence) or meaning. In speaking, you would pause before and after these words, phrases, and clauses.

The survey showed, however, that we need to redesign our website.

Ms. Linda Salus, the vice president, will speak at the conference.

Our group, which had never lost a debate, won the grand prize.

If a nonessential element does not interrupt the flow of a sentence, no comma is used. (In speaking, you would not pause before or after it.)

I updated the records accordingly.

5. Use commas to separate three or more items in a series.

Companies seek employees with dependability, trustworthiness, ambition, and judgment.

6. Use a comma to separate *coordinate adjectives* (adjectives that independently modify a noun).

She had a large, receptive audience.

To determine whether adjectives are coordinate, try using *and* between them.

a *large and receptive* audience

Compare the adjectives above to the adjectives in this sentence:

The *old clock* tower is being repaired.

Could you say *old and clock tower*? *Old* and *clock* are not coordinate adjectives, and a comma should not be used.

7. Use a comma to set off quotations from the rest of the sentence.

Viola suggested, "Let's have a face-to-face conference."

"The committees have agreed," Leo said, "to work together on the project."

"Sirena will handle that responsibility," Travis said.

8. Use a comma to set off the name of a city from the name of a state or country.

Our southern branch is located in Atlanta, Georgia.

9. Use commas to set off the second and all following items in complete dates and in addresses.

The anniversary party was planned for June 18, 201-, at the Hill Hotel.

Marguerite's new address is 19 State Street, Skagway, Alaska.

Do not use a comma when the date has only two parts or uses the word *of*.

I earned my degree in June 2012.

The wedding will take place on the 5th of May.

10. Use a comma after the complimentary close in a business letter when mixed punctuation is used.

Sincerely yours,

11. Use a comma to separate personal and professional titles that follow names. The personal titles *Jr.* and *Sr.* may appear without the comma if that is the person's preference.

William R. Warner, Jr.

Ramona Sanchez, Ph.D.

12. For numbers greater than zero, use a comma to separate the digits into groups of three. Do not use a comma in parts of a number that are less than zero (decimals), street names and numbers, and years.

	50,000 members	$3,575,000
But	3.14159	1930 (year)

Comma Splice The *comma splice*, a common grammatical error, occurs when a sentence contains two or more independent clauses joined by a comma.

I walked home, then I had dinner.

Here are three ways to correct a comma splice:

- Make two sentences.
  I walked home. Then I had dinner.
- Add a coordinating conjunction.
  I walked home, and then I had dinner.
- Replace the comma with a semicolon.
  I walked home; then I had dinner.

Semicolon

1. Use a semicolon to separate independent clauses that are not joined by a coordinating conjunction (such as *and, but, or, nor, for,* or *yet*).

   Everyone enjoyed the meal; many of us did not enjoy the movie.

2. Use a semicolon between independent clauses that are joined by a conjunctive adverb, such as *besides, however, nevertheless, still, then,* or *therefore,* or by a phrase such as *as a result* or *for example.*

   I ordered all three DVDs; however, only two were in stock.

   Max is considerate of his employees; for example, he got us ergonomic chairs.

3. Use semicolons to separate a series of items that contain commas.

   This year's outstanding employees are Anna Wang, Personnel; Henry Wright, Technical Support; and Emaan Yazdan, Marketing.

Colon

The colon is most often used to direct the reader's attention to what comes after it, usually a list.

1. Use a colon after introductory expressions such as *the following, thus,* or *as follows.*

   Please send the following by parcel post: books, magazines, and newspapers.

   A colon must always be preceded by an independent clause, except when the listed items are on separate lines.

2. Use a colon after the salutation in a business letter when mixed punctuation is used.

   Dear Ms. Carroll:

3. Use a colon to separate hours and minutes when indicating time.

   2:10 p.m.

Dash

The dash is most often used in place of commas, parentheses, a colon, or a semicolon when special emphasis is desired.

This is not a revision of an old book—it is a totally new book.

These sales arguments—and every one of them is important—should get us the order.

A short dash, known as an en dash, is used to separate ranges of numbers.

pages 32–35

Parentheses

Parentheses are used to set off additions to a sentence that are not necessary to its meaning. Unlike the dash, parentheses tend to de-emphasize what they set off. Use parentheses to enclose explanations, references, directions, and numbers and letters of listed items.

Our personnel costs (including benefits) are much too high.

An additional 45 percent of our customers (Figure 1) would like a live chat feature.

To download the software, (1) go to the Downloads page of the company intranet, (2) click *Interoffice Scheduler,* (3) create a six-character password that includes letters and numbers, and (4) follow the instructions on the screen.

Hyphen

1. The hyphen is used in most compound adjectives that precede a noun and in some compound nouns and verbs.

That was a time-consuming project.

My brother-in-law works at the Pentagon.

Try not to second-guess your decision.

2. The hyphen is also used in spelled out compound numbers; phone numbers; nine-digit ZIP Codes; and spelled-out, simple fractions.

Thirty-five employees attended the meeting.

555-0175 45213-1419 two-thirds

Apostrophe

1. Use an apostrophe to show ownership or possession.

the assistant's tablet the paralegals' request

See "Possessives" for additional examples.

2. Use an apostrophe to indicate the omission of a letter or letters in a contraction.

it's (it is) you're (you are) we'll (we will)

Quotation Marks

1. Use quotation marks to enclose a person's exact words (a direct quotation).

The author writes, "Too-frequent use of certain words weakens the appeal."

Jessup said that Ms. Carrero was "truly the best teacher I have ever had."

When you interrupt a quoted sentence to identify the speaker, end the first part of the sentence at a logical place, and start the second part with a lowercase letter.

"Do you think," said Lisa, "that we should take a second look at the figures?"

When the break occurs between sentences, end the first part with a period. Begin the new quoted sentence with a quotation mark and a capital letter.

"That sounds like a good idea," said Fabrizio. "Can you explain it in more detail?"

2. Do not use quotation marks for an indirect quotation. The statement must be the exact words of a person for quotation marks to be used.

Jack said that he would have the report ready by 10:30.

3. Use quotation marks to set off the titles of parts of works such as these:

Chapters of books

Newspaper or magazine articles

Songs or television episodes

Sections of websites

4. Use italics to set off titles of complete works such as these:

Books

Newspapers or magazines

Music CDs or television series

5. Follow these guidelines for punctuation with quotation marks:

Place commas and periods inside quotation marks.

"I took a class in medical law and ethics," she replied.

Garrett said, "I completed an internship in the public defender's office."

Place semicolons and colons outside quotation marks.

I downloaded "Ashokan Farewell"; have you heard that song?

Place question marks and exclamation points inside quotation marks if they are part of the quoted matter and outside quotation marks if they punctuate the entire sentence.

Jaecar asked, "Are you coming with us to the seminar?"

Did you read the part that said, "Listening is the communication skill that many people use most"?

Respectful Speech and Writing

When addressing anyone, use terms that show respect. Remember that all assistants are not female and all executives are not male. If you answer the telephone and hear a woman's voice, do not assume she is an assistant and ask to speak to her supervisor. Do not refer to a woman as a girl or a young lady or use any other term that can sound gender-biased. Do not refer to a man as a boy or a guy.

Avoid statements such as *Each manager should submit his timesheet* by doing one of the following:

- Use the plural of the noun and pronoun.
  All managers should submit *their* timesheets.
- Delete the pronoun or replace it with an article.
  Each manager should submit *a* timesheet.
- Use *he or she* (this use is awkward, so try to avoid it).
  Each manager should submit *his or her* timesheet.

Spelling

1. Use this guide to determine which comes first, *i* or *e*:

   Put *i* before *e* except after *c* or when sounded like *a* as in *neighbor* or *weigh*.

   convenient receive freight

   This rule has numerous exceptions, such as *either, neither, foreign,* and *height*.

2. Words ending in a silent *e* generally drop the *e* before a suffix that begins with a vowel.

   guide guidance
   use usable

   They retain it before a suffix that begins with a consonant unless another vowel precedes the final *e*.

   care careless
   argue argument

   As with most spelling rules, there are a few exceptions, such as *nine/ninth*. See also the next rule.

3. Words ending in *ce* or *ge* generally retain the silent *e* before the suffixes *able* and *ous* but drop it before the suffixes *ible* and *ing*.

   manage manageable
   force forcible

4. When a word ends in *y* preceded by a consonant, the *y* is usually changed to *i* before adding a suffix, except for suffixes beginning with *i*.

   easy easily
   try tries trying

5. When adding a suffix that begins with a vowel, double the final consonant if a single vowel precedes it and if (for words with more than one syllable) the consonant ends an accented syllable.

   bag baggage
   occur occurrence

   If the first syllable of a multisyllable word is accented, don't double the consonant (*differ/different*). And don't double it if the accent shifts to the first syllable when the suffix is added (*refer/reference*).

   These rules have several exceptions, such as not doubling the final consonant *w, x,* or *y* (*fix/fixed*) and doubling the *m* in *program* (*programmed*).

6. When a word ends in two consonants or a single consonant preceded by two vowels, do not double the final consonant before any suffix.

   act acting
   look looked

   An exception is *equip* (*equipped*).

Subject-Verb Agreement

1. Verbs must agree with their subjects in person and number. A singular subject takes a singular form of a verb. A plural subject takes a plural form of a verb.

   Andrew works in our New Orleans office.

   Ishan and Kelsey work in our San Diego office.

2. Disregard intervening words, phrases, and clauses when establishing agreement between subject and verb.

   One of the men *needs* additional training.

3. The following pronouns are always singular and require a singular verb:

   another either neither other
   anybody everybody no one somebody

anyone	everyone	nobody	someone
anything	everything	nothing	something
each	much	one	

Everyone plans to attend the meeting.

Neither is an ideal solution.

4. *Both, few, many, others,* and *several* are always plural and require a plural verb.

   Both were asked to make presentations.

5. *All, any, none, some, more,* and *most* may be singular or plural depending on the noun or pronoun to which they refer.

   Most of the paper *was* recycled.

   Most of them *are* useful.

6. When the subject consists of two singular nouns and/or pronouns connected by *or, either–or, neither–nor,* or *not only–but also,* use a singular verb if the nouns and/or pronouns are singular and a plural verb if they are plural.

   Jane or *Bob has* the letter.

   Neither the *managers* nor the *administrative assistants have* access to that information.

7. When the subject is made up of both singular and plural nouns and/or pronouns connected by *or, either–or, neither–nor,* or *not only–but also,* the verb agrees with the noun or pronoun that is closer to the verb.

   Either *Ms. Salazar* or the *assistants have* access to that information.

   Neither the *men* nor *Jo* is working.

8. *There* and *here* are never the subjects of a sentence. When a sentence begins with one of these words, look elsewhere for the subject, and choose the appropriate form of the verb.

   There *are* a memo and a letter.
   (*a memo and a letter* is the subject)

9. Use a singular verb with words or phrases that express periods of time, weights, measurements, and amounts of money.

   Three hours *is* a very long delay.

   Two hundred dollars *is* my limit.

10. *The number* has a singular meaning and requires a singular verb; *a number* has a plural meaning and requires a plural verb.

    The number of requests *is* surprising.

    A *number* of people *are* planning to attend.

11. Geographic locations are considered singular and are used with a singular verb when referring to one location. When reference is made to separate states or islands, the plural form is used with a plural verb.

    The United Arab Emirates *is* made up of seven states.

    The Cocos Islands *were* not inhabited until the 1800s.

Document Formats

Letters

Business letters are typically formatted in block or modified block style. Open or mixed punctuation can be used with both letter styles. Figure 1 shows a block letter with open punctuation, and Figure 2 on page 432 shows a modified block letter with mixed punctuation.

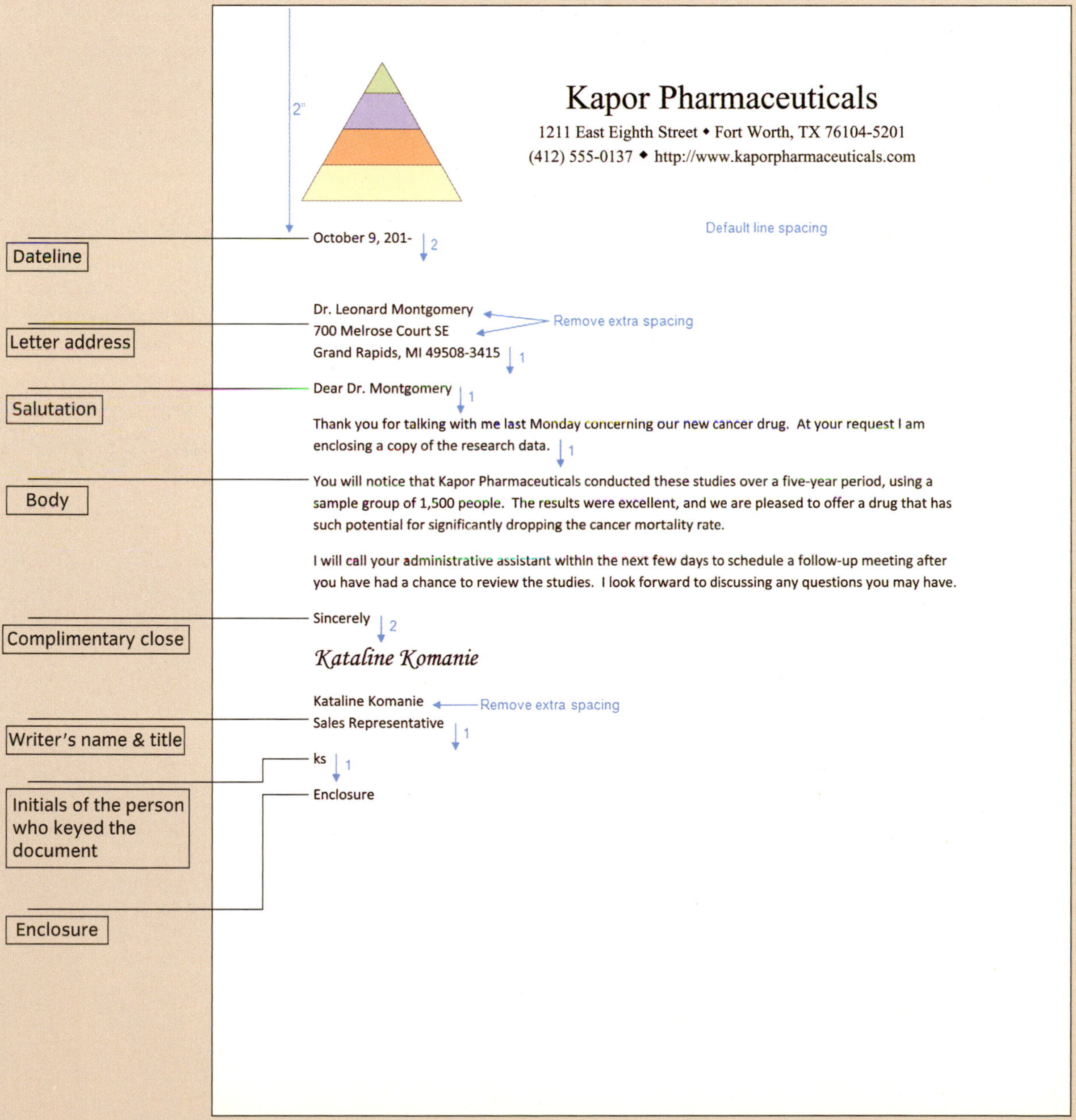

Kapor Pharmaceuticals
1211 East Eighth Street • Fort Worth, TX 76104-5201
(412) 555-0137 • http://www.kaporpharmaceuticals.com

October 9, 201-

Dr. Leonard Montgomery
700 Melrose Court SE
Grand Rapids, MI 49508-3415

Dear Dr. Montgomery

Thank you for talking with me last Monday concerning our new cancer drug. At your request I am enclosing a copy of the research data.

You will notice that Kapor Pharmaceuticals conducted these studies over a five-year period, using a sample group of 1,500 people. The results were excellent, and we are pleased to offer a drug that has such potential for significantly dropping the cancer mortality rate.

I will call your administrative assistant within the next few days to schedule a follow-up meeting after you have had a chance to review the studies. I look forward to discussing any questions you may have.

Sincerely

Kataline Komanie

Kataline Komanie
Sales Representative

ks

Enclosure

FIGURE 1 Block Letter With Open Punctuation

Palm Atlantic Airlines

1720 East Higgins Road
Schaumburg, IL 60173-5114
(847) 555-0197
http://www.palmatlanticair.com

Tab at about 3.25" → November 14, 201-

Ms. Grace Edwardson
Maximum Media Production
243 High Street
Marquette, MI 49855-2345

Same top margin and spacing as in Figure 1

Dear Ms. Edwardson:

Thank you for asking me to speak at your conference in December. I greatly enjoy my association with your group; you truly provide an excellent growth opportunity for managers.

The demands on my time for the next several months are extremely heavy. In addition to a new planning process that I must implement, we have recently employed two managers who are looking to me for assistance in learning their jobs. As you might expect, I am extremely busy. I must say no to your request at this time. However, if you need a speaker in the future, please contact me again. I always enjoy talking with your group.

I look forward to working with you in the future. Best wishes for success with the conference.

Sincerely,

Rachel Portales

Rachel Portales
Chief Operating Officer

es

FIGURE 2 Modified Block Letter With Mixed Punctuation

Envelopes

Many word processing programs have an envelopes feature that automatically inserts a delivery address on an envelope, placing it properly according to USPS guidelines. The software may allow you to include a return address for your organization or to omit it if you will be using envelopes with a printed return address.

The address on an envelope should be located in an area that can be read by USPS automated equipment, such as an optical character reader. Figure 3 shows the OCR area for a letter-sized envelope.[1] When you place a label on an envelope or address an envelope manually, be sure the address is placed in the OCR read zone.

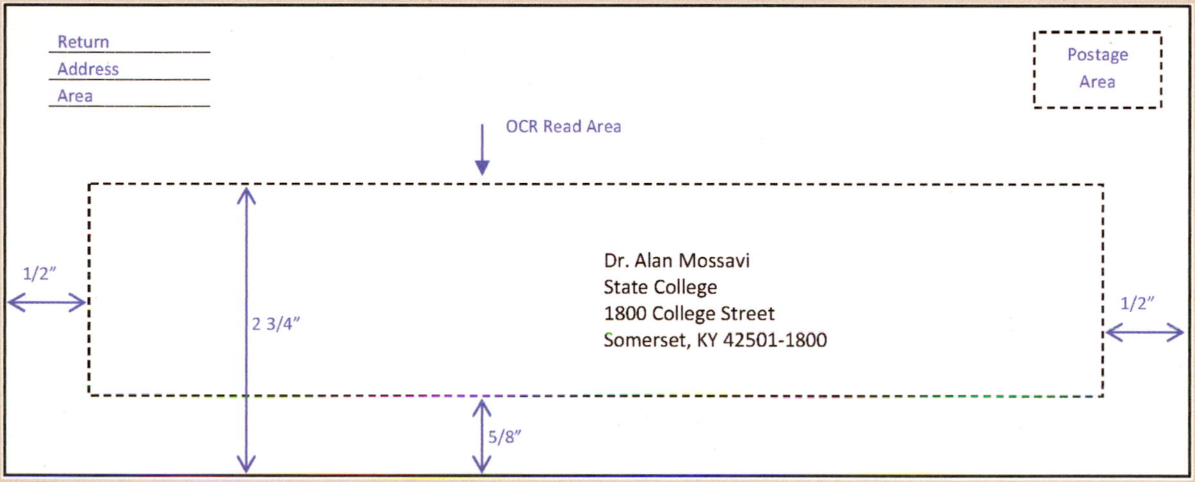

FIGURE 3 OCR Read Area for Letter Envelope

Place notations that affect postage (for example, REGISTERED and CERTIFIED) below the stamp position (line 8). Place other special notations (such as HOLD FOR ARRIVAL, CONFIDENTIAL, and PLEASE FORWARD) two lines below the return address.

Large Envelopes (No. 10, 9, 7 3/4)

Fold a letter for insertion in a large envelope in the following manner:

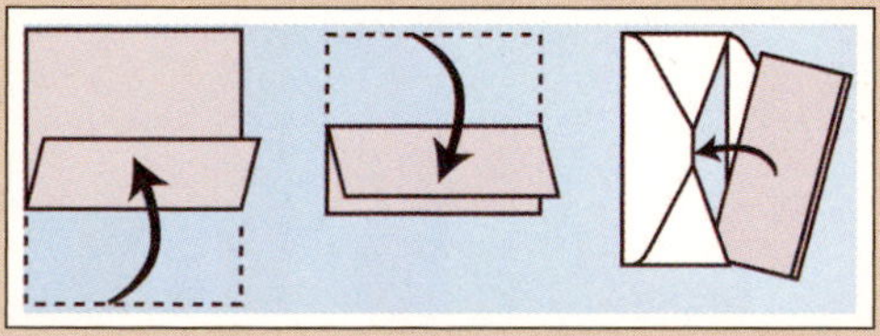

Small Envelopes (No. 6 3/4, 6 1/4)

Fold a letter for insertion in a small envelope in the following manner:

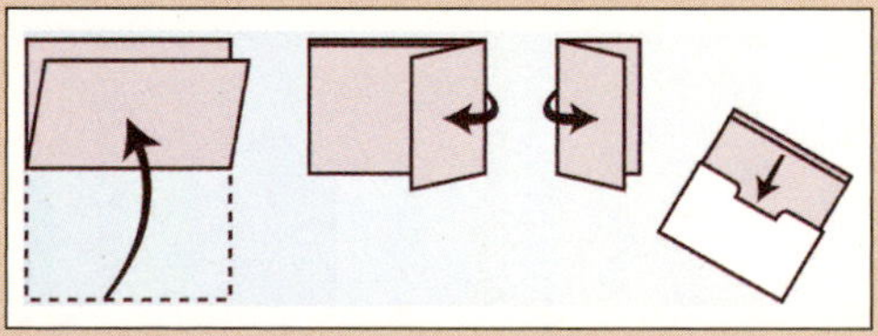

[1] U.S. Postal Service, *Domestic Mail Manual*, "Address Placement," http://pe.usps.com/text/dmm300/202.htm#1064332.(accessed September 26, 2011).

Memorandums

Memorandums (memos) are short messages that may be printed on letterhead or plain paper. Figure 4 shows a memorandum.

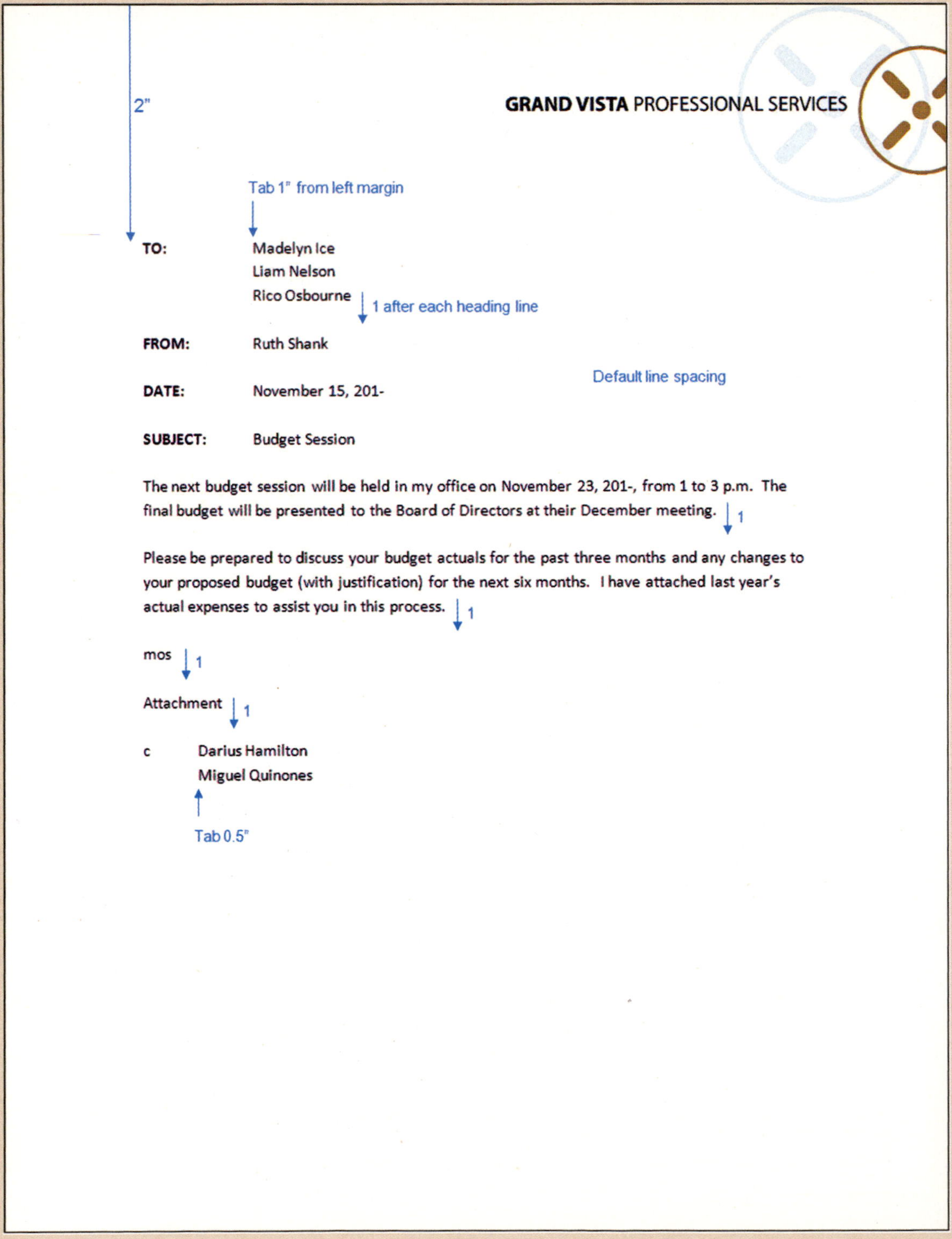

GRAND VISTA PROFESSIONAL SERVICES

TO: Madelyn Ice
Liam Nelson
Rico Osbourne

FROM: Ruth Shank

DATE: November 15, 201-

SUBJECT: Budget Session

The next budget session will be held in my office on November 23, 201-, from 1 to 3 p.m. The final budget will be presented to the Board of Directors at their December meeting.

Please be prepared to discuss your budget actuals for the past three months and any changes to your proposed budget (with justification) for the next six months. I have attached last year's actual expenses to assist you in this process.

mos

Attachment

c Darius Hamilton
Miguel Quinones

FIGURE 4 Memorandum

Second-Page Headings

If a memo or letter is more than one page long, a heading should be placed on the second and following pages. The heading should include the recipient's name, Page 2 (or the appropriate number), and the date. Figure 5 shows a sample second-page heading.

Business Reports

Formal business reports usually contain several parts as listed below. Not all reports will contain all these parts.

- Executive summary
- Title page (Figure 6 on page 436)
- Table of contents (Figure 7 on page 437)
- Body (Figures 9–11 on pages 438–440)
- Bibliography or reference section (Figure 8 on page 437)
- One or more appendices

Formal business reports are typically prepared in manuscript style. The body of the report includes a main title and side headings to identify parts of the report. Software features, such as the Title and Heading styles in *Word*, are typically used to format titles and headings. The report paragraphs are formatted using the default 1.15 line spacing. The paragraphs are not indented. Tables, charts, or other visual aids may be included in the report body or an appendix. A bibliography or reference page lists sources at the end of the report. One or more appendices may be included to provide additional details or related information.

Documentation must be provided for sources of information used in a business report that are not the author's own. This rule applies whether the material is quoted or paraphrased. Unless the material is considered general knowledge, documentation must be provided.

Documentation may follow several different styles using footnotes, endnotes, or internal citations and a reference page. Three frequently used styles are the Modern Language Association (MLA) style, the American Psychological Association (APA) style, and the Chicago style (named for *The Chicago Manual of Style* produced by the University of Chicago Press). Your company may use one of those styles for its formal reports, or it may have another format that you will be expected to use.

- **Footnotes** appear at the bottom of the page. A superscript number in the report body marks the referenced material (...others.[2]). A bibliography at the end of the report lists all the footnote references in a slightly different format in alphabetical order. The bibliography, which may be titled "References" or something similar, can appear on the last page of the report if it will fit or can be on a separate page. The sample report in this Reference Guide uses footnotes.
- **Endnotes** appear at the end of the report in numerical order. Titled "Notes" or something

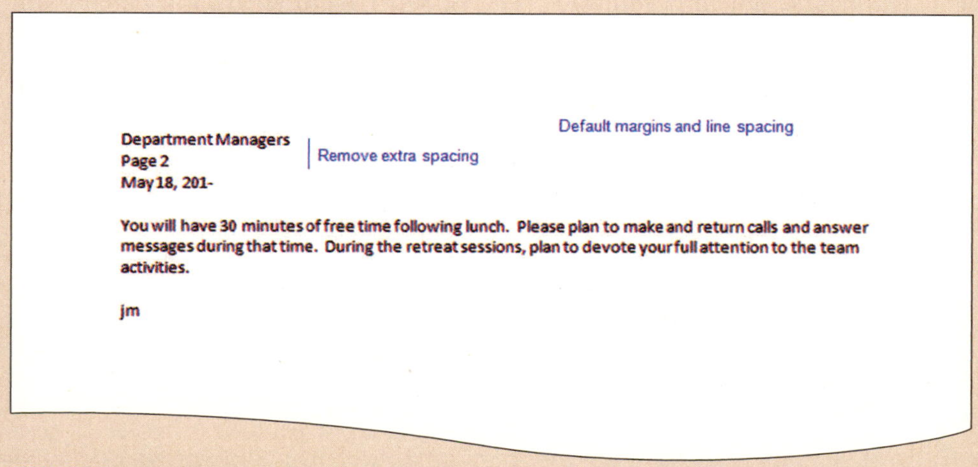

Department Managers
Page 2
May 18, 201-

You will have 30 minutes of free time following lunch. Please plan to make and return calls and answer messages during that time. During the retreat sessions, plan to devote your full attention to the team activities.

jm

FIGURE 5 Second-Page Heading

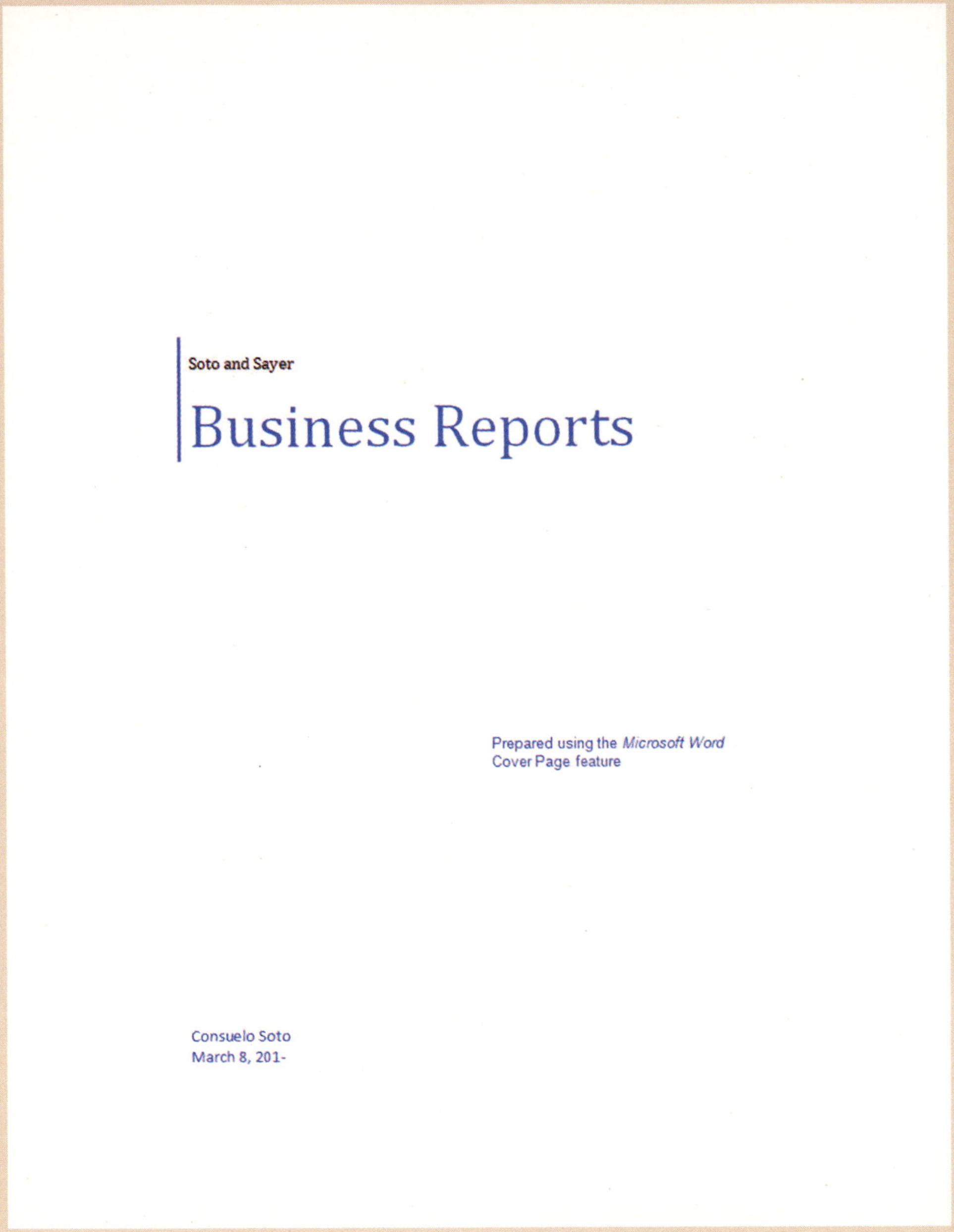
Soto and Sayer

Business Reports

Prepared using the *Microsoft Word* Cover Page feature

Consuelo Soto
March 8, 201-

FIGURE 6 Report Title Page

similar, they can appear on the last page of the report if they will fit or on a separate page. A superscript number in the report body marks the referenced material (…around the globe.[3]). The Notes page is followed by a references page in which the sources appear in alphabetical order.

- **Internal citations** appear in the body of the report, in parentheses. They include the name of the author(s) and, depending on the citation style used, the publication date, page number, or both. The MLA and APA styles use internal citations. A section or page at the end of the report lists the references in alphabetical order.

  Rice's mother taught the baseball legend Willie Mays, who remembers her as a woman who recognized his abilities and encouraged him to pursue them (Rice 21).

Microsoft Word and other word processing programs provide features that automate many of

Table of Contents

Determine the Purpose or Goal 1

Analyze the Reader 1

Consider the Tone 2

Gather the Appropriate Information 2

Organize the Content 2

Draft and Edit the Message 2

Proofread and Prepare the Final Product 3

FIGURE 7 Report Table of Contents

5

Bibliography

Fulton-Calkins, Patsy J., Rankin, Dianne S., and Shumack, Kellie A. *The Administrative Professional*, 14e. Cincinnati, OH: South-Western Cengage Learning, 2011.

Stolley, Karl. "Avoiding Plagiarism." *The OWL at Purdue*. August 24, 2011. http://owl.english.purdue.edu/owl/resource/589/01/ (accessed September 26, 2011).

FIGURE 8 Report Bibliography

the tasks involved in documenting sources. These programs can number and place footnotes and endnotes for you. *Word* automatically formats references in MLA, APA, Chicago, and several other styles. You can also use word processing software to generate a bibliography.

For complete information about using MLA, APA, or Chicago styles, you can purchase the appropriate style manual, consult a library reference copy, or borrow a circulating copy from a library. The latest editions as of the time of this writing are listed below. Online and library resources also provide information about formatting internal citations, notes, and bibliographies in these and other commonly used styles.

- *The Chicago Manual of Style,* 16th edition. Chicago: The University of Chicago Press, 2010.
- *MLA Handbook for Writers of Research Papers,* 7th edition. New York: The Modern Language Association of America, 2009.
- *Publication Manual of the American Psychological Association,* 6th edition. New York: American Psychological Association, 2009.

Business Reports

Organizations produce many different types of reports. They may be informal reports of two or three pages (sometimes in memo format), or they may be formal reports containing a table of contents, body (with footnotes or endnotes), bibliography or reference page(s) or section, and one or more appendices. Because reports are often presented orally, in addition to distribution of the written copy, *PowerPoint* slides can be an effective visual.[1]

Like all effective writing, effective report writing is based on determining the goal or purpose, analyzing the audience/reader, considering the tone, gathering the appropriate information, organizing the content, drafting and editing the message, and proofreading and preparing the final product. An effective report is complete, clear, correct, concise, courteous, and considerate.

Determine the Purpose or Goal

Business messages are written to inform the reader, request information, provide information, establish a record of facts, promote goodwill, or persuade the reader to take or forego some action. Some business messages have more than one objective. For example, the objectives may be to inform and persuade. To determine the goal of a report or any type of written message, ask yourself what your purpose in writing is and what you hope to accomplish.

Analyze the Reader

If your employer is not clear with you concerning who is receiving the correspondence, do not be afraid to ask. It is important that you analyze the reader before you begin to write. Ask questions such as these about the reader:

- How much does the person receiving the report know about the subject?
- What is the educational level of the reader? Is the reader familiar with technical jargon that might be used?
- What effect will the message have on the reader? Will the reader react favorably or unfavorably to the message?
- Does the reader come from a different background? If so, what is that background? When the reader is from another country, you need to take additional steps to make certain that you are clear and not offending the reader in any way.

[1] Patsy J. Fulton-Calkins, Dianne S. Rankin, and Kellie A. Shumack, *The Administrative Professional*, 14e (Cincinnati: South-Western, Cengage Learning, 2011.

FIGURE 9 Report Body, Page 1

Consider the Tone

To give an appropriate tone to a business report, think about the reader as you write. Use the *you* approach to put yourself in the place of the reader. Business reports are frequently written in a formal tone, but you will also use your analysis of the reader to tailor the writing to that particular audience.

Gather the Appropriate Information

You may check the organization's files on the subject, talk with your employer concerning any background information, and/or research the topic. Most reports involve some type of research. The research may be primary research—the collecting of original data through surveys, observations or experiments. The research may also be secondary research—data or material that other people have discovered and reported via the Internet, books, periodicals, and various other publications. Be sure to give credit to sources of the material used in the report. Purdue University's Online Writing Lab offers this advice:

> While some cultures may not insist so heavily on documenting sources of words, ideas, images, sounds, etc., American culture does. A charge of plagiarism can have severe consequences, including expulsion from a university or loss of a job, not to mention a writer's loss of credibility and professional standing.[2]

Organize the Content

Make an outline of the key points that should be covered; arrange your points logically. Brainstorm with others if the project is a collaborative one. Write down everything that comes to mind. Then group your ideas, getting all similar ideas together. Next, determine which idea logically goes first, which second, and so on. The basic organizational structure uses a three-pronged approach. The first part of the document conveys the purpose of the report. The second part supports, informs, and/or convinces the reader. The last part states the desired results, the action, or a summary of the findings. Table 1 on page 3 lists the parts of a typical report.

Draft and Edit the Message

Follow your outline as you write the first draft of your report. If you are writing collaboratively, some group members may draft different parts of the report. Remember that in the first draft, your goal should be to write down everything you want to say. Do not allow yourself to be distracted by exact word choices and other items that can be checked later. You do not have to write every part of the report in order. Write the parts in the order that works best for you.

You should keep several things in mind while editing the report. Edit for the C characteristics of effective communication. Look for unity, coherence, and parallel structure in paragraphs. Does the

---

[2] Karl Stolley, "Avoiding Plagiarism," *The OWL at Purdue*, http://owl.english.purdue.edu/owl/resource/589/01/ (accessed September 26, 2011).

FIGURE 10 Report Body, Page 2

3

TABLE 1 Parts of a Formal Business Report	
Executive summary	A one- or two-page summary of the document.
Title page	Includes information such as the report title, the name and title of the person for whom the report is prepared, the name and title of the preparer, and the date the report is submitted.
Table of contents	Lists each major section of the report and the page number of the first page of that section. Although not required, it can be helpful for the reader.
Body	Divided into sections using side headings.
Bibliography or reference section	Lists all references in alphabetical order by authors' last names. May appear on the last page of the report if all references fit on the page; if not, list on a separate, numbered page.
Appendix	Supporting information such as tables and statistics can be provided in one or more appendices at the end of the report. Label multiple appendices as Appendix A, Appendix B, etc.

report flow from one page or section to the next? Be especially alert to this question if you have written the sections out of order or if several people have written parts of the report. One person should be responsible for making sure that the parts of the report are consistent in detail of content and tone. Check that sentences are varied in structure and that, if the passive voice is used, it is used appropriately. Make sure the report is grammatically correct, and verify facts.

Proofread and Prepare the Final Product

Now you are ready to prepare the final draft of the report. Remember to plan sufficient time for this stage and not to rush through it. Make any necessary adjustments to the format. Read for consistency in formatting, style, and facts. Run grammar and spelling checks. Then proofread the report, first on the screen and then as a printed copy.

FIGURE 11 Report Body, Page 3

Proofreaders' Marks

When proofreading printed documents, use proofreaders' marks to indicate changes or corrections. Figure 12 shows commonly used proofreaders' marks.

PROOFREADERS' MARKS

SYMBOL		MARKED COPY	CORRECTED COPY
||	Align	|| $298,000 || $117,000	$298,000 $117,000
	Bold	The meaning is important.	The **meaning** is important.
≡	Capitalize	bobbie caine	Bobbie Caine
	Close up space	Use con cise words.	Use concise words.
	Delete	They are happpy.	They are happy.
∧	Insert	Please make a copy.	Please make a copy.
#	Space	Show alot of examples.	Show a lot of examples.
	Italicize	The Sacramento Bee	The *Sacramento Bee*
stet	Ignore correction	He is an effective writer.	He is an effective writer.
/	Lowercase	Sincerely Yours	Sincerely yours
	Move as shown	I am only going tomorrow.	I am going only tomorrow.
	Move left, right, up, or down	Mr. Herschel King 742 Wabash Avenue Skokie, IL 60077	Mr. Herschel King 742 Wabash Avenue Skokie, IL 60077
	Paragraph	The file is attached.	The file is attached.
sp	Spell out	7209 E. Darrow Avenue	7209 East Darrow Avenue
	Transpose	The down up and motion	The down and up motion
	Use initial cap only	FORMATTING A MEMO	Formatting a Memo

FIGURE 12 Proofreaders' Marks

Glossary

401(k) account A tax-deferred retirement plan for employees of private companies and corporations

403(b) account A tax-deferred retirement plan for employees of nonprofit organizations or educational institutions

A

accession log A file containing a list of numbers that have been used in a numeric filing system

active voice A form of the verb in which the subject performs the action

advertising-supported software (adware) Software that displays advertising

agenda A document that lists the topics to be discussed at a meeting

annotate To add explanatory notes to a document

annual percentage rate (APR) A credit card interest rate expressed as an annual rate

archive record A record that has historical value to an organization and should be preserved permanently

audio conference A meeting in which a number of people participate via telephone or some other device

autocratic leadership style A leadership style that involves complete control

B

backup A copy of electronic files or folders made as a precaution against loss or damage of the original data

balance sheet A financial document that shows an organization's assets, liabilities, and owner's equity at a given point in time

blog A website, or part of a website, where an individual can share his or her thoughts and ideas on a variety of topics

body language Nonverbal messages transmitted through gestures and posture using the eyes, face, hands, arms, and legs

bond A loan that a buyer makes to a bond issuer

brainstorming A technique used to generate ideas

budget A spending and saving plan based on anticipated income and expenses

business casual dress A style of professional dress that is less formal than traditional, conservative professional dress and that varies by organization

business ethics The application of ethical standards in the workplace

bylaws Written policies and procedures that clearly define how board meetings are to be conducted

C

cash flow statement A financial document that shows incoming and outgoing cash for a given period

character Your consistent personal standards of behavior

chief executive officer (CEO) The highest-ranking person in a company who reports to the board of directors and develops and implements strategic plans, makes major corporate decisions, and (often) oversees company operations

chronological resume A resume that gives an applicant's work experience in order with the most recent work experience listed first

cloud computing The use of computer services from virtual servers available on demand over the Internet

coding The process of marking a record to indicate the filing segment and indexing units

coherence A quality achieved in a paragraph when the sentences relate to each other in content, grammatical construction, and choice of words

committee A team set up to solve a problem, monitor an issue, or complete a task

compressed workweek An alternative to a traditional workweek that increases the number of hours per day and decreases the number of days worked

computer output to microfilm (COM) The process of converting computer data to a microform without first printing the records

computer virus A malicious program that attaches itself to files or software in order to spread to other files or programs

confidentiality Secrecy, privacy, or discretion

conflict A state of opposition or disagreement

consulate An office of a government in a foreign city that acts to assist and protect citizens of the represented country

corporation A type of business that is a legal entity formed by following a process of incorporation set forth by state statutes

credibility Believability or trustworthiness

cross-functional team A team composed of individuals from a number of different functional groups within an organization

cross-reference A note or document that shows an alternate name or subject by which a record might be requested and indicates the storage location of the original record

cross-training Training personnel to complete differing tasks within a department or unit

customer focus A commitment to providing high-quality customer service to all customers

customer service The ability of an organization to consistently give customers what they want and need

D

database A collection of records about one topic or related topics

defined benefit plan A retirement plan for an employee that is paid for by the employer

delegate To give the responsibility for a task to another person

democratic leadership style A leadership style that involves sharing authority, decisions, and plans with subordinates

demographics Characteristics of a group of people such as age, gender, and educational level

direct approach A message strategy in which the main idea is presented first

director An officer of a company who is charged with the management of its affairs and conduct. A group of directors is referred to as a board of directors.

dividend A share of a company's profits distributed to stockholders

document imaging The process of scanning paper documents and converting them to digital images

downward communication Messages that flow from management to employees

duplexing Copying on both sides of a sheet of paper

E

electronic record A record stored on an electronic medium that can be accessed or changed

electronic resume A resume in an electronic (rather than printed) format

electronic whiteboard A device that has the ability to electronically scan images drawn or written on it and transfer the data to a computer where it can be edited, printed, or e-mailed

empathy Understanding or concern for someone's feelings or position

Equal Employment Opportunity Commission (EEOC) The federal agency that enforces laws related to discrimination in the workplace

ethical road map A set of personal qualities and practices that help individuals determine the right direction ethically

ethics The standards that help a person determine right from wrong

e-ticket An electronic ticket that represents the purchase of a seat on a passenger airline

etiquette Code developed through customs that governs acceptable behavior

executive summary A one- or two-page summary of a document, such as a report

exit interview A meeting between an employee who is leaving the company and a company representative

external customers People or organizations that buy or use the products and services provided by the organization

external team A team formed when individuals within an organization work with individuals outside the organization to achieve specified goals

F

Family Educational Rights and Privacy Act of 1974 (FERPA) A federal law that protects the privacy of student education records

filing segment The name, subject, number, or geographic location by which a record is stored and requested

financial goal A plan for how you will pay for what you want to achieve

financial plan A guide that points you in the direction to meet your financial goals

firewall Software that monitors information as it enters and leaves a computer

flextime A variable work schedule in which all employees do not work a standard 9 a.m. to 5 p.m. day

flip chart A tablet of large paper for drawing pictures or recording notes during a presentation

formal communication Communication through official channels

Fortune 500 company One of the top 500 American public corporations as measured by gross revenue

frequent flyer program An incentive program that provides a variety of awards after the accumulation of a certain number of mileage points

fringe benefit An employment benefit given in addition to wages

functional resume A resume that focuses on the skills and qualifications of an applicant for a particular job rather than on work experience

G

government entity An organization funded and managed by a local, state, or national government in order to carry out its functions

green handout Handout information provided on a website rather than on paper

H

Health Insurance Portability and Accountability Act of 1996 (HIPAA) A federal law that protects the privacy of personal health information

heterogeneous group A group of individuals having dissimilar backgrounds and experiences

homogeneous group A group of individuals having similar backgrounds and experiences

horizontal communication Messages that flow from coworker to coworker, from manager to manager, or within a team

human relations skills Abilities that allow one to interact with others effectively

hyperlink Text or a graphic that links to another place in a file, a website, or another file

I

image record A digital or photographic representation of a record stored on electronic or microform media

important record A record necessary to the orderly continuation of a business and replaceable only at a considerable cost of time and money

incentive An intrinsic or extrinsic reward or encouragement

income statement A financial document that shows the income, expenses, and profit or loss of an organization for a given period of time

index A list of all the names or titles used in a filing system

indexing The process of determining the filing segment to be used in storing a record

indirect approach A message strategy in which the opening is pleasant but neutral and the main idea is presented later

individual retirement arrangement (IRA) A plan that permits individuals to save and invest for retirement

informal communication Communication through unofficial channels

inspecting The process of checking a record to determine whether it is ready to be filed

intelligent mobile hotspot A traveling Internet connection

interactive whiteboard A large display board connected to a computer that is used to capture images and notes or access computer programs or the Internet

interference Anything that stands in the way of progress

internal customers Departments or employees within an organization who use the products or services provided by others within the organization

itinerary A document that gives travel information such as flight numbers, arrival and departure times, hotel and car reservations, and appointments

J

jet lag A feeling of exhaustion following a flight through several time zones

job agent A software program that automatically searches job listings and retrieves jobs matching criteria you set

job board A website that allows you to browse job listings and sometimes to post your resume and allows employers to post job openings and review resumes

job sharing An arrangement in which two or more people complete the duties of one job position

K

key operator A person responsible for copier maintenance and simple copier repairs

key unit The first unit of the filing segment

L

laissez-faire leadership style A leadership style that allows subordinates to lead themselves

leadership The act of inspiring and motivating people to achieve organizational goals

leadership styles Patterns of behavior associated with leadership

letter of application A letter sent to a potential employer that states your interest in a job, provides general information about and sells your skills, transmits your resume, and requests an interview

limited liability company (LLC) A business form that combines the tax advantages of a partnership with the limited liability of a corporation

liquidity How easily an investment is converted into cash

M

mail merge A feature of word processing programs that allows you to create personalized letters, labels, or envelopes for large mailings

manners Standards of conduct that show us how to behave in a cultured, polite, or refined way

microform A general term for several types of microimage media such as roll microfilm, microfiche, and aperture cards

minutes A written record of a meeting

mobile application Software that runs on a handheld device or computer

motion A proposal presented for discussion and voting in a meeting

mutual fund An investment fund that consists of stocks, bonds, and other investments focused on a particular investment strategy

N

networking The process of exchanging information with other people and building positive business relationships

nonessential record A record that has no future value to an organization and that may be destroyed after current use

nonprofit corporation A corporation formed to promote a civic, charitable, or artistic purpose whose profits benefit that purpose

nonverbal communication The sharing of information through body language, gestures, voice quality, or proximity

O

organizational culture The key values, beliefs, and attitudes that drive the organization and the way it conducts business

organizational structure The way that lines of authority, responsibility, and communication are arranged in order to accomplish the work of the business

outsourcing Using outside firms to perform certain functions of an organization

P

parallel structure The expression of parallel ideas in parallel form

paraphrase To restate a concept in different words

partnership An association of two or more people as co-owners of a business

passive voice A form of the verb in which the subject receives the action

passport An official government document that certifies the identity and citizenship of an individual and grants the person permission to travel abroad

peer-to-peer file sharing A system of sharing files on an informal network with others who have the same software

periodic transfer The movement of materials from active to inactive files after a stated period of time

perpetual transfer The movement of materials from active to inactive files once they are no longer needed for frequent reference

persuasive approach A message strategy that builds interest and closes by asking for the desired action

phishing Using an online message that seems to be from a legitimate source to gather personal information

pitch An attribute of sound that can be described as high or low

portfolio A compilation of samples of your work and other career-related information

prescreening The process of gathering information about an applicant prior to a formal in-person interview

primary research The collection of original data through surveys, observations, or data review and analysis

priority Something that merits your attention ahead of other tasks

procrastination The act of trying to avoid a task by putting it aside with the intention of doing it later

professional image The way a person is perceived in the business world relating to integrity, work ethic, skills, personal appearance, and etiquette

project team A team that is developed for a clearly defined project that has a beginning and an end

Q

QR code A two-dimensional bar code that can be read with a mobile device to yield a URL, text message, phone number, or other information

R

record Information that is evidence of an event, activity, or business transaction created or received by an organization and stored on any medium

records management Systematic control of records from creation or receipt to final disposition

resume A concise statement of your background, education, skills, and work experience

retention period Time that records must be kept according to operational, legal, regulatory, and fiscal requirements

role ambiguity An absence of clarity concerning work objectives and expectations

S

secondary research The process of finding data or material that other people have discovered and reported via the Internet, books, periodicals, and other publications

self-discipline Your control over what you do, as well as how and when you do it

servant leadership A philosophy and style of leadership that focuses on serving others

sexual harassment Sexual conduct that is unwelcome by the recipient and that may be either physical or verbal in nature

simplified employee pension plan (SEP) A retirement plan for small business owners (including self-employed persons) and their employees

situational leadership The changing of leadership styles for different situations

smartphone A full-featured cellular phone with many of the functions of a handheld computer

social bookmarking The practice of saving bookmarks to a public website so they are organized and easy to access

sole proprietorship A type of business that is owned and controlled by an individual

spyware Software that tracks the websites you view and collects information about you

stakeholder A person or group that has an interest in the outcome of a decision or situation

stock A share of ownership in a corporation

stockholder A person who owns shares of stock in a company

stress The worry and anxiety you feel when you react to pressure from others or yourself

suspension folder A file folder with metal extensions that allow it to hang on file-drawer frames

T

targeted job search A job search that involves targeting companies where you wish to work rather than specific positions

task force A project team set up to deal with a specific issue or problem

team A group that works together toward a common goal

telecommunications The transmission of text, data, voice, video, and images electronically from one location to another

tone The attitude your words express to the reader

topic sentence The sentence that contains the main idea of a paragraph

traditional job search A job search that involves applying at many organizations with job openings that match your career goals

Trojan horse Malicious software designed to look like something interesting or useful

U

unity A quality achieved in a paragraph when the sentences clarify or support the main idea

upward communication Messages that travel from employees to management

useful record A record needed for the smooth, effective operation of an organization that is slow or inconvenient to replace

V

values Personal beliefs about right and wrong

verbal communication The process of exchanging information through words

verbal pauses Words used to fill silent spaces in conversation

verbatim Word for word

video conference A meeting in which two or more people at different locations use equipment such as computers, video cameras, and microphones to see and hear each other

virtual office professional An administrative professional who works remotely on a contractual basis for one or more clients

virtual team A team that primarily meets electronically and crosses the boundaries of time and distance to operate

visa An approval granted by a government that permits a traveler to enter and in some cases to travel within that particular country

visionary Able to see what is possible

visual aid An object or image used to help an audience understand a spoken or written message

visualization The creation of a mental picture

vital record A record that cannot be replaced and should never be destroyed

Voice over Internet Protocol The transmitting of voice over the Internet

W

Web 2.0 Interactive web resources

web conferencing Holding a conference via the Internet

web meeting A meeting in which two or more people at different locations communicate and share information via computers and a network connection, such as the Internet or a local area network

webcast A broadcast similar to a television broadcast that takes place over the World Wide Web

webinar A seminar presented over the World Wide Web

wiki A website that can be easily set up and used and that is collaborative in nature

work ethic A set of values based on the merits of hard work and diligence

workaholic A person who is addicted to work or has a compulsive need to work

workplace politics The relationships within an office and the nature of the networks established in a workplace

worm A malicious, self-replicating program that does not need human interaction to multiply

Index

C

Q

R

S

U

V

W

X